Collins Dictionary
for Writers and Editors

Collins, part of HarperCollins Publishers
77–85 Fulham Palace Road, London W6 8JB
www.collins.co.uk

First published in Great Britain in 2006 by
HarperCollins Publishers

1

Copyright © Collins, 2007

A catalogue record for this book is available from
the British Library.

ISBN 978-0-00-720351-2

Typeset by Rowland Phototypesetting Ltd,
Bury St Edmunds, Suffolk

Printed and bound in Great Britain by
Clays Ltd, St Ives plc

Visit the author's website: www.martinmanser.com

Permission to reproduce extracts from the
BS5261:2005 is granted by BSI

Collins
Dictionary for Writers and Editors

Martin H. Manser
Associate Editor Rosalind Fergusson

Collins

Contents

Introduction

The aims of this dictionary

Is the verb spelt *practice* or *practise*? Should you write *the dog is wagging its tail* or *the dog is wagging it's tail*? Which is correct: *hypocrisy* or *hypocracy*? Should you write *website, web site,* or *Website?*, *online, on line* or *on-line; loveable* or *lovable, well-known* or *well known*? Can all *-ise* variants (e.g. *criticise/criticize* and *organise/organize*) also be spelt *-ize*? And is it *spelled* or *spelt*? What about the comma before *or* and *and* at the end of a list? When is the plural of *formula formulas* and when is it *formulae*? Is it *Mother's Day* or *Mothers' Day*? You will find the answer to these and many more matters of written usage in this new dictionary.

The *Collins Dictionary for Writers and Editors* is an authoritative A–Z reference source for all those who work with the written word, giving reliable guidance on problematic words, names, etc., stylistic conventions, and usage. Issues are dealt with under individual words and phrases wherever possible. Where more general comment is required, e.g. for the use of semicolons, split infinitives, or *-ize/-ise* spellings, entries are inserted at the appropriate position in the alphabetical list, rather than as separate appendices. *Collins English Dictionary* is used as a basis for preferred forms and spellings.

This book is intended primarily for professional writers and editors, as the title suggests, but anybody whose work involves the writing of reports, essays, web content, etc., will find it gives definitive guidance.

Content

The following categories are covered:

1. Misspellings. Words that are frequently misspelt are listed with a brief comment drawing attention to the part of the word where errors are made. Note that the misspelt words themselves are not included, either as headwords or within the entry of the correct spelling. Inflections and derivatives of the headword are not shown unless they have a separate problem of their own, in which case they have their own entry (but entries showing whether a final single consonant is doubled in past and present participle are combined if alphabetically adjacent). Definitions are only given if they are needed for some other purpose, e.g. to distinguish between confusibles.

>**accommodate** (double **c**, double **m**)
>**analyse** (**-yze** in US English)
>**capsize** (never **-ise**)
>**changeable** (**e** after **g**)
>**galloped, galloping** (not **-pp-**)
>**gauge** measure or estimate (not **-ua-**; compare **gage**)
>**permissible** permitted (not **-able**)
>**televise** (never **-ize**)

2. Variant spellings. The preferred spelling in *Collins English Dictionary* is given first, followed by variants that are generally acceptable in UK English. The variant has its own entry if not alphabetically adjacent. Inflections and derivatives of the headword are not shown unless the suffix has a variant spelling of its own, in which case it has a separate entry. Archaic or obsolete variants are not shown.

>**ageing** (the spelling **aging** is not incorrect, but it is less common)
>**gaol** less common variant of **jail**
>**judgement** variant of **judgment**
>**judgment** (also **judgement**)
>**mediaeval** rare variant of **medieval**
>**medieval** (rarely **mediaeval**)
>**organize** (also **organise**)

3. Compound words. Guidance is given on whether these should be spelt as one or two words, solid or hyphenated. For compounds that are not hyphenated, the guidance comment is 'one word' or 'two words' unless the absence of a hyphen is considered more relevant (e.g. at **dining room** and **wellbeing** below). Headwords are listed separately, for clarity. Difficulty and/or frequency are the main criteria for inclusion.

> **ad lib** (adverb; adjective after noun)
> **ad-lib** (verb; noun; adjective before noun)
> **dining room** (no hyphen unless used before another noun, as in *dining-room furniture*)
> **game bird** (two words)
> **gamecock** (one word)
> **website** (one word; lower-case **w**)
> **wellbeing** (no hyphen)
> **well-known** (hyphenated before noun (as in *a well-known author*) and two words after noun (as in *the author is well known*); the same principle applies to other **well-** compounds)

4. Abbreviations and acronyms. The two main issues here are: (a) the use of full stops and (b) capitalization. The headword follows the style of *Collins English Dictionary*, with minimal treatment of variance (e.g. *PhD* does not show *Ph.D.* as a variant, but *plc* shows *PLC* as a variant). However, where scientific (or other) convention does not allow variance, this point is made in the entry.

> **AIDS** acquired immune deficiency syndrome (no full stops; also **Aids**)
> **flu** influenza (no apostrophe; no full stop; compare **flew** and **flue**)
> **km** kilometre or kilometres (no full stop; no **s** in plural)
> **Ltd** limited (company)
> **PhD** Doctor of Philosophy (from Latin *Philosophiae Doctor*; the variant **DPhil**, an abbreviation of the English form, is less common but not incorrect)
> **plc** public limited company (also **PLC** or **Plc**)

5. Homophones and other confusibles. This area is particularly important in modern writing, with the increasing reliance on spellcheck software, which does not highlight incorrectly used confusibles as errors. There is an entry for each member of a confusible pair or set, with a brief definition or part-of-speech label and cross-references to the other members unless alphabetically adjacent.

> **envelop** (verb)
> **envelope** (noun)
> **flaunt** display ostentatiously (compare **flout**)
> **flout** disregard openly (compare **flaunt**)
> **their** of them (compare **there; they're**)
> **there** in that place (compare **their; they're**)
> **they're** contraction of **they are** (compare **their** and **there**)

6. Foreign words and phrases. Guidance is given on whether the word or phrase is normally italicized in English text, and whether anglicized words have accents. A brief definition of the term is also supplied.

> **ad hoc** for a particular purpose (not italic; no hyphen)
> *fait accompli* something done that cannot be changed
>   (italic; plural *faits accomplis*)
> **premiere** first public performance (not italic; no accent)
> *Schadenfreude* pleasure gained from others' misfortune
>   (italic; capital **S**)

7. Plurals. Nouns with irregular and/or problematic plurals are shown, but very common words such as **tooth/teeth** are not included.

> **gateau** cake (not italic; also **gâteau**; plural **gateaux, gateaus,**
>   or **gâteaux**)
> **gallows** (same form for singular and plural)
> **octopus** (plural **octopuses**)
> **referendum** (single **f** then single **r**; plural **referendums** or
>   **referenda**)

8. Capitalization. Words and phrases where capitalization is unexpected, optional, or otherwise problematic are listed, with separate headwords where appropriate.

> **Bath chair** (capital **B**)
> **bible** an authoritative text, as in *the sailors' bible* (lower-case **b**)

Bible the sacred writings of Christianity (capital **B**; not italic)

biblical of the Bible (lower-case **b**)

French windows (capital **F**)

galaxy any of a number of star systems, or figurative use of the noun (lower-case **g**)

Galaxy the galaxy that contains the solar system (capital **G**)

roman describing the standard vertical type used for most text, as in these words (lower-case **r**; compare **italic**)

Roman of Rome (capital **R**)

9. Apostrophes. Names of companies, institutions, medical disorders, etc., with potentially problematic apostrophes, or with no apostrophe where one might be expected, are listed, together with lexical items such as **its/it's** and **theirs**. There is also a general entry at **apostrophe** covering the main uses (and misuses) of this punctuation mark.

Alzheimer's disease (capital **A**; apostrophe)

Barclays banking and finance company (no apostrophe)

Earls Court London (no apostrophe)

its of it (no apostrophe, as in *wagging its tail*)

it's contraction of **it is** or **it has**, as in *it's too late* or *it's stopped raining* (apostrophe)

Mother's Day fourth Sunday in Lent (in the UK and South Africa) or second Sunday in May (in the USA, Canada, and Australia) (**-'s** not **-s'**; also **Mothering Sunday** in the UK and South Africa)

St Andrews Scottish city and university (no apostrophe)

St Giles' Oxford street name (**-s'** not **-s's**)

St James's Palace London (**-s's** not **-s'**)

theirs of them (no apostrophe)

Waterstone's bookseller (apostrophe)

10. Style, usage, and grammar. Some of the more common problems of style and usage (in addition to the 'confusible' items and others mentioned above) are dealt with, as concisely as possible.

-ize/-ise see individual entries for words with these endings. Most dictionaries of UK English now list the **-ize** form (of verbs such as *organize* and their derivatives) as the preferred spelling, but many periodicals still use the **-ise** form: follow the publisher's house style. In any writing it is important to maintain consistency: do not use *organize* and *realise*, for example, within the same text. Note that some verbs (e.g. *televise* and *capsize*) have only one correct spelling. See also **-yse/-yze**.

semicolon punctuation mark used to separate two clauses, each of which could form a sentence in its own right (e.g. *They squandered their winnings; their children never forgave them.*) Semicolons are also used to separate divisions of a complex list that are further subdivided by commas (e.g. *I had cereal, toast, and coffee for breakfast; soup and sandwiches for lunch; and chicken, pasta, and salad for dinner.*)

split infinitive infinitive in which an adverb (or other word) is placed between *to* and the verb, as in *to boldly go*. Split infinitives are best avoided if the adverb can be placed elsewhere without ambiguity or inelegance.

11. Sensitive terms. Advice is given on the potential offensiveness of terms relating to disability, sex, race, etc., with acceptable alternatives.

Down's syndrome genetic disorder (former name **mongolism** now considered offensive)

firefighter (no hyphen; use instead of gender-specific **fireman** where appropriate)

fireman (use **firefighter** instead where appropriate)

mongol offensive former name for person with Down's syndrome (lower-case **m**)

Mongol person from Mongolia (capital **M**)

mongolism offensive former name for **Down's syndrome**

12. Titles. Titles of well-known books, plays, poems, etc., that have unconventional spellings, or that are otherwise problematic, are included. There are also general entries at **titles of works**, covering the use of italics or quotation marks, and **titles of periodicals** commenting on use of *The*. Books of the Bible are individually listed, with their standard abbreviations, which also have individual entries of their own.

Compleat Angler, The book by Izaak Walton (not ***Complete***)
Faerie Queene, The poem by Edmund Spenser
Gen. Genesis (full stop; not italic)
Genesis book of the Bible (not italic; abbreviation **Gen.**)
Through the Looking-Glass novel by Lewis Carroll (not ***Alice through . . .*** ; the full title is ***Through the Looking-Glass and What Alice Found There***)
Times, The (italic ***The*** with capital *T*; see also **titles of periodicals**)

13. Place names. Names of towns, countries, mountains, streets, etc., are included, e.g. if the spelling is unpredictable from the pronunciation, or where part of the name is spelt differently in different names (e.g. *-borough/brough/burgh; -sted/stead*), or where variant spellings exist, or where the local (foreign) name is also sometimes encountered.

Glamis Castle Scotland
Leicester English city (**-ei-, -ces-**)
Majorca Mediterranean island (Spanish name **Mallorca**)
Mallorca Spanish name for **Majorca**
Marseilles French city (French name **Marseille**)
Middlesbrough English town (not **-borough**)
Romania European country (the spellings **Rumania** or **Roumania** are less common, especially in modern usage, but not incorrect)

14. Institutions. Names of educational institutions, political institutions, etc., are included, e.g. where variant spellings exist, or where two homophonic names have different spellings.

al-Qaeda Islamic fundamentalist organization (lower-case **a**, hyphen, not **Qu-**; also **al-Qaida, al-Qa'ida**)
Magdalen College Oxford
Magdalene College Cambridge

15. People. Names of famous people are included, e.g. where variant spellings of either the first name or surname exist, or where the surname is spelt differently from a homophonic place name or other word. For transliterated Russian, Arabic, or Chinese names, variants are only shown if they are as frequent or important as the main form. (Pinyin is used as the main form for Chinese transliterations of people and places unless another form is better-known or more appropriate for historical reasons.) Some fictional characters are also included, e.g. if their name has entered the language as a generic.

> **Brueghel, Jan, Pieter** (the Elder), and **Pieter** (the Younger)
> Flemish painters (also **Breughel** for all three painters, but
> the spelling **Bruegel** is used only for Pieter the Elder)
> **Dostoevsky, Fyodor Mikhailovich** Russian novelist
> **Gaddafi, Moamar al** Libyan statesman (also **Qaddafi**)
> **Luxembourg** European country or its capital city
> **Luxemburg, Rosa** German socialist leader
> **Mao Tse-tung** Chinese statesman (also **Mao Ze Dong**)
> **Qaddafi** variant of **Gaddafi**
> **Romeo** Shakespearean hero, hence any male lover (capital **R**;
> plural **Romeos**)
> **Streisand, Barbra** US singer (**-ei-**; not **Barbara**)

16. Typographical terms. Those typographical terms that are likely to be encountered by writers and editors unfamiliar with the production process are defined. These are given a *typog.* label, where appropriate, to distinguish them from definitions at confusibles etc. The names of accents, diacritics, and special sorts are also included.

> **galley** (*typog.*) printer's proof, usually unpaginated (also **galley
> proof**; compare **page proof**)
> **widow** (*typog.*) short last line of paragraph, especially when
> occurring undesirably at top of page or column

17. Trademarks. The trademark status of certain words and names is shown, especially where the trademark has entered the language as a generic noun and/or verb. (In such cases the use of a synonym is recommended.)

> **Biro** trademark for a ballpoint pen (capital **B**)
> **Hoover** trademark for a vacuum cleaner (capital **H**, sometimes

lower-case when used as a verb; in generic use better replaced
by a synonym)

Xerox trademark for a photocopying process (capital **X**,
sometimes lower-case when used as a verb; in generic use
better replaced by a synonym)

Yale trademark for a type of lock (capital **Y**)

18. Appendices. The following items are included as appendices:

proofreading marks (BSI 2005)
mathematical and scientific symbols that are likely to be
encountered outside specialist texts (e.g. $>$, $<$, $\approx$, $\neq$, ∞)
transliteration of Greek, Cyrillic, and Hebrew alphabets
Beaufort scale
diacritics used in European languages (e.g. French: à, â, ç, é, è, ê)

World Englishes

Although this dictionary primarily describes standard British
English spelling, coverage is also given of other English variants
and usages, e.g. US, Canadian, Australian, and South African
English, where relevant.

counselled, counselling (single l in US English)
Foxe Basin Canada (not **Fox**)
vlei area of marshy ground in South Africa (not italic; **-ei**)
wrapped past tense and past participle of **wrap**, or variant of **rapt**
in Australian informal sense 'delighted' (compare **rapped**)

US spellings do not usually have their own cross-reference
headwords. But where the US headword is some distance away,
and the user might wonder if this is a permissible British variant,
a cross-reference headword has been added:

estrogen US spelling of **oestrogen**

Typefaces

1. bold: used for headwords; variants; cross-references; individual
letters, partwords and words in spelling and usage guides:

aggravate (double **g**, single **v**; use **annoy** instead where appropriate)

2. *italic:* used for examples; foreign words and phrases as appropriate:

ABS antilock braking system (no full stops; originally an abbreviation of German *Antiblockiersystem*)

titles of works as appropriate:

The Economist

the label (*typog.*):

ligature (*typog.*) character made up of two or more joined letters, such as fi, æ

collocating prepositions:

affinity (double **f**, single **n**; may be followed by *with* or *for*)

Punctuation

apostrophe: in spelling guides, where it is necessary to pluralize single letters, -'s is used:

abracadabra (all the vowels are **a**'s)

hyphen: in spelling guides, hyphens are used for partwords:

troubadour (**-ou-** twice)

but not for single letters when preceded by 'single', 'double', 'ending in', 'beginning with', etc.:

acquittance settlement of a debt (**-cq-**; double **t**)

Elsewhere, hyphens may occasionally be used for single letters:

agma the phonetic symbol (ŋ), representing the **-ng** of *thing* or the **-n-** of *think* (also **eng**)

Arrangement of entries

Headwords are ordered according to the following conventions: letter-by-letter alpha order; lower-case precedes capital; unpunctuated form precedes punctuated form; solid form precedes two-word form but two-word form precedes hyphenated form:

ad lib (adverb; adjective after noun)
ad-lib (verb; noun; adjective before noun)
bath wash in bath (compare **bathe**)
Ba'th Arab political party (also **Ba'ath** or **Baath**)
bible an authoritative text, as in *the sailors' bible* (lower-case **b**)
Bible the sacred writings of Christianity (capital **B**; not italic)

Names beginning with **Mac-** and **Mc-** are alphabetized together as if they all began with **Mac-**; names and phrases beginning with **Saint** and **St** are alphabetized together as if they all began with **Saint.**

Conclusion

In compiling and editing this book we have been fortunate in being able to draw on the vast resources of the Collins Word Web database as well as *Collins English Dictionary*.

We wish to thank the following for their encouragement and help in the book's production: Edwin Moore, Christopher Riches, Martin Toseland, and Elaine Higgleton.

We trust this dictionary will prove an authoritative guide to troublesome points of English spelling and usage, and to stylistic conventions of writing and editing.

Martin H. Manser
Rosalind Fergusson

a the form of the indefinite article used before an initial consonant sound, regardless of spelling, as in *a yacht, a European, a UFO*. In modern usage it also precedes *hotel, historic, hereditary, heroic, habitual*, etc. Compare **an**.

Å angstrom unit

a- (hyphen before *-ing* forms, as in *go a-begging*, but not in such words as *afoot, ablaze*, etc.)

@ at (symbol used in commerce and e-mail addresses)

A1 first class (also **A-1**)

A3 paper size, twice A4

A4 paper size, 210 × 297 mm

A5 paper size, half A4

AA Alcoholics Anonymous; Automobile Association (no full stops)

Aachen German city (French name **Aix-la-Chapelle**)

Aalborg Danish city (also **Ålborg**)

Aalesund variant of **Ålesund**

Aalto, Alvar Finnish architect

A & E Accident and Emergency (hospital department)

A & M Ancient and Modern (hymn book)

A & R artists and repertoire

aardvark (double **a** in first syllable, single **a** in second syllable)

Aarhus Danish city (also **Århus**)

Aaron (double **a** for the biblical character; **Aaron** or **Aron** as Elvis Presley's middle name)

A'asia Australasia (apostrophe)

AB able-bodied seaman; Bachelor of Arts (in USA, from Latin *Artium Baccalaureus*); blood group (no full stops)

abacus (plural **abaci** or **abacuses**)

Abadan Iranian port

Abaddon Hell or the Devil

abalone (-**bal**-, not -**bel**-)

abandoned, abandoning (not -**nn**-)

abattoir (single **b**, double **t**)

Abbasid dynasty of caliphs (double **b**, single **s**)

abbé French cleric (not italic; acute accent)

Abbotsinch Airport Glasgow

abbr. abbreviation (full stop)

abbrev. abbreviation (full stop)

abbreviate (double **b**)

abbreviations see individual entries for common abbreviations. As a general rule, do not use full stops for abbreviations that consist of a string of capital initial letters (*BBC, UN*), for those that end with the last letter of the full word (*Dr, Ltd*), or for metric units of measurement (*km, g*). Short forms that have entered the language as words in their own right do not need full stops or apostrophes (*ad, vet, flu, phone*). See also **acronyms** and **contraction**.

ABC rudiments of a subject (no full stops)

abdomen (not -**min**)

abdominal (not -men-)

abductor (not -er)

à Becket see **Becket**

Abednego biblical character (not -nd-, not -igo)

Abel biblical character (not -le)

Abelard, Peter French philosopher and theologian (no accent in English; French name **Pierre Abélard**; see also **Héloïse**)

Aberdonian of Aberdeen, or a person from Aberdeen

Aberfan Welsh coal-mining village (not -van)

abernethy biscuit (lower-case a)

aberration (single b, double r)

Aberystwyth Welsh town (not -ist- or -ith)

abetter (the variant **abettor** is chiefly used in legal contexts)

abided variant of **abode**

Abidjan legislative capital of Côte d'Ivoire (-dj-; compare **Yamoussoukro**)

Abingdon town in Oxfordshire (not -ton)

ab initio from the start (italic)

abjure renounce, retract, or abstain from (compare **adjure**)

-able/-ible see individual entries for words with these endings. Note that new coinages are usually formed by adding **-able**, as in *microwavable*. See also **-eable**.

able-bodied (hyphen)

ableism (-ei-)

Åbo Swedish name for **Turku**

aboard on or in a ship, train, etc. (compare **abroad**)

abode past tense of **abide** (also **abided**)

A-bomb atomic bomb (capital A; hyphen)

aboriginal indigenous, or existing in a place from the earliest time (lower-case a)

Aboriginal (as adjective) of the native peoples of Australia; (as noun) variant of **Aborigine** (capital A)

aborigine original inhabitant of a place (lower-case a)

Aborigine member of native people of Australia (also **Aboriginal**; capital A)

ABO system blood classification system (capital **ABO**, lower-case **s**; no full stops)

Aboukir Bay Egypt (also **Abukir Bay**; Arabic name **Abu Qîr**)

aboulia variant of **abulia**

about face (interjection)

about-face (noun and verb)

about turn (interjection)

about-turn (noun and verb)

aboveboard (adjective before noun)

above board (adverb; adjective after noun)

above-mentioned (hyphen)

ab ovo from the beginning (italics)

abracadabra (all the vowels are a's)

abridgment (also **abridgement**)

abroad in or to a foreign place (compare **aboard**)

abrogate cancel or repeal (compare **arrogate**)

ABS antilock braking system (no full stops; originally an abbreviation of German *Antiblockiersystem*)

abscess (-sc- then -ss)

abscissa (-sc- then -ss; plural **abscissas** or **abscissae**)

abseil (-ei-)

absent-minded (hyphen)

absit omen may the presentiment not become fact (italics)

absorb soak up or take in (compare **adsorb**)

absorbable (not -ible)

absorbent (not -ant)

absorption (-orp-, not -orb-)

absorptive (-orp-, not -orb-)

abstention withholding one's vote

abstinence refraining from sex, alcohol, etc.

abstractedly in a preoccupied manner

abstractly in an abstract way

ABTA Association of British Travel Agents (no full stops)

Abu Dhabi capital of United Arab Emirates

Abukir Bay variant of **Aboukir Bay**

abulia inability to make decisions (also **aboulia**)

Abu Qîr Arabic name for **Aboukir Bay**

Abu Simbel former Egyptian village (also **Ipsambul**)

abysmal very great or very bad (compare **abyssal**)

abyss (single **b**, double **s**)

abyssal of the ocean depths (compare **abysmal**)

Abyssinia former name for **Ethiopia**

Ac actinium (no full stop)

AC alternating current; athletic club; Member of the Welsh Assembly (from Welsh *Aelodau'r Cynulliad*; also **AM**)

academe place of learning, such as a university (capital **A** in *the groves of Academe*)

academia the academic world (lower-case **a**)

Académie française (capital **A**, lower-case **f**; **-é-**, **-ç-**)

Academy Award official name for **Oscar** (capital **A** twice)

Acadia Atlantic Provinces of Canada or their French-speaking areas (French name **Acadie**; compare **Arcadia**)

Acadian of Acadia (compare **Accadian** and **Arcadian**)

Acadie French name for **Acadia**

a cappella without instrumental accompaniment (not italic)

ACAS Advisory Conciliation and Arbitration Service (also **Acas**; no full stops)

Accad variant of **Akkad**

Accademia Venetian art gallery (double **c**)

Accadian variant of **Akkadian** (compare **Acadian**)

accede assent or attain, as in *accede to the throne* (compare **exceed**)

accelerate (double **c**, single **l**)

accelerator (not **-er**)

accent (as verb) put an accent or stress on; (as noun) stress, characteristic pronunciation of a particular area, or mark placed over vowel in some languages (see **acute**, **grave**, **circumflex**, and other names of accents; individual entries for words with accents; and Appendix v). For the use of accents on English words and capital letters, see **diacritic**.

accentuate emphasize

accept take or receive (compare **except**)

acceptance (not **-ence**)

access means or right of approach or entry (compare **accession** and **excess**)

accessary less common variant of **accessory** in the sense 'person who incites or assists a criminal'

accessible (not **-able**)

accession acceding (e.g. to the throne) or an addition (e.g. to a collection) (compare **access**)

accessorize (also **accessorise**; see **-ize/-ise**)

accessory (the spelling **accessary** is not incorrect in legal contexts, meaning 'person who incites or assists a criminal', but it is less common in this sense and should not be used in any other sense)

accidentally (not **-ently**)

accidie apathy or spiritual sloth (also **acedia**)

acclamation (double **c**, single **m**)

acclimatize (also **acclimatise**; also **acclimate**)

accommodate (double **c**, double **m**)
accompanist (no **y**)
accordion (not **-ian**)
accouchement childbirth (italics)
accountable (not **-ible**)
accoutre (**-er** in US English)
accoutrement (**-er-** in US English)
Accra capital of Ghana (double **c**)
accumulate (double **c**, single **m**)
acedia variant of **accidie**
acer (lower-case **a** in general use: *Acer* is the genus name)
acetic of an acid or vinegar (compare **ascetic**)
Acheson, Dean US statesman
Acheulian period of ancient culture (also **Acheulean**)
achieve (**-ie-**)
Achilles heel (capital **A**, no apostrophe)
Achilles tendon (capital **A**, no apostrophe)
achy (not **-ey**)
acid rain (two words)
acknowledgment (also **acknowledgement**)
acme culmination or peak
acne skin disorder
acolyte (not **-ite**)
Açores Portuguese name for the **Azores**
acoustics (single **c**; use singular verb in the sense 'science of sound', use plural verb in the sense 'sound qualities of a room')
acquiesce (**-cq-**, **-sc-**; may be followed by *in* or *to*)
acquirement abstract thing acquired, such as a skill (**-cq-**)
acquisition material thing acquired, such as a painting (**-cq-**)
acquittal discharge or release from a criminal charge or an obligation (**-cq-**, double **t**)
acquittance settlement of a debt (**-cq-**; double **t**)
Acre city in Israel

acriflavine (not **-in**)
Acrilan trademark for an acrylic fibre or fabric (capital **A**, not **-ryl-**)
acronyms abbreviations comprising a string of initial letters that is pronounced as a word, as in *AIDS*, *NATO*. Acronyms do not have full stops, and sometimes only the first letter is a capital (as in the variant forms *Aids*, *Nato*). Acronyms that have become fully established as words in their own right (e.g. *laser*, *radar*) do not have capital initials. See individual entries for common acronyms.
acrophobia fear of heights (compare **agoraphobia**)
acrylic (not **-ril-**)
Act (capital **A** for named acts of legislation, as in *the Stamp Act of 1765*, or numbered acts of a play, as in *Act 5, Scene 3*)
ACT Australian Capital Territory
Actaeon hunter in Greek mythology (**-aeo-**)
ACTH adrenocorticotrophic hormone
actinium (symbol **Ac**)
activate make active (compare **actuate**)
active see **passive**
act of God (lower-case **a**, capital **G**)
actor (may be used for males and females)
actress (note that many modern serious actresses prefer to be called actors)
Acts book of the Bible (not italic; not abbreviated; full name **The Acts of the Apostles**)
actualize (also **actualise**)
actuate motivate (compare **activate**)
acute denoting the accent used on é, ó, etc. (compare **grave**), or describing a disease that is sudden and severe or of short duration (compare **chronic**)

ad advertisement (no full stop; compare **add**)

A.D. anno Domini (also **AD**; usually printed or typeset in small capitals). The abbreviation is used for dates after the birth of Christ (compare **B.C.**; see also **CE**). It traditionally precedes year numbers, as in A.D. 346, but follows centuries, as in *the 2nd century* A.D. Although the full form literally means 'in the year of our Lord', the word *in* may precede the abbreviation where appropriate, as in *he died in* A.D. 59.

Ada computer programming language (not **ADA**)

adagio music term (not italic; plural **adagios**)

Adam, Robert Scottish architect and furniture designer (compare **Adams** and **Addams**)

Adams, Gerry Northern Ireland politician (not **Jerry**); **Henry** US writer; **John Quincy** US president (compare **Addams** and **Adam**)

Adam's apple (capital **A** for first word; apostrophe)

adaptable (not **-ible**)

adaptor (sometimes **adapter**, especially with reference to a person rather than a device)

ADC aide-de-camp; analogue-digital converter

add combine (compare **ad**)

Addams, Jane US social reformer (compare **Adams** and **Adam**)

Addenbrooke's Hospital Cambridge (apostrophe)

addendum (plural **addenda**)

Add. Esth. Additions to Esther (full stops; not italic)

Addis Ababa capital of Ethiopia (double **d**, single **b** twice)

addition the act of adding, or something added (compare **edition**)

Additions to Esther book of the Apocrypha (not italic; abbreviation **Add. Esth.**)

addresses (use minimal punctuation in addresses, especially on envelopes)

Adélie Land part of Antarctica (acute accent)

Adenauer, Konrad German statesman (not **Conrad**)

à deux of or for two people (italics; grave accent)

adherence adhering to rules, a political party, etc. (not **-ance**)

adhesion physically adhering or sticking together

ad hoc for a particular purpose (not italic; no hyphen)

adieu (plural **adieus** or **adieux**)

Adi Granth another name for **Guru Granth**

ad infinitum to infinity (not italic)

ad interim in the meantime (not italic)

Adirondack Mountains USA (capital **A** & **M**; also **Adirondacks**)

adj. adjective (full stop)

adjudicator (not **-er**)

adjure command or urge (compare **abjure**)

adjutant general (no hyphen)

Adler, Alfred Austrian psychiatrist; **Larry** US harmonica player

ad lib (adverb; adjective after noun)

ad-lib (verb; noun; adjective before noun)

admin administration (no full stop when used informally as a word in its own right)

administer apply, dispense, execute, or direct

administrate manage or direct the affairs of a business or institution

administrator (not **-er**)

admiralty office or jurisdiction of an admiral (lower-case **a**)

Admiralty former department of Ministry of Defence (capital **A**)

admissible (not **-able**)

admission permission to enter, price of entry, confession, or acknowledgment

admittance right or authority to enter

admittedly (not **-ably**)

ad nauseam to a tedious or sickening extent (not italic; not **-um**)

adolescent (**-sc-**; not **-ant**)

Adonai a Hebrew name for God

Adonais poem by Shelley, an elegy on the death of Keats

Adonis handsome youth in Greek mythology, hence any handsome young man (capital **A**)

adopted denoting the child of **adoptive** parents

adoptive denoting the parents of an **adopted** child

ad rem to the point (italics; no hyphen)

adrenalin variant of **adrenaline** (lower-case **a**)

Adrenalin trademark for a synthetic form of adrenaline used as a drug (capital **A**)

adrenaline (also **adrenalin**)

Adrianople former name for **Edirne**

adsorb accumulate on the surface of a solid (compare **absorb**)

adv. adverb (full stop)

ad valorem in proportion to estimated value (not italic; no hyphen)

advance forward movement, pro-gress, or money paid before it is due

advancement promotion

advantageous (**e** after **g**)

adversary (not **-ery** or **-ory**)

adverse hostile, unfavourable, or contrary (compare **averse**)

advertise (never **-ize**)

advice (noun; compare **advise**)

advisable (not **-ible**)

advise (verb; compare **advice**; never **-ize**)

adviser (also **advisor**)

advisory (not **-ary** or **-ery**)

advocaat (not **-cat**)

ae rarely represented by the character **æ** in modern English, but note that it is wrong to replace **æ** with **ae** in Old English words (see **ash**). See individual entries for the use of **ae** versus **e**.

A.E. pen name of George William **Russell** (also **AE** or **Æ**)

Aegean of Aegean Sea or its islands (**Ae-** then **-ea-**)

Aegean Sea part of Mediterranean Sea (capital **A** & **S**)

aegis (always **ae-**)

aegrotat (not italic; **ae-**)

Ælfric English writer (not **Ae-** or **E-**)

Aeneas Trojan prince in classical mythology (not **Æ-**)

Aeneid epic poem by Virgil (italics; not **Æ-**, not **-ead**)

aeolian of the wind (lower-case **a**)

Aeolian of an ancient Hellenic people (capital **A**; also **Eolian**)

aeolian harp (lower-case **a**)

aeon extremely long time (compare **eon**)

AER annual equivalent rate (of interest on savings account; compare **APR**)

aerate (not **air-**)

aerial (**ae-**, **-ia-**; compare **Arial**)

aerie less common variant of **eyrie**

aerobatics (not **air-**)

aerobics (not **air-**)

aerodrome (**airdrome** in US English)

aerodynamics (one word; not **air-**)

aero engine (two words)

aerofoil (one word; not **air-**)

aerogram (also **aerogramme**)

aeronautical (one word; not **air-**)

aeroplane (**airplane** in US English)

aerosol (not **air-**)

aerospace the atmosphere and outer space, or of spacecraft, rockets, missiles, etc. (one word; compare **airspace**)

aery[1] rare variant of **airy**

aery[2] rare variant of **eyrie**

Aeschylus ancient Greek dramatist (not Æ-)

Aesculapius Roman god of healing (not Æ-; compare **Asclepius**)

Aesop ancient Greek writer of fables (not Æ-)

aesthete (not **es-**)

aesthetic artistic or relating to good taste (not **es-**; compare **ascetic**)

aether less common variant of **ether** in the sense 'air, atmosphere'

aethereal rare variant of **ethereal**

aetiology (also **etiology**)

Aetna Latin name for **Etna**

affect (as verb) act on, influence, move emotionally, make a pretence of, or adopt; (as noun) technical term in psychology (compare **effect**)

affectation assumed manner or false display

affection fondness or emotion

affidavit (not italic)

affiliate (double **f**, single **l**)

affinity (double **f**, single **n**; may be followed by *with* or *for*)

afflict cause distress or suffering to, as in *he afflicted them with taxes* (compare **inflict**)

afflicted by (avoid this phrase when describing people with a specified illness or disorder: use **with** or **who has/have** instead)

affluent wealthy (compare **effluent**)

affront insult (compare **effrontery**)

afghan sheepskin coat or knitted blanket (lower-case **a**)

Afghan person from Afghanistan (capital **A**; the variant **Afghani** is less common but not incorrect)

Afghan hound (capital **A**)

afghani monetary unit of Afghanistan (lower-case **a**)

Afghani less common variant of **Afghan** (capital **A**)

AFL Australian Football League

aficionado (single **f**; plural **aficionados**)

aforementioned (one word)

a fortiori for similar reasons (not italic)

afreet demon or monster in Arabian mythology (the spelling **afrit** is not incorrect, but it is less common)

African-American the preferred term for an American of African descent (hyphen)

African-Caribbean variant of **Afro-Caribbean**

Africander variant of **Afrikander**

Afrikaans language (compare **Afrikaner**)

Afrikander breed of cattle or sheep of southern Africa (also **Africander**)

Afrikaner person (compare **Afrikaans**)

afrit less common variant of **afreet**

Afro-American (use **African-American** instead)

Afro-Caribbean (hyphen; also **African-Caribbean**)

afterbirth (one word)

aftercare (one word)

aftereffect (one word)

afterimage (one word)

afterlife (one word)

aftertaste (one word)

afterthought (one word)

afterward variant of **afterwards**, rarely used in UK English but the more common form in US English

afterwards (rarely **afterward** in UK English)

Ag silver (no full stop; from Latin *argentum*)

AG *Aktiengesellschaft* (used in German company names; no full stops)

Aga trademark for a cooking range (capital **A**)

Agadir Moroccan port

Aga Khan (capital **A** & **K**)

age (capital **A** for named periods of history, as in *Stone Age, Middle Ages*)

age group (two words)

ageing (the spelling **aging** is not incorrect, but it is less common)

ageism (the spelling **agism** is not incorrect, but it is less common)

agenda (use singular verb in the sense 'list of things to be dealt with'; plural **agendas**)

Agent Orange (capital **A** & **O**)

agent provocateur person employed to provoke suspected offender to commit crime (italics; two words; plural *agents provocateurs*)

age-old (hyphen)

aggrandize (also **aggrandise**; see **-ize/-ise**)

aggravate (double **g**, single **v**; use **annoy** instead where appropriate)

aggressive (double **g**, double **s**)

aggressor (not **-er**)

aging less common variant of **ageing**

agism less common variant of **ageism**

agitator (not **-er**)

AGM annual general meeting

agma the phonetic symbol (ŋ), representing the **-ng** of *thing* or the **-n-** of *think* (also **eng**)

agnail rare variant of **hangnail**

agnostic person who claims that knowledge of a Supreme Being is impossible (compare **atheist**)

à gogo as much as one likes (grave accent; not italic; no hyphens)

agonize (also **agonise**; see **-ize/-ise**)

agoraphobia fear of public places (not **agra-**; compare **acrophobia**)

Agram German name for **Zagreb**

agriculturist (the variant **agriculturalist** is less common but not incorrect)

Agulhas, Cape South Africa (**h** after **l**, not **-gh-**)

aha (no hyphen)

ahead of (use **before** instead where appropriate)

Ahern, Bertie Irish statesman (not **-erne**)

-aholic the more common form of the suffix when added to a full word, as in *shopaholic* (compare **-oholic**)

Ahvenanmaa Finnish name for the **Åland Islands**

AI artificial insemination; artificial intelligence

aid help or support

aide helper or assistant

aide-de-camp military assistant (not italic; hyphens; plural **aides-de-camp**)

aide-mémoire memory aid (italics, acute accent, plural *aides-mémoire*; may be anglicized to **aide-memoire**, plural **aide-memoires**, but note that both italics and accent must be dropped)

AIDS acquired immune deficiency syndrome (no full stops; also **Aids**)

aigrette plume of feathers worn as ornament (the spelling **aigret** is not incorrect, but it is less common; compare **egret**)

ail be ill (compare **ale**)

Ain department in central France (compare **Aisne**)

aïoli garlic mayonnaise (not italic; diaeresis)

air atmosphere (compare **heir**)

Air, Point of headland in N Wales (compare **Aire, Ayre, Ayr**, and **Eyre**)

air bag (two words)

air base (two words)

air bed (two words)

airborne (one word)

Airbus trademark for a commercial aircraft (capital **A**)

air-conditioned (hyphen)

air conditioning (no hyphen unless used before another noun, as in *air-conditioning unit*)

aircraft (use capital initial for types

of aircraft, such as Spitfire; use italics for names of individual aircraft, e.g. Lindbergh's *Spirit of St Louis*; use hyphen in B-52, F-106, etc., but not in Boeing 747)

aircraft carrier (two words)

aircraftman serviceman in RAF (compare **airman**)

aircraftwoman servicewoman in RAF (compare **airwoman**)

aircrew (one word)

airdrop (one word)

Aire English river (compare **Air, Ayre, Ayr,** and **Eyre**)

Airedale breed of dog (capital **A**)

airfield (one word)

airflow (one word)

air force (two words; capital **A** & **F** in names of national air forces, as in *Royal Air Force*)

air gun (two words)

air hostess (use **flight attendant** instead where appropriate)

airlift (one word)

airline (one word)

airlock (one word)

airmail (one word)

airman male pilot (compare **aircraftman;** use gender-neutral **pilot** or **aviator** instead where appropriate)

air mile unit of length equal to nautical mile (lower-case **a** & **m**)

Air Miles points awarded with purchases that can be used to pay for flights (capital **A** & **M**)

air pocket (two words)

airport (one word; capital **A** as part of name, as in *Manchester Airport*)

air raid (no hyphen unless used before another noun, as in *air-raid warden*)

air-sea rescue (one hyphen)

airship (one word)

airshow (one word)

airsick (one word)

airspace the atmosphere above a particular part of the earth (one word; compare **aerospace**)

airstrip (one word)

airtight (one word)

air-to-air (hyphens)

air-traffic control (one hyphen)

air vice-marshal (one hyphen; capital **A, V,** & **M** when followed by name)

airwaves (one word)

airwoman female pilot (compare **aircraftwoman;** use gender-neutral **pilot** or **aviator** instead where appropriate)

airy (rarely **aery**)

aisle passageway separating seats (compare **isle**)

Aisne department in NE France (compare **Ain**)

ait islet (also **eyot**)

Aix-en-Provence city in SE France

Aix-la-Chapelle French name for **Aachen**

Aix-les-Bains town in E France

Ajaccio capital of Corsica (double **c**)

AK Alaska (US postal code)

a.k.a. also known as

Akaba less common variant of **Aqaba**

Akkad Babylonian city (also **Accad**)

Akkadian member of ancient Semitic people (also **Accadian;** compare **Acadian**)

Akmola former name for **Astana**

akvavit variant of **aquavit**

Al aluminium (no full stop)

AL Alabama (US postal code)

al- (Arabic article, used in names, e.g. *al-Qaeda;* lower-case **a,** hyphen)

à la in the manner or style of (not italic; grave accent)

à la carte with dishes individually priced (not italic; grave accent)

Aladdin character in *The Arabian Nights' Entertainments* (single **l,** double **d**)

Aladdin's cave (capital **A**)

Alamein see **El Alamein**

Alanbrooke, Viscount British field marshal

Åland Islands island group in Gulf of Bothnia (capital **Å** & **I**; Finnish name **Ahvenanmaa**)

Al-Anon association for friends and relatives of alcoholics (compare **Alcoholics Anonymous**)

alarm clock (two words)

alarums and excursions (not **alarms**)

Albee, Edward US dramatist

albeit (one word)

Albert Hall London (capital **A** & **H**; full name **Royal Albert Hall**)

albinism (not **-oism**)

albino (plural **albinos**)

Ålborg variant of **Aalborg**

Albright, Madeleine US diplomat

albumen egg white (not **-in**)

albumin protein found in blood plasma and egg white (also **albumen**)

Albuquerque US city

Alcantara trademark for upholstery fabric (capital **A**; no accent)

Alcántara Spanish town (capital **A**; acute accent)

Alcatraz US island and former prison

alcheringa another name, from a native Australian language, for **Dreamtime**

Alcoholics Anonymous association for alcoholics (compare **Al-Anon**)

Alcoran the Koran (one word; also **Alkoran**)

Alcott, Louisa May US novelist (double **t**)

Aldeburgh town in Suffolk, site of annual music festival (**-deb-**; not **-borough** or **-brough**)

al dente cooked so as to be firm when eaten (italic; two words)

Alderney one of the Channel Islands (not **-ny**; French name **Aurigny**)

Aldis lamp (capital **A**)

ale beer (compare **ail**)

alef variant of **aleph**

Alembert, Jean le Rond d' French mathematician, physicist, and philosopher

Alençon French town (cedilla)

Aleppo Syrian city (single **l**; double **p**)

aleph Hebrew letter transliterated by the special sort (') (also **alef**)

Ålesund Norwegian town (also **Aalesund**)

Aleutian Islands island group off Alaska (capital **A** & **I**)

A level (no hyphen unless used before another noun, as in *A-level maths*)

Alexandrian of Alexander the Great or Alexandria in Egypt (**-ian**; always capital **A**)

Alexandrine line of verse (**-ine**; also **alexandrine**)

Alfa Romeo Italian motor manufacturer, or any of their vehicles (no hyphen; capital **A** & **R**; not **Alpha**)

alfresco in the open air (not italic; one word)

algae (plural noun; singular **alga**)

algebra (not **-gib-**)

Algol computer programming language, or star (also **ALGOL** for the programming language)

Algonkian former name for the **Proterozoic**, or less common variant of **Algonquian**

Algonkin less common variant of **Algonquin**

Algonquian North American Indian people or language (the spelling **Algonkian** is not incorrect, but it is less common)

Algonquin North American Indian people or language (the spelling **Algonkin** is not incorrect, but it is less common)

Algonquin Hotel New York City, USA (not **-kin**; not **-ian**)

Algonquin Park Canada (not **-kin**; not **-ian**)

Algonquin Round Table group of literary wits, notably Dorothy Parker, who met at the **Algonquin Hotel** in the 1920s and 1930s (not **-kin**; not **-ian**)

Ali see **Mehemet Ali** and **Muhammad Ali**

alibi (plural **alibis**)

Alice band (capital **A**)

Alice's Adventures in Wonderland novel by Lewis Carroll (not *Alice in Wonderland*; see also *Through the Looking-Glass*)

Alice Springs Australian town (sometimes shortened to **Alice** or **the Alice**)

Aligarh Indian city

Alighieri surname of **Dante**

align (rarely **aline**)

A-line denoting flared style of dress or skirt (capital **A**; hyphen)

Alitalia Italian airline (capital **A**; not **All-**; one word)

al-Jazeera TV station in Qatar

alkali (plural **alkalis** or **alkalies**)

Alkoran variant of **Alcoran**

all every one (compare **awl**)

Allah Muslim name for God (**-ah**)

Allahabad Indian city (double **l**)

Allahu Akbar exclamation used in Islam, literally meaning 'God is most great' (capital **A** twice; double **l**; not italic)

Allan-a-Dale member of Robin Hood's band (hyphens; not **Alan** or **Allen**; not **-A-**)

allay relieve (compare **alley**)

all clear (two words)

all-comers (hyphen)

allege (not **-edge**)

Allegheny Mountains USA (capital **A** & **M**; **-gh-**; also **Alleghenies**)

allegiance (not **-ence**)

allegory (double **l**)

allegretto music term (not italic; plural **allegrettos**)

allegro music term (not italic; plural **allegros**)

alleluia variant of **hallelujah**, more common in liturgical contexts

allemande music or dance (lower-case **a**; not italic)

Allen, Ethan American soldier; **Woody** US actor and director (not **Allan**)

Allende, Isabel Chilean novelist; **Salvador** Chilean politician

Allen key (capital **A**; not **Allan**)

allergy (double **l**)

alley passage (compare **allay**)

All Fools' Day (always **-s'** not **-'s**)

Allhallows another name for **All Saints' Day** (the variant **All-Hallows** is less common but not incorrect)

Allhallows Eve another name for **Halloween** (no apostrophe; the variant **All-Hallows Eve** is less common but not incorrect)

allied united or related (lower-case **a**)

Allied of the Allies (capital **A**)

allies allied countries or people (lower-case **a**)

Allies in World Wars I and II, Britain and allied countries (capital **A**)

alligator (not **-er**)

all in (no hyphen unless used before a noun, as in *all-in wrestling*)

Allingham, Margery British writer of detective stories (not **Marjorie**)

all mouth and trousers (not . . . **no trousers**)

allot (double **l**; single **t**)

allotment (single **t**)

allotted, allotting (double **t**)

allowed permitted (compare **aloud**)

all ready completely ready (compare **already**)

all right (use instead of **alright**)

all-round (hyphen; **all-around** in US English)

All Saints' Day (**-s'** not **-'s**)

All Souls College Oxford (no apostrophe)

All Souls' Day (apostrophe)
allspice (one word)
all-time (hyphen)
all together at the same time or as a group (compare **altogether**)
allude refer indirectly (compare **elude**)
allusion indirect reference (compare **illusion** and **delusion**)
allusive containing allusions (compare **elusive** and **illusive**)
Al Madinah Arabic name for **Medina**
alma mater one's place of education (two words; lower-case **a** & **m**)
almanac (rarely **almanack**; capital **A** in titles)
almanack rare or archaic variant of **almanac**, spelt with capital **A** in some titles, e.g. *Whitaker's Almanack*)
almighty omnipotent or very great (lower-case **a**)
Almighty, the God (capital **A**)
Alnwick town in Northumberland (not **An-**)
aloe vera (lower-case **a** & **v** in general use: *Aloe vera* is the genus name)
a lot (two words)
aloud audibly (compare **allowed**)
ALP Australian Labor Party
Alpes-de-Haute-Provence French department (not **Alps-**)
alphabetization may be word-by-word (thus **act**, **act of God**, **activate**) or letter-by-letter (thus **act**, **activate**, **act of God**); the latter is used in this book. Note that in foreign-language dictionaries and indexes, some accented characters and digraphs may be placed at the end of the letter, or even at the end of the alphabet.
alphabetize (also **alphabetise**; see **-ize/-ise**)
alphanumeric (not **-ical**)
alpine of high mountains, or growing on mountains (lower-case **a**)

Alpine of the Alps (capital **A**)
alpinist (lower-case **a**)
Alps European mountain range (capital **A**)
al-Qaeda Islamic fundamentalist organization (lower-case **a**, hyphen, not **Qu-**; also **al-Qaida**, **al-Qa'ida**)
already by this time (compare **all ready**)
alright less acceptable variant of **all right** in the sense 'OK'
Alsace region of France (German name **Elsass**)
Alsace-Lorraine area of France (hyphen; German name **Elsass-Lothringen**)
Alsatian (as noun) breed of dog, or person from Alsace; (as adjective) of Alsace (not **-ion**; capital **A**; the dog is now often called a **German shepherd** or **German shepherd dog**)
also-ran (hyphen)
altar place or structure where religious rites are performed
alter change
alteration change
altercation argument
alter ego second self or intimate friend (two words; not italic; plural **alter egos**)
alternate occurring by turns
alternative (as noun) one of two (or sometimes more) possible things, courses of action, etc.; (as adjective) being an alternative (for the noun, use **choice** or **option** instead if there are more than two possibilities)
alternator (not **-er**)
Althing Icelandic parliament (capital **A**)
Althorp seat of the Spencer family and burial place of Diana, Princess of Wales (not **-thorpe** or **-throp**)
alto (plural **altos**)
altogether completely or in total (compare **all together**)

alto-relievo high relief (also **alto-rilievo**; hyphen; not italic)

aluminium (symbol **Al**; **-num** in US English)

alumna female graduate of place of education (plural **alumnae**)

alumnus graduate of place of education (may be used for males or females; plural **alumni**)

Alzheimer's disease (capital **A**; apostrophe)

Am americium (no full stop)

AM Master of Arts (in USA, from Latin *Artium Magister*); Member of the Welsh Assembly (also **AC**)

a.m. ante meridiem (full stops; used for times from midnight to midday. Note that 12 *a.m.* usually means 'midnight' but may be ambiguous, and 8 *a.m. in the morning* is tautological)

amanuensis (plural **amanuenses**)

amaretto Italian liqueur (compare **amoretto**)

amaryllis (lower-case **a** in general use: *Amaryllis* is the genus name)

amateur not professional (a neutral term; compare **amateurish**)

Amateur Athletic Association (not **Athletics**)

amateurish lacking skill or expertise (always derogatory; compare **amateur**)

Amazon South American river, female warrior, or tall strong woman (capital **A**; also **amazon** in the sense 'tall strong woman')

Ambala Indian city

ambassador (may be used for males and females)

ambassadress (use **ambassador** instead to avoid offence)

ambergris waxy secretion of sperm whale (not **-grease**)

ambiance less common variant of **ambience**

ambidextrous (not -ter-)

ambience (the spelling **ambiance** is not incorrect, but it is less common)

ambient (not -ant)

ambiguous having more than one possible meaning

ambivalent having conflicting attitudes or feelings simultaneously (not -ant)

amend alter, improve, or correct, as in *amend the legislation* (compare **emend**)

America (use **USA** instead where appropriate for clarity)

American (as adjective, use **US** instead where appropriate for clarity)

American Indian (also **Native American** or **Amerindian**; former name **Red Indian** now considered offensive)

Americanize (also **Americanise**; see -ize/-ise)

American Revolution US name for **War of American Independence**

American spelling As a general rule, in US English the **-yse** ending of *analyse, paralyse*, etc. becomes **-yze**; the **-our** ending of *colour, honour*, etc. becomes **-or**; the **-ll-** of *traveller, modelling*, etc. becomes **-l-**; the **-re** of *centre, fibre*, etc. becomes **-er**; and **-ae-** and **-oe-** become **-e-**. There are, however, numerous exceptions (especially in the case of **-ae-** and **-oe-**) and other examples: use an American dictionary to check individual words.

American Standard Version revision of **Authorized Version** of Bible, published by committee of American scholars in 1901

American War of Independence variant of **War of American Independence**

America's Cup (apostrophe)

americium (symbol **Am**)

Amerindian variant of **American Indian**

Amharic official language of Ethiopia (**-mh-**)

amiable having a friendly nature, as in *an amiable chap*

amicable characterized by friendliness, as in *an amicable agreement*

Amicus trade union (not **AMICUS**)

amicus curiae person who advises a court of law (not italic; plural **amici curiae**)

amid (the variant **amidst** is less common but not incorrect)

amidships (one word)

amidst less common variant of **amid**

amigo friend (not italic; plural **amigos**)

Amis, Sir Kingsley and **Martin** British novelists

Amish Mennonite sect of North America

Amman capital of Jordan (not **-on**)

ammeter instrument for measuring current in amperes (double **m**; not **amp-**)

amoeba (**-oe-**)

amok (not **-ock**; the spelling **amuck** is not incorrect, but it is less common)

among (use instead of **between** when more than two are involved, as in *agreement among the committee members*; the variant **amongst** is less common but not incorrect)

amoral having no moral quality or standards (compare **immoral**)

amoretto cupid (compare **amaretto**)

amortize (also **amortise**; see **-ize/-ise**)

Amos book of the Bible (not italic; not abbreviated)

amour-propre self-respect (italics)

amp ampere or amplifier (no full stop)

ampere unit of electric current (lower-case **a**; no accent)

Ampère, André Marie French physicist (grave accent)

ampersand the symbol (&), used in place of **and** in some company names and abbreviations, e.g. *Marks & Spencer, R & D*

amphetamine (**-ph-, -ine**)

amphibian (**-ph-, -ian**)

Amritsar Indian city (**-ar**)

amuck less common variant of **amok**

Amundsen, Roald Norwegian explorer (not **-son**, not **Ron-**)

an the form of the indefinite article used before an initial vowel sound, regardless of spelling, as in *an uncle, an hour, an MP*. It is now rarely used before *hotel, historic, hereditary, heroic, habitual*, etc. Compare **a**.

AN Anglo-Norman

anabolic (single **n**)

Anacreon ancient Greek poet

anaemia (**-nem-** in US English)

anaerobic (**-ae-**)

anaesthetic (**-nes-** in US English)

anaesthetize (also **anaesthetise**; see **-ize/-ise**)

analog variant of **analogue** used in computing and in US English

analog computer (not **-gue**)

analogue the UK spelling for most senses and uses (see **analog**)

analogue clock (**-gue**)

analogue watch (**-gue**)

analogue recording (**-gue**)

analyse (**-yze** in US English)

analysis (plural **analyses**)

anapaest metrical foot (the spelling **anapest** is not incorrect, but it is less common)

anaphora the use of a word, e.g. a pronoun, that refers to something previously mentioned (compare **cataphora**)

Anapurna variant of **Annapurna**

anat. anatomical; anatomy (full stop)

anathema (plural **anathemas**)

ANC African National Congress

ancestor (may be used for males and females)

ancestress (use **ancestor** instead to avoid offence)

anchorite (not -et)

anchylosis less common variant of **ankylosis**

ancien régime former regime (italics; acute accent; plural *anciens régimes*)

Ancient Greek language (capital **A** & **G**)

Ancient Mariner, The Rime of the poem by Coleridge (not *Rhyme*)

ancillary (double **l**; not -iary)

and (may be used at the beginning of a sentence for effect, but sparingly; see also **and/or**)

Andalucía Spanish name for **Andalusia**

Andalusia region of Spain (Spanish name **Andalucía**)

Andersen, Hans Christian Danish writer of fairy tales (not -son)

Anderson shelter (capital **A**)

Andhra Pradesh Indian state (-dhr-)

and/or (avoid outside legal and commercial contexts by paraphrasing, e.g. replace *cars and/or buses* with *cars, buses, or both*)

Andorra European principality (double **r**)

Androcles in Roman legend, slave not killed by lion he had once helped (rarely **Androclus**)

androgenous producing only male offspring

androgynous having male and female characteristics

Andropov, Yuri Soviet statesman

anemone (not -nome)

aneurysm (not -ism)

angel spiritual being (compare **angle**)

angelfish (one word)

Angelico, Fra Italian painter and friar

Angers French city

angina chest disorder (full name **angina pectoris** in this sense)

angle corner (compare **angel**; lower-case **a**)

Angle early Germanic settler of England (capital **A**)

angle brackets the characters < and >, which have various specialist uses. Used alone as symbols, < means 'less than' and > means 'greater than'.

Anglesey Welsh island (not -gel-, not -sy or -sea; Welsh name **Ynys Môn**)

Angleterre French name for England

Anglican of the Church of England (capital **A**)

anglicize (also **anglicise**; lower-case **a**)

Anglo- attached with hyphen, not en dash, to words with capital initial, as in *Anglo-French*; no hyphen elsewhere, as in *Anglophile*. It may denote England or the UK, though the latter use can cause offence.

Anglophile (no hyphen; capital **A**)

Anglophobe (no hyphen; capital **A**)

Anglophone (no hyphen; the spelling **anglophone**, with lower-case **a**, is less common but not incorrect)

Anglo-Saxon (hyphen)

angora yarn (lower-case **a**)

Angora former name for **Ankara**, or breed of cat, goat, or rabbit (capital **A**)

Angostura former name for **Ciudad Bolívar**

angostura bark bark formerly used medicinally (lower-case **a** & **b**)

Angostura bitters trademark for tonic used to flavour drinks (capital **A**, lower-case **b**)

angst anxiety (not italic; lower-case **a**)

angstrom unit of length used for wavelengths of electromagnetic radiation (lower-case **a**; no diacritics)

Ångström, Anders Swedish physicist

animal breeds see individual entries for capitalization. As a general rule, animal breeds linked to place names retain the capital initial. Where the word is more readily associated with the animal than with the place (e.g. **Chihuahua**), the use of a lower-case initial is not incorrect, but the capital form remains more common and is preferred in specialist contexts (e.g. when writing about animal shows or farming).

Ankara capital of Turkey (former name **Angora**)

ankh cross with loop (**-kh**)

anklebone (one word)

ankle sock (two words)

ankylosis (the spelling **anchylosis** is not incorrect, but it is less common)

annals historical records (compare **annuals**)

Annapurna Himalayan massif (also **Anapurna**)

Ann Arbor US city (not **Anne**, not **-our**)

Anne, Princess daughter of Elizabeth II (title **Princess Royal**); **Queen** British monarch; **St** mother of Virgin Mary (not **Ann**)

Anne of Cleves fourth wife of Henry VIII (not **Ann**)

annex (verb)

annexe (noun)

anno Domini full form of **A.D.** (not italic; capital **D**)

annotate (double n)

annuals books published once a year (compare **annals**)

annul (double n; single l)

annulment (single l)

annulled, annulling (double l)

Annunzio see **D'Annunzio**

annus horribilis terrible year (not italics; double **n**, **-bilis**)

annus mirabilis year of wonders or notable events (italics; double *n*, *-bilis*)

anodize (also **anodise**; see **-ize/-ise**)

anodyne (not **-ine**)

anoint (not **ann-**)

anon soon (no full stop)

anon. anonymous (full stop)

anonymous (not **-nim-**)

anorectic variant of **anorexic**

anorexia disorder characterized by refusal of food (full name **anorexia nervosa** in this sense)

anorexic (also **anorectic**)

Anouilh, Jean French dramatist

Ansafone see **answerphone**

Ansaphone see **answerphone**

answerphone telephone answering machine (lower-case **a**; the spellings **Ansaphone** and **Ansafone** are sometimes used in names)

-ant/-ent see individual entries for words with these endings.

Antaeus African giant in Greek mythology

antagonize (also **antagonise**; see **-ize/-ise**)

Antananarivo capital of Madagascar

Antarctic (**-arct-**)

Antarctica continent around South Pole

Antarctic Ocean sea around Antarctica, consisting of southernmost parts of Atlantic, Pacific, and Indian Oceans (also **Southern Ocean**)

ante gaming stake (not **-i**)

ante- before (compare **anti-**; attached without hyphen, except to words beginning with **e** or capital letter)

antecedent (not **-ant**)

antechamber (one word; not **anti-**)

antediluvian (one word; not **anti-**)

antemeridian (one word; **-ian**)

ante meridiem full form of **a.m.** (not italic; two words; **-iem**)

antenatal (one word; not **anti-**)

antenna (plural **antennae** in the sense 'insect appendage' or **antennas** in the sense 'aerial')

antepenultimate (one word; not anti-)

anteroom (one word; not anti-)

ant hill (two words)

Anthony, St Egyptian hermit (not -ton-)

Anthony of Padua, St Franciscan friar (not -ton-)

anthropomorphize (also **anthropomorphise**; see -ize/-ise)

anti- against or opposite to (compare **ante-**; attached without hyphen, except to words beginning with **i** or capital letter, as in *anti-inflationary*, *anti-Catholic*)

antibody (one word; not ante-)

Antichrist (one word; not ante-; capital **A**, lower-case **c**)

anticipate (use **expect** instead where appropriate)

anticlimax (one word; not ante-)

anticlockwise (one word; not ante-)

antidepressant (one word; not ante-, not -ent)

antifreeze (one word; not ante-)

Antigua Caribbean island (-gua)

antihero (one word; not ante-; plural **antiheroes**)

antihistamine (one word; not ante-, not -in)

antimacassar (one word; not ante-, single **c**, double **s**, not -er)

antimatter (one word; not ante-)

antimony (symbol **Sb**)

antipodes diametrically opposite place or region (often **Antipodes** with reference to Australia and New Zealand)

antiquated outmoded or obsolete

antique valued for its age and quality

antirrhinum (-rrh-; lower-case **a** in general use: *Antirrhinum* is the genus name)

anti-Semitism (hyphen; not ante-; capital **S**)

antisocial injurious to other people,

as in *antisocial behaviour* (compare **asocial**, **unsociable**, and **unsocial**)

antithesis (plural **antitheses**)

antiwar (one word; not ante-)

Antoninus Pius Roman emperor (not **Antonius**)

Antonius, Marcus Latin name for **Mark Antony** (not -inus)

Antony, Mark Roman general and statesman (not -thon-; Latin name **Marcus Antonius**)

Antony and Cleopatra play by Shakespeare (not -thon-)

antonym (not -nim)

Antwerp (Flemish name **Antwerpen**; French name **Anvers**)

anybody (one word; interchangeable with **anyone**)

anyhow (one word)

any more (two words)

anyone (one word; interchangeable with **anybody**)

anything (one word)

anyway in any case, nevertheless, or anyhow (one word)

any way in any manner or by any means (two words)

anywhere (one word)

Anzac Australian and New Zealand Army Corps (not **ANZAC**; now used to refer to any Australian or New Zealand soldier)

AOB any other business (the variant **a.o.b.** is not incorrect, but it is less common in modern times)

A-OK perfect or excellent (hyphen)

aorta (plural **aortas** or **aortae**)

Aotearoa Maori name for New Zealand

apache Parisian gangster or ruffian (lower-case **a**)

Apache North American Indian people (capital **A**)

apartheid former policy of racial segregation in South Africa (lower-case **a**; not italic; -heid)

Apelles ancient Greek painter (single **p**, double **l**)

Apennines Italian mountain range (single **p**, double **n**)

apéritif alcoholic drink before meal (not italic; acute accent)

apex (plural **apexes** or **apices**)

APEX Advance Purchase Excursion (reduced fare; also **Apex**); Association of Professional, Executive, Clerical, and Computer Staff (former trade union; not **Apex**)

Apex Club Australian business and professional association (not **APEX**)

aplomb (single **p**; **-mb**)

apocalypse prophetic disclosure or event of great importance (lower-case **a**)

Apocalypse in the Vulgate and Douay Bible, the book of Revelation (capital **A**)

Apocrypha, the appendix to Old Testament in some versions of the Bible (capital **A**)

apocryphal of questionable authenticity, or of the Apocrypha (also **Apocryphal** in the sense 'of the Apocrypha')

apogee (single **p**, double **e**)

Apollinaire, Guillaume French poet (single **p**, double **l**, single **n**)

Apollo god in classical mythology, or US spacecraft (single **p**, double **l**)

apologize (also **apologise**; see **-ize/ -ise**)

apophthegm (not **-pth-**; not **-em**; the spelling **apothegm** is not incorrect, but it is less common)

apostasy (not **-acy**)

apostatize (also **apostatise**; see **-ize/ -ise**)

a posteriori involving reasoning from facts or effects to a general principle (two words; not italic; compare **a priori**)

apostle one of the 12 disciples chosen by Christ, or any Christian missionary or ardent supporter of a cause (often **Apostle** in the sense 'disciple chosen by Christ')

Apostles' Creed (capital **A** & **C**; **-s'** not **-'s**)

apostrophe punctuation mark used to indicate possession, as in *the horse's saddle, the twins' birthday, for old times' sake*. It is followed by **s** after singular nouns (whether or not they end in **s**, e.g. *the princess's car*) and irregular plural nouns that do not end in **s** (e.g. *women's clothing*). The following **s** is optional in some set phrases (e.g. *for conscience'(s) sake*) and after some names ending in **s** (e.g. *Dickens'(s) novels*). Note the apostrophe in such phrases as *three days' work* and *in five hours' time*, and the **-'s** in *a book of my father's* (see also **possessive**) and *I object to Jack's using the computer* (see also **-ing**). The apostrophe also indicates a missing letter or letters in contractions such as *haven't* and *'twas*, but is not needed in short forms such as *flu* and *phone*. (Beware of computer software that automatically substitutes an opening quotation mark (see **turned comma**) for the apostrophe at the beginning of words such as *'twas*.) Note that **-'s** is not used to form the plural of words, names, or dates (*videos, Kennedys, the 1950s*), but may be used to form the plural of single letters, as in *mind your p's and q's*. See individual entries for problematic examples and established exceptions in the use of the apostrophe.

apothecaries' weight (lower-case **a** & **w**; apostrophe)

apotheosis (plural **apotheoses**)

appal (double **p**, single **l**)

Appalachian Mountains (double **p**, single **l**; capital **A** & **M**; also **Appalachians**)

appalled, appalling (double **p**, double **l**)

apparatchik (**-tch-**, **-ik**)

apparatus (double **p**, single **r**; plural **apparatuses**)

apparatus criticus textual notes in scholarly edition (not italic)

appeasement (not **-sm-**)

appellation (double **p**, double **l**)

appendicitis (not **-us**)

appendix (plural **appendices**, especially in the sense 'additional material in book', or **appendixes**, especially in the anatomical sense)

appertain (double **p**)

appetizer (also **-iser**; see **-ize/-ise**)

appetizing (also **-ising**; see **-ize/-ise**)

apple pie (two words)

apple-pie bed (one hyphen)

apple-pie order (one hyphen)

appliqué (acute accent)

appliquéd (not **-éed**)

appraise assess value or quality of (compare **apprise** and **apprize**)

apprehend arrest, dread, or understand (compare **comprehend**)

apprise inform (rarely **apprize**; compare **appraise**)

apprize rare variant of **apprise**, or archaic Scottish legal term (compare **appraise**)

appro approval (no full stop)

approx. approximate or approximately (full stop)

APR annual percentage rate (of interest on loan, credit card, etc.; compare **AER**)

Apr. April (full stop)

après-ski social activity after skiing (not italic; grave accent; hyphen)

April Fools' Day (also **April Fool's Day** or **All Fools' Day**)

a priori involving reasoning from a general principle to facts or effects (two words; not italic; compare **a posteriori**)

apropos (one word; no accent; often

followed by *of* when used as a preposition meaning 'with regard to')

Apulia region of Italy (Italian name **Puglia**)

Aqaba port in Jordan (not **-qu-**; the spelling **Akaba** is not incorrect, but it is less common)

Aqaba, Gulf of Middle East (capital **G**; not **-qu-**; the spelling **Gulf of Akaba** is not incorrect, but it is less common)

aquaerobics (also **aquarobics**)

aquarium (plural **aquariums** or **aquaria**)

aquarobics variant of **aquaerobics**

aquavit Scandinavian alcoholic spirit (one word; also **akvavit**)

aqua vitae archaic name for brandy (two words; not italic)

aqueduct (not **aqui-**)

aquilegia flowering plant (lower-case **a** in general use: *Aquilegia* is the genus name)

Aquileia Italian town (**-eia**)

Ar argon (no full stop)

AR Arkansas (US postal code)

Arab member of Middle Eastern people, or breed of horse; also used adjectivally, as in *the Arab nations* (compare **Arabian** and **Arabic**)

Arabia Asian peninsula between Red Sea and Persian Gulf

Arabian of Arabia or the Arabs (compare **Arab** and **Arabic**)

Arabian Nights' Entertainments, The collection of stories (apostrophe; also ***The Thousand and One Nights***)

Arabian Sea part of Indian Ocean (capital **A** & **S**)

Arabic language of the Arabs, or of this language (compare **Arab** and **Arabian**)

Arabic numerals the symbols 0, 1, 2, 3, etc. (the use of lower-case **a** is not incorrect in this context, but capital **A** should be retained when it occurs in close proximity to the phrase

Roman numerals, which always has capital **R**)

arachnid (-ch-)

Arafat hill in Saudi Arabia (single **r**, single **f**; compare **Ararat**)

Arafat, Yasser Palestinian leader (also **Yassir**)

Aragon region of Spain (single **r**)

Araldite trademark for a strong glue (capital **A**)

Aramaean of ancient Syria, or a person from ancient Syria (also **Aramean**)

Aramaic ancient Middle Eastern language, or of this language (-aic)

Aramean variant of **Aramaean**

Aran of Aran Islands, or denoting a type of thick sweater (capital **A**; compare **Arran** and **Arun**)

Aran Islands island group off Ireland (capital **A** & **I**; compare **Arran**)

Ararat extinct volcano in Turkey (compare **Arafat**)

arbiter person empowered to judge, as in *arbiter of fashion* (not -or; compare **arbitrator**)

arbitrary (-ary)

arbitrator person who settles a dispute (not -er; compare **arbiter**)

arbor rotating shaft of tool, or US spelling of **arbour**

Arbor Day (not -our)

arboreal (not -ial)

arboretum (plural **arboreta** or **arboretums**)

arbour leafy glade or bower (**arbor** in US English)

arc curve (compare **ark**)

Arc see **Joan of Arc**

Arcadia department of Greece, or idealized rural setting in poetry (compare **Acadia**)

Arcadian of Arcadia (compare **Acadian**)

Arc de Triomphe monument in Paris, France (capital **A** & **T**)

arced formed an arc (the spelling **arcked** is not incorrect, but it is less common)

arch. archaic; archaism; architecture (full stop)

Archaean division of Precambrian era (-aea-; former name **Archaeozoic**)

archaeology (the spelling **archeology** is not incorrect, but it is less common, even in US English)

archaeopteryx (-aeo-, -yx)

Archaeozoic former name for **Archaean** (-aeo-)

archangel principal angel (lower-case **a** unless part of name)

Archangel Russian port (Russian name **Arkhangelsk**)

archenemy (one word)

archeology less common variant of **archaeology**

Archer, Geoffrey British novelist and former TV news reporter; **Jeffrey** British novelist and former MP

archetypal (not archi-; the variant **archetypical** is less common but not incorrect)

archetype (not archi-)

archetypical less common variant of **archetypal**

archiepiscopal (-ie-)

Archimedean of the ancient Greek mathematician Archimedes (not -ian)

Archimedes' principle (-s' not -s's)

archipelago (plural **archipelagos** or **archipelagoes**)

Archipiélago de Colón Spanish name for **Galápagos Islands** (acute accents; not -pel-)

arcing forming an arc (the spelling **arcking** is not incorrect, but it is less common)

arcked (less common variant of **arced**)

arcking (less common variant of **arcing**)

arctic very cold, or of the Arctic

(lower-case **a**; also **Arctic** in the sense 'of the Arctic')

Arctic, the northernmost regions of the earth (capital **A**)

Arctic Circle (capital **A** & **C**)

arctic fox (lower-case **a**)

arc welding (two words)

Ardoyne district of Belfast (not **the Ardoyne**)

areola pigmented ring around nipple (compare **aureola**)

Arequipa Peruvian city

arête mountain ridge (single **r**; circumflex; not italic)

Argentine of Argentina, or a person from Argentina (also **Argentinian**)

Argentine, the less common name for **Argentina**

Argentinian variant of **Argentine**

argon (symbol **Ar**)

argot slang or jargon (not italic)

arguable (not **-uea-**)

argyle with diamond-shaped pattern (lower-case **a**; not **-yll**)

Argyll and Bute Scottish council area

Argyll and Sutherland Highlanders Scottish regiment

Argyll and the Isles Scottish diocese

Argyllshire former Scottish county

Århus variant of **Aarhus**

Arial typeface (compare **aerial**)

Arian follower of the ancient Greek heretic Arius, or variant of **Arien**, or less common variant of **Aryan**

Arien person born under Aries (also **Arian**)

arise originate or result (compare **rise**)

Aristotelian of the ancient Greek philosopher Aristotle (not **-ean**)

ark vessel (capital **A** in names, e.g. *Noah's Ark* and *the Ark of the Covenant*; compare **arc**)

Arkansas US state

Arkhangelsk Russian name for **Archangel**

armada large number of ships or aircraft (lower-case **a**)

Armada, the fleet sent by Spain against England in 1588 (capital **A**)

armadillo (plural **armadillos**)

Armageddon (capital **A**; double **d**)

Armagh county, district, and town of Northern Ireland (not **-argh**)

armchair (one word)

armed forces (lower-case **a** & **f**)

Armenian of the NW Asian country Armenia (compare **Arminian**)

armful (not **-full**; plural **armfuls**)

armhole (one word)

Armidale Australian town

Arminian of the Dutch theologian Arminius (compare **Armenian**)

Armistice Day November 11 (compare **Remembrance Sunday**)

armorial (not **-our-**)

armour-bearer (hyphen)

armpit (one word)

arm's length (**-'s**; no hyphen in the phrase **at arm's length**, but hyphenated when used before noun, as in *arm's-length negotiations*)

army (sometimes capital **A** with reference to a particular national army, as in *the French Army* or *join the Army*, but the lower-case form is more common, especially in the second example; always capital **A** in names, as in *the Salvation Army* or *the Territorial Army*)

Arnhem Dutch city

Arnhem Land region of Australia

Aron see **Aaron**

arouse elicit or stimulate (compare **rouse**)

arpeggio notes of chord played in rapid succession (not italic; double **g**; plural **arpeggios**)

arquebus (also **harquebus**)

arraign (double **r**; **-aign**)

Arran island off Scotland (compare **Aran** and **Arun**)

arrant utter (compare **errant**)

arras wall hanging (lower-case **a**)

Arras French town

Arrhenius, Svante August Swedish chemist (**-rrh-**)

arriviste unscrupulously ambitious person (not italic; not **-ist**)

arrogate claim or appropriate (compare **abrogate**)

arrondissement administrative subdivision or municipal district in France (not italic; double **r**, double **s**)

arrowhead (one word)

arrowroot (one word)

arsenic (symbol **As**)

ars poetica art of poetry (not italic; not **art**)

art. article (full stop)

Art Deco (capital **A** & **D**)

artefact (also **artifact**)

Artex trademark for a textured coating for ceilings (capital **A**)

artifact variant of **artefact**

artillery (not **-ary**)

artisan (not **-zan**)

artist person with artistic or other expertise

artiste entertainer, as in *music-hall artiste* (use **artist** instead for modern performers)

Art Nouveau (capital **A** & **N**; also *Jugendstil*)

Arts and Crafts movement (capital **A** & **C**, lower-case **m**)

artwork (one word)

Arun English river (compare **Aran** and **Arran**)

Arundel English town (not **-dle** or **-dell**)

Aryan in Nazi ideology, non-Jewish white person (the spelling **Arian** is not incorrect in this sense, but it is less common)

as (do not drop the second **as** in phrases of the following type: *as good as or better than, as old as if not older than*)

As arsenic (no full stop)

AS Anglo-Saxon (see also **AS level**)

asafoetida unpleasant-smelling resin (single **s**; the spelling **asafetida** is not incorrect, but it is less common)

a.s.a.p. as soon as possible

ASBO Anti-Social Behaviour Order (no full stops; plural **ASBOs**)

ascendancy (the spelling **ascendency** is not incorrect, but it is less common)

ascendant (the spelling **ascendent** is not incorrect, but it is less common)

ascendency less common variant of **ascendancy**

ascendent less common variant of **ascendant**

ascender (*typog.*) upper part of letters such as *b*, *d*, or *h*

ascension act of ascending (lower-case **a**)

Ascension passing of Christ into heaven (capital **A**)

ascent upward movement (compare **assent**)

ascetic practising self-denial or religious austerity (compare **acetic** and **aesthetic**)

Ascham, Roger English writer (not **Ask-**)

ASCII American standard code for information interchange (computer code; all capitals; no full stops)

Asclepius Greek god of healing (compare **Aesculapius**)

ASEAN Association of Southeast Asian Nations (no full stops)

as from (use **from** instead where appropriate)

Asgard dwelling place of the gods of Norse mythology (also **Asgarth**)

ash (*typog.*) the character (æ) or (Æ), used in Old English and in the International Phonetic Alphabet. See also **ae**.

Ashanti region of Ghana, or a person from this region

Ashby-de-la-Zouch English town (three hyphens; not **Zouche**)
Ashes, the cricket trophy (capital **A**)
Ashkenazi Jew of German or E European descent (**-i**; plural **Ashkenazim**)
Ashkenazy, Vladimir Soviet-born pianist and conductor (**-y**)
Ashmolean Museum Oxford (capital **A** & **M**; not **-ian**)
Ashton-under-Lyne English town (hyphens; lower-case **u**; not **Lyme**)
ashtray (one word)
Asiatic (use **Asian** instead with reference to people)
A-side more important side of record (hyphen)
as if see **like**
asinine (single **s**)
Asir region of Saudi Arabia
askance (not **-ant**)
ASLEF Associated Society of Locomotive Engineers and Firemen (no full stops; also **Aslef**)
AS level (no hyphen unless used before another noun, as in *AS-level maths*)
ASLIB Association of Information Management (formerly Association of Special Libraries and Information Bureaux; no full stops; also **Aslib**)
asocial withdrawn from or hostile to society (compare **antisocial**, **unsocial**, and **unsociable**)
as of (use **from** instead where appropriate)
Asperger's syndrome (capital **A**; apostrophe)
asphalt (not **ash-**)
asphyxia (**-phy-**)
aspidistra (lower-case **a** in general use: *Aspidistra* is the genus name)
assagai less common variant of **assegai**
assailant (not **-ent**)
assassinate (double **s** twice, single **n**)

assay analysis of impurities in metal or of metal in ore (compare **essay**)
assegai African tree or spear (the spelling **assagai** is not incorrect, but it is less common)
assent agreement (compare **ascent** and **consent**)
assertion positive statement
assertiveness confidence or aggression
assessor (not **-er**)
asset-stripping (hyphen)
assignation secret meeting
assignment task or mission
assimilate (double **s**, single **m**, single **l**)
Assiniboine Canadian river or North American Indian people
Assisi Italian town (double **s** then single **s**)
assistant (not **-ent**)
assize (never **-ise**)
assuage (not **-auge**)
Assuan less common variant of **Aswan**
assume take for granted, undertake, or feign (compare **presume**, which is virtually synonymous in the sense 'take for granted')
assurance financial protection in the event of death (compare **insurance**)
assure convince or promise (compare **ensure**)
Astana capital of Kazakhstan (former name **Akmola**)
astatine (symbol **At**)
asterisk the symbol (*), used to represent an omitted letter (as in *f*** off*), to cross-refer to a footnote, etc.
Asterix cartoon character created by René Goscinny and Albert Uderzo (French spelling **Astérix**, with acute accent)
asthma (**-sth-**)
as though see **like**

Asti spumante (capital **A**, lower-case **s**)

astrakhan fur or cloth with curled pile (lower-case **a**, **-kh-**)

Astrakhan Russian city

astrol. astrology (full stop)

astrology study of the effect of planetary movements on human affairs (compare **astronomy**)

astron. astronomy (full stop)

Astronomer Royal (capital **A** & **R**)

astronomy scientific study of celestial bodies and the universe (compare **astrology**)

Asturias region of Spain

Asunción capital of Paraguay (acute accent)

Aswan Egyptian town (the spelling **Assuan** is not incorrect, but it is less common)

asylum seeker (two words)

asymmetry (single **s**, double **m**)

asymptote (**-mpt-**)

At astatine (no full stop)

Atalanta maiden in Greek mythology (compare **Atlanta**)

Atatürk, Kemal Turkish general and statesman (single **t** twice, diaeresis)

ate past tense of **eat** (compare **eaten**)

atelier artist's studio or workshop (not italic)

Athabaska Canadian lake and river (also **Athabasca**)

atheist person who denies the existence of a Supreme Being (compare **agnostic**)

atheling Anglo-Saxon prince (not **ae-**)

Athena Greek goddess of wisdom (also **Athene** or **Pallas Athena**)

Athenaeum London club, or building in ancient Greece or imperial Rome (not **-neum**)

Atlanta US city (compare **Atalanta**)

Atlantic Ocean (capital **A** & **O**; also **the Atlantic**)

Atlantic Provinces four Canadian provinces: New Brunswick, Nova Scotia, Prince Edward Island, and Newfoundland (see also **Maritime Provinces**)

ATM automated teller machine (cash dispenser)

at. no. atomic number (full stops)

atoll (single **t**, double **l**)

atomize (also **atomise**; see **-ize/-ise**)

attach (not **-atch**)

attaché person on diplomatic mission, or member of embassy staff (not italic; acute accent)

attaché case briefcase (not italic; acute accent; two words)

Attic salt refined incisive wit (capital **A**; also **Attic wit**)

Attila (double **t**, single **l**)

Attlee, Clement British statesman (double **t**, double **e**)

attn attention (no full stops)

attorney (not **-ny**)

Attorney General (two words; lower-case **a** & **g** with reference to law officers of US states)

Atwood, Margaret Canadian writer (not **Att-**)

at. wt. atomic weight (full stops)

Au gold (no full stop; from Latin *aurum*)

aubergine (US, Canadian, and Australian name **eggplant**)

aubrietia (lower-case **a** in general use: *Aubrietia* is the genus name; also **aubretia** or **aubrieta**)

Aubusson French town, or denoting a tapestry or carpet made there (double **s**)

Auchinleck, Sir Claude British field marshal

au contraire on the contrary (italics)

au courant up to date with current affairs (italics)

audio book (two words)

audio frequency (two words)

audiotypist (one word)

audiovisual (one word)

audited, auditing (not -tt-)

Audubon, John US ornithologist and artist (**-dub-**)

au fait informed or expert (italics)

Aufklärung the Enlightenment, especially in Germany (italics; capital **A**; umlaut)

auf Wiedersehen goodbye (italics; capital **W**; not **-sehn**)

Aug. August (full stop)

Augean very dirty (capital **A**; **-gean**)

Augean stables in Greek mythology, stables of King Augeas cleaned by Hercules (capital **A**, lower-case **s**)

auger tool (compare **augur**)

aught anything, as in *for aught I know* (the spelling **ought** is not incorrect in this sense, but it is less common)

au gratin with a browned topping (not italic)

Augsburg (not **-berg**)

augur (as noun) prophet; (as verb) predict, presage, or bode (compare **auger**)

Augustan of the Roman emperor Augustus

Augustine either of two saints (St Augustine of Hippo, one of the Fathers of the Christian Church, or a 6th-century missionary to Britain who became the first archbishop of Canterbury), or a member of religious order

Augustinian of St Augustine of Hippo, or a member of a religious order

auld lang syne old times remembered with affection (lower-case **a**, **l**, & **s**)

'Auld Lang Syne' Scottish song (capital **A**, **L**, & **S**; quotation marks)

Auld Reekie nickname for Edinburgh (capital **A** & **R**)

au naturel naked, or plainly cooked (italics)

Aung San Suu Kyi Burmese politician

auntie aunt (also **aunty**; capital **A** when followed by name)

Auntie informal name for the BBC (capital **A**; not **-ty**)

Aunt Sally fairground game, or target of attack (capital **A** & **S**)

aunty variant of **auntie**

Aunty informal name for the Australian Broadcasting Association (capital **A**; not **-tie**)

au pair foreigner working for family to learn language (not italic; no hyphen, even when used before another noun, as in *au pair girl*)

aural of the ear (compare **oral**)

Aurangzeb Mogul emperor

aureola variant of **aureole** (compare **areola**)

aureole halo (also **aureola**)

au revoir goodbye (italics)

Aurigny French name for **Alderney**

aurochs extinct ancestor of modern cattle (**-s** in singular and plural)

aurora australis southern lights (lower-case **a** twice)

aurora borealis northern lights (lower-case **a** & **b**)

Auschwitz Polish town and Nazi concentration camp (Polish name **Oświęcim** for the town only)

auspicious (**-ci-**)

Aussie informal word for Australian

Austen, Jane English novelist; see also **Chamberlain**

Austin, Herbert British engineer, founder of the Austin Motor Company

Australasia Australia, New Zealand, and neighbouring Pacific islands (compare **Austrasia** and **Austronesia**)

Australian Labor Party (not **Labour**)

australopithecine (lower-case **a**)

Austrasia region of Frankish kingdom in 6th–8th centuries (compare **Australasia**)

Austria European country (German name **Österreich**)

Austria-Hungary former European empire (hyphen, not en dash; not **Austro-**)

Austro-Hungarian of Austria-Hungary (hyphen; not **Austrian-**)

Austronesia the Pacific islands of Indonesia, Melanesia, Micronesia, Polynesia, etc. (compare **Australasia**)

autarchy autocracy or self-government

autarky self-sufficiency

auteur creative film director (not italic; not **-th-**)

author (as noun, may be used for males and females; as verb, use **write** instead where appropriate)

author–date system reference system giving the author's name and year of publication of the relevant source title; in the bibliography, the publication date directly follows the author's name (also **Harvard system**; compare **author–number system** and **author–title system**)

authoress (use **author** instead to avoid offence)

authoritarian demanding strict obedience to authority

authoritative supported by authority or exercising authority

authorize (also **authorise**; see **-ize/-ise**)

Authorized Version English translation of the Bible published in 1611 (also **King James Version**)

author–number system reference system giving the author's name and a number designating the relevant source title, a numbered list being given in the bibliography (also **Vancouver system**; compare **author–date system** and **author–title system**)

author–title system reference system giving the author's name and a short version of the title of the relevant source after the first mention of the full title (compare **author–date system** and **author–number system**)

autism (**au-**)

autobahn German motorway (not italic; lower-case **a**)

Autocue trademark for a television prompting device (capital **A**)

auto-da-fé ceremony or execution of Spanish Inquisition (not italic, hyphens, not **-de-**, acute accent; plural **autos-da-fé**)

autogiro (plural **autogiros**; also **autogyro**)

automatize (also **automatise**; see **-ize/-ise**)

automaton (plural **automata**)

autopista Spanish motorway (not italic)

autoroute French motorway (not italic)

autostrada Italian motorway (not italic)

autumn (**-mn**)

Auvergne region of France (not **the Auvergne**)

auxiliary (single **l**, **-iary**)

AV audiovisual; Authorized Version (of the Bible)

Avalon island paradise of Arthurian legend

avant-garde (as noun) experimental artists, writers, etc.; (as adjective) of the avant-garde (not italic; hyphen)

Ave Avenue (in addresses; no full stop)

Averroës Arab philosopher (also **Averroes**, without diaeresis; Arabic name **ibn-Rushd**)

averse opposed or disinclined, as in *not averse to the idea* (compare **adverse**)

Avestan ancient Iranian language of the sacred writings of Zoroastrianism

aviator (use instead of gender-

specific **airman, airwoman,** or
aviatrix)
aviatrix (use **aviator** or **pilot** instead)
Aviemore Scottish winter sports
resort (**-ie-**)
Avignon French city (**-gn-**)
avocado (plural **avocados**)
Avogadro, Amedeo Italian physicist
Avogadro's constant (**-'s**)
avoid keep out of the way of or
refrain from (compare **evade**)
avoidance/evasion see **tax avoidance**
and **tax evasion**
avoirdupois system of weights (one
word)
await (usually transitive, as in
awaiting your response: compare
wait)
awake (as verb) wake up or become
aware; (as adjective) not asleep
(compare **awaken** and **wake**)
awaken arouse (compare **awake** and
waken)
Awdry, Wilbert Vere British
clergyman and writer (usually
known as **the Rev. W. Awdry**, creator
of Thomas the Tank Engine)
aweigh describing an anchor raised
from the bottom (not **away**)
awe-inspiring (hyphen)
awesome (one word)
awe-stricken (hyphen)
awestruck (one word)
awful (not **awe-**, not **-full**)
awhile for a short time, as in *wait
awhile*
a while a short time, as in *wait for a
while*

awl pointed tool (compare **all**)
AWOL absent without leave
axel skating jump (compare **axle**)
axes plural of **axe** or **axis**
axis line about which something can
rotate or is symmetrical (lower-case
a; plural **axes**)
Axis, the in World War II, the alliance
of Germany, Italy, and Japan (capital
A)
axle shaft on which a wheel revolves
(compare **axel**)
ay ever (also **aye**)
ayatollah Iranian religious leader
(capital **A** when followed by name)
Ayckbourn, Sir Alan English
dramatist
aye yes (also **ay**)
Ayers Rock former name for **Uluru**
(no apostrophe; capital **A** & **R**)
ayin Hebrew letter transliterated by
the special sort (ʿ)
Aylesbury English town (not **Ail-** or
Ayls-)
Ayr Scottish port (compare **Ayre, Air,
Aire,** and **Eyre**)
Ayre, Point of headland in the Isle of
Man (compare **Air, Aire, Ayr,** and
Eyre)
Azerbaijan NW Asian country, or
region of NW Iran
Azerbaijani person from Azerbaijan
(also **Azeri**)
Azores, the three groups of Atlantic
islands (Portuguese name **Açores**)
Azov, Sea of part of Black Sea
Azrael Jewish and Islamic angel of
death (not **As-**)

B

B bel; boron (no full stop)
Ba barium (no full stop)
BA Bachelor of Arts; British Airways
Baader-Meinhof Gang (hyphen may be replaced by en dash; capital **G**)
Baal ancient god (compare **Basle**)
Baalbek Lebanese town (ancient name **Heliopolis**)
baas South African word for **boss** (in the sense 'manager or overseer')
baaskap in South Africa, control of non-Whites by Whites (also **baasskap**)
Baath variant of **Ba'th**
Ba'ath variant of **Ba'th**
Babbitt central character of the novel *Babbitt* by Sinclair Lewis, hence any narrow-minded complacent middle-class person (capital **B** then double **b**, double **t**)
babel confusion of noises or voices (usually lower-case **b**; an allusion to the **Tower of Babel**)
Babel biblical city or the **Tower of Babel** (always capital **B**)
babu Indian title or form of address for men (**-bu**)
baby-boomer (hyphen)
Babygro trademark for an all-in-one garment for babies (capital **B**; not **-ow**)
baby-minder (hyphen)
baby-sit (hyphen)
baby-sitter (hyphen)
Baccalauréat French school-leaving exam (the use of lower-case **b** is less common but not incorrect; acute accent; not **-ate**)
baccalaureate international school-leaving exam equivalent to A level, or university degree of BA, BSc, etc (capital **B** as part of name, as in *International Baccalaureate*)
baccarat card game (double **c**, single **r**)
bacchanalia drunken revelry, or rites associated with the god Bacchus (also **Bacchanalia** in the sense 'rites of Bacchus')
Bach, Johann Christian, Johann Christoph, Johann Sebastian, Karl (or **Carl**) **Philipp Emanuel,** and **Wilhelm Friedemann** German composers (in general texts, the surname alone usually refers to Johann Sebastian Bach)
Bacharach, Burt US composer of popular songs (not **Bert**)
bachelor (not **-tch-**)
bacillus (plural **bacilli**)
backache (one word)
backbencher (one word)
backbreaking (one word)
back burner (two words; chiefly used in the phrase *on the back burner*)
back formation a word coined from another word that is wrongly assumed to be derived from it (e.g. *burgle* from *burglar*), or the process of coining such words

backlash (one word)

backlog (one word)

back matter the parts of a book (e.g. appendices or index) that follow the main text (two words; also **end matter**)

back-pedal (hyphen; single **l**)

back-pedalled, back-pedalling (single **l** in US English)

backsheesh variant of **baksheesh**

backslash the symbol (\ ), used in computing (compare **solidus**)

backstreet (one word)

backup (noun; the verb is **back up**)

backward (adjective, sometimes adverb (see **-ward** and **-wards**); adjectival use to describe a person with learning difficulties may be considered offensive)

backwards (adverb only)

backyard (one word)

baclava variant of **baklava**

BACS Bankers Automated Clearing System (no full stops)

bacteria (plural noun; singular **bacterium**)

bad not good

bade past tense of **bid**, especially in the senses 'utter', 'order', and 'invite' (compare **bid** and **bidden**)

Baden-Powell, Robert, 1st Baron Baden-Powell British general and founder of the Boy Scouts (hyphen)

Baden-Württemberg German state (hyphen; umlaut, double **t**, **-berg**)

bad hair day (no hyphen)

badinage repartee or banter (not italic)

Baedeker travel guidebook (capital **B**)

Baedeker, Karl German publisher of travel guidebooks

Baffin Island Canada (capital **B** & **I**)

BAFTA British Academy of Film and Television Arts, or award for achievement in cinema or television (no full stops; plural **BAFTAs**)

bagatelle (single **g**, single **t**, double **l**)

Bagdad less common variant of **Baghdad**

Bagehot, Walter English economist and journalist

bagel ring-shaped bread roll (**-el**; also **beigel**)

Baghdad capital of Iraq (the spelling **Bagdad** is not incorrect, but it is less common)

baguette French stick loaf (**-gu-**, double **t**)

Baha'i Faith religious system (apostrophe, capital **B** & **F**; also **Baha'ism**)

Baha'ism another name for **Baha'i Faith**, not used by members of the religion

Bahamas, the Caribbean island group (also **Bahama Islands**)

Bahamian of the Bahamas, or a person from the Bahamas

Bahasa Indonesia official language of Indonesia

Bahrain Middle Eastern sheikhdom (**h** before **r**; also **Bahrein**)

bail money paid as security to release person from custody, or bar placed on cricket stumps (compare **bale**; see also **bail out**)

bailey outer wall or court of castle (lower-case **b**, but see also **Old Bailey**; compare **bailie**)

Bailey, David British photographer (compare **Baillie**)

Bailey bridge temporary bridge made of prefabricated panels (capital **B** then lower-case **b**)

bailie Scottish magistrate (single **l**; compare **bailey**)

bailiwick bailiff's area of jurisdiction (single **l**; capital **B** as part of name, as in **Bailiwick of Guernsey**)

bailiff landlord's agent or officer serving writ (single **l**, double **f**)

Baillie, Dame Isobel British soprano (double **l**; compare **Bailey**)

bail out (also **bale out** in the senses 'remove water from boat', 'jump from aircraft', and 'help out of a predicament', but note that the sense 'release from custody by paying security' can only be spelt **bail out**)

bain-marie cooking or warming vessel (italics; plural *bains-marie*)

Bairam Muslim festival

Baisakhi Sikh festival

bait food used to attract fish, birds, etc., or temptation (compare **bate**)

baited fitted with bait, teased, or tempted (compare **bated**)

Bakelite trademark for resin used to make plastic ware (capital **B**)

Bakewell tart (capital **B**)

baklava Middle Eastern cake (also **baclava**)

baksheesh money given as tip (also **backsheesh**)

balaclava close-fitting hood (not -klava; also **balaclava helmet**; the use of capital **B** is less common but not incorrect in this sense)

Balaklava Ukrainian port, scene of battle in Crimean War (also **Balaclava**)

balalaika Russian musical instrument (single **l** twice, -aik-)

balanceable (**e** after **c**)

Balboa Panamanian port (-oa)

bale bundle (compare **bail**)

Bâle French name for **Basle**

Balearic Islands Mediterranean island group including Majorca, Minorca, and Ibiza (Spanish name **Baleares**)

baleful menacing, as in *a baleful stare* (compare **baneful**)

bale out variant of **bail out** in the senses 'remove water from boat', 'jump from aircraft', and 'help out of a predicament'

Bali Indonesian island

balk (as verb) stop short, thwart, or avoid deliberately; (as noun) timber beam or deceptive motion in sport (also **baulk** in all senses)

Balkan States the European countries of the former Yugoslavia, Romania, Bulgaria, Albania, Greece, and part of Turkey

ball round object, or dance (compare **bawl**)

ballad narrative song or poem

ballade verse form or instrumental composition

Ballarat Australian town

ball bearing (two words)

ballet dancer (two words)

ball game used in the phrase *a whole new ball game* (two words; compare **ballpark**)

Balliol College Oxford (double **l** then single **l** in first word)

ballon d'essai project or policy put forward experimentally to gauge reactions (not italic; single **o**; plural **ballons d'essai**)

balloted, balloting (not -tt-)

ballpark used in the phrases *in the right ballpark, a ballpark figure*, etc (one word; compare **ball game**)

ballpoint (one word; also **ballpoint pen**)

ballroom (one word)

Balmoral royal residence in Scotland (single **l** twice)

balmy mild or soothing, or less common variant of **barmy**

Balochistan variant of **Baluchistan**

baloney nonsense (also **boloney**)

Baluchistan province of Pakistan, or mountainous region in Pakistan and Iran (also **Balochistan**)

baluster post supporting rail (compare **banisters**)

Balzac, Honoré de French writer

Bamberg German town (not -burg)

Bamburgh Castle England (not -borough or -brough)

Banaras variant of **Benares**

bandanna (also **bandana**)

Bandaranaike, Sirimavo Sri Lankan stateswoman

B & B bed and breakfast (spaces around ampersand)

band names (for names of rock groups and bands, e.g. *the Beatles*, use lower-case **t**, not **The**)

B&Q do-it-yourself store (no spaces around ampersand)

baneful destructive or fatal (compare **baleful**)

Banff Scottish town or Canadian town (double **f**)

Bangalore Indian city

Bangkok capital of Thailand (Thai name **Krung Thep**)

Bangladesh S Asian country (one word; see also **Pakistan**)

banian variant of **banyan**

banisters railing beside stairs (also **bannisters**; compare **baluster**)

banjo (plural **banjos**)

bank holiday (capital **B** & **H** in names, e.g. *Bank Holiday Monday*)

banknote (one word)

Bank of England (capital **B**)

bannisters variant of **banisters**

banns formal public announcement of intended marriage (the spelling **bans** is not incorrect, but it is less common)

banquet lavish meal (compare **banquette**)

banqueted, banqueting (not -tt-)

banquette upholstered bench (compare **banquet**)

bans plural of **ban**, or less common variant of **banns**

banshee (-ee)

banyan (also **banian**)

banzai Japanese battle cry or salutation (not italic)

Baptist member of Christian sect, or denoting this sect (capital **B**)

baptistry (also **baptistery**)

baptize (also **baptise**; see -ize/-ise)

Bar, the barristers or their profession, as in *called to the Bar* (capital **B**)

Bar. Baruch (full stop; not italic)

Barbadian of Barbados, or a person from Barbados

Barbados Caribbean island (not -oes)

barbarize (also **barbarise**; see -ize/-ise)

Barbary region of Africa (not -ery)

Barbary ape (capital **B**)

barbecue (not -que)

barbecuing (not -ueing)

Barbirolli, Sir John English conductor

Barbour trademark for waterproof waxed jacket (capital **B**)

barcarole (also **barcarolle**)

BArch Bachelor of Architecture

Barclays banking and finance company (no apostrophe)

bar code (two words)

Barcoo River Australia

bard poet (lower-case **b**)

Bard, the William Shakespeare (capital **B**; also **the Bard of Avon**)

bare (as verb) expose; (as adjective) naked (compare **bear**)

Barenboim, Daniel Israeli pianist and conductor

Barents Sea part of Arctic Ocean (capital **B** & **S**; not -ent's or -entz)

bargepole (one word)

barium (symbol **Ba**)

bark dog's cry, outer layer of tree trunk, or less common variant of **barque**

barmaid see **bartender**

barman see **bartender**

Bar Mitzvah ceremony for Jewish boy attaining religious majority (two words; the use of lower-case **b** & **m** is less common but not incorrect; compare **Bat Mitzvah**)

barmy mad (the spelling **balmy** is not incorrect in this sense, but it is less common)

Barnard, Christiaan South African surgeon (not **Christian**)

Barnardo, Dr Thomas John British philanthropist

Barnardo's children's charity (apostrophe; former name **Dr Barnardo's**)

Barnstaple English town (not **-able**)

Barolo Italian wine (single **r**, single **l**; the use of lower-case **b** is less common but not incorrect)

baron male member of nobility (compare **barren**; for capitalization see **titles of people**)

baroness female member of nobility or wife of baron

baronet person ranking below baron

Barons Court London (no apostrophe)

baroque highly ornamented style of art, architecture, or music (also **Baroque**)

barque sailing vessel (the spelling **bark** is not incorrect in this sense, but it is less common)

barracuda (double **r**, single **c**)

barratry legal term (the spelling **barretry** is not incorrect, but it is less common)

Barrault, Jean-Louis French actor and director

barre rail used in ballet (italics)

barré technique used in playing guitar chords (not italic; acute accent)

barrel (double **r**, single **l**)

barrelled, barrelling (single **l** in US English)

barren sterile or unproductive (compare **baron**)

barretry less common variant of **barratry**

Barrie, Sir James Matthew Scottish writer (not **Barry**)

barrister (double **r**)

Barrow-in-Furness English town (hyphens)

Barry see **du Barry**

Bart. Baronet (full stop)

bartender (one word; may be used instead of gender-specific **barmaid** or **barman**)

Barth, Karl Swiss theologian

Barthes, Roland French writer and critic

Bartók, Béla Hungarian composer (acute accents)

Bartolommeo, Fra Italian painter (single **l**, double **m**)

Bart's St Bartholomew's Hospital, London (apostrophe)

Baruch book of the Apocrypha (not italic; abbreviation **Bar.**)

base bottom (compare **bass**)

Basel variant of **Basle**

bases plural of **base** or **basis**

BASIC computer programming language (no full stops; also **Basic**)

Baskerville typeface

Basle Swiss city and canton (also **Basel**, French name **Bâle**; compare **Baal**)

Bas Mitzvah variant of **Bat Mitzvah**

basque women's bodice (lower-case **b**)

Basque member of people living in Spain and France (capital **B**)

Basra Iraqi port (the spelling **Basrah** is not incorrect, but it is less common)

bas-relief low relief (also **basso-rilievo**; hyphen; not italic)

Bas-Rhin French department (not **-Rhine**)

bass low voice or sound (compare **base**)

bassinet wickerwork cradle (double **s**, not **-ette**)

basso-rilievo variant of **bas-relief**

Bass Strait channel between mainland Australia and Tasmania (capital **B** & **S**)

Bastille French fortress and former prison (**-ille**)

Bastille Day July 14 (capital **B** & **D**)

bastinado beating on soles of feet (not italic; plural **bastinadoes**)

Basutoland former name for **Lesotho**

Batavia former name for **Jakarta**

bate bad temper (compare **bait**)

bated used in the phrase *with bated breath* (compare **baited**)

bath wash in bath (compare **bathe**)

Ba'th Arab political party (also **Ba'ath** or **Baath**)

Bath and Wells English diocese

bath bun (lower-case **b**)

Bath chair (capital **B**)

bath cube (two words)

bathe swim or cleanse (compare **bath**)

Bath Oliver (capital **B** & **O**)

bathos sudden ludicrous descent in style (compare **pathos**)

bathrobe (one word)

Bathurst Australian city or Canadian port

batik (the spelling **battik** is not incorrect, but it is less common)

Bat Mitzvah ceremony for Jewish girl attaining religious majority (two words; the use of lower-case **b** & **m** is less common but not incorrect; also **Bas Mitzvah**; compare **Bar Mitzvah**)

baton stick used by conductor, police officer, etc. (compare **batten**)

Baton Rouge US city

battalion (double **t**, single **l**)

batten (as noun) strip of wood; (as verb) strengthen or secure with battens, as in *batten down the hatches*, or thrive (compare **baton**)

Battenberg German village (not **-burg**)

Battenburg cake (capital **B**; not **-berg**)

battened, battening (not **-nn-**)

batter (*typog.*) damaged piece of type

Battersea Dogs' Home (**-s'** not **-'s**)

battik less common variant of **batik**

Battle (capital **B** for names of specific battles, as in *the Battle of Hastings*)

battle-axe (hyphen)

battle cry (two words)

battledress (one word)

battlefield (one word)

battleground (one word)

battleship (one word)

Batum city in Georgia, Asia (also **Batumi**)

baud unit used in computing (not **-aw-**)

Baudelaire, Charles Pierre French poet (not **Beau-**)

Bauhaus German school of architecture (capital **B**; **-au-** twice)

baulk billiards term, or variant of **balk** in all its senses

Bavaria German state (German name **Bayern**)

bawl shout (compare **ball**)

Bayern German name for **Bavaria**

Bayeux tapestry (capital **B**, lower-case **t**)

Bayreuth German city, site of annual Wagner festival (compare **Beirut**)

bazaar market or fair (also **bazar**; compare **bizarre**)

BBC British Broadcasting Corporation (note that there is no space before the number in the channel names **BBC1**, **BBC2**, etc.)

B.C. before Christ (also **BC**; usually printed or typeset in small capitals). The abbreviation is used for dates before the birth of Christ (compare **A.D.**; see also **BCE**). It always follows the year number or century, as in *647 B.C.*, *the 5th century B.C.* Note that in year spans B.C. the second number cannot be unambiguously
. abbreviated: 258–236 B.C. is a period of 22 years; 258–36 B.C. is a period of 222 years.

BCE Before Common Era (used instead of **B.C.**, e.g. in non-Christian contexts)

BCG bacille Calmette-Guérin (antituberculosis vaccine or vaccination)

BCh Bachelor of Surgery (from Latin *Baccalaureus Chirurgiae*)

BCL Bachelor of Civil Law

BCom Bachelor of Commerce

BD Bachelor of Divinity

BDS Bachelor of Dental Surgery

Be beryllium (no full stop)

BE Bachelor of Education; Bachelor of Engineering

beach shore (compare **beech**)

Beach-la-Mar creole language spoken in Fiji and Vanuatu (capital **B** & **M**; also **Biche-la-mar**)

be-all and end-all (two hyphens)

bean edible seed or pod (compare **been**)

bean sprout (two words)

bear (as verb) support, bring, or tolerate; (as noun) large mammal, or stock- exchange speculator (compare **bare**)

bear hug (two words)

Béarnaise rich sauce (not italic; capital **B**, acute accent)

bearskin (one word)

beat past tense of beat (in standard English, used as past participle in adjectival sense 'exhausted' only)

beaten past participle of **beat**

Beatles, the British rock group (-ea-; not **The**)

beatnik (-ik)

Beaton, Cecil British photographer (compare **Beeton**)

Beatrix, Queen Dutch monarch (not -ice)

beau sweetheart or dandy (plural **beaux** or **beaus**; compare **bow**)

Beaufort scale (capital **B**, lower-case **s**; see Appendix iv)

Beaujolais French wine (the spelling **beaujolais**, with lower-case **b**, is less common but not incorrect)

Beaulieu English village, site of Lord Montagu's house and the National Motor Museum

beau monde world of fashionable society (not italic)

Beaune French wine (capital **B**)

beautician (-eau-, -cian)

beautiful (-eau-, single **l**)

Beauvoir, Simone de French writer

beaux-arts fine arts (not italic; hyphen)

beaver amphibious rodent, or part of medieval helmet (lower-case **b**)

Beaver member of the youngest group of boys in the Scout Association (capital **B**; see also **Cub**)

became past tense of **become** (compare **become**)

because of (may be used instead of **due to** where appropriate, to avoid controversy)

béchamel white sauce (not italic; lower-case **b**, acute accent)

bêche-de-mer another name for **trepang** (circumflex, hyphens; plural **bêches-de-mer**)

Bechstein, Karl German piano maker

Bechuanaland former name for **Botswana**

Becket, St Thomas à English martyr (also **St Thomas Becket**)

Beckett, Samuel Irish writer

become past participle of **become** (compare **became**)

becquerel unit of radioactivity (lower-case **b**, -cqu-)

Becquerel, Antoine Henri French physicist

bed (*typog.*) flat part of printing press on which the type is placed

BEd Bachelor of Education

bed-blocking (hyphen)

bedbug (one word)

Bede, St English monk and historian (known as **the Venerable Bede**)

Bedouin member of nomadic Arab

people (the spelling **Beduin** is not incorrect, but it is less common)

bedpan (one word)

bedridden (no hyphen)

bedsit (one word)

Beduin less common variant of **Bedouin**

bed-wetting (hyphen)

beech tree (compare **beach**)

beefburger another name for **hamburger**

beefsteak (one word)

beef stroganoff (lower-case **s**, **-gan-**, **-off**)

beehive (one word)

been past participle of **be** (compare **bean**)

beer alcoholic drink (compare **bier**)

beestings cow's first milk after giving birth (also **biestings**)

beeswax (one word)

Beethoven, Ludwig van German composer (not **von**)

beetle insect (compare **betel**)

Beeton, Isabella Mary British cookery writer (known as **Mrs Beeton**; compare **Beaton**)

befitted, befitting (double **t**)

began past tense of **begin** (compare **begun**)

beggar (not **-er**)

Beggar's Opera, The opera by John Gay (**-'s** not **-s'**)

Begin, Menachem Israeli statesman

beg the question (use **raise the question** instead in the context of a question that needs to be asked)

beguile (**-gui-**)

begun past participle of **begin** (compare **began**)

behavioural (**-or-** in US English)

behemoth (not **-him-**)

Behn, Aphra English writer

beholden indebted or obliged (not **-ing**)

behove be necessary or fitting for (**-oove** in US English)

Behring, Emil von German bacteriologist (not **Ber-**)

beige (**-ei-**)

beigel variant of **bagel**

Beijing capital of China (former name **Peking**)

Beirut capital of Lebanon (the spelling **Beyrouth** is less common but not incorrect; compare **Bayreuth**)

bel unit of sound (compare **bell** and **belle**)

Bel god of the earth in Babylonian and Assyrian mythology, or abbreviation for Bel and the Dragon

Bel and the Dragon book of the Apocrypha (not italic; abbreviation **Bel**)

Belarus European country (also **Byelorussia** or **Belorussia**)

Belarussian (as adjective) of Belarus; (as noun) the language of Belarus or a person from Belarus (also **Belarusian**)

bel canto style of singing (not italic; two words)

beleaguer (**-guer**)

Belgian Congo a former name of **Democratic Republic of Congo**

Belgrade capital of Serbia and Montenegro (Serbo-Croat name **Beograd**)

beliefs plural of noun **belief** (compare **believes**)

believable (not **-eable**)

believes third person present tense of **believe** (compare **beliefs**)

Belisha beacon (capital **B** then lower-case **b**)

Belitung another name for **Billiton**

Belize Central American country (former name **British Honduras**)

bell ringing instrument or device (compare **belle** and **bel**)

belladonna deadly nightshade (one word)

belle beautiful woman (compare **bell** and **bel**)

belle époque comfortable period before World War I (italics; acute accent)

Belle Isle, Strait of channel between Labrador and Newfoundland (not hyphenated; not **Île**; capital **S**)

belles-lettres literary works of aesthetic value (hyphen; not italic)

bellow shout or roar (compare **below**)

bell-ringer (hyphen)

Bell's whisky (apostrophe)

bellwether (one word; **-weth-**)

Belorussia another name for **Belarus**

below under (compare **bellow**)

Belshazzar biblical king

Beltane Celtic festival on May 1 (not **-ain**)

belvedere (all the vowels are **e**'s)

Benares former name for **Varanasi** (also **Banaras**)

benchmark (one word)

Ben Day process in printing, method of adding shading or detail to drawings

Bendigo Australian city

Benedick character in Shakespeare's *Much Ado about Nothing*

Benedict, St Italian monk

benefactor (not **-ni-**, not **-er**)

beneficent charitable or generous (compare **beneficial** and **benevolent**; not **-ni-**)

beneficial advantageous (compare **beneficent**)

benefited, benefiting (single **t**)

Benelux the countries of Belgium, the Netherlands, and Luxembourg

Benenden School English public school for girls, in Kent (**-en-** three times)

Benét, Stephen Vincent US poet and novelist (single **n** & **t**, acute accent)

Benetton clothing company (single **n**, double **t**)

benevolent kindly or charitable (compare **beneficent** and **benign**)

BEng Bachelor of Engineering

Bengali (as noun) member of people of Bangladesh and West Bengal, or their language; (as adjective) of Bengal, Bengali, or the Bengalis

Benghazi Libyan port (also **Bengasi**)

Ben-Gurion, David Israeli statesman (hyphen)

Ben-Hur novel by Lew Wallace and film (hyphen)

benign not malignant, as in *a benign tumour*, or kindly (compare **benevolent**)

Benin African country (single **n** twice; former name **Dahomey**)

Bennett, Alan British writer and actor; **Arnold** British novelist; **Richard Rodney** British composer (double **n**, double **t**)

Bentham, Jeremy British philosopher

benzene liquid used as a solvent and insecticide

benzine mixture of hydrocarbon constituents of petroleum

Beograd Serbo-Croat name for **Belgrade**

Beowulf Old English poem (not **-wolf**)

Berber member of N African Muslim people, or their language

Berchtesgaden German town, site of Hitler's mountain retreat (not **-garden**)

bereaved deprived of somebody through death, as in *the bereaved parents*

bereft deprived of something abstract, as in *bereft of hope*

beret hat (compare **berry**)

berg short for **iceberg**, or South African word for **mountain** (compare **burg**)

Bergerac French town (see also **Cyrano de Bergerac**)

Bergman, Ingmar Swedish film director; **Ingrid** Swedish actress
beriberi (one word)
Bering Sea part of Pacific Ocean (not **Behr-**)
Bering Strait channel between Alaska and Russia (not **Behr-**)
berk fool (the spelling **burk** is not incorrect, but it is less common)
Berkeley US city
Berkeley Square London
berkelium (symbol **Bk**)
Berkhamsted English town (not **-hamp-**, not **-stead**)
Berkshire English county
Bermuda shorts (capital **B**)
Bermuda Triangle (capital **B & T**)
Bermudian of Bermuda, or person from Bermuda (not **-dan**)
Bern capital of Switzerland (French name **Berne**)
Bernabéu Spanish football stadium, home ground of Real Madrid (acute accent; full name **Santiago Bernabéu Stadium**)
Bernadette of Lourdes, St French peasant girl who had visions of Virgin Mary (not **-nard-**; original name **Marie Bernarde Soubirous**)
Bernard, Claude French physiologist; **St** French monk (see also **St Bernard**)
Bernard of Clairvaux, St French abbot and theologian
Berne French name for **Bern**
Berne Convention agreement concerning copyright (not **Bern**)
Bernhardt, Sarah French actress
Bernoulli, Daniel Swiss mathematician and physicist; **Jacques** and **Jean** Swiss mathematicians (not **-oui-**)
berretta less common variant of **biretta**
berry fruit (compare **beret** and **bury**)
berserk (**s** not **z**)

berth bed or mooring (compare **birth**)
Berwick-upon-Tweed English town (hyphens; lower-case **u**; not **-on-**)
beryllium (symbol **Be**)
Besançon French city (cedilla)
beside next to or at the side of
besides apart from, moreover, or as well
besiege (**-ie-**)
besotted (single **s**, double **t**)
Bessarabia region of Europe
Bessemer process (capital **B**, lower-case **p**)
bestseller (no hyphen)
beta-blocker (hyphen)
beta-test (hyphen for both noun and verb)
betatron (one word)
betel Asian plant (compare **beetle**)
Betelgeuse star (the spelling **Betelgeux** is not incorrect, but it is less common)
bête noire pet hate (italics; circumflex)
Betjeman, Sir John English poet
better person who bets (not **-or**)
between (use instead of **among** when only two are involved, as in *agreement between her parents*)
Betws-y-Coed Welsh village
Bevan, Aneurin British statesman and minister of health (compare **Bevin**)
bevel (single **l**)
bevelled, bevelling (single **l** in US English)
beverage drink
Beveridge, William Henry, 1st Baron Beveridge British economist
Beverley English town (**-ley**)
Beverly Hills USA (**-ly**)
Bevin, Ernest British statesman and minister of labour (compare **Bevan**)
bevvy drink
bevy flock

Bewick, Thomas English wood engraver

Bexleyheath Greater London (one word)

Beyrouth less common variant of **Beirut**

BFPO British Forces Post Office

Bh bohrium (no full stop)

Bhagavad-Gita sacred Hindu text, part of the ***Mahabharata*** (the spelling ***Bhagavadgita*** is not incorrect, but it is less common)

bhaji Indian vegetable dish (**bh-**, **-ji**)

bhangra Asian pop music (**bh-**)

Bhopal Indian city

bhp brake horsepower

Bhs British Home Stores (lower-case **h** & **s**)

Bhutto, Benazir Pakistani stateswoman

bi- two, as in *bifocal* (never attached with hyphen; compare **by-**)

Bi bismuth (no full stop)

Biafra region of Nigeria

biannual occurring twice a year (compare **biennial**)

Biarritz French resort

biased, biasing (also **biassed, biassing**)

bible an authoritative text, as in *the sailors' bible* (lower-case **b**)

Bible the sacred writings of Christianity (capital **B**; not italic)

Bible Belt (capital **B** twice)

biblical of the Bible (lower-case **b**)

biblical references (use full form or standard abbreviation of the Bible book, not italic; chapter and verse numbers are usually separated by a colon)

bibliography list of works consulted or cited, printed at the end of a book before the index. References usually follow a fixed pattern, according to the publisher's house style, typically: name of author or editor, *title of book* (place of publication, year of publication).

biblio page another name for **imprint page**

Bibliothèque nationale national library of French-speaking country (capital **B**, lower-case **n**; grave accent)

bicentenary (as noun) 200th anniversary; (as adjective) marking a bicentenary or occurring every 200 years (**bicentennial** for both noun and adjective in US English)

biceps (same form for singular and plural)

Biche-la-mar variant of **Beach-la-Mar** (lower-case **l** & **m**)

bid past tense and past participle of **bid**, especially in the senses 'offer' and 'declare (expected number of tricks in bridge)' (compare **bade** and **bidden**)

bidden past participle of **bid**, especially in the senses 'utter', 'order', and 'invite', except in fixed phrases such as *do as you are bid* (compare **bid** and **bade**)

biennial occurring every two years (compare **biannual**)

bier platform or stand for coffin or corpse (compare **beer**)

Bierce, Ambrose US writer

biestings variant of **beestings**

Big Apple, the informal name for New York City (capital **B** & **A**)

big bang (no hyphen unless used before another noun, as in *big-bang theory*)

Big Brother person or organization with total control (capital **B** twice)

bigheaded (no hyphen)

big-hearted (hyphen)

bight large bay (compare **bite** and **byte**)

Bight, the informal name for **Great Australian Bight**

bigoted (not **-tt-**)

bijou small and elegant (not italic)

Bilbao Spanish port (**-ao**)

bilberry (single **l**)

Bildungsroman novel about person's formative years (italics; capital *B*)

Billericay English town

billet-doux love letter (not italic; hyphen; plural **billets-doux**)

billeted, billeting (not **-tt-**)

billiard ball (not **-ards**)

billiard table not **-ards**)

billion one thousand million (formerly, one million million; compare **trillion**)

Billiton Indonesian island (also **Belitung**)

bill of rights any summary of basic human rights (lower-case **b** & **r**)

Bill of Rights English (1689), US (1791), or Canadian (1960) statute guaranteeing human rights and liberty (capital **B** & **R**)

Billy Elliot film (not *Eliot* or *Elliott*)

biltong (single **l**)

bimbo (plural **bimbos** or **bimboes**)

bimonthly every two months or twice a month (replace with synonym or paraphrase to avoid ambiguity)

bin Laden, Osama Saudi Arabian terrorist (lower-case **b**; the spellings **Ladin** and **Usama** are not incorrect, but both are less common)

binnacle (double **n**)

binoculars (single **n**)

binomial (also **binominal**) denoting the system of nomenclature in which plants, animals, and other organisms have two Latin names, as in *Parus caeruleus* (bluetit). Both are italic; the first is the genus, with a capital initial, and the second is the species, with a lower-case initial. The genus name is sometimes abbreviated, as in *E. coli* (the bacterium *Escherichia coli*). See also **taxonomic names.**

Binyon, Laurence British poet

biodegradable (not **-eable**)

biological nomenclature see **binomial** and **taxonomic names**

birdbath (one word)

birdcage (one word)

Birds Eye frozen food company (no apostrophe, no hyphen)

bird's-eye view (apostrophe, one hyphen)

birdsong (one word)

bird-watcher (hyphen)

biretta cap worn by Roman Catholic priests, bishops, and cardinals (the spelling **berretta** is not incorrect, but it is less common)

Biro trademark for a ballpoint pen (capital **B**)

birth being born (compare **berth**)

birth control (two words)

birthplace (one word)

birth rate (two words)

birthright (one word)

biriani variant of **biryani**

Birtwistle, Sir Harrison English composer (not **-whistle**)

biryani Indian dish (also **biriani**)

bis twice or encore (not italic)

BIS Bank for International Settlements

bisect (single **s**)

Bishop Auckland English town (not **Bishop's**)

Bishopbriggs Glasgow (**-pbr-**, double **g**)

Bishopsgate London (one word)

Bishop's Stortford English town (**-'s**)

Bishop's Waltham English town (**-'s**)

Bismarck, Prince Otto von German statesman (**-ck**)

Bismillah Muslim blessing used in Islam, literally meaning 'in the name of God' (capital **B**, **-ah**)

bismuth (symbol **Bi**)

bison (plural **bison**)

bisque soup, colour, or pottery (not italic)

bissextile denoting a leap year (double **s**)

bistro (not italic; plural **bistros**)

bit past tense of **bite**, small amount, or binary digit in computing (compare **bitten** and **byte**)

bite grip or cut with teeth (compare **bight** and **byte**)

bitten past participle of **bite** (compare **bit**)

bivouac (not **-ck**)

bivouacked, bivouacking (**-ck-**)

biweekly every two weeks or twice a week (replace with synonym or paraphrase to avoid ambiguity)

bizarre strange (compare **bazaar**)

Bizet, Georges French composer

Bk berkelium (no full stop)

BL Bachelor of Law; Bachelor of Letters; British Library

black colour of coal (lower-case **b**)

Black of a dark-skinned race (capital **B**; avoid noun use: replace with more specific term, such as **Afro-Caribbean**, **African-American**, or **Aborigine**)

black-and-white (hyphenated with reference to photographs, films, etc.; no hyphens in the phrase *in black and white* meaning 'in print or writing')

Black Country central England (capital **B** & **C**)

Black Death plague (capital **B** & **D**)

blackfly plant pest (one word)

Black Forest, the hilly wooded region of Germany (capital **B** & **F**; German name **Schwarzwald**)

black hole astronomy term (lower-case **b** & **h**)

Black Hole of Calcutta dungeon (capital **B** & **H**)

black letter (*typog.*) another name for **Gothic** (the typeface)

blacklist (one word)

Black Maria police van (capital **B** & **M**)

Blackmore, R(ichard) D(oddridge) English novelist (not **-moor**)

blackout (noun; the verb is **black out**)

Black Rod officer of House of Lords (capital **B** & **R**)

Blackshirt member of fascist organization (capital **B**; one word)

black spot (two words)

blad promotional booklet of sample pages from forthcoming publication

Blaenau Ffestiniog Welsh town (**Ffe-**; compare **Festiniog Railway**)

Blairgowrie Scottish town

blamable (also **blameable**)

blanch plunge food in boiling water, or make or become white or pale (compare **blench**)

blancmange jelly-like dessert (**-ncm-**)

blanketed, blanketing (not **-tt-**)

Blasco Ibáñez, Vicente Spanish novelist (acute accent, tilde)

blasé indifferent (not italic; acute accent)

blastoff (noun; the verb is **blast off**)

blatant glaringly conspicuous, as in *a blatant lie* (compare **flagrant**)

bleed (*typog.*) print so that text or illustrations run off the trimmed page, or the resulting printed matter, page, etc.

blench quail, or make or become white or pale (compare **blanch**)

Blenheim German village, site of battle; or English palace, birthplace of Sir Winston Churchill

Blériot, Louis French aviator (acute accent, single **r**)

blesbok antelope (the spelling **blesbuck** is not incorrect, but it is less common)

blessed[1] past tense and past participle of **bless** (the spelling **blest** is not incorrect, but it is less common)

blessed[2] holy (not **blest**)

blest less common variant of **blessed¹**

blew past tense of **blow** (compare **blown** and **blue**)

Blighty England (the spelling **blighty**, with lower-case **b**, is less common but not incorrect)

blind (*typog.*) another name for **pilcrow**

blind, the (use **blind people** instead to avoid offence)

BLit Bachelor of Literature

BLitt Bachelor of Letters (from Latin *Baccalaureus Litterarum*)

blitz sustained or intensive attack (lower-case **b**)

Blitz, the German bombing of the UK in World War II (capital **B**)

blitzkrieg intensive military attack (**-ie-**)

Blixen, Karen Danish author (pen name **Isak Dinesen**)

BLL Bachelor of Laws

bloc group of people or countries with common interest (compare **block**)

Bloch, Ernest US composer (**-ch**)

block solid piece of wood or stone, large building, or group of buildings (compare **bloc**)

Bloc Quebecois Canadian political party (**Bloc Québécois**, with acute accents, in French contexts)

Bloemfontein South African city (**-oe-**, **-ein**)

blokeish (also **blokish**)

blond describing fair hair in males, or denoting a man with blond hair

blonde describing fair hair in females, or denoting a woman with blonde hair

blood poisoning (two words)

blood sport (two words)

bloodstain (one word)

bloodstained (one word)

bloodstream (one word)

blood vessel (two words)

Bloody Mary tomato juice and vodka, or nickname of **Mary I** (capital **B** & **M**)

Bloomingdale's US department store (apostrophe)

Bloomsbury Group group of writers and artists of early 20th century (capital **B** & **G**)

blow-dry (hyphen for both verb and noun)

blowed past participle of **blow** in the sense 'damn', as in *I'll be blowed!* (compare **blown**)

blow-in (noun; the verb is **blow in**)

blown past participle of **blow** in all senses except 'damn' (compare **blew** and **blowed**)

blowout (noun; the verb is **blow out**)

blowsy slovenly or sluttish (not **-ou-**; also **blowzy**)

blow-up (noun; the verb is **blow up**)

blowzy variant of **blowsy**

Blücher, Gebhard Leberecht von Prussian field marshal (umlaut)

blue colour of sky (compare **blew**)

blue-chip company (one hyphen)

blue-collar of manual industrial workers (hyphen; compare **white-collar**)

blue-eyed boy (one hyphen)

blueing (also **bluing**)

blueish variant of **bluish**

blueprint (one word)

bluey (as adjective) bluish; (as noun) Australian informal word for a blanket, a swagman's bundle, or a red-haired person (**-ey**; also **Bluey** in the sense 'red-haired person')

bluing variant of **blueing**

bluish (also **blueish**)

blurb promotional text on book jacket

blush go red in the face because of embarrassment, modesty, or similar emotion (compare **flush**)

Blu-Tack trademark for malleable material used to stick posters to walls (capital **B** & **T**, hyphen, not **Blue-**)

Blvd Boulevard (in addresses; no full stop)

Blyth English town (not **-the**)

Blyth, Sir Chay British yachtsman (not **-the**)

BM Bachelor of Medicine; British Museum

BMus Bachelor of Music

BMW Bayerische Motorenwerke (German motor manufacturer), or any of their vehicles (no full stops; plural **BMWs**)

BMX bicycle motocross, or denoting a bicycle designed for this (no full stops)

B'nai B'rith Jewish fraternal organization (apostrophes)

Boadicea another name for **Boudicca**

Boanerges fiery preacher (capital **B**)

boar animal of pig family (compare **bore**, **boor**, **Bohr**, and **Boer**)

board flat piece of wood, meals, or group of directors (compare **bored**)

boarding house (two words)

boarding school (two words)

boardroom (one word)

boat small sailing, rowing, or motor vessel, or submarine (compare **ship**; use italics for names of individual boats, e.g. Sir Francis Chichester's *Gypsy Moth IV*)

boathouse (one word)

boatswain (also **bosun** or **bo's'n**)

bobbejaan South African word for a baboon, spider, or monkey wrench (double **b**, double **a**)

bobby socks ankle socks worn by US teenage girls in 1940s (two words)

bobbysoxer girl wearing bobby socks (one word; **-sox-**)

bobsleigh (one word)

Boccaccio, Giovanni Italian writer (double **c** twice)

Boccherini, Luigi Italian composer (**-cch-**)

Boche derogatory name for Germans in World Wars I and II (compare **Bosch**)

Boddingtons brewery (no apostrophe)

Bodensee German name for Lake **Constance**

Bodh Gaya variant of **Buddh Gaya** (single **d**)

Bodhisattva in Mahayana Buddhism, divine being worthy of nirvana who remains among humans (single **d**, double **t**)

Bodhi Tree sacred peepul (bo tree) under which the Buddha attained enlightenment (single **d**)

Bodleian Library Oxford (capital **B** & **L**, **-eia-**)

Bodoni typeface

body (*typog.*) measurement of type from top to bottom

body building (two words)

bodyguard (one word)

body mass index (three words, no hyphen)

Boeotia region of ancient Greece, or Modern Greek name for **Voiotia**

Boer South African of Dutch or Huguenot origin (compare **boor**, **boar**, **bore**, and **Bohr**)

boerbul South African dog (**-ul**)

Boer War (capital **B** & **W**)

Boethius, Anicius Roman philosopher and statesman

Bogarde, Sir Dirk British actor

Bogart, Humphrey US actor (nickname **Bogie**)

bogey evil spirit, golfing term, piece of dried nasal mucus, or Australian word for bathe or swim (also **bogy** in the first three senses, also **bogie** in the sense 'bathe or swim')

bogeyman (one word; **-ey-**)

bogie railway wheelbase, or variant of **bogey** in the sense 'bathe or swim' (also bogy in the sense 'railway wheelbase')

Bogie nickname of Humphrey **Bogart**

Bogotá capital of Colombia (acute accent)

bog-standard (hyphen)

bogy variant of **bogey** in the senses 'evil spirit', 'golfing term', or 'piece of dried nasal mucus', or variant of **bogie** in the sense 'railway wheelbase'

Bohème, La opera by Puccini (grave accent)

Bohemia region of Czech Republic, or former kingdom of central Europe

Bohemian (as noun) person from Bohemia, or artistic person living unconventional life; (as adjective) of Bohemia, or unconventional (also **bohemian** with reference to unconventional person or lifestyle)

Bohr, Aage and **Niels** Danish physicists (compare **boar, bore, boor,** and **Boer**)

bohrium (symbol **Bh**)

boilermaker (one word)

boiler room (two words)

boiler suit (two words)

boiling point (two words)

Bokhara variant of **Bukhara**

Bokmål one of the official forms of written Norwegian, related to Danish (former name **Riksmål**; see also **Nynorsk**)

bold (*typog.*) describing type with thicker lines, as in **these words** (indicated with a wavy underline in proofreading and editing)

boldface (adjective)

bold face (noun)

bole tree trunk (compare **bowl**)

bolero (plural **boleros**)

Boleyn, Anne second wife of Henry VIII (**-eyn**; not **Ann**)

Bolingbroke, Henry St John, 1st Viscount English politician (single **l**, not **-brook**)

bolívar monetary unit of Venezuela (lower-case **b**, acute accent)

Bolívar, Simon South American soldier (acute accent)

Bologna Italian city

bologna sausage (lower-case **b**)

bolognese denoting sauce for pasta, as in *spaghetti bolognese* (lower-case **b**; **-gnese**)

Bolognese of Bologna, or a person from Bologna

boloney variant of **baloney**

Bolshevik Russian communist in former times, or any political radical (also **bolshevik** in the sense 'any political radical')

bolshie rebellious, or a political radical (lower-case **b**; also **bolshy**)

bolt in printing, folded edge of sheet before trimming to page size

Bolt, Robert British playwright (compare **Boult**)

bomb explosive device (compare **bombe**)

bombasine variant of **bombazine**

Bombay Indian city (official name **Mumbai**)

bombazine fabric (also **bombasine**; not **-een**)

bombe ice-cream dessert (compare **bomb**)

bombshell (one word)

bona fide genuine (not italic; two words)

bona fides good faith (not italic; two words)

Bonaparte surname of **Napoleon I** (Italian spelling **Buonaparte**)

bonbon a sweet (not italic; one word)

Bondi Beach Australia (capital **B** twice)

bone-dry (hyphenated unless used after noun, as in *the washing was bone dry*)

Bo'ness Scottish town

Bowness English town

Bonham Carter, Helena British actress (no hyphen; not **Helen**)

Bonhams auction house (no apostrophe)

bonhomie geniality (not italic)

bon mot clever remark (not italic; plural **bons mots**)

Bonnie Prince Charlie nickname of Charles Edward **Stuart**, also known as the **Young Pretender** (**-ie** twice)

bon vivant person who enjoys good food and drink (italics; also **bon viveur**, which is not used in French and therefore not italic)

bony (not **-ey**)

booby trap (noun)

booby-trap (verb)

Boodle's London club (apostrophe)

boogie-woogie (hyphen; not **-y**)

bookbinder (one word)

bookcase (one word)

book end (two words)

Booker Prize annual award for fiction (capital **B** & **P**; official name (from 2002) **Man Booker Prize**)

book-keeper (hyphen)

bookmaker (one word)

Book of Common Prayer (capital **B**, **C**, & **P**; also **Prayer Book**)

bookseller (one word)

Booksellers Association (no apostrophe)

bookshelf (one word)

bookshop (one word)

book titles see **titles of works**

Boolean algebra (capital **B**; **-ean**)

Boone, Daniel American pioneer (**-ne**)

boor ill-mannered or insensitive person (compare **boar**, **bore**, **Boer**, and **Bohr**)

bootee baby's soft shoe (compare **booty**)

Boötes constellation (**-oö-**)

Boothia, Gulf of Canada

bootstrap (one word)

booty loot (compare **bootee**)

Bophuthatswana former Bantu homeland in South Africa

Bordeaux French port, or wine produced nearby (capital **B**)

Border collie (capital **B**)

bore (as verb) produce hole, fail to interest, or past tense of **bear**; (as noun) hole, diameter, hollow part of cylinder, dull person or thing, or large wave in estuary (compare **boar**, **boor**, **Bohr**, and **Boer**)

bored not interested (compare **board**; use *with* or *by*, rather than *of*, after **bored**)

Borehamwood English town

Borges, Jorge Luis Argentine writer

Borghese surname of noble Italian family of 16th–19th centuries

Borgia surname of notorious Italian family of 15th century: **Rodrigo** (Pope Alexander VI), his son **Cesare**, and his daughter **Lucrezia**

born past participle of bear in passive use with reference to birth, as in *he was born in France*

borne past participle of **bear** in active use with reference to birth, as in *she has borne three children*, and in active or passive use in other senses, as in *the seeds are borne on the wind*

boron (symbol **B**)

borough town, constituency, or division of city (compare **burgh**)

borrow take for temporary use, as in *he borrowed her car* (compare **lend**)

borscht beetroot soup (also **borsch** or **borshch**)

borstal former name for **young offender institution** (lower-case **b**)

Bosch company manufacturing electric appliances and tools (compare **Boche**)

Bosch, Hieronymus Dutch painter

bo's'n variant of **boatswain**

Bosnia region of Bosnia-Herzegovina

Bosnia-Herzegovina European
country

Bosporus strait between European
and Asian Turkey (also **Bosphorus**;
not **-ous**)

Boston Tea Party (capital **B**, **T**, & **P**)

bosun variant of **boatswain**

botanical name see **binomial** and
taxonomic names

Botany wool (capital **B**)

botfly (one word)

both (use plural verb, as in *both were
carrying briefcases*; compare **each**)

Bothnia, Gulf of part of Baltic Sea

bo tree another name for **peepul**

Botswana African country (former
name **Bechuanaland**)

Botticelli, Sandro Italian painter

bottle bank (two words)

bottle-feed (hyphen)

bottleneck (one word)

Boucicault, Dion Irish dramatist
and actor

Boudicca queen of the Iceni in
ancient Britain (also **Boadicea**)

boudoir woman's bedroom or
private sitting room (not italic)

bouffant puffed out (not italic)

bougainvillea (lower-case **b** in
general use: *Bougainvillea* is the
genus name; also **bougainvillaea**)

bough branch of tree (compare **bow**)

bouillabaisse fish soup or stew
(not italic; **-oui-**, double **l**, double **s**)

bouillon broth or stock (not italic;
-oui-, double **l**)

boulevard (**-lev-**; capital **B** when part
of name, as in **Sunset Boulevard**)

Boulez, Pierre French composer

Boulogne French port (official name
Boulogne-sur-Mer)

Boult, Adrian English conductor
(compare **Bolt**)

bouncy (not **-ey**)

bound tied, destined, obliged, or
going towards (compare **-bound** and
bounded)

-bound restricted to or by, as in
housebound, fogbound (not attached
with hyphen)

Boundary Commission (capital **B**
& **C**)

bounded limited or having a
boundary (compare **bound** and
-bound)

bouquet bunch of flowers or aroma
(not italic; **-ou-**, **-et**)

bourbon US whiskey (lower-case **b**)

Bourbon member of former
European ruling family (capital **B**)

Bourbon biscuit (capital **B**)

bourgeois middle class (not italic;
-ou-, **-eoi-**)

bourgeoisie middle classes (not
italic; **-sie**)

Bourgogne French name for
Burgundy

Bournemouth English resort (**-nem-**)

Bournville Birmingham (**-nv-**)

Boutros-Ghali, Boutros Egyptian
diplomat, former secretary-general
of the UN

bow¹ curved weapon for shooting
arrows (compare **beau**)

bow² bend as sign of respect, or front
of boat (compare **bough**)

bowdlerize (also **bowdlerise**; see
-ize/-ise)

bowl round container, ball rolled in
game, throw ball in cricket, or move
rapidly (compare **bole**)

bow tie (two words)

Boxing Day (capital **B** & **D**)

box number (two words)

box office (no hyphen unless used
before another noun, as in *a box-
office success*)

boxroom (one word)

boy male child (compare **buoy**)

boycott (double **t**)

boyfriend (one word)

Boyne Irish river

Boys' Brigade (**-s'** not **-'s**)

Boy Scouts former name for **Scout**

Association (note that a member of the senior branch of this association is now simply called a **Scout** or **scout**)

Boy's Own Paper, The former publication (**-'s** not **-s'**)

BP British Petroleum; British Pharmacopoeia

BPC British Pharmaceutical Codex

BPharm Bachelor of Pharmacy

BPhil Bachelor of Philosophy

Br bromine (no full stop)

bra woman's undergarment (no full stop)

braaivleis South African barbecue (**-aai-**, **-ei-**)

braces the characters { and }, which have various specialist uses (also **curly brackets**). A larger single brace may be used to group items in a list.

bracketed, bracketing (not **-tt-**)

brackets a pair of punctuation marks used to enclose words or characters or to separate them from surrounding text. The characters (and) are called **parentheses** or **round brackets**; the characters [and] are called **square brackets**; the characters < and > are called **angle brackets**; and the characters { and } are called **braces** or **curly brackets**. See those entries for further information. Note that in UK usage the term *brackets* used alone generally denotes parentheses, whereas in US usage it generally denotes square brackets.

brae Scottish hillside (compare **bray**)

braggadocio boasting (double **g**, single **c**)

Brahe, Tycho Danish astronomer

Brahman member of highest Hindu caste (former name **Brahmin**)

Brahmaputra S Asian river

Brahmin in the USA, highly intelligent or socially superior person, or former name for **Brahman**

Braille system of writing for blind people (capital **B**)

brainchild (one word)

Braine, John English novelist (**-ne**)

braise cook slowly in closed pan (compare **braze**)

brake (as noun) slowing or stopping device, or area of dense undergrowth, or open horse-drawn carriage; (as verb) slow down (compare **break**)

Brandenburg German city and state (not **-berg**)

brand-new (hyphen)

Brands Hatch (no apostrophe)

Brandt, Willy German statesman (**-ndt**)

Brasenose College Oxford (**-ase-**)

brasier less common variant of **brazier**

Brasília capital of Brazil (acute accent; not **-az-**)

brasserie bar or cheap restaurant (not italic)

brassiere woman's undergarment (not italic; no accent; compare **brazier**)

Braun, Eva mistress of Adolf Hitler; **Karl Ferdinand** German physicist (see also **von Braun**; compare **Brown** and **Browne**)

Braunschweig German name for **Brunswick**

bravado swagger

bravery courage

bravura brilliance

bray make sound of donkey (compare **brae**)

braze make of or like brass, or solder (compare **braise**)

brazier portable fire or cooker (the spelling **brasier** is less common but not incorrect; compare **brassiere**)

brazil nut (two words; lower-case **b**)

Brazzaville capital of Congo-Brazzaville (double **z**)

breach break, gap, or violation (compare **breech**)

bread food made from dough (compare **bred**)

breadboard (one word)

breadcrumb (one word)

breadline (one word)

break (as verb) separate, fracture, pause, or violate; (as noun) fracture, pause, or variant of **brake** in the sense 'open horse-drawn carriage' (compare **brake**)

breakdown (noun; the verb is **break down**)

break-in (noun; the verb is **break in**)

breakthrough (noun; the verb is **break through**)

break-up (noun; the verb is **break up**)

breast-feed (hyphen)

breath (noun; compare **breathe**)

Breathalyser trademark for device measuring amount of alcohol in breath (capital **B**; also **Breathalyzer**)

breathalyse give a Breathalyser test to (**-yze** in US English)

breathe (verb; compare **breath**)

Brecht, Bertolt German dramatist

Brecon Beacons Welsh national park (not **-eck-**)

bred past tense and past participle of **breed** (compare **bread**)

breech lower part, e.g. of the human body (as in *breech delivery*), or part of gun behind barrel (compare **breach**)

Br'er Rabbit character in US folk tale (apostrophe)

Breslau German name for **Wrocław**

Bretagne French name for **Brittany**

Breton (as adjective) of Brittany; (as noun) a person from Brittany or the indigenous Celtic language of Brittany (single **t**)

Bretton Woods Conference international monetary conference

in USA in 1944 (double t; capital **B, W,** & **C**)

Breughel variant of **Brueghel**

breve the symbol (˘), placed over a short vowel or used as a diacritic

Brezhnev, Leonid Ilyich Soviet statesman (**-zhn-**)

briar shrub of heath family, or tobacco pipe made from its root (also **brier**)

bribable (also **bribeable**)

bric-a-brac (hyphens; not **-ck**)

brickbat (one word)

bridal of a bride or wedding (compare **bridle**)

Bridgend Welsh town and county borough (one word)

Bridge of Sighs Venice (capital **B** & **S**)

Bridget Jones's Diary novel by Helen Fielding and film (**-s's** not **-s'**)

Bridgetown capital of Barbados (**-dge-**)

Bridgnorth English town (not **-dge-**)

Bridgwater English town (not **-dge-**)

bridle horse's headgear (compare **bridal**)

bridle path path suitable riding horses (two words)

bridleway official term for public right of way where horses can be ridden (one word)

Brie cheese (capital **B**)

brier thorny shrub, e.g. *sweetbrier* (also **briar**)

Brillat-Savarin, Anthelme French politician and gourmet

brimful (also **brimfull**)

brio liveliness or vigour (not italic)

briquette small brick of coal, ice cream, etc.(not italic; also **briquet**; not **-ck-**)

Brit (informal; use **Briton** instead where appropriate)

Britain another name for **Great Britain** or the **United Kingdom**. See also **British Isles**.

Britannia (single **t**, double **n**)

Britart late 20th-century movement in British art (one word)

Briticism linguistic feature peculiar to British English (the variant **Britishism** is less common but not incorrect)

British (use instead of **English** with reference to Great Britain or the UK in general, but note that is sometimes more appropriate to use English, Scottish, or Welsh for specific people or places)

British Columbia Canadian province (not **-lom-**)

British Council (capital **B** & **C**)

British Empire (capital **B** & **E**)

British Guiana former name for **Guyana**

British Honduras former name for **Belize**

British Isles group of islands comprising Great Britain, all of Ireland, the Isle of Man, and most of the Channel Islands. See also **Great Britain** and **United Kingdom**.

Britishism less common variant of **Briticism**

British Library (capital **B** & **L**)

British Museum (capital **B** & **M**)

British Standards Institution (not **Institute**)

British Summer Time (capital **B, S,** & **T**)

Briton person from the UK

Britpop British pop music of the mid-1990s (one word)

Brittain, Vera English writer, feminist, and pacifist (double **t**; compare **Brittan** and **Britten**)

Brittan, Sir Leon British politician (compare **Brittain** and **Britten**)

Brittany (double **t**, single **n**; French name **Bretagne**)

Britten, Benjamin English composer (compare **Brittan** and **Brittain**)

Brittonic less common variant of **Brythonic**

Britvic soft drinks company (capital **B**)

broach open (compare **brooch**)

Broads, the group of shallow lakes in E England (capital **B**)

broadsheet (one word)

Brobdingnag country of giants in *Gulliver's Travels* by Jonathan Swift

broccoli (double **c**, single **l**)

broderie anglaise open embroidery on fabric (not italic)

Broederbond secret society of Afrikaner nationalists

broke (as verb) past tense of **break**; (as adjective) having no money

broken (as verb) past participle of **break**; (as adjective) fractured, intermittent, imperfect, or not working

broken-down (hyphen)

brokenhearted (one word)

bromine (symbol **Br**)

bronchitis (**-ch-**, **-is**)

bronco wild horse (the spelling **broncho** is not incorrect, but it is less common)

Brontë, Anne, Charlotte, and Emily, English novelists (diaeresis)

Bronx, the borough of New York City

brooch piece of jewellery (compare **broach**)

Brook, Peter British stage and film director

Brooke, Rupert British poet

Brooklyn borough of New York City

Brookner, Anita British writer (compare **Bruckner**)

broomstick (one word)

Bros. Brothers (in company name; full stop)

brother-in-law (plural **brothers-in-law**)

brougham closed horse-drawn carriage (**-am**)

brouhaha (one word)

Brown, Sir Arthur Whitten British aviator; **George, Lord George-Brown** British politician; **Gordon** British politician; **John** US abolitionist leader; **Lancelot** British landscape gardener (known as **Capability Brown**); **Robert** Scottish botanist after whom the **Brownian movement** of particles in fluid is named (compare **Browne** and **Braun**)

Browne, Coral Australian actress; **Sir Thomas** English physician and author (compare **Brown** and **Braun**)

brownfield denoting a site previously built on (one word; compare **greenfield**)

Brownian movement see **Brown**

brownie helpful elf or chocolate cake (lower-case **b**)

Brownie member of the junior branch of the Guide Association (full name **Brownie Guide**; see also **Rainbow**)

Brownie points (capital **B**)

Bruce, Robert (the) see **Robert I**

Bruckner, Anton Austrian composer (compare **Brookner**)

Brueghel, Jan, Pieter (the Elder), and **Pieter** (the Younger) Flemish painters (also **Breughel** for all three painters, but the spelling **Bruegel** is used only for Pieter the Elder)

Bruges Belgian city (Flemish name **Brugge**)

Brummell, George Bryan English dandy (known as Beau Brummell; double **m**, double **l**)

Brunei country on Borneo (**-ei**)

Brunel, Isambard Kingdom English engineer (single **l**)

Brunelleschi, Filippo Italian architect (double **l**, **-sch-**)

brunette woman with dark brown hair (not **-net**)

Brunhild in German legend, queen won for King Gunther by magic of Siegfried (also **Brünnhilde**; compare **Brynhild**)

Brunswick German city and state (German name **Braunschweig**)

brushoff (noun; the verb is **brush off**)

Brussels capital of Belgium (French name **Bruxelles**)

Brussels sprout (capital **B**; **-els**)

brut denoting dry champagne (not italic)

brutalize (also **brutalise**; see **-ize/-ise**)

Bruyère see **La Bruyère**

Bruxelles French name for **Brussels**

Brylcreem trademark for men's hair cream (capital **B**; not **-il**, not **-eam**)

Brynhild in Norse mythology, Valkyrie won for Gunnar by magic of Sigurd (compare **Brunhild**)

Brythonic group of Celtic languages comprising Welsh, Cornish, and Breton (the variant **Brittonic** is less common but not incorrect; compare **Goidelic**)

BS Bachelor of Surgery; British Standard

BSc Bachelor of Science

BSE bovine spongiform encephalopathy (informal name **mad cow disease**)

BSI British Standards Institution

B-side less important side of record (hyphen)

BST bovine somatotrophin (growth hormone); British Summer Time

BT British Telecommunications

BTEC Business and Technology Council, or a vocational certificate awarded by this body (no full stops)

BTech Bachelor of Technology

BTW by the way

buccaneer (double **c**, single **n**)

Bucharest capital of Romania (Romanian name **Bucureşti**)

Buckingham Palace (capital **B** & **P**)

buckminsterfullerene form of carbon (one word)

Bucureşti Romanian name for
Bucharest

buddha image of the Buddha (lower-
case **b**)

Buddha, the Gautama Siddhartha,
the founder of Buddhism (capital **B**)

Buddh Gaya Indian village and
sacred site (double **d**; also **Bodh
Gaya**)

Buddhism (-**ddh**-)

budget estimate of income and
expenditure (lower-case **b**)

Budget, the British government's
financial plans for the coming year
(capital **B**)

budgeted, budgeting (not -**tt**-)

Buenos Aires capital of Argentina

Buerk, Michael British TV journalist
(compare **Burke**)

buffalo (plural **buffaloes** or **buffalo**)

buffeted, buffeting (not -**tt**-)

Bugatti (single **g**, double **t**)

Buggins' turn (capital **B**; the more
cumbersome variant **Buggins's term**
is less common but not incorrect)

builder's merchant (-'**s** not -**s**')

build-up (noun; the verb is **build up**)

built-in (hyphen)

built-up (hyphen)

Bukhara city in Uzbekistan (also
Bokhara)

bulbul songbird (single **l** twice)

bulgur wheat (-**ur**)

bullet (*typog.*) the symbol (•), used to
introduce items in a list (also
centred dot)

bulletin (double **l**, single **t**)

bullfight (one word)

bullring (one word)

Bullring new Birmingham shopping
centre (capital **B**, one word)

Bull Ring old Birmingham shopping
centre (capital **B** & **R**, two words)

bull's-eye (-'**s**- not -**s**'-, hyphen)

bull terrier (two words)

bulrush (single **l**)

bulwark (single **l**, not -**work**)

bum bag (two words)

bumblebee (one word; the variant
humblebee is less common but not
incorrect)

bumf (the spelling **bumph** is not
incorrect, but it is less common)

bumpkin simple rustic person (not
-**mk**-)

buncombe less common variant of
bunkum

Bundesbank central bank of
Germany (capital **B**; full name
Deutsche Bundesbank)

Bundesrat German council of state
ministers (capital **B**)

Bundestag German parliament of
elected members (capital **B**)

bungee jumping (the spelling **bungy
jumping** is not incorrect, but it is
less common)

bunk bed (two words)

bunkum (the spelling **buncombe** is
not incorrect, but it is less common)

Bunsen burner (capital **B** then
lower-case **b**)

Buñuel, Luis Spanish film director
(tilde)

Buonaparte Italian spelling of
Bonaparte

buoy float (compare **boy**)

buoyant (-**uo**-)

buoy up (-**uo**-)

BUPA British United Provident
Association (company providing
private medical insurance; no full
stops)

bur clinging seed vessel (also **burr**)

Burberry trademark for raincoat
(capital **B**; -**ur**- then -**err**-)

bureau (plural **bureaus** or **bureaux**)

bureaucracy (not -**asy**)

burg in former times, a fortified
town (compare **berg** and **burgh**)

burger another name for **hamburger**
(compare **burgher**)

burgh in Scotland, a town that
formerly had a degree of self-

government (compare **borough** and **burg**)

burgher citizen (compare **burger**)

Burghley, William Cecil, 1st Baron Burghley English statesman, chief adviser to Elizabeth I (also **Burleigh**)

burgundy purplish-red colour (the use of capital **B** is less common but not incorrect in this sense)

Burgundy region of France or wine produced there (always capital **B** for the region; the use of lower-case **b** for the wine is less common but not incorrect; French name **Bourgogne** in both senses)

burial ground (two words)

burk less common variant of **berk**

burka variant of **burqa**

Burke, Edmund British statesman; **Robert O'Hara** Irish explorer of Australia; **William** Irish body snatcher (compare **Buerk**)

Burkinabé of Burkina-Faso, or a person from Burkina-Faso (acute accent)

Burkina-Faso African country (former name **Upper Volta**)

Burleigh variant of **Burghley**

Burma former name for **Myanmar**

Burmah Oil company (**-ah**)

Burmese (as adjective) of Myanmar; (as noun) the language of Myanmar or a person from Myanmar (plural **Burmese**)

Burmese cat (capital **B**)

burned variant of **burnt**

Burne-Jones, Sir Edward English artist (hyphen)

Burnet, Sir Alastair British journalist and broadcaster (not **Alistair**)

Burnett, Frances Hodgson US novelist

burnous Arab hooded cloak (also **burnouse**)

Burns Night January 25 (no apostrophe; capital **B** & **N**)

burnt past tense and past participle of **burn** (also **burned**)

Burntisland Scottish town (one word)

burqa Muslim woman's garment (not **-qua**; also **burka**)

burr file, rough edge, dialectal articulation of r, or variant of **bur**

burrito Mexican dish (double **r**, single **b**)

Burroughs, Edgar Rice and William S(eward) US novelists (not **-ows**)

bursar (not **-er**)

burton used in the phrase *gone for a burton* (lower-case **b**)

Burton-upon-Trent English town (hyphens; lower-case **u**; not **-on-**)

Burundi African country (former name **Urundi**)

bury inter or hide (compare **berry**)

Bury St Edmunds English town

bus passenger-carrying vehicle, or to transport or travel by bus (no apostrophe; plural **buses** or **busses**; compare **buss**)

bused past tense and past participle of **bus** (also **bussed**)

buses plural or third person present tense of **bus** (also **busses**)

Bushey English town (**-ey**)

Bushido code of samurai (the spelling **bushido**, with lower-case **b**, is less common but not incorrect)

bushranger (one word)

business commercial activity, matter, affair, or concern (compare **busyness**)

businesslike (no hyphen)

businessman (use **businessperson** or **executive** instead where appropriate)

businessperson (use instead of gender-specific **businessman** or **businesswoman** where appropriate)

businesswoman (use **businessperson** or **executive** instead where appropriate)

busing present participle of **bus** (also **bussing**)

buss archaic or dialect word for **kiss** (compare **bus**)

bussed variant of **bused**, or past tense and past participle of **buss**

busses variant of **buses**, or plural or third person present tense of **buss**

bussing variant of **busing**, or present participle of **buss**

busybody (one word)

busyness being busy (compare **business**)

but (conjunction, preposition, and adverb; compare **butt** and **butte**; may be used at the beginning of a sentence for effect, but sparingly; see also **not only . . . but also**)

Buthelezi, Mangosuthu Gatsha Zulu leader

Butlins holiday company (no apostrophe)

butt blunt or unused end, target, cask, strike with head, or intrude (compare **but** and **butte**)

butte flat-topped hill (compare **butt** and **but**)

buttonhole (one word)

buy purchase (compare **by** and **bye**)

buyers' market (-s' not -'s)

buy-in (noun; the verb is **buy in**)

buyout (noun; the verb is **buy out**)

buzz word (two words)

by (preposition and adverb; compare **bye** and **buy**)

by- near or secondary, as in *bystander*, *by-product* (often attached with hyphen; also **bye-** in some words (see individual entries); compare **bi-**)

by and by presently (**by** twice; compare **by the bye**)

by and large on the whole (not . . . in . . .)

bye sporting term or farewell (compare **by** and **buy**)

bye- variant of **by-** in some words (see individual entries)

bye-election variant of **by-election**

bye-law variant of **bylaw**

by-election (hyphen; also **bye-election**)

Byelorussia another name for **Belarus**

bygone (one word)

bylaw (no hyphen, but also **bye-law** with hyphen)

by-line (hyphen)

bypass (one word)

by-product (hyphen)

bystander (one word)

byte in computing, group of bits (compare **bite**, **bight**, and **bit**)

by the bye incidentally (not . . . the by; compare **by and by**)

Byzantine (capital **B** in all senses)

Byzantium ancient name for **Istanbul**

C

c centi-, as in **cm** centimetre (no full stop)

C carbon; Celsius; centigrade; century; name of computer programming language; Roman numeral for 100 (no full stop)

c. circa (used before an approximate date, as in *c. 1450*; the abbreviation may also be italic, and the following full stop and/or space may be dropped: follow publisher's house style)

© symbol for **copyright** (used before the name of the copyright-holder)

Ca calcium (no full stop)

CA California (US postal code)

ca. circa (used before an approximate date, as in *ca. 1450*; the abbreviation may also be italic, and the following full stop and/or space may be dropped: follow publisher's house style)

Caaba variant of **Kaaba**

CAB Citizens Advice Bureau

cabal group of political intriguers, conspiracy, or clique (lower-case **c**)

Cabal group of ministers of Charles II (capital **C**)

cabala variant of **cabbala**

cabaret (not **-ber-**)

cabbala ancient Jewish mystical tradition, or any esoteric doctrine (also **cabala**, **kabbala**, or **kabala**)

cabbie (also **cabby**)

caber tree trunk thrown in Highland games (not **-re**)

Cabernet Sauvignon grape or wine (not **-bin-**; the use of lower-case **c** & **s** is less common but not incorrect)

cabinet piece of furniture, or executive body of government ministers (also **Cabinet** in the sense 'body of ministers')

cabinet-maker (hyphen)

cabochon polished but unfaceted gem (not italic)

cacao tree bearing cocoa beans, or less common variant of **cocoa**

cache hidden store, or small area of computer memory (compare **cash**)

cachet official seal, distinguishing mark, or prestige (not italic)

cachou lozenge that sweetens breath (compare **cashew**)

cacodemon evil spirit (also **cacodaemon**)

cacophony (**caco-**)

cactus (plural **cacti** or **cactuses**)

CAD computer-aided design

caddie golfer's attendant (also **caddy**)

caddis fly (two words)

caddy container for tea, or variant of **caddie**

cadi Muslim judge (plural **cadis**; also **kadi** or **qadi**)

Cádiz Spanish port (acute accent)

Cadmean victory another name for **Pyrrhic victory** (not **-ian**)

cadmium (symbol **Cd**)

cadre nucleus of trained people or experts (not italic; not **-er**)

caecum (**cec-** in US English)

Cædmon Anglo-Saxon poet (not **Cae-** or **Ce-**)

Caenozoic variant of **Cenozoic**

Caernarfon Welsh port and resort (the spellings **Caernarvon** and **Carnarvon** are not incorrect in this sense, but both are less common in modern usage)

Caernarvonshire former Welsh county

Caerphilly Welsh town, or cheese (capital **C**)

Caesar, Gaius Julius Roman general and statesman (the title **Caesar** was also born by other Roman emperors)

Caesarean of Julius Caesar or any of the other Caesars, or denoting a surgical operation (full name **Caesarean section**) to deliver a baby (also **Caesarian**; lower-case **c** may be used for the surgical sense only)

Caesars Palace Las Vegas, USA (no apostrophe)

caesium (symbol **Cs**)

caesura (plural **caesuras** or **caesurae**; the spelling **cesura** is not incorrect, but it is less common, even in US English)

café (acute accent)

cafeteria (**-teria**; no accents)

cafetiere (**-tiere**; no accents)

caffeine (double **f**, **-ei-**; the spelling **caffein** is not incorrect, but it is less common)

caftan variant of **kaftan**

cagey (also **cagy**)

cagoule (also **kagoule** or **kagoul**)

cagy variant of **cagey**

Caiaphas biblical priest (**-aia-**)

caiman variant of **cayman** (plural **caimans**)

Cain biblical character

Caine, Michael British actor

Cainozoic variant of **Cenozoic**

Cairngorm Mountains Scotland (capital **C** & **M**; also **Cairngorms**)

Cairns Australian port

cairn terrier (lower-case **c**)

Caius variant of **Gaius** (as the name of the Roman jurist; note that the forename of Julius Caesar and others is always **Gaius**)

Caius College Cambridge (full name **Gonville and Caius College**)

Cajun US ethnic group (capital **C**)

calamari squid cooked for eating (**-ari**)

calcareous chalky (not **-ious**)

calceolaria (lower-case **c** in general use: *Calceolaria* is the genus name)

calcium (symbol **Ca**)

calculator (not **-er**)

calculus (plural **calculuses** in the sense 'branch of mathematics' or **calculi** in the sense 'stonelike concretion in body')

Calcutta Indian city (official name **Kolkata**)

Calderón de la Barca, Pedro Spanish dramatist

caldron less common variant of **cauldron**

calendar table showing dates of year (compare **calender** and **colander**)

calender machine for rolling paper or cloth (compare **calendar** and **colander**)

calf (noun, plural **calves**; compare **calve**)

calfskin (one word)

Calgary Canadian city

Caliban Shakespearean character, hence any brutish man (capital **C**)

calibre (**-er** in US English; single **l**)

calico (single **l**; plural **calicoes** or **calicos**)

calif less common variant of **caliph**

californium (symbol **Cf**)

caliph (the spellings **calif**, **kalif**, and **khalif** are less common but not incorrect)

calisthenics less common variant of **callisthenics**

calix chalice (plural **calices**; compare **calyx**)

calk transfer by tracing, spike or spikes to prevent slipping, or variant of **caulk** (compare **cork**)

Callaghan, James, Baron British statesman

calligraphy (double **l**)

calliper (single **l** in US English)

callisthenics (the spelling **calisthenics** is not incorrect, but it is less common)

callous unfeeling, or describing hardened and thickened skin (compare **callus**)

call-up (noun; the verb is **call up**)

callus area of hard or thick skin or bony tissue (compare **callous**)

Calor trademark for liquefied gas (capital **C**)

calorie unit of heat equal to 4.1868 joules, now rarely used, or nonscientific spelling of **Calorie** (lower-case **c**)

Calorie unit of heat equal to 1000 calories, used to express energy value of food (capital **C**; also **kilocalorie**). In nonscientific contexts, e.g. *counting calories, low-calorie diet,* **Calorie** is now usually spelt with a lower-case **c**.

Caltech California Institute of Technology (one word)

calvary any experience involving great suffering (lower-case **c**; compare **cavalry**)

Calvary place of Christ's crucifixion (capital **C**; also **Golgotha**)

calve (verb; compare **calf**)

calypso West Indian song with syncopated beat (lower-case **c**)

Calypso nymph in Greek mythology (capital **C**)

calyx part of flower or kidney (plural **calyxes** or **calyces**; compare **calix**)

camaraderie comradeship (not italic; -**mar**-)

Camargue, la region of S France (also **the Camargue**)

Cambodia SE Asian country (former names **Khmer Republic** (1970–76) and **Kampuchea** (1976–89))

Camborne English town (not -**our**-)

Cambridgeshire English county (-**dge**-)

Camden borough of Greater London (not -**mpd**-)

came past tense of **come** (compare **come**)

camellia (single **m**, double **l**; lower-case **c** in general use: *Camellia* is the genus name)

Camembert cheese (capital **C**)

cameo (plural **cameos**)

cameraman (use **camera operator** instead where appropriate)

camera obscura darkened chamber for projecting images of outside objects (not italic)

camera operator (use instead of gender-specific **cameraman** or **camerawoman** where appropriate)

camera-ready copy material ready to be photographed for printing (also **mechanical**)

camerawoman (use **camera operator** instead where appropriate)

Cameroon African country (not -**oons**; French name **Cameroun**, German name **Kamerun**)

Cammell Laird shipyard (double **m**, double **l**)

camomile (also **chamomile**)

camouflage (-**ou**-, -**ge**)

Campari trademark for alcoholic drink (capital **C**)

Campbell, Alastair former British press secretary (not **Alistair**)

Campbell-Bannerman, Sir Henry British statesman (hyphen)

Campbeltown Scottish town (single **l**)

campfire (one word)

camp follower (two words)

campsite (one word)

CAMRA Campaign for Real Ale (no full stops)

can (in the sense 'be permitted', use **may** instead for formality or politeness)

Canaan ancient region: the Promised Land of the Israelites (single **a** then double **a**)

Canadian Shield area of Precambrian rock extending over much of Canada (capital **C** & **S**; also **Laurentian Shield** or **Laurentian Plateau**)

canaille mob or rabble (italics)

Canaletto Italian artist (single **n** & **l**, double **t**; original name **Giovanni Antonio Canale**)

canapé (acute accent)

canasta card game (compare **canaster** and **canister**)

canaster tobacco (compare **canasta** and **canister**)

Canaveral, Cape Florida, USA (**-ver-**; former name **Cape Kennedy**)

cancan (one word)

cancel (*typog.*) new page or section of book replacing defective or missing one (single **l**)

cancelled, cancelling (single l in US English)

candela unit of luminous intensity

candelabrum branched candle-holder (**-del-**; plural **candelabra** or **candelabrums**; the plural form **candelabra** is also used as a singular noun with the same meaning, plural **candelabras**)

Candia Italian name for **Iráklion**

Candide satire by Voltaire

candlelight (one word; when used before another noun, as in *candlelight dinner, candlelight vigil*, may be replaced by **candlelit**)

Candlemas February 2 (**-dle-**; single **s**)

candlestick (one word)

candlewick (one word)

candour (**-or** in US English)

C & W country and western (music)

candyfloss (one word)

Canea variant of **Chania**

canister container (compare **canaster** and **canasta**; single **n**)

cannabis (double **n**)

cannelloni (double **n**; the spelling **canneloni** is not incorrect, but it is less common)

Cannes French port and resort

cannibalize (also **cannibalise**; see **-ize/-ise**)

cannon gun, billiards shot, rebound, or collide (compare **canon**)

cannonball (one word)

cannoned (not **-nn-**)

cannon fodder (two words)

cannoning (not **-nn-**)

cannot (one word; more formal than **can't**, though the latter is generally acceptable in writing)

canoeing (**-oei-**)

canoeist (**-oei-**)

canon rule, piece of music, author's works, or cleric (compare **cannon** and **cañon**)

cañon variant of **canyon** (compare **canon**)

canonize (also **canonise**; see **-ize/-ise**)

can-opener (hyphen)

Canossa ruined castle in Italy, scene of the penance done by Holy Roman Emperor Henry IV (double **s**)

cant insincere talk, stock phrases, jargon, or slant

can't (less formal than **cannot**, but generally acceptable in writing)

Cantab. of Cambridge (from Latin *Cantabrigiensis*)

cantabile music term (not italic)

Cantabrigian of Cambridge, or a person from Cambridge (not **-dg-**)

cantaloupe (also **cantaloup**)

canter gait of horse, or person who uses cant (compare **cantor**)

Canterbury English city or council area of New Zealand (**-bury**)

Canticle of Canticles another name for **Song of Solomon**

cantilever (**-tile-**)

canton political division of Switzerland or administrative subdivision in France (lower-case **c**; not italic)

Canton Chinese port (also **Kwangchow**, Pinyin **Guangzhou**) or US city

cantor leader of synagogue service or church singing (compare **canter**)

Cantuar. of Canterbury (from Latin *Cantuariensis*)

Canute Danish king of England (note that Canute's failed attempt to turn back the tide was not intended to prove his omnipotence, but to prove to his courtiers that he was not omnipotent; also **Cnut** or **Knut**)

canvas heavy cloth

canvass solicit votes, conduct survey, or investigate thoroughly

canyon gorge or ravine (also **cañon**)

caoutchouc rubber (**-aout-, -ouc**)

Cap French word for **Cape**

cap. capital; capital letter

Cape (capital **C** as part of name, as in *Cape Cod, Cape Canaveral*; **the Cape** denotes the SW region of South Africa)

Cape Horn South America (also **the Horn**)

Čapek, Josef and Karel Czech writers

Cape of Good Hope South Africa

capercaillie (also **capercailzie**)

Cape Province former South African province, replaced by **Northern Cape**, **Western Cape**, and **Eastern Cape**

Cape Town capital of South Africa

Cape Verde country comprising a group of Atlantic islands off W Africa (see also **Verde**)

Cape Verdean of Cape Verde (the country), or a person from Cape Verde (not **-ian**)

capillary (single **p**, double **l**; not **-iary**)

capital (as noun) seat of government, money, assets, upper part of column, or another word for **capital letter**; (as adjective) punishable by death, very serious, principal, excellent, or denoting a capital letter (compare **Capitol**; also **upper-case** in the sense 'denoting a capital letter')

capitalization see **capital letter**

capitalize (also **capitalise**; see **-ize/ -ise**)

capital letter any of the letters A, B, C, D, etc., used at the beginning of sentences, as the initial letter of proper nouns, and in many abbreviations. Capital letters are indicated with a triple underline in proofreading and editing. For the use of initial capital letters see individual entries, **animal breeds**, **eponym**, **ranks**, **titles of people**, **titles of works**, **trademark**, etc. Capital initials are rarely used in modern English for personal pronouns relating to God (e.g. *he, him,* and *his*), but the preference of the author should be taken into account and consistently applied when editing religious texts. See also **capital**, **full capital**, and **small capital**.

Capitol main building of US Congress, or temple on Capitoline (compare **capital**)

Capitoline one of the hills on which ancient Rome was built

cappuccino coffee with steamed milk (not italic; double **p**, double **c**; plural **cappuccinos**)

capriccio lively piece of music (not italic; single **p**, double **c**)

caps. capital letters

capsize (never **-ise**)
captain (**-ain**)
caption title or comment accompanying an illustration
captor (not **-er**)
capuchin monkey or hooded cloak (lower-case **c**)
Capuchin Franciscan friar (capital **C**)
carabineer variant of **carbineer**
carabiner variant of **karabiner**
carabinier variant of **carbineer**
carabiniere Italian police officer (italics; plural *carabinieri*)
caracal animal resembling lynx, or its reddish fur (compare **caracul** and **caracole**)
Caracas capital of Venezuela
caracole half turn in dressage (also **caracol**; compare **caracal** and **caracul**)
Caractacus variant of **Caratacus**
caracul variant of **karakul** (compare **caracal** and **caracole**)
Caradoc another name for **Caratacus**
carafe (**-afe**)
carageen variant of **carrageen**
caramelize (also **caramelise**; see **-ize/-ise**)
carat measure of weight of precious stones or quality of gold (compare **caret** and **carrot**)
Caratacus British chieftain who led resistance against Romans (also **Caractacus** or **Caradoc**)
Caravaggio, Michelangelo Merisi da Italian painter (single **r**, single **v**, double **g**)
caravanserai (also **caravanseray**)
caraway (single **r**)
carbineer soldier with carbine (also **carabineer** or **carabinier**)
carbon (symbol **C**)
carbon-14 dating variant of **radiocarbon dating** (one hyphen; also **carbon dating**)
carboniferous yielding coal or carbon (lower-case **c**)

Carboniferous period of the Palaeozoic era, or of this period (capital **C**)
carbonize (also **carbonise**; see **-ize/-ise**)
car-boot sale (one hyphen)
carburettor (double **t**; the spelling **carburetter** is not incorrect, but it is less common)
carcass (also **carcase**)
Carcassonne French city (double **s**, double **n**)
cardamom (also **cardamum** or **cardamon**)
cardigan knitted jacket (lower-case **c**)
Cardigan, 7th Earl of British cavalry officer
Cardigan Bay Wales
Cardiganshire former Welsh county (abolished in 1974 and reinstated in 1996 as **Ceredigion**)
card index (noun)
card-index (verb)
careen sway or keel over
career rush headlong, or chosen profession
caret the symbol (⁁), used in proofreading and editing to indicate where something is to be inserted (compare **carat** and **carrot**)
caretaker (one word)
Carey, George English prelate; **Peter** Australian novelist (compare **Cary**)
carfuffle less common variant of **kerfuffle**
cargo (plural **cargoes** or **cargos**)
Caribbean (as adjective) of Caribbean Sea or its islands; (as noun) Caribbean Sea, or states and islands of Caribbean Sea (single **r**, double **b**, **-ean**)
Caribbean Sea part of Atlantic Ocean between Central and South America (capital **C & S**)
Cariboo Mountains Canada (capital **C & M**; **-oo**)
caribou reindeer (**-ou**)

Carinthia Austrian state (German name **Kärnten**)

Carisbrooke Castle Isle of Wight

Carleton, William Irish novelist (**-let-**)

Carlile, Richard English reformer (compare **Carlisle** and **Carlyle**)

Carlisle English city (compare **Carlile** and **Carlyle**)

Carlist supporter of Don Carlos (in Spain) or Charles X (in France) or their descendants

Carlovingian variant of **Carolingian**

Carlsbad variant of **Karlsbad**, German name for **Karlovy Vary**

Carlton English town, London club, or hotel in various locations

Carlyle, Robert Scottish actor; **Thomas** Scottish essayist and historian (compare **Carlile** and **Carlisle**)

Carmarthen Welsh town (not **Caer-**, not **-on**)

Carnac French village noted for menhirs and other megaliths (compare **Karnak**)

Carnarvon Australian town, or less common variant of **Caernarfon**

Carnatic region of India (not **Kar-**)

Carnegie Hall New York (capital **C** & **H**)

carnival (**-niv-**)

carol song (single **r**, single **l**; compare **carrel** and **Carroll**)

Carolean variant of **Caroline**

Caroline of Charles I or Charles II (also **Carolean** or **Carolinian**)

Carolingian of Frankish dynasty founded in 8th century, or a member of this dynasty (also **Carlovingian** or **Carolinian**)

Carolinian of North or South Carolina, a person from either of these US states, or a variant of **Caroline** or **Carolingian**

carolled, carolling (single **l** in US English)

Carothers, Wallace Hume US chemist (**-aro-**)

carousal merry drinking party

carousel circular slide magazine, rotating conveyor belt, or merry-go-round

carpal bone of wrist (compare **carpel**)

car park (two words)

carpe diem seize the day (italics)

carpel reproductive organ of flower (compare **carpal**)

carpetbagger (one word)

carpeted, carpeting (not **-tt-**)

carpet-sweeper (hyphen)

carport (one word)

carrageen edible seaweed (also **carragheen** or **carageen**)

Carrantuohill Irish mountain (one word; also **Carrauntoohill**)

Carrara Italian town, famous for its marble (double **r** then single **r**)

Carrauntoohill variant of **Carrantuohill**)

Carré see **Le Carré**

carrel small study room or desk (also **carrell**; compare **carol**)

carriageway (one word)

Carroll, Lewis pen name of Charles Lutwidge **Dodgson** (double **r**, double **l**; compare **carol**)

carrot vegetable (compare **carat** and **caret**)

Carrott, Jasper English comedian (double **r**, double **t**; real name **Robert Davies**)

carrycot (one word)

carry-on (noun; the verb is **carry on**)

carsick (one word)

cart vehicle used for transport, or carry with effort (compare **kart**)

carte blanche complete authority (not italic)

Cartesian of French philosopher and mathematician René Descartes (capital **C**)

carthorse (one word)

cartilage (-ti-, -age)

carton box

cartoon humorous drawing, comic strip, animated film, or preparatory sketch for work of art

cartouche ornamental tablet in form of scroll, or case for combustible material in firework (also **cartouch**)

cartwheel (one word)

Cary, Joyce British novelist (compare **Carey**)

caryatid column in form of female figure (**-ry-**; plural **caryatids** or **caryatides**; compare **telamon**)

'Casabianca' poem by Mrs Hemans, containing the line 'The boy stood on the burning deck' (not **-bl-**; quotation marks)

Casabianca, Louis de French naval officer (not **-bl-**)

Casablanca Moroccan port

Casablanca title of film starring Humphrey Bogart (italics)

Casals, Pablo Spanish cellist

Casanova man noted for amorous adventures (capital **C**)

Casanova, Giovanni Jacopo Italian adventurer

Casaubon, Isaac French theologian

casbah variant of **kasbah**

case in bookbinding, the cover of a book; in typography, either of the sets of capital (upper-case) or lower-case letters; in grammar, a form of nouns, pronouns, and adjectives used to indicate their relation to other words (English has only two cases, the **subjective** and **objective**)

casebound another word for **hardback** (adjective)

case history (two words)

casein milk protein (**-ein**)

caseload (one word)

cash money (compare **cache**)

cash-and-carry (hyphens)

cashback (one word)

cash dispenser (two words)

cashew nut or tree (compare **cachou**)

cash flow (two words)

cashmere fine soft wool obtained from Kashmir goat (lower-case **c**; rarely **kashmir**)

Cashmere rare variant of **Kashmir** (capital **C**)

casino (plural **casinos**)

Cassandra in Greek mythology, woman whose prophecies were never believed, hence anyone who predicts disaster but is unheeded (capital **C**)

cassata ice cream

cassava plant or starch derived from its root

Cassel variant of **Kassel** (single **l**)

Cassell publishing company (double **l**)

Cassiopeia constellation (**-peia**)

cast (as noun) actors in play, plaster casing, mould, form, etc.; (as verb) throw, shed, mould, etc. (compare **caste**)

castaway (noun and adjective; the verb is **cast away**)

caste social class (compare **cast**)

caster person or thing that casts, bottle for sprinkling sugar, or small swivelling wheel (also **castor** in the senses 'bottle' and 'wheel')

caster sugar (not **-or**)

Castile former kingdom comprising most of modern Spain (single **l**; the variant **Castilla** is less common but not incorrect)

cast iron (no hyphen unless used before another noun, as in *a cast-iron pan*)

castoff (noun)

cast off (*typog.*) estimate how much space text will occupy in a particular typesize and font (verb)

cast-off (adjective)

castor beaver, its fur, or a secretion used in perfumery and medicine, or a variant of **caster** in the senses 'bottle for sprinkling sugar' or 'small swivelling wheel'

Castor and Pollux twins in classical mythology (not **-er**)

castor oil (not **-er**)

castrato (plural **castrati** or **castratos**)

casual chance, offhand, or informal (compare **causal**)

cataclysm violent upheaval (**-ysm**)

Catalan (as noun) the language of Catalonia or a person from Catalonia; (as adjective) of Catalonia, its people, or their language

cataloging in publication referring to the US Library of Congress's record of or data about a publication; these words (or their abbreviation **CIP**) often appear on the imprint page of a book, usually with capital **C** & **P**, and the US spelling is retained in UK publications (**-gi-**; see also **cataloguing in publication**)

catalogue (**-log** in US English)

catalogue raisonné descriptive catalogue, e.g. of works in art exhibition (italics)

cataloguing (**-gi-** in US English)

cataloguing in publication referring to the British Library's record of or data about a publication; these words (or their abbreviation **CIP**) often appear on the imprint page of a book, usually with capital **C** & **P** (**-gui-**; see also **cataloging in publication**)

Catalonia region of Spain (**-onia**; Catalan name **Catalunya**, Spanish name **Cataluña**)

catalyse (**-yze** in US English)

catamaran (all the vowels are **a**'s and all the consonants are single)

cataphora the use of a word, e.g. a pronoun, that refers to something subsequently mentioned (compare **anaphora**)

catarrh (**-rrh**)

catch phrase (two words)

catch-22 situation in which paradoxical rules or circumstances prevent escape (lower-case **c**; hyphen)

Catch-22 title of novel by Joseph Heller (capital **C**; hyphen; italics)

catchup less common variant of **ketchup**

catchword (*typog.*) word printed as **running head** in reference book, or first word of next page printed or typed at bottom of page (one word)

catechism (**-tech-**)

categorize (also **categorise**; see **-ize/-ise**)

category (**-te-**, **-ory**)

cater (may be followed by *for* or *to*)

cathartic (not **-arctic**)

Cathay archaic name for **China**

Cathedral (capital **C** for names of specific cathedrals, as in *Canterbury Cathedral*)

Catherine, St Christian martyr (not **-ar-**)

Catherine II Russian empress (known as **Catherine the Great**; not **-ar-**)

Catherine de' Medici French queen (not **Catharine**; lower-case **d**; apostrophe followed by space; also **Catherine de Médicis**)

Catherine of Aragon first wife of Henry VIII (not **Catharine**)

Catherine of Braganza wife of Charles II (not **Catharine**)

Catherine of Siena, St Italian mystic (not **Catharine**)

Catherine wheel (not **-ar-**; capital **C**, lower-case **w**)

cathode-ray tube (one hyphen)

catholic universal, comprehensive, or liberal (lower-case **c**)

Catholic (as adjective) of the Roman Catholic Church or of the Christian Church before separation into Eastern and Western Churches;

(as noun) a member of the Roman Catholic Church (capital **C**; use **Roman Catholic** instead where necessary to avoid ambiguity)

cat-o'-nine-tails (three hyphens; apostrophe)

cats see **animal breeds** and individual entries

CAT scan computerized axial tomography scan: former name for **CT scan**

cat's cradle (-**'s** not -**s'**; no hyphen)

Catseye trademark for reflective stud in road (capital **C**; one word)

cat's-eye gemstone (apostrophe; hyphen)

catsuit (one word)

catsup less common variant of **ketchup**

Cattegat rare variant of **Kattegat**

cattle-grid (hyphen)

Catullus, Gaius Valerius Roman poet (single **t**, double **l**)

Caucasia region of NW Asia (also **the Caucasus**)

Caucasian (as adjective) of a light-skinned race or of Caucasia; (as noun) light-skinned person, person from Caucasia, or language of Caucasia (capital **C**; also **Caucasoid** with reference to light-skinned people, but **White** is the usual term in UK English)

Caucasus, the mountain range in SW Russia (also **Caucasus Mountains**), or another name for **Caucasia**

caucus (plural **caucuses**)

cauldron (the spelling **caldron** is not incorrect, but it is less common)

caulk fill cracks or crevices (also **calk**; compare **cork**)

causal being or stating a cause (compare **casual**)

cause célèbre (not italic; acute accent then grave accent; plural **causes célèbres**)

cauterize (also **cauterise**; see **-ize/-ise**)

cavalier (not **-eer**; capital **C** for supporter of Charles I in Civil War)

Cavalleria rusticana opera by Mascagni (double **l**; not **-iera**; lower-case **r**)

cavalry mounted or armoured part of army (compare **calvary**)

caveat warning (not italic; not **-iat**)

caveat emptor let the buyer beware (not italic; not **-iat**, not **-er**)

cave-in (noun; the verb is **cave in**)

caviar (also **caviare**)

cavil (single **l**)

cavilled, cavilling (single **l** in US English)

Cawnpore former name for **Kanpur** (also **Cawnpur**)

cayenne hot red pepper (lower-case **c**; also **cayenne pepper**)

Cayenne capital of French Guiana

cayman animal of crocodile family (lower-case **c**; plural **caymans**; also **caiman**)

Cayman Islands Caribbean island group (capital **C & I**)

CB Citizens' Band (radio)

CBE Commander of the Order of the British Empire

CBI Confederation of British Industry

cc carbon copy (also **c.c.**); cubic centimetre or cubic centimetres (no full stops)

CCTV closed-circuit television (no full stops)

Cd cadmium (no full stop)

CD compact disc (no full stops; plural **CDs**)

CD-ROM compact disc read-only memory (hyphen; no full stops; plural **CD-ROMs**)

Ce cerium (no full stop)

CE Church of England; Common Era (used instead of **A.D.**, e.g. in non-Christian contexts); Communauté Européenne

Ceadda variant of **Chad** (the saint)

cease-fire (hyphen)

Ceauşescu, Nicolae Romanian statesman (**ş** then **s**)

CED *Collins English Dictionary* (italics)

cedar tree (compare **ceder**)

cede transfer or surrender (compare **seed**)

ceder person who cedes (compare **cedar**)

cedilla the diacritic used under **ç**, etc.

Ceefax trademark for television text service of BBC (capital **C**; compare **Teletext**)

ceilidh social gathering with folk music and dancing (**cei-**, **-dh**)

ceiling upper surface of room or upper limit (compare **sealing**)

cel transparent sheet bearing drawing for animated film (also **cell**; compare **sell**)

Celebes another name for **Sulawesi**

cell small room, cavity, or group of people, or variant of **cel** (compare **sell**)

cellar underground room (compare **seller**)

Cellini, Benvenuto Italian sculptor (double **l**, single **n**)

cello (no apostrophe; plural **cellos**; see also **violoncello**)

Cellophane trademark for thin transparent sheeting (capital **C**)

Celsius denoting temperature scale in which ice melts at 0° and water boils at 100° (capital **C**; formerly also **centigrade**; compare **Fahrenheit**)

Celt (rarely **Kelt**)

cemetery (all the vowels are **e**'s)

CEng chartered engineer

cenotaph monument honouring person or people buried elsewhere (lower-case **c**)

Cenotaph, the London monument honouring dead of World Wars I and II (capital **C**)

Cenozoic most recent geological era, or of this era (also **Caenozoic** or **Cainozoic**)

censer container for burning incense)

censor remove part of letter, publication, film, etc., or a person who does this

censure criticize or condemn, or severe criticism or disapproval

census (plural **censuses**)

cent monetary unit (compare **scent** and **sent**)

centenarian 100-year-old person (compare **centenary**)

centenary (as noun) 100th anniversary; (as adjective) of 100-year period or occurring every 100 years (also **centennial** for adjective in UK English and for both adjective and noun in US English)

centennial lasting for 100 years, or variant of **centenary**

Center (use this spelling in UK texts for names of US buildings, institutions, etc., such as the Lincoln Center, New York)

Center Parcs holiday company (not **Centre**, not **Parks**)

centigrade another word, now rarely used, for **Celsius** (lower-case **c**)

centilitre (**-er** in US English; abbreviation **cl**, without full stop)

centimetre (**-er** in US English; abbreviation **cm**, without full stop)

Central America isthmus joining North and South America (capital **C & A**)

centralize (also **centralise**; see **-ize/-ise**)

Central Provinces two Canadian provinces: Ontario and Quebec

Central Provinces and Berar former Indian province, now comprising Madhya Pradesh and part of Maharashtra

centre (**-er** in US English)

centre around (use **centre on** instead)

centred (-tr-)

centred dot dot placed above the line, as formerly in decimals (e.g. 14·796), or another name for **bullet**

centrefold (one word)

centre on (use instead of **centre around**)

centrepiece (one word)

centring (-tr-)

centurion (not -ian)

Cephalonia Greek island in Ionian Sea (Modern Greek name **Kephallinía**)

ceramic (rarely **keramic**)

Cerberus three-headed dog in Greek mythology

cereal plant, grain, or breakfast food (compare **serial**)

cerebrospinal (one word)

cerecloth waxed cloth used as shroud (**cere-**)

Ceredigion Welsh county (see also **Cardiganshire**)

ceremonial of ceremony or ritual

ceremonious excessively formal or polite, or observing ceremony

Cerenkov variant of **Cherenkov**

cerium (symbol **Ce**)

CERN European Laboratory for Particle Physics (acronym of its former name, Conseil Européen pour la Recherche Nucléaire; no full stops)

cert certainty, as in *a dead cert* (no full stop)

CertEd Certificate in Education

cerulean (not **caer-**; not -ian)

Cervantes, Miguel de Spanish writer (full surname **Cervantes Saavedra**)

Cervin, Mont French name for **Matterhorn**

Cervino, Monte Italian name for **Matterhorn**

cervix (plural **cervixes** or **cervices**)

cessation ceasing (compare **cession**)

cession ceding (compare **cessation** and **session**)

c'est la vie that's life (italics)

cesura less common variant of **caesura**

ceteris paribus other things being equal (not italic)

Ceylon former name for **Sri Lanka** (note that the island occupied by Sri Lanka is still called Ceylon)

Cézanne, Paul French painter (acute accent)

Cf californium (no full stop)

cf. compare (from Latin *confer*)

CFC chlorofluorocarbon (no full stops; plural **CFCs**)

cgs units metric system of units based on centimetre, gram, and second (replaced by **SI units** in science and technology; see also **fps units** and **mks units**)

Chablis French wine (the spelling **chablis**, with lower-case **c**, is less common but not incorrect)

cha-cha-cha ballroom dance (also **cha-cha**)

chacun à son goût each to his own taste (italics)

Chad African country (French name **Tchad**)

Chad, St Anglo-Saxon churchman (also **Ceadda**)

chador garment covering Muslim or Hindu woman from head to foot (also **chuddar**)

chafe make sore by rubbing, warm, or irritate

chaff tease, or husks separated from seeds during threshing

Chagall, Marc French artist (single **g**, double **l**)

chagrined (not -nn-)

chain-smoke (hyphen)

chain smoker (no hyphen)

chair (use instead of gender-specific **chairman** or **chairwoman** where appropriate)

chairman (use **chair** or **chairperson** instead where appropriate)

chairperson (use instead of gender-specific **chairman** or **chairwoman** where appropriate)

chairwoman (use **chair** or **chairperson** instead where appropriate)

chaise longue (not italic; not **lounge**; plural **chaise longues** or **chaises longues**)

chalcedony (not -cid-)

Chaldea ancient region of Babylonia, or another name for Babylonia itself (also **Chaldaea**)

Châlons-sur-Marne city in NE France (-âlons-)

Chalon-sur-Saône city in central France (-alon-)

Chamberlain, Sir Austen British statesman (not **Austin**)

chambermaid (one word)

chamber pot (two words)

Chambers publishing company (no apostrophe; part of **Chambers Harrap**)

Chambertin French wine (capital **C**)

chambray fabric

chambré at room temperature (not italic; acute accent)

chameleon (not -mae-, not -ion)

chamois leather (the spelling **shammy leather** is not incorrect, but it is less common)

chamomile variant of **camomile**

Chamonix French town

champagne French sparkling wine (the use of capital **C** is less common but not incorrect in this sense)

champaign expanse of level or undulating country

champignon mushroom (not italic; -gnon)

Champs Elysées street in Paris, France (capital **C** & **E**; no hyphen; also **Champs Élysées**)

chancellery office of chancellor (also **chancellory**)

chancellor (not -er)

Chancellor of the Exchequer (capital **C** & **E**)

chancellory variant of **chancellery**

chandelier (single **l**; -ier)

Chandler's Ford English town (apostrophe)

Chanel, Coco French couturier (real name **Gabrielle Chanel**; single **n**, single **l**)

Chang Pinyin name for **Yangtze**

changeable (**e** after **g**)

changeover (noun; the verb is **change over**)

Chang Jiang Pinyin name for **Yangtze Jiang**

Chania Greek port, in NW Crete (also **Hania** or **Canea**; Greek name **Khaniá**)

channel strait, watercourse, path, means of access or communication, frequency band (lower-case **c**; double **n**, single **l**)

Channel of or short for **English Channel**, as in *swim the Channel* (capital **C**)

Channel Islands (capital **C** & **I**; not **Isles**)

channelled, channelling (single l in US English)

Channel Tunnel (capital **C** & **T**)

chanson de geste Old French epic poem (italics; plural *chansons de geste*)

Chantilly French town, or denoting sweetened whipped cream or delicate lace

Chanukah variant of **Hanukkah**

chaparral (double **r**)

chapati (also **chapatti**)

chapel (*typog.*) the trade-union members of a printing or publishing company

Chapel-en-le-Frith English town (hyphens; lower-case **e** & **l**)

chaperon (also **chaperone** for both noun and verb)

Chappell music publishing company (double **p**, double **l**)

char burn, clean, fish, or tea (also **charr** for the fish only)

charabanc (one word, no accent)

character (*typog.*) any single letter, number, punctuation mark, or symbol (also **sort**)

characterize (also **characterise**; see **-ize/-ise**)

Chardonnay grape or wine (the spelling **chardonnay**, with lower-case **c**, is less common but not incorrect)

chargeable (**e** after **g**)

chargé d'affaires ambassador's deputy (not italic; acute accent; plural **chargés d'affaires**)

char-grilled (hyphen)

charisma (**ch-**)

charivari (**-ari-** twice)

Charlemagne Frankish king and Holy Roman Emperor (**-agne**)

Charles's Wain another name for the **Plough** (**-s's** not **-s'**)

charleston dance (lower-case **c**)

Charleston US city in West Virginia or port in South Carolina

charlotte russe dessert (not italic; lower-case **c** & **r**)

Charolais breed of cattle (capital **C**, single **l**)

Charollais breed of sheep (capital **C**, double **l**)

Charon ferryman of the dead in Greek mythology (**Ch-**)

charr variant of **char** (the fish)

charred, charring (double **r**)

charted mapped or plotted on a chart

chartered hired, professionally qualified, or having a charter

Charters Towers Australian city

Chartres French city

chartreuse liqueur (lower-case **c**)

Charybdis whirlpool or sea monster in classical mythology (compare **Scylla**)

Chas. short for Charles (full stop in formal contexts, e.g. *Mr Chas. E. Jones*, but no full stop in informal use, e.g. *his friends call him Chas*)

chased pursued (compare **chaste**)

Chasidic variant of **Chassidic**

chassé dance step (acute accent; compare **chassis**)

Chassidic denoting Jewish sect (also **Chasidic**, **Hassidic**, or **Hasidic**)

chassis frame, wheels, etc. of motor vehicle (plural **chassis**; compare **chassé**)

chaste pure or virginal (compare **chased**)

chastise (never **-ize**)

chateau (also **château**; plural **chateaus**, **chateaux**, or **châteaux**; **Château** or **Chateau** in wine names)

Chateaubriand steak (no circumflex)

Chateaubriand, François René, Vicomte de French writer (no circumflex)

Châteaubriant French town (circumflex; **-ant**)

Château d'Yquem variant of **Yquem**, used especially for the wine

chatline (one word)

chatroom (one word)

chat show (two words)

Chattanooga US city

Chaucer, Geoffrey English poet

chauffeur (may be used for males and females)

chauffeuse (use **chauffeur** instead to avoid offence)

chauvinist fanatical patriot, or person who smugly believes his or her race, party, sex, etc. is superior (use **male chauvinist** where appropriate to avoid ambiguity)

ChB Bachelor of Surgery (from Latin *Chirurgiae Baccalaureus*)

cheap inexpensive (compare **cheep**)

Chechen member of Russian people inhabiting Chechen Republic

Chechen Republic constituent republic of Russia (also **Chechnya**; the variant **Chechenia** is less common but not incorrect)

check (as verb) examine, restrain, pause, or US word for tick; (as noun) examination, restraint, square in pattern, chess term, US word for bill, or US spelling of **cheque**

checked past tense and past participle of **check**, or patterned with squares (compare **chequered**)

checkers US and Canadian name for **draughts** (compare **Chequers**)

check-in (noun; the verb is **check in**)

check list (two words)

checkmate (one word)

checkout (noun; the verb is **check out**)

checkup (noun; the verb is **check up**)

Cheddar English village, or cheese (the use of lower-case **c** for the cheese is not incorrect, but it is less common)

Cheddar Gorge England (capital **C & G**)

cheep cry of young bird (compare **cheap**)

cheerleader (one word)

cheeseboard (one word)

cheesecake (one word)

cheesecloth (one word)

cheetah (-ee-, -ah)

chef cook (not italic)

chef-d'oeuvre masterpiece (also *chef-d'oeuvre*; italics; hyphen; plural *chefs-d'oeuvre*)

Cheiron variant of **Chiron**

Chekhov, Anton Pavlovich Russian writer (also **Chekov**)

Chelyabinsk Russian city

chemin de fer gambling game (not italic, no hyphens)

Chemnitz German city (former name (1953–90) **Karl-Marx-Stadt**)

Chennai official name for **Madras**

cheongsam Chinese dress (one word)

cheque means of paying money from bank account (**check** in US English)

chequebook (one word)

chequered marked by fluctuating fortune (compare **checked**)

Chequers British prime minister's country residence, in Buckinghamshire (compare **checkers**)

Cherbourg French port (not **-burg**)

Cherenkov, Pavel Alekseyevich Soviet physicist (also **Cerenkov**)

Chernenko, Konstantin Soviet statesman

Chernobyl town in Ukraine, site of accident at nuclear power station

Cherokee North American Indian people or language

cherub (plural **cherubs**, especially in the sense 'child', or **cherubim** in the sense 'angel')

Cherwell English river (not **Char-**)

Chesapeake Bay USA (capital **C & B**; single **s**)

che sarà sarà what will be, will be (Italian proverb; compare **que sera sera**)

chesterfield overcoat or sofa (lower-case **c**)

Chesterfield English town

Chester-le-Street English town (hyphens; lower-case **l**)

chestnut (-stn-)

cheval glass (two words)

Chevalier, Albert British music-hall entertainer; **Maurice** French singer and actor

Chevallier, Gabriel French novelist

Chevrolet US motor manufacturer, or any of their vehicles (capital **C**)

chevy less common variant of **chivy**

Chevy informal name for **Chevrolet** (capital **C**)

Cheyenne North American Indian people or language

chez at the home of, or among (italics)

chi[1] Greek letter

chi[2] energy in Oriental medicine, martial arts, etc. (also **ch'i** or **qi**)

Chiang Kai-shek Chinese general and statesman (Pinyin **Jiang Jieshi**)

Chianti Italian mountain range, or wine produced in the region (often **chianti** for the wine

chiaroscuro artistic use of light and dark (not italic)

chic stylish (not italic)

chiccory less common variant of **chicory**

Chichén Itzá Mexican village, site of Mayan ruins

chick young bird (compare **chicken**)

Chickasaw North American Indian people or language

chicken domestic fowl or its flesh (compare **chick**)

chickenpox (one word)

chicory (the spelling **chiccory** is not incorrect, but it is less common)

chignon roll of hair at back of head (not italic; **-gn-**)

Chihuahua Mexican city or state, or breed of dog (the use of lower-case **c** for the dog is not incorrect, but it is less common; see also **animal breeds**)

chi kung variant of **qigong**

child-bearing (hyphen)

childbirth (one word)

childcare (one word)

Childe Harold's Pilgrimage poem by Byron (not *Child . . .*)

childish like a child, especially in being puerile

childlike like a child, especially in being innocent

ChildLine (one word; capital **C & L**)

child minder (two words)

Children's Society, The (capital **T**)

chile rare variant of **chilli**

Chile South American country

Chilean of Chile, or a person from Chile (not **-ian**)

chilli hot pepper (also **chili**, rarely **chile**)

chilly cool

chimaera fish, or variant of **chimera**

chimera fire-breathing monster in Greek mythology, fabulous beast, or unrealistic dream (also **chimaera**; often capital **C** in Greek mythology)

China see **People's Republic of China** and **Republic of China**

Chinaman offensive former name for Chinese person, or cricket term (often **chinaman** in cricket sense)

Chinese names for the transliteration of Chinese names and other words, the **Pinyin** system (as in *Mao Zedong*) has largely replaced the **Wade-Giles** system (as in *Mao Tse-tung*). However, in English texts the earlier form is often retained for historical figures who were active before the introduction of the Pinyin system, such as Mao himself.

Chinghai variant of **Qinghai**

Chingtao variant of **Qingdao**

chinoiserie imitation Chinese style or object (not italic)

chinook wind (lower-case **c**)

Chinook North American Indian people or language, or type of helicopter (capital **C**)

Chipping Campden English town (not **-md-**)

chiromancy (**chir-**)

Chiron centaur in Greek mythology (also **Cheiron**)

chiropodist (**chir-**)

chiropractor (**chir-**, **-or**)

chirruped, chirruping (not **-pp-**)

chisel (**-sel**)

chiselled, chiselling (single l in US English)

chivy harass or nag (also **chivvy**; the variant **chevy** is less common but not incorrect)

chlamydia disease-causing bacteria (**chl-**, **-myd-**)

chlorine (symbol **Cl**)

chlorophyll (**chl-**, **-phyll**)

ChM Master of Surgery (from Latin *Chirurgiae Magister*)

chocaholic less common variant of **chocoholic**

chock-a-block (**-ck-** twice)

chocoholic (the spelling **chocaholic** is not incorrect, but it is less common)

choir group of singers (compare **quire**)

cholesterol (**chol-**, **-ster-**)

Chomsky, Noam US linguist

Chomskyan (not **-ian**)

choose infinitive and present tense (compare **chose**)

choosy (not **-sey**)

Chopin, Frédéric Polish composer and pianist

chop suey (two words)

choral sung by choir, or less common variant of **chorale**

chorale stately hymn tune, or choir (the variant **choral** is less common but not incorrect in this sense)

chord simultaneous sounding of notes, line connecting points on curve, or less common variant of **cord** in the anatomical sense

choreography composition of dance steps (the variant **choregraphy** is less common but not incorrect)

chorography technique of mapping regions

chorused, chorusing (not **-ss-**)

chose past tense of **choose** (compare **choose** and **chosen**)

chosen past participle of **choose** (compare **chose**)

Chosen Japanese name for **Korea** while it was annexed to Japan (1910–45)

Chosŏn Korean name for **North Korea**

Chou En-lai Chinese statesman (Pinyin **Zhou Enlai**)

choux denoting type of pastry (compare **shoe** and **shoo**)

chow dog or food (compare *ciao*)

chow mein (two words)

Chr. Christ; Christian; Chronicles (full stop; not italic)

Chrétien de Troyes French poet

Christ see **Jesus**

Christchurch city in New Zealand or English town (one word)

Christ Church Oxford college (two words)

christen (lower-case **c**)

christened, christening (not **-nn-**)

Christian (the use of lower-case **c** is not incorrect for the adjectival meaning 'kind or good', but it is less common in this sense and should not be used in any other sense)

Christiania former name (1624–1877) for **Oslo**

Christianize (capital **C**; also **Christianise**, see **-ize/-ise**)

Christian name (use **first name** or **forename** instead where appropriate, e.g. on official forms, to avoid offending non-Christians)

Christiansand variant of **Kristiansand**

Christian Scientist member of the **Church of Christ, Scientist** (capital **C & R**)

Christie's auction house (apostrophe)

Christmas Day December 25 (capital **C & D**)

Christmas Eve December 24 (capital **C & E**)

chromium (symbol **Cr**)

chromosome (**-mos-**)

Chron. Chronicles (full stop; not italic)

chronic describing a disease that develops slowly or is of long duration (compare **acute**)

1 Chronicles book of the Bible (not italic; abbreviation **1 Chron.** or **1 Chr.**; also **I Chronicles**)

2 Chronicles book of the Bible (not italic; abbreviation **2 Chron.** or **2 Chr.**; also **II Chronicles**)

chrysalis (**-ys-** then **-is**)

chrysanthemum (not **-is-**; lower-case **c** in general use, *Chrysanthemum* is the genus name)

Chrysler US motor manufacturer, or any of their vehicles (capital **C**; compare **Kreisler**)

Chrysostom, St John Greek churchman (**Chrys-**)

Chubb trademark for a type of lock (capital **C**, double **b**)

chuddar variant of **chador**

chukka period of play in polo (**-kka**)

church (lower-case **c** with reference to a specific building or an occasion of public worship, as in *the village church, go to church*)

Church (capital **C** in names of denominations, e.g. *the Baptist Church*, or with reference to institutionalized religion, e.g. *the conflict between Church and State*)

churchgoer (no hyphen)

Church of Christ, Scientist official name for the Christian Scientists' Church

Church of Jesus Christ of Latter-day Saints official name for the Mormon Church (lower-case **d** for **-day**; not **... the Latter-day ...**)

churchwarden (one word)

churinga sacred amulet of Aborigines (**chu-**)

chute slope, slide, or informal name for parachute (compare **shoot**)

chutney (**-ney**)

chutzpah (the spelling **hutzpah** is not incorrect, but it is less common)

CIA Central Intelligence Agency

ciao hello or goodbye (italics; compare **chow**)

Cibber, Colley English actor and writer

cicada (also **cicala**)

cicerone guide for tourists (not italic; plural **cicerones** or **ciceroni**)

CID Criminal Investigation Department

Cid, El Spanish soldier and hero

cider (the spelling **cyder** is not incorrect, but it is less common)

Cie *Compagnie* (used in French company names; no full stop)

cilium (plural **cilia**)

Cincinnati US city (**-nc-** then double **n**, single **t**)

cine camera (two words)

cinemagoer (no hyphen)

CinemaScope trademark for wide-screen projection (one word; capital **C & S**)

cinéma vérité film realism (not italic; three acute accents)

cinquecento 16th century, especially with reference to Italian art, literature, etc. (not italic; **-que-**)

Cinque Ports association of towns in SE England, originally the ports of Hastings, Romney, Hythe, Dover, and Sandwich (capital **C & P**; **-que**)

CIP catalog(u)ing in publication, as in *CIP data, CIP record* (see **cataloguing in publication** and **cataloging in publication**)

cipher (also **cypher**)

circa (used before an approximate date; abbreviation **c.** or **ca.** (see those entries); the use of italics for the full form is less common but not incorrect)

Circe enchantress in Greek mythology

circuit (**-uit**)

circuit breaker (two words)

circumcise (never **-ize**)

circumflex the accent used on â, î, etc.

Cirencester English town

cirrhosis liver disease (**-rrh-**)

cirrus cloud (plural **cirri**)

CIS Commonwealth of Independent States

cissy variant of **sissy**

cist ancient Greek or Roman box, or burial chamber (also **kist** in the sense 'burial chamber'; compare **cyst**)

Cistercian denoting a monastic order (**-cian**)

cite quote, mention, commend, or list (compare **sight** and **site**)

Citizens Advice Bureau (no apostrophe; plural **Citizens Advice Bureaux**)

Citizens' Band (**-s'** not **-'s**)

Citizen's Charter (**-'s** not **-s'**)

Citlaltépetl Mexican volcano (Spanish name **Pico de Orizaba**)

Citroën French motor manufacturer, or any of their vehicles (capital **C**; **-oë-**)

City, the financial centre of London, or the institutions located there (capital **C**)

Ciudad Bolívar Venezuelan port (former name **Angostura**)

Ciudad Juárez Mexican city (former name **El Paso del Norte**)

civic of a city or citizenship, as in *civic centre, civic reception*

civil of or between citizens, as in *civil rights, civil war*, or polite

civilize (also **civilise**; see **-ize/-ise**)

civil service (sometimes capital **C & S**, especially with reference to the civil service of a particular country)

Civil War (capital **C & W** with reference to the 17th-century

conflict in England or the 19th-century conflict in the USA)

CJD Creutzfeldt-Jakob disease (use **variant CJD** or **vCJD** for the form that is thought to be linked to eating contaminated beef)

cl centilitre or centilitres (no full stop; no **s** in plural)

Cl chlorine (no full stop)

clack short sharp sound (compare **claque**)

Clackmannan Scottish town (double **n** then single **n**)

claimant (not **-ent**)

clamorous (not **-our-**)

clamour (**-or** in US English)

clampdown (noun; the verb is **clamp down**)

clandestine (**-ine**)

clangorous (not **-our-**)

clangour (**-or** in US English)

claptrap (one word)

claque group of hired applauders or fawning admirers (compare **clack** and **clique**)

claret Bordeaux wine (lower-case **c**)

Claridge's London hotel (apostrophe)

clarinettist (also **clarinetist**)

Clark, Kenneth, Baron English art historian

Clarke, Sir Arthur C(harles) British writer; **Kenneth Harry** British politician

class in the hierarchy of **taxonomic names**, the group that comes above an order and below a phylum or division. The class name has a capital initial and is not italic.

classic of highest class in art or literature, of lasting significance or appeal, serving as a standard or model, or pure and simple in style

classical of ancient Greeks and Romans, denoting serious music, pure and simple in style, or serving as a standard or model

Claude Lorrain French painter (not **Claud**, not **Lorraine**; real name **Claude Gelée**)

clause a subdivision of a sentence, usually containing a verb. In the sentence *we'll go for a walk if it stops raining*, for example, *we'll go for a walk* is the **main clause**, because it can stand alone as a sentence in its own right, and *if it stops raining* is the **subordinate clause**. See also **relative clause**.

Clausewitz, Karl von Prussian general

claustrophobia fear of being in a confined space (**-aus-**)

Clay, Cassius original name of **Muhammad Ali**

clayey (**-ey**)

clean-shaven (hyphen)

cleanup (noun; the verb is **clean up**)

clear-cut (hyphenated unless used after noun, as in *the evidence is not clear cut*)

clear-headed (hyphen)

clearstory variant of **clerestory**

clearway (one word)

Clemenceau, Georges Eugène Benjamin French statesman (no accent on surname)

Clemens, Samuel Langhorne US writer (pen name **Mark Twain**)

clementine citrus fruit (lower-case **c**)

clench grip or close tightly, as in *clench the teeth* (compare **clinch**)

clerestory row of windows in upper part of church wall (not **-ey**; also **clearstory**)

clergyman (use gender-neutral **member of the clergy** or more specific noun instead where appropriate)

clergywoman (use gender-neutral **member of the clergy** or more specific noun instead where appropriate)

clerihew form of comic verse (lower-case **c**)

clerk office worker (not **-ar-**)

Clermont-Ferrand French city (hyphen)

Cleveland former English county

clew ball of thread or corner of sail (compare **clue**)

cliché (acute accent)

clichéd (acute accent; not **-éed**)

click short light sound (compare **clique**)

Clicquot see **Veuve Clicquot**

clientele clients collectively (not italic; no accent)

cliffhanger (one word)

climacteric critical event or period, or menopause

climactic causing or involving a climax

climatic of climate

climb ascend or ascent (compare **clime**)

climb-down (noun; the verb is **climb down**)

clime poetic word for a region or its climate (compare **climb**)

clinch settle, as in *clinch an argument*, or hold boxing or wrestling opponent (compare **clench**)

clingfilm (one word)

Clio the Muse of history in Greek mythology

clip-on (adjective; the verb is **clip on**)

clique small exclusive group of friends (compare **claque** and **click**)

cliquey (also **cliquy**)

Clitheroe English town (**-oe**)

cloak-and-dagger (hyphens)

cloche cover for plants or hat (not italic; **-che**)

clock-watcher (hyphen)

clockwise (one word)

clockwork (one word)

cloisonné enamel design (not italic; single **s**, double **n**; acute accent)

close corporation type of small company in South Africa, or variant of **closed corporation**

closed-circuit television (one hyphen)

closed corporation type of small company in the USA (also **close corporation**)

close-down (noun; the verb is **close down**)

closed season variant of **closed season**

close-fisted (hyphen)

close season (also **closed season**)

closeted, closeting (not -tt-)

close up (*typog.*) remove space between words or lines (verb)

close-up (noun)

cloth (noun)

clothe (verb)

clothes garments

cloths fabrics

cloud-cuckoo-land (lower-case **c**'s & **l**; hyphens)

cloze test comprehension test with missing words (not **close**)

club foot (two words)

club-footed (hyphen)

clubhouse (one word)

clue hint (compare **clew**)

Cluniac of Benedictine order founded at Cluny

Cluny French town

Clwyd former Welsh county

Clytemnestra wife of Agamemnon in Greek mythology (also **Clytaemnestra** or **Clytaemestra**)

cm centimetre or centimetres (no full stop; no **s** in plural)

Cm curium (no full stop)

CMG Companion of the Order of St Michael and St George

CND Campaign for Nuclear Disarmament

Cnossus less common variant of **Knossos**

Cnut variant of **Canute**

Co cobalt (no full stop)

CO Colorado (US postal code)

Co. Company; County (as part of name)

c/o care of (used in addresses)

co- (rarely attached with hyphen; see individual entries)

coal black solid fuel (compare **kohl**)

coalface (one word)

coalfield (one word)

coal mine (two words)

coal miner (two words)

coarse rough or vulgar (compare **course**)

coarse fishing (not **course**)

coastguard (one word)

coastline (one word)

coat hanger (two words)

coat of arms (three words)

coauthor (no hyphen)

coaxial cable (no hyphen)

cobalt (symbol **Co**)

cobblestone (one word)

Coblenz variant of **Koblenz**

COBOL computer programming language (also **Cobol**)

coca plant containing cocaine (lower-case **c**)

Coca-Cola trademark for carbonated drink (capital **C** twice; hyphen)

cocaine (rarely **cocain**)

coccyx bone at end of spine (plural **coccyges**)

cochineal (-**eal**)

cochlear implant device to alleviate deafness (not -**lea**)

Cockaigne legendary land of luxury and idleness (also **Cockayne**)

cock-and-bull story (two hyphens)

cockatiel (the spelling **cockateel** is not incorrect, but it is less common)

Cockayne variant of **Cockaigne**

cockfight (one word)

cockney (often **Cockney** with reference to a person)

cock of the walk (no hyphens)

cockswain less common variant of **coxswain**

cockup (noun; the verb is **cock up**)

cocoa powdered beans of cacao tree, or drink made from this (the variant **cacao** is less common but not incorrect in this sense)

coconut (rarely **cocoanut**)

cocoon (single **c** twice, single **o** then double **o**)

Cocos Islands island group in Indian Ocean (also **Keeling Islands**)

cocotte (single **c** twice, double **t**)

COD cash on delivery

COD *Concise Oxford Dictionary* (italics)

codeine (**-eine**)

codex (plural **codices**)

cod-liver oil (one hyphen)

co-driver (hyphen)

co-ed (hyphen)

coeducational (no hyphen)

coefficient (no hyphen)

coelacanth primitive fish (**-oe-**, **-lac-**)

coeliac (**cel-** in US English)

coequal (no hyphen)

coercion (**-cion**)

Coeur de Lion Lion-Heart (applied to Richard I; not italic; see also **oe**)

coeval contemporary (no hyphen; never **-ae-**)

coexist (no hyphen)

coextensive (no hyphen)

C of E Church of England

coffee bar (two words)

coffeepot (one word)

coffee table (no hyphen unless used before another noun, as in *coffee-table book*)

cogito, ergo sum I think, therefore I am (italics)

Cognac French town or brandy produced in the area (the use of lower-case **c** for the brandy is not incorrect, but it is less common)

cognizant (also **cognisant**; see **-ize/-ise**)

cognoscenti people with informed appreciation (not italic; singular **cognoscente**)

coheir (no hyphen)

coherent logical

cohesive sticking together

COI Central Office of Information

coiffeur hairdresser (may be used for males and females; compare **coiffure**)

coiffeuse (use **hairdresser** or **stylist** instead to avoid causing offence or sounding pretentious)

coiffure hairstyle (compare **coiffeur**)

Cointreau trademark for orange-flavoured liqueur (capital **C**; **-eau**)

coke solid fuel or slang name for **cocaine** (lower-case **c**)

Coke trademark for carbonated drink (capital **C**; short for **Coca-Cola**)

Coke, Sir Edward English jurist (not **Cook**)

Col. Colossians (full stop; not italic)

cola tropical tree, or drink flavoured with its seeds (lower-case **c**; also **kola**)

colander strainer (single **l**; the variant **cullender** is less common but not incorrect; compare **calendar** and **calender**)

cold-blooded (hyphen)

Coldstream Guards (capital **C** & **G**)

cold war state of hostility between countries without open warfare (lower-case **c** & **w**)

Cold War state of hostility between US and Soviet blocs after World War II (capital **C** & **W**)

Coleraine town and district in Northern Ireland

Coleridge, Samuel Taylor English poet

Coleridge-Taylor, Samuel British composer

coleslaw (one word; **cole-**)

Colette pen name of French novelist

Sidonie Gabrielle Claudine Colette (single **l**, double **t**)

coleus (lower-case **c** in general use: *Coleus* is the genus name)

colicky (**-ck-**)

coliseum large stadium or theatre (lower-case **c**; single **l**, single **s**; also **colosseum**)

Coliseum London theatre (capital **C**; compare **Colosseum**)

collaborator (not **-er**)

collage artistic composition of pieces or objects pasted onto surface (compare **college**)

collapsible (the spelling **collapsable** is not incorrect, but it is less common)

collarbone (one word)

colleague (double **l**, **-gue**)

collectable (also **collectible**)

collectanea miscellany or anthology (not italic; **-ea**)

collectible variant of **collectable**

collective nouns with nouns such as *committee, family, jury, team,* etc., use a singular verb or pronoun when the group is considered as a single entity and a plural verb or pronoun when it is considered as a set of individuals. Do not mix singular and plural forms within the same sentence, e.g. *the team has won all its* [not *their*] *home matches this season, the team have* [not *has*] *apologized for their behaviour after the match.*

collectivize (also **collectivise**; see **-ize/-ise**)

collector (not **-er**)

college educational institution (compare **collage**)

collegiate of a college (**-giate**)

Colles' fracture (**-s'** not **-s's**)

collie (lower-case **c**; **-ie**)

Collins publishing company (no apostrophe; part of **HarperCollins**)

colloquium gathering for discussion (plural **colloquiums** or **colloquia**)

colloquy conversation or dialogue (**-quy**)

cologne perfume (lower-case **c**; **-gn-**; also **eau de Cologne**)

Cologne German city (German name **Köln**)

Colombia South American country (not **-lum-**)

Colombo capital of Sri Lanka (not **-lum-**)

Colombo, Cristoforo Italian name for Christopher **Columbus** (not **-lum-**)

colon punctuation mark used to introduce a list, a quotation, or an explanation of what precedes it (e.g. *He has never been to Australia: he is afraid of flying.*). Colons are also used in ratios (e.g. *10:1*) and sometimes in expressions of time (e.g. *12:45*).

Colón Panamanian port (acute accent; see also **Archipiélago de Colón**)

Colón, Cristóbal Spanish name for Christopher **Columbus** (acute accents)

colonel officer (compare **kernel**)

colonize (also **colonise**; see **-ize/-ise**)

colonnade (single **l**, double **n**)

colophon publisher's emblem

Colorado beetle (capital **C**, lower-case **b**)

colorant (the spelling **colourant** is not incorrect, but it is less common)

coloration (also **colouration**)

coloratura soprano or virtuoso passage (not italic; not **-lour-**; plural **colorature**)

colossal (single **l**, double **s**)

colosseum variant of **coliseum** (lower-case **c**; single **l**, double **s**)

Colosseum Roman amphitheatre (capital **C**; compare **Coliseum**)

Colossians book of the Bible (not italic; single **l**, double **s**; abbreviation **Col.**)

colossus something very large (lower-case **c**; single **l**, double **s**; plural **colossi** or **colossuses**)

Colossus of Rhodes former statue, one of the **Seven Wonders of the World** (capital **C** & **R**)

colourant less common variant of **colorant**

colouration variant of **coloration**

colour-blind (hyphen)

Coloured in South Africa, a person of mixed parentage or descent (capital **C**; note that the use of the word elsewhere to denote a non-White person may cause offence)

Colquhoun surname (the **-lqu-** is silent)

Columbia US city and spacecraft (not **-lom-**; see also **British Columbia** and **District of Columbia**)

Columbo TV detective (not **-lom-**)

Columbus, Christopher Italian explorer in the service of Spain (not **-lom-**; Italian name **Cristoforo Colombo**, Spanish name **Cristóbal Colón**)

column (**-mn**)

coma unconscious state or cloud surrounding head of comet (single **m**)

combated, combating (not **-tt-**)

come past participle of **come** (compare **came**)

comeback (noun; the verb is **come back**)

comedian (may be used for males and females)

Comédie-Française, La French national theatre (hyphen)

Comédie Humaine, La series of novels by Balzac (no hyphen)

comedienne (use **comedian** instead to avoid offence)

comedown (noun; the verb is **come down**)

come-hither look (one hyphen)

come-on (noun; the verb is **come on**)

comeuppance (one word)

comfit sweet

comfort ease

comfrey (**-ey**)

comic of comedy, humorous, comedian, or children's magazine

comical causing laughter or ludicrous

Comintern Communist International: former international Communist organization (also **Komintern** or **Third International**)

comma punctuation mark used in lists and sometimes between phrases or clauses (e.g. *if you're not here by 10 o'clock, we'll go without you*). It should not be used to separate a lengthy subject from its verb (e.g. *the van used to transport the stolen goods was later found abandoned* [no comma after *goods*]). A pair of commas is used around incidental material, such as a nonrestrictive **relative clause** or phrase (e.g. *the kiwi, a flightless bird, lives in New Zealand*). Note that commas are not used around material that is essential to the text (e.g. *the actor Mel Gibson was among the guests* [no comma after *actor* or *Gibson*]). For the use of a comma before *and* or *or* in lists, see **serial comma**. See also **direct speech** and **quotation marks**.

commandant officer commanding place or establishment

commandeer seize arbitrarily or for public or military use

commander officer commanding military unit or operation, naval officer, or high-ranking member of knightly order

commandment (lower-case **c**; see also **Ten Commandments**)

commando (plural **commandos** or **commandoes**)

commedia dell'arte Italian comedy

of 16th–18th centuries (not italic; double **m**, double **l**)

comme il faut correct (italics)

commemorate (double **m** then single **m**)

commentary (-ary)

commentator (not -er)

commercialize (also **commercialise**; see -ize/-ise)

commingle (double **m**)

commissaire referee in cycle racing

commissar former Soviet Union official

commissionaire doorman

commissioner person with particular authority or power, or member of a commission

commit (double **m**, single **t**)

commitment (single **t**)

committed (double **t**)

committee (double **m**, double **t**, double **e**; see also **collective nouns**)

committing (double **t**)

commodore (-ore)

common law (no hyphen unless used before another noun, as in *his common-law wife*)

Common Market informal name for **European Economic Community** (capital **C** & **M**)

common or garden (not **commonal**)

commonplace (one word)

Commons, the short for **House of Commons** (capital **C**)

common sense (noun)

common-sense (adjective)

commonwealth the body politic, or a republic (lower-case **c**)

Commonwealth association of sovereign states ruled or formerly ruled by Britain (official name **Commonwealth of Nations**), or republic of 1649–1660 in Britain (capital **C**)

Commonwealth of Independent States organization of former Soviet republics

Commonwealth of Nations see **Commonwealth**

communard member of commune (lower-case **c**)

Communard supporter of Paris Commune (capital **C**)

commune converse intimately, take Communion, group living together, or administrative unit of some European countries (lower-case **c**)

Commune committee that governed Paris during French Revolution, suppressed in 1794 (capital **C**; see also **Paris Commune**)

communications satellite (-tions)

communion exchange of thoughts, sharing or participation, religious group, or spiritual union between Christians and Christ (lower-case **c**)

Communion celebration of or participation in the Christian sacrament of the Eucharist (capital **C**)

communiqué official announcement (not italic; acute accent)

communism any political movement or doctrine advocating classless society with no private ownership (lower-case **c**)

Communism political movement based on philosophy of Karl Marx, or social order established by Communist Party, e.g. in former Soviet Union or China (sometimes lower-case **c**, especially in Marxist sense)

communist supporter of communism (lower-case **c**)

Communist supporter of Communism or member of Communist Party (capital **C**)

Communist Party (capital **C** & **P**)

community service (no hyphen unless used before another noun, as in *community-service order*)

commutator device reversing flow of electric current (not -er)

commuter person travelling to and from work (not **-or**)

compact disc (not **disk**)

Companies Act (no apostrophe)

comparative (not **-rit-**) denoting the form of an adjective or adverb marked by the addition of **-er** or the use of **more** before the word. Most one-syllable and some two-syllable words take **-er** (e.g. *faster, happier*); others take **more** (e.g. *more careful, more comfortably*). Do not use **more** and **-er** together, and do not use either with *unique, perfect, complete, equal, impossible*, etc. Compare **superlative**.

compare (followed by *to* in the sense 'liken', as in *she compared the experience to giving birth*; followed by *with* in the sense 'observe similarity or difference', as in *compare the copy with the original*, or 'be similar', as in *this novel doesn't compare with his earlier work*)

compartmentalize (also **compartmentalise**; see **-ize/-ise**)

compass points see individual entries for capitalization of **north**, **south**, **east**, **west**, etc. Do not abbreviate these words when they form part of a place name (e.g. *East Anglia, South Africa, Northwest Territories*). Do not hyphenate or separate *northwest, southeast*, etc. in general lower-case use, but note that some place names have the hyphenated or two-word form (e.g. the unitary authority *North East Lincolnshire*). Intermediate compass points have the following style: *north-northeast* (one hyphen), *northeast by north* (no hyphens).

compatible (not **-able**)

compeer person of equal status, or companion (compare **compere**)

compel force or exact (compare **impel**)

compelled, compelling (double **l**)

compendium (plural **compendiums** or **compendia**)

compere person who introduces entertainment (not italic; no accent; compare **compeer**)

competent (not **-ant**)

Competition Commission (former name **Monopolies and Mergers Commission**)

competitor (not **-er**)

Compiègne French city, scene of the armistice (grave accent)

compiler (not **-or**)

complacent smug or self-satisfied (not **-ant**)

complaisant obliging or polite (not **-ent**)

compleat archaic spelling of **complete**

Compleat Angler, The book by Izaak Walton (not ***Complete***)

complement (as noun) part that completes or makes up a whole; (as verb) make complete (compare **compliment** and **supplement**). In grammar, the complement is a word, phrase, or clause that follows a verb such as *be* or *feel* (see **copula**) or a preposition (e.g. *nervous* and *the room* in *I felt nervous as I walked into the room*).

complementary completing or making up a whole (compare **complimentary**)

complete (always **-ete** in modern English; archaic spelling **compleat**; do not use with *more, most*, or *very*)

complex composite or intricate (compare **complicated**)

complexion (not **-ect-**)

complicated difficult to understand or analyse (compare **complex**)

compliment (as noun) flattering remark or respectful greeting; (as verb) congratulate or flatter (compare **complement**)

complimentary congratulatory, flattering, or given free, as in *complimentary tickets* (compare **complementary**)

compose make up, as in *Great Britain, Ireland, and various other islands compose the British Isles* (compare **comprise**)

composer person who writes music or machine that sets type (not **-or**)

compositor person who sets type (not **-er**)

compos mentis sane (italics)

compote dish of fruit in syrup (not italic; no accent)

compound word made up of two or more other words. See individual entries for the use of hyphens and spaces in compounds and the plural of compound nouns. Two-word compounds are often hyphenated when used before a noun, e.g. *a first-class performance* (but *the performance was first class*), *a coffee-table book* (but *the book is on the coffee table*).

comprehend understand or include (compare **apprehend**)

comprehensible understandable (not **-able**)

comprehensive all-inclusive

comprise consist of, as in *the British Isles comprise Great Britain, Ireland, and various other islands* (never **-ize**; not followed by *of*; compare **compose**)

compromise (never **-ize**)

compte rendu review, statement, or report (italics; not **-mte**; plural *comptes rendus*)

Compton-Burnett, Dame Ivy English novelist (hyphen; **-ett**)

comptroller variant of **controller** in the sense 'financial officer or executive', used in some official titles (capital **C** as part of title)

compulsive forced by internal urge, as in *a compulsive gambler*

compulsory obligatory, as in *compulsory education*

computer (not **-or**)

computerize (also **computerise**; see **-ize/-ise**)

comte French title equivalent to **count** (italics; not **-mpte**)

Comte, Auguste French mathematician and philosopher (not **-mpte**)

Conakry capital of Guinea (also **Konakry** or **Konakri**)

Conan Doyle, Sir Arthur British writer, creator of Sherlock Holmes (no hyphen; also alphabetized as **Doyle**)

concede (not **-ceed**)

conceivable (not **-eable**)

Concepción Chilean city (acute accent; not **-tion**)

conceptualize (also **conceptualise**; see **-ize/-ise**)

Concertgebouw concert hall in Amsterdam, the Netherlands (not **-bow**)

Concertgebouw Orchestra (capital **C & O**)

concertgoer (one word)

concertinaed, concertinaing (no apostrophe or hyphen)

concerto (plural **concertos** or **concerti**)

concessionaire (single **n**)

concierge caretaker of block of flats or hotel (not italic)

Concord US town in Massachusetts or city in New Hampshire

Concorde supersonic aircraft

concours competition for best-looking car (italics; full form *concours d'élégance*)

concourse crowd, coming together, or open space in public space

concur (single **r**)

concurred (double **r**)

concurrent (double **r**; not **-ant**)

concurring (double **r**)

condemn express strong disapproval of (**-mn**; compare **condone**)

condensed (*typog.*) denoting type that is narrower than usual for its height

condone overlook or forgive (compare **condemn**)

conductor (not **-er**; may be used for males and females)

conductress (use **conductor** instead to avoid offence)

coney variant of **cony**

Coney Island New York, USA (capital C & I; not **-ny**)

confectionery (not **-ary**)

Confederacy the 11 Southern states of the USA that seceded in 1861 (capital C; also **Confederate States of America**)

Confederation the 13 original states of the USA, constituted in 1777 (capital C)

confer (single r)

conference (single r)

Conference pear (capital C)

conferment (single r)

conferred, conferring (double r)

confessor (not **-er**)

confetti (double t)

confidant person (usually male) to whom secrets are confided

confidante person (usually female) to whom secrets are confided

confident sure of oneself, bold, or certain

confrère fellow member (not italic; grave accent)

Confucius Chinese philosopher (Chinese names **K'ung Fu-tzu**, **K'ung Fu-tse**, **Kong Zi**, or **Kongfuzi**)

confusable (sometimes **confusible**, especially in the titles of books about words that are often confused)

congé permission to depart, dismissal, or farewell (not italic; acute accent)

congenial pleasant and friendly, as in *a congenial atmosphere*, or compatible (compare **congenital** and **genial**)

congenital existing from birth (compare **congenial** and **genital**)

Congo African river or variant of **Kongo** (see also **Democratic Republic of Congo, Congo-Brazzaville**, and **Zaïre**)

Congo-Brazzaville African country (former names **Middle Congo** and **Republic of Congo**)

Congo Free State a former name for **Democratic Republic of Congo**

Congo-Kinshasa a former name for **Democratic Republic of Congo**

Congolese of the Democratic Republic of Congo or Congo-Brazzaville, or a person from either of these countries (compare **Kongo**)

congregational of a congregation (lower-case c)

Congregational denoting a Protestant Christian Church that is now largely part of the United Reformed Church in England and Wales (capital C)

congress conference, national legislative assembly, society, or sexual intercourse (lower-case c)

Congress US legislature, comprising the House of Representatives and the Senate (capital C)

congruent denoting triangles with identical shapes, agreeing, or corresponding

congruous suitable, appropriate, agreeing, or corresponding

conjoined twins (nontechnical name **Siamese twins**)

conjunction part of speech used to join words, phrases, or clauses, e.g. *and, but, or, if, because, although* (see also **and** and **but**)

conjunctivitis (not **-us**)

conjuror (the spelling **conjurer** is not incorrect, but it is less common)

conker horse chestnut (compare **conquer**)

con man (two words)

Connacht Irish province (former name **Connaught**)

Connah's Quay Welsh town (apostrophe)

Connaught former name for **Connacht**

connecter less common variant of **connector**

Connecticut US state and river (-ect-)

connection (the spelling **connexion** is not incorrect, but it is less common in modern usage)

connector (the spelling **connecter** is not incorrect, but it is less common)

connexion less common variant of **connection**

connivance (not -ence)

connoisseur person with informed appreciation (not italic; double **n**, double **s**)

Connolly, Billy Scottish comedian; **Cyril** British critic and writer (double **n**, double **l**)

connote imply or suggest (double **n**; compare **denote**)

conquer defeat (compare **conker**)

conquistador Spanish adventurer or conqueror (not italic; plural **conquistadors** or **conquistadores**)

Conrad, Joseph Polish-born British novelist (real name **Teodor Josef Konrad Korzeniowski**)

conscience sense of right and wrong (note that the phrase *for conscience sake* is also written *for conscience' sake* or *for conscience's sake*)

conscientious diligent or painstaking (-nsci- then -nti-)

conscious awake or aware, or part of the human mind

consensus general agreement (thus *general* and *of opinion* in the phrases *general consensus* and *consensus of opinion* are redundant; -ns- twice)

consent permission (compare **assent**)

consequent following as a result (compare **consequential** and **subsequent**)

consequential significant, self-important, or following as a result (especially an indirect result, as in *consequential loss*; compare **consequent**)

conservative opposing change and innovation, moderate, or conventional, or a person who opposes change and innovation (lower-case **c**)

Conservative of a Conservative Party, or a member of a Conservative Party (capital **C**)

Conservative Party right-wing political party (capital **C & P**)

conservatoire institution for the study of music (not italic; also **conservatory** or **conservatorium**)

conservatory greenhouse, or variant of **conservatoire**

consistent (not -ant)

consommé clear soup (not italic; acute accent)

consortium (plural **consortia**)

Constance German city (German name **Konstanz**)

Constance, Lake W Europe (German name **Bodensee**)

Constantinople former name for **Istanbul**

constrain compel or oblige (compare **restrain**)

Consumers' Association (-s' not -'s)

containerize (also **containerise**; see -ize/-ise)

contemporary (use **modern** instead where appropriate to avoid ambiguity)

contemptible deserving contempt (not -able)

contemptuous showing or feeling contempt

continent large land mass (lower-case **c**)

Continent, the mainland Europe (capital **C**)

continental of a continent (lower-case **c**)

Continental of mainland Europe (capital **C**)

continental breakfast (lower-case **c** & **b**)

continental quilt (lower-case **c** & **q**)

continual recurring frequently, or occurring without interruption (compare **continuous**)

continuance act of continuing, or duration of an action or condition

continuation sequel, resumption, or act of continuing

continuity logical sequence, or a continuous whole

continuous occurring without interruption (compare **continual**)

continuum (plural **continua** or **continuums**)

contraction shortening of a word or words by omitting letters from the middle, as in *St* for *Saint* (or *Dept* for *Department*, *Ltd* for *Limited*, etc.) and *let's* for *let us* (or *haven't* for *have not*, *they're* for *they are*, etc.). Contractions of the first type, used to form **abbreviations**, usually do not have a full stop. Contractions of the second type are mainly used in speech and informal writing; note that the space between the words is removed and the **apostrophe** replaces the missing letter (or letters).

contractor (not **-er**)

contralto (plural **contraltos** or **contralti**)

contretemps awkward situation of slight disagreement (not italic; not **-tra-**; plural **contretemps**)

contributor (not **-er**)

control (single **l**)

controlled (double **l**)

controller person who directs or controls, or financial officer (the variant **comptroller** is used in the titles of some financial officers)

controlling (double **l**)

conundrum (plural **conundrums**)

convalescence (**-esc-** then **-enc-**)

convector (not **-er**)

convenance propriety (italics; not *-ence*)

convener (also **convenor**)

conversazione social gathering for learned discussion (italics; not *-tio-*; plural *conversazioni* or *conversaziones*)

converter (the spelling **convertor** is not incorrect, but it is less common)

convertible (not **-able**)

convertor less common variant of **converter**

conveyor (also **conveyer**, especially in the sense 'person who conveys')

conveyor belt (two words; not **-er**)

convolvulus (lower-case **c** in general use: *Convolvulus* is the genus name; plural **convolvuluses** or **convolvuli**)

Conwy Welsh town, river, and county borough (former name **Conway** for the town)

cony (also **coney**)

coo call of dove or pigeon, or exclamation of surprise (compare **coup**)

Cooch Behar Indian city and former state (also **Kuch Bihar**)

Cook, Captain James British explorer; **Peter** British comedy actor; **Sir Joseph** Australian statesman; **Robin** British politician; **Thomas** British travel agent

Cooke, Alistair US journalist and broadcaster

cookie (rarely **cooky**)

Cookstown district of Northern Ireland

Cooktown Australian town

cooky rare variant of **cookie**

coolabah Australian tree (also **coolibah**)

cooling-off period (one hyphen)

coop¹ a cage, or to confine (compare **coup** and **coupe**)

coop² a cooperative (also **co-op**)

Co-op supermarket: a member of the **Co-operative Group** (hyphen; capital **C**)

cooperate (also **co-operate**)

coopt (also **co-opt**)

coordinate (also **co-ordinate**)

cop slang word for police officer, catch, steal, or get, and used in such phrases as *a fair cop, cop out, cop it sweet, not much cop*, etc. (compare **kop**)

copeck variant of **kopeck**

Copenhagen capital of Denmark (Danish name **København**)

copier (not **-py-**)

Copland, Aaron US composer (not **Cope-**)

copper (symbol **Cu**)

copula verb such as *be, become, seem, look, feel, taste, sound*, or *smell* (see also **complement**)

copy (*typog.*) material to be typeset or printed, especially text

copycat (one word)

copy-edit (hyphen)

copy editor (two words)

copyist (**-yi-**)

copyright right to produce copies of original text, artwork, etc. (symbol **(c)**; not **-write**)

copyright page another name for **imprint page**

copywriter person who writes promotional material for an advertisement (not **-right-**)

coq au vin chicken stewed in red wine (italics; not *coque*)

coquetry flirtation (single **t**)

coquette woman who flirts (not italic; double **t**)

Cor. Corinthians (full stop; not italic)

coral marine animal, its skeleton, or rocklike aggregation of these (compare **corral**)

cor anglais woodwind instrument of oboe family (not italic; plural **cors anglais**)

Corbusier see **Le Corbusier**

Corcyra ancient name for **Corfu**

cord string or rope, or anatomical part resembling this, as in *spinal cord, vocal cords* (the spelling **chord** is less common but not incorrect in the anatomical sense)

Corday, Charlotte French revolutionary

cordillera series of parallel mountain ranges (not italic; double **l**; not **-iera**)

Cordilleras, the complex of mountain ranges from Alaska to Cape Horn (capital **C**; **-as**)

Córdoba Spanish city (English name **Cordova**)

cordon bleu denoting high standard of cookery (not italic)

Cordova English name for **Córdoba**

corduroy (**-dur-**)

core central part (compare **corps**)

Corelli, Arcangelo Italian composer (single **r**, double **l**)

co-respondent alleged partner in adultery (compare **correspondent**)

Corfu Greek island in Ionian Sea (Modern Greek name **Kérkyra**, ancient name **Corcyra**)

Corinth Greek port or region of ancient Greece (Modern Greek name **Kórinthos** for the port)

Corinth, Gulf of Greece (also **Gulf of Lepanto**)

1 Corinthians book of the Bible (not italic; abbreviation **1 Cor.**; also **I Corinthians**; full name **The First Epistle of Paul the Apostle to the Corinthians**)

2 Corinthians book of the Bible (not italic; abbreviation **2 Cor.**; also **II**

Corinthians; full name **The Second Epistle of Paul the Apostle to the Corinthians**)

cork light material used for stoppers, insulation, etc. (compare **caulk** and **calk**)

Corneille, Pierre French dramatist

cornerstone (one word)

cornet brass instrument of trumpet family or cone-shaped container (compare **coronet**)

cornetist (also **cornettist**)

cornflour starchy maize flour (one word)

cornflower plant with blue flowers (one word)

Cornish pasty (capital **C**)

Corn Laws (capital **C** & **L**)

coronary (-**ary**)

coronet small crown (compare **cornet**)

Corot, Jean Baptiste Camille French painter

corporal (as adjective) of the body; (as noun) military officer

corporeal physical or material rather than spiritual

corps body of people (compare **core** and **corpse**; plural **corps**)

corps de ballet members of ballet company who dance together (not italic)

corpse dead body (compare **corps**)

corpus body of writings or data (plural **corpora**)

Corpus Christi Christian festival, US port, or college at Oxford and Cambridge

corral enclosure for livestock (compare **coral**)

Correggio, Antonio Allegri da Italian painter (double **r**, double **g**)

correspondent letter-writer or journalist (compare **co-respondent**)

Corrèze French department (grave accent)

corrida bullfight (not italic)

corrigendum error to be corrected, or book insert listing such errors (not italic; plural **corrigenda**)

corroborate (double **r** then single **r**, single **b**, three o's)

corroboree Aboriginal sacred or festive assembly (-**ree**)

Corsica Mediterranean island, a region of France (French name **Corse**)

cortege (also **cortège**)

Cortes national assembly of Spain (capital **C**; no accent)

Cortés, Hernando or **Hernán** Spanish conquistador (acute accent on surname and shorter form of first name; also **Cortez**)

cortex (plural **cortices**)

Cortez variant of **Cortés** (no accent)

Corunna English name for **La Coruña** (double **n**)

coruscating sparkling (sometimes wrongly used in the sense 'harshly critical')

cos variety of lettuce (lower-case **c**)

Cos variant of **Kos**

Cosa Nostra US branch of Mafia (capital **C** & **N**)

Così fan tutte opera by Mozart (grave accent; lower-case *f* & *t*; not *-tti*)

cosignatory (no hyphen)

Cosmas, St martyred physician, twin brother of St **Damian** (not **-mos**)

cosseted, cosseting (not -**tt**-)

cost past tense and past participle of **cost** in the senses 'be priced at' or 'cause the loss of', as in *the car cost £20,000* (compare **costed**)

co-star (hyphen)

cost-benefit analysis (hyphen may be replaced by en dash)

costed past tense and past participle of **cost** in the sense 'estimate cost of', as in *have you costed the project?* (compare **cost**)

cost-effective (hyphen)

cost of living (no hyphens unless used before another noun, as in *cost-of-living index*)

cote shelter for birds (also **cot**)

Côte d'Azur Mediterranean coast of France (circumflex; no hyphen)

Côte d'Ivoire African country (circumflex; no hyphen; former name **Ivory Coast**)

Côte-d'Or French department (circumflex; hyphen)

coterie small exclusive group of friends (not italic)

Côtes-d'Armor French department (circumflex; hyphen; not **Côte-**; former name **Côtes-du-Nord**)

cotillion (also **cotillon**; single t, double l)

cotoneaster (lower-case c in general use: *Cotoneaster* is the genus name; not **cott-**)

cotton wool (no hyphen unless used before another noun, as in *cotton-wool ball*)

Coué, Émile French psychologist (acute accents)

cougar (-**ar**)

could've contraction of **could have** (**'ve** not **of**)

coulee lava flow, dry stream valley, or intermittent stream (no accent)

coulis purée of fruit or vegetables (not italic)

coulomb unit of electric charge (lower-case c)

Coulomb, Charles Augustin de French physicist

council administrative body (compare **counsel**; capital C as part of name, as in *Oxford City Council*)

councillor member of council (compare **counsellor**)

Council of Trent council of Roman Catholic Church that met in mid-16th century in what is now **Trento**

counsel advice, barrister, advise, or recommend (compare **council**)

counselled, counselling (single l in US English)

counsellor adviser or diplomatic officer (compare **councillor**; single l in US English)

countdown (noun; the verb is **count down**)

countenance (-**ten**-)

counter- (rarely attached with hyphen; see individual entries)

counterattack (no hyphen)

counterbalance (no hyphen)

counterespionage (no hyphen)

counterintelligence (no hyphen)

counterproductive (no hyphen)

Counter-Reformation 16th-century Roman Catholic reform movement (capital C & R; hyphen)

counter-revolution (hyphen)

counter-revolutionary (hyphen)

countertenor (no hyphen)

countrified (the spelling **countryfied** is not incorrect, but it is less common)

country dance (two words)

countryfied less common variant of **countrified**

coup brilliant stroke, or short for **coup d'état** (compare **coo**, **coupe**, and **coop**)

coup de grâce death blow or decisive stroke (italics; circumflex; plural *coups de grâce*)

coup d'état sudden seizure of government (not italic; acute accent; plural **coups d'état**)

coup de théâtre dramatic turn of events, sensational theatrical device, or stage success (italics; acute accent and circumflex; plural *coups de théâtre*)

coupe dessert or dish in which it is served (compare **coop** and **coup**; no accent)

coupé car or carriage (acute accent)

Couperin, François French composer

courageous (-ge-)

Courchevel French ski resort (not -al)

courgette (US, Canadian, and Australian name **zucchini**)

courier (single **r** twice)

course progression, route, path, duration, series of lessons, or part of meal (compare **coarse**)

coursework (one word)

Courtauld Institute of Art London (-auld)

Courtenay, Tom English actor (not **Courtney**)

courteous (not **cur-**, not **-ti-**)

courtesan (the spelling **courtezan** is not incorrect, but it is less common)

courtesy politeness (compare **curtsy**)

courtezan less common variant of **courtesan**

courthouse (one word)

court martial (noun; plural **court martials** or **courts martial**)

court-martial (verb)

court-martialled, court-martialling (single **l** in US English)

Court of Appeal (capital **C & A**)

Court of Session (capital **C & S**)

Court of St James's (capital **C**; -s's not -s')

Courtrai Belgian town (Flemish name **Kortrijk**)

courtroom (one word)

courtyard (one word)

couscous type of semolina or dish made with it (compare **cuscus** and **khuskhus**)

cousin-german first cousin (hyphen)

Coutts banking and finance company (double **t**; no apostrophe)

couturier (may be used for males and females)

couturière (grave accent; use **couturier** instead to avoid offence)

covenanter variant of **covenantor** (lower-case **c**)

Covenanter upholder of 17th-century bond between Scotland and England to defend Presbyterianism (capital **C**; not -or)

covenantor person who performs what is promised in a covenant (also **covenanter**)

Coverley see **Sir Roger de Coverley**

cover-up (noun; the verb is **cover up**)

coveted, coveting (not -tt-)

Coward, Sir Noël English dramatist, actor, and composer (also **Noel**, without diaeresis)

co-worker (hyphen)

Cowper, William English poet (not **Cooper**; see also **Powys**)

cowrie (the spelling **cowry** is not incorrect, but it is less common)

Cox variety of apple (capital **C**; full name **Cox's Orange Pippin**)

coxswain (not -xw-; the spelling **cockswain** is not incorrect, but it is less common)

CPR cardiopulmonary resuscitation

CPU central processing unit

Cr chromium (no full stop)

Crabbe, George English poet

crackdown (noun; the verb is **crack down**)

crackup (noun; the verb is **crack up**)

Cracow Polish city (Polish name **Kraków**, German name **Krakau**)

craft skill, handiwork, cunning, or vessel (compare **kraft**)

crampon (not -oon)

crane fly insect with long thin legs (two words; informal name **daddy-longlegs**)

cranesbill (one word; no apostrophe)

cranium (plural **craniums** or **crania**)

crape black fabric used for mourning clothes, or variant of **crepe**

crash helmet (two words)

crash-landing (hyphen)

crayfish freshwater crustacean, or spiny lobster (a marine crustacean) (also **crawfish**, especially in the sense 'spiny lobster')

CRC camera-ready copy

creak harsh squeak (compare **creek**)

creation act of creating, something created, or the whole universe (lower-case **c**)

Creation God's act of creating the universe, or the universe thus created (capital **C**)

creator person or thing that creates (not **-er**; lower-case **c**)

Creator God (capital **C**)

crèche nursery or play area for children (not italic; grave accent)

Crécy French village, site of battle (English name **Cressy**, now rarely used)

credence acceptance or belief (not **-ance**; compare **credibility** and **credulity**)

credibility quality of being believed or trusted (compare **credence** and **credulity**)

credible believable or trustworthy (not **-able**; compare **creditable** and **credulous**)

creditable praiseworthy (not **-ible**; compare **credible** and **credulous**)

credit card (two words)

creditor (not **-er**)

creditworthy (one word)

credo any formal statement of beliefs or principles (lower-case **c**; plural **credos**)

Credo the Apostles' Creed or the Nicene Creed (capital **C**; plural **Credos**)

credulity gullibility (compare **credence** and **credibility**)

credulous willing to believe on little evidence (compare **credible** and **creditable**)

creek narrow inlet or small stream (compare **creak**)

creepy-crawly (hyphen)

Creighton, Mandell English bishop and historian (compare **Crichton**)

crematorium (plural **crematoriums** or **crematoria**)

crème brûlée cream dessert topped with crisp caramelized sugar (italics; three accents)

crème caramel custard dessert with liquid caramel (not italic; grave accent)

crème de la crème the very best (italics; two grave accents)

crème de menthe peppermint-flavoured liqueur (not italic; grave accent)

crème fraîche soured cream (not italic; two accents)

creole language incorporating features from two others that is a community's mother tongue (lower-case **c**; compare **pidgin**)

Creole native-born person of European ancestry or native-born Black person in Caribbean and Latin America, native-born person of French ancestry in Louisiana, or French creole spoken in Louisiana (capital **C**)

crepe fabric with crinkled surface, or very thin pancake (also **crape**, especially in the sense 'fabric', or **crêpe**, especially in the sense 'pancake')

crepe de Chine (lower-case **c** then capital **C**; no hyphen unless used before another noun, as in *crepe-de-Chine blouse*)

crepe paper (two words)

crepe rubber (two words)

crêpe suzette orange-flavoured flambéed pancake (not italic; circumflex; lower-case **s**; plural **crêpes suzettes**)

crescendo gradual increase in loudness or intensity (to avoid controversy, do not use in the sense 'peak of noise or intensity')

Cressy English name for **Crécy**, now rarely used

Cretaceous last period of Mesozoic era, or of this period (**-ce-**)

Creuset see **Le Creuset**

Creusot see **Le Creusot**

Creutzfeldt-Jakob disease (hyphen may be replaced by en dash; abbreviation **CJD**; see also **variant CJD**)

crevasse deep fissure, e.g. in a glacier

crevice narrow crack or split

Crichton, James Scottish scholar (known as **the Admirable Crichton**); **Michael** US writer (compare **Creighton**)

cricketer (not **-tt-**)

cri de coeur heartfelt appeal (not italic; plural **cris de coeur**; see also **oe**)

crier (not **-yer**)

crime passionnel crime of passion (not italic; double **n**, single **l**; plural **crimes passionnels**)

Crimplene trademark for crease-resistant synthetic fabric (capital **C**)

cringing (not **-ge-**)

cripple (to avoid offence, do not use as noun or verb in literal senses)

crisis (plural **crises**)

criterion (plural **criteria**; do not use plural form with singular meaning)

critic judge or reviewer (compare **critique**)

criticize (also **criticise**; see **-ize/-ise**)

critique critical commentary (compare **critic**)

Croat person from Croatia or variant of **Croatian**

Croatia European country (Croatian name **Hrvatska**)

Croatian (as adjective) of Croatia; (as noun) the dialect of Serbo-Croat used in Croatia, or variant of **Croat**

Croato-Serb variant of **Serbo-Croat**

crochet loop and intertwine thread with hook, or work done in this way (compare **crotchet**)

crocheted, crocheting (not **-tt-**)

Crockford's Clerical Directory list of Anglican clergy (often shortened to *Crockford*)

crocus (plural **crocuses**)

Croesus Lydian king noted for wealth, hence any very rich person (capital **C**; **-oe-**)

croissant flaky roll (not italic; double **s**)

Croix de Guerre French military decoration (italics; capital **C & G**)

Cro-Magnon man (capital **C & M** then lower-case **m**; hyphen)

Crome Yellow novel by Aldous Huxley (not *Chrome . . .*)

Cronus Titan in Greek mythology (also **Cronos** or **Kronos**)

Crookes, Sir William English scientist (**-kes**)

croquet ball game with hoops and mallets

croquette cake of minced meat or fish

crosier (also **crozier**)

Cross structure on which Christ was crucified, as in *make the sign of the Cross*, or the Crucifixion itself (capital **C**; use lower-case **c** for the verb *cross oneself* or for any representation of the Cross (see also **crucifix**), but note that capital **C** is used in names of awards, e.g. *George Cross*)

crossbar (one word)

cross-Channel (hyphen; lower-case **c** then capital **C**)

cross-examine (hyphen)

cross-match (hyphen)

crossover (noun and adjective; the verb is **cross over**)

cross-reference (hyphen)

crossroads (one word; same form for singular and plural)

cross section (two words)

cross the Rubicon (capital **R**)

crossways variant of **crosswise**

crosswind (one word)

crosswise (also **crossways**)

crotch angle between inner legs, genital area, or corresponding part of garment (also **crutch**)

crotchet musical note, hook, or perverse notion (compare **crochet**)

croupier (-ou-, -ier)

crouton small piece of toasted or fried bread (not italic, no accent)

Crowley, Aleister English writer and magician

Crown (capital C with reference to the government or sovereignty of a monarch)

crow's-foot (apostrophe; hyphen; plural **crow's-feet**)

crow's-nest (apostrophe; hyphen)

crozier variant of **crosier**

CRT cathode-ray tube

cru French vineyard or wine-producing region (not italic)

crucifix representation of the Cross with Christ on it (lower-case **c**)

crucifixion method of execution by nailing or tying to a cross (lower-case **c**)

Crucifixion the execution of Christ, or a representation of this (capital **C**)

Crufts (no apostrophe)

Cruickshank, Andrew Scottish actor

Cruikshank, George English illustrator and caricaturist

cruise pleasure trip by sea (compare **cruse**)

cruise missile (lower-case **c** & **m**)

crumby full of crumbs, or variant of **crummy** in the sense 'inferior'

crumhorn medieval woodwind instrument (also **krummhorn**)

crummy inferior, or Canadian loggers' lorry (also **crumby** in the sense 'inferior')

crusade holy war or vigorous campaign (lower-case **c**)

Crusade any of the Christian expeditions to recapture the Holy Land from the Muslims in the 11th–13th centuries (the use of lower-case **c** in this sense is less common but not incorrect)

cruse container for liquids (see **widow's cruse**; compare **cruise**)

Cruse charity for bereavement care (not **CRUSE**)

crutch support, or variant of **crotch**

cryptic (cry-)

crystal (cry-; single **l**)

crystallize (also **crystallise**, see -ize/-ise; the spellings **crystalize** and **crystalise** are less common but not incorrect)

Cs caesium (no full stop)

CSE Certificate of Secondary Education (replaced by **GCSE** in 1988)

CT Connecticut (US postal code)

CT scan computerized tomography scan (former name **CAT scan**)

Cu copper (no full stop; from Latin *cuprum*)

cub young animal or inexperienced person (lower-case **c**)

Cub member of the junior branch of the Scout Association (full name **Cub Scout**, former name **Wolf Cub**; see also **Beaver**)

cubism (often **Cubism**)

Cub Scout full name for **Cub**

Cuchulain hero of Ulster in Celtic mythology (also **Cuchulainn** or **Cuchullain**)

cudgel (single **l**)

cudgelled, cudgelling (single **l** in US English)

cue signal, reminder, stick used in billiards and snooker, give a cue to, or hit with a cue (compare **queue**)

cueing (-uei-)

cui bono for whose benefit, or for what purpose (italics)

Cuillins, the Scottish mountain range on Skye (also **the Cuillin**)

cuirass (single **r**, double **s**)

cuisine style of cookery or food (not italic)

cul-de-sac (two hyphens; plural **culs-de-sac** or **cul-de-sacs**)

cullender less common variant of **colander** (double l)

Cullinan South African village or diamond found there (double l, single **n** twice)

Culpeper, Nicholas English herbalist (single l, single **p** twice)

cum (not italic and attached with hyphens when used between nouns to denote something of a combined nature, as in *workshop-cum-gallery*)

Cumberland former English county

Cumbernauld Scottish town (-**au**-)

Cumbria English county

cum grano salis with a grain of salt, i.e. not literally (italics)

cumin (also **cummin**)

cummerbund (double **m**; not -**band**; rarely **kummerbund**)

cummin variant of **cumin**

cummings, e e US poet whose work is characterized by a lack of capital letters and punctuation (full name **Edward Estlin Cummings**)

cumquat variant of **kumquat**

cumulus (plural **cumuli**)

cuneiform (-**ei**-)

Cunninghame Graham, R(obert) B(ontine) Scottish traveller, writer, and politician (-**hame** then -**ham**; no hyphen)

CUP Cambridge University Press

cupbearer (one word)

Cup Final (capital **C** & **F** for final of FA Cup or Scottish Cup)

cupful (not -**full**; plural **cupfuls**)

Cupid's bow shape of upper lip (capital **C**)

cupronickel (no hyphen)

cup tie (lower-case **c** & **t**)

Curaçao Caribbean island, or liqueur originally made there (capital **C**; cedilla; -**ao**)

curare (the spelling **curari** is not incorrect, but it is less common)

curb (as verb) restrain or control; (as noun) something that restrains or controls, stones around top of well, horse's bit, or US and Canadian spelling of **kerb**

curable (not -**eable**)

curé French parish priest (not italic; acute accent)

curie unit of radioactivity (lower-case **c**)

Curie, Marie and **Pierre** French scientists

curio (plural **curios**)

curium (symbol **Cm**)

curlicue (-**li**-)

curly brackets another name for **braces**

currant dried grape or shrub (compare **current**)

current (as adjective) present, up-to-date, or valid; (as noun) flow of air, water, electricity, etc. (compare **currant**)

curriculum (plural **curricula** or **curriculums**)

curriculum vitae (plural **curricula vitae**; US and Canadian name **résumé**)

curser person who curses

cursor flashing line on computer screen or sliding part of measuring instrument

cursory (not -**ary** or -**ery**)

curtain-raiser (hyphen)

curtsy gesture of respect made by women or girls (also **curtsey**; compare **courtesy**)

curvilinear (no hyphen)

cuscus Australian animal (compare **couscous** and **khuskhus**)

custom house (also **customs house**)

customize (also **customise**; see -**ize/ -ise**)

customs import or export duty, government department, or part of port, airport, etc. (use singular or plural verb)

customs house variant of **custom house**

cut and dried (three words)

cutback (noun; the verb is **cut back**)

Cutch variant of **Kutch**

cutoff (noun; the verb is **cut off**)

cutout (noun; the verb is **cut out**)

cut-throat (hyphen)

Cutty Sark sailing ship (italics)

CV curriculum vitae

Cwmbran Welsh town

cwt hundredweight

cybercafé (one word; acute accent)

cyberspace (one word)

Cyclades Greek island group in Aegean Sea (Modern Greek name **Kikládhes**)

Cyclops any of a race of one-eyed giants in classical mythology (capital **C**; plural **Cyclopes** or **Cyclopses**)

cyder less common variant of **cider**

cygnet young swan (compare **signet**)

cymbal percussion instrument (compare **symbol**)

Cymru Welsh name for **Wales**

Cynewulf Anglo-Saxon poet (not -**wolf**; also **Kynewulf** or **Cynwulf**)

cypher variant of **cipher**

cypress tree (compare **Cyprus**)

Cyprian less common variant of **Cypriot**

Cyprian, St bishop of Carthage

Cypriot of Cyprus, or a person from

Cyprus (the variant **Cyprian** is less common but not incorrect)

Cyprus Mediterranean island (compare **cypress**)

Cyrano de Bergerac, Savinien French writer and soldier, famous for his large nose

Cyrillic alphabet used for Russian, Bulgarian, and Serbian (see Appendix iii)

cyst abnormal fluid-filled sac in body (compare **cist**)

czar variant of **tsar**

czarevitch variant of **tsarevitch**

czarevna variant of **tsarevna**

czarina variant of **tsarina**

czaritza another name for **tsarina**

Czech (as adjective) of the Czech Republic; (as noun) the language of the Czech Republic or a person from the Czech Republic. In historical contexts, the term may be used to refer to the former Czechoslovakia and its people, specifically the regions of Bohemia and Moravia, their people, and their language.

Czechoslovak of the former Czechoslovakia

Czechoslovakia former European country, created in 1918 and divided into the **Czech Republic** and **Slovakia** in 1993

Czechoslovakian of the former Czechoslovakia, or a person from the former Czechoslovakia

Czech Republic European country

D

d deci-, as in **dB** decibel (no full stop)

D Roman numeral for 500 (no full stop)

d', D' for capitalization and alphabetization of names beginning with **d'** or **D'**, see individual entries. As a general rule, names of French people usually have lower-case **d'** and are alphabetized under the following capital initial.

'd contraction of **would** or **had** (as in *I'd have told her if she'd asked me*). It is also sometimes used instead of **-ed**, especially to form the past tense or past participle of abbreviations (as in *KO'd, OD'd*).

ð, Ð characters used in Serbo-Croat

đ, Ð see **edh**

da (names containing **da** as a separate word with lower-case **d** are usually alphabetized under the following or preceding capital initial)

Dacca former name for **Dhaka**

dacha Russian country house (not italic; also **datcha**)

Dachau German town and Nazi concentration camp

dachshund (lower-case **d**; **-chsh-**)

Dada artistic movement (capital **D**; also **Dadaism**)

dadah slang word for illegal drugs

daddy-longlegs informal name for **crane fly** (in the UK) or **harvestman** (in the USA, Canada, and Australia) (one hyphen, no space)

dado (plural **dadoes** or **dados**)

Daedalus architect and inventor in Greek mythology (compare **Dedalus**)

daemon demigod or guardian spirit (also **daimon**; compare **demon**)

Dafydd ap Gruffudd Welsh leader of revolt against Edward I

da Gama see **Gama**

Dagestan Republic constituent republic of Russia (also **Dagestan** or **Daghestan**)

dagger (*typog.*) the symbol †), used to indicate a cross reference to a footnote or for various other purposes (also **obelisk** or **obelus**; see also **double dagger**)

Daghestan another name for **Dagestan Republic**

Daguerre, Louis Jacques Mandé French inventor

daguerreotype (not **-rro-**)

Dahl, Roald British writer (not **Ron-**)

dahlia (lower-case **d** in general use: *Dahlia* is the genus name)

Dahomey former name for **Benin**

Dáil Éireann lower chamber of Irish parliament (two acute accents; also **Dáil**; compare **Seanad Éireann**; see also **Oireachtas**)

Daimler motor manufacturer, or any of their vehicles (capital **D**)

daimon variant of **daemon**

daiquiri drink containing rum and lime juice (lower-case **d**; **-qu-**)

dairy place where milk and milk products are stored, produced, or sold (compare **diary**)

dais (**-ai-**)

Dakar capital of Senegal (compare **Dhaka**)

dal variant of **dhal**

Dalai Lama title of spiritual head of Tibetan Buddhism (capital **D** & **L**)

d'Alembert see **Alembert**

Dales, the another name for the **Yorkshire Dales**

Dali, Salvador Spanish painter (also **Dalí**, with acute accent)

Dalmatia region of Croatia

Dalmatian (as noun) breed of dog, or person from Dalmatia; (as adjective) of Dalmatia (not **-ion**; capital **D**)

dam (as noun) barrier across river, reservoir, female parent; (as verb) obstruct with dam; (as interjection, adverb, or adjective) variant of **damn** used in combination, as in *damfool*, *dammit*

damageable (**e** after **g**)

damascene decorate metal by etching or inlaying, or denoting something produced by this process (lower-case **d**; **-scene**)

Damascene of Damascus, or a person from Damascus (capital **D**)

Dame (capital **D** when used as title)

Dame aux camélias, La play by Dumas *fils* (lower-case *c*, acute accent, single *l*)

Damian, St martyred physician, twin brother of St **Cosmas** (compare **Damien** and **Damon**)

Damien character in film *The Omen* and its sequels (compare **Damian** and **Damon**)

Damien, Joseph Belgian missionary (known as **Father Damien**; not **-ian**)

damn condemn, exclamation of annoyance, or intensifier (see also **dam**)

Damon one of two loyal friends (**Damon and Pythias**) in classical legend (compare **Damian** and **Damien**)

Dan. Daniel (book of the Bible; full stop; not italic)

Danaë mother of Perseus in Greek mythology (diaeresis)

D and C dilation and curettage

Dandie Dinmont breed of dog (capital **D** twice; not **-dy**)

dandruff (rarely **dandriff**)

Danegeld (also **Danegelt**)

Danelaw (also **Danelagh**)

dangling participle see **misplaced modifier**

Daniel book of the Bible (not italic; abbreviation **Dan.**)

Daniell cell (capital **D**; not **Daniel**)

Danish blue cheese (capital **D**, lower-case **b**)

Danish pastry (capital **D**)

danke schön thank you (italics; umlaut)

D'Annunzio, Gabriele Italian writer (capital **D**)

danse macabre dance of death (italics; capital *D* for the symphonic poem by Saint-Saëns)

Dante Italian poet (full name **Dante Alighieri**)

Danube European river (German name **Donau**)

Danzig German name for **Gdańsk**

daphne shrub (lower-case **d** in general use: *Daphne* is the genus name)

Daphne nymph in Greek mythology

daphnia water flea (lower-case **d** in general use: *Daphnia* is the genus name)

Daphnis shepherd in Greek mythology

Darby, Abraham British iron manufacturer (not **Derby**)

Darby and Joan ideal elderly married couple (not **Derby**)

d'Arc see **Joan of Arc**

Dardanelles strait separating European from Asian Turkey (single **n**, double **l**, **-es**; ancient name **Hellespont**)

dare (no **-s** in third person present tense when used negatively, as in *she dare not ask*, or interrogatively, as in *dare he refuse?*)

daredevil (one word)

dare say (also **daresay**)

Dar es Salaam chief port and former capital of Tanzania (lower-case **e**; **-aam**)

Darien E part of Isthmus of Panama, or former name for the Isthmus (not **-ian**; Spanish name **Darién**)

Darjeeling Indian town or tea grown in the region (capital **D**)

dark ages any comparatively unenlightened period, e.g. that preceding the introduction of new technology (lower-case **d** & **a**)

Dark Ages the 5th–10th centuries A.D. (capital **D** & **A**; note that this is not universally regarded as an unenlightened period)

darkroom (one word)

Darwen English town

Darwin Australian port (former name **Palmerston**)

Darwin, Charles English naturalist

dash punctuation mark sometimes used in place of a comma or colon (but not in combination with the latter). An en dash (–) usually has a space before and after it; an em dash (—) does not. Pairs of dashes may be used to enclose parenthetical material (e.g. *the trapdoor in the ceiling – his only means of escape – was securely padlocked*); single dashes may be used sparingly for effect (e.g. *I did not reply to her letter – in fact I threw it away unopened*). See also en dash, em dash, hyphen, and swung dash.

dashboard (one word)

data (plural noun now often used with singular verb or pronoun, especially when considered as a body of information; singular **datum**)

data bank (two words)

database (one word)

datable (also **dateable**)

data processing (no hyphen unless used before another noun, as in *data-processing software*)

datcha variant of **dacha**

dateline date and location of newspaper story (one word; lower-case **d**)

Dateline dating agency (one word; capital **D**)

date line another name for **International Date Line** (two words, lower-case **d** & **l**)

dates month may precede or follow day number in UK English, depending on publisher's house style (i.e. *May 10* or *10 May*; rarely *May 10th* or *10th May* in modern usage). Where the month comes first, the day number is usually separated from the year number by a comma (i.e. *May 10, 2005* but *10 May 2005*). Use **en dash** rather than hyphen for date spans (e.g. *the period 1985–91*), but replace with *to* or *and* after *from* or *between* (e.g. *from 1985 to 1991, between 1985 and 1991*). Note that the year number following the en dash may be abbreviated (see **numbers**); in other contexts, abbreviated year numbers require an apostrophe in place of the century digits (e.g. *the winter of '64*). See also **A.D., B.C., BCE, CE**, and **decades**.

datum singular of **data**, used to denote a single piece of information or a proposition on which something is based

Daudet, Alphonse French writer

daughter-in-law (plural **daughters-in-law**)

Davies, Sir Peter Maxwell English composer; **Robertson** Canadian writer (compare **Davis**)

da Vinci see **Leonardo da Vinci**

Davis, Bette US actress (not **Betty**); **Sir Colin** English conductor; **Steve** English snooker player (compare **Davies**)

Davis Cup tennis championship or trophy (capital **D** & **C**; not **Davies**)

Davison, Emily English suffragette; **Peter** English actor (not **Davidson**)

Davis Strait channel between Baffin Island and Greenland (capital **D** & **S**; not **Davies**)

Davy, Sir Humphry English chemist (not **-phrey**)

Davy Jones's locker (capital **D** & **J**, lower-case **l**; **-s's** not **-s'**)

Davy lamp (capital **D**, lower-case **l**)

Dawson Creek Canadian town

Dawson's Creek TV series

Day (capital **D** in names of festivals, holidays, etc., as in *New Year's Day*, *Day of Judgment*)

Dayak variant of **Dyak**

Dayan, Moshe Israeli soldier and statesman

day bed (two words)

daybreak (one word)

daycare (one word)

daydream (one word)

Day-Glo trademark for fluorescent colouring material (capital **D** & **G**; hyphen)

Day-Lewis, Cecil British writer (pen names **C. Day Lewis**, without hyphen, and **Nicholas Blake**); **Daniel** British actor

daylight-saving time any system whereby time is set ahead of local standard time to provide extra daylight in the evening (one hyphen; lower-case **d**, **s**, & **t**)

Daylight Saving Time US and Canadian equivalent of **British Summer Time** (three words; capital **D**, **S**, & **T**; reduced to **Daylight Time** in specific time zones, as in *Eastern Daylight Time*)

daylong (one word)

Day of Atonement another name for **Yom Kippur** (capital **D** & **A**)

Day of Judgment another name for **Judgment Day** (capital **D** & **J**)

day-to-day (two hyphens)

Dayton US city in Ohio

Daytona Beach US city in Florida

day trip (two words)

day-tripper (hyphen)

dB decibel or decibels (no full stops; also **db**)

DBE Dame Commander of the Order of the British Empire

DC direct current; District of Columbia (US postal code, also used as general abbreviation (as in *Washington, DC*) and often **D.C.** in such contexts)

DCL Doctor of Civil Law

DCMG Dame Commander of the Order of St Michael and St George

DD direct debit; Doctor of Divinity

D-day June 6, 1944 (the beginning of the Allied invasion of Europe in World War II), or the planned starting day for any large-scale operation (hyphen; also **D-Day** for June 6)

DDR Deutsche Demokratische Republik (German name for the former **East Germany**; see also **GDR**)

DDS Dewey Decimal System; Doctor of Dental Surgery

DDSc Doctor of Dental Science

DDT dichlorodiphenyltrichloroethane (insecticide, now banned in UK; no full stops)

de, De for capitalization and alphabetization of names containing **de** or **De** as a separate word, see individual entries. As a general rule, names of French people usually have lower-case **de** and are alphabetized under the following capital initial, **de Gaulle** being a notable exception.

DE Delaware (US postal code)

de- (rarely attached with hyphen; see individual entries)

deadbeat (noun)

dead beat (adjective)

deadhead (one word)

dead heat (two words)

deadline (one word)

deadlock (one word)

deadly likely to cause death, as in *deadly combat*, or very boring (compare **deathly**)

deadwood (one word)

deaf, the (use **deaf people** instead to avoid offence)

deaf-and-dumb offensive former term referring to people who cannot hear or speak

deaf-mute person who cannot hear or speak, or describing such a person (now widely considered offensive)

deaf without speech denoting people who cannot hear or speak

dear beloved or expensive (compare **deer**)

deathbed (one word)

deathly resembling death, as in *a deathly silence* (compare **deadly**)

death rate (two words)

death's-head (-'s-, hyphen)

death trap (two words)

deathwatch beetle (two words, no hyphen)

deb debutante (no full stop)

debacle disastrous collapse or (not italic; no accents)

debatable (the spelling **debateable** is not incorrect, but it is less common)

debited, debiting (not -tt-)

debonair (the spelling **debonnaire** is not incorrect, but it is less common)

Debrett's Peerage list of British aristocracy (often shortened to *Debrett* or **Debrett**; full name *Debrett's Peerage and Baronetage*)

debris rubble (not italic; also **débris**)

debut first public appearance (not italic; no accent)

debutant person of either sex making first appearance in particular role or activity

debutante young upper-class woman being presented to society

Dec. December (full stop)

deca- ten, as in *decametre* (10 m) (abbreviation **da**; compare **deci-**)

decades use *1820s*, *1960s*, etc., without apostrophe. Century digits may be replaced by apostrophe (e.g. *during the '40s and '50s*) in less formal contexts, or the shortened number may be spelt out, especially in names, which may have capital initials (e.g. *the Roaring Twenties*).

Decalogue another name for the **Ten Commandments**

Decameron collection of short stories by Boccaccio

decanter (not -or)

Deccan Indian plateau (double **c**)

deceitful describing somebody who intentionally or habitually deceives (compare **deceptive**)

decelerate (single **c**, single **l**)

decentralize (also **decentralise**; see -ize/-ise)

deceptive describing something that is misleading or likely to deceive (compare **deceitful**)

deceptively (beware of ambiguity when followed by adjective: is a *deceptively simple* task more or less simple than it looks?)

deci- one tenth, as in *decimetre* (0.1 m) (abbreviation **d**; compare **deca-**)

decibel (not **-bell**; abbreviation **dB** or **db**)

decided unmistakable or determined (compare **decisive**)

decimalize (also **decimalise**; see **-ize/-ise**)

decimals (use full stop rather than centred dot for the decimal point, but note that in some countries a comma is used instead)

decisive conclusive, or able to make quick decisions (compare **decided**)

deckchair (one word)

Decker rare variant of **Dekker**

Declaration of Independence (capital **D** & **I**)

déclassé having lost status (not italic; two acute accents)

declension (not **-tion**)

décolletage low-cut neckline (not italic; acute accent; double **l**, single **t**)

décolleté low-cut, or wearing a low-cut garment (not italic; two acute accents; double **l**, single **t**)

décor style of decoration (not italic; also **decor**)

decorator (not **-er**)

decorous (not **-our-**)

decrepit (not **-id**)

decry disparage or denounce (compare **descry**)

Dedalus, Stephen character in James Joyce's *A Portrait of the Artist as a Young Man* and *Ulysses* (compare **Daedalus**)

deduce conclude by reasoning, or infer (compare **deduct**)

deducible (not **-able**)

deduct take away or subtract (compare **deduce**)

deductible (not **-able**)

deer animal (compare **dear**)

deerstalker (one word)

de-escalate (hyphen)

de facto existing in fact, whether legal or not (not italic; two words)

de Falla see **Falla**

defecate (rarely **defaecate**)

defective imperfect (compare **deficient**)

defector (not **-er**)

defence (**-ense** in US English)

defendable (not **-ible**)

defendant (not **-ent**)

defensible (not **-enc-**; not **-able**)

defensive (not **-enc-**)

deference (single f, single r, not **-ance**)

deferential (single f, single r)

deferred, deferring (single f, double r)

defibrillator (double l; not **frib-**, not **-ul-**, not **-er**)

deficient incomplete (compare **defective**)

definable (not **-eable**)

definite explicit, precise, or sure (not **-ate**; compare **definitive**)

definitely (not **-ate-**)

definitive conclusive or authoritative (compare **definite**)

deflection (rarely **deflexion**)

Defoe, Daniel English writer (surname is one word)

deforestation (no hyphen)

Defra Department for Environment, Food and Rural Affairs (no full stops; not **DEFRA**)

defunct (**-nct**)

defuse remove fuse or cause of tension from, as in *defuse a bomb*, *defuse a crisis* (compare **diffuse**)

dégagé casual, relaxed, uninvolved, or detached (italics; two acute accents)

Degas, Hilaire Germain Edgar French artist (no accent)

de Gaulle, Charles French general and statesman (lower-case **d**; not **Gaul**)

de Havilland, Olivia US actress (lower-case **d**)

De Havilland, Sir Geoffrey British aircraft designer (capital **D**)

dehumanize (also **dehumanise**; see **-ize/-ise**)

de-ice (hyphen)

Dei gratia by the grace of God (italics; capital **D**, lower-case **g**; compare *Deo gratias*)

de-ionize (hyphen; also **de-ionise**, see **-ize/-ise**)

déjà vu perception that new situation has occurred before (not italic; acute accent then grave accent)

de jure according to law (not italic; two words)

Dekker, Thomas English writer (the spelling **Decker** is not incorrect, but it is less common)

de Klerk, F(rederik) W(illem) South African statesman (lower-case **d**)

de Kooning see **Kooning**

Delacroix, Eugène French painter (surname is one word)

de la Mare, Walter English writer (lower-case **d** & **l**)

Delaroche, Paul French painter (surname is one word)

de la Tour, Frances English actress (lower-case **d** & **l**; see also **Latour** and **La Tour**)

Delaware US state or river, North American Indian people, or variety of grape (capital **D**)

De La Warr, Baron English administrator in America (known as **Lord Delaware**)

dele the symbol (⌀), used in proofreading and editing to indicate that something is to be deleted

de Lesseps see **Lesseps**

Delft Dutch town or pottery made there (capital **D**)

delftware Delft pottery (lower-case **d**)

Delibes, Léo French composer (no accent on surname)

delicatessen (single **l**, double **s**; **-en**)

Delilah biblical character (**-ah**)

delirious (**e** then **i** twice; single **l**, single **r**)

deliverance rescue, salvation, or formal pronouncement

delivery delivering of goods, mail, etc., giving birth, manner of public speaking, or manner of bowling a ball

Deloitte financial and tax consultancy (single **l**, double **t**)

DeLorean US motor manufacturer, or any of their vehicles (one word; capital **D** & **L**; **-ean**)

Delors, Jacques French politician and economist (surname is one word)

Delphi ancient Greek city, site of oracle

Delphic of Delphi or its oracle, obscure, or ambiguous (capital **D**)

delusion mistaken idea, as in *delusions of grandeur*, or belief held despite evidence to the contrary (compare **illusion** and **allusion**)

de luxe (two words)

demagogue (**-gog** in US English)

demarcate (not **-mark-**)

dematerialize (also **dematerialise**; see **-ize/-ise**)

demeanour (**-or** in US English)

demerara sugar or rum (lower-case **d**)

Demerara river or region of Guyana (capital **D**)

demigod (no hyphen)

demilitarize (also **demilitarise**; see **-ize/-ise**)

DeMille, Cecil B(lount) US film producer and director (capital **D** & **M**; also **De Mille**)

demimonde group considered to be outside respectable society (not italic; no hyphen)

demise (never **-ize**)

demisemiquaver (no hyphens)

demitasse small coffee cup (not italic; no hyphen)

demo demonstration (no full stop; plural **demos**)

demobilize (also **demobilise**; see -ize/-ise)

Democrat member of US Democratic Party (capital **D**)

Democratic Party US or South African political party (capital **D** & **P**)

Democratic Republic of Congo African country (former names **Congo Free State, Belgian Congo, Congo-Kinshasa**, and **Zaïre**)

démodé outmoded (italics; two acute accents)

demon evil spirit, wicked person, bad habit or obsession, or highly skilled person (compare **daemon**)

demonstrable (not -atable)

demonstrator (not -er)

de Montfort see **Montfort**

demoralize (also **demoralise**; see -ize/-ise)

demotic of the common people, or denoting a form of ancient Egyptian hieroglyphics (lower-case **d**)

Demotic denoting the spoken form of Modern Greek (capital **D**)

demur (single **m**, single **r**)

demurral (double **r**)

demurred, demurring (double **r**)

demy any of various sizes of paper or book (not -mi)

denationalize (also **denationalise**; see -ize/-ise)

Den Bosch another name for 's Hertogenbosch

Dench, Dame Judi British actress (not **Judy**)

DEng Doctor of Engineering

Deng Xiaoping Chinese statesman (also **Teng Hsiao-Ping**)

Den Haag a Dutch name for The Hague (capital **D** & **H**, double **a**)

deniable (not -ny-)

De Niro, Robert US actor

Denis, St patron saint of France (also **Denys**; single **n**)

Denktaş, Rauf Cypriot politician (cedilla; not -ash)

Dennis, C(larence) J(ames) Australian poet (double **n**)

denote designate or have as the literal meaning (compare **connote**)

denouement final outcome or resolution of plot (not italic; -oue-; also **dénouement**)

Denys variant of **Denis**

deodorize (not -our-; also **deodorise**, see -ize/-ise)

Deo gratias thanks be to God (italics; capital **D**, lower-case **g**; compare *Dei gratia*)

département administrative division in France (not italic, acute accent, -tem-; also **department** in English texts, including this book)

Department for Education and Skills (not ... of ...; abbreviation **DfES**)

Department for Environment, Food and Rural Affairs (not ... of the ...; abbreviation **Defra**)

Department for Transport (not ... of ...; abbreviation **DfT**)

Department for Work and Pensions (not ... of ...; abbreviation **DWP**)

Department of Employment former UK government department

Department of Health (not ... for ...; abbreviation **DH**)

Department of Health and Social Security former UK government department

Department of Social Security former UK government department

Department of Trade and Industry (not ... for ...; abbreviation **DTI**)

dependant (noun; compare **dependent**)

dependence state of being dependent on somebody (not -ance)

dependency territory subject to nonadjacent country, or overreliance on a drug (not -ancy)

dependent (adjective; compare **dependant**)

depersonalize (also **depersonalise**; see **-ize/-ise**)

depositary person to whom something is entrusted (also **depository**), or variant of **depository**

depository store (also **depositary**), or variant of **depositary**

depot (no accents)

deprecate express disapproval of, or disparage

depreciate decline in value, or disparage

depression mental disorder, economic slump, or meteorology term (lower-case **d**)

Depression worldwide economic slump of early 1930s (capital **D**)

depressurize (also **depressurise**; see **-ize/-ise**)

deputize (also **deputise**; see **-ize/-ise**)

De Quincey, Thomas English critic and essayist (capital **D**; not **-cy**)

derailleur gear-changing mechanism on bicycle (not italic; double **l**, **-eur**)

derby US and Canadian name for bowler hat (lower-case **d**)

Derby English city, cheese, horse race, or football match between local teams (capital **D**; not **Darby**)

Derbyshire English county

de rigueur required (italics; two words; *-ueu-*)

derisible ridiculous

derisive scornful

derisory worthy of derision

Derry district in Northern Ireland (in Co. Londonderry), or another name for **Londonderry**

derv (no capitals or full stops)

Derwent English or Australian river

Derwentwater English lake (one word; note that the name is not preceded by **Lake**)

Descartes, René French philosopher and mathematician (note the **-'s** in such phrases as *Descartes's birthplace*, needed because the final **s** of the name is silent)

descendant (noun)

descendent (adjective)

descender (*typog.*) lower part of letters such as *g*, *p*, or *y*

descent downward movement or slope, lineage, or decline (compare **dissent**)

descry discern (compare **decry**)

deselect (no hyphen)

desensitize (also **desensitise**; see **-ize/-ise**)

desert[1] dry region (compare **dessert**)

desert[2] abandon, abscond, or something deserved, as in *get one's just deserts* (compare **dessert**)

deshabille state of being partially or carelessly dressed (not italic; also **dishabille**)

desiccated (single **s**, double **c**)

desirable worthy of or arousing desire (not **-eable**)

desirous having or expressing desire

desktop (one word)

Des Moines US city and river

despatch variant of **dispatch**

desperado (plural **desperadoes** or **desperados**)

desperate (not **-par-**)

despise (never **-ize**)

despoiled (not **-spoilt**)

despoliation (**-spoli-**)

des res desirable residence (no full stops)

dessert sweet course of meal (compare **desert**)

dessertspoon (one word)

dessertspoonful (not **-full**; plural **dessertspoonfuls**)

De Stijl group of Dutch artists and architects (capital **D** & **S**; **-ij-**)

destructible (not **-able**)

desuetude (**-suet-**)

desultory (**-tory**)

detach (not **-atch**)

detectable (the spelling **detectible** is not incorrect, but it is less common)

detector (the spelling **detecter** is less common but not incorrect in the sense 'person who detects', but it should not be used for mechanical or electronic devices; a person using a metal detector is informally known as a **detectorist**)

détente relaxing of tension between nations (not italic; acute accent)

deter (single **r**)

detergent (not **-ant**)

deterred (double **r**)

deterrent (double **r**; not **-ant**)

deterring (double **r**)

detestable (not **-ible**)

detonator (not **-er**)

detract diminish, as in the noise detracted from my enjoyment (compare **distract**)

detractor (not **-er**)

de trop in the way or superfluous (italics; two words)

Dettol trademark for antiseptic and disinfectant products (capital **D**; double **t**, single **l**)

Deut. Deuteronomy (full stop; not italic)

deuterocanonical referring to the books of the Apocrypha (one word)

Deuteronomy book of the Bible (not italic; abbreviation **Deut.**)

Deutsch, Otto Erich Austrian music historian and art critic (**-tsch**)

Deutsche Bundesbank full name for **Bundesbank** (capital **D** & **B**; **-tsche**)

Deutschland German name for **Germany** (**-tsch-**)

de Valera, Eamon Irish statesman (lower-case **d**; single **n** in first name)

de Valois see **Valois**

Devanagari syllabic script of Indian languages (**e** then three **a**'s)

developed, developing (not **-pp-**)

development (**-pm-**)

device (noun; compare **devise**)

devil (often **Devil** with reference to the evil adversary of God)

devilish (single **l**)

devilled (single **l** in US English)

devil's advocate (**-'s**)

Devil's Island island off French Guiana (**-'s**; French name **Île du Diable**)

devise (verb; compare **device**; never **-ize**)

DeVito, Danny US actor (surname is one word; capital **D** & **V**)

devon Australian processed meat (lower-case **d**)

Devon English county (also **Devonshire**)

De Vries, Hugo Dutch botanist (capital **V**)

dew drops of condensed water (compare **due**)

Dewar flask (capital **D**)

Dewey Decimal System library classification system (all capital initials; **-wey**)

de Witt see **Witt**

dexterous (also **dextrous**)

DF Defender of the Faith

DFC Distinguished Flying Cross

DfES Department for Education and Skills (no full stops; lower-case **f**)

DFM Distinguished Flying Medal

DfT Department for Transport (no full stops; lower-case **f**)

DG *Deo gratias*; director-general

DH Department of Health (no full stops)

Dhaka capital of Bangladesh (former name **Dacca**; compare **Dakar**)

dhal curry made from split pulses (also **dal**)

dhobi washerman

dhoti loincloth

dhow Arab sailing vessel (**dh-**)

DHSS Department of Health and Social Security (former UK government department)

diacritic mark placed on or under a letter to indicate that it has different sound or stress. See **accent**, **cedilla**, **háček**, **tilde**, and other names of diacritics; **dots**; individual entries for words with diacritics; and Appendix v. Most English words of foreign origin lose their diacritics over time (e.g. *début* is now usually spelt *debut*). However, some are retained, especially if pronunciation is affected, as in *café*. If a word originally had more than one diacritic, either all or none should be dropped (i.e. *melee* can be spelt *mêlée*, but not *mêlee* or *melée*). Note that diacritics are retained when letters are capitalized, as in the French name *Émile*.

diaeresis the diacritic used on ë, ï, etc. following another vowel, to indicate that the two vowels are pronounced separately, as in the variant spelling *naïve* (plural **diaereses**; also **dieresis**; compare **umlaut**). The diaeresis is falling out of use in English, but is still used in French and other languages.

Diaghilev, Sergei Pavlovich Russian ballet impresario (**-gh-**, **-ev**)

diagnosis identification of disease through examination of symptoms, or conclusion reached through analysis of facts (plural **diagnoses**; compare **prognosis**)

diagrammatic (double **m**)

dialect form of language spoken in a particular area

dialectal of dialect

dialectic debate

dialectical of dialectic or dialectics

dialectics study of reasoning

dialled, dialling (single **l** in US English)

dialogue (not **-log**, except as a less common variant in US English)

dialyse (**-yze** in US English)

diamanté decorated with jewels, sequins, etc. (not italic; acute accent)

diameter (**-er**)

Diana, Princess of Wales title of Prince Charles's first wife (maiden name **Lady Diana Frances Spencer**)

diaphanous (**-phan-**)

diaphragm (**-ph-**, **-gm**)

diarrhoea (**-rrh-**; **-oe-**)

diary record of daily events or appointments (compare **dairy**)

Diaspora (capital **D** for the dispersion of Jews or Christians)

DiCaprio, Leonardo US actor (surname is one word; capital **D** & **C**; not **De-**)

dice (used for both singular and plural: the original singular form **die** is now rare in UK English, except in the phrase *the die is cast*)

dicey (not **-cy**)

dichotomy division into two parts (do not use with reference to paradox or ambivalence; **-ch-**)

Dickens, Charles English novelist (**-ens**)

dickey variant of **dicky**

dickeybird variant of **dickybird**

Dickins & Jones department store (**-ins**; ampersand)

dicky (also **dickey**)

dickybird (one word; also **dickeybird**)

Dictaphone trademark for tape recorder used for dictation and subsequent audiotyping (capital **D**)

dictator (not **-er**)

dictum (plural **dicta**)

did past tense of **do** (compare **done**)

didgeridoo (also **didjeridu**)

die cease to live or exist, block used to cut or form metal, or original singular form of **dice** (compare **dye**)

died past tense and past participle of **die** (compare **dyed**)

die-hard (hyphen)

Dien Bien Phu Vietnamese village, scene of French defeat

dieresis variant of **diaeresis**

diesel (-ie, -el)

diesis another name for **double dagger**

dietary (-tary)

dietician (also **dietitian**)

differed (not -rr-)

different (double **f**, single **r**, -ent; to avoid controversy, use **different from** rather than . . . **to** or . . . **than** in UK English)

differing (not -rr-)

diffuse spread, disperse, or scatter (compare **defuse**)

diffuser (the spelling **diffusor** is not incorrect, but it is less common)

digestible (not -able)

Digibox trademark for device enabling reception of digital TV signals (capital **D**)

digitalize administer drug for treatment of heart disorder to (also **digitalise**; see -ize/-ise)

digitize convert into digital form for computer processing (also **digitise**; see -ize/-ise)

dignitary (-tary)

digraph combination of two letters to represent single sound, e.g. the -**gh** of *rough* or the -**oe**- of *amoeba* (compare **diphthong** and **ligature**)

dike variant of **dyke**

diktat decree or dogmatic statement (not italic; lower-case **d**; -kt-)

dilapidated (dil-, -pid-)

dilation (also **dilatation**)

dilatory (single **l**, -tory)

dilettante person with superficial rather than professional interest, or person who loves the arts (not italic; -lett-, -te)

diligent (single **l**; not -ant)

DiMaggio, Joe US baseball player (surname is one word; capital **D** & **M**; not De-; double **g**)

dimension (not -tion)

dim sum Chinese dumplings (not italic; two words)

Dinan French town

Dinant Belgian town

dinar monetary unit of various countries (not de-)

d'Indy, Vincent French composer (lower-case **d**)

Dinesen, Isak pen name of Karen Blixen

dinghy small boat (compare **dingy**)

dingo (plural **dingoes**)

dingy dark, drab, or dirty (compare **dinghy**)

dining room (no hyphen unless used before another noun, as in *dining-room furniture*)

Dinky trademark for model cars and similar toys (capital **D**)

dinner-dance (hyphen)

dinner jacket (two words)

diocese (**c** then **s**)

Dionysius tyrant of Syracuse

Dionysus Greek god of wine (also **Dionysos**)

dioptre (-er in US English)

DipEd Diploma in Education

diphtheria (-phth-)

diphthong vowel sound that changes during the articulation of a single syllable (as in *lane, site, foul*, and *roam*), a **digraph** or **ligature** representing such a sound, or (loosely) any digraph or ligature made up of two vowels (-phth-)

dip switch device for dipping car headlights (lower-case; two words)

DIP switch switch that controls settings on electronic devices (**DIP** is acronym of *dual in-line package*)

diplomat official engaged in diplomacy, or diplomatic person

diplomate person with diploma

diptych (**i** then **y**)

direct object person or thing that receives action of verb and usually follows it, e.g. *a present* in *they gave* *me a present* (compare **indirect object** and **subject**)

Directoire denoting a decorative style or style of women's dress of late 18th-century France (italics; capital **D**)

Director of Public Prosecutions (all capital initials)

director-general (hyphen)

direct speech the reporting of something said by repeating the exact words (compare **indirect speech**). Direct speech is usually enclosed in **quotation marks**, with a capital letter at the beginning of what is said and relevant punctuation inside the quotation marks, as in '*If he leaves,' she asked, 'will you go too?*' or *I replied, 'Probably not.'*. In dialogue, each change of speaker usually requires a new paragraph.

dirigible (not -**able**)

dirndl gathered skirt or dress with gathered skirt (not italic; -**dl**)

dis- indicating reversal, negation, or removal (compare **dys-**)

disabled, the (use **disabled people** instead to avoid offence)

disappear (single **s**, double **p**)

disappoint (single **s**, double **p**)

disassemble take apart (single **s** then double **s**; compare **dissemble**)

disassociate less common variant of **dissociate** (single **s** then double **s**)

disastrous (not -**ter**-)

disbelief (noun)

disbelieve (verb)

disburse pay out (compare **disperse**)

disbursement (-**sem**-)

disc the UK spelling for most senses and uses, as in *disc jockey, a slipped disc*. The variant **disk** is used in computing (as in *hard disk, floppy disk*, but note the spelling of **compact disc**) and in US English.

discernible (not -**able**)

disciplinary (not -**ery**)

discipline (-**sc**-)

disco (plural **discos**)

discoloration (also **discolouration**)

discolour (-**or** in US English)

discolouration variant of **discoloration**

discomfit make uneasy, disconcert, or thwart (compare **discomfort**)

discomfited, discomfiting (not -**tt**-)

discomfort (as noun) inconvenience, distress, or lack of comfort; (as verb) make uncomfortable (compare **discomfit**)

disconnection (the spelling **disconnexion** is not incorrect, but it is less common in modern usage)

discotheque full form of **disco** in the sense 'place for dancing to pop records' (not italic; no accent)

discreet tactful or judicious (compare **discrete**)

discrepancy conflict or variation between things that should be the same (compare **disparity**)

discrete separate or distinct (compare **discreet**)

discriminating showing discrimination in matters of taste, i.e. discerning

discriminatory showing discrimination in the treatment of people, i.e. biased

discus disc thrown in athletics (plural **discuses** or **disci**)

discuss talk or write about (compare **discus**)

disenfranchise (also **disfranchise**; never -**ize**)

disenthral (double **l** in US English)

disenthralled, disenthralling (double **l**)

disfranchise variant of **disenfranchise** (never -**ize**)

dishabille variant of **deshabille**

dishevelled (single **s**, double **l**)

dishonour (-**or** in US English)

dishonourable (**-or-** in US English)
dishwasher (no hyphen)
disillusion (single **s**, double **l**)
disinterested free from bias or involvement (compare **uninterested**)
disk see **disc**
disk drive (not **disc**)
diskette (not **disc-**)
Disneyland theme park in California, Paris, and Tokyo (one word; see also **Euro Disney**)
Disney World theme park in Florida (two words; full name **Walt Disney World**)
disorganize (also **disorganise**; see **-ize/-ise**)
disorientate (also **disorient**)
disparate (**-par-**)
disparity difference or inequality, e.g. in age or pay (compare **discrepancy**)
dispassionate objective or impartial (compare **impassive** and **impassioned**)
dispatch (also **despatch**)
dispensable (not **-ible**)
dispensary (not **-ery**)
dispenser (not **-or**)
dispense with do away with or manage without (compare **dispose of**)
dispensing optician see **optician**
disperse scatter, dissipate, or separate (compare **disburse**)
display (*typog.*) denoting printed matter set apart from running text (e.g. long quotations or equations), usually with spacing and indents, or given prominence (e.g. headings or advertisements), usually with eye-catching typefaces
disposable (not **-ible**)
dispose of deal with or throw away (compare **dispense with**)
disputable (not **-ible**)
Disraeli, Benjamin British statesman and novelist (not **D'Israeli**)

dissect (double **s**)
dissemble conceal real feelings by pretence (double **s**; compare **disassemble**)
dissension (not **-tion**)
dissent disagree, or difference of opinion (compare **descent**)
dissenter person who dissents (lower-case **d**)
Dissenter Protestant who does not conform to the Church of England (capital **D**)
dissertation (double **s**)
dissimilar (double **s**)
dissimulate conceal real feelings by pretence (double **s**; compare **simulate**)
dissociate (double **s**; the variant **disassociate** is less common but not incorrect)
distension (also **distention**)
distil (single **l**)
distilled, distilling (single **l** in US English)
distinct clear, separate, different, or definite
distinctive characteristic or distinguishing
distingué distinguished (italics; acute accent)
distract turn away the attention of, as in *the noise distracted me from my work*, entertain, or make mad (compare **detract**)
distrait absent-minded or abstracted (not italic)
distraught greatly troubled or agitated
distributor (the spelling **distributer** is not incorrect, but it is less common)
District of Columbia US federal district covering the same area as the city of **Washington** (not **-lom-**)
dithyramb (**i** then **y**; **-mb**)
dive-bomb (hyphen)
dive bomber (two words)

divers various or sundry (an archaic or literary word)

diverse assorted or distinct

divine (not **de-**)

divisible (not **-able**)

division in the hierarchy of **taxonomic names** of plants, the group that comes above a class and below a kingdom (compare **phylum**). The division name has a capital initial and is not italic.

divisor (not **-er**)

divorcé divorced man (not italic; acute accent)

divorcee divorced person of either sex (no accent)

divorcée divorced woman (not italic; acute accent)

Diwali Hindu festival of lights

Dixie southern states of USA, a song adopted by these states during the Civil War, or of these states (also **Dixieland** in the sense 'southern states')

Dixieland form of jazz, or variant of **Dixie** in the sense 'southern states'

DIY do-it-yourself

DJ dinner jacket; disc jockey

Djakarta variant of **Jakarta**

djellaba hooded cloak (also **djellabah**, **jellaba**, or **jellabah**)

Djibouti African country or its capital (also **Jibouti**)

djinni variant of **jinni** (plural **djinn**)

DLit Doctor of Literature

DLitt Doctor of Letters (from Latin *Doctor Litterarum*)

DMus Doctor of Music

DNA deoxyribonucleic acid (no full stops)

DNB *Dictionary of National Biography* (italics)

Dneiper European river, rising in Russia (Russian name **Dnepr**)

D-notice (capital **D**, lower-case **n**; hyphen)

do see **did**, **done**, and **do's and don'ts**

Doberman pinscher (capital **D**, lower-case **p**; **-sch-**; also **Doberman** or **Dobermann pinscher**)

Docklands E London (capital **D**, **-lands**)

dockyard (one word)

Doc Martens trademark for lace-up boots with lightweight soles (capital **D** & **M**; no apostrophe; not **-tins**; full name **Doctor Martens**)

Dr Barnardo's former name for **Barnardo's**

Dr Dolittle see **Dolittle**

Dr Faustus play by Christopher Marlowe

Doctor Martens full name for **Doc Martens**

Doctor Who TV series

doctrinaire (single **n**; not **-air**)

docudrama (no hyphen)

documentary (**-tary**)

Dodgem trademark for bumper car (capital **D**; **-em**)

Dodgson, Charles Lutwidge (pen name **Lewis Carroll**)

dodo (plural **dodos** or **dodoes**)

doe female deer, rabbit, etc. (compare **dough**)

doek African headscarf (**-oe-**)

dog-eared (hyphen)

dog-end (hyphen)

dogey variant of **dogie**

dogfight (one word)

Dogger Bank North Sea (capital **D** & **B**)

doggerel (double **g**, single **r** & **l**; rarely **dogrel**)

doggy (as noun) children's word for dog; (as adjective) of or like a dog (also **doggie**)

doghouse (one word)

dogie motherless calf (also **dogy** or **dogey**)

do-gooder (hyphen)

dogrel rare variant of **doggerel**

dogs see **animal breeds** and individual entries

dogy variant of **dogie**

doily (the spelling **doyley** is not incorrect, but it is less common)

Dolby trademark for noise reduction system in recording (capital **D**)

Dolcelatte Italian cheese (capital **D**; one word)

dolce vita life of luxury (not italic; two words)

Dolgellau Welsh town (**-ell-**; **-au**)

Dolittle, Dr hero of series of children's books by Hugh Lofting (compare **Doolittle**)

Dollfuss, Engelbert Austrian statesman (double **l**, double **s**)

doll's house (**-'s** not **-s'**)

dolman robe, jacket, cloak, or denoting wide sleeve tapering to wrist

dolmen megalithic tomb or stone formation

Dolomites Italian mountain range (single **l** & **m**; **-lom-**)

dolorous (**-or-**)

dolour (**-or** in US English)

dom title given to some monks and formerly borne by royalty and nobles in Portugal and Brazil (also **Dom**; compare **don** and **Don**)

domain in the hierarchy of **taxonomic names**, the highest classification, above a kingdom (also **superkingdom**)

domesday less common variant of **doomsday**

Domesday Book (also **Doomsday Book**; capital **D** & **B**)

domiciliary (single **l**, **-iary**)

dominate control, rule, tower above, or overlook

domineer behave imperiously

Dominica Caribbean country occupying island in Lesser Antilles

Dominican Republic Caribbean country occupying half of the island of Hispaniola in the Greater Antilles (former name **Santo Domingo**)

domino (plural **dominoes**)

don university teacher, Spanish nobleman, or head of Mafia family (capital **D** as part of name)

Don Spanish title of respect for men

Dona Portuguese title of respect for women

Doña Spanish title of respect for women (tilde)

Donatello Florentine sculptor (single **n** & **t**, double **l**; original name **Donato di Betto Bardi**)

Donau German name for **Danube**

done past participle of **do** (compare **did**)

Donegal (not **-gall**)

doner kebab (lower-case **d**; **-er**)

Donets Russian river (**-ets**)

Donizetti, Gaetano Italian composer (single **n**, double **t**)

donjon central tower or keep of medieval castle (the spelling **dungeon** is not incorrect in this sense, but it is less common)

Donna Italian title of respect for women

Donne, John English poet (not **Dunn**)

donor (**-or**)

Don Quixote hero of the novel *Don Quixote* by Cervantes, hence any impractical idealist (capital **D** & **Q**)

donut variant of **doughnut**, especially in US English

doodlebug another name for **V-1** (one word)

Doolittle, Eliza character in George Bernard Shaw's *Pygmalion*; **Hilda** US poet (compare **Dolittle**)

doomsday day of Last Judgment, any day of reckoning, or characterized by predictions of disaster, as in *doomsday scenario* (the spelling **domesday** is less common but not incorrect in these senses; capital **D** may be used with either spelling in the sense 'day of Last Judgment')

Doomsday Book variant of **Domesday Book**

doona Australian name for continental quilt (**doo-**)

doorkeeper (one word)

Doornik Flemish name for **Tournai**

dopey (also **dopy**)

doppelgänger ghostly double of living person (not italic; lower-case **d**; umlaut)

Doppler effect (capital **D**)

dopy variant of **dopey**

Dorchester, The London hotel (capital **T**; not . . . **Hotel**)

Doré, Gustave French illustrator (acute accent)

Dorian (as noun) member of ancient Greek people; (as adjective) of this people, or denoting a mode in music

Doric (as adjective) of the Dorians, or denoting an order of architecture; (as noun) dialect of Ancient Greek, or rural dialect of Scotland

dormouse (not **door-**; plural dormice)

Dorset English county (not **-shire**)

dory fish or boat (not **-ey**)

DOS disk-operating system

dos-à-dos seat on which people sit back to back, or variant of **do-si-do** (not italic; two hyphens; grave accent)

dosage (not **-eage**)

do's and don'ts (two apostrophes; not **-nt's** or **-n't's**)

do-si-do figure in square dancing, or call instructing dancers to perform it (also **dos-à-dos**)

Dos Passos, John US novelist (capital **D**)

dossier collection of papers (not italic)

Dostoevsky, Fyodor Mikhailovich Russian novelist

dotcom (also **dot.com**)

dots see **ellipsis** for the use of (. . .). See also **bullet**, **centred dot**, and **full stop**. A dot below a letter is used as a diacritic in some African languages, transliterations of Sanskrit, etc.

Douai French city (**-ai**)

Douay Bible English translation of the Bible completed in 1610 (**-ay**; also **Douay Version**)

double-barrelled (hyphen; single l in US English)

double check (noun)

double-check (verb)

double cross technique for producing hybrid stock (two words)

double-cross cheat or betray, or an instance of this (hyphen)

double dagger (*typog.*) the symbol (‡), used to indicate a cross reference to a footnote or for various other purposes (also **diesis** or **double obelisk**)

double-dealing (hyphen)

double-decker (hyphen)

double entendre ambiguous word or phrase, or humour arising from this (not italic; two words)

double Gloucester cheese (capital **G**)

double negative nonstandard use of two negatives where only one is needed, as in *I didn't tell nobody*, or acceptable use of **not** to reduce the negative force of the following adjective, as in *a not unfriendly reception.*

double obelisk (*typog.*) another name for **double dagger**

double talk (two words)

doublethink (one word)

doubt (may be followed by *whether, if,* or *that* in positive contexts)

doubting Thomas (capital **T**)

douche stream of water directed onto or into body (not italic)

dough mixture used to make bread or pastry, or slang word for money (compare **doe**)

doughnut (sometimes **donut**, especially in US English)

Douglas fir (capital **D**)

Douglas-Home, Sir Alec, Baron Home of the Hirsel British statesman (not **-Hume** or **-Hulme**)

Doukhobor member of Christian sect of Russian origin (also **Dukhobor**)

Dounreay Scottish site of nuclear power station (**-ou-**, **-ea-**)

douse plunge into or drench with water, or extinguish (also **dowse**)

dovecote (also **dovecot**)

Dow-Jones denoting index of US stock-exchange prices (hyphen)

down-and-out (two hyphens)

downgrade (one word)

downhearted (one word)

down-market (also **downmarket**)

downpour (one word)

downs rolling upland in Britain, or grassy area in Australia and New Zealand (lower-case **d**)

Downs, the range of chalk hills in S England (capital **D**)

Down's syndrome genetic disorder (former name **mongolism** now considered offensive)

downstairs (adverb, adjective, and noun; never **-stair**)

downtime (one word)

downtown (one word)

downturn (one word)

down under (noun and adverb; lower-case **d** & **u**)

downward (adjective; sometimes adverb (see **-ward** and **-wards**))

downwards (adverb only)

downwind (one word)

dowry (not **-ery**)

dowse search for underground water, or variant of **douse**

Doyle see **Conan Doyle**

doyley less common variant of **doily**

D'Oyly Carte, Richard British producer of operettas of Gilbert and Sullivan (capital **D**; apostrophe; not **-ley**)

DP data processing; displaced person

DPhil less common variant of **PhD**

Dr Doctor (before name; entries beginning with this abbreviation are alphabetized under the full form); Drive (in addresses)

Draconian (sometimes lower-case **d**, especially in figurative use)

draft plan, sketch, preliminary version, selection for military service (in USA), detachment of military personnel, group of livestock separated from herd or flock (in Australia and New Zealand), verb related to these noun senses (as in *draft a speech*, *draft military personnel*, etc.), or US spelling of **draught**

drafter person who draws up a legal document, speech, etc. (compare **draughtsman**, **draughtsperson**, and **draughtswoman**)

dragée sweet (not italic; acute accent)

dragoman (plural **dragomans** or **dragomen**)

dragon mythical monster or fierce person (compare **dragoon**)

dragonfly (one word)

dragoon soldier, or coerce (compare **dragon**)

Dragoon Guards (capital **D** & **G**)

dramatis personae list of characters (not italic)

dramatize (also **dramatise**; see **-ize/-ise**)

Drambuie trademark for liqueur based on Scotch whisky (capital **D**)

drank past tense of **drink** (compare **drunk**)

draught current of air, load or act of pulling it, amount to be drunk, air or smoke inhaled, beer stored in cask, depth of vessel in water (**draft** in US English; see also **draughts**)

draughtboard (one word; not **-tsb-**)

draughts board game (use singular

verb; not **-afts**; US and Canadian name **checkers**)

draughtsman person who prepares drawings of machines, buildings, etc., person skilled in drawing, or piece used in playing draughts (may be used for males or females in the senses 'person who draws', but use **draughtsperson** instead where appropriate)

draughtsperson (use instead of gender-specific **draughtsman** or **draughtswoman** where appropriate, e.g. in job advertisements)

draughtswoman (use **draughtsperson** instead where appropriate, e.g. to avoid offence)

drawback (noun; the verb is **draw back**)

drawbridge (one word)

drawing board (two words)

drawing pin (two words)

dray low cart for carrying loads, or variant of **drey**

dreadnought (the spelling **dreadnaught** is not incorrect, but it is less common)

dreamed past tense and past participle of **dream** (also **dreamt**)

Dreamtime in Aboriginal mythology, a mythical Golden Age of the past (one word; capital **D**; also **alcheringa**)

Dreiser, Theodore US novelist (-ei-)

Dresden German city, or denoting china made there (capital **D**; -den)

dressing-down (hyphen)

dressing gown (two words)

dressing room (two words)

dressing table (two words)

drey squirrel's nest (also **dray**)

drier comparative of **dry** (also **dryer**), or variant of **dryer**

drily in a dry manner (also **dryly**)

drink-driving (hyphen)

drip-dry (hyphen)

drivable (also **driveable**)

drive-in (hyphen)

driving licence (not **driver's . . .**)

Drogheda Irish port (-ogh-)

droit du seigneur right of feudal lord to have sex with vassal's bride (not italic; also **. . . de . . .**)

dromedary (-med-, -ary)

drop initial (*typog.*) large first letter of text (e.g. in chapter opening) that descends for two or more lines

drop kick (noun)

drop-kick (verb)

drop-leaf table (one hyphen)

dropout person who drops out of college or society (one word)

drop out (verb; two words)

drop-out electronics or rugby term (hyphen)

drought (not -outh)

drug squad (two words; not **drugs . . .**)

drugstore (one word)

druid (also **Druid** in both ancient and modern senses)

drumbeat (one word)

drumstick (one word)

drunk past participle of **drink** (compare **drank**). When used adjectivally, it usually refers to a single episode of intoxication and follows the verb, as in *her husband was drunk so she drove home* (compare **drunken**).

drunken may refer to habitual intoxication and usually precedes the noun, as in *she finally divorced her drunken husband* (compare **drunk**)

drunkenness (double **n** before -ess)

Druze member of religious sect in Syria, Lebanon, and Israel (also **Druse**)

dry-clean (hyphen)

dryer person or thing that dries (also **drier**), or variant of **drier**

dryly variant of **drily**

dry-stone wall (one hyphen)

DSc Doctor of Science

DSC Distinguished Service Cross

DSM Distinguished Service Medal

DSO Distinguished Service Order

DSS Department of Social Security (former UK government department)

DTI Department of Trade and Industry (no full stops)

DT's delirium tremens (apostrophe)

du (for capitalization and alphabetization of names containing **du** as a separate word, see individual entries)

dual double (compare **duel**)

Dual Alliance alliance between French and Russia from 1893 to 1917 (capital **D** & **A**)

Dual Monarchy monarchy of Austria Hungary from 1867 to 1918 (capital **D** & **M**)

dual-purpose (hyphen)

du Barry, Comtesse mistress of Louis XV (lower-case **d**)

dubbin substance used on leather (also **dubbing**)

Dubček, Alexander Czechoslovak statesman (**-ček**)

Dublin Bay prawn (capital **D** & **B**)

Dubonnet trademark for apéritif wine (capital **D**; double **n**)

Duce, Il title assumed by Benito **Mussolini**

duchess (not -tch-, but see also **Dutchess County**; for capitalization see **titles of people**)

duchesse potatoes (lower-case **d**; -esse)

duckbill short for **duck-billed platypus** (no hyphen in short form)

duck-billed platypus (one hyphen; -ty-, -us; plural **duck-billed platypuses**)

duckfoot quotes the characters « » used as quotation marks in some European languages (also **guillemets**)

dudgeon anger or resentment, chiefly used in the phrase *in high dudgeon* (compare **dungeon**)

due owing, proper, or expected to arrive (compare **dew**; see also **due to**)

duel fight (compare **dual**)

duelled, duelling (single **l** in US English)

duenna Spanish or Portuguese governess and chaperon (not italic; double **n**)

due to (may be used adjectivally without controversy, as in *diseases due to poor hygiene*; as preposition, may be replaced by **owing to** or **because of**)

Dufay, Guillaume French composer

duffel bag (two words; double **f**, single **l**)

duffel coat (two words; double **f**, single **l**)

Dufy, Raoul French artist

du Gard see **Martin du Gard**

dugout canoe, military excavation, or covered bench at sports ground (one word)

duiker antelope or cormorant (also **duyker**)

Duisburg German city (-ui- then -ur-)

Duke of Edinburgh's Award (capital **D, E,** & **A**; -'s)

Dukhobor variant of **Doukhobor**

dullness (rarely **dulness**)

dully in a dull manner (compare **duly**)

dulness rare variant of **dullness**

duly in the due manner or at the due time (compare **dully**)

Dumas, Alexandre (known as **Dumas *père***) French writer, author of *The Count of Monte Cristo* and *The Three Musketeers*; **Alexandre** (known as **Dumas *fils***) French writer, author of *La Dame aux camélias* (note the -'s in such phrases as *Dumas's birthplace*, needed because the final **s** of the name is silent)

Du Maurier, Dame Daphne and
George English novelists (capital **D**)

dumb (to avoid offence, do not use
with reference to people who
cannot speak because of physical or
mental disorder; see also **deaf-and-
dumb**, **deaf-mute**, and **deaf without
speech**)

Dumbarton Scottish town (not
Dun-)

dumbbell (one word; double **b**)

dumbfound (rarely **dumfound**)

Dumfries and Galloway Scottish
council area

Dumfriesshire former Scottish
county

dummy (*typog.*) prototype of
proposed book, or designer's layout
of page

Dunbartonshire Scottish county
(not **Dum-**)

Dundonian of Dundee, or a person
from Dundee

dungarees (**-gar-**)

dungeon underground prison cell,
or less common variant of **donjon**
(**-ge-**; compare **dudgeon**)

dunghill (one word)

Dunkerque French port (English
name **Dunkirk**)

Dún Laoghaire Irish port (acute
accent; **-aogh-**)

Duns Scotus, John Scottish
theologian

duodecimo book size with twelve
leaves (i.e. 24 pages) per sheet (also
twelvemo or **12mo**)

duplication duplicating or being
duplicated

duplicity deception or double-
dealing

du Pré, Jacqueline English cellist
(lower-case **d**; acute accent; surname
is two words)

Dupré, Marcel French organist and
composer (acute accent; surname is
one word)

Dürer, Albrecht German painter
(umlaut)

duress (not **-esse**)

Durex trademark for condom in
UK or adhesive tape in Australia
(capital **D**)

d'Urfé see **Urfé**

D'Urfey, Thomas English playwright and songwriter (capital **D'**;
-fey)

Durham English city and county (use
County Durham or **Co. Durham** for
the county if necessary to avoid
ambiguity)

Dushanbe capital of Tajikistan
(former name (1929–61) **Stalinabad**)

Düsseldorf German city (umlaut,
double **s**, single **l**)

dustbin (one word)

dust bowl semiarid area (lower-case
d & **b**)

Dust Bowl, the area of south central
USA (capital **D** & **B**)

dust jacket (two words)

dustman (use **refuse collector**
instead where appropriate)

dustsheet (one word)

dutch slang word for wife (lower-case
d)

Dutch of the Netherlands, or the
language or people of the
Netherlands (capital **D**, also in such
phrases as *double Dutch*, *go Dutch*,
Dutch courage, *Dutch treat*)

Dutch East Indies former name for
Indonesia

Dutchess County New York, USA
(**-utch-**; compare **duchess**)

Dutch Guiana former name for
Surinam

Dutch New Guinea former name
for **Irian Jaya**

duteous (not **-ti-**)

dutiful (not **-ty-**)

duty-free (hyphen)

dux top pupil (not italic)

duyker variant of **duiker**

DVD digital versatile disk or digital video disk (no full stops; plural **DVDs**)

DVLA Driver and Vehicle Licensing Agency (not Authority)

Dvořák, Antonin Czech composer (two diacritics)

DVM Doctor of Veterinary Medicine

DVT deep vein thrombosis

dwarf (plural **dwarfs** or **dwarves**)

dwelt past tense and past participle of **dwell** (also **dwelled**)

DWP Department for Work and Pensions (no full stops)

Dy dysprosium (no full stop)

Dyak Malaysian people of Borneo (also **Dayak**)

Dyck see **Van Dyck**

dye colour or stain (compare **die**)

dyed past tense and past participle of **dye** (compare **died**)

dyeing present participle of **dye** (compare **dying**)

Dyfed former Welsh county

dying present participle of **die** (compare **dyeing**)

dyke (also **dike**)

dynamo (plural **dynamos**)

dys- bad, abnormal, or difficult (compare **dis-**)

dysentery (not **dis-**, not **-try**)

dyslexia (not **dis-**)

dyslexic (the variant **dyslectic** is less common but not incorrect)

dyspepsia (not **dis-**)

dysprosium (symbol **Dy**)

Dzongka official language of Bhutan (also **Dzongkha**)

E

E east or East

è see **grave**

e- electronic (usually attached with hyphen; see individual entries)

-eable used for words ending in **-ge** or **-ce** (e.g. *changeable, replaceable*), the **e** being required to retain the soft sound of the **g** and **c**. (Note that the **e** is not required before **-ible**, as the **i** serves this purpose.) Most other words drop their final **e** before **-able** is added, but sometimes two spellings are possible (e.g. *likable* or *likeable*). See also **-able/-ible**.

each (use singular verb, as in *each was carrying a briefcase*; compare **both**)

each other (may be used regardless of the number of people or things involved: synonymous with **one another**)

E & OE errors and omissions excepted

EAP English for academic purposes

earache (one word)

eardrum (one word)

Earhart, Amelia US aviator (**Ear-** then **-ar-**)

Earl Grey tea (capital **E** & **G**; not **Gray**)

ear lobe (two words)

Earls Court London (no apostrophe)

earned past tense and past participle of **earn** (not **-nt**)

earplug (one word)

earring (no hyphen)

ear-splitting (hyphen)

earth (also **Earth** in astronomical contexts, referring to the planet as a whole)

earthly of the planet earth, worldly, or possible (compare **earthy**)

earthworm (one word)

earthy of earth or soil, lusty, or crude (compare **earthly**)

east (as noun) direction or compass point opposite west, or area lying in this direction; (as adjective or adverb) in, to, or from the east (sometimes capital **E** in the sense 'area lying in the east'; see also **compass points**)

East Asia regarded as culturally distinct from Europe, America, etc.; formerly, the Communist countries; or denoting the eastern part of a particular country, continent, etc. (sometimes lower-case **e** in adjectival use, but always capital **E** in names; also **Orient** in the sense 'Asia'; see also **Far East**, **Middle East**, and **Near East**)

East Anglia region of England (do not abbreviate **East**)

East Cape easternmost point of New Guinea or New Zealand (capital **E** & **C**; compare **Eastern Cape**)

East End part of London containing former industrial and dock areas (capital **E** twice)

East Ender person from the East End (two words; capital **E** twice)

EastEnders TV series (one word; capital *E* twice)

Easter Island Pacific island off Chile (also **Rapa Nui**)

eastern of, in, or to the east (lower-case **e**)

Eastern of, in, or to the East (capital **E**)

Eastern Cape South African province (capital **E** & **C**; also **Eastern Province**; compare **East Cape**)

Eastern Ghats Indian mountain range (capital **E** & **G**)

Eastern Orthodox Church another name for **Orthodox Church**

Eastern Province variant of **Eastern Cape**

East Friesland region of Germany (**-ies-**)

East Germany former European country, created in 1949 and reunited with **West Germany** in 1990 (do not abbreviate **East** in this sense; see also **DDR** and **GDR**)

East India Company (capital **E**, **I**, & **C**)

east-northeast (one hyphen)

east-southeast (one hyphen)

eastward (adjective; sometimes adverb (see **-ward** and **-wards**))

eastwards (adverb only)

easy-going (hyphen)

easyJet airline company (one word; lower-case **e**, capital **J**)

eatable fit to eat, especially in the sense 'palatable' (**-able**; compare **edible**)

eaten past participle of **eat** (compare **ate**)

eau de Cologne another name for **cologne** (not italic; lower-case **e**, capital **C**; three words)

eau de nil pale green (not italic; also **eau de Nil**; no hyphen unless used before another noun, as in *an eau-de-nil rug*)

eau de toilette another name for **toilet water** (not italic; three words)

eau de vie brandy (not italic; three words)

EB *Encyclopaedia Britannica* (italics; see also that entry)

eBay Internet auction site (no hyphen; lower-case **e**, capital **B**)

Ebbw Vale Welsh town

e-book (hyphen)

ebullient (not **-ant**)

EC European Community (see that entry)

eccentric (double **c** then single **c**)

Eccl. Ecclesiastes (full stop; not italic)

Eccles. Ecclesiastes (full stop; not italic)

Eccles cake (capital **E**)

Ecclesiastes book of the Bible (not italic; abbreviation **Eccl.** or **Eccles.**)

Ecclesiasticus another name for **Sirach** (book of the Apocrypha; not italic)

ECG electrocardiogram; electrocardiograph (no full stops)

echelon level of responsibility or military formation (not italic; no accent)

echo (plural **echoes**)

éclair finger-shaped cake (not italic; acute accent)

éclat brilliant or conspicuous success, effect, or display (not italic; acute accent)

eclipse obscuring of sun, moon, etc.; loss of power or importance; surpass; or overshadow (compare **ellipse**)

Eco, Umberto Italian writer (single **c**)

eco- (rarely attached with hyphen; see individual entries)

E. coli *Escherichia coli* (bacterium; italics; capital *E*, lower-case *c*)

e-commerce (also **ecommerce**)

economic relating to economics or an economy, profitable, or cheap

economical not wasteful of resources, frugal, or used in the phrase *economical with the truth*

economize (also **economise**; see -ize/-ise)

ecosystem (no hyphen)

ecotourism (no hyphen)

eco-warrior (hyphen)

ecru colour of unbleached linen (not italic; no accent)

ecstasy (not **ex-**, not **-cy**; lower-case **e** in all senses, including the drug (see also **MDMA**))

ECT electroconvulsive therapy (no full stops)

Ecuador South American country (not **Equ-**)

Ecuadorean of Ecuador, or a person from Ecuador (not **-ian**)

ecumenical (rarely **oecumenical**)

eczema (**-cz-**)

ed. edited; edition; editor (plural **eds**)

-ed/-t (see individual entries for the use of **-ed** versus **-t** to form the past tense and past participle of verbs such as *burn, dream, leap,* and *spell*)

Edam Dutch town or cheese (capital E)

Eddystone denoting group of rocks or lighthouse in English Channel

edelweiss (**-del-**, **-ei-**, double **s**)

edema US spelling of **oedema**

Edgbaston Birmingham (not **Edge-**)

Edgehill battle site in Warwickshire (one word; **Edge-**)

Edgeworth, Maria Anglo-Irish novelist (**Edge-**)

Edgware London (not **Edge-**)

edh the symbol ð or Đ, used in Old English, Old Norse, modern Icelandic, and the International Phonetic Alphabet (also **eth**)

edible fit to eat, especially in the sense 'not poisonous' (**-ible**; compare **eatable**)

Edinburgh (not **-borough**)

Edinburgh, Duke of husband of Elizabeth II (also **Prince Philip**)

Edirne Turkish city (former name **Adrianople**)

Edison, Thomas Alva US inventor

edition first version of publication, or a subsequent revised, enlarged, or abridged version (compare **impression** (for meaning) and **addition** (for spelling))

editor (not **-er**)

edn edition

eds editions; editors

educable (also **educatable**)

educationalist (also **educationist**)

-ee indicates recipient of action, as in *employee, lessee* (compare **-er** and **-or**). The use of **-ee** in place of **-er**, as in *escapee, attendee, standee,* is controversial.

EEC European Economic Community (see that entry)

EEG electroencephalogram; electroencephalograph (no full stops)

e'er ever (compare **ere** and **err**)

eerie weird or ghostly (compare **eyrie** and **Erie**)

effect (as noun) result, efficacy, condition of being operative, impression, or scientific phenomenon; (as verb) cause to occur (compare **affect**)

effendi Turkish title of respect (double **f**; **-di**)

effervescent (**-erv-**, **-scent**)

effluent liquid or radioactive waste, or flowing out (compare **affluent**)

effrontery impudence or audacity (compare **affront**)

E-FIT trademark for computer-generated image of police suspect, or the technique used to produce such images (acronym of Electronic Facial Identification Technique; hyphen; no full stops)

EFL English as a foreign language

(for people in non-English-speaking country; compare **ESL**; see also **ESOL**)

EFTA European Free Trade Association (no full stops)

e.g. for example (from Latin *exempli gratia*; compare **i.e.**)

egg cup (two words)

eggplant US, Canadian, and Australian name for **aubergine**

eggshell (one word)

ego (plural **egos**)

egoism concern for one's own welfare

egotism inflated sense of self-importance

egregious (egr- then -egi-)

egret bird (compare **aigrette**)

Eid-ul-Adha Muslim festival marking end of pilgrimage to Mecca

Eid-ul-Fitr Muslim festival marking end of Ramadan

Eifel German plateau region (single **f & l**)

Eiffel, Alexandre Gustave French engineer (double **f**, single **l**)

Eiffel Tower monument in Paris, France (capital **E & T**)

Eigg Scottish island

eighteenmo book size with 18 leaves (i.e. 36 pages) per sheet (also **18mo** or **octodecimo**)

eighth (-hth)

eightvo another name for **octavo** (also **8vo**)

Eilean Donan Castle Scotland

Einstein, Albert German-born US physicist

einsteinium (symbol **Es**)

Eire former name for **Republic of Ireland** or Irish Gaelic name for **Ireland**

eirenic variant of **irenic**

eirenicon peace proposition (also **irenicon**)

Eisenhower, Dwight David US general and statesman

Eisenstein, Sergei Soviet film director

eisteddfod (double **d** then single **d**; plural **eisteddfods** or **eisteddfodau**; capital **E** in names, e.g. *Royal National Eisteddfod*)

either use singular verb with singular subject, as in *either spelling is acceptable* and *either of the spellings is acceptable*. In the **either . . . or** construction, use singular verb if both subjects are singular (as in *either Jack or Emma is the culprit*) and use plural verb if one or both subjects are plural (as in *if either the box or its contents are damaged*). Beware of ambiguity in contexts where the meaning could be 'one or the other' or 'both', as in *at either end of the line*.

ejector (not -er)

Ekaterinburg variant of **Yekaterinburg**

El Alamein Egyptian village, scene of Allied victory in World War II (two words)

élan style and vigour (not italic; acute accent)

élan vital life force (italics; acute accent)

elbowroom (one word)

Elbrus Russian mountain (-brus)

Elburz Mountains Iranian mountain range (-burz)

elder describing person born earlier than another, as in *my elder brother, the elder of my two daughters* (compare **eldest**; use **older** instead as comparative with *than*, as in *my brother is older than I am*)

elderly, the (use **elderly people** or a more appropriate synonym instead to avoid offence)

eldest describing person born earlier than more than one other, as in *the eldest of my three daughters* (compare **elder**)

El Dorado fabled South American city rich in treasure, or any place of great riches (two words; capital **E** & **D**; also **eldorado** in the sense 'any place of great riches')

elector (not **-er**)

electoral college body of electors chosen by voters (lower-case **e** & **c**)

Electoral College body that elects US president (the use of lower-case **e** & **c** is less common but not incorrect)

Electra complex sexual attachment of girl to father (compare **Oedipus complex**)

electric of, derived from, producing, or powered by electricity, as in *electric blanket*, or emotionally charged, as in *the atmosphere was electric*

electrical of or concerned with electricity, as in *electrical engineering*

electrocardiogram tracing made by electrocardiograph

electrocardiograph instrument for recording electrical activity of the heart

electrocute (use only where the result is death; not **-tric-**)

electroencephalogram tracing made by electroencephalograph

electroencephalograph instrument for recording electrical activity of the brain

electrolyse (**-yze** in US English)

electrolyte (**-yte**)

electromagnetic (no hyphen)

elegiac (**-iac**)

elegy mournful poem or lament (**-leg-**; compare **eulogy**)

elementary (**-tary**)

elevator (not **-er**)

elf (plural **elves**)

elfish (also **elvish**)

El Gîza Egyptian city (circumflex)

El Greco Spanish painter born in Crete (real name **Domenikos Theotocopoulos**)

Eli biblical priest

Elia pen name of Charles **Lamb**

Elias variant of **Elijah**

elicit evoke (compare **illicit**)

eligible qualified or worthy (compare **illegible**)

Elijah biblical prophet (also **Elias**)

Eliot, George English novelist (real name **Mary Ann Evans**, later **Marian Evans**); T(homas S(tearns) British poet and dramatist (compare **Elliot**)

elision omission of letters or syllables, as in *th'* for *the* (compare **ellipsis**)

elite most powerful, rich, or gifted members of a group (not italic; also **élite**)

Elizabeth, Queen English monarch (**Elizabeth I**) or British monarch (**Elizabeth II**) (not **-lis-**)

Ellice Islands a former name for **Tuvalu** (not **Ellis**)

Elliot surname of characters in Jane Austen's *Persuasion* (compare **Eliot**)

ellipse oval (plural **ellipses**; compare **eclipse** and **ellipsis**)

ellipsis (plural **ellipses**) group of three dots indicating that text has been omitted (as in *'I have a dream that one day ... the sons of former slaves and the sons of former slave owners will be able to sit down together'*) or used for effect (as in *it sounded plausible, but ...*). If the last part of a sentence within a quotation is replaced by an ellipsis, it is not necessary to add a fourth dot as a full stop; however, if a whole sentence is omitted, the sentence preceding the ellipsis should have a full stop as usual. An ellipsis may be enclosed in square brackets to show that it has been inserted by the editor rather than the original author of the quoted text. The term **ellipsis** also denotes the omission of a word or words to avoid repetition, e.g. a second *he* after *and* in *he tore up the letter and threw it away* (compare **elision**). Beware of omitting words that are required, e.g. *been* in *it has not been and probably never will be found.*

El Niño meteorological phenomenon (capital **E** & **N**; tilde)

'Eloisa to Abelard' poem by Alexander Pope about the love of Peter **Abelard** and **Héloïse**

El Paso US city (two words; single **s**)

El Paso del Norte former name for **Ciudad Juárez**

El Salvador Central American country (two words; compare **Salvador** and **San Salvador**)

Elsass German name for **Alsace**

Elsass-Lothringen German name for **Alsace-Lorraine**

Elsevier publishing company (not **Elz-**, not **-vir**)

Elsinore English name for **Helsingør**

ELT English language teaching

elude escape by cunning, or fail to be discovered, achieved, or understood by (compare **allude** and **evade**)

elusive difficult to catch, achieve, or remember (compare **allusive** and **illusive**)

elvish variant of **elfish**

Elysée palace in Paris, France (also **Élysée**)

Elysium in Greek mythology, dwelling place of blessed after death (also **Elysian fields**)

em (*typog.*) unit of measurement originally equivalent to the width of capital M in any size of type, or another name for **pica** (compare **en**; see also **em dash** and **em space**)

'em them (apostrophe)

e-mail (also **email**, **E-mail**, or **Email**)

Emanuel, David and **Elizabeth** fashion designers (single **m**)

Emanuel School London (single **m**)

embargo (plural **embargoes**)

embarkation (not **-arc-**)

embarras de richesses abundance of good things, options, etc. (italics; single **s** at end of first word)

embarrass (double **r**, double **s**)

embed (rarely **imbed**)

embezzlement (not **-lment**)

embodiment (not **-dyment**)

embonpoint plumpness (italics)

embroil (not **im-**)

embryo (plural **embryos**)

em dash (also **em rule**) the symbol (—), longer than an **en dash**, used as a punctuation mark (see **dash**) and sometimes to represent omitted letters, as in *the Duke of G—*

emend correct or improve by critical editing, as in *emend a text* (compare **amend**)

emigrant person leaving country to settle elsewhere (compare **immigrant**)

emigration act of leaving country as emigrant (compare **immigration**)

émigré emigrant, especially one leaving native country for political reasons (not italic; two acute accents)

Emilia-Romagna region of Italy (hyphen)

Emin, Tracey British artist (not **Tracy**)

eminent distinguished or noteworthy (compare **imminent** and **immanent**)

emissary (single **m**, double **s**, **-ary**)

emission act of discharging, or something discharged (compare **omission**)

emit (single **m**, single **t**)

emitted, emitting (single **m**, double **t**)

Emmanuel variant of **Immanuel**

Emmanuel College Cambridge (double **m**)

Emmenthal cheese (capital **E**; also **Emmental**)

Emmy US award for achievement in television (plural **Emmys** or **Emmies**)

emollient softening or soothing (single **m**, double **l**, not **-ant**)

emolument fee or wage (single **l**)

emotional of, expressing, or affected by emotion

emotive arousing emotion

empathize (also **empathise**; see **-ize/ -ise**)

emperor (**-er-** then **-or**; for capitalization see **titles of people**)

emphasis (plural **emphases**)

emphasize (also **emphasise**; see **-ize/-ise**)

Empire (capital **E** when the word is used alone with reference to the British Empire, or in names of other empires, e.g. *Second Empire, Holy Roman Empire*)

employment tribunal (former name **industrial tribunal** still used in Northern Ireland)

empty-handed (hyphen)

empty-headed (hyphen)

em rule another name for **em dash**

EMS European Monetary System

em space a space one em wide

EMU European Monetary Union

emulate (in human contexts use **imitate** instead if there is no rivalry or competition involved)

en (*typog.*) unit of measurement equal to half an **em** (see also **en dash** and **en space**)

enamel (single **l**)

enamelled, enamelling (single **l** in US English)

enamoured (**-ored** in US English; followed by *of*)

en bloc all together (italics)

encapsulate (rarely **incapsulate**)

encase (rarely **incase**)

encephalitis (not **enk-**, not **-us**)

enchilada Mexican dish (not italic; single **l** & **d**)

enclose (rarely **inclose**)

encode (not **in-**)

encore extra or repeated performance (not italic)

encrust (the spelling **incrust** is not incorrect, but it is less common)

encrustation (also **incrustation**)

encrypt (not **-ipt**)

encumber (rarely **incumber**)

encyclopaedia variant of **encyclopedia**

Encyclopaedia Britannica (not **-ped-**; the books themselves have **æ**)

encyclopedia (also **encyclopaedia**; if the word is part of the title, use capital **E** and retain original spelling)

en dash (also **en rule**) the symbol (–), longer than a **hyphen** but shorter than an **em dash**, used as a punctuation mark (see **dash**) and in place of *to* (e.g. 10–15%, 1939–45, *May–September, Dover–Calais*; see also **numbers** and **dates**). It is sometimes used instead of a hyphen when the words or names so linked denote separate entities, as in *cost–benefit analysis, parent–child relationship, Creutzfeldt–Jakob disease, the French–German border.*

endear (not **in-**)

endemic present within a particular area (compare **epidemic** and **pandemic**)

endgame (one word)

end matter another name for **back matter** (two words)

endnote note printed at end of chapter or book (compare **footnote**)

endorse (the spelling **indorse** is not incorrect, but it is less common)

endpaper leaf at beginning or end of book, one half pasted inside the front or back cover and the other half forming the **flyleaf** (one word)

Endymion poem by Keats or novel by Disraeli

energize (also **energise**; see **-ize/-ise**)

enervate weaken (compare **innervate** and **innerve**)

enfant terrible unconventional or indiscreet person (italics; plural *enfants terribles*)

enfold (the spelling **infold** is not incorrect, but it is less common)

enforceable (**e** after **c**; not **-cible**)

enfranchise (never **-ize**)

eng another name for **agma**

engagé committed (italics; acute accent)

Engels, Friedrich German socialist leader and political philosopher (**-gels**)

engender (not **in-**)

engine room (two words)

England part of **Great Britain** and the **United Kingdom** (do not use with reference to Britain in general)

English (use **British** instead with reference to Great Britain or the UK in general)

English Channel part of Atlantic Ocean between England and France (capital **E** & **C**; French name **La Manche**)

engrain less common variant of **ingrain**

engross (not **in-**)

engulf (the spelling **ingulf** is not incorrect, but it is less common)

en masse all together (not italic)

enmesh (rarely **inmesh** or **immesh**)

enmity (**-nm-**)

Enniskillen Northern Ireland town (former name **Inniskilling**)

ennui listless discontent (not italic; double **n**)

enormity outrageousness or atrocity (to avoid controversy, do not use in the sense 'enormous size, extent, or degree')

en passant in passing (not italic)

enquire variant of **inquire** (often preferred in the sense 'ask')

enquiry variant of **inquiry** (often preferred in the sense 'request for information')

enrol (double **l** in US English)

enrolled, enrolling (double **l**)

enrolment (double **l** in US English)

en route on the way (not italic)

en rule another name for **en dash**

ensconce (**-nsc-** then **-nc-**)

ensemble group, outfit, or general effect (not italic)

enshrine (the spelling **inshrine** is not incorrect, but it is less common)

ensnare (rarely **insnare**)

en space a space one en wide

ensuing (not **-uei-**)

ensure make sure or guarantee (compare **assure** and **insure**)

ENT ear, nose, and throat

-ent/-ant see individual entries for words with these endings.

entail (not **in-**)

entente cordiale friendly understanding or relationship between states (not italic; lower-case **e** & **c**)

Entente Cordiale understanding reached between France and Britain in 1904 (not italic; the use of lower-case **e** & **c** is less common but not incorrect)

enterprise (never **-ize**)

enthral (double **l** in US English)

enthralled, enthralling (double **l**)

enthralment (double **l** in US English)

entomb (not **in-**)

entomology study of insects (compare **etymology**)

entourage attendants or retinue (not italic)

entr'acte interval or entertainment during interval (not italic; apostrophe)

entrap (not **in-**)

entreaty (not **in-**)

entrechat ballet leap (not italic)

entrecôte beefsteak (not italic; circumflex)

Entre-Deux-Mers French wine (capital **E**, **D**, & **M**; two hyphens)

entrée dish served before main course, main course itself, or right of entry (not italic; acute accent)

entrench (the spelling **intrench** is not incorrect, but it is less common)

entrepôt warehouse or trading centre for import and re-export (not italic; circumflex)

entrepreneur owner of business who takes risks or uses initiative (not italic; **-eur**)

entrust (the spelling **intrust** is not incorrect, but it is less common)

E number (capital **E**; no hyphen; note that E numbers may indicate natural as well as artificial substances used as additives)

enure less common variant of **inure**

envelop (verb)

envelope (noun)

enviable arousing envy

envious feeling or showing envy

envisage form mental image of, or foresee

envision foresee

enwrap (rarely **inwrap**)

enzyme (**-yme**)

Eocene geological epoch, or of this epoch (capital **E**; **-cene**)

Eolian variant of **Aeolian**

eon longest unit of geological time (compare **aeon**)

epaulette ornament on shoulder of garment (not italic; **-let** in US English)

épée sword (not italic; two acute accents)

Épernay French town (acute accent; **-ay**)

Eph. Ephesians (full stop; not italic)

ephemeral (**-ph-**, **-mer-**)

Ephesians book of the Bible (not italic; abbreviation **Eph.**)

epicure gourmet or person devoted to sensual pleasures (lower-case **e**)

epicurean (as adjective) hedonistic or suitable for an epicure; (as noun) epicure (lower-case **e**; not **-ian**)

Epicurean of the philosophy of Epicurus, or a follower of Epicurus (capital **E**; not **-ian**)

Epicurus ancient Greek philosopher who held that pleasure is the highest good

epidemic affecting many people at the same time within a particular area (compare **endemic** and **pandemic**)

epidural (**-dur-**)

epiglottis (double **t**)

epigram short, witty remark or poem (compare **epigraph**, **epithet**, and **epitaph**)

epigraph quotation at beginning of book or chapter, or inscription on monument (compare **epigram**, **epitaph**, and **epithet**)

epilogue (**-gue**)

epiphany divine or supernatural manifestation, or moment of sudden revelation (lower-case **e**; **-phan-**)

Epiphany Christian festival on Jan 6 (capital **E**; **-phan-**)

episcopal of a bishop or bishops (lower-case **e**)

Episcopal of the Episcopal Church (capital **E**)

Episcopal Church Scottish and US Church that belongs to the same group as the Church of England (capital **E** & **C**)

episcopalian advocating Church government by bishops (lower-case **e**)

Episcopalian of the Episcopal Church (capital **E**)

epitaph inscription on tombstone (compare **epigraph**, **epithet**, and **epigram**)

epithalamion variant of **epithalamium**

Epithalamion poem by Edmund Spenser

epithalamium poem or song written to celebrate a marriage (also **epithalamion**)

epithet descriptive word or phrase used with or in place of a name (compare **epigram**, **epigraph**, and **epitaph**)

epitome (not -omy)

epitomize (also **epitomise**; see -ize/-ise)

eponym word or name derived from name of person, or the person after whom something is named. See individual entries for the capitalization of eponyms. As a general rule, the more frequent the word, or the more distant its relationship in form or meaning to the original name, the more likely it is to have a lower-case initial (e.g. *sandwich, diesel, guillotine, pasteurize*). However, eponyms used before another noun often retain their capital initial, as in *Morse code, Bunsen burner, Wellington boots* (but *wellingtons*).

eponymous being an eponym, e.g. Titus Andronicus is the *eponymous hero* of Shakespeare's play of that name (-nym-)

EPOS electronic point of sale

Epsom salts (capital E)

Epstein, Sir Jacob British sculptor

equable even-tempered or unvarying (compare **equitable** and **equatable**)

equal (do not use with *more, most,* or *very*)

equalize (also **equalise**; see -ize/-ise)

equalled, equalling (single l in US English)

equally (do not use with *as*)

equal sign the symbol (=), usually set with a space before and after it (also **equals sign**)

equatable able to be equated (compare **equable** and **equitable**)

equator (lower-case e; not -er)

Equatorial Guinea African country

equerry (double r)

equestrian (may be used for males and females)

equestrienne (use **equestrian** instead to avoid offence)

equilibrium (single l; plural **equilibriums** or **equilibria**)

equinoctial (not -ox-)

equitable impartial, fair, or just (compare **equatable** and **equable**)

equity fairness, justice, value of property in excess of debt, or ordinary shareholders' interest in company (lower-case e)

Equity actors' trade union (capital E)

equivalent (not -velant)

Er erbium (no full stop)

ER Emergency Room (US equivalent of **A & E**); Queen Elizabeth (from Latin *Elizabetha Regina*)

-er indicates performer of action, as in *employer* (compare **-ee**). Some words end in **-or** rather than **-er**, or have both spellings with slightly different meanings: where both spellings exist, the **-er** form is often less specific or specialized than the **-or** form (see also individual entries). For adjectives and adverbs ending in **-er**, see **comparative**.

eraser (not -or)

Erasmus, Desiderius Dutch humanist

Erato the Muse of love in Greek mythology (single r)

erbium (symbol **Er**)

ere before (compare **err** and **e'er**; no apostrophe)

Erechtheum temple on Acropolis in Athens, Greece (also **Erechtheion**)

Eretria ancient Greek city (compare **Eritrea**)

Erevan variant of **Yerevan**

Erewhon novel by Samuel Butler (not -*hw*-)

ergo therefore (not italic)

ergotism fungal poisoning (also **St Anthony's fire**)

Erie, Lake North America (compare **eerie** and **eyrie**)

Erimanthos Modern Greek name for **Erymanthus**

Erin poetic name for **Ireland**

Eritrea African country (compare **Eretria**)

erlking malevolent spirit in German mythology (one word; lower-case **e**)

ERM Exchange Rate Mechanism

Ernie machine for random selection of winning Premium Bond numbers (capital **E**; not **ERNIE**; acronym of Electronic Random Number Indicator Equipment)

erogenous (-**gen**-)

Eroica symphony by Beethoven

Eros Greek god of love

erotic of or arousing sexual desire (compare **erratic**)

err make mistake or stray (compare **ere** and **e'er**)

errant wandering, as in *knight errant,* or erring (compare **arrant**)

erratic irregular or inconsistent (compare **erotic**)

erratum printing error, or book insert listing such errors (not italic; plural **errata**)

erroneous (not -**ious**)

ersatz produced in imitation of something natural or genuine (not italic; -**atz**)

erupt eject volcanic material or break out on the skin (compare **irrupt**)

Erymanthus Greek mountain (Modern Greek name **Erimanthos**)

erysipelas skin disease (ery-, -las; also **St Anthony's fire**)

Es einsteinium (no full stop)

escalade assault on fortified place using ladders, or gain access in this way

escalate increase

escalator (not -**er**)

escallop rare variant of **scallop** (double **l**)

escalope thin slice of meat (not italic; single l, -**pe**)

escapable (not -**eable**)

escapee see -**ee**

escapement clock mechanism (compare **escarpment**)

escargot edible snail (italics)

escarpment steep face of ridge (compare **escapement**)

Escaut French name for **Scheldt**

Escher, Maurits Cornelius Dutch artist noted for drawings that trick the eye (-**sch**-)

Escherichia coli full name for *E. coli* (capital *E,* lower-case *c; -sch-* then -*ch*-)

escritoire writing desk (not italic)

escutcheon (-**tch**-; the variant **scutcheon** is less common but not incorrect)

Esd. Esdras (full stop; not italic)

1 Esdras book of the Apocrypha (not italic; abbreviation **1 Esd.**; also **I Esdras**)

2 Esdras book of the Apocrypha (not italic; abbreviation **2 Esd.**; also **II Esdras**)

Eskimo (use **Inuit** instead for peoples of Canada, Greenland, and Alaska; plural **Eskimos** or **Eskimo**)

ESL English as a second language (for people in English-speaking country; compare **EFL**; see also **ESOL**)

ESOL English for speakers of other languages (see also **EFL** and **ESL**)

esophagus US spelling of **oesophagus**

ESP extrasensory perception

espadrille light canvas shoe with cord sole (not italic; -**ille**)

España Spanish name for **Spain** (tilde)

especially in particular, as in *especially when it rains*, or very much, as in *especially useful* (compare **specially**)

espionage (single **n**)

espresso strong coffee (not italic; not **exp-**; plural **espressos**)

esprit de corps sense of fellowship (not italic; three words)

Esq. esquire (follows name only when no title precedes it)

essay written composition, or attempt (compare **assay**)

essay titles see **titles of works**

-est see **superlative**

Established Church (capital **E** & **C**)

establishment act of establishing, business, organization, institution, or building (lower-case **e**)

Establishment group of people who have authority within a society (capital **E**)

esteem (as noun) high regard; (as verb) regard highly or deem (compare **estimate** and **estimation**)

Esth. Esther (full stop; not italic)

Esther book of the Bible (not italic; abbreviation **Esth.**)

Esthonia rare variant of **Estonia**

estimate (as verb) gauge; (as noun) approximate calculation or statement of likely cost of work (compare **estimation** and **esteem**)

estimation act of estimating, judgment, or respect (compare **estimate** and **esteem**)

Estonia European country (rarely **Esthonia**)

estrogen US spelling of **oestrogen**

estrous US spelling of **oestrous**

estrus US spelling of **oestrus**

estuary (-ua-)

Eszett the character (ß), used in German in place of **-ss-** (italics; capital **E**)

ETA¹ estimated time of arrival

ETA² Euskadi ta Askatasuna (Basque separatist organization; no full stops; also **Eta**)

et al. and others: used to avoid listing or repeating all the names of joint authors, editors, etc. (not italic; from Latin *et alii*)

etc. et cetera

et cetera and other things (not italic; also **etcetera**)

ETD estimated time of departure

Eternal City, the informal name for Rome (capital **E** & **C**)

eth variant of **edh**

ether (the spelling **aether** is less common but not incorrect in the sense 'air, atmosphere, heavens'; however, it should not be used in the chemical sense 'colourless liquid with characteristic odour')

ethereal (rarely **aethereal**; not **-ial**)

ethics (use singular verb in the sense 'philosophical study of moral values', use plural verb in the senses 'code of conduct' and 'morality of a decision, action, etc.')

Ethiopia African country (former name **Abyssinia**)

ethnic (beware of ambiguity when used alone with reference to people from ethnic minorities)

etiology variant of **aetiology**

etiquette conventions or rules of correct behaviour (not italic)

Etna Italian volcano in Sicily (Latin name **Aetna**)

Eton College English public school for boys (not **Ea-**; not ... **School**)

et seq. and the following (not italic; from Latin *et sequens*; plural **et seqq.**, from Latin *et sequentia*)

étude musical composition (not italic; acute accent)

étui case for small articles (not italic; acute accent)

etymology study of the sources and

development of words (compare **entomology**)

Eu europium (no full stop)

EU European Union (see that entry)

Euboea Greek island in Aegean Sea (Modern Greek name **Évvoia**)

eucalyptus (not **-lip-**)

Eucharist (capital E; **-char-**)

euchre (not **-er**)

Euclid ancient Greek mathematician or his works

Euclidean (also **Euclidian**)

Eugénie, Empress wife of Napoleon III

Eulenspiegel see **Till Eulenspiegel**

eulogize (also **eulogise**; see **-ize/-ise**)

eulogy speech or writing expressing high praise (**-log-**; compare **elegy**)

eunuch (**-uch**)

euonymus (lower-case **e** in general use: *Euonymus* is the genus name; the spelling **evonymus** is less common but not incorrect)

euphemism inoffensive substitute word or phrase, e.g. *pass away* for *die* (compare **euphuism**)

euphorbia plant (lower-case **e** in general use: *Euphorbia* is the genus name)

euphoria elation

euphuism stylish affectation in speech or writing (compare **euphemism**)

Eure department in N France

Eure-et-Loir department in central France (hyphens; not **-Loire**)

eureka triumphant exclamation on discovering or solving something (not italic)

Eureka Stockade incident between miners and military in Australia (capital **E & S**)

eurhythmics training through movement to music (**-ry-** in US English; see also **Eurythmics**)

euro monetary unit (lower-case **e**; plural **euros** or **euro**)

euro- of Europe or the euro (also **Euro-**; sometimes attached with hyphen; see individual entries)

Eurocentric (capital E; no hyphen)

eurocheque (the use of capital **E** is less common but not incorrect; no hyphen)

eurocrat (the use of capital **E** is less common but not incorrect; no hyphen)

eurocurrency (the use of capital **E** is less common but not incorrect; no hyphen)

Euro Disney company that operates **Disneyland** Paris (two words)

eurodollar (the use of capital **E** is less common but not incorrect; no hyphen)

Euroland countries that use the euro (capital **E**; no hyphen; also **Eurozone**)

Euro MP informal name for **MEP** (two words)

European Commission executive body of European Union (capital **E & C**)

European Community (created in 1967, became part of **European Union** in 1993)

European Convention on Human Rights (not **for**)

European Court of Human Rights (not **for**)

European Economic Community (created in 1957, became part of **European Community** in 1967; informal name **Common Market**)

European Monetary System system for stabilizing exchange rates in European Union

European Monetary Union agreement to adopt single currency of European Union

European Parliament assembly of European Union (capital **E & P**)

European Union (created in 1993)

Europhile (capital E; no hyphen)

Europhobic (capital **E**; no hyphen)

europium (symbol **Eu**)

Europoort Dutch port (**-oor-**)

Euro-sceptic (capital **E**; hyphen)

Eurotunnel company that owns and operates the Channel Tunnel and runs the vehicle shuttle service through it, or this service or the tunnel itself (capital **E**; no hyphen)

Eurostar company that runs fast passenger trains through the Channel Tunnel, or this rail service itself (capital **E**; no hyphen)

Eurovision song contest (capital **E**, lower-case **s** & **c**)

Eurozone another name for **Euroland** (capital **E**; no hyphen)

Eurydice wife of Orpheus in Greek mythology (**y** then **i**)

eurythmics US spelling of **eurhythmics**

Eurythmics rock band (not **-rhy-**)

Eustachian tube (capital **E**)

eV electronvolt or electronvolts (no full stops)

evade get away from or shirk (compare **avoid** and **elude**)

evangelist preacher, especially of the Christian gospel, or zealous advocate (lower-case **e**)

Evangelist any of the writers of the New Testament Gospels (capital **E**)

evangelize (also **evangelise**; see **-ize/ -ise**)

Evans, Mary Ann or **Marian** see **Eliot**

evaporate (not **-pour-**)

evasion/avoidance see **tax evasion** and **tax avoidance**

even-handed (hyphen)

evensong (one word; lower-case **e**)

even-tempered (hyphen)

Everglades marshy region of Florida, USA (capital **E**)

evermore (one word)

everybody (one word; interchangeable with **everyone**)

everyday daily or ordinary, as in *an everyday occurrence* (adjective; one word)

every day on each day, as in *he phones her every day* (adverb; two words)

everyman the ordinary person (the use of capital **E** in this sense is less common but not incorrect)

Everyman central character of medieval English morality play, representing mankind (always capital **E**)

everyone (one word; interchangeable with **everybody**)

evildoer (no hyphen)

evonymus less common variant of **euonymus**

Évvoia Modern Greek name for **Euboea**

ewe female sheep (compare **yew** and **you**)

ex without, as in *ex dividend* (not italic)

ex- (attached with hyphen in the sense 'former', as in *ex-husband*)

Ex. Exodus (full stop; not italic)

exacerbate (**-cer-**)

exaggerate (double **g**, single **r**)

exalt raise in rank, praise, excite, or fill with joy (compare **exult**)

exam examination (no full stop)

exasperate (**-per-**)

Excalibur King Arthur's magic sword (capital **E**; **-bur**)

ex cathedra with authority, or defined by the pope (not italic)

excavator (not **-er**)

exceed be superior to or go beyond (**-xc-**; compare **accede**)

excel (single **l**)

ExCel London exhibition centre (capital **E** & **C**)

excellence quality of being excellent (lower-case **e**; double **l**, not **-ance**, not **-cy**)

Excellency title of address for person of high rank (capital **E**; preceded by

Your, His, or *Her;* the variant **Excellence** is less common but not incorrect)

except apart from, or exclude (**-xc-**; compare **accept**)

excepting (to avoid controversy, do not use as preposition in place of **except** unless preceded by *not*)

exceptionable objectionable

exceptional not ordinary, or more than average

excerpt (**-xc-**, **-rpt**)

excess surplus (**-xc-**; compare **access**)

exchangeable (**e** after **g**)

exchequer (**-qu-**; often **Exchequer** with reference to the government department)

excise (never **-ize**)

excitable (not **-eable**)

exclamation mark punctuation mark used after commands or to express strong feeling, as in *look out!* (use very sparingly; note that in Spanish, exclamations are enclosed in a pair of marks, the first being inverted)

exclamatory (**-ama-**, **-ory**)

excusable (not **-eable**)

ex-directory (hyphen)

exeat leave of absence (not italic)

executioner person who carries out death sentence (not **-or;** compare **executor**)

executive (use instead of gender-specific **businessman** or **businesswoman** where appropriate)

executor person who carries out wishes expressed in will (may be used for males and females; not **-er;** compare **executioner**)

executrix (may be replaced by **executor** in general usage)

exegesis (plural **exegeses**)

exemplar (not **-am-**, not **-er**)

exemplary (not **-ory**)

exempt (**-mpt**)

exequies funeral rites (use plural verb, even when the word has singular sense denoting the ceremony as a whole)

exercise (as verb) use, exert oneself, or practise; (as noun) exertion, practice, or set of questions or tasks (compare **exorcize**; not **-xc-**; never **-ize**)

exeunt they go out (stage direction; italics)

ex gratia given as a favour without legal obligation (not italic; two words)

exhaust (**-xh-**)

exhausting tiring

exhaustive comprehensive or thorough

exhibit (**-xh-**)

exhibitor (not **-er**)

exhilarate (**-xh-**, single **l**, **-ar-**)

existence (not **-ance**)

existentialism (not **-enc-**)

exit way out, departure, go away, or go offstage (not italic)

ex libris from the collection of (printed on bookplates; not italic; two words)

ex-libris bookplate bearing owner's name (not italic; hyphen)

Exocet trademark for missile (capital **E**)

exodus act of going out (lower-case **e**)

Exodus departure of Israelites from Egypt led by Moses (capital **E**), or book of the Bible (not italic; abbreviation **Ex.**)

ex officio by right of office (not italic; two words)

exorbitant (not **-xh-**, not **-ent**)

exorcize rid of evil spirits (also **exorcise**, see **-ize/-ise**; compare **exercise**)

expand enlarge or increase (compare **expend**)

expandable (not **-ible**)

expanded (*typog.*) denoting type that is wider than usual for its height

expansible (not **-able**)

expansive tending to expand, wide, extensive, or talkative (compare **expensive**)

expatriate (no hyphen; not **-iot**)

expectorant (not **-er-**, not **-ent**)

expedient appropriate in the circumstances (not **-ant**)

expeditious prompt or speedy

expel (single **l**)

expend spend or use up (compare **expand**)

expendable (not **-ible**)

expense (not **-ence**)

expensive costly (compare **expansive**)

expertise special skill (not **-ize**), or variant of **expertize**

expertize act as expert (also **expertise**; see **-ize/-ise**)

explanatory (**-ana-**, **-ory**)

explicit clearly or openly expressed (compare **implicit**)

Explorer Scout member of the oldest group of boys in the Scout Association (also **Explorer**; former name **Venture Scout**)

exposé disclosure of scandal, crime, etc. (not italic; acute accent)

expositor (not **-er**)

expressible (not **-able**)

extant still in existence (compare **extent** and **extinct**)

extempore without planning or preparation (not italic; one word)

extemporize perform extempore, or improvise (also **extemporise**, see **-ize/-ise**; compare **temporize**)

extendible (also **extendable**)

extensible (not **-able**)

extension (not **-tion**)

extent range, scope, area, or length (compare **extant**)

externalize (also **externalise**; see **-ize/-ise**)

extinct no longer in existence (compare **extant**)

extol (single **l**)

extolled, extolling (double **l**)

extract (as verb) withdraw or remove; (as noun) quoted passage or concentrated essence (compare **extricate**)

extractable (not **-ible**)

extractor (not **-er**)

extracurricular (**-ar**; no hyphen)

extramarital (no hyphen)

extramural (no hyphen)

extraneous (not **-ious**)

extraordinary (not **-tror-**; no hyphen

extrasensory (**-ory**; no hyphen)

extraterrestrial (no hyphen)

extravert variant of **extrovert**

extricate remove or free from complication or difficult (compare **extract**)

extrovert (also **extravert**)

exuberant (not **-xh-**, not **-ent**)

exult rejoice or triumph (compare **exalt**)

ex voto in accordance with vow, or offering made to fulfil vow (italics; two words)

Exxon oil company (double **x**)

Eyck see **van Eyck**

eyeball (one word)

eyebrow (one word)

eye-catching (hyphen)

eyeing (also **eying**)

eyelash (one word)

eyelid (one word)

eyeliner (one word)

eye-opener (hyphen)

eye shadow (two words)

eye socket (two words)

eyestrain (one word)

eyetooth (one word)

eyewitness (one word)

eying variant of **eyeing**

eyot variant of **ait**

Eyre Australian lake and peninsula (compare **Ayre**, **Air**, **Aire**, and **Ayr**)

eyrie eagle's nest (the spelling **aerie**

is less common and the spelling **aery** is rare, but neither is incorrect; compare **eerie** and **Erie**)

Ezek. Ezekiel (full stop; not italic)

Ezekiel book of the Bible (not italic; abbreviation **Ezek.**)

Ezra book of the Bible (not italic; not abbreviated)

F Fahrenheit; fluorine (no full stop)
f. folio (followed by page number); following page (preceded by page number) (plural **ff.**)
FA Football Association
Fabianism advocacy of democratic socialism introduced through gradual reform (capital **F**)
Fablon trademark for self-adhesive plastic (capital **F**)
façade (also **facade**)
face (*typog.*) printing surface of piece of type, or style or design of font (also **typeface**)
face-lift (hyphen)
face pack (two words)
face-saving (hyphen)
faceted, faceting (the spellings **facetted, facetting** are less common but not incorrect)
face value (two words)
facia variant of **fascia**
facility ease or amenity (compare **faculty**)
facsimile (-cs-, -le)
factious producing or characterized by dissension, as in *a factious dispute* (compare **fractious** and **factitious**)
factitious artificial or sham, as in *factitious enthusiasm* (compare **fictitious** and **factious**)
factor (not **-er**)
factorize (also **factorise**; see **-ize/ -ise**)
factotum (plural **factotums**)

faculty ability, power, or university department (compare **facility**)
FA Cup (capital **C**)
faecal (**fecal** in US English)
faeces (**feces** in US English)
faerie poetic word for fairyland or enchantment, or archaic spelling of **fairy**
Faerie Queene, The poem by Edmund Spenser
Faeroes island group between Iceland and the Shetland Islands (also **Faroes, Faeroe Islands**, or **Faroe Islands**)
Faeroese (as adjective) of the Faeroes; (as noun) the language of the Faeroes or a person from the Faeroes (also **Faroese**)
Fahrenheit denoting temperature scale in which ice melts at 32° and water boils at 212° (capital **F**; **-hr-**, **-eit**; compare **Celsius**)
faïence tin-glazed earthenware (not italic; **-aïe-**)
fain archaic word for willingly or gladly, as in *I would fain rest awhile* (compare **feign**)
faint (as adjective) weak, pale, low, or dizzy; (as noun) loss of consciousness; (as verb) lose consciousness (compare **feint**)
faint-hearted (hyphen)
fair (as adjective) just, light in colour, attractive, or moderately good; (as noun) entertainment with

sideshows, event where goods are sold, or commercial exhibition (compare **fare**; see also **fayre**)

fair and square (three words)

fairground (one word)

Fair Isle one of the Shetland Islands, or multicoloured pattern in knitting (capital **F** & **I**)

fair play (two words)

fairway (one word)

fair-weather friend (one hyphen)

fairy (archaic spelling **faerie**)

fairyland (one word)

fairy lights (two words)

fairy story (two words)

fairy tale (noun)

fairy-tale (adjective)

Faisal, King Iraqi monarch (also **Feisal**)

fait accompli something done that cannot be changed (italic; plural *faits accomplis*)

faith healing (two words)

fakir (also **faqir** or **fakeer**)

Falangist member of Spanish fascist movement (compare **Phalangist**)

falderal (also **falderol** or **folderol**)

Falkirk Scottish town and council area

Falkland Islands island group in S Atlantic Ocean (Spanish name **Islas Malvinas**)

Falkner see **Faulkner**

Falla, Manuel de Spanish composer (lower-case **d**)

fallacious illogical, erroneous, or misleading (compare **fallible**)

fallible capable of making mistakes or being wrong (not **-able**; compare **fallacious**)

Fallopian tubes (capital **F**)

fallout (noun; the verb is **fall out**)

falsehood quality of being untrue, or a lie

falseness quality of being untrue, fake, artificial, or disloyal

falsity falseness or falsehood

familiarize (also **familiarise**; see **-ize/-ise**)

family in the hierarchy of **taxonomic names**, the group that comes above a genus and below an order. The family name has a capital initial and is not italic. The term is also used to denote a group of related languages. For the use of singular or plural verb with **family** in the sense 'people related by blood', see **collective nouns**.

fanbase (one word)

fan belt (two words)

fan club (two words)

fancy-free (hyphen)

fandango (plural **fandangos**)

fanlight (one word)

fantail (one word)

fan-tailed (hyphen)

fantasize (also **fantasise**; see **-ize/-ise**)

fantasm archaic spelling of **phantasm**

fantasy (**-asy**; archaic spelling **phantasy**)

fanzine (one word)

FAO Food and Agriculture Organization (of the UN); for the attention of

FAQ frequently asked question or questions (also **FAQs** for the plural form)

faqir variant of **fakir**

FAQs frequently asked questions (lower-case **s**)

Faraday, Michael English scientist (**-rad-**)

fare (as noun) charge paid by passenger, or food and drink; (as verb) get on, as in *how did you fare?*, or turn out, as in *it fared badly with us* (compare **fair**; see also **fayre**)

Far East the countries of E Asia, including China, Japan, etc. (see also **Middle East** and **Near East**)

Fareham town in S Hampshire (compare **Farnham**)

farewell (one word; not **fair-**)
far-fetched (hyphen)
far-flung (hyphen)
Far from the Madding Crowd novel by Thomas Hardy (not *Maddening*)
farinaceous (not **-ious**)
farm hand (two words)
farmhouse (one word)
farmyard (one word)
Farnborough town in NE Hampshire (not **-brough**)
Farnham town in Surrey (compare **Fareham**)
faro gambling game (lower-case **f**; compare **Pharaoh**)
Faro Portuguese port and resort
Faroe Islands variant of **Faeroe Islands**
Faroes variant of **Faeroes**
Faroese variant of **Faeroese**
Farquhar, George Irish-born dramatist (**-quhar**)
farrago (double **r**, single **g**; plural **farragos** or **farragoes**
Farsi language of modern Iran
far-sighted (hyphen)
farther more distant, or to or at a greater distance (use for literal senses only; compare **further**)
farthest most distant, or to or at the greatest distance (use for literal senses only; compare **furthest**)
fascia (plural **fascias**, especially in the senses 'surface above shop window' and 'dashboard', or **fasciae**; also **facia**)
fascicle bundle, or variant of fascicule
fascicule one part of work published in instalments (also **fascicle** or **fasciculus**)
fascinate (**-sc-**)
fascism any right-wing nationalist or authoritarian ideology or movement (the use of capital **F** is less common but not incorrect in this sense)
Fascism the political movement or doctrine of Benito Mussolini in Italy (always capital **F**)
Fassbinder, Rainer Werner German film director (double **s**)
fatal causing death, or disastrous (compare **fateful**)
fate (as noun) destiny, final result, or calamitous outcome; (as verb) destine or doom (compare **fête**)
fateful decisively important, or controlled by fate (compare **fatal**)
Fates three goddesses of destiny in Greek mythology (capital **F**)
Father (capital **F** with reference to God or as title of Christian priest)
father-in-law (plural **fathers-in-law**)
fatherland (one word)
Father's Day (**-'s** not **-s'**)
Father Time (capital **F** & **T**)
fathomed, fathoming (not **-mm-**)
fatiguing (**-gui-**)
fatwa religious decree issued by Muslim leader (not italic; also **fatwah**; note that the word does not necessarily denote a death sentence)
Faulkner, William US writer (originally **Falkner**)
fault-finding (hyphen)
faun rural deity in legend (compare **fawn**)
fauna animal life of region (compare **flora**)
Fauré, Gabriel French composer (acute accent)
Fauvism artistic movement (capital **F**)
faux pas social blunder (not italic; same form for singular and plural)
favour (**-or** in US English)
favourable (**-or-** in US English)
favourite (**-or-** in US English)
Fawkes, Guy English conspirator (**-aw-**)
fawn young deer or light greyish-brown colour (compare **faun**)
fayre pseudo-archaic spelling of the nouns **fair** or **fare**

faze disconcert (compare **phase**)

FBI Federal Bureau of Investigation

FCA Fellow of the Institute of Chartered Accountants

FCCA Fellow of the Chartered Association of Certified Accountants

FCII Fellow of the Chartered Insurance Institute

FCO Foreign and Commonwealth Office

FD *Fidei Defensor* (Defender of the Faith)

Fe iron (no full stop; from Latin *ferrum*)

fearful afraid (to avoid confusion, do not use in the less common sense 'frightening')

fearsome frightening (to avoid confusion, do not use in the less common sense 'afraid')

feasible (not **-able**)

feat remarkable exploit (compare **feet**)

featherbed (verb)

feather bed (noun)

featherbrained (one word)

Feb. February (full stop)

February (**-ruar-**)

fecal US spelling of **faecal**

feces US spelling of **faeces**

fedayeen Arab commandos (not italic; singular **fedayee**; the use of capital **F** is less common but not incorrect)

federal with power divided between central and regional governments, or of the central government of a federation (capital **F** in names)

Federal of or supporting the northern states of the USA in the American Civil War (capital **F**)

Federal Republic of Germany official name for **Germany** and formerly for **West Germany**

federation union of provinces, states, or countries in which each retains some autonomy, or the act of forming such a union (capital **F** in names)

Federation the federation of the Australian colonies in 1901, or a style of architecture of that period (capital **F**)

fed up (followed by *with*)

feedback (noun; the verb is **feed back**)

feel-good factor (one hyphen)

feet plural of **foot** (compare **feat**)

feign put on a show of, as in *feign ignorance* (compare **fain**)

feint (as noun) misleading action or movement, e.g. mock attack in boxing or fencing, or narrow line on ruled paper; (as verb) make a misleading action or movement (compare **faint**)

Feisal variant of **Faisal**

feisty (**-ei-**)

feldspar (also **felspar**)

Felixstowe English port (**-xs-**, **-we**)

fell cut or knock down, or past tense of **fall** (compare **felled**)

fellah Arab peasant (plural **fellahs**, **fellahin**, or **fellaheen**; compare **feller**)

felled past tense and past participle of **fell**

feller person or thing that fells (compare **fellah**)

Fellini, Federico Italian film director (double l, single n; not **Fred-**)

fellow person, companion, or member of university governing body or teaching staff (lower-case f; no hyphen when used before another noun, as in *fellow citizen, fellow traveller*)

Fellow member of society, academy, institute, etc. (capital **F**)

fellow feeling (two words)

felo de se suicide (not italic; three words)

felon (single l)

felspar variant of **feldspar**

felt-tip pen (one hyphen)
fem. feminine
female of women or girls, or denoting sex of animals, plants, etc.
feminine characteristic of women or girls, or denoting gender of nouns
feminize (also **feminise**; see **-ize/-ise**)
femme fatale seductive woman (italics; *-ale*; plural *femmes fatales*)
femur (-ur)
Fénelon, François de Salignac de La Mothe French theologian and writer (not **Féné-**)
feng shui Chinese art of design for maximum harmony (not italic; two words)
fennel (double **n**, single **l**)
feral wild (compare **ferial**)
Fergana region of Asia or city in Uzbekistan (also **Ferghana**)
ferial of weekday (compare **feral**)
Fermanagh county and district of Northern Ireland (-**agh**)
Fermat, Pierre de French mathematician
ferment see **foment**
Fermi, Enrico Italian physicist
fermium (symbol **Fm**)
Ferrara Italian city
Ferrari Italian motor manufacturer, or any of their vehicles (capital **F**)
ferreted, ferreting (not -**tt**-)
Ferris wheel (capital **F**)
ferrule cap or ring for end of stick or post (also **ferule**)
fertilize (also **fertilise**; see **-ize/-ise**)
ferule ruler formerly used to punish schoolchildren, or variant of **ferrule**
fervour (-**or** in US English)
Fès Moroccan city (grave accent; also **Fez**)
Festiniog Railway Wales (**Fe-**; compare **Blaenau Ffestiniog**)
Festival Hall London (capital **F** & **H**; full name **Royal Festival Hall**)
festschrift collection of essays to honour eminent scholar (not italic;

lower-case **f**; -**stschr-**; plural **festschriften** or **festschrifts**)
feta Greek cheese (not italic; single **t**)
fetal (also **foetal**)
fête (as noun) gala, bazaar, or feast day; (as verb) honour or entertain with festivity (not italic; also **fete**; compare **fate**)
fetich less common variant of **fetish**
fetid (also **foetid**)
fetish (the spelling **fetich** is not incorrect, but it is less common)
fetor (also **foetor**; not -**our**)
fetus (plural **fetuses**; also **foetus**)
Feuchtwanger, Lion German writer
feuilleton part of European newspaper containing reviews, serialized fiction, etc. (not italic; -**eui-**)
fewer (use with plural nouns, as in *fewer cars, fewer than five people*; use **less** with singular nouns or with units of measurement, time, money, etc., as in *less traffic, less than five hours*)
fez brimless cap (plural **fezzes**)
Fez variant of **Fès**
ff. folios (followed by page numbers); following pages (preceded by page number)
Ffestiniog Welsh town (**Ffe-**; see also **Blaenau Ffestiniog**; compare **Festiniog Railway**)
FIA Fédération Internationale de l'Automobile; Fellow of the Institute of Actuaries
fiancé man who is engaged to be married (-**é**)
fiancée woman who is engaged to be married (-**ée**)
Fianna Fáil Irish political party (capital **F** twice; acute accent)
fiasco (plural **fiascos** or **fiascoes**)
fiat official permission, or arbitrary decree (not italic; lower-case **f**)
Fiat Italian motor manufacturer, or any of their vehicles (capital **F**)

Fibonacci, Leonardo Italian mathematician (single **b** & **n**; double **c**)

fibre (**-er** in US English)

fibreglass (one word)

fibreoptic (one word)

fibre optics (two words)

fibrillation (double **l**; not **frib-**, not **-ul-**)

fibula one of two bones between knee and ankle (compare **tibia**)

fictional of fiction, as in *a fictional character* (compare **fictitious**)

fictionalize (also **fictionalise**; see **-ize/-ise**)

fictitious false or invented, as in *a fictitious address* (compare **factitious** and **fictional**)

Fid. Def. *Fidei Defensor* (Defender of the Faith; also **FID DEF**)

fiddlesticks (one word)

Fidei Defensor Defender of the Faith (italics)

fidgeted, fidgeting (not **-tt-**)

fidgety (not **-tt-**)

fidus Achates faithful friend (not italic; capital **A**)

field day (two words)

field glasses (two words)

field marshal (two words; for capitalization see **ranks**)

Fiennes, Sir Ranulph Twisleton-Wykeham English explorer

fierce (**-ie-**)

fieri facias writ (not italic)

FIFA Fédération Internationale de Football Association (no full stops)

Fife, Duncan see **Phyfe**

fifth columnist (two words)

fifty-fifty (hyphen)

fig. figurative; figure

Fighting Téméraire, The picture by J. M. W. Turner (italics; two acute accents)

figurehead (one word)

figures see **numbers**

figure skating (two words)

Fiji country comprising 844 islands in Pacific Ocean

filagree less common variant of **filigree**

filbert (not **ph-**)

file (as noun) folder, documents, line, or tool used for smoothing, shaping, etc.; (as verb) put in a file, walk in a file, or use a file on (compare **phial**)

filename (one word)

filet variant of **fillet** in culinary senses of noun, especially in French names of cuts or dishes, e.g. *filet mignon*

filibuster (single **l**)

filigree (single **l**; the spelling **filagree** is not incorrect, but it is less common)

Filipina woman or girl from the Philippines (not **Ph-**; single **l**, single **p**)

Filipino of the Philippines, or a person from the Philippines (not **Ph-**; single **l**, single **p**; also **Philippine** for the adjective)

fillet (double **l**, single **t**; also **filet** in culinary senses of noun)

filleted, filleting (not **-tt-**)

fill-in (noun; the verb is **fill in**)

filling station (two words)

fillip source of stimulation or enjoyment, or flick or snap of fingers (double **l**; compare **Philip** and **Phillip**)

fill-up (noun; the verb is **fill up**)

filmsetting typesetting in which printing plates are made from photographic film (one word)

film star (two words)

film strip (two words)

film titles see **titles of works**

filo very thin pastry (not italic)

Filofax trademark for loose-leaf ring binder used as personal organizer (capital **F**; **-ax**) *fils* added to French surname to specify son rather than father, as in Dumas *fils* (italics; compare *père*)

filter (as noun) substance or device that prevents the passage of solid particles, impurities, certain frequencies or wavelengths, etc.; (as verb) pass through a filter (**-er**; compare **philtre**)

filterable (also **filtrable**)

filter tip (two words)

filter-tipped (hyphen)

filtrable variant of **filterable**

fin appendage of aquatic animal, or part with similar form or function (single **n**; compare **Finn**)

finable (also **fineable**)

final (as adjective) concluding or conclusive; (as noun) contest that decides ultimate winner

finale concluding part of performance, musical composition, etc.

finalize (also **finalise**; see **-ize/-ise**)

Finchley district of London (**-ley**)

fin de siècle end of 19th century as time of social, moral, and artistic transition (italics; grave accent; hyphenated when used adjectivally)

fine ordinary brandy (italics; compare **fino**)

fineable variant of **finable**

Fine Gael Irish political party (capital **F** & **G**)

finesse elegant skill, subtlety, or trick (not italic; single **n**, double **s**, **-e**)

fine-tooth comb (hyphen then space; also **fine-toothed comb**; do not use **fine toothcomb**)

Fingal's Cave Scotland (capital **F** & **C**; apostrophe)

finger bowl (two words)

fingermark (one word)

fingernail (one word)

fingerprint (one word)

fingertip (one word)

finicky (also **finicking** or **finical**)

finish end or surface (single **n**; compare **Finnish**)

Finistère French department (grave accent; single **r**)

Finisterre, Cape Spanish headland (no accent; double **r**)

Finland European country (single **n**; Finnish name **Suomi**)

Finn person from Finland (double **n**; compare **fin**)

finnan haddock (lower-case f; double **n** then single **n**)

Finnegans Wake novel by James Joyce (**-inne-**; no apostrophe)

Finney, Albert British actor (**-ey**)

Finnish of Finland, or the language of Finland (double **n**; compare finish)

fino very dry sherry (not italic; compare *fine*)

fiord variant of **fjord**

fir tree (compare **fur**)

fire alarm (two words)

firearm (one word)

fire drill (two words)

fire-extinguisher (hyphen)

firefighter (no hyphen; use instead of gender-specific **fireman** where appropriate)

fireguard (one word)

fireman (use **firefighter** instead where appropriate)

Firenze Italian name for **Florence**

fireplace (one word)

fire station (two words)

firewood (one word)

firing line (two words; do not use *in the firing line* to mean 'in the line of fire', i.e. being attacked)

first (either **first . . .** or **firstly . . .** may be used in a sequence followed by **secondly . . .** and **thirdly . . .**, but only **first . . .** should be used in a sequence followed by **second . . .** and **third . . .**)

first aid (no hyphen unless used before another noun, as in *a first-aid kit*)

first-born (hyphen)

first class (noun; adverb; adjective after noun)

first-class (adjective before noun)

first-footing (hyphen)

first-hand (hyphen in adjective and adverb, but space in the phrase *at first hand*)

first lady (often capital **F** & **L** in the sense 'wife of US president or state governor')

firstly see **first**

First Minister chief minister of Northern Ireland Assembly, Scottish Parliament, or Welsh Assembly (capital **F** & **M**)

first name (use instead of **Christian name** where appropriate, e.g. on official forms, to avoid offending non-Christians)

first-rate (hyphen)

First Sea Lord see **Sea Lord** (capital initials)

First World War another name for **World War I**

firth (**-ir-**)

Fischer, Bobby US chess player (compare **Fisher**)

Fischer-Dieskau, Dietrich German baritone

fish (plural **fish** in most contexts, sometimes **fishes** in technical contexts)

fish and chips (three words)

fish-and-chip shop (two hyphens; not **-chips**)

Fisher, Andrew Australian statesman (compare **Fischer**)

fish-hook (hyphen)

fishing rod (two words)

fishwife (one word)

fission the act of splitting

fissure a crack, split, cleft, or groove

fist (*typog.*) another name for **index**

in the sense 'mark indicating note or paragraph'

fisticuffs (not **-ty-**)

fit (past tense and past participle **fitted** in UK English)

Fitzgerald, Edward English poet (also **FitzGerald**); **Ella** US jazz singer; **F(rancis) Scott (Key)** US writer; **Garret** Irish politician

Fitzwilliam Museum Cambridge (capital **F** & **M**)

five-a-side (two hyphens)

fizz (double **z**)

fjord (also **fiord**)

FL Florida (US postal code)

fl. *floruit* (flourished: used to indicate period when person whose birth and death dates are not known was most active; italics; also ***flor.***)

flabbergasted (double **b**; **-er-**)

flaccid (double **c**)

flack less common variant of **flak**

flag day day on which flags or stickers are sold for charity (lower-case **f** & **d**)

Flag Day June 14 (US holiday celebrating adoption of Stars and Stripes; capital **F** & **D**)

flageolet musical instrument or bean (not italic; **-geo-**)

flagpole (one word)

flagrant openly outrageous, as in *flagrant violation of the rules* (compare **blatant**)

flagship (one word)

flagstaff (one word)

flagstone (one word)

flair aptitude, discernment, or stylishness (compare **flare**)

flak (the spelling **flack** is not incorrect, but it is less common)

Flamborough Head England (capital **F** & **H**; not **-brough**)

flamboyant (not **-ent**)

flamenco (plural **flamencos**)

flameproof (no hyphen)

flame-thrower (hyphen)

flamingo (plural **flamingos** or **flamingoes**)

flammable (use instead of **inflammable** to avoid misunderstanding; the opposite is **nonflammable**)

Flamsteed, John English astronomer (not **-stead**)

flannel (double **n**, single **l**)

flannelette (double **n**, single **l**, double **t**)

flannelled, flannelling (single **l** in US English)

flare burn suddenly and brightly, spread outwards, device producing blaze of light, or spreading shape (compare **flair**)

flare-up (noun; the verb is **flare up**)

flashback (noun; the verb is **flash back**)

flashbulb (one word)

flashlight (one word)

flash point (two words)

flatfish (one word)

flatfoot (one word)

flat-footed (hyphen)

flatulence (not **-ance**)

Flaubert, Gustave French writer

flaunt display ostentatiously (compare **flout**)

flautist (US and Canadian name **flutist**)

flavour (**-or** in US English)

flea insect (compare **flee**)

fledgling (also **fledgeling**)

flee run away (compare **flea**)

Fleming, Sir Alexander Scottish bacteriologist; **Ian** English writer, creator of James Bond

fleshly of the body, carnal, or worldly

fleshy of or like flesh, plump, or pulpy

fleur-de-lys three-petalled heraldic device (not italic; two hyphens; plural **fleurs-de-lys**; also **fleur-de-lis**)

flew past tense of **fly** (compare **flu** and **flue**)

flexible (not **-able**)

flexitime (also **flextime**)

flibbertigibbet (double **b** twice, **-er-** then **-et**)

flick knife (two words)

flier variant of **flyer**

flight attendant (use instead of gender-specific **air hostess** or **stewardess**)

flight path (two words)

floatation variant of **flotation**

floe sheet of ice (compare **flow**)

Flood, the biblical flood from which Noah and his family and animals were saved (capital **F**)

floodgate (one word)

floodlight (one word; past tense and past participle **floodlit**)

flood plain (two words)

floorboard (one word)

floor show (two words)

flor. variant of *fl.*

flora plant life of region (compare **fauna**)

floreat may (he, she, or it) flourish (italics; compare *floruit*)

Florence (Italian name **Firenze**)

florescence process or period of flowering (**-sc-** then **-nc-**; compare **fluorescence**)

floruit flourished (italics; see *fl.*; compare *floreat*)

flotation (also **floatation**)

flotsam wreckage from ship found floating (compare **jetsam**; see also **flotsam and jetsam**)

flotsam and jetsam useless or discarded objects in general

flounder struggle (compare **founder**)

flour powder used in cooking (compare **flower**)

flout disregard openly (compare **flaunt**)

flow stream (compare **floe**)

flow chart (two words)

flower bloom (compare **flour**)

flowerbed (one word)
flower head (two words)
flowerpot (one word)
flu influenza (no apostrophe; no full stop; compare **flew** and **flue**)
flue shaft of chimney (compare **flu** and **flew**)
fluent (not -ant)
flugelhorn (lower-case f; no umlaut; -gel-)
fluky (also **flukey**)
flummox (double **m**, **-ox**)
flunky (also **flunkey**)
fluorescence emission of light (-sc- then -nc-; compare **florescence**)
fluorescent (not -our-, not -ant)
fluoride substance added to water to reduce tooth decay
fluorine chemical element (symbol F)
flush (as verb) go red in the face because of emotion, fever, alcohol, etc. (compare **blush**); (as adjective) (*typog.*) aligned with margin and not indented
Flushing Dutch port (Dutch name **Vlissingen**)
flutist US and Canadian name for **flautist**
flyer (also **flier**)
flyleaf leaf at beginning or end of book (see **endpaper**; one word)
flyover (one word)
fly-past (hyphen)
fly spray (two words)
fly-tipping (hyphen)
flywheel (one word)
Fm fermium (no full stop)
f-number photography term (lower-case f; hyphen may be replaced by space)
FO Foreign Office (use **FCO** for the current UK government department)
Foch, Ferdinand French marshal (-ch)
foci a plural of **focus**

fo'c's'le variant of **forecastle** (also fo'c'sle)
focus (plural **focuses** or **foci**)
focused (also **focussed**)
focuses a plural or a form of the third person present tense of **focus** (also **focusses** for the verb)
focusing (also **focussing**)
focussed variant of **focused**
focusses variant of **focuses** (verb)
focussing variant of **focusing**
foehn variant of **föhn**
foetal variant of **fetal**
foetid variant of **fetid**
foetor variant of **fetor**
foetus variant of **fetus**
fogey (also **fogy**)
Fogg, Phileas hero of Jules Verne's *Around the World in Eighty Days* (double **g**)
fogy variant of **fogey**
föhn warm dry wind in Alps (not italic; umlaut; also **foehn**)
foie gras see **pâté de foie gras**
folderol variant of **falderal**
Fokker, Anthony Herman Gerard Dutch aircraft designer (not -ck-)
-fold (attached without hyphen to numbers spelt out as words, as in *fourfold*)
Folies Bergère, Les French cabaret (no hyphen; capital F & B; single l; grave accent)
folio book size with two leaves (i.e. four pages) per sheet, leaf of paper numbered on one side only, or page number in book (plural **folios**)
folk dancing (two words)
Folkestone English port (-lke-, -one)
Folketing Danish parliament (not -thing)
folklore (one word)
folk song (two words)
following (use **after** instead where appropriate)
follow-on (noun; the verb is **follow on**)

follow-through (noun; the verb is **follow through**)

follow-up (noun; the verb is **follow up**)

foment (interchangeable with **ferment** only in the transitive verb sense 'stir up', as in *foment trouble*)

fondant (not **-ent**)

font baptismal bowl, or style of type (also **fount** in the sense 'style of type')

Fontainebleau French town (not **-bleu**)

fontanelle membranous gap in skull of fetus or baby (**-tan-**)

Fontenelle, Bernard le Bovier de French philosopher (**-ten-**)

Fonteyn, Dame Margot English ballet dancer (**-eyn**)

foodstuff (one word)

foolproof (no hyphen)

foolscap size of paper (one word; no apostrophe)

fool's cap dunce's cap, or jester's cap with bells and tassels (apostrophe; two words)

foot (plural **feet**, but for the unit of measurement **foot** is used before another noun, as in *a 24-foot yacht*, and may be used elsewhere, as in *six foot tall*)

foot-and-mouth disease (two hyphens)

footbridge (one word)

foothill (one word)

footnote note printed at foot of page (compare **endnote**)

footpath (one word)

footprint (one word)

footrest (one word)

foot soldier (two words)

footstool (one word)

for- indicating rejection, prohibition, etc. (compare **fore-**)

forasmuch as (one space only: not four words)

forbade past tense of **forbid** (the spelling **forbad** is less common but not incorrect; compare **forbidden**)

forbear refrain, or less common variant of **forebear**

forbidden past participle of **forbid** (the variant **forbid** is less common but not incorrect; compare **forbade**)

force-feed (hyphen)

forceful powerful or persuasive (compare **forcible**)

force majeure irresistible force or compulsion preventing fulfilment of contract (not italic)

forceps (same form for singular and plural)

Forces armed services (capital **F**)

forcible done by, using, or involving force (not **-eable**; compare **forceful**)

fore- before, or at the front (compare **for-**)

forearm (one word)

forebear ancestor (the spelling **forbear** is not incorrect in this sense, but it is less common)

foreboding (not **-rb-**)

forecast (not **-rc-**; past tense and past participle **forecast** or **forecasted**)

forecastle (not **-rc-**; also **fo'c's'le** or **fo'c'sle**)

fore-edge outer edge of pages of book (hyphen)

forefinger (one word)

forego precede, or less common variant of **forgo**

foregoing preceding (not **forg-**)

foregone conclusion (not **forg-**)

forehead (one word)

foreign (**-eign**)

foreign titles of works for French titles mentioned in English texts, capitalize only the first word and any proper nouns (e.g. *Une vie*), unless the first word is the definite article, in which case the following noun is capitalized (e.g. *La Peau de chagrin*), as is any adjective that precedes it (e.g. *Le Petit Prince*), but not any adjective that follows it (e.g. *Les Mains sales*). For German titles, capitalize only the first word and any nouns or proper nouns (e.g. *Die Leiden des jungen Werthers*). For titles in Italian, Spanish, and other languages, capitalize only the first word and any proper nouns (e.g. *Il nome della rosa*, *El ingenioso hidalgo don Quijote de la Mancha*). See also **titles of works**.

foreleg (one word)

forename (use instead of **Christian name** where appropriate, e.g. on official forms, to avoid offending non-Christians)

foreordain (no hyphen)

foresee (not **-rs-**)

foreshorten (not **-rsh-**)

forestall (not **-rst-**)

Forester, C(ecil) S(cott) English novelist (compare **Forster**)

forever eternally, incessantly, or for a very long time (also **for ever** in the sense 'eternally')

foreword introductory statement written by somebody other than author or editor of book (compare **forward** (for spelling) and **preface** (for meaning))

forgeable (**e** after **g**)

forget-me-not (hyphens)

forgivable (not **-eable**)

forgo give up or do without (the spelling **forego** is not incorrect in this sense, but it is less common)

forgot past tense or archaic past participle of **forget**

forgotten past participle of **forget**

fork-lift truck (one hyphen)

formalize (also **formalise**; see **-ize/ -ise**)

formally in a formal manner (compare **formerly**)

format (*typog.*) general appearance or approximate size of publication

formatted, formatting (double t)

forme type matter assembled and ready for printing (**-me**)

former of an earlier time, or denoting the first of two previously mentioned (compare **latter**; do not use if there are more than two)

formerly in the past (compare **formally**)

Former Yugoslav Republic of Macedonia official name for **Macedonia** (European country; abbreviation **FYROM**)

Formica trademark for laminated plastic sheet (capital **F**)

Formosa former name for **Taiwan**

formula (plural **formulas**, especially in general contexts, or **formulae**, especially in mathematical and scientific contexts)

forsake (not **fore-**)

Forster, E(dward) M(organ) English novelist (compare **Forester** and **Foster**)

forswear (not **fore-**)

forsythia (lower-case **f** in general use: *Forsythia* is the genus name)

fort fortified building or position (compare **forte**)

Fort-de-France capital of Martinique (hyphens)

forte strong point, or music instruction to play loudly (compare **fort** and **forty**)

forth forward, out, or away (compare **fourth**)

Forth Scottish river

Fort Knox site of US Gold Bullion Depository (capital **F** & **K**)

Fort Lamy former name for **Ndjamena**

Fortnum & Mason English department store (ampersand; not **-sons**)

FORTRAN computer programming language (no full stops; also **Fortran**)

fortuitous happening by chance

fortunate lucky

forty 40 (not **four-**; compare **forte**)

forum meeting for open discussion, or open space for public business, market trading, etc. in ancient Italian city (plural **forums** or **fora**; lower-case **f**)

Forum the forum of ancient Rome (capital **F**)

forward (adjective, sometimes adverb (especially in phrasal verbs such as *come forward* and *put forward*; see also **-ward** and **-wards**), verb; compare **foreword**)

forwards (adverb only)

forward slash see **solidus**

Fosbury flop (capital **F**)

fossilize (also **fossilise**; see **-ize/-ise**)

Foster, Jodie US actress; **Stephen Collins** US songwriter (compare **Forster**)

Foucault, Jean Bernard Léon French physicist (**-ault**)

Foucquet variant of **Fouquet** (for Nicolas)

foul offensive, against the rules, violation of rules, or make dirty (compare **fowl**)

foul-up (noun; the verb is **foul up**)

found establish, cast, or past tense and past participle of **find** (compare **founded**)

founded past tense and past participle of **found**

founder sink or fail (compare **flounder**)

fount spring, fountain, source or variant of **font** in the sense 'style of type'

fountainhead (one word)

Fountains Abbey England (capital **F** & **A**; no apostrophe)

Fouqué, Friedrich Heinrich Karl German writer

Fouquet, Jean French painter; **Nicolas** French statesman (also **Foucquet** for Nicolas)

Fourier, Charles French social reformer; **Jean Baptiste Joseph** French mathematician

four-letter word (one hyphen)

four-poster (hyphen; also **four-poster bed**)

fourth 4th (compare **forth**)

fourth estate journalists (the use of capital **F** & **E** is less common but not incorrect)

Fourth of July US holiday celebrating adoption of Declaration of Independence (capital **F** & **J**; official name **Independence Day**)

four-wheel drive (one hyphen)

Fowey resort and fishing village in Cornwall (not **Foy**)

fowl bird (compare **foul**)

Fowler, Henry Watson English lexicographer

Fowles, John British novelist

Fox, Charles James British statesman; **George** English religious leader, founder of the Quakers; **Sir William** New Zealand statesman

Foxe, John English clergyman, author of the *Book of Martyrs*

Foxe Basin Canada (not **Fox**)

foxhole (one word)

foxhound (one word)

fox hunt (two words)

fox-hunting (hyphen)

fox terrier (two words)

foxtrot (one word)

fps units imperial system of units based on foot, pound, and second (replaced by **SI units** in science and technology; see also **cgs units**)

Fr francium (no full stop)

Fr. Father; Frau

Fra title of Italian monk or friar (no full stop)

Fra Angelico see **Angelico**

fracas (same form for singular and plural)

fractious irritable or unruly, as in *a fractious child* (compare **factious**)

fragmentary (**-ary**)

fragrant (not **-ent**)
frame-up (noun; hyphen)
framework (one word)
franc monetary unit (compare **frank**)
Frances feminine spelling of first name (compare **Francis**)
Franche-Comté region of France (**-che-**; hyphen; acute accent)
franchise (never **-ize**)
Francis masculine spelling of first name (compare **Frances**)
Francis of Assisi, St Italian monk
Francis Xavier see **Xavier**
francium (symbol **Fr**)
Franck, César French composer (acute accent on first name; compare **Frank**)
Franco, Francisco Spanish general
Franco- (attached with hyphen, not en dash, to adjectives with capital initial, as in *Franco-German*; no hyphen elsewhere, as in *Francophile*)
Franco-Prussian War (one hyphen; capital **F**, **P**, & **W**)
Francophile (no hyphen; capital **F**)
Francophobe (no hyphen; capital **F**)
Francophone (no hyphen; the spelling **francophone**, with lower-case **f**, is less common but not incorrect)
frangipane almond-flavoured pastry
frangipani shrub or tree
Franglais informal French containing many English words (not italic; capital **F**)
frank honest, blunt, or put postage mark on (compare **franc**)
Frank member of Germanic people who conquered Gaul and Germany
Frank, Anne German girl whose *Diary* recorded life as Jew under Nazis (not **Ann**; compare **Franck**)
Frankenstein creator of monster in Mary Shelley's novel *Frankenstein*, hence anybody who creates something that brings about his or her ruin (capital **F**; note that Frankenstein is not the name of the monster)
Frankfurt am Main city in central Germany (lower-case **a**; also **Frankfurt**)
Frankfurt an der Oder city in E Germany (lower-case **a** & **d**; also **Frankfurt**)
frankfurter sausage (lower-case **f**)
Frankfurter person from Frankfurt (capital **F**)
Fraser Canadian river (not **-zer**)
Fraser, Malcolm Australian statesman; **Peter** New Zealand statesman (compare **Frazer**)
fraternize (also **fraternise**; see **-ize/-ise**)
Frau German equivalent of **Mrs** (no umlaut; abbreviation **Fr.**)
fraught (**-augh-**)
Fräulein German equivalent of **Miss** (umlaut; **-ei-**; abbreviation **Frl.**)
Frazer, Sir James George Scottish anthropologist (compare **Fraser** and **Frazier**)
Frazier, Joe US boxer (compare **Frazer**)
FRCM Fellow of the Royal College of Music
FRCOG Fellow of the Royal College of Obstetricians and Gynaecologists
FRCP Fellow of the Royal College of Physicians
FRCS Fellow of the Royal College of Surgeons
FRCVS Fellow of the Royal College of Veterinary Surgeons
Fredericton Canadian city (not **-ick-** or **-ik-**)
Frederiksberg Danish city (not **-ick-** or **-ic-**, not **-burg**)
Free Church (capital **F** & **C**)
free fall (two words)
Freefone trademark for telephone system in which recipient pays for calls (capital **F**; not **-ph-**)
free-for-all (hyphens)

freemason member of medieval guild (one word; lower-case **f**)

Freemason member of secret order (one word; capital **F**)

Freepost trademark for mail system in which recipient pays for postage (capital **F**)

free-range (hyphen)

freestanding (one word)

Free State South African province, which replaced **Orange Free State** in 1994

freethinker (one word)

freeze change to ice, or spell of very cold weather (compare **frieze**)

freeze-up (noun; the verb is **freeze up**)

freezing point (two words)

Freiberg German city in Saxony

Freiburg German city in Baden-Württemberg (official name **Freiburg im Breisgau**), or German name for **Fribourg**

Fremantle Australian port (not **Free-**)

French Canadian (noun)

French-Canadian (adjective)

French Guiana French overseas region in South America (not **Guy-**)

French horn (capital **F**)

French kiss (capital **F**)

French leave (capital **F**)

French polish (noun; capital **F**; two words)

French-polish (verb; capital **F**; hyphen)

French Revolution (capital **F** & **R**)

French windows (capital **F**)

frenetic (**fren-**)

fresco (plural **frescoes** or **frescos**)

freshwater (one word)

Fresnel, Augustin Jean French physicist

Freud, Anna Austrian psychiatrist; **Lucian** British painter (not **Lucien**); **Sigmund** Austrian psychiatrist

Freudian slip (capital **F**)

Freytag, Gustav German novelist

FRG Federal Republic of Germany (official name for **Germany** and formerly for **West Germany**)

friable crumbly (compare **fryable**)

friar member of religious order (compare **fryer**)

friar's balsam (**-'s** not **-s'**)

Fribourg Swiss town and canton (German name **Freiburg**)

fricassee meat in white sauce (not italic; double **s**, double **e**; no accent)

FRICS Fellow of the Royal Institution of Chartered Surveyors

friend (**-ie-**)

frier variant of **fryer**

Friesian breed of cattle, or variant of **Frisian**

Friesland Dutch province (Frisian name **Fryslân**), or area comprising this province along with **East Friesland** and **North Friesland** in Germany (**-ies-**)

frieze ornamental band on upper wall (compare **freeze**)

frigid (not **-dg-**)

Frisbee trademark for plastic disc thrown for recreation (capital **F**; **-bee**)

Frisian (as noun) language of NW Netherlands and parts of N Germany, speaker of Frisian, or person from Friesland; (as adjective) of Frisian or Friesland (also **Friesian**)

Frisian Islands island chain off the Netherlands, Germany, and Denmark (capital **F** & **I**; not **Friesian**)

frisson shudder, shiver, or thrill (italics)

Friuli-Venezia Giulia region of Italy (one hyphen; **-iuli-** then **-iulia**)

frivolity (single **l**)

frizz (double **z**)

Frl. Fräulein

Froebel, Friedrich German educator (also **Fröbel**)

frogman (one word)

frogmarch (one word)

frolic (not **-ck**)

frolicked, frolicking (**-ck-**)

frolicsome (not **-ck-**)

fromage frais soft cheese with light texture (not italic)

Fronde rebellious movement in 17th-century France (not italic; capital F; **-de**)

frontbencher (one word)

frontier (**-ier**)

frontispiece illustration facing title page of book

front line (two words as noun, e.g. *in the front line*, but one word when used before another noun, e.g. *frontline troops*)

front matter another name for **prelims** (two words)

frontrunner (one word)

frostbite (one word)

frowsy variant of **frowzy**

frowsty musty

frowzy unkempt (also **frowsy**)

FRPS Fellow of the Royal Photographic Society

FRS Fellow of the Royal Society

fruitcake (one word)

fruit machine (two words)

frustum part of cone or pyramid (not **-trum**)

fryable able to be fried (compare **friable**)

fryer person or thing that fries (also **frier**; compare **friar**)

frying pan (two words)

Fryslân Frisian name for **Friesland**

FSA Financial Services Authority

ft foot or feet (also **ft.**)

Fuad, King Egyptian monarch

fuchsia (lower-case f in general use: *Fuchsia* is the genus name; **-chs-**)

fuddy-duddy (hyphen)

fuelled, fuelling (single l in US English)

fugacious (**-ious**)

fugal (not **-ual**)

fugue (**-gue**)

Führer leader, especially Adolf Hitler (italics; umlaut; *h* before first *r*; also **Fuehrer**)

Fuji, Mount Japanese volcano (also **Fujiyama** or **Fuji-san**, neither of which should be preceded by **Mount**)

-ful (single l when part of word, as in *add a bucketful of water to the cement*; plural **-fuls**, not **-sful**; compare **full**)

Fulbright, J(ames) William US politician after whom a scholarship programme is named (single **l**)

fulcrum (plural **fulcrums** or **fulcra**)

fulfil (single l twice)

fulfilled, fulfilling (single l before **-ed** and **-ing** in US English)

fulfilment (single l twice)

full (double l when separate word, as in *keep a bucket full of water beside the fire* compare **-ful**)

full-blown (hyphen)

full capital capital letter of normal size, as opposed to a **small capital**

fuller's earth (**-'s** not **-s'**)

full-fledged variant of **fully fledged** (hyphen)

full-length (hyphen)

fullness (double l)

full out (*typog.*) aligned with margin and not indented

full stop punctuation mark used at end of sentence and sometimes in **abbreviations** (see that entry). It is sometimes called a **full point** in UK English; in US and Canadian English it is called a **period**; when used in Internet domain names it is called a **dot**.

full time (noun; adverb)

full-time (adjective)

full-title page another name for **title page**, as opposed to **half-title page**

fully fledged (two words; also **full-fledged**, with hyphen)

fulmar bird (not **-er**)

fulsome (single **l**; note that *fulsome praise*, for example, is offensively excessive or insincere: to avoid controversy, do not use the adjective in the sense 'highly complimentary')

fundraising (one word)

funeral burial ceremony, or of such a ceremony, as in *a funeral cortege*

funereal gloomy or mournful, as in *a funereal atmosphere*

funfair (one word)

fungus (plural **fungi** or **funguses**)

funnel (double **n**, single **l**)

funnelled, funnelling (single **l** in US English)

fur animal hair or skin (compare **fir**)

Furness region of NW England (not **-iss**)

furore (**-re**)

further (as adjective) additional, or more distant; (as adverb) in addition, to a greater degree or extent, or to or at a greater distance; (as verb) assist the progress of (compare **farther**)

furthest most distant, to the greatest degree or extent, or to or at the greatest distance (compare **farthest**)

Furtwängler, Wilhelm German conductor (umlaut)

furze (**-ze**)

fuse (**-se**)

fuselage (**-sel-**)

fusilier (single **l**; capital **F** when part of name)

fusillade (double **l**)

fwd forward

f.w.d. four-wheel drive; front-wheel drive

FYI for your information

Fylde region of NW England

FYROM Former Yugoslav Republic of Macedonia (see **Macedonia**)

G

g gram or grams (no full stop; no **s** in plural)

G giga-, as in **GHz** gigahertz (no full stop)

Ga gallium (no full stop)

GA Georgia (US postal code)

gabardine (the spelling **gaberdine** is not incorrect, but it is less common)

gabble speak rapidly and indistinctly (compare **garble**)

gaberdine less common variant of **gabardine**

Gaborone capital of Botswana (former name **Gaberones**)

Gabriel biblical archangel (not **-ial**)

Gabrieli, Andrea and **Giovanni** Italian composers (also **Gabrielli**)

Gabrieli String Quartet (not **-elli**; capital **G, S, & Q**)

gadabout (one word)

Gadarene of or in a headlong rush (capital **G**; alluding to the *Gadarene swine* of the Bible (Matt. 8))

Gaddafi, Moamar al Libyan statesman (also **Qaddafi**)

Gadhelic less common variant of **Goidelic**

gadolinium (symbol **Gd**)

Gaea variant of **Gaia**

Gaedhealtacht variant of **Gaeltacht**

Gael speaker of Gaelic

Gaelic Celtic language of Scotland and Ireland (compare **Gallic**)

Gaeltacht region of Ireland where Gaelic is spoken (also

Gaedhealtacht; compare **Gaidhealtachd**)

gaff angling or nautical term; also used in the phrase *blow the gaff* meaning 'divulge a secret'

gaffe social blunder

Gagarin, Yuri Soviet cosmonaut

gage pledge (compare **gauge**)

Gaia Greek goddess or personification of the earth (also **Gaea**)

Gaia hypothesis (capital **G**; not **Gaea**)

Gaidhealtachd region of Scotland where Gaelic is spoken (compare **Gaeltacht**)

gaiety being carefree and merry (**-aie-**; compare **gayness**)

gaily (not **gay-**)

Gainsborough, Thomas English painter (not **-brough**)

gait way of walking (compare **gate**)

Gaitskell, Hugh British politician (not **-kill**)

Gaius Roman jurist (also **Caius**, but note that the forename of Julius Caesar and others is always **Gaius**)

gal. gallon (full stop; also **gall.**)

Gal. Galatians (full stop; not italic)

gala festive or sporting occasion (compare **galah**)

galactic of a galaxy or the Galaxy (lower-case **g**)

galah Australian cockatoo (compare **gala**)

Galahad Arthurian knight, hence any pure or noble man (capital **G**)

galantine (not **gall-**)

Galápagos Islands Pacific Ocean (Spanish name **Archipiélago de Colón**)

Galatea statue in Greek mythology

Galatia region in Asia Minor

Galatians book of the Bible (not italic; abbreviation **Gal.**)

galavant rare variant of **gallivant**

galaxy any of a number of star systems, or figurative use of the noun (lower-case **g**)

Galaxy the galaxy that contains the solar system (capital **G**)

Galilean of Galilee or Galileo

Galilee region of Israel

Galileo Italian astronomer (full name **Galileo Galilei**)

galivant rare variant of **gallivant**

gall. gallon (full stop; also **gal.**)

gall bladder (two words)

galleon ship (double **l**; not **-ion**; compare **gallon**)

galley (*typog.*) printer's proof, usually unpaginated (also **galley proof**; compare **page proof**)

gallic of gallium or galls (lower-case **g**)

Gallic of France or Gaul (capital **G**; compare **Gaelic**)

Gallicize (also **Gallicise**; see **-ize/-ise**)

Gallipoli Turkish port and peninsula, scene of battle in World War I (Turkish name **Gelibolu** for the port)

gallium (symbol **Ga**)

gallivant (rarely **galivant** or **galavant**)

gallon unit of capacity (compare **galleon** and **galloon**)

galloon trimming on clothing or upholstery (compare **gallon**)

gallop horse's gait (compare **galop**)

galloped, galloping (not **-pp-**)

Gallovidian of Galloway (also **Galwegian**)

Galloway area of SW Scotland or breed of cattle (capital **G**)

gallows (same form for singular and plural)

gallstone (one word)

Gallup Poll (capital **G** & **P**; not **-op**)

galop 19th-century dance or music for it (compare **gallop**)

galoshes (rarely **goloshes**)

Galsworthy, John English novelist (single **l**)

galumph (not **-umf**)

galvanize (also **galvanise**; see **-ize/-ise**)

Galway Irish county and port (single **l**)

Galwegian person from Galway, or variant of **Gallovidian**

Gama, Vasco da Portuguese navigator (lower-case **d**)

Gambia, The African country

gambit opening move (thus *opening* in the phrase *opening gambit* is redundant)

gamble wager

gambol frolic

gambolled, gambolling (single **l** in US English)

game bird (two words)

gamecock (one word)

gamekeeper (one word)

game plan (two words)

game show (two words)

game warden (two words)

gamey of game (also **gamy**; compare **gammy**)

gamin street urchin (not italic)

gamine boyish girl (not italic)

gamma globulin (two words)

gamma ray (no hyphen unless used before another noun, as in *gamma-ray astronomy*)

gammy lame (compare **gamey**)

gamut (single **m**)

Gand French name for **Ghent**

Gandhi, Indira and **Rajiv** Indian prime ministers; **Mohandas**

Karamchand (known as **Mahatma**) Indian leader (**h** after **d**, not **Gh-**; in general texts, the surname alone usually refers to Mahatma Gandhi)

ganglion (plural **ganglia** or **ganglions**)

gangplank (one word)

gangrene (not **-een**)

gangway (one word)

gantlet section of overlapping railway track, or variant of **gauntlet** in the sense 'heavy glove'

Ganymede cupbearer to the gods in mythology, or satellite of Jupiter

gaol less common variant of **jail**

gaolbird less common variant of **jailbird**

gaoler less common variant of **jailer**

Garamond typeface

garble jumble, or distort the meaning of (compare **gabble**)

García Lorca, Federico Spanish poet and dramatist (acute accent; also alphabetized as **Lorca**)

García Márquez, Gabriel Colombian novelist (two acute accents; also alphabetized as **Márquez**)

garçon waiter (not italic)

Gard see **Martin du Gard**

garda member of the Garda Síochána (lower-case **g**; plural **gardaí**)

Garda Síochána Irish police force (capital **G** & **S**; two acute accents)

gardener (not **-dn-**)

Gardeners' Question Time radio programme (**-s'** not **-'s**)

gardenia (lower-case **g** in general use; *Gardenia* is the genus name)

Gardner, Ava US actress; **Erle Stanley** US crime writer (not **-den-** or **-din-**)

Gargantua giant with large appetite in Rabelais's *Gargantua and Pantagruel*

gargantuan huge (the use of capital

G is less common but not incorrect in this sense)

gargoyle (**-oyle**)

garibaldi biscuit (lower-case **g**)

Garibaldi, Giuseppe Italian patriot, leader of the Risorgimento

garish (not **gair-**)

garlic (not **-ick**)

garlicky (**-ick-**)

garrotte (also **garotte** or **garrote**)

Gascogne French name for **Gascony**

Gascoigne, Paul English footballer

Gascony former province of SW France (French name **Gascogne**)

gas (plural **gases** or **gasses**)

gaseous (not **-ious**)

gases plural or third person present tense of **gas** (also **gasses**)

Gaskell, Mrs English novelist (born **Elizabeth Cleghorn Stevenson**)

gasoline (also **gasolene**)

Gaspé Canadian peninsula (acute accent)

gassed (double s)

gasses variant of **gases**

gassing (double s)

gastroenteritis (no hyphen; **-is**)

gate movable barrier or opening (compare **gait**)

gateau cake (not italic; also **gâteau**; plural **gateaux, gateaus**, or **gâteaux**)

gate-crash (hyphen)

gatehouse (one word)

gatepost (one word)

gather in printing, assemble (book sections) in correct sequence for binding

Gatling gun (capital **G** then lower-case **g**)

GATT General Agreement on Tariffs and Trade

gauche awkward or tactless (not italic)

gaucho South American cowboy (not italic; plural **gauchos**)

gauffer less common variant of **goffer**

gauge measure or estimate (not **-ua-**; compare **gage**)

Gauguin, Paul French painter (**-au-** then **-ui-**)

Gaul ancient region of Europe (corresponding to France, Belgium, and parts of Italy, Germany, and the Netherlands), or person from this region

Gauleiter provincial governor in Hitler's Germany, or any overbearing person in similar position of authority (not italic; **-ei-**; also **gauleiter** in the sense 'overbearing person')

Gaulle see **de Gaulle**

Gaullist supporter of de Gaulle or his policies (double **l**)

Gauloise trademark for French cigarette (capital **G**)

Gaultier, Jean-Paul French fashion designer (compare **Gautier**)

gaumless rare variant of **gormless**

gauntlet heavy glove, or used in the phrases *throw down the gauntlet* and *run the gauntlet* (also **gantlet** in the sense 'heavy glove')

Gautier, Théophile French philosopher (compare **Gaultier**)

gauss unit of magnetic flux density (lower-case **g**)

Gauss, Karl Friedrich German mathematician

gave past tense of **give** (compare **given**)

gay (beware of ambiguity when used in senses other than 'homosexual')

Gay-Lussac, Joseph Louis French scientist (hyphen)

gayness being homosexual (compare **gaiety**)

Gaza Strip region on SE Mediterranean coast (capital **G** & **S**; single **z**)

gazebo (plural **gazebos**)

gazpacho Spanish soup (not italic; **gaz-**)

GB Great Britain

GBE Grand Cross of the Order of the British Empire

GBH grievous bodily harm

GBS George Bernard Shaw

GC George Cross

GCB Grand Cross of the Order of the Bath

GCE General Certificate of Education

GCHQ Government Communications Headquarters

GCMG Grand Cross of the Order of St Michael and St George

GCSE General Certificate of Secondary Education (replaced **CSE** and **O level** in 1988; plural **GCSEs**)

GCVO Grand Cross of the Royal Victorian Order

Gd gadolinium (no full stop)

Gdańsk Polish port (German name **Danzig**)

Gdns Gardens (in addresses; no full stop)

GDP gross domestic product

GDR German Democratic Republic (English name for the former **East Germany**; see also **DDR**)

Ge germanium (no full stop)

gearbox (one word)

gear lever (two words)

gecko (plural **geckos** or **geckoes**)

Geelong Australian port (double **e**)

geezer man (compare **geyser**)

Geiger counter (capital **G**)

geisha (**-ei-**)

gel jelly-like substance, or variant of **jell**

gelatine (also **gelatin**)

Gelderland Dutch province (also **Guelderland** or **Guelders**)

Geldof, Bob Irish rock singer and philanthropist (not **-orf**; his knighthood is honorary, so he does not officially have the title *Sir*)

Gelibolu Turkish name for **Gallipoli** (the port)

gemsbok (also **gemsbuck**)

gemütlich friendly or cosy (italics; umlaut)

Gen. Genesis (full stop; not italic)

gendarme French police officer (not italic; **-arme**)

gender avoid using a gender-specific word (e.g. **authoress** or **fireman**) where a gender-neutral alternative (e.g. **author** or **firefighter**) is more appropriate or less likely to offend (see individual entries for these and other examples). For the use of he, he or she, they, etc. as words of common gender, see **he**, **his** and **their**. Note that **gender** is primarily a grammatical term (denoting the categorization of nouns as masculine, feminine, or neuter); do not use in place of **sex** unless the latter would be ambiguous in the context.

gene unit of heredity (compare **jeans**)

genealogy (not **-ology**)

genera a plural of **genus**

General Assembly (capital **G** & **A** with reference to the UN or other specific governing bodies)

generalissimo supreme commander (single **l** & **m**, double **s**; plural **generalissimos**)

generalize (also **generalise**; see **-ize/-ise**)

generator (not **-er**)

generic applicable to whole class, nonproprietary, or of a genus (compare **genetic**)

genesis beginning or origin (lower-case **g**)

Genesis book of the Bible (not italic; abbreviation **Gen.**)

genetic of genes or the study of heredity (compare **generic** and **genital**)

Geneva Swiss city and canton (French name **Genève**, German name **Genf**)

Geneva, Lake lake between Switzerland and France (French name **Lac Léman**, German name **Genfersee**)

Geneva Convention (capital **G** & **C**)

Genève French name for **Geneva**

Geneviève, St French nun (grave accent)

Genf German name for **Geneva**

Genfersee German name for Lake **Geneva**

Genghis Khan Mongol ruler (**Ge-**, **-gh-**, **Kh-**; the variants **Jinghis Khan** and **Jenghis Khan** are less common but not incorrect)

genial cheerful and easy-going, as in *our genial host* (compare **congenial** and **genital**)

genie magic servant in fairy tales (plural **genies**; compare **genius**)

genii plural of **genius** in mythological senses

genital of the sexual organs or reproduction (compare **congenital**, **genetic**, **genial**, and **genitive**)

genitive denoting case of nouns used to indicate possession (compare **genital**)

genius brilliant person, exceptional ability, distinctive spirit of place or time, guardian spirit in Roman mythology, or demon in Arabic mythology (plural **geniuses** in non-mythological senses or **genii** in mythological senses; compare **genie** and **genus**)

genius loci guardian spirit or special atmosphere of place (italics)

genoa sail (lower-case **g**)

Genoa Italian port (Italian name **Genova**)

Genoa cake (capital **G**)

Genova Italian name for **Genoa**)

genre category or sort (not italic; **-re**)

Gent Flemish name for **Ghent**

genteel polite, proper, or refined (compare **gentle**)

gentile denoting words used to designate places or their inhabitants, such as *Danish* and *Dane* (lower-case **g**)

Gentile (as noun) person who is not a Jew, person who is not a Mormon, or a heathen; (as adjective) not Jewish, not Mormon, or pagan (capital **G**)

gentle kindly, mild, or gradual (compare **genteel**)

gentlemen's agreement (also **gentleman's agreement**)

gents lavatory (no apostrophe)

genuflection (also **genuflexion**)

genus (plural **genera** or **genuses**) in the hierarchy of **taxonomic names**, the group that comes above a species and below a family. The genus name has a capital initial and is italic (see also **binomial**). Compare **genius**.

Geoffrey of Monmouth Welsh chronicler

geographical (also **geographic**)

geological (also **geologic**)

geometric (also **geometrical**)

Geordie (as noun) person from Tyneside or dialect of Tyneside; (as adjective) of the people or dialect of Tyneside

George-Brown, Lord see **Brown**

George Cross (capital **G** & **C**)

Georgetown capital of Guyana or capital of the Cayman Islands (one word)

George Town Malaysian port, capital of Penang state (two words; also **Penang**)

Georgia NW Asian country or US state

Georgian (as adjective) of any of the six kings of Britain called George or their reigns (especially denoting 18th-century architecture), of the Asian country of Georgia, or of the US state of Georgia; (as noun) the language of the country of Georgia, or a person from the country or state of Georgia

geranium (lower-case **g** in general use; *Geranium* is one of the genus names)

gerbil rodent kept as pet (the spelling **jerbil** is less common but not incorrect; compare **jerboa**)

geriatric (to avoid offence, use only in medical contexts with reference to old people)

Géricault, Théodore French painter (acute accent on surname and first name)

german having same parents as oneself (as in *brother-german*), having a parent who is a brother or sister of one's father or mother (as in *cousin-german*), or less common variant of **germane** (lower-case **g**)

German (as adjective) of Germany; (as noun) the language of Germany or a person from Germany (capital **G**)

germane relevant (the variant **german** is less common but not incorrect)

germanic of germanium (lower-case **g**)

Germanic group of languages, of this group of languages, or of Germany or German (capital **G**)

germanium (symbol **Ge**)

German measles (capital **G**)

German shepherd dog another name for **Alsatian** (the dog), preferred by breeders, dog clubs, etc. (capital **G**; also **German shepherd**)

Germany European country (German name **Deutschland**; official English name **Federal Republic of Germany**; see also **East Germany** and **West Germany**)

Geronimo North American Indian chieftain, or exclamation (capital **G**)

gerrymander (lower-case **g**; double **r**)

gerund noun formed from verb to denote action or state. In English, gerunds end in **-ing** (see that entry).

Gestalt whole perceived as more than sum of parts (not italic; not -sht-; the use of lower-case **g** is less common but not incorrect in English)

Gestalt psychology (capital **G**)

Gestapo (capital **G**)

gesundheit said to somebody who has sneezed (italics)

get-at-able (two hyphens)

getaway (noun; the verb is **get away**)

Gethsemane garden where Christ was betrayed

get-out (noun; the verb is **get out**)

get-together (noun; the verb is **get together**)

Getty, J(ean) Paul US millionaire

Gettysburg US town, site of national cemetery (double **t**, **-ys-**, **-burg**)

get-up (noun; the verb is **get up**)

get-up-and-go (three hyphens)

Gewürztraminer grape or wine (capital **G**; **-würz-**)

geyser hot spring (compare **geezer**)

Ghana African country (**Gh-**)

Ghanaian (also **Ghanian**)

ghastly (**gh-**)

ghat in India, mountain range or pass, or stairs or passage leading down to river (**gh-**)

Ghats either of two Indian mountain ranges, the **Eastern Ghats** and the **Western Ghats**

ghee clarified butter in Indian cookery (not italic)

Ghent Belgian city (Flemish name **Gent**, French name **Gand**)

gherkin (**gh-**)

ghetto (plural **ghettos** or **ghettoes**)

Ghibelline member of medieval Italian faction originally supporting German emperor (**Gh-**, single **b**, double **l**; compare **Guelph**)

ghillie laced shoe, or variant of **gillie**

Ghirlandaio, Domenico Italian painter (also **Ghirlandajo**)

ghost (**gh-**)

ghostwrite (one word)

ghoulish (**gh-**, **-ou-**)

GHQ General Headquarters

ghyll variant of **gill**[1] in the sense 'narrow stream, ravine, or pothole'

GI US soldier (from abbreviation of *government issue*; plural **GIs**)

Giacometti, Alberto Swiss sculptor and painter

Giant's Causeway promontory of basalt pillars in Northern Ireland (capital **G** & **C**; **-'s** not **-s'**)

gibber prattle or chatter (compare **jibber**)

gibberish (double **b**, single **r**)

gibbet (**-et**)

Gibbon, Edward English historian; **Lewis Grassic** Scottish writer

Gibbons, Grinling English sculptor and carver; **Orlando** English organist and composer

gibe jeer (also **jibe**; compare **gybe**)

Gibeon ancient town of Palestine (compare **Gideon**)

Gibraltar city on Rock of Gibraltar (not **-er**)

Gibraltar, Rock of promontory at tip of S Spain (capital **R** & **G**)

Gibraltar, Strait of channel between S Spain and NW Africa (capital **S** & **G**; not **Straits**)

Gide, André French writer (acute accent on first name)

Gideon biblical judge (compare **Gibeon**)

Gideon Bible (capital **G** & **B**)

Gielgud, Sir John English actor (**-ie-**; not **-good**)

giga- thousand million, as in *gigahertz*; or 2^{30}, as in *gigabyte*

GIGO garbage in, garbage out (no full stops)

gigolo (plural **gigolos**)

gild cover with gold or give falsely

attractive appearance to, or less common variant of **guild** in medieval sense

gilded past tense and past participle of gild (also **gilt**)

Gilead mountainous region east of River Jordan, or biblical character (single **l**, **-ead**)

gill[1] respiratory organ, or dialect word for narrow stream, ravine, or pothole (also **ghyll** in dialect sense)

gill[2] unit of liquid measure

Gillette, King Camp US inventor of safety razor (double **l**, double **t**)

gillie hunting or fishing guide or attendant (also **ghillie** or **gilly**)

gilliflower less common variant of **gillyflower**

Gillray, James English caricaturist (double **l**)

gillyflower (the spelling **gilliflower** is not incorrect, but it is less common)

gilt (as verb) variant of **gilded**; (as adjective) covered with gold; (as noun) gold applied as covering, or young female pig (compare **guilt**)

gilt-edged (hyphen)

gimbals (not **-bles**)

gimmick (double **m**; **-ck**)

ginger ale (two words)

ginger beer (two words)

gingerbread (one word)

gingham (**gi-** then **-gh-**)

ginkgo (also **gingko**)

Ginsberg, Allen US poet (not **Alan**)

Ginzburg, Natalia Italian writer

Gioconda, La another name for *Mona Lisa*

Giotto Florentine painter (also **Giotto di Bondone**)

Gipsy variant of **Gypsy** (the use of lower-case **g** is less common but not incorrect)

girlfriend (one word)

Girl Guides former name for **Guide Association** (note that a member of the senior branch of this association is now simply called a **Guide** or **guide**)

Girlguiding UK UK branch of the Guide Association (capital **G** then lower-case **g** without space)

Girls' Brigade (**-s'** not **-'s**)

giro (lower-case **g**; plural **giros**)

Girobank (capital **G**; one word)

Giscard d'Estaing, Valéry French politician

gismo less common variant of **gizmo**

gîte French self-catering cottage (not italic; circumflex)

Giuseppe Italian first name (not **Gui-**)

givable (also **giveable**)

give (past tense **gave**, past participle **given**)

giveable variant of **givable**

giveaway (noun; the verb is **give away**)

given past participle of **give** (compare **gave**)

Gîza see **El Gîza**

gizmo (the spelling **gismo** is not incorrect, but it is less common)

GLA Greater London Authority (comprising Mayor of London and London Assembly)

glacé crystallized, candied, or covered in icing (not italic; acute accent)

glacier mass of ice (compare **glazier**)

gladiolus (lower-case **g** in general use; *Gladiolus* is the genus name; plural **gladioli** or **gladioluses**)

Glamis Castle Scotland

glamorize (not **-our-**; also **glamorise**, see **-ize/-ise**)

glamorous (the spelling **glamourous** is not incorrect, but it is less common)

glamour (not **-or**)

glamourous less common variant of **glamorous**

glasnost public openness and accountability (not italic)

glass-blowing (hyphen)
glassful (not **-full**; plural **glassfuls**)
glasshouse (one word)
Glaswegian of Glasgow, or a person from Glasgow
Glauber's salt (capital **G**; **-au-**; also **Glauber salt**)
glaucoma (**-au-**)
glazier person who glazes windows (compare **glacier**)
Glazunov, Aleksandr Konstantinovich Russian composer
Glen, Esther New Zealand children's writer (compare **Glenn**)
Glencoe Scottish town and mountain valley (also **Glen Coe** for the valley)
Glendower, Owen Welsh chieftain (Welsh name **Owain Glyndŵr**)
glengarry Scottish cap (lower-case **g**)
Glenlivet, The Scotch whisky (capital **T** & **G**)
Glenn, John US astronaut (compare **Glen**)
Glennie, Evelyn Scottish percussionist
Glenrothes Scottish town (**-thes**)
globetrotter (one word)
glockenspiel (**-ck-**, **-ie-**)
Glorious Twelfth August 12 (start of grouse-shooting season; capital **G** & **T**)
Glos. Gloucestershire
Gloucester English city
Gloucestershire English county
glove puppet (two words)
glow-worm (hyphen)
glueing variant of **gluing**
glue-sniffing (hyphen)
gluing (also **glueing**)
gluten (not **-tin**)
glutinous (not **-ten-**)
glycerine (also **glycerin**)
Glyndŵr, Owain Welsh name for Owen **Glendower**
GM genetically modified; George Medal

GmbH *Gesellschaft mit beschränker Haftung* (used in German company names; lower-case **m** & **b**)
GMT Greenwich Mean Time (see also **UTC**)
gnocchi Italian dumplings (not italic; **gn-**, **-cch-**)
gnostic possessing knowledge (lower-case **g**)
Gnostic of heretical religious movement, or an adherent of this movement (capital **G**)
GNP gross national product
gnu (plural **gnus** or **gnu**)
GNVQ general national vocational qualification
go-ahead (noun and adjective; the verb is **go ahead**)
goalkeeper (one word)
goalpost (one word)
goatee beard (compare **goaty**)
goatherd (one word)
goatskin (one word)
goaty like a goat (compare **goatee**)
gobbledegook (also **gobbledygook**)
Gobelin denoting tapestry with vivid pictorial scenes (capital **G**)
go-between (hyphen)
Gobi Asian desert (compare **goby**)
gobsmacked (one word)
goby fish (compare **Gobi**)
go-cart another name for **kart**
god any of various deities worshipped in polytheistic societies (lower-case **g**)
God sole Supreme Being worshipped in monotheistic religions (capital **G**; for the use of capital initials for personal pronouns relating to God, see **capital letter**)
goddaughter (one word)
godfather (one word)
God-fearing (capital **G**; hyphen)
godforsaken (lower-case **g**; one word)
godmother (one word)
godsend (one word)
godson (one word)

Godthaab former name for **Nuuk**
Godwin Austen another name for **K2**
(**-in** then **-en**)
Goebbels, Paul Joseph German
Nazi politician (**-oe-** not **-ö-**,
double **b**)
-goer (attached without hyphen, as
in *partygoer*)
Goering see **Göring**
Goethe, Johann Wolfgang von
German writer (**-oe-** not **-ö-**)
gofer assistant who runs errands
(compare **goffer** and **gopher**)
goffer (as noun) pleated frill or
decorated edge of book; (as verb)
pleat (frill) or decorate (edges of
book) (the spelling **gauffer** is not
incorrect, but it is less common;
compare **gofer**)
Gogh see **Van Gogh**
go-go dancer (one hyphen)
Goidelic group of Celtic languages
comprising Irish Gaelic, Scottish
Gaelic, and Manx (the variants
Goidhelic and **Gadhelic** are less
common but not incorrect; compare
Brythonic)
goings-on (hyphen)
go-kart variant of **kart**
gold (symbol **Au**)
gold-digger (hyphen)
gold dust (two words)
Golden Delicious apple (capital
G & **D**)
Golden Gate strait between Pacific
Ocean and San Francisco Bay
Golders Green London (no
apostrophe)
goldfish bowl (two words)
gold mine (two words)
gold-mining (hyphen)
Goldsmiths College London (no
apostrophe)
golem artificially created human
being in Jewish legend (compare
Gollum)
golf ball (two words)

golf club (two words)
golf course (two words)
Golgotha another name for **Calvary**
Gollancz, Sir Victor British
publisher (**-ncz**)
golliwog (not **golly-**)
Gollum character in Tolkien's *The
Lord of the Rings* (compare **golem**)
goloshes rare variant of **galoshes**
Gomorrah biblical city destroyed by
God in the Old Testament, hence
any place of vice or depravity (single
m, double **r**, also **Gomorrha** in New
Testament references to the city in
the Authorized Version)
gonorrhoea (**-orrh-**; **-oe-**)
Gonville and Caius College
Cambridge
goodbye (no hyphen)
good day (two words)
Good Friday Friday before Easter
Sunday (capital **G** & **F**)
good-humoured (hyphen)
good-looking (hyphen)
good-natured (hyphen)
goodness (note that the phrase *for
goodness sake* is also written *for
goodness' sake* but rarely *for goodness's
sake*)
good night (two words)
Good Samaritan biblical character,
hence person who helps another in
distress (capital **G** & **S**)
goodwill (one word)
goose (plural **geese** in the senses
'bird' and 'silly person' or **gooses** in
the senses 'iron used by tailors' and
'playful prod in the behind')
goose flesh (two words)
goose step (noun)
goose-step (verb)
Goossens, Sir Eugene British
composer and conductor; **Leon**
British oboist (double **o** then
double **s**)
gopher burrowing animal (compare
gofer)

Gorbachov, Mikhail Sergeevich
Soviet statesman (also **Gorbachev**)
Gordian knot (capital **G**)
Gordonstoun School Scotland (not
-**town**)
Gore-Tex trademark for breathable
waterproof fabric (capital **G** & **T**;
hyphen)
Gorgon any of three monstrous
sisters in Greek mythology, hence
a fierce or unpleasant woman (also
gorgon in the non-mythological
sense)
Gorgonzola cheese (capital **G**)
gorilla ape or brutal-looking man
(compare **guerrilla**)
Göring, Hermann Wilhelm German
Nazi leader (also **Goering**)
Gorki former name for **Nizhni
Novgorod** (also **Gorky**)
Gorki, Maxim Russian writer (also
Gorky)
gormand less common variant of
gourmand
gormandize eat greedily (also
gormandise, see -**ize**/-**ise**; compare
gourmandise)
gormless (rarely **gaumless**)
Gorsedd Welsh bardic institution
(capital **G**; double **d**)
go-slow (noun; the verb is **go
slow**)
gospel story narrated in Gospels,
religious doctrine, unquestionable
truth, or Black religious music
(lower-case **g**)
Gospel any of the first four books
of the New Testament, or a reading
from one of these in church
(capital **G**)
Gosse, Sir Edmund William English
critic and poet (-**sse**)
gossiped, gossiping (not -**pp**-)
gossipy (not -**pp**-)
got (do not use **has got** or **have got**
in formal contexts where **has** or
have can stand alone, as in *he has*

[not *has got*] *three children* or *we have*
[not *have got*] *to make a decision*)
Göteborg Swedish port (umlaut; not
-**burg**; also **Gothenburg**)
Goth member of East Germanic
people from Scandinavia, or
denoting style of rock music or
fashion (also **goth** or **Gothic** for the
music or fashion)
Gothenburg variant of **Göteborg**
(-**burg**)
Gothic of the Goths; of style of
architecture, sculpture, painting, etc.
of 12th–16th centuries; of literary
style characterized by gloom,
grotesque, and supernatural (also
gothic or **Gothick**); language of
Goths; heavy script typeface (also
black letter); or variant of **Goth** with
reference to the music or fashion
gotten past participle of **get** used in
US English or in such phrases as
ill-gotten gains in UK English
Götterdämmerung twilight of the
gods in German mythology (not
italic; capital **G**; two umlauts)
Göttingen German city (umlaut;
double **t**)
Gouda Dutch town or cheese
(capital **G**)
goujon deep-fried strip of fish or
chicken (not italic; -**jon**)
gourmand glutton (the spelling
gormand is less common but not
incorrect; compare **gourmet**)
gourmandise love of good food
(compare **gormandize**)
gourmet person with discriminating
palate for good food and drink (not
gor-; compare **gourmand**)
Government (capital **G** with
reference to the government of a
specific country, as in *the British
Government*)
governor (not -**er**)
Gower, David English cricketer; **John**
English poet

Gowers, Sir Ernest English civil servant, author of *Plain Words*

goy Jewish word for Gentile (not italic; plural **goyim** or **goys**)

Goya, Francisco de Spanish painter (full name **Francisco José de Goya y Lucientes**)

GP general practitioner (plural **GPs**)

GPS global positioning system

Graaff see **Van de Graaff**

Graafian follicle (capital **G**; double **a** then single **f**)

Gracchus, Gaius Sempronius and **Tiberius Sempronius** Roman tribunes and reformers (**-cch-**; known as **the Gracchi**)

grace-and-favour (two hyphens)

graceful characterized by beauty of style or movement (compare **gracious**)

grace note (two words)

Graces three goddesses of charm and beauty in Greek mythology (capital **G**)

gracious kind, courteous, or condescending (compare **graceful**)

gradable (not **-eable**)

gradation gradual progression or transition, or the act of arranging in grades

graduation act of graduating from university, college, etc.; ceremony at which degrees are conferred; or marking that indicates measure

Graeco- (**Greco-** in US English)

Graf German title equivalent to **count** (italics; capital **G**)

graffiti (plural noun now often used with singular verb or pronoun, especially with reference to such drawings or messages in general; singular **graffito**)

Graham, Billy US evangelist; **Martha** US dancer and choreographer; **Thomas** British physicist

Grahame, Kenneth Scottish author of *The Wind in the Willows*

Graian Alps mountains in France and Italy (**-aia-**)

Grail see **Holy Grail**

Grainger, Percy Aldridge Australian pianist and composer (compare **Granger**)

gram (not **gramme**; abbreviation **g**, without full stop)

grammar (not **-er**)

Grammy US award for achievement in the record industry (plural **Grammys** or **Grammies**)

gramophone (**-amo-**)

Granada former kingdom of Spain, Spanish or Nicaraguan city, or TV company (compare **Grenada**)

Gran Canaria Spanish name for **Grand Canary** (not **Grand**)

Gran Chaco South American plain (not **Grand**)

grand- (attached without hyphen to form words denoting parent's parent or child's child, as in *grandmother, grandson*, etc., or to form less common variants of words beginning with **great-**, as in grandaunt for great-aunt)

grandad (also **granddad**)

Grand Canary Atlantic island in the Canaries (Spanish name **Gran Canaria**)

Grand Canyon Arizona, USA (capital **G** & **C**)

Grand Coulee Dam Washington State, USA (capital **G**, **C**, & **D**; **-ou-**, **-ee**)

granddad variant of **grandad** (no hyphen)

granddaughter (double **d**; no hyphen)

grandeur (**-eur**)

Grand Guignol short sensational horrifying play (italics; **-uign-**)

grand mal form of epilepsy with violent convulsions (not italic; compare **petit mal**)

Grand Marnier trademark for

orange-flavoured liqueur (capital **G** & **M**)

grandmaster top chess player (one word; capital **G** as part of title)

Grand Master title of head of society or organization such as Freemasons (two words; capital **G** & **M**)

Grand Prix (not italic; capital **G** & **P**; plural **Grands Prix**)

Granger, Stewart English actor (not **Stuart**; compare **Grainger**)

Granny Smith apple (capital **G** & **S**)

Granth see **Guru Granth**

grant-maintained (hyphenated unless used after noun, as in *the school is grant maintained*)

gran turismo full form of **GT** (not italic; not **grand**; not **tour-**)

Granville-Barker, Harley English dramatist and theatre director

grapefruit (plural **grapefruit** or **grapefruits**)

graphics (use singular verb in the senses 'art of drawing' and 'study of writing systems', use plural verb in the sense 'pictures, diagrams, symbols, etc.')

Grasmere English lake (single **s**; note that the name is not preceded by **Lake**)

Grass, Günter German writer (umlaut on first name)

grasshopper (one word)

grass roots (no hyphen unless used before another noun, as in *grass-roots support*)

grate shred, scrape, framework of metal bars, or fireplace (compare **great**)

gratin see **au gratin**

gravadlax another name for **gravlax**

grave denoting the accent used on à, è, etc. to indicate that the vowel has a different sound (compare **acute**). It is also sometimes used in English to indicate that the **-ed** ending of a past tense or past participle is to be pronounced as a separate syllable, as in *blessèd*, but this usage is now rare.

gravelled, gravelling (single **l** in US English)

Gravenhage see **'s Gravenhage**

Graves French wine (the spelling **graves**, with lower-case **g**, is less common but not incorrect)

Graves' disease (-s' not -s's)

gravestone (one word)

graveyard (one word)

gravitas seriousness (not italic)

gravlax marinated dry-cured salmon (not italic; also **gravadlax**)

gravy boat (two words)

gravy train (two words)

gray unit of radiation, or US spelling of **grey**

Gray, Simon British writer; **Thomas** English poet (compare **Grey**)

grayling (not **grey-**)

Gray's Inn London (apostrophe)

Graz Austrian city (not **-atz**)

great large, important, extreme, or excellent (compare **grate**)

great- attached with hyphen to form words denoting parent's aunt or uncle, or child of nephew or niece, as in *great-aunt*, *great-nephew*, etc. (The use of **grand-** for this purpose, attached without a hyphen, is less common but not incorrect.) The prefix **great-** is also used to form words denoting relatives of older or younger generations, as in *great-granddaughter*, *great-great-grandfather*.

Great Australian Bight large inward curve on S coast of Australia (informal name **the Bight**)

Great Barrier Reef coral reef off NE Australia (capital **G**, **B**, & **R**)

Great Britain England, Wales, and Scotland, including most adjacent islands but excluding self-governing islands such as the Isle of Man. The term came into use in 1603. See also **British Isles** and **United Kingdom**.

Great Dane (capital **G** & **D**)
great-grandchildren (one hyphen)
great-grandparents (one hyphen)
Great Lakes Lakes Superior, Huron, Erie, Ontario, and Michigan in North America (capital **G** & **L**)
Great Ormond Street Hospital for Children London (not **Ormonde**)
Great Power nation with exceptional political influence and military strength (capital **G** & **P**)
Great Wall of China (capital **G, W,** & **C**)
Great Yarmouth port and resort in Norfolk (sometimes shortened to **Yarmouth**, but see also that entry)
Grecian classically simple in design or beauty (compare **Greek**)
Greco see **El Greco**
Greco- US spelling of **Graeco-**
Greek (as adjective) of Greece; (as noun) the language of Greece or a person from Greece (compare **Grecian**)
Greek Orthodox Church established Church of Greece, or another name for **Orthodox Church**
Greeley, Horace US journalist and political leader (**-ley**)
Green of the Green Party, or a member of the Green Party (capital **G**; to avoid ambiguity, use **green** with general reference to environmental issues or politicians from other parties who support such issues)
Green, John Richard British historian (compare **Greene**)
green belt (two words)
Greene, Graham English writer (compare **Green**)
greenfield denoting a site not previously built on (one word; compare **brownfield**)
Green Goddess army fire engine (capital **G** twice)
greengrocer (no hyphen)

greenhouse (one word)
Green Party political party concerned with environment (capital **G** & **P**)
Greenwich borough of Greater London (not **Gren-**)
Greenwich Mean Time (capital **G, M,** & **T**; not **Gren-**; see also **UTC**)
greetings card (not **-ing**)
Gregorian calendar calendar in use today, introduced by Pope Gregory XIII to replace **Julian calendar** (capital **G**; see also **New Style**)
Grenada Caribbean island (compare **Granada**)
Grenadian of Grenada, or a person from Grenada
grenadier member of infantry regiment (**-ier**)
grenadine pomegranate syrup or light thin fabric (lower-case **g**)
Grenadines, the chain of islets in Caribbean Sea
Gresham's law economic hypothesis that bad money drives good money out of circulation (lower-case **l**)
grey colour (compare **gray**)
Grey, Charles, 2nd Earl Grey British statesman; **Sir Edward, 1st Viscount Grey of Fallodon** British statesman; **Sir George** British statesman and colonial administrator; **Lady Jane** queen of England for ten days; **Zane** US writer (compare **Gray**)
Grey Friar Franciscan friar (two words; capital **G** & **F**)
Greyfriars College Oxford (no apostrophe)
greyhound (one word)
greyhound racing (two words)
grey matter (two words)
gridiron (one word)
gridlock (one word)
grief (**-ie-**)
Grieg, Edvard Norwegian composer (not **Greig**, not **Edward**)
grievous (**-ie-**; not **-ious**)

griffin winged monster (also **griffon** or **gryphon**)

griffon dog, vulture, or variant of **griffin**

grike fissure in limestone (also **gryke**)

Grikwa variant of **Griqua**

grill cooking device, food cooked on or under grill, cook on or under grill, interrogate, or variant of **grille**

grille metal framework, grating, or screen, as in *radiator grille* (also **grill**)

grillroom (one word)

Grimm, Jakob Ludwig Karl and **Wilhelm Karl** German philologists and folklorists who compiled collection of fairy tales (double **m**)

Grindelwald Swiss valley and resort (-**del**-, -**wald**)

grindstone (one word)

Griqua South African people of mixed European and Khoikhoi ancestry (also **Grikwa**)

grisaille monochrome painting technique (not italic)

grisly gruesome, as in *a grisly murder*

gristly having gristle, as in *gristly meat*

grizzly partly grey, as in *a grizzly beard*, whining fretfully, as in *a grizzly child*, or short for **grizzly bear**

groan moan (compare **grown**)

groin part of body where legs join abdomen (compare **groyne**)

Grolier denoting decorative style of bookbinding (capital **G**)

Gromit dog in *Wallace and Gromit* animations

grommet ring or tube (rarely **grummet**)

Gropius, Walter US architect (compare **Grotius**)

gros point large needlepoint stitch (not italic; compare **petit point**)

Grotius, Hugo Dutch jurist and statesman (compare **Gropius**)

grotto (plural grottoes or **grottos**)

ground (as noun) land, position, reason, etc.; (as verb) establish, instruct in fundamentals, confine to ground or house, run aground, or past tense and past participle of **grind**

grounded past tense and past participle of **ground**

ground floor (two words)

Groundhog Day February 2 (capital **G** & **D**)

ground plan (two words)

ground rent (two words)

groundsheet (one word)

groundswell (one word)

groundwork (one word)

grovelled, grovelling (single **l** in US English)

grown past participle of **grow** (compare **groan**)

grown-up (hyphen)

groyne breakwater (compare **groin**)

Grozny Russian city, capital of Chechen Republic

Grub Street world of literary hacks (capital **G** & **S**)

gruelling (single **l** in US English)

gruesome (-**ue**-)

grummet rare variant of **grommet**

Gruyère Swiss cheese (capital **G**, grave accent)

gryke variant of **grike**

gryphon variant of **griffin**

grysbok (not -**buck**)

gsm grams per square metre (specifying weight of paper)

GST goods and services tax (Australian, New Zealand, and Canadian equivalent of **VAT**)

G-string (capital **G**; hyphen)

GT gran turismo (great touring: denoting high-performance luxury sports car)

Guadalajara Mexican or Spanish city (five **a**'s)

Guadalupe Hidalgo Mexican city (-**dalu**-)

Guadeloupe French overseas region in Caribbean (**-delou-**)

Guangdong Chinese province (also **Kwangtung**)

Guangzhou Pinyin name for **Canton** (the Chinese port)

Guantánamo Cuban city and site of US naval base (acute accent)

guarantee (**-au-**, single **r**, double **e**)

guardhouse (one word)

guardrail (one word)

guard's van (**-'s** not **-s'**; two words)

Guatemala Central American country (not **-tam-**)

gudgeon (**-dge-**)

Guelderland variant of **Gelderland**

guelder-rose (hyphen; not **gel-**)

Guelders another name for **Gelderland**

Guelph member of medieval Italian faction originally supporting pope (also **Guelf**; compare **Ghibelline**), or Canadian city (not **-elf**)

Guenevere variant of **Guinevere**

guerilla variant of **guerrilla**

Guernica Spanish town

Guernica painting by Picasso depicting destruction of Guernica in Spanish Civil War

Guernesey French spelling of **Guernsey** (the island)

guernsey sleeveless woollen shirt or jumper worn by Australian footballer, or variant of **Guernsey** (the sweater)

Guernsey one of the Channel Islands, breed of dairy cattle, or sailor's knitted woollen sweater (also **guernsey** for the sweater; French spelling **Guernesey** for the island)

guerrilla member of irregular armed force (also **guerilla**; compare **gorilla**)

guesstimate (also **guestimate**)

guesswork (one word)

guesthouse (one word)

guestimate variant of **guesstimate**

Guevara, Ernesto Latin American politician and soldier (known as **Che Guevara**; no accent; not **Gua-**)

Guggenheim Museum New York City, USA (capital **G** & **M**; double **g**, **-ei-**)

Guiana region of South America including **Guyana**, **Surinam**, and **French Guiana**

Guide member of the senior branch of the Guide Association (the use of lower-case **g** in this sense is not incorrect but may cause confusion with other senses of **guide**; see also **Ranger Guide**)

Guide Association worldwide youth movement for girls

guidebook (one word)

guide dog (two words)

guideline (one word)

guild organization or fellowship, or medieval association of merchants or artisans (the spelling **gild** is less common but not incorrect in the medieval sense; however, it should not be used in the modern sense)

Guildenstern character in Shakespeare's *Hamlet* (**-en-** then **-ern**)

Guildford English city (not **-lf-**)

guildhall (one word)

guillemets another name for **duckfoot quotes** (not italic)

guillemot sea bird (**-ui-**, double **l**, **-em-**)

guillotine (**-ui-**, **-ot-**)

guilt responsibility for wrong or offence (compare **gilt**)

Guinea African country, adjacent to Guinea-Bissau

Guinea-Bissau African country, adjacent to Guinea

guinea fowl (two words)

guinea pig (two words)

Guinevere wife of King Arthur in Arthurian legend (also **Guenevere**)

Guinness brewing company (double **n**, double **s**)

guipure type of lace or trimming (not italic)

Guisborough English town (**Gui-**; not **-brough**)

Gujarat Indian state or region (also **Gujerat**)

Gujarati Indian language, Indian people, or of this language or people (also **Gujerati**)

Gujerat variant of **Gujarat**

Gujerati variant of **Gujarati**

Gulag former Soviet department responsible for prisons and labour camps (capital **G**)

gulf deep bay or chasm (lower-case **g**)

Gulf, the the Persian Gulf, (in Australia) the Gulf of Carpentaria, or (in New Zealand) the Hauraki Gulf (capital **G**)

Gulf States the oil-producing countries around the Persian Gulf, or the US states around the Gulf of Mexico

Gulf Stream warm ocean current (capital **G** & **S**)

Gulf War (capital **G** & **W**)

gullible (not **-able**)

gum arabic (two words)

gumboil (one word)

gumboots (one word)

gumption (**-mpt-**)

gumshield (one word)

gumtree (one word)

gunboat (one word)

gun dog (two words)

gunfire (one word)

gung ho (two words)

gunmetal (one word)

Gunn, Thom(son William) British-born poet (double **n**; not **Tom**)

Gunnar in Norse mythology, king of Burgundy and husband of Brynhild (compare **Gunther**)

gunnel variant of **gunwale**

gunpoint (one word)

gunpowder (one word)

Gunpowder Plot (capital **G** & **P**)

gunrunning (one word)

gunshot (one word)

Gunter's chain (capital **G**; **-ter's**)

Gunther in German legend, king of Burgundy and husband of Brunhild (**-ther**; compare **Gunnar**)

Guntur Indian city (**-tur**)

gunwale (also **gunnel**)

gurdwara Sikh place of worship (not italic)

Gurkha member of Nepalese Hindu people, especially one serving in British army (**-kh-**)

guru (not **-oo-**)

Guru Granth sacred scripture of the Sikhs (also **Guru Granth Sahib** or **Adi Granth**)

Gutenberg, Johann German printer (not **-burg**)

gutta-percha (hyphen)

gutter (*typog.*) space between text of facing pages of book or between columns of type

guttural (not **-er-**)

Guyana South American country (former name **British Guiana**)

Guy's Hospital London (apostrophe)

Gwyn, Nell English actress and mistress of Charles II (not **Gwynne**, though this was the original spelling of her surname)

Gwynedd Welsh county (single **n**, double **d**)

gybe move sail across boat (also **jibe**; compare **gibe**)

gymkhana (**-kh-**)

gymnasium (plural **gymnasiums** or **gymnasia**)

gymslip (one word)

gynaecology (**-nec-** in US English)

Gypsy (the use of lower-case **g** is less common but not incorrect; also **Gipsy**; see also **Roma** and **Romany**)

gyrate (not **gir-**)

gyratory (not **gir-**)

gyroscope (not **gir-**)

H

H hydrogen (no full stop)
Ha hahnium (no full stop)
Haag see **Den Haag**
Häagen-Dazs trademark for ice cream (capital **H** & **D**; hyphen; **-äa-**; **-zs**)
Haarlem Dutch city
Hab. Habakkuk (full stop; not italic)
Habakkuk book of the Bible (not italic; abbreviation **Hab.**)
Habana Spanish name for **Havana**
habeas corpus writ ordering person to be brought before court (not italic)
Haberdashers' Aske's School (-s' then -'s)
habitual (use *a*, not *an*, before this word)
habitué frequent visitor (not italic; acute accent)
Habsburg German name for **Hapsburg**
háček the diacritic used on č, ř, etc.
hacienda ranch in Spanish-speaking country (not italic)
Hackney borough of Greater London
hackney carriage (lower-case **h**)
hackneyed (not **-nied**)
Hades abode of the dead (capital **H**)
hadj variant of **hajj**
hadji variant of **hajji**
Hadrian's Wall (capital **H** & **W**)
Haeckel, Ernst Heinrich German biologist and philosopher

haemoglobin (not **-ma-**; **hem-** in US English)
haemophilia (**hem-** in US English)
haemorrhage (**-rrh-**; **hem-** in US English)
haemorrhoids (**-rrh-**; **hem-** in US English)
haeremai Maori expression of welcome (not italic)
hafnium (symbol **Hf**)
Hag. Haggai (full stop; not italic)
Haggai book of the Bible (not italic; abbreviation **Hag.**)
haggard (double **g**; **-ard**)
Haggard, Sir Rider British writer of adventure stories (not **Ryder**)
Hagiographa last of three parts into which Hebrew Scriptures are divided
hagiography biography of the saints, or biography that idealizes its subject
Hague, The seat of government of the Netherlands (capital **T**; Dutch names **Den Haag** and **'s Gravenhage**)
Hague, William Jefferson British politician (compare **Haig**)
ha-ha representation of laughter, or wall set in ditch (hyphen)
hahnium (symbol **Ha**)
Haig, Douglas, 1st Earl Haig British field marshal (compare **Hague**)
haiku Japanese verse form (not italic)

hail ice pellets, greet, acclaim, attract the attention of (as in *hail a taxi*), or originate (as in *he hails from New Zealand*) (compare **hale**)

Haile Selassie title of **Ras Tafari Makonnen**, emperor of Ethiopia

hail-fellow-well-met (three hyphens; not **hale-**)

Hail Mary (capital **H** & **M**; plural **Hail Marys**)

hailstone (one word)

Hainault district of London, or variant of **Hainaut**

Hainaut Belgian province (also **Hainault**)

hair threadlike outgrowth from skin (compare **hare**)

hairbrained less common variant of **harebrained**

hairbrush (one word)

haircut (one word)

hairdo (plural **hairdos**)

hairdresser (no hyphen)

hairdryer (no hyphen; also **hairdrier**)

hairlike (no hyphen)

hairpiece (one word)

hair's-breadth (-'s-; hyphen)

hair shirt (two words)

hair slide (two words)

hair space (*typog.*) very thin space used to separate characters

hairsplitting (one word)

hairspray (one word)

hairstyle (one word)

Haiti Caribbean country occupying half of the island of Hispaniola in the Greater Antilles, or a former name for **Hispaniola**

haji variant of **hajji**

hajj pilgrimage to Mecca (also **hadj**)

hajji Muslim who has made a pilgrimage to Mecca (also **hadji** or **haji**)

haka Maori war chant with gestures (not italic)

Hakluyt, Richard English geographer

halal denoting meat slaughtered according to Muslim law (not italic; the spelling **hallal** is not incorrect, but it is less common)

halcyon (not **-ion**)

hale healthy and robust, or to haul (compare **hail**)

Halesowen English town (one word)

Halévy, Jacques François Fromental French composer (acute accent; **-vy**)

Haley, Bill US rock-and-roll singer (compare **Halley**)

half (noun (plural **halves**), adjective, adverb; compare **halve**)

half a dozen (no hyphens)

half-and-half (two hyphens; not **-in-**)

half an hour (no hyphens)

halfback (one word)

half-binding bookbinding in which spine and corners are bound in different material from sides (hyphen)

half-brother son of either of one's parents by another partner (hyphen; compare **stepbrother**)

half-dozen (hyphen)

half-hearted (hyphen)

half-hitch (hyphen)

half holiday (two words)

half-hour (hyphen)

half-mast (hyphen)

halfpenny (one word; also **ha'penny**)

halfpennyworth (one word; also **ha'p'orth**)

half-price (hyphen)

half-sister daughter of either of one's parents by another partner (hyphen; compare **stepsister**)

half term (no hyphen unless used before another noun, as in *half-term holiday*)

half-timbered (hyphen)

half-time (hyphen)

half-title title of book printed on half-title page, often in smaller type and without subtitle, name of author, etc.; or another name for **half-title page** (hyphen)

half-title page page bearing half-title, usually the right-hand page preceding the **title page** (also **half-title**)

halftone illustration reproduced by breaking it up into dots (one word)

half-truth (hyphen)

halfway (one word)

halfwit (one word)

halitosis (single l)

hallal less common variant of **halal**

Halle German city (no accent)

Hallé, Sir Charles German conductor (acute accent; compare **Halley**)

hallelujah (also **halleluiah** or **alleluia**)

Hallé Orchestra Manchester (acute accent; capital H & O)

Halley, Edmund English astronomer (compare **Hallé** and **Haley**)

Halley's Comet (capital H & C; double l)

halliard rare variant of **halyard**

hallo variant of **hello** or **halloo** (compare **hallow**)

halloo shout to attract attention (also **hallo**)

hallow consecrate (compare **hallo**)

Halloween October 31 (also **Hallowe'en** or **Allhallows Eve**)

halo (plural **haloes** or **halos**)

halogen (single l)

Hals, Frans Dutch painter

halve (verb; compare **half**)

halved (not -lfed)

halyard (single l; rarely **halliard**)

hamadryad nymph in classical mythology, or another name for **king cobra**

hamadryas baboon

Hambros Bank (no apostrophe)

Hamburg German city

hamburger fried cake of minced beef (lower-case h; also **burger** or **beefburger**)

Hamelin English name for **Hameln**, as in Robert Browning's poem 'The Pied Piper of Hamelin' (compare **Hamlyn**)

Hameln German town (English name **Hamelin**)

ham-fisted (hyphen)

Hamlyn publishing company (compare **Hamelin**)

Hammarskjöld, Dag Swedish statesman (not **Hammer-**)

hammerhead (one word)

Hammerstein II, Oscar US librettist

Hammett, Dashiell US writer of detective novels (double **m**, double **t**, double **l**)

Hampden, John English statesman (not -don; compare **Hampton**)

Hampstead district of London (-mp-; -ead)

Hampton, Christopher James British playwright (compare **Hampden**)

Hampton Court Palace Richmond-upon-Thames capital H, C, & P)

hamstring (past tense and past participle **hamstrung**)

handbill (one word)

handbook (one word)

handbrake (one word)

Handel, George Frederick German composer, resident in England (German name **Georg Friedrich Händel**, with umlaut)

handful (not -full; plural **handfuls**)

hand-held (hyphen)

handicapped (replace with **disabled** (for adjective) or **disabled people** (for noun) where appropriate to avoid offence)

handiwork (not -dy-)

handkerchief (-dk-, -ie-; plural **handkerchiefs**)

handmade (one word)

hand-me-down (two hyphens)

hand-out (noun; the verb is **hand out**)

handover (noun; the verb is **hand over**)

hand-picked (hyphen)

handrail (one word)

handshake (one word)

handsome good-looking (compare **hansom**)

hand-to-hand (two hyphens)

hand-to-mouth (two hyphens)

handwriting (one word)

handyman (one word; not **-di-**)

hangar aircraft building (compare **hanger**)

hangdog (no hyphen)

hanged past tense and past participle of **hang** in the senses 'suspend by the neck until dead' and 'damn', as in *I'll be hanged!* (compare **hung**)

hanger support for hanging something, person who hangs something, or a wood on a hillside (compare **hangar**)

hanger-on (hyphen; plural **hangers-on**)

hang-glider (hyphen)

hanging denoting a style of paragraph indentation in which the first line is aligned with the margin and subsequent lines are indented

hangnail (one word; rarely **agnail**)

hangover (one word)

Hanguk Korean name for **South Korea**

hang-up (noun; the verb is **hang up**)

Hania variant of **Chania**

hanky-panky (hyphen)

Hannover German city (English spelling **Hanover**)

Hanoi capital of Vietnam

Hanover royal house of Germany and Britain, or English spelling of **Hannover**

Hanoverian of Hannover or the house of Hanover (single **n**)

Hansa variant of **Hanse**

Hansard report of parliamentary proceedings (capital **H**; not italic)

Hanse another name for **Hanseatic League**, or any medieval guild of merchants (capital **H**; also **Hansa**)

Hanseatic League medieval commercial association of German towns (capital **H** & **L**; also **Hanse** or **Hansa**)

hansom horse-drawn carriage (also **hansom cab**; the use of capital **H** is less common but not incorrect; compare **handsome**)

Hants Hampshire

Hanukkah Jewish festival of lights (also **Hanukah** or **Chanukah**)

ha'penny variant of **halfpenny** (apostrophe)

ha'p'orth variant of **halfpennyworth** (two apostrophes)

happy-go-lucky (two hyphens)

happy hunting ground (three words)

Hapsburg German royal family (German name **Habsburg**)

hara-kiri (hyphen; the variant **hari-kari** is an anglicized form that is best avoided)

harangue (**-gue**)

Harare capital of Zimbabwe (single **r** twice; former name **Salisbury**)

harass (single **r**, double **s**)

harbour (**-or** in US English)

harbour master (two words)

hardback book with stiff cover, or denoting such a book or edition (also **casebound** or **hardcover** for adjective; compare **paperback**)

hardboard (one word)

hard-boiled (hyphen)

hard copy computer output on paper

hardcore type of rock music or dance music (one word)

hard core intransigent nucleus of group, or broken stones used as foundation (two words)

hard-core denoting explicit pornography or extreme commitment (hyphen)

hardcover another word for
  hardback (adjective)
hard disk (not **disc**)
Hardecanute variant of
  Harthacanute
hard-hit (hyphen)
Hardicanute variant of **Harthacanute**
Hardie, Keir British politician
  (compare **Hardy**)
hardihood (not **-dy-**)
hard line (two words as noun, e.g.
  take a hard line, but one word when
  used before another noun, e.g. *a
  hardline policy*)
hard shoulder (two words)
hardwood (one word)
hard-working (hyphen)
Hardy, Oliver US film comedian;
  Thomas British novelist and poet;
  Sir Thomas Masterman British
  naval officer (compare **Hardie**)
hare animal resembling large rabbit
  (compare **hair**)
harebrained (the spelling
  hairbrained is not incorrect, but it is
  less common)
hareem rare variant of **harem**
Hare Krishna Hindu sect (single **r**
  and final **e** in first word)
harem (rarely **hareem**)
haricot French bean (not italic)
hari-kari see **hara-kiri**
Haringey borough of Greater
  London (see also **Harringay**)
harken variant of **hearken**, especially
  in US English
Harlech Welsh town (**-lech**)
harlequin (also **Harlequin** with
  reference to the comic character,
  but lower-case **h** in other senses
  and uses)
Harley-Davidson US motorcycle
  manufacturer, or any of their
  motorcycles (hyphen; not **Davison**)
harlot (not **-let**)
harmattan dry wind from Sahara
  (double **t**; all the vowels are **a**'s)

harmonize (also **harmonise**; see
  -ize/-ise)
HarperCollins publishing company
  (one word; capital **H & C**)
Harpers & Queen magazine (no
  apostrophe; ampersand)
Harper's Ferry US village
  (apostrophe)
harquebus variant of **arquebus**
harridan (double **r**)
Harringay place within the borough
  of **Haringey**
Harris Tweed trademark for tweed
  made in Outer Hebrides (capital **H
  & T**)
Harrods (no apostrophe)
Harrogate English town (not **-ow-**)
Harrovian of Harrow School, or a
  person educated there
hart deer (compare **heart**)
Hart, Lorenz US lyricist; **Moss** US
  dramatist (compare **Harte**)
hartbeest less common variant of
  hartebeest
Harte, (Francis) Bret US writer
  (compare **Hart**)
hartebeest (not **-beast**; the spelling
  hartbeest is not incorrect, but it is
  less common)
Hartford US port (compare
  Hertford)
Harthacanute Danish and English
  king (also **Hardecanute** or
  Hardicanute)
Hart's Rules style guide widely used
  in printing and publishing (full title
  *Hart's Rules for Compositors and
  Readers at the University Press,
  Oxford*; replaced by *Oxford Guide
  to Style*)
harum-scarum (hyphen; not **-em-**)
Harvard system another name for
  author–date system
harvestman arachnid with long thin
  legs (one word; US, Canadian, and
  Australian informal name **daddy-
  longlegs**)

Harwich English port (-rw-)

Harz Mountains Germany (not -tz)

has-been (hyphen)

hashish (the variant **hasheesh** is less common but not incorrect)

Hasidic variant of **Chassidic**

Haslemere town in Surrey (compare **Hazlemere**)

Hassidic variant of **Chassidic**

hassium (symbol **Hs**)

hatband (one word)

hatbox (one word)

hatchback (no hyphen)

hatpin (one word)

Hatshepsut Egyptian queen (also **Hatshepset**)

hat stand (two words)

Hattersley, Roy, Baron Hattersley of Sparkford British politician

hat trick (two words)

Hauptmann, Gerhart German naturalist and writer (double **n**)

Hausa W African people or their language (not **Hou-**)

hausfrau German housewife (not italic)

Haussmann, Georges-Eugène, Baron French town planner (double **s**, double **n**)

haute couture high fashion (italics)

haute cuisine high-class cookery (italics)

Hautes-Alpes French department (-tes-)

Haute-Saône French department (-te-; circumflex)

Haute-Savoie French department (-te-, -oie)

Hautes-Pyrénées French department (-tes-; two acute accents)

hauteur haughtiness (not italic)

haut monde high society (italics)

Haut-Rhin French department (not **Haute-**, not **-Rhine**)

Hauts-de-Seine French department (two hyphens; -ts-)

Havana capital of Cuba (Spanish name **Habana**)

Havel, Václav Czech dramatist and statesman

Haverfordwest Welsh town (one word)

haversack (-ver-, -ck)

Havilland see **de Havilland** and **De Havilland**

Havisham, Miss character in Dickens' *Great Expectations* (not -ver-)

havoc (not -ck)

Havre see **Le Havre**

Hawaii US state

Hawaiian (as adjective) of Hawaii; (as noun) person from Hawaii or a language of Hawaii (double **i**)

Haw-Haw, Lord British broadcaster of Nazi propaganda (hyphen; real name **William Joyce**)

hawk-eyed (hyphen)

hawksbill turtle (not **hawk's-**)

Hawthorne, Nathaniel US writer (not -thorn)

Haydn, (Franz) Joseph Austrian composer

hay fever (two words)

haymaking (one word)

hayrick (one word)

haystack (one word)

hazelnut (one word)

Hazlemere village in Buckinghamshire (not -zel-; compare **Haslemere**)

Hazlitt, William English critic and essayist (not **Has-**; double **t**)

H-beam (capital **H**; hyphen)

H-bomb (capital **H**; hyphen)

HCF highest common factor (also **hcf**)

he (when gender is unspecified, use **he or she** in formal contexts and **they** elsewhere, or rephrase to avoid the problem; for the use of capital initial with reference to God, see **capital letter**)

He helium (no full stop)

head see **running head**

headache (one word)

headachy (the spelling **headachey** is not incorrect, but it is less common)

head butt (noun)

head-butt (verb)

headdress (one word)

headed for (use **heading for** instead in intransitive contexts)

head-hunter (hyphen)

heading for (use instead of **headed for** in intransitive contexts, as in *they are heading* [not *headed*] *for disaster* or *we were heading* [not *headed*] *for the exit*)

headlamp (one word)

headlight (one word)

headline heading at top of newspaper or magazine article, printed in larger and heavier type, or line at top of page bearing title, page number, etc. (one word; see also **running head**)

headmaster (one word; use **head teacher** instead where appropriate)

headmistress (one word; use **head teacher** instead where appropriate)

head-on (hyphen)

headphones (one word)

headquarters (same form for singular and plural; use singular or plural verb in singular sense, as in *the company's headquarters is* [or *are*] *in Dover*)

headrest (one word)

headroom (one word)

headscarf (one word)

head start (two words)

headstone (one word)

head teacher (two words; use instead of gender-specific **headmaster** or **headmistress** where appropriate)

headwind (one word)

headword key word at beginning of entry in reference book, printed in larger and heavier type (one word)

heal cure (compare **heel**)

health centre (two words)

health farm (two words)

health food (no hyphen unless used before another noun, as in *health-food shop*)

hear perceive sound, receive information, or used in the phrase *hear, hear!* (compare **here**)

heard past tense and past participle of **hear** (compare **herd**)

hearken (sometimes **harken**, especially in US English)

hearsay gossip or rumour (one word; no apostrophe, unlike the short-lived pop group of this name)

Hearst, William Randolph US newspaper publisher (compare **Hirst** and **Hurst**)

heart organ of body, centre, pity, courage, etc. (compare **hart**)

heartbeat (one word)

heartbreaking (one word)

heartbroken (one word)

heartburn (one word)

hearth rug (two words)

heart-rending (hyphen)

heartsease (also **heart's-ease**)

heartstrings (one word)

heart-throb (hyphen)

heart-to-heart (two hyphens)

heart-warming (hyphen)

Heath Robinson denoting absurdly complicated mechanical device (see also **Robinson**)

heatproof (one word)

heat-resistant (hyphen)

heatstroke (one word)

heat wave (two words)

heaved past tense and past participle of **heave** in most non-nautical senses (compare **hove**)

heave-ho (hyphen)

heaven (also **Heaven** with reference to God, his abode, or the state of communion with him after death; always lower-case **h** and often **heavens** in the sense 'sky'; note the position of the apostrophe in the phrase *for heaven's sake*, which may also have capital *H*)

heaven-sent (hyphen)

Heaviside layer (capital H; not -vy-)

heavy-duty (hyphen)

heavy-handed (hyphen)

heavy metal (no hyphen unless used before another noun, as in *heavy-metal band*)

heavyweight (one word)

Heb. Hebrews (full stop; not italic)

Hebrews book of the Bible (not italic; abbreviation **Heb.**)

Hebridean of the Hebrides, or a person from the Hebrides (rarely **Hebridian**)

Hebrides, the island group off W Scotland, divided into the **Inner Hebrides** and the **Outer Hebrides** (see also **Western Isles**)

Hebridian rare variant of **Hebridean**

Hedda Gabler play by Ibsen (double *d*, single *b*)

hedgehog (one word; -dge-)

hedgerow (one word; -dge-)

heel back of foot, part of shoe, contemptible person, or lean over (compare **heal**)

Heep, Uriah character in Dickens' *David Copperfield* (not **Heap**)

Hegel, Georg Wilhelm Friedrich German philosopher (not **George**)

Hegira starting point of Muslim era, or emigration or flight (often lower-case **h** in the sense 'emigration or flight'; also **Hejira** or **Hijrah**)

Heidegger, Martin German philosopher

Heidelberg German city (-del-; not -burg)

heifer (-ei-, single **f**)

Heifetz, Jascha Russian-born US violinist

heigh-ho exclamation of weariness, disappointment, or surprise (not hey-)

height (-ei-; not -th)

Heilongjiang Chinese province (also **Heilungkiang**)

Heimlich manoeuvre (capital H; -ei-, -ich)

Heine, Heinrich German poet and essayist

Heineken brewing company (-eke-)

Heinemann publishing company (-nem-; double **n** at end)

heinous (-ei-, not -ious)

heir person who inherits or succeeds to something (compare **air**)

heir apparent (plural **heirs apparent**)

Heisenberg, Werner Karl German physicist (-eis-; not -burg)

Hejira variant of **Hegira**

Helensburgh Scottish town (not -borough)

Heliopolis ancient name for **Baalbek**

helipad (no hyphen)

heliport (no hyphen)

helium (symbol **He**)

helix (plural **helices** or **helixes**)

hell (also **Hell** with reference to the abode of the spirits of the dead or the place of punishment of the wicked after death)

Hellas Ancient Greek name for Greece

hellbent (one word)

Hellespont ancient name for **Dardanelles**

hellfire (one word)

hello (also **hallo** or **hullo**)

Hell's Angels (capital H & A; apostrophe)

helmeted (not -tt-)

Helmholtz, Baron Hermann Ludwig Ferdinand von German physiologist, physicist, and mathematician

Héloïse pupil and mistress of Peter **Abelard** (acute accent and diaeresis; see also **'Eloisa to Abelard'**)

help (when followed by infinitive, the *to* is optional, as in *she helped him (to)* *clean the flat* or *the rain will help (to) clear the air*, but the latter case – with no direct object – is more widely acceptable with *to*)

helpline (one word)

Helsingfors Swedish name for **Helsinki**

Helsingør Danish port (English name **Elsinore**)

Helsinki capital of Finland (Swedish name **Helsingfors**)

helter-skelter hyphen

Helvellyn English mountain (single **l** then double **l**; **-yn**)

Helvetia Latin name for **Switzerland**

Helvetica typeface

Hemel Hempstead English town (single **m**, single **l**, **-mp-**, **-ead**)

hemidemisemiquaver (**h** then **d** then **s**)

hemisphere (lower-case **h** in all uses, including *northern hemisphere, western hemisphere*, etc.)

hemistich half line of verse (not **-stitch**)

hemoglobin US spelling of **haemoglobin**

hemophilia US spelling of **haemophilia**

hemorrhage US spelling of **haemorrhage**

hemorrhoids US spelling of **haemorrhage**

hemstitch (one word)

hence for this reason, following from this, or from this time or place (thus *from* in the phrase *from hence* is redundant and should be avoided)

henhouse (one word)

Henley-on-Thames (two hyphens; not **-upon-**; also **Henley**)

hennaed (not **-a'd**)

henpecked (one word)

Henri, Adrian English poet

Henry[1]**, Joseph** US physicist; **O.** US writer (real name **William Sydney Porter**)

Henry[2]**, Thierry** French footballer

Hepburn, Audrey and **Katharine** US actresses (not **Katherine**)

Hephaestus god of fire and metal-working in Greek mythology (also **Hephaistos**)

Heptateuch first seven books of Old Testament (capital **H**; **-euch**)

Heracles Greek name for **Hercules** (also **Herakles**)

Heraklion variant of **Iráklion** (also **Herakleion**)

herbaceous (not **-cious**)

herbarium (plural **herbariums** or **herbaria**)

Hercegovina variant of **Herzegovina**

Herculaneum ancient city in Italy (not **-ium**)

herculean requiring great strength or effort, or resembling Hercules (also **Herculean** in the sense 'resembling Hercules')

Hercules hero of classical mythology who performed twelve labours, hence any man of great strength or size (capital **H**; Greek name **Heracles** or **Herakles**)

hercules beetle (lower-case **h**)

herd large group, or move in large group (compare **heard**)

here in this place (compare **hear**)

hereafter (one word)

hereditary (adjective; use *a*, not *an*, before this word)

heredity (noun)

Hereford English city or breed of cattle (capital **H**)

Hereford and Worcester former English county

Herefordshire English county

herein (one word)

hereinafter (one word)

hereinbefore (one word)

heresy unorthodox opinion or doctrine (**-sy**)

heretofore (one word)

herewith (one word)

Heriot-Watt University Edinburgh (hyphen; single **r** and single **t** in first word)

hero (plural **heroes**; may be used for males or females)

Herodotus ancient Greek historian

heroic (use *a*, not *an*, before this word)

heroin drug (compare **heroine**)

heroine principal female character, or girl or woman with heroic qualities (compare **heroin**; use **hero** instead where appropriate to avoid offence, especially with reference to real people in the modern world)

hero worship (noun)

hero-worship (verb)

herpesvirus (one word)

Herr German equivalent of **Mr**

Herrenvolk master race (italics; capital *H*; not *-folk*)

herringbone (one word)

herring gull (two words)

Herriot, James British vet and writer (double **r**, single **t**; real name **James Alfred Wight**)

hers (no apostrophe)

Herschel, Caroline Lucretia, Sir John Frederick William, and **Sir (Frederick) William** British astronomers (William, born **Friedrich Wilhelm Herschel** in Germany, was the father of Caroline and John)

Herstmonceux English village, former site of the Royal Observatory (the spelling **Hurstmonceux** is less common in modern usage but not incorrect; not **Hearst-**, not **-ceaux**)

Hertford English town (compare **Hartford**)

Hertfordshire English county

Herts Hertfordshire

hertz unit of frequency (lower-case **h**; **-tz**; abbreviation **Hz**, with capital **H** and no full stop)

Hertz, Gustav and **Heinrich Rudolph** German physicists (the unit of frequency is named after Heinrich, who was Gustav's uncle)

Hertzog , James Barry Munnik South African statesman (compare **Herzog**)

Herzegovina region of Bosnia-Herzegovina (also **Hercegovina**)

Herzog, Roman German politician; **Werner** German film director (compare **Hertzog**)

hesitance state of being hesitant (also **hesitancy**)

hesitation act of hesitating

Hess, Dame Myra English pianist; **Rudolf** German Nazi leader; **Victor Francis** Austrian-born US physicist

Hesse German state

Hesse, Hermann German writer

hessian fabric (lower-case **h**)

Hessian of Hesse, person from Hesse, or German mercenary in British army in War of American Independence or Napoleonic Wars (capital **H**)

hetaera ancient Greek courtesan (not italic; plural **hetaerae**; also **hetaira**, plural **hetairai**)

heterogeneous (not **-nous**)

Hever Castle England

hew cut (compare **hue**)

hewed past tense and past participle of **hew** (also **hewn** for the past participle)

hexameter line of verse (not **-tre**)

Hexateuch first six books of Old Testament (capital **H**; **-euch**)

heyday (**hey-**)

Heyerdahl, Thor Norwegian anthropologist

Heyhoe Flint, Rachael English cricketer (not **Rachel**)

Heysham English port (**Hey-**)

Hezbollah militant Shiite Muslim organization (also **Hizbollah**)

Hf hafnium (no full stop)

Hg mercury (no full stop; from Latin *hydrargyrum*)

HGV heavy goods vehicle (former name, still widely used, for **LGV**)

HH Her Highness; His Highness; His Holiness

HI Hawaii (US postal code)

hiatus (plural **hiatuses**)

hibernate (not **hy-**)

Hibernian of Ireland, person from Ireland, or name of Scottish football team

hiccup (the spelling **hiccough** is not incorrect, but it is less common)

hiccuped, hiccuping (also **hiccupped, hiccupping**)

hic jacet here lies (italics)

hid past tense of **hide** or variant of **hidden**

hidalgo member of lower nobility in Spain (lower-case **h**)

Hidalgo Mexican state

hidden past participle of **hide** (also **hid**)

hide-and-seek (two hyphens)

hideaway (one word)

hidebound (one word)

hierarchy (-ier-, -chy)

hieroglyphic (-ier-, -yph-)

hifalutin variant of **highfalutin**

hi-fi high fidelity, or a set of high-fidelity equipment (hyphen; not **high-**)

higgledy-piggledy (hyphen)

highbrow (one word)

highchair (one word)

High Church (capital **H** & **C**)

High Court (capital **H** & **C**)

higher more high (compare **hire**)

Higher Scottish equivalent of **A level** (the use of lower-case **h** in this sense is not incorrect but may cause confusion)

highfalutin (also **hifalutin** or **highfaluting**)

high fidelity (no hyphen unless used before another noun, as in *high-fidelity equipment*)

high-flier variant of **high-flyer**

high-flown (hyphen)

high-flyer (hyphen; also **high-flier**)

highjack less common variant of **hijack**

high jinks (not **jinx**)

high jump (two words)

highland relatively high ground (lower-case **h**)

Highland Scottish council area, or of the Highlands (capital **H**)

Highlands, the northern part of Scotland (capital **H**)

high-minded (hyphen)

high pressure (noun)

high-pressure (adjective)

high-rise (hyphen)

high street (capital **H** & **S** as street name, and also sometimes in other uses; no hyphen unless used before another noun, as in *high-street prices*)

high tech variant of **hi tech**

high-tech variant of **hi-tech**

high-water mark (one hyphen)

High Wycombe English town (not **Wickham** or **Wykeham**)

hijack (the spelling **highjack** is not incorrect, but it is less common)

Hijrah variant of **Hegira**

Hilary term (capital **H**; not **Hillary**)

Hillary, Sir Edmund New Zealand mountaineer (not **Hilary**)

hillbilly (one word)

hillfort (one word)

hillside (one word)

hilltop (one word)

him masculine singular objective pronoun (compare **hymn**). When gender is unspecified, use **him or her** in formal contexts and **them** elsewhere, or rephrase to avoid the problem. For the use of capital initial with reference to God, see **capital letter**.

Himachal Pradesh Indian state

Himalayas, the Asian mountain range (also **Himalaya**)

himself (when gender is unspecified, use **himself or herself** in formal contexts and **themselves** elsewhere, or rephrase to avoid the problem)

Hinckley English town (not **-nk-**, not **-ly**)

Hindenburg German name for **Zabrze** (not **-berg**)

Hindenburg, Paul von Beneckendorff und von German field marshal and statesman (not **-berg**)

Hindi Indian language, or native speaker of this language (compare **Hindu**)

hind leg (two words)

Hindoo old or rare variant of **Hindu**

hindquarters (one word)

hindrance (not **-der-**; not **-ence**)

hindsight (one word)

Hindu adherent of Hinduism or person from Hindustan (rarely **Hindoo**; compare **Hindi**)

Hinduism dominant religion of India

Hindustan area of India where Hinduism predominates or where Hindi is the predominant language

Hindustani (as noun) dialect of Hindi used in Delhi and spoken throughout India, or language group comprising all forms of Hindi and Urdu; (as adjective) of Hindustan or Hindustani

hinging (the spelling **hingeing** is not incorrect, but it is less common)

hinterland (one word)

hipbone (one word)

hip flask (two words)

hippie variant of **hippy** (noun)

Hippocratic oath (capital H; double **p**)

hippogriff monster in Greek mythology (lower-case **h**; also **hippogryph**)

hippopotamus (double **p** then single **p**; plural **hippopotamuses** or **hippopotami**)

hippy (as noun) member of 1960s culture rejecting conventional values; (as adjective) having large hips (also **hippie** for the noun)

hire rent or employ (compare **higher**)

hirable (also **hireable**)

hire-purchase (hyphen)

hirsute (**hir-**, **-ute**)

Hirst, Damien British artist (not **Damian**; compare **Hurst** and **Hearst**)

his (when gender is unspecified, use **his or her** or **his or hers** in formal contexts and **their** or **theirs** elsewhere, or rephrase to avoid the problem; for the use of capital initial with reference to God, see **capital letter**)

Hispaniola Caribbean island in Greater Antilles divided between Haiti and the Dominican Republic (former names **Santo Domingo** and **Haiti**)

historic significant, or likely to become famous in history (use *a*, not *an*, before this word)

historical of or concerned with history, or based on history or fact (use *a*, not *an*, before this word)

Historical Manuscripts Commission (not **Historic**; part of The **National Archives** since 2003)

histrionic (not **hyst-**)

hitchhike (one word)

Hitchin English town (not **-en**)

hi tech (noun; also **high tech**)

hi-tech (adjective; also **high-tech**)

Hitler, Adolf German dictator (not **Adolph**)

hit list (two words)

hit man (two words)

HIV human immunodeficiency virus (thus *virus* in the phrase *HIV virus* is redundant)

Hizbollah variant of **Hezbollah**

HM Her (or His) Majesty ; Her (or His) Majesty's

h'm used to indicate hesitation, doubt, etc. (apostrophe)

HMI Her (or His) Majesty's Inspector (of schools)

H.M.S. Her (or His) Majesty's Ship (also **HMS**; note that in ship names, the abbreviation is not italic: H.M.S. *Sheffield*)

HMSO Her (or His) Majesty's Stationery Office (former name for **TSO**)

HNC Higher National Certificate

HND Higher National Diploma (equivalent to ordinary degree)

Ho holmium (no full stop)

hoard store or cache, or gather or accumulate (compare **horde**)

hoarfrost (one word; not **hore-**)

hoarse harsh or husky (compare **horse**)

Hobbes, Thomas English political philosopher (compare **Hobbs**)

hobbledehoy (one word)

Hobbs, Sir John Berry English cricketer (known as **Jack Hobbs**; compare **Hobbes**)

hobbyhorse (one word)

hobnailed (no hyphen)

hobnob (no hyphen)

hobnobbed, hobnobbing (double **b**)

hobo (plural **hobos** or **hoboes**)

Hobson's choice (capital **H**; apostrophe)

Hochheimer German wine (capital **H**; **-chh-**)

Ho Chi Minh Vietnamese statesman (original name **Nguyen That Tan**)

Ho Chi Minh City Vietnamese port (former name **Saigon**)

Hockney, David English painter (**-ney**)

hocus-pocus (hyphen)

hodgepodge variant of **hotchpotch**, especially in US and Canadian English

Hodgkin's disease (capital **H**; not **-dge-**; apostrophe)

hoeing (**-oei-**)

Hoek van Holland Dutch name for **Hook of Holland**

Hoff see **van't Hoff**

Hoffman, Dustin US actor (double **f**, single **n**; compare **Hoffmann** and **Hofmann**)

Hoffmann, Ernst Theodor Amadeus (originally **Wilhelm**) German writer and composer, on whose stories Offenbach's opera *Tales of Hoffmann* is based (double **f**, double **n**; compare **Hoffman** and **Hofmann**)

Hoffnung, Gerard German-born British cartoonist and musician (double **f**; not **Gerald**)

Hofmann, Hans German-born US painter (single **f**, double **n**; compare **Hoffmann** and **Hoffman**)

Hofmannsthal, Hugo von Austrian poet and dramatist (single **f**, double **n**)

Hogmanay (capital **H**; **-nay**)

hogshead cask or unit of capacity for alcoholic drinks (no apostrophe; no hyphen)

Hohenstaufen German royal family (single **f**; **-en**)

Hohenzollern German noble family (double **l**; **-ern**)

hoiden variant of **hoyden**

hoi polloi the masses (not italic; as *hoi* is Greek for *the*, the latter word is technically redundant in the phrase *the hoi polloi*, but its omission would be unidiomatic in many contexts)

hokey cokey (two words)

Hokkaido one of four main islands of Japan (double **k**)

hokum (not **-cum**)

Holbein, Hans (known as **Holbein the Elder**) German painter; **Hans** (known as **Holbein the Younger**) German painter, court painter to Henry VIII

hold-up noun; the verb is **hold up**)
hole opening (compare **whole**)
hole-and-corner (two hyphens)
holey full of holes (compare **holy** and **wholly**)
Holi Hindu festival (capital **H**)
Holiday, Billie US jazz singer (compare **Holliday**)
holiday-maker (hyphen)
holier-than-thou (two hyphens)
Holinshed, Raphael English chronicler (the spelling **Holingshed** is less common but not incorrect; not **-head**)
holism (not **wh-**)
holistic (not **wh-**)
Holland another name for the **Netherlands**
hollandaise sauce (not italic; lower-case **h**; **-aise**)
Hollands Dutch gin (capital **H**)
Holliday, Judy US actress (compare **Holiday**)
hollowware (no hyphen)
hollyhock (no hyphen)
Hollywood suburb of Los Angeles, or the US film industry (capital **H** in all uses)
Holmes, Oliver Wendell US writer; **Oliver Wendell** US jurist (son of the writer of the same name); **Sherlock** fictional detective created by Sir Arthur Conan Doyle (**-lm-**)
holmium (symbol **Ho**)
holocaust great destruction or loss of life (lower-case **h**)
Holocaust, the mass murder of Jews by Nazis during World War II (the use of lower-case **h** is less common but not incorrect in this sense)
Holocene most recent geological epoch, or of this epoch (capital **H**; single **l**)
Holofernes Assyrian general killed by biblical heroine Judith (single **l**)
hologram photographic image with three-dimensional effect (single **l**)

holograph original manuscript (single **l**)
holy sacred (compare **holey** and **wholly**)
Holy Communion (capital **H** & **C**)
Holy Ghost (capital **H** & **G**)
Holy Grail according to legend, the drinking vessel used by Christ at the Last Supper, which became the quest of medieval knights; hence any desired ambition or goal (capital **H** & **G**)
Holyhead Welsh town (single **l**)
Holyoake, Sir Keith Jacka New Zealand politician (**-oake**)
holy of holies any place of special sanctity (lower-case **h** twice)
Holy of Holies innermost compartment of Jewish tabernacle (capital **H** twice)
Holy Roman Empire (capital **H**, **R**, & **E**)
Holyroodhouse royal palace in Scotland (one word)
Holy Spirit (capital **H** & **S**)
holystone (one word)
Holy Week (capital **H** & **W**)
homage (single **m**)
homburg hat (lower-case **h**)
Homburg German town
home (as noun) residence, place of origin, etc.; (as verb) return home, provide with a home, or be directed, as in *home in on a target* (compare **hone**)
Home see **Douglas-Home** (compare **Hume** and **Hulme**)
home-brew (hyphen)
Home Counties English counties surrounding London (capital **H** & **C**)
home-grown (hyphen)
Home Guard (capital **H** & **G**)
homeland (one word)
homely (in UK English) pleasantly characteristic of the ordinary home, or denoting a person who is warm

and domesticated; (in US and Canadian English) unattractive (beware of possible ambiguity when used with reference to people; compare **homy**)

home-made (hyphen)

Home Office (capital **H** & **O**)

homeopathy (also **homoeopathy**)

homeowner (one word)

home page (two words)

home rule self-government or partial autonomy (lower-case **h** & **r**)

Home Rule self-government for Ireland, sought by Irish nationalists in the late 19th and early 20th centuries

homesick (no hyphen)

homespun (no hyphen)

homeward (adjective; sometimes adverb (see **-ward** and **-wards**))

homewards (adverb only)

homework (one word)

homeworker (one word)

homey variant of **homy**

homoeopathy variant of **homeopathy**

homogeneity state of being homogeneous (compare **homogeny**)

homogeneous uniform, composed of similar elements, or having a constant property throughout (also **homogenous**)

homogenize (also **homogenise**; see **-ize/-ise**)

homogenous of or exhibiting homogeny, or variant of **homogeneous**

homogeny similarity in biological structure due to common ancestry (compare **homogeneity**)

homograph word with the same spelling as another or others of different meaning or origin, e.g. *bow* in the senses 'bend', 'weapon for shooting arrows', or 'front of boat or ship'. Homographs may have the same or different pronunciations;

in dictionaries and reference books (such as this one) they may be separately listed with a superscript number after the headword. Compare **homophone**; see also **homonym**.

homologue (-gue)

homonym a **homograph** or **homophone** (-nym)

homophone word with the same pronunciation as another or others of different spelling, meaning, or origin, e.g. *cite*, *sight*, and *site*, or *bow* in the senses 'bend', and 'front of boat or ship'. Homophones are a common source of spelling errors, as they are not picked up by computer spellcheckers. Compare **homograph**; see also **homonym**.

Homo sapiens (italics; capital **H**, lower-case **s**)

homy like a home in being comfortable, cosy, informal, unpretentious, etc. (also **homey**; compare **homely**)

Hon. Honorary; Honourable (as title)

honcho (plural **honchos**)

Honduran of Honduras, or a person from Honduras

Honduras Central American country (-as)

hone (as noun) stone or tool for sharpening or smoothing; (as verb) sharpen or polish (compare **home**)

Honecker, Erich German statesman

Honegger, Arthur French composer

honeybee (one word)

honeycomb (one word)

honey-eater (hyphen)

honeyed (the spelling **honied** is not incorrect, but it is less common)

honeymoon (one word)

Hong Kong partly autonomous region of China and former British colony, or main island of this region (two words; Pinyin **Xianggang**)

Hongkong and Shanghai Banking Corporation (not **Hong Kong...**; abbreviation **HSBC**)

honied less common variant of **honeyed**

honi soit qui mal y pense shamed be he who thinks evil of it (motto of the Order of the Garter; italics)

Honolulu Hawaiian port (two **o**'s then two **u**'s)

honorarium (not **-our-**; plural **honorariums** or **honoraria**)

honorary given as an honour (as in *honorary degree*) or unpaid (as in *honorary secretary*) (not **-our-**; compare **honorific** and **honourable**)

honorific denoting a term that shows honour or respect (not **-our-**; compare **honorary** and **honourable**)

honoris causa for the sake of honour (italics)

honour (**-or** in US English)

honourable having or showing high principles, or worthy of honour or respect (**-our-**; compare **honorary** and **honorific**)

Hons honours (with reference to university degree, as in *BA Hons*)

hoof (plural **hooves** or **hoofs**)

Hooghly Indian river (**-oo-**, **-gh-**)

hoo-ha (hyphen)

Hook, Theodore Edward English writer (compare **Hooke**)

hookah pipe for smoking marijuana, tobacco, etc. (also **hooka**; compare **hooker**)

Hooke, Robert English scientist and inventor (compare **Hook**)

hooker rugby player, or slang word for prostitute (compare **hookah**)

Hook of Holland cape or port in the Netherlands (capital **H** twice; Dutch name **Hoek van Holland**)

hook-up (noun; the verb is **hook up**)

hoop ring (compare **whoop**)

hoopoe (**-oo-** then **-oe**)

hooray variant of **hurrah**, or term of farewell in Australia and New Zealand

Hooray Henry (capital **H** twice; not **Hurrah**; plural **Hooray Henries** or **Hooray Henrys**)

Hoover trademark for a vacuum cleaner (capital **H**, sometimes lowercase when used as a verb; in generic use better replaced by a synonym)

hopefully (the controversial use of this adverb in the sense 'it is hoped that', as in *hopefully it won't rain*, is now acceptable in informal contexts)

Hopkins, Sir Anthony British actor (not **Antony**); **Gerard Manley** British poet (not **Gerald**); **Johns** US businessman and philanthropist (not **John**)

hopscotch (one word)

horde large crowd or nomadic group (compare **hoard**)

Hormuz island off Iran (also **Ormuz**)

Horn, the another name for **Cape Horn**

hornblende (**-de**)

hornpipe (no hyphen)

hors concours unrivalled, or excluded from competing (italics)

hors de combat disabled or injured (italics)

hors d'oeuvre appetizer (not italic; plural **hors d'oeuvre** or **hors d'oeuvres**)

horse animal (compare **hoarse**)

horsebox (one word)

horse chestnut (two words)

Horse Guards (capital **H** & **G**)

Horse Guards Parade London (no apostrophe)

horsehair (one word)

horseplay (one word)

horsepower (one word)

horse race (two words)

horseradish (one word)

horseshoe (one word)

horsewhip (one word)

horsey (also **horsy**)

horticulturist (the variant **horticulturalist** is less common but not incorrect)

Hos. Hosea (full stop; not italic)

hosanna (single **s**, double **n**, not **-ah**)

Hosea book of the Bible (not italic; abbreviation **Hos.**)

hospitalize (also **hospitalise**; see **-ize/-ise**; paraphrase to avoid controversy)

Hospitaller member of Knights Hospitallers, a military religious order (capital **H**; **-aler** in US English; never **-alier**)

host (may be used for males and females)

hosteller person who stays at youth hostels, or archaic word for innkeeper (single **l** in US English; compare **hostler**)

hostelling (single **l** in US English)

hostess (use **host** instead where appropriate, e.g. with reference to person introducing TV show; see also **air hostess**)

hostler variant of **ostler** (archaic word for stableman; compare **hosteller**)

hot-air balloon (one hyphen)

hotbed (one word)

hotchpotch (no hyphen; sometimes **hodgepodge**, especially in US and Canadian English)

hot cross bun (three words)

hot-desking (hyphen)

hot dog (noun)

hot-dog (verb)

hotel (use *a*, not *an*, before this word)

hotelier (single **l**; **-ier**)

hotfoot (one word)

hothead (one word)

hot-headed (hyphen)

hothouse (one word)

hot metal (*typog.*) cast metallic type (no hyphen unless used before another noun, as in *hot-metal printing*)

hotplate (one word)

hotpot (one word)

hot seat (two words)

hotshot (one word)

hot spot (two words)

Hottentot offensive former name for **Khoikhoi**

hot-water bottle (one hyphen)

hot-wire (hyphen)

houdah variant of **howdah**

Houdini, Harry US escapologist (real name **Ehrich Weiss**)

Houghton-le-Spring English town (two hyphens; lower-case **l**)

hoummos variant of **hummus** (also **houmous**)

Hounslow borough of Greater London (not **Hounds-**)

hour period of time (compare **our**)

hourglass (one word)

houseboat (one word)

housebreaking (one word)

housecoat (one word)

housemaid's knee (**-'s** not **-s'**)

House of Commons (capital **H** & **C**)

House of Lords (capital **H** & **L**)

House of Representatives (capital **H** & **R**)

house party (two words)

house-proud (hyphen)

Houses of Parliament (capital **H** & **P**)

house style the preferred spellings, capitalization, punctuation, and typographical conventions of a particular publishing or printing company

house-to-house (two hyphens)

house-trained (hyphen)

house-warming (hyphen)

Housman, A(lfred) E(dward) English poet (not **House-**)

Houston US city (compare **Huston**)

Houyhnhnms talking horses in *Gulliver's Travels* by Jonathan Swift

hove past tense and past participle of **heave** in chiefly nautical phrases meaning 'appear' or 'stop', as in *they hove in sight* and *the yacht was hove to* (compare **heaved**)

Howards End novel by E. M. Forster (no apostrophe)

howdah (also **houdah**)

however (also two words as emphatic form of **how**, as in *how ever did they find out?*; always one word in the senses 'no matter how', 'nevertheless', 'by whatever means', etc.)

howitzer (not -ts-)

howsoever (one word)

hoyden (also **hoiden**)

HP hire purchase; horsepower

HQ headquarters

HR human resources

HRH Her Royal Highness; His Royal Highness

HRT hormone replacement therapy

Hrvatska Croatian name for **Croatia**

Hs hassium (no full stop)

Hsi variant of Xi

Hsian variant of **Xi An**

Hsiang variant of **Xiang**

Hsining variant of **Xining**

HTML hypertext mark-up language

HTTP hypertext transfer protocol

Huang Hai Pinyin name for **Yellow Sea**

Huang Ho Pinyin name for **Yellow River**

Hubble telescope (capital **H**; also **Hubble space telescope**)

hubcap (one word)

hubris pride, or (in Greek tragedy) excessive pride causing downfall (not italic; rarely **hybris**)

Hudibras poem by Samuel Butler (single **s**)

hudibrastic mock-heroic (lower-case **h**)

Hudson Bay Canada (not **Hudson's**)

Hudson's Bay Company (-'s; capital **C**)

hue shade of colour (compare **hew**)

hue and cry (three words; not **hew**)

Hughenden Manor England (not -don)

Huguenot French protestant (-**gue**-)

Hull English city and port (official name **Kingston upon Hull**), or Canadian city

hullabaloo (also **hullaballoo**)

hullo variant of **hello**

Hulme, Keri New Zealand writer (compare **Hume** and **Home**)

humanize (also **humanise**; see -**ize**/ -**ise**)

humankind (to avoid controversy or offence, use instead of **mankind** with reference to the human race)

humblebee less common name for **bumblebee** (one word)

humble pie (two words)

Humboldt, Baron Alexander von German scientist (-**ldt**)

Hume, Basil English prelate of the Roman Catholic Church; **David** Scottish philosopher; **John** Northern Ireland politician (compare **Hulme** and **Home**)

humerus bone of arm (compare **humorous**)

humiliation loss of dignity or pride

humility humbleness

hummingbird (one word)

hummus chickpea purée used as dip (also **hoummos** or **houmous**; compare **humus**)

humorist (not -**our**-)

humorous (not -**our**-; compare **humerus**)

humour (-**or** in US English)

humus organic matter in soil (compare **hummus**)

humpback (no hyphen)

Humperdinck, Engelbert German composer, or stage name of British popular singer (real name **Arnold Dorsey**, original stage name **Gerry Dorsey**) (not -**dink**, not **Engle**-)

Humphries, Barry Australian comedian and writer (not **-phreys**; compare **Humphrys**)

Humphry Clinker novel by Smollett (not *-phrey*)

Humphrys, John Welsh journalist and broadcaster (not **-phreys**; compare **Humphries**)

hunchback (no hyphen)

hundredweight (one word)

Hundred Years' War series of wars between England and France, 1337–1453 (capital **H**, **Y**, and **W**; apostrophe)

hung past tense and past participle of **hang** in all senses except 'suspend by the neck until dead' and 'damn' (compare **hanged**)

Hungary European country (**-gary**; Hungarian name **Magyarország**)

hunky-dory (hyphen)

Huntingdon town in Cambridgeshire (not **-ton**)

Huntington's disease (former name **Huntington's chorea**; capital **H**; apostrophe; not **-don's**)

Hurd, Douglas, Baron Hurd of Westwell British politician (not **Herd**)

hurdy-gurdy (hyphen)

hurly-burly (hyphen)

hurrah (also **hooray** or **hurray**)

Hurst, Geoff(rey) English footballer (compare **Hirst** and **Hearst**)

Hurstmonceux less common variant of **Herstmonceux**

Hurstpierpoint English town (not **Herst-**)

Hus, Jan Czech name of John **Huss**

Husain Islamic caliph, or variant of **Hussein** (king of Jordan)

hush-hush (hyphen)

Huss, John Bohemian religious reformer (Czech name **Jan Hus**)

Hussein, King Jordanian monarch (also **Husain**); **Saddam** Iraqi statesman

Huston, Anjelica US actress (not **Angelica**); **John** US film director (compare **Houston**)

hutzpah less common variant of **chutzpah**

Huxley, Aldous British writer (**-ous**); **Sir Andrew Fielding**, **Sir Julian**, and **Thomas Henry** English biologists

Huygens, Christiaan Dutch physicist (**Huy-**, **-ens**; double **a** in first name)

Huysmans, Joris Karl French novelist (**Huy-**, **-ans**)

HW high water

Hwang Hai Chinese name for **Yellow Sea** (Pinyin **Huang Hai**)

Hwang Ho Chinese name for **Yellow River** (Pinyin **Huang Ho**)

hyacinth (**hy-**)

hyaena rare variant of **hyena**

hybrid (**hy-**)

hybris rare variant of **hubris**

Hyde Park London (not **Hide**)

Hyderabad Indian city, former Indian state, or Pakistani city

hydrangea (not **-gia**; lower-case **h** in general use: *Hydrangea* is the genus name)

hydroelectric (no hyphen)

hydrogen (symbol **H**)

hydrolyse (**-yze** in US English)

hydrometer instrument for measuring relative density of liquid (compare **hygrometer**)

hyena (rarely **hyaena**)

hygiene (**hy-**, **-gie-**)

hygrometer instrument for measuring humidity (compare **hydrometer**)

hymn song of praise (compare **him**)

hyper- high, above, or denoting excess (compare **hypo-**)

hyperactive (no hyphen)

hyperbola curve

hyperbole exaggeration

hypercritical excessively critical (compare **hypocritical**)

hyperglycaemia abnormally high level of blood sugar (**-cem-** in US English; compare **hypoglycaemia**)

hyperlink (not **hypo-**)

hypermarket (not **hypo-**)

hypertension abnormally high blood pressure (compare **hypotension**)

hyperthermia abnormally high fever (compare **hypothermia**)

hyphen punctuation mark used in some compound words (e.g. *brother-in-law*, *double-dealing*); see individual entries. A hyphen is used to attach a prefix to a word beginning with a capital letter (e.g. *anti-Semitism*) and sometimes to a word beginning with the last letter of the prefix (e.g. *re-enter*, *step-parent*). As a general rule, use hyphens sparingly, but note that many nouns formed from phrasal verbs are hyphenated (e.g. *a break-in*, *a hold-up*), as are most compounds used adjectivally before a noun (e.g. *a well-known remedy*, *a coffee-table book*). Hyphens are also used to avoid ambiguity (e.g. to distinguish between *40-odd people* and *40 odd people*, or between *a black-cab driver* and *a black cab-driver*). Compound adjectives in which the second element is a participle or other word ending in **-ed** (e.g. *labour-saving*, *time-honoured*, *absent-minded*) are usually hyphenated; however, there is no hyphen when the first element is an adverb ending in **-ly**, as in *a neatly written letter*. For the use of hyphens in end-of-line word division, see **soft hyphen**. See also **en dash**.

hypnotize (also **hypnotise**; see **-ize/-ise**)

hypo- low, below, or denoting deficiency (compare **hyper-**)

hypochondria (not **hyper-**; **-ch-**)

hypocrisy (not **-acy**)

hypocritical insincere (compare **hypercritical**)

hypodermic (not **hyper-**)

hypoglycaemia abnormally low level of blood sugar (**-cem-** in US English; compare **hyperglycaemia**)

hypotension abnormally low blood pressure (compare **hypertension**)

hypotenuse (not **-tin-**)

hypothermia abnormally low body temperature (compare **hyperthermia**)

hypothesis (plural **hypotheses**)

hypothesize (also **hypothesise**; see **-ize/-ise**)

hysterectomy (not **hist-**)

hysterical (not **hist-**)

Hz hertz (capital **H**; no full stop)

I

I iodine; Roman numeral for 1 (no full stop); first person singular pronoun used as subject of verb, as in *I need a drink* or *Peter and I left earlier* (compare **me**)

IA Iowa (US postal code)

IAEA International Atomic Energy Agency (not Authority)

iamb metrical foot comprising short syllable followed by long syllable (also **iambus**)

Iaşi Romanian city (cedilla; German name **Jassy**)

IATA International Air Transport Association

ib. variant of **ibid.**

IBA Independent Broadcasting Authority

Ibáñez see **Blasco Ibáñez**

Ibarruri, Dolores real name of La Pasionara (double **r** then single **r**)

I-beam (capital **I**; hyphen)

Iberian Peninsula European peninsula comprising Spain and Portugal (also **Iberia**)

ibex wild goat (plural **ibexes**, **ibices**, or **ibex**; compare **ibis**)

ibid. in the same place: used in footnotes, bibliographies, etc. with reference to a source cited in the preceding entry, to avoid repeating the author's name, the title of the work, etc. (not italic; also **ib.**; from Latin *ibidem*)

ibis wading bird (plural **ibises** or **ibis**; compare **ibex**)

Ibiza Mediterranean island, or its capital (not **-tha**; rarely **Iviza**)

-ible see **-able/-ible** and **-eable**

ibn (in Arabic names, usually lower-case **i** and attached with hyphen)

ibn-Rushd Arabic name for **Averroës**

ibn-Saud, Abdul-Aziz first king of Saudi Arabia

Ibo W African people or their language (also **Igbo**)

iBook trademark for portable computer (one word; lower-case **i**, capital **B**)

IBRD International Bank for Reconstruction and Development (official name for World Bank)

Ibsen, Henrik Norwegian dramatist (not **-son**)

ibuprofen (lower-case **i**)

ICBM intercontinental ballistic missile

iceberg (one word)

icebox (one word)

icecap (one word)

ice cream (no hyphen unless used before another noun, as in *ice-cream cone*)

ice cube (two words)

ice hockey (two words)

Iceni ancient British tribe

ice pack (two words)

ice pick (two words)

ice rink (two words)
ice skate (noun)
ice-skate (verb)
ice-skater (hyphen)
I Ching ancient Chinese book of divination (not italic; two words; capital **I** & **C**)
ichthyology study of fishes (**-chth-**; not **-iol-**)
Icknield Way ancient English road
icon (sometimes **ikon**, especially in the sense 'religious image')
ICU intensive care unit; I see you (used in text messaging)
ID Idaho (US postal code); identification (document)
IDB illicit diamond buying
idealize (also **idealise**; see **-ize/-ise**)
idée fixe obsession (italics; acute accent; plural *idées fixes*)
idée reçue generally held opinion or concept (italics; acute accent, cedilla; plural *idées reçues*)
Identikit trademark denoting picture of police suspect built up from transparencies of facial characteristics, or the set of transparencies used for this (capital **I**; one word)
ideogram symbol representing concept or thing, e.g. in Chinese or Japanese writing system (not **idio-**; also **ideograph**)
ideologist (also **ideologue**)
ideology (not **ideal-** or **idiol-**)
ides 15th day of March, May, July, and October, or 13th day of other months, in Roman calendar (lower-case **i**)
idiolect linguistic usage of an individual (not **ideo-**)
idiom phrase with meaning other than that of constituent words (e.g. *dog in the manger*), linguistic usage of native speakers or of a particular group, or characteristic artistic style
idiomatic (not **ideo-**)

idiosyncrasy (not **ideo-**, not **-acy**)
idle inactive, lazy, do nothing, or tick over (compare **idol** and **idyll**)
Ido artificial language
idol worshipped object or revered person (compare **idle** and **idyll**)
idolater (not **-or**)
idolatrous (not **-ter-**)
idolize (also **idolise**; see **-ize/-ise**)
idyll pastoral poem or prose work, or charming scene or event (compare **idle** and **idol**)
idyllic (**-dy-**, double **l**)
i.e. that is (from Latin *id est*; compare **e.g.**)
IEA International Energy Agency
Ieper Flemish name for **Ypres**
if (beware of ambiguity when used to mean 'though', as in *it is difficult, if not impossible*)
IFC International Finance Corporation
Igbo variant of **Ibo**
igneous (not **-ious**)
ignis fatuus phosphorescence seen over marshy ground (not italic)
ignitable (rarely **ignitible**)
ignominy (not **-mony**)
ignoramus (plural **ignoramuses**)
Igraine mother of King Arthur (the spelling **Ygerne** is not incorrect, but it is less common)
iguana tropical lizard
iguanodon dinosaur (not **-adon**)
IJmuiden Dutch town (capital **I** & **J**; **-ui-**; the spelling **Ymuiden** is now less common but it is not incorrect)
IJssel Dutch river (capital **I** & **J**; double **s**; the spelling **Yssel** is now less common but it is not incorrect)
IJsselmeer Dutch lake (capital **I** & **J**; double **s**; not **-mere**; the spelling **Ysselmeer** is now less common but it is not incorrect; see also **Zuider Zee**)
ikebana Japanese art of flower arrangement (not italic)

ikon less common variant of **icon**, chiefly used in the sense 'religious image'

IL Illinois (US postal code)

Île-de-France region of France (circumflex; **-de-**; two hyphens)

Île du Diable French name for **Devil's Island** (circumflex; . . . **du** . . .; no hyphens)

ileum part of intestine (compare **ilium**)

ilex (lower-case **i** in general use; *Ilex* is the genus name)

Iliad epic poem attributed to Homer (italics; single *l*)

Ilion Greek name for ancient **Troy**

ilium part of hipbone (compare **ileum**)

Ilium Latin name for ancient **Troy**

ilk (in Scottish usage *of that ilk* means 'of the place of the same name'; the adoption of **ilk** into general English usage in the sense 'class or sort' was formerly controversial but is now generally accepted)

ill- (usually forms hyphenated compound adjectives (e.g. *ill-humoured*) and two-word compound nouns (e.g. *ill humour*), but see also individual entries below)

ill-advised (hyphen)

ill-assorted (hyphen)

ill at ease (three words)

ill-behaved (hyphen)

ill-bred (hyphen)

ill-disposed (hyphen)

Ille-et-Vilaine French department (no circumflex; double **l** in first word and single **l** in last word; two hyphens)

illegal forbidden by law, or against the rules, as in *an illegal tackle in football* (compare **illegitimate** and **illicit**)

illegible unable to be read, especially because of poor handwriting, small print, faint lettering, etc. (compare **unreadable** (for meaning) and **eligible** (for spelling))

illegitimate forbidden by law, or born out of wedlock, as in *an illegitimate child* (compare **illegal** and **illicit**)

ill fame (two words)

ill-fated (hyphen)

ill feeling (two words)

ill-gotten (hyphen)

ill health (two words)

illicit forbidden by law, or not approved by common custom, as in *illicit sexual relations* (compare **illegal** and **illegitimate** (for meaning) and **elicit** (for spelling))

illimitable (double **l**; not **-ible**)

Illinois US state and river (double **l**, single **n**)

illiterate (double **l**, single **t**)

ill-judged (hyphen)

ill-mannered (hyphen)

ill-natured (hyphen)

ill-tempered (hyphen)

ill-treat (hyphen)

ill-treatment (hyphen)

illus. illustrated; illustration

ill-use (hyphen for both noun and verb)

illusion false or misleading appearance or perception, as in *optical illusion* (compare **allusion** and **delusion**)

illusive variant of **illusory** (compare **allusive** and **elusive**)

illusory deceptive or unreal (also **illusive**)

illustrator (not **-er**)

ill will (two words)

iMac trademark for computer (one word; lower-case **i**, capital **M**)

imaginable (not **-ible**)

imaginary existing in the imagination

imaginative having or produced by a creative imagination

imam Muslim leader (not italic; also **imaum**)

imbed rare variant of **embed**

Imbolc ancient Celtic festival on February 1 or February 2 (the spelling **Imbolg** is not incorrect, but it is less common)

imbroglio confused or perplexing situation (not italic; plural **imbroglios**)

imbue (not **em-**)

IMF International Monetary Fund

imitator (not **-er**)

Immaculate Conception (capital **I** & **C**)

immanent inherent, or present throughout universe (compare **imminent** and **eminent**)

Immanuel child whose birth was foretold by Isaiah (also **Emmanuel**)

immemorial (double **m** then single **m**)

immesh rare variant of **enmesh**

immigrant person entering country to settle there (compare **emigrant**)

immigration act of entering country as immigrant, or part of port or airport where foreigners' passports or visas are examined (compare **emigration**)

imminent likely to happen soon (compare **eminent** and **immanent**)

immobilize (also **immobilise**; see **-ize/-ise**)

immoral contrary to accepted moral standards (compare **amoral** and **immortal**)

immortal everlasting, or having perpetual life (compare **immoral**)

immortalize (also **immortalise**; see **-ize/-ise**)

immortelle flower that retains colour when dried (not italic)

immovable (also **immoveable**, which is the preferred spelling in legal senses relating to property)

immune (followed by *to* in the sense 'unsusceptible', followed by *from* in the sense 'exempt')

immunity ability to resist disease, or exemption from obligation or liability (compare **impunity**)

immunize (also **immunise**; see **-ize/-ise**)

imp. imperative; imperfect; imperial; imprimatur

impassable not able to be travelled along, through, or over (compare **impassible**)

impasse stalemate or deadlock (not italic; **-sse**)

impassible not susceptible to pain or emotion (compare **impassable**)

impassioned filled with passion (compare **dispassionate** and **impassive**)

impassive not feeling or showing emotion (compare **dispassionate** and **impassioned**)

impeccable (double **c**; not **-ible**)

impedance (not **-ence**)

impedimenta (plural noun)

impel drive or urge (compare **compel**)

impelled, impelling (double **l**)

impenetrable (not **-nit-**; not **-atable** or **-ible**)

impenitent (not **-ant**)

imperial (sometimes capital **I** with reference to a specific empire; lower-case **i** with reference to the system of British weights and measures including the foot, pound, and gallon)

Imperial College London (no comma)

imperil (single **l**)

imperilled, imperilling (single **l** in US English)

impermeable (not **-mia-**)

impersonate imitate or pretend to be (compare **personate** and **personify**)

impetuous impulsive or rash

impetus impelling force, incentive, or stimulus (plural **impetuses**)

impinge encroach, or collide (followed by *on* and interchangeable with **infringe** in the sense 'encroach')

impinging (not **-geing**)

implement (not **-plim-**)

implicit implied, indirect, or unreserved (compare **explicit**)

imply suggest (compare **infer**)

impose (*typog.*) arrange pages on sheet so that they will be in correct order after printing and folding

impossible (do not use with *more*, *most*, or *very*)

impostor (also **imposter**)

impregnable unable to be taken by force or overcome, or able to be impregnated (also **impregnatable** in the sense 'able to be impregnated')

impresario (single **s**; plural **impresarios**)

impression (*typog.*) first printing of publication in a particular setting, or a subsequent printing from the same setting with no or few alterations (compare **edition**)

impressionable (not **-ible**)

impressionist entertainer who impersonates famous people (lowercase **i**)

Impressionist member of group of 19th-century French painters including Monet and Renoir (rarely lower-case **i**)

imprimatur official approval of something to be printed or published (not italic)

imprint (*typog.*) name of publisher or publishing division, usually printed on title page of book, or other details such as place and date of publication, printer's name and address, etc.

imprint page verso of title page, bearing details such as name and address of publisher and printer,

date of publication, copyright notice, ISBN, CIP data, etc. (also **copyright page** or **biblio page**)

impromptu without planning or preparation (not italic; **-mptu**)

improvise (never **-ize**)

impugn challenge or attack (compare **impute**)

impunity exemption from punishment or other unpleasant consequences (compare **immunity**)

impute attribute (compare **impugn**)

In indium (no full stop)

IN Indiana (US postal code)

in. inch or inches

in absentia in his or her absence (italics)

inaccessible (not **-able**)

inadmissible (not **-able**)

inadvertent (not **-ant**)

in aeternum forever (italics; two words; *ae-*)

inamorata female lover (not italic; single **n**; plural **inamoratas**)

inamorato male lover (not italic; single **n**; plural **inamoratos** or **inamorati**)

inapt inappropriate or lacking skill (the primary meaning is 'inappropriate'; compare **inept**)

inasmuch as (one space only: not four words)

in-between (hyphen)

inboard (no hyphen)

inbred (no hyphen)

in-built (hyphen)

Inc. Incorporated (used in US company names)

in camera not in public (not italic)

incandescent (**-sc-**; not **-ant**)

incapsulate rare variant of **encapsulate**

incase rare variant of **encase**

incense (**-nc-** then **-ns-**)

incentivize (also **incentivise**, see **-ize/-ise**; paraphrase to avoid controversy)

incessant (not **-ent**)
incidentally (not **-dently**)
incinerator (not **-er**)
incipient (not **-sip-**, not **-ant**)
incise (never **-ize**)
incisor (not **-er**)
inclose rare variant of **enclose**
incognito (as adjective) under an assumed name or in disguise; (as noun) assumed name or disguise, or person who is incognito (not italic; plural **incognitos**)
incoming (no hyphen)
incommunicado deprived of communication with others (not italic)
incompatible (not **-able**)
incompetent (not **-ant**)
inconsistent (not **-ant**)
incontrovertible (not **-able**)
incorrigible (not **-able**)
incredible unbelievable (not **-able**)
incredulous unbelieving
increment (not **-crim-**)
incrust less common variant of **encrust**
incrustation variant of **encrustation**
incubator (not **-er**)
incur (single **r**)
incurred, incurring (double **r**)
Ind Coope brewing company
indebted (not **en-**)
indefensible (not **-able**)
indefinable (not **-ible**)
indefinite (not **-ate**)
indelible (single **l**; not **-able**)
indent (*typog.*) (as verb) leave space between margin and written or printed matter, e.g. when starting a paragraph or when setting a long quotation; (as noun) variant of **indentation**
indentation (*typog.*) act of indenting or amount of space left (also **indent**)
independence (not **-ance**)
Independence Day official name for **Fourth of July**

independent (not **-ant**)
in-depth (hyphen)
indescribable (not **-eable** or **-ible**)
indestructible (not **-able**)
index alphabetical list at back of book, indicator, ratio, or (*typog.*) the symbol (☞ or ☞), used to indicate notes, paragraphs, etc. (also **fist**) (plural **indexes**, especially in the sense 'alphabetical list', or **indices**)
Indian of India, or a person from India (use **American Indian** or **Native American** for the indigenous peoples of the Americas)
Indian ink (capital **I** then lower-case **i**)
Indian summer (capital **I**)
India rubber (capital **I**)
indicator (not **-er**)
indict charge with crime (**-ct**; compare **indite**)
indictable (not **-ible**)
indie independent film or record company (not **-dy**)
indigenous native
indigent poor
indigestible (not **-able**)
indirect object person or thing that receives action of verb and direct object and usually lies between them, e.g. *me* in *they gave me a present* (compare **direct object** and **subject**)
indirect speech (also **reported speech**) the reporting of something said without repeating the exact words, e.g. *she said she didn't mind* or *I asked how much it was* (compare **direct speech**, in which the corresponding examples would be *she said, 'I don't mind'* or *I asked, 'How much is it?'*). Note the change of tense (and sometimes of pronoun, word order, or closing punctuation) and the lack of quotation marks in indirect speech.
indiscreet imprudent or tactless
indiscrete not divided into parts

indiscriminate random (compare **undiscriminating**)

indispensable (not **-ible**)

indistinguishable (not **-ible**)

indite archaic word for write (compare **indict**)

indium (symbol **In**)

individualize (also **individualise**; see **-ize/-ise**)

Indochina Asian peninsula between India and China (also **Indo-China**)

Indo-European of family of languages including English and Latin (hyphen; capital **I** & **E**)

Indonesia Asian country (former name **Dutch East Indies**)

indoor (adjective before noun)

indoors (adverb)

indorse less common variant of **endorse**

indubitable (not **-ible**)

industrial of, derived from, or used in industry (compare **industrious**)

industrialize (also **industrialise**; see **-ize/-ise**)

Industrial Revolution (capital **I** & **R**)

industrial tribunal former name for **employment tribunal** in England, Scotland, and Wales

industrious hard-working (compare **industrial**)

Indy see **d'Indy**

inedible not fit to be eaten, especially in the sense 'dangerous or impossible to eat' (**-ible**; compare **uneatable**)

ineducable (not **-atable**)

ineffaceable (**e** after **c**)

ineligible (not **-able**)

inept incompetent or not suitable (the primary meaning is 'incompetent'; compare **inapt**)

inequality disparity (compare **inequity**)

inequity unfairness (compare **inequality** and **iniquity**)

inescapable (not **-eable**)

inexplicable (not **-ible**)

in extremis in dire straits or at the point of death (italics)

inf. infinitive

infallible (not **-able**)

infantryman (one word)

infer deduce by reasoning or indicate as logical consequence (compare **imply**; to avoid controversy do not use in place of that verb)

inference (single **r**)

inferior (*typog.*) another word for **subscript**

inferno (plural **infernos**)

inferred, inferring (double **r**)

infighting (no hyphen)

infinite unlimited

infinitesimal extremely small

infinitive see **split infinitive**

in flagrante delicto red-handed (not italic)

inflammable liable to catch fire (replace with **flammable** to avoid misunderstanding; compare **nonflammable** and **inflammatory**)

inflammatory tending to arouse strong emotion, or characterized by inflammation (compare **inflammable**)

inflatable (not **-eable**)

inflection modulation of voice, or change in form of word showing different tense, person, number, gender, etc. (the spelling **inflexion** is not incorrect, but it is less common)

inflexible (not **-able**)

inflexion less common variant of **inflection**

inflict impose, as in *he inflicted taxes on them* (compare **afflict**)

in-flight (hyphen)

infold less common variant of **enfold**

informant person who gives information of any kind

informer person who gives police information about a crime or criminal, or person who gives information of any kind

infra dig beneath one's dignity (not italic)

infrared (one word)

infrastructure (one word)

infringe violate, or encroach (followed by *on* and interchangeable with **impinge** in the sense 'encroach')

infringement (not -gm-)

infringing (not -geing)

-ing ending of **gerund** and **present participle**. The -ing form may function as noun (e.g. *skiing is fun*), adjective (e.g. *a boring film*), or part of verb (e.g. *it's raining*). Note the use of the **possessive** in the following examples: *I object to Jack's using the computer* and *I object to his using the computer*. In modern English, *Jack* and *him* may be used instead, especially in informal contexts. However, for non-personal nouns or complex noun phrases the possessive is best avoided, e.g. *I object to Jack and Emma using the computer* or *I object to inexperience being used as an excuse for incompetence.*

Inge, William Ralph English theologian (known as **the Gloomy Dean**)

ingenious clever (compare **ingenuous**)

ingénue innocent or inexperienced young woman (not italic; acute accent; -ue)

ingenuity cleverness or inventiveness (compare **ingenuousness**)

ingenuous naive, innocent, or candid (compare **ingenious**)

ingenuousness state of being ingenuous (compare **ingenuity**)

Ingleborough English mountain (not -gel-, not -brough)

ingrain (the spelling **engrain** is not incorrect, but it is less common)

Ingres, Jean Auguste Dominique French painter

ingulf less common variant of **engulf**

inhaler (not -or)

in-house (hyphen)

iniquity wickedness (compare **inequity**)

initialize (also **initialise**; see -ize/-ise)

initialled, initialling (single l in US English)

initials there is an increasing tendency to omit full stops after initials in people's names, thus either *D. H. Lawrence* or *D H Lawrence* is permissible, according to the publisher's house style. Such initials are usually separated by spaces, but it is undesirable to have a line break between them. Where the whole name is reduced to initials, as in *GBS* for *George Bernard Shaw*, there are usually no full stops or spaces. See also **abbreviations** and **acronyms**.

Initiatives of Change worldwide movement for moral and spiritual renewal leading to social, economic, and political change (not **for**; former name **Moral Rearmament**, original name **Oxford Group**)

inkblot (one word)

ink-jet printer (one hyphen)

inkstand (one word)

inkwell (one word)

Inland Revenue (capital **I** & **R**)

in-laws (hyphen)

in-line skate (one hyphen)

in loco parentis in place of a parent (italics)

in memoriam in memory of (not italic)

inmesh rare variant of **enmesh**

inner city (no hyphen unless used before another noun, as in *inner-city schools*)

innervate supply nerves to (compare **enervate** and **innerve**)

innerve stimulate (compare **enervate** and **innervate**)

innings (same form for singular and plural)

Inniskilling former name for **Enniskillen**

innkeeper (one word)

innocuous (double **n**, single **c**)

innovative (double **n**)

Innsbruck Austrian city (not **-brook**)

innuendo (plural **innuendos** or **innuendoes**)

Innuit variant of **Inuit**

inoculate introduce vaccine or other substance into body to induce immunity, introduce bacteria into culture medium, or figurative use of the verb (single **n**, single **c**; compare **vaccinate**)

inpatient (one word)

in perpetuum forever (italics)

input (the past tense and past participle is **inputted** or **input**)

inputted, inputting (double **t**)

inquire ask or investigate (also **enquire**, especially in the sense 'ask')

inquiry request for information, or investigation (also **enquiry**, especially in the sense 'request for information')

inquisition investigation or inquiry (lower-case **i**)

Inquisition former institution of Roman Catholic Church founded to suppress heresy (capital **I**)

inquisitive (not **-quiz-**)

in re in the matter of (not italic)

INRI Iesus Nazarenus Rex Iudaeorum (inscription placed over Christ's head during Crucifixion)

inroad (no hyphen)

inscrutable (not **-ible**)

inseparable (not **-per-**)

insert in printing, folded section placed in another and bound into book, or loose sheet placed between pages (also **inset**)

in-service (hyphen)

inset in printing, small map or diagram set within borders of larger one, or variant of **insert**

inshrine less common variant of **enshrine**

insignia (same form for singular and plural)

insistent (not **-ant**)

in situ in the original or appropriate position (italics)

insnare rare variant of **ensnare**

in so far as (also **insofar as**)

insolvent (not **-ant**)

insouciant carefree or unconcerned (not italic)

inspector (not **-er**)

install (also **instal**)

installation (double **l**)

installed, installing (double **l**)

instalment (double **l** in US English)

instantaneous (not **-nious**)

instil (double **l** in US English)

instilled, instilling (double **l**)

Institute/Institution see individual entries or their abbreviations to ascertain which is the correct form for the names of learned societies, charities, professional bodies, etc. In general senses and uses, with lower-case initial, **institution** is the more frequent, e.g. *an educational institution* or *hospitals, prisons, and other institutions.*

institutionalize (also **institutionalise**; see **-ize/-ise**)

instructional intended to instruct, but not necessarily fulfilling that purpose, as in *an instructional leaflet*

instructive serving to instruct, whether intentionally or not, as in *an instructive experience*

instructor (not **-er**)

insurance financial protection in

the event of death, illness, damage, fire, theft, etc. (compare **assurance**)

insure protect with insurance (compare **ensure**)

intaglio incised ornamentation, or printing technique using etched or engraved plate (not italic)

integer (-**ege**-)

intelligent having capacity for understanding (not -**ant**; compare **intelligible**)

intelligentsia intelligent or educated people (not italic)

intelligible able to be understood (not -**able**; compare **intelligent**)

intense of extreme force, strength, etc. (compare **intensive**)

intensely extremely (compare **intently**)

intensive involving maximum use of time, land, or some other resource (compare **intense**)

intently with concentration or determination (compare **intensely**)

inter- between or among (compare **intra-**; usually attached without hyphen)

interactive (no hyphen)

inter alia among other things (italics; two words)

inter alios among other people (italics; two words)

interbank (no hyphen)

intercalary (not -**ory**)

intercede (not -**ceed**)

interchangeable (**e** after **g**)

intercity (no hyphen)

intercontinental (no hyphen)

interdependent (not -**ant**)

interdictory (not -**ary**)

interleaf blank or protective leaf inserted between leaves of book (noun; plural **interleaves**)

interleave intersperse or provide with interleaves (verb; not -**leaf**)

interlibrary loan (no hyphen)

interlocutor (not -**er**)

intermarriage (no hyphen)

interment burial (compare **internment**)

intermezzo (plural **intermezzos** or **intermezzi**)

intermittent (not -**ant**)

internal-combustion engine (one hyphen)

internalize (also **internalise**; see -**ize/-ise**)

International Bank for Reconstruction and Development official name for **World Bank** (abbreviation **IBRD**)

International Date Line (capital **I**, **D**, & **L**; also **date line**)

Internationale, the revolutionary socialist hymn (not italic; the use of capital **T** and/or quotation marks is not necessary but not incorrect)

internationalize (also **internationalise**; see -**ize/-ise**)

International Olympic Committee (not **Olympics**)

International Phonetic Alphabet letters and symbols representing speech sounds, used to transcribe pronunciation of words (capital **I**, **P**, & **A**)

Internet (the use of lower-case **i** is less common but not incorrect)

internment imprisonment (compare **interment**)

interplanetary (no hyphen)

Interpol International Criminal Police Organization (capital **I**)

interpretative (also **interpretive**)

interpreter (not -**or**)

interpretive variant of **interpretative**

interred (double **r**)

interregnum (no hyphen; plural **interregnums** or **interregna**)

interrelate (no hyphen)

interring (double **r**)

interrogate (double **r**)

interrogator (not -**er**)

interwar (no hyphen)

intifada Palestinian uprising against Israel (not italic)

into (one word as preposition (e.g. *he jumped into the lake*); two words as preposition plus infinitive marker (e.g. *he jumped in to rescue the drowning child*))

in toto totally (italics)

intr. intransitive

intra- within or inside (compare **inter-**; usually attached without hyphen)

intramuscular (no hyphen)

intransigent (not -ant)

intransitive denoting verb used without direct object, e.g. *interfere* (compare **transitive**)

intrauterine (no hyphen)

intravenous (no hyphen)

in-tray (hyphen)

intrench less common variant of **entrench**

intriguing (-gui-)

introvert (not -tra-)

intrust less common variant of **entrust**

Inuit (use instead of **Eskimo** for peoples of Canada, Greenland, and Alaska; also **Innuit**)

Inuktitut language of the Inuit

inure (the spelling **enure** is not incorrect, but it is less common)

in utero within the womb (italics)

inveigh speak vehemently (followed by *against*)

inveigle cajole (-ei-)

invent (use **design** or **discover** instead where appropriate)

inventor (not -er)

inventory (not -try)

Inveraray Scottish town (not -ary)

Inverness-shire former Scottish county (hyphen)

invertebrate animal without backbone (compare **inveterate**)

inverted commas see **quotation marks**

inverter (also **invertor**)

investable (also **investible**)

investigator (not -er)

investor (not -er)

inveterate long established, deep-rooted, or hardened (compare **invertebrate**)

invigilator (not -er)

invincible (not -able)

in vino veritas in wine there is truth: i.e. people speak the truth when drunk (italics)

invisible (not -able)

in vitro fertilization (no hyphen, no italics; abbreviation **IVF**)

involuntary (not -try)

invulnerable (-vuln-)

inward (adjective; sometimes adverb (see -**ward** and -**wards**))

inwards (adverb only)

inwrap rare variant of **enwrap**

Ioánnina Greek city (also **Yanina**; Serbian name **Janina**)

IOC International Olympic Committee

iodine (symbol **I**)

IOM Isle of Man (also **IoM**)

ion electrically charged atom (compare **iron**)

Iona island off Scotland

Ionia ancient region of Asia Minor

Ionian (as noun) member of ancient Greek people; (as adjective) of this people, of Ionia, of the Ionian Sea or its islands, or denoting a mode in music (compare **Ionic**)

Ionian Sea part of Mediterranean Sea (capital **I** & **S**)

Ionic (as adjective) of the Ionia or the Ionians, or denoting an order of architecture; (as noun) dialect of Ancient Greek, or type of metrical foot (compare **Ionian**)

ionize (also **ionise**, see -**ize/-ise**; not **iron-**)

IOU written promise to pay debt (plural **IOUs**)

IOW in other words; Isle of Wight (also **IoW** for the Isle of Wight)

IPA International Phonetic Alphabet

ipecacuanha (single **p**, single **c** twice, **-nha**)

iPod trademark for portable electronic music player (one word; lower-case **i**, capital **P**)

Ipsambul variant of **Abu Simbel**

ipso facto by that very fact (not italic)

IQ intelligence quotient (plural **IQs**)

Iqbal, Sir Muhammad Indian Muslim poet, philosopher, and political leader

Ir iridium (no full stop)

IR infrared; Inland Revenue

IRA Irish Republican Army

Iráklion Greek port, in N Crete (also **Heraklion** or **Herakleion**; Italian name **Candia**)

Iran Asian country (former name **Persia**)

Iraq Asian country

Iraqi (not **-qui**)

irascible (single **r**, **-sc-**, not **-able**)

Ireland island comprising **Northern Ireland** and the **Republic of Ireland**, part of the British Isles (may be used to denote the Republic of Ireland alone when the context is clear, e.g. in listing European countries; Irish Gaelic name **Eire**; poetic name **Erin**)

irenic promoting peace (also **eirenic**)

irenicon variant of **eirenicon**

Irian Jaya Indonesian province occupying W part of island of New Guinea (former name **Dutch New Guinea**; English name **West Irian**)

iridescent (single **r**, **-sc-**, not **-ant**)

iridium (symbol **Ir**)

Irish Republic another name for **Republic of Ireland**

Irish whiskey (capital **I**; **-key**)

iron metallic element (symbol **Fe**), appliance for pressing clothes, linen, etc., or golf club (compare **ion**)

ironclad (one word)

Iron Curtain (capital **I** & **C**)

ironic (also **ironical**)

ironing board (two words)

Irons, Jeremy British actor

ironware (one word)

irradiate (double **r**)

Irrawaddy Myanmar river (double **r**, double **d**)

irredeemable unable to be redeemed, bought back, reformed, or recovered (compare **irremediable**)

irreg. irregular

irregardless (use **regardless** or **irrespective** instead)

irrelevant (double **r**; not **-vel-**, not **-ent**)

irremediable unable to be remedied or put right (compare **irredeemable**)

irreparable (double **r**; not **-pair-**)

irreplaceable (**e** after **c**)

irresistible (double **r**; not **-able**)

irresponsible (double **r**; not **-able**)

irreverent (double **r** then single **r**; not **-ant**)

irreversible (not **-able**)

irrupt enter suddenly or forcibly (double **r**; compare **erupt**)

Irtysh Asian river (also **Irtish**)

Irvine Scottish town

Irving, Sir Henry English actor and theatre manager (real name **John Henry Brodribb**); **Washington** US writer

ISA individual savings account (no full stops; plural **ISAs**)

Isa. Isaiah (full stop; not italic)

Isaac biblical patriarch (double **a**)

Isaiah book of the Bible (not italic; abbreviation **Isa.**)

ISBN International Standard Book Number (thus *number* in the phrase *ISBN number* is redundant

ISDN integrated services digital network

-ise/-ize see **-ize/-ise**

Iseult princess in Arthurian legend

(also **Yseult** or **Isolde**; see also **Tristan**)

Ishmael biblical character, or narrator of Herman Melville's *Moby-Dick*

Isidore of Seville, St Spanish archbishop and scholar

isinglass gelatine (one word; not **ic-**, single **g**)

Islam religion of Muslims, Muslims collectively, or Muslim countries

island (capital **I** in names, e.g. *Easter Island, Aran Islands*)

Islas Malvinas Spanish name for **Falkland Islands**

isle island (compare **aisle**; capital **I** in names, e.g. *Isle of Man, Scilly Isles*)

Ismaili member of Shiah sect (also **Isma'ili**)

ISO International Organization for Standardization (not International Standards Organization)

Isolde variant of **Iseult**

isosceles (single **s** then **-sc-**)

ISP Internet service provider

I-spy (hyphen)

Israeli of the present-day republic of Israel, or a person from this republic

Israelite member of biblical ethnic group or citizen of the biblical kingdom of Israel

ISSN International Standard Serial Number (of periodical)

Istanbul Turkish city (single **l**; ancient name **Byzantium**, former name **Constantinople**)

isthmus (**-sth-**; plural **isthmuses** or **isthmi**)

IT information technology

ital. italic or italics

Italia Italian name for **Italy**

italic describing type with lines that slope to the right, as in *these words* (lower-case **i**; compare **roman**). Italic type is used for emphasis, foreign words, many titles (see **titles of works** and **titles of periodicals**), the name of an **aircraft**, **boat**, **ship**, etc., and the Latin names of plants and animals (see **binomial**). Italic type is indicated with a single underline in proofreading and editing. Where a word or phrase that would normally be italic (e.g. a book title) occurs in a sentence or passage set in italics for some other reason, the word or phrase may be made roman to provide the necessary contrast, as in *I watched* Casablanca *for the umpteenth time last night.* Either italics or **quotation marks** may be used to highlight a particular word or phrase under discussion (e.g. the word *vulnerable* is often mispronounced/the word 'vulnerable' is often mispronounced).

Italic denoting group of languages (capital **I**)

italicize (also **italicise**; see **-ize/-ise**)

italics italic type (lower-case **i**)

Italy European country (Italian name **Italia**)

ITAR-TASS news agency serving Russia, E Europe, and central Asia, created in 1992 to replace **TASS** (acronym of Information Telegraph Agency of Russia-Telegraph Agency of Sovereign States)

ITC Independent Television Commission

itemize (also **itemise**; see **-ize/-ise**)

It girl (two words; capital **I**)

itinerary (not **-ery**)

ITN Independent Television News

its of it, as in *wagging its tail* (no apostrophe)

it's contraction of **it is** or **it has**, as in *it's too late* or *it's stopped raining* (apostrophe)

ITV Independent Television

IUCD intrauterine contraceptive device

IUD intrauterine device

IVF in vitro fertilization

Iviza rare variant of **Ibiza**

Ivorian of Côte d'Ivoire, or a person from Côte d'Ivoire

Ivory Coast former name for **Côte d'Ivoire**

Ivy League group of prestigious US universities: Brown, Columbia, Cornell, Dartmouth College, Harvard, Princeton, the University of Pennsylvania, and Yale (capital **I** & **L**)

-ize/-ise see individual entries for words with these endings. Most dictionaries of UK English now list the **-ize** form (of verbs such as *organize* and their derivatives) as the preferred spelling, but many periodicals still use the **-ise** form: follow the publisher's house style. In any writing it is important to maintain consistency: do not use *organize* and *realise*, for example, within the same text. Note that some verbs (e.g. *televise* and *capsize*) have only one correct spelling. See also **-yse/-yze**.

J

J joule or joules (no full stop)

Jabalpur Indian city (also **Jubbulpore**)

jacaranda (lower-case **j** in general use; *Jacaranda* is the genus name)

jackanapes (one word)

jackaroo variant of **jackeroo**

jackass (one word in all senses)

jackboot (one word)

jackeroo (also **jackaroo**)

jacketed, jacketing (not -tt-)

Jack Frost personification of winter frost (capital **J** & **F**)

jackhammer (one word)

jack-in-the-box (three hyphens; plural **jack-in-the-boxes** or **jacks-in-the-box**)

jackknife (one word; double **k**)

jackknifes third person present tense of **jackknife** (verb)

jackknives plural of **jackknife** (noun)

jack of all trades (four words; plural **jacks of all trades**)

jack-o'-lantern (two hyphens; apostrophe)

jack rabbit (two words)

Jack Russell breed of dog (capital **J** & **R**; also **Jack Russell terrier**)

jackstay (one word)

Jack Tar any sailor (capital **J** & **T**)

Jack-the-lad (two hyphens; capital **J**)

Jacobean (as adjective) of James I of England and Ireland (James VI of Scotland) or his reign (1603–25), or of a style of furniture or architecture of this period; (as noun) writer or other person who lived in the Jacobean period (compare **Jacobian**, **Jacobin**, and **Jacobite**)

Jacobi, Derek British actor; **Karl Gustav Jacob** German mathematician

Jacobian mathematical term, named after Karl Gustav Jacob Jacobi (compare **Jacobean** and **Jacobin**)

Jacobin member of most radical club in French Revolution, any extreme radical, French Dominican friar, or variety of fancy pigeon (also **jacobin** for the pigeon; compare **Jacobean**, **Jacobian**, and **Jacobite**)

Jacobite supporter of James II of England and Ireland (James VII of Scotland) after his overthrow in 1688, or of his descendants in their attempts to regain the throne (compare **Jacobean** and **Jacobin**)

Jacobite Rebellion (capital **J** & **R**)

Jacob's ladder (capital **J**; apostrophe)

Jacob's staff (capital **J**; apostrophe)

Jacquard fabric or loom (capital **J**; -cqu-)

Jacuzzi trademark for system of underwater jets in bath, or bath equipped with this system (capital **J**)

j'adoube chess term (italics)

jaeger soldier, hunter, or bird (lower-case **j**; also **jager** or **jäger** for the soldier and hunter)

Jaeger clothing manufacturer (capital **J**)

Jaffa port in Israel, or variety of orange (capital **J**; biblical name **Joppa**, Hebrew name **Yafo**, for the port)

Jagannath another name for **Juggernaut** (also **Jagannatha**)

jager variant of **jaeger** (also **jäger**)

jaguar animal (lower-case **j**; **-uar**)

Jaguar motor manufacturer, or any of their vehicles (capital **J**; **-uar**)

Jahweh less common variant of **Yahweh** (also **Jahveh**)

jai alai ball game (not italic; two words

jail (the spelling **gaol** is not incorrect, but it is less common in modern times)

jailbait (one word)

jailbird (one word; the spelling **gaolbird** is less common but not incorrect)

jailer (the spellings **jailor** and **gaoler** are less common but not incorrect)

Jain adherent of Hindu religion of Jainism (also **Jaina**)

Jaipur Indian city (**-ur**)

Jakarta capital of Indonesia (also **Djakarta**; former name **Batavia**)

Jalandhar Indian city (**-dh-**)

jalapeño hot chilli pepper (not italic; lower-case **j**; tilde)

jalopy (rarely **jaloppy**)

jalousie window blind or shutter with angled slats (not italic)

jam cram, wedge, block, congestion, difficult situation, or fruit preserve

jamb side of door frame or window frame (rarely **jambe**)

jambalaya Creole dish (not italic; not **-lya**)

jambe rare variant of **jamb**

jamboree (**-bor-**)

James book of the Bible (not italic; abbreviation **Jas.**)

James, Henry US-born British

writer; **Jesse** US outlaw (not **Jessie**); **P(hyllis) D(orothy), Baroness James of Holland Park** British detective novelist; **William** US philosopher and psychologist

Jameson, Sir Leander Starr British administrator in South Africa

Jameson Raid (capital **J** & **R**)

Jammu and Kashmir part of Kashmir under Indian control

Jan. January (full stop)

Janáček, Leoš Czech composer (diacritics)

Jane Eyre novel by Charlotte Brontë

Jane's any of various books about aircraft, ships, etc. (apostrophe; italics when part of book title)

Janina Serbian name for **Ioánnina**

janissary (also **janizary**)

janitor (not **-er**)

janizary variant of **janissary**

Jansen, Cornelis Dutch Roman Catholic theologian (not **-son**; Latin name **Cornelius Jansenius**)

Jansenism religious movement or doctrine of Cornelis Jansen (capital **J**; not **-son-**)

Janus-faced (hyphen; capital **J**)

japan glossy black lacquer (lower-case **j**)

Japan Asian country (capital **J**; Japanese name **Nippon** or **Nihon**)

japanned, japanning (double n)

Japheth biblical character (**-ph-**, **-th**)

japonica (lower-case **j**)

Jaques-Dalcroze, Émile Swiss composer, teacher, and inventor of eurhythmics (not **-cqu-**)

jardinière ornamental plant container, or garnish of fresh vegetables (not italic; grave accent)

jargonize (also **jargonise**; see **-ize/ -ise**)

Jas. James (full stop)

jasmine (the variant **jessamine** is less common and is restricted to plants of the genus *Jasminum*, as opposed to similar shrubs such as yellow jasmine and red jasmine)

jaspé mottled or variegated (not italic; acute accent)

Jassy German name for **Iași**

jaundice (-au-; -ice)

Java Indonesian island, or trademark for computer programming language (capital **J**)

Javan of Java, or a person from **Java**

Javanese (as adjective) of Java; (as noun) the language of Java or a person from Java

Javel water (capital **J**; also **Javelle water**)

jawbone (one word)

Jaycee member of junior chamber of commerce in Australia, New Zealand, the USA, or Canada (capital **J**)

jaywalk (one word)

JCB trademark for construction machine with shovel and excavator (no full stops)

JCR junior common room

Jdt. Judith (book of the Apocrypha; full stop; not italic)

jealous (-eal-)

Jeanne d'Arc French name of **Joan of Arc**

Jean Paul German novelist (real name **Johann Paul Friedrich Richter**)

jeans casual trousers (compare **gene**)

Jedda variant of **Jidda**

Jedi order of knights in *Star Wars* films (capital **J**; single **d**)

Jeep trademark for road vehicle with four-wheel drive (capital **J**)

Jefferies, Richard British writer and naturalist

Jeffrey, Francis, Lord Scottish judge and literary critic

Jeffreys, George, 1st Baron Jeffreys of Wem English judge, notorious for his brutality

Jeffries, Lionel English actor and director

jehad variant of **jihad**

Jehoshaphat biblical king, or site of Jehovah's apocalyptic judgment (-sh-, -ph-)

Jehovah see **Tetragrammaton**

Jehovah's Witness (capital **J** & **W**; apostrophe)

Jekyll and Hyde person with dual personality, both good and evil, from character in Robert Louis Stevenson's *The Strange Case of Dr Jekyll and Mr Hyde* (no hyphens unless used before another noun, as in *a Jekyll-and-Hyde personality*)

jell become gelatinous, congeal, or assume definite form (also **gel**)

jellaba variant of **djellaba** (also **jellabah**)

Jell-o trademark for jelly in the USA and Canada (capital **J**; hyphen)

jelly baby (two words)

jellybean (one word)

jellyfish (one word)

je ne sais quoi indefinable quality (italics; four words)

Jenghis Khan less common variant of **Genghis Khan**

jeopardize (not jep-; also **jeopardise**, see -ize/-ise)

Jer. Jeremiah (full stop; not italic)

jerbil less common variant of **gerbil**

jerboa rodent with long hind legs (compare **gerbil**)

jeremiad long lamentation or complaint (lower-case **j**)

Jeremiah book of the Bible (not italic; abbreviation **Jer.**)

Jerez Spanish town, famous for sherry (official name **Jerez de la Frontera**; former name **Xeres**)

jeroboam large wine bottle (lower-case **j**)

Jeroboam biblical king

jerry informal word for chamber pot (lower-case **j**)

Jerry slang word for German soldier, any German, or Germans collectively (capital **J**)

jerry-built (lower-case **j**; hyphen)

jerry can (lower-case **j**; two words)

jersey knitted garment, knitted fabric, or football shirt (lower-case **j**)

Jersey one of the Channel Islands, or breed of dairy cattle (capital **J**)

Jerusalem artichoke (capital **J**)

jessamine less common variant of **jasmine** (for plants of the genus *Jasminum*)

Jesse father of David in the Bible

Jesus founder of Christianity (the possessive form is traditionally **Jesus'**; also **Jesus Christ** or **Christ**)

jet black (no hyphen unless used before another noun, as in *jet-black hair*)

jet lag (two words)

jet-propelled (hyphen)

jet propulsion (two words)

jetsam things thrown overboard to lighten ship, e.g. during storm (compare **flotsam**; see also **flotsam and jetsam**)

jet set (two words)

jet-setting (hyphen)

Jet Ski trademark for small self-propelled watercraft resembling scooter (capital **J** & **S**; no hyphen)

jettison (double **t**, single **s**)

jeunesse dorée rich and fashionable young people (italics; acute accent)

Jew (may be used for males and females)

jeweller's rouge (-'s not -s')

jewellery (-**elry** in US English)

Jewess offensive name for Jewish woman or girl

jew's-harp (lower-case **j**; -'s not -s'; hyphen)

Jezebel biblical character, hence any shameless or scheming woman (the use of lower-case **j** in the non-biblical sense is less common but not incorrect)

Jiang Jieshi variant of **Chiang Kai-shek**

jib sail, arm of crane, be reluctant, or stop short (not **gib**; compare **jibe**)

jibber person or animal that jibs (compare **gibber**)

jibe agree or harmonize, or variant of **gibe** or **gybe** (compare **jib**)

Jibouti variant of **Djibouti**

Jidda Saudi Arabian port (also **Jedda**)

jiggery-pokery (hyphen)

jigsaw (one word)

jigsaw puzzle (two words)

jihad (also **jehad**)

Jiménez, Juan Ramón Spanish poet (acute accents; not **Xim-**)

Jiménez de Cisneros, Francisco Spanish cardinal and statesman (also **Ximenes de Cisneros** or **Ximenez de Cisneros**)

Jinghis Khan less common variant of **Genghis Khan**

jinks used in the phrase *high jinks* (compare **jinx**)

jinni supernatural being (plural **jinn**; also **djinni**)

jinrikisha less common name for **rickshaw** (also **jinriksha**)

jinx unlucky or malevolent force, or put a jinx on (compare **jinks**)

JIT just-in-time (method used in manufacturing industry)

jitterbug (one word)

jiujitsu variant of **jujitsu** (also **jiujutsu**)

Jn John (books of the Bible; no full stop; not italic)

Jnr Junior

Joan of Arc, St French national heroine (French name **Jeanne d'Arc**)

Job book of the Bible (not italic; not abbreviated)

Jobcentre (one word; capital **J**)

job lot (two words)

jobseeker's allowance (-'s not -s')

jobsworth (one word)
Joburg informal name for
Johannesburg (no apostrophe)
Jockey Club (capital **J** & **C**)
jockstrap (one word)
Jodhpur Indian city and former state
(**-dhp-**)
jodhpurs riding breeches (lower-case
j; **-dhp-**)
Joel book of the Bible (not italic; not
abbreviated)
Jogjakarta variant of **Yogyakarta**
Johannesburg South African city
Johannisberg German town or
wine
John book of the Bible, one of the
Gospels (not italic; abbreviation **Jn**)
1 John book of the Bible (not italic;
abbreviation **1 Jn**; also **I John**)
2 John book of the Bible (not italic;
abbreviation **2 Jn**; also **II John**)
3 John book of the Bible (not italic;
abbreviation **3 Jn**; also **III John**)
John Dory fish (capital **J** & **D**)
Johnny-come-lately (two hyphens;
capital **J**; plural **Johnny-come-
latelies** or **Johnnies-come-lately**)
John o' Groats village at
northeasternmost tip of Scottish
mainland (not **-'s**; variants such as
John o' Groats (with space) and **John
O'Groats** (with capital **O**) are less
common but not incorrect)
Johns Hopkins University
Baltimore, USA (not **John**)
Johnson, Amy British aviator;
Lyndon Baines US statesman
(known as **LBJ**); **Samuel** British
lexicographer (known as **Dr
Johnson**) (compare **Jonson**)
John the Baptist, St biblical
character (capital **B**)
joie de vivre joy of living (italics)
joint stock (no hyphen unless used
before another noun, as in *joint-stock
company*)
jojoba (**j**, not **h**, twice)

jokey (also **joky**)
Jon. Jonah (full stop; not italic)
Jonah book of the Bible (not italic;
abbreviation **Jon.**)
Jonathan biblical character (not
John-, not **-thon**)
Joneses used in the phrase *keeping up
with the Joneses* (not **-s's**)
Jönköping Swedish city (two
umlauts)
Jonson, Ben English writer (compare
Johnson)
Joplin, Janis US singer (not **Janice**);
Scott US pianist and composer
Joppa biblical name for **Jaffa** (the
port)
Jordaens, Jacob Flemish painter
(**-ae-**)
Joseph of Arimathea, St biblical
character (not **-thaea**)
Josh. Joshua (full stop; not italic)
Joshua book of the Bible (not italic;
abbreviation **Josh.**)
joule unit of work or energy (lower-
case **j**, but abbreviation is **J**)
Joule, James Prescott English
physicist
Jove another name for the god
Jupiter
Joyce, James Irish writer; **William**
real name of Lord **Haw-Haw**
Joycean of or like James Joyce or his
works (not **-ian**)
joyrider (one word)
joyriding (one word)
joystick (one word)
JP Justice of the Peace
Jr Junior
Juárez see **Ciudad Juárez**
Jubbulpore variant of **Jabalpur**
Judaea part of ancient Palestine
(also **Judea**)
Judaeo- relating to Judaism (**Judeo-**
in US English)
judas peephole in door (the use of
capital **J** is less common but not
incorrect in this sense)

Judas apostle who betrayed Christ (full name **Judas Iscariot**), hence a traitor (capital **J**)

Jude book of the Bible (not italic; not abbreviated)

Judea variant of **Judaea**

Judg. Judges (full stop; not italic)

judgement variant of **judgment**

Judges book of the Bible (not italic; abbreviation **Judg.**)

judgment (also **judgement**)

Judgment Day (capital **J** & **D**; also **Day of Judgment**)

judicial relating to the administration of justice

judicious having or showing good judgment

Judith book of the Apocrypha (not italic; abbreviation **Jdt.**)

Jugendstil another name for **Art Nouveau** (italics; capital **J**)

jugful (not **-full**; plural **jugfuls**)

juggernaut large lorry, or destructive force (lower-case **j**)

Juggernaut Hindu idol or form of Krishna (capital **J**; also **Jagannath** or **Jagannatha**)

Juilliard name of US school of music or string quartet (**-illi-**)

jujitsu (one word; also **jiujitsu** or **jiujutsu**)

juju (one word)

jukebox (one word)

Jul. July (full stop)

Julian calendar calendar introduced by Julius Caesar, subsequently replaced by **Gregorian calendar** (capital **J**; see also **Old Style**)

julienne denoting finely shredded vegetables, or soup containing such vegetables (not italic)

Juliet cap (capital **J**)

jumbo jet (two words)

jump-off (noun; the verb is **jump off**)

jump-start (hyphen)

jump suit (two words)

Jun. June (full stop)

junction place where roads, lines, etc. meet or cross

juncture point in time

Jung, Carl Gustav Swiss psychologist

Jungfrau Swiss mountain

Junior (used to distinguish son from father; usually preceded by comma and abbreviated to **Jnr** or **Jr**, as in *Douglas Fairbanks, Jnr*)

junk food (two words)

junkie (also **junky**)

junk mail (two words)

junk shop (two words)

junkyard (one word)

Juno queen of Olympian gods, hence a woman of stately beauty (capital **J**)

Junoesque (capital **J**)

junta military group holding power in country; cabal, faction, or clique; or Latin American council (not italic; the variant **junto** is less common but not incorrect in the sense 'cabal, faction, or clique' but it should not be used in the other senses)

Jurassic last period of Mesozoic era, or of this period (single **r**, double **s**)

juror (not **-er**)

jury see **collective nouns**

jury-rigged (hyphen)

jus canonicum canon law (not italic)

jus divinum divine law (not italic)

just deserts (not **desserts**)

justify (*typog.*) adjust spaces between words to align text with both margins

Jutland peninsula forming main part of Denmark (Danish name **Jylland**)

juvenilia works produced in author's, artist's, or composer's youth (not italic; plural noun)

Jylland Danish name for **Jutland**

K

k kilo-, as in **kg** kilogram (no full stop)

K kelvin or kelvins (no full stop); **Köchel** (indicating serial number of works of Mozart); potassium (no full stop; from Latin *kalium*)

K2 mountain in Karakoram range (also **Godwin Austen**)

Kaaba sacred shrine at Mecca containing black stone toward which Muslims turn in prayer (also **Caaba**; Arabic name **Ka'bah**)

kabala variant of **cabbala** (also **kabbala**)

Kabinett dry German wine (capital **K**; double **t**; not italic)

kabob rare variant of **kebab**

kabuki form of Japanese drama (not italic)

Kabul capital of Afghanistan

kadi variant of **cadi**

Kaffir offensive name for Black African or non-Muslim, or former name for Xhosa (the language) (also **Kafir**)

kaffir corn (lower-case **k**)

kaffiyeh variant of **keffiyeh**

Kafir variant of **Kaffir** or another name for **Nuri** (the people)

Kafiri another name for **Nuri** (the language)

Kafiristan former name for **Nuristan**

Kafka, Franz Czech novelist whose works portrayed nightmarish dehumanized world

Kafkaesque (capital **K**)

kaftan (also **caftan**)

kagoul variant of **cagoule** (also **kagoule**)

kaiak less common variant of **kayak**

kail variant of **kale**

kailyard school variant of **kaleyard school**

Kaiser any German emperor, especially Wilhelm II (sometimes lower-case **k**: see **titles of people**)

kaizen philosophy underlying total quality management (italics)

kakapo New Zealand parrot (plural **kakapos**)

kala-azar disease (hyphen)

kalanchoe (lower-case **k** in general use; *Kalanchoe* is the genus name)

Kalashnikov (capital **K**)

kale cabbage (also **kail**)

kaleidoscope (-ei-)

Kalevala national epic of Finnish legend, set in Kalevala, land of the hero Kaleva

kaleyard school group of Scottish writers including J. M. Barrie (lower-case **k** & **s**; also **kailyard school**)

Kalgoorlie Australian city (double **o**)

kalif less common variant of **caliph**

Kalimantan Indonesian part of Borneo

Kaliningrad Russian port (not -linig-; former name **Königsberg**)

Kama Russian river, or Hindu god of love (compare **karma**)

Kama Sutra Hindu text on erotic pleasure (two words; not **-arm-**)

Kamerun German name for **Cameroon**

kamikaze (one word; not **-zi**)

Kampuchea a former name (1976–89) for **Cambodia**

kanban manufacturing management system using cards to record progress of materials, or card used in this system (italics)

Kanchenjunga variant of **Kangchenjunga**

Kandahar Afghan city (**-har**)

Kangchenjunga Himalayan mountain (also **Kanchenjunga**)

Kanpur Indian city (former name **Cawnpore** or **Cawnpur**)

Kant, Immanuel German philosopher (not **Emmanuel**)

KANU Kenya African National Union

kaolin (the spelling **kaoline** is not incorrect, but it is less common)

kapok (not **-ock**)

kaput (single **t**)

karabiner clip used in mountaineering (also **carabiner**)

Karachi capital of Pakistan

Karajan, Herbert von Austrian conductor

Karakoram mountain range in Kashmir (also **Karakorum**)

Karakorum ruined city in Mongolia, or variant of **Karakoram**

karakul sheep with dark hair, or black curly fur obtained from karakul lamb (also **caracul**)

karaoke (not **-ri-**, not **-ki**)

karate (not **-ti**)

Karl-Marx-Stadt former name (1953–90) for **Chemnitz**

Karloff, Boris English actor known for horror films (real name **William Pratt**)

Karlovy Vary Czech city (German name **Karlsbad** or **Carlsbad**)

Karlsbad German name for **Karlovy Vary**

Karlsruhe German city

karma Hindu or Buddhist principle of retributive justice determining state of life and reincarnation (compare **Kama**)

Karnak Egyptian village noted for ruins of ancient Thebes (compare **Carnac**)

Karnataka Indian state (former name (1956–73) **Mysore**)

Kärnten German name for **Carinthia**

Karoo any of several high arid plateaus in South Africa, or geological period in southern Africa (also **Karroo**; sometimes lower-case **k** in nonspecific references to the plateaus)

Karpov, Anatoly Russian chess player

Karroo variant of **Karoo**

karst denoting characteristic scenery of limestone region (not italic; lower-case **k**)

kart vehicle used for racing (also **go-kart** or **go-cart**; compare **cart**)

kasbah (also **casbah**)

kashmir rare variant of **cashmere** (lower-case **k**)

Kashmir region of Asia (capital **K**; rarely **Cashmere**; see also **Jammu and Kashmir**)

Kashmir goat breed of goat from which cashmere is obtained (capital **K**)

Kasparov, Gary Armenian-Jewish chess player (real name **Gary Weinstein**)

Kassel German city (also **Cassel**)

Katar rare variant of **Qatar**

Katmandu capital of Nepal (also **Kathmandu**)

Kattegat strait between Denmark and Sweden (rarely **Cattegat**)

Kauffmann, Angelica Swiss painter

Kaufman, George S(imon) US dramatist

Kaválla Greek port (acute accent)

kayak (the spelling **kaiak** is not incorrect, but it is less common)

Kazakhstan central Asian country (also **Kazakstan**)

KB Knight Bachelor

KBE Knight Commander of the Order of the British Empire

KC King's Counsel

KCB Knight Commander of the Order of the Bath

KCMG Knight Commander of the Order of St Michael and St George

KCVO Knight Commander of the Royal Victorian Order

kebab (rarely **kabob**)

kedgeree (-dg-, -ree)

Keele English town (-le)

keelhaul (one word)

Keeling Islands another name for **Cocos Islands**

keep fit (no hyphen unless used before another noun, as in *keep-fit classes*)

keepsake (one word)

keeshond (lower-case k; not -hound)

keffiyeh Arab headdress (not italic; also **kaffiyeh**)

Keighley English town (not -th-)

Kellogg's manufacturer of breakfast cereals (double l, double g, apostrophe)

kelpie Australian sheepdog, or water spirit in Scottish folklore (also **kelpy** for the dog)

Kelt rare variant of **Celt**

kelvin unit of thermodynamic temperature (lower-case k, but abbreviation is **K**)

Kelvin denoting thermodynamic temperature scale in which zero is absolute zero (capital **K**)

Kempis, Thomas à German monk

Kendal English town

Kendal, Felicity English actress

Kendall, Edward Calvin US biochemist

Keneally, Thomas Australian writer (single **n**, double **l**)

Kenilworth English town (single **n**, single **l**)

Kennedy, Cape former name for Cape **Canaveral**

kennelled, kennelling (single l in US English)

Kenyatta, Jomo Kenyan statesman (double **t**)

Kephallinía Modern Greek name for **Cephalonia**

kepi military cap (not italic; no accent)

Kepler, Johannes German astronomer (single **p**)

keramic rare variant of **ceramic**

kerb edge of pavement (**curb** in US and Canadian English)

kerb crawling (two words)

kerfuffle (the spellings **kurfuffle** and **carfuffle** are less common but not incorrect)

Kérkyra Modern Greek name for **Corfu**

kernel central part of nut (compare **colonel**)

kerning adjustment of space between characters to allow for their shape and improve appearance of text, e.g. increasing space to prevent ascender of italic letter from touching tip of a round bracket, or reducing space between drop initial and next letter of word

kerosene (also **kerosine**, especially in technical and industrial usage)

Kerouac, Jack US writer

ketchup (the variants **catchup** and **catsup** are less common but not incorrect)

kettledrum (one word)

key (the spelling used for most senses of the word with this sound: compare **quay**)

keyboard (one word)

keyhole (one word)

Keynes, John Maynard, 1st Baron Keynes English economist

keynote (one word)

keypad (one word)

key ring (two words)

key signature (two words)

keystone (one word)

keystroke (two words)

keyword (one word)

kg kilogram or kilograms (no full stop; no **s** in plural)

KG Knight of the Order of the Garter

KGB former Soviet secret police (from Russian *Komitet Gosudarstvennoi Bezopasnosti*)

Kgs Kings (books of the Bible; no full stop; not italic)

Khachaturian, Aram Ilich Russian composer

khaki (**h** after **k**)

khalif less common variant of **caliph**

Khalkha official language of Mongolia (**h** after **k** twice)

Khaniá Greek name for **Chania**

Khartoum capital of Sudan (the spelling **Khartum** is not incorrect, but it is less common)

Khayyám see **Omar Khayyám**

khazi slang word for toilet (**h** after **k**)

Khirbet Qumran archaeological site in Jordan where Dead Sea Scrolls were found

Khmer (as noun) member of a people of Cambodia, or official language of Cambodia; (as adjective) of the Khmers or Khmer)

Khmer Republic a former name (1970–76) for **Cambodia**

Khmer Rouge Kampuchean communist party

Khoikhoi S African people or their language (former name **Hottentot** now considered offensive)

Khomeini, Ruholia Iranian religious and political leader (known as **Ayatollah Khomeini**)

Khrushchev, Nikita Sergeyevich Soviet statesman (**Kh-, -sh-, -ch-**)

khuskhus Indian grass (compare **cuscus** and **couscous**)

Khyber Pass mountain pass between Afghanistan and Pakistan (capital **K** & **P**)

kHz kilohertz (capital **H**; no full stop)

kibbutz collective settlement in Israel (double **b**; plural **kibbutzim**)

kibitz interfere (single **b**)

kiblah direction of Mecca (also **kibla** or **qibla**)

kibosh (also **kybosh**)

kickback (noun; the verb is **kick back**)

kickoff (noun; the verb is **kick off**)

kick-start (hyphen for both noun and verb)

Kid, Thomas see **Kyd**

Kidd, William Scottish pirate (known as **Captain Kidd**; compare **Kyd**)

kiddy (also **kiddie**)

kidnapped (double **p**)

kidnapper (double **p**)

kidnapping (double **p**)

kids' stuff (-s' not -'s)

Kierkegaard, Søren Aabye Danish philosopher and theologian (**-ier-** then **-aar-** in surname; **ø** in first name)

Kiev capital of Ukraine

Kikládhes Modern Greek name for **Cyclades**

Kikuyu E African people or their language

Kilimanjaro Tanzanian massif (single **l**)

Kilkenny Irish county and its county town (single **l**; **-nny**)

Killarney Irish town (double **l**; **-ney**)

Killiecrankie Scottish mountain pass and battle site (**-ie-** twice)

killjoy (one word)

Kilmarnock Scottish town (single **l**)

Kilner jar trademark for preserving jar with airtight lid (capital **K**, lower-case **j**)

kilo (no full stop; plural **kilos**)

kilo- 1000, as in *kilogram*; or 1024, as in *kilobyte*

kilocalorie another name for **Calorie**

kilogram (not **-gramme**; abbreviation **kg**, without full stop)

kilometre (**-er** in US English; abbreviation **km**, without full stop)

kilowatt-hour (hyphen; abbreviation **kWh**, with capital **W**)

Kimberley South African city (**-ley**)

Kim Il Sung North Korean statesman (capital **K**, **I**, & **S**)

kimono (plural **kimonos**)

kinaesthesia (**-nes-** in US English)

kind (use *this/that kind of book*, *these/those kinds of books*, or *these/those kinds of book*, but do not use plural *these/those* with singular *kind*)

kinfolk variant of **kinsfolk**, especially in US and Canadian English

king (for capitalization see **titles of people**)

King Charles spaniel (capital **K** & **C**; no apostrophe)

king cobra (also **hamadryad**)

kingdom in the hierarchy of **taxonomic names**, the group that comes above a phylum or division and below a domain. The kingdom name has a capital initial and is not italic.

kingfisher (one word)

King James Version another name for **Authorized Version** (no apostrophe)

kingmaker (one word)

kingpin (one word)

1 Kings book of the Bible (not italic; abbreviation **1 Kgs**; also **I Kings**)

2 Kings book of the Bible (not italic; abbreviation **2 Kgs**; also **II Kings**)

King's College, Cambridge (apostrophe; comma)

King's College London (apostrophe; no comma)

King's Counsel (capital **K** & **C**; apostrophe; not **-cil**)

King's Cross station in London (apostrophe)

King's English (capital **K** & **E**; apostrophe)

King's Guide (capital **K** & **G**; apostrophe)

king-size (hyphen; also **king-sized**)

Kings Langley English town (no apostrophe)

King's Lynn English town (apostrophe)

King's Scout (capital **K** & **S**; apostrophe)

King's speech another name for **speech from the throne** (capital **K**, lower-case **s**)

Kingston capital of Jamaica, Canadian port, or short for **Kingston upon Thames**

Kingston upon Hull official name for **Hull** (England) (no hyphens; not ... **on** ...)

Kingston upon Thames borough of Greater London (no hyphens; not ... **on** ...; sometimes shortened to **Kingston**)

Kingstown capital of St Vincent and the Grenadines

Kinross-shire former Scottish county (hyphen)

kinsfolk (also **kinfolk**, especially in US and Canadian English)

Kinshasa capital of Democratic Republic of Congo (former name **Léopoldville**)

Kintyre Scottish promontory (not **-tire**)

Kioto less common variant of **Kyoto**

kirby grip (two words; lower-case **k**; not **-rkby**)

Kirchhoff, Gustav Robert German physicist (double **h**, double **f**)

Kirghiz variant of **Kyrgyz**

Kirghizia former Russian name for **Kyrgyzstan**

Kirghizstan variant of **Kyrgyzstan**

Kirgiz variant of **Kyrgyz**

Kirgizia former Russian name for **Kyrgyzstan**

Kirgizstan variant of **Kyrgyzstan**

Kirkby town in Merseyside (not -rby)

Kirkcaldy Scottish town (-kc-)

Kirkcubright Scottish town (-kc-)

Kirov Russian city (former name **Vyatka**)

Kirsch cherry brandy (not italic; capital K; -sch; also **Kirschwasser**)

kissagram (also **kissogram**)

kiss-and-tell (two hyphens)

kist variant of **cist** in the sense 'burial chamber'

Kistna another name for **Krishna** (the river)

Kiswahili variant of **Swahili** (the language)

kitbag (one word)

Kitchener, Horatio Herbert, 1st Earl Kitchener of Khartoum British field marshal (-ener)

kitchen sink (no hyphen unless used before another noun, as in *kitchen-sink drama*)

Kitemark official mark of quality of British Standards Institution (capital K; one word)

kitesurfing (one word)

kitsch (-tsch)

kittiwake (double t)

Kitzbühel Austrian town (umlaut)

Kiushu rare variant of **Kyushu**

kiwi (plural **kiwis**)

KKK Ku Klux Klan

Kleenex trademark for paper tissue used as handkerchief (capital K)

Klein bottle (capital K; -ei-)

Klemperer, Otto German-born conductor (not -or)

kleptomania (not clept-)

Klerk see **de Klerk**

klieg light (lower-case k; -ie-)

Klondike region and river of Canada (not -dyke)

km kilometre or kilometres (no full stop; no s in plural)

knapsack (one word; not nap-)

knar variant of **knur**

knave rogue or playing card (compare **nave**)

knead squeeze or press (compare **kneed** and **need**)

kneecap (one word)

kneed past tense and past participle of **knee** (compare **knead** and **need**)

kneejerk (one word when used before another noun, as in *a kneejerk reaction*)

knees-up (hyphen)

knelt past tense and past participle of **kneel** (also **kneeled**)

Knesset parliament of Israel (also **Knesseth**)

knew past tense of **know** (compare **new**)

knickerbockers (one word)

knick-knack (hyphen; the spelling **nick-nack** is not incorrect, but it is less common)

knife edge (two words)

knife-point (hyphen)

knifes third person present tense of **knife** (verb; compare **knives**)

knight man bearing title *Sir*, or serving medieval lord (compare **night**)

knight errant (plural **knights errant**)

knightly of or resembling a knight (compare **nightly**)

Knights Hospitallers see **Hospitaller**

Knight Templar another name for **Templar** (plural **Knights Templars** or **Knights Templar**)

knit variant of **knitted**; compare **nit**)

knitted past tense and past participle of **knit** (also **knit**)

knitting machine (two words)

knitting needle (two words)
knives plural of **knife** (noun; compare **knifes**)
knobkerrie (one word; not **-rry**)
knockabout (noun and adjective; the verb is **knock about**)
knockdown (noun and adjective; the verb is **knock down**)
knock-knee (hyphen; not **-knees**)
knock-kneed (hyphen)
knock-on (adjective and noun; the verb is **knock on**)
knockout (noun; the verb is **knock out**)
Knole mansion in Kent (not **Knowle**)
Knossos ruined city in Crete (the spelling **Cnossus** is not incorrect, but it is less common)
knot tied fastening, lump on tree trunk, or unit of speed (compare **not**)
know be aware of, certain of, or familiar with (compare **no**)
know-all (hyphen)
know-how (hyphen)
knowledgeable (the spelling **knowledgable** is not incorrect, but it is less common)
Knox-Johnston, Sir Robin British yachtsman (hyphen; not **-son**)
knur protuberance in tree trunk or wood (also **knurr** or **knar**)
knurl one of a series of ridges providing gripping surface, or to impress with such ridges (the spelling **nurl** is not incorrect, but it is less common)
knurr variant of **knur**
Knut variant of **Canute**
Knutsford English town (**Kn-**)
KO knockout or knock out (third person present tense **KO's**, past tense and past participle **KO'd**)
koala (also **koala bear**)
København Danish name for **Copenhagen**
Koblenz German city (also **Coblenz**)

Koch, Robert German bacteriologist (compare **Kock**)
Köchel, Ludwig von Austrian musicologist who catalogued Mozart's works (see **K**)
Kock, Charles Paul de French novelist (compare **Koch**)
Kodak manufacturer of photographic equipment, film, etc. (compare **Kodiak**)
Kodály, Zoltán Hungarian composer (acute accent on surname and first name)
Kodiak island in Gulf of Alaska (compare **Kodak**)
Kodiak bear (capital **K**)
Koestler, Arthur Hungarian-born British writer (**-oe-**)
Koh-i-noor very large diamond (capital **K**; the spellings **Kohinor** and **Kohinur** are less common but not incorrect)
kohl dark cosmetic powder (compare **coal**)
Kohl, Helmut German statesman
kohlrabi cabbage (one word; **-oh-**; plural **kohlrabies**)
kola variant of **cola**
Kolkata official name for **Calcutta**
kolkhoz Russian collective farm (the variants **kolkhos** and **kolkoz** are less common but not incorrect)
Köln German name for **Cologne**
Komintern variant of **Comintern**
Komodo dragon (capital **K**; also **Komodo lizard**)
Konakry variant of **Conakry** (also **Konakri**)
Kong Zi a Chinese name of **Confucius** (also **Kongfuzi**)
Kongo African people inhabiting forests of the Democratic Republic of Congo, Congo-Brazzaville, and Angola, or the language of this people (compare **Congolese**)
Königsberg former name for **Kaliningrad** (umlaut)

Konstanz German name for Constance (the city)

koodoo variant of **kudu**

kookaburra (double **o**, double **r**)

Kooning, Willem de Dutch-born US painter

kop prominent isolated hill or mountain (compare **cop**)

Kop, the stand at Liverpool Football Club stadium (capital **K**)

kopeck Russian coin (also **kopek** or **copeck**)

kopje small isolated hill (not italic; also **koppie**)

Koran sacred book of Islam (also **Qur'an**)

Korea former NE Asian country, divided in 1948 into **North Korea** and **South Korea** (see also **Chosen**)

Kórinthos Modern Greek name for **Corinth** (the port)

Kortrijk Flemish name for **Courtrai**

Kos Greek island in Aegean Sea (also **Cos**)

Kosciusko, Mount Australia

Kosciusko, Thaddeus Polish general (Polish name **Tadeusz Kościusko**)

Kosovo autonomous province of Serbia and Montenegro (full name **Kosovo-Metohija**)

Kosygin, Aleksei Nikolayevich Soviet statesman (**y** then **i**)

Kowait less common variant of **Kuwait**

kowtow (one word)

kph kilometres per hour

Kr krypton (no full stop)

kraal village or enclosure in S Africa (not italic; double **a**)

Krafft-Ebing, Richard, Baron von Krafft-Ebing German neurologist and psychiatrist (hyphen; double **f**, single **b**)

kraft strong wrapping paper (lower-case **k**; compare **craft**)

Kraft food processing company

Krakatoa volcanic island in Indonesia (also **Krakatau** or **Rakata**)

Krakau German name for **Cracow**

kraken legendary Norwegian sea monster (not italic; lower-case **k**)

Kraków Polish name for **Cracow**

Krasnodar Russian city (former name **Yekaterinodar**)

Kreisler, Fritz German-born US violinist (compare **Chrysler**)

kremlin citadel of any Russian city (lower-case **k**)

Kremlin citadel of Moscow, or (formerly) the government of the Soviet Union (capital **K**)

kriegspiel war game, or variation of chess (not italic; also **Kriegspiel**; **-ie-** twice; single **s** in English usage)

Krishna Hindu deity, or Indian river (also **Kistna** for the river)

Kristiania former name (1877–1924) for **Oslo**

Kristiansand Norwegian port (also **Christiansand**)

kromesky meat or fish croquette (not italic; not **-ski**)

krona monetary unit of Sweden (plural **kronor**)

króna monetary unit of Iceland (acute accent; plural **krónur**)

krone monetary unit of Norway, Denmark, the Faeroes, and Greenland (plural **kroner**)

Kronos variant of **Cronus**

Kropotkin, Prince Peter Russian anarchist

Kruger National Park South Africa (capital **K**, **N**, & **P**)

Krugerrand (capital **K**; double **r**)

krummhorn variant of **crumhorn**

Krung Thep Thai name for **Bangkok**

krypton (symbol **Kr**)

KS Kansas (US postal code)

KStJ Knight of the Order of St John

kt knot (unit of speed)

Kt knight

KT Knight of the Order of the Thistle; Knight Templar

Ku kurchatovium (no full stop)

Kuala Lumpur Malaysian city (**-pur**)

Kublai Khan Mongol emperor of China (not **-bla**)

'Kubla Khan' poem by Coleridge (not **-blai**)

Kuch Bihar variant of **Cooch Behar**

kudos acclaim, glory, or prestige (not italic)

kudu African antelope (also **koodoo**)

Ku Klux Klan (capital initials; no hyphens; no **l** in first word; not **Clan**)

Kulturkampf struggle of Prussian state against Roman Catholic Church (not italic; one word; capital initial; **-pf**)

Kulun Chinese name for **Ulan Bator**

Kum variant of **Qom**

Kumbh Mela Hindu festival

kümmel aniseed-flavoured liqueur (lower-case **k**; umlaut)

kummerbund rare variant of **cummerbund**

kumquat (also **cumquat**)

kung fu martial art (not italic; two words)

K'ung Fu-tzu a Chinese name of **Confucius** (also **K'ung Fu-tse**)

Kuomintang political party formerly dominant in China and now the official ruling party of Taiwan

kurchatovium (symbol **Ku**)

Kurd member of nomadic people of Turkey, Iraq, and Iran

Kurdistan region between Caspian Sea and Black Sea (also **Kurdestan**)

kurfuffle less common variant of **kerfuffle**

kursaal public room at health resort, or amusement park (not italic; **-ur-**, double **a**)

Kutch (also **Cutch**)

Kuwait Middle Eastern country or its capital (the variant **Kowait** is less common but not incorrect)

kV kilovolt or kilovolts (capital **V**; no full stop)

kW kilowatt or kilowatts (capital **W**; no full stop)

Kwangchow another name for **Canton** (the Chinese port)

Kwangtung variant of **Guangdong**

KwaZulu/Natal South African province, which replaced Natal in 1994 (no spaces; capital **K**, **Z**, & **N**)

kWh kilowatt-hour or kilowatt-hours (capital **W**; no full stop)

KWIC key word in context

KWOC key word out of context

KY Kentucky (US postal code)

kybosh variant of **kibosh**

Kyd, Thomas English dramatist (single **d**; also **Kid**; compare **Kidd**)

Kynewulf variant of **Cynewulf**

Kyoto Japanese city (the spelling **Kioto** is not incorrect, but it is less common)

Kyrgyz central Asian people or their language (also **Kirghiz** or **Kirgiz**)

Kyrgyzstan central Asian country (also **Kirghizstan** or **Kirgizstan**; former Russian name **Kirghizia** or **Kirgizia**)

Kyrie eleison part of liturgy or musical setting of this (capital **K**, lower-case **e**; **-ie** then **-ei-**)

Kyushu one of four main islands of Japan (rarely **Kiushu**)

Kyzyl Kum desert in Kazakhstan and Uzbekistan (also **Kyzylkum**)

L

l litre or litres (no full stop; no **s** in plural)

l. line (plural **ll.**)

L Roman numeral for 50

La lanthanum (no full stop)

LA Los Angeles; Louisiana (US postal code)

laager African camp, or place where military vehicles are parked (also **lager**)

lab laboratory or Labrador retriever (lower-case **l**; no full stop in informal use)

Lab. Labour

label (single **l**)

labelled, labelling (single **l** in US English)

laboratory (**-or-** twice)

Labor Day public holiday in USA, Canada, and Australia (capital **L** & **D**; compare **Labour Day**)

Labor Party Australian political party (capital **L** & **P**; compare **Labour Party**)

labour (**-our** in UK English; capital **L** with reference to the Labour Party, as in *Labour ministers*)

Labour Day public holiday in UK and elsewhere (capital **L** & **D**; compare **Labor Day**)

labour-intensive (hyphen)

Labour Party British political party (capital **L** & **P**; compare **Labor Party**)

Labrador region of Canada, or short for **Labrador retriever** (the use of lower-case **l** for the dog is not incorrect, but it is less common; see also **animal breeds**)

Labrador retriever breed of dog (capital **L** for full name)

La Bruyère, Jean de French moralist and writer (capital **L** & **B**, lower-case **d**; grave accent

laburnum (lower-case **l** in general use; *Laburnum* is the genus name)

labyrinth (**y** then **i**; capital **L** for the original maze containing the Minotaur in Greek mythology)

lac resin secreted by insects, or variant of **lakh** (compare **lack**)

Laccadive, Minicoy, and Amindivi Islands former name for **Lakshadweep Islands**

lace-up (noun and adjective; the verb is **lace up**)

lacewing (one word)

Lachaise see **Père Lachaise**

Lachlan Australian river (not **Loch-**)

lachrymal variant of **lacrimal**

lachrymose tearful or mournful (**-chry-**; compare **lacrimal**)

lack shortage, or be deficient in (compare **lac** and **lakh**)

lackadaisical (one word; **-ck-**, **-dais-**)

lacker rare variant of **lacquer**

lackey (rarely **lacquey**)

lacklustre (one word; **-er** in US English)

Laconia ancient Greek country of which Sparta was the capital, corresponding to modern **Lakonia**

Laconian of Laconia, or a person from Laconia

laconic terse (also **laconical**)

La Coruña Spanish port (English name **Corunna**)

lacquer (rarely **lacker**)

lacquey rare variant of **lackey**

lacrimal of tears or the glands that secrete them (also **lachrymal** or **lacrymal**; compare **lachrymose**)

Lacroix, Christian French couturier (surname is one word)

lacrosse ball game (one word; -sse)

lacrymal variant of **lacrimal**

lacuna (plural **lacunae** or **lacunas**)

lacy (not -cey)

Ladbrokes gambling company (no apostrophe; not -brooks)

lade put cargo or freight on, or burden (compare **laid**)

la-de-da variant of **la-di-da**

laden past participle of **lade**, used adjectivally in the sense 'weighed down with a load' (compare **loaded**)

Laden see **bin Laden**

la-di-da (two hyphens; also **lah-di-dah** or **la-de-da**)

ladies lavatory (no apostrophe)

ladies' man (also **lady's man**)

ladies' room (apostrophe; not -dy's)

lady woman of high social position or good breeding (lower-case l; as general synonym of **woman**, use only in contexts where you would use **gentleman** for a member of the opposite sex)

Lady title borne by various women of the peerage (capital L; see also **Our Lady**)

ladybird (one word)

Lady Chapel chapel dedicated to Virgin Mary within church or cathedral (capital **L** & **C**)

Lady Day March 25 (capital **L** & **D**)

lady-in-waiting (two hyphens; plural **ladies-in-waiting**)

lady-killer (hyphen)

ladylike (one word)

lady's maid (not -dies')

lady's man variant of **ladies' man**

Ladysmith South African city besieged by Boers during Boer War (not -di-)

lady's-slipper orchid (apostrophe; hyphen; not -dies'-)

Lafayette, Comtesse de French novelist; **Marquis de** French general and statesman (also **La Fayette** for both)

Laffitte, Jacques French statesman (double f, double t)

Lafite, Chateau French wine (single f, single t; also **Château**)

La Fontaine, Jean de French poet, known for his *Fables* (capital **L** & **F**, lower-case **d**)

lager light beer, or variant of **laager**

Lagoon Islands a former name for **Tuvalu**

Lagrange, Comte Joseph Louis French mathematician and astronomer (surname is one word)

La Guardia, Fiorello H(enry) US politician, mayor of New York (also **LaGuardia**, with capital **L** & **G** but no space)

LaGuardia Airport New York (capital **L** & **G** but no space)

lah-di-dah variant of **la-di-da**

Lahore Pakistani city (-hore)

laid past tense and past participle of **lay**, as in *I laid the blanket on the ground* or *the rain has laid the dust* (compare **lade**, **lay**, and **lain**)

laid-back (hyphen)

laid paper paper with mesh impressed on it that is visible when held to the light (compare **wove paper**)

Lailat-ul-Qadr Muslim night of

study and prayer (two hyphens; lower-case **u**)

lain past participle of **lie** in the senses 'be prostrate or horizontal', 'be situated', or 'remain', as in *she had lain in the sun for too long* (compare **lane**, **laid**, **lay**, and **lied**)

Laine, Cleo British jazz singer (not **Lane**)

Laing, R(onald) D(avid) Scottish psychiatrist (compare **Lang** and **Lange**)

laisser allez variant of *laissez aller*

laisser faire variant of **laissez faire**

laisser passer variant of *laissez passer*

laissez allez freedom or lack of constraint (italics; two words; also *laisser aller*)

laissez faire freedom in commerce, or noninterference in the affairs of others (not italic; two words; also **laisser faire**)

laissez passer document giving unrestricted access or movement (italics; two words; also *laisser passer*)

Lake (capital **L** as part of name, as in *Lake Erie*)

Lake District England (capital **L** & **D**)

Lake Poets Wordsworth, Coleridge, and Southey (capital **L** & **P**)

Lake Wobegon fictional US town in stories by Garrison Keillor (not **Woebegone**)

lakh in India and Pakistan, one hundred thousand, especially 100 000 rupees (also **lac**; compare **lack**)

Lakonia region of modern Greece, corresponding to ancient **Laconia**

Lakshadweep Islands island group off India (former name **Laccadive, Minicoy, and Amindivi Islands**)

lam thrash or escape (compare **lamb**)

Lam. Lamentations (full stop; not italic)

lama Buddhist priest or monk (capital **L** in titles, e.g. *Dalai Lama*; compare **llama**)

Lamarck, Jean Baptiste Pierre Antoine de Monet, Chevalier de French naturalist (surname is one word; **-rck**)

Lamartine, Alphonse Marie Louis de Prat de French poet (surname is one word)

lamb young sheep (compare **lam**)

Lamb, Charles English writer (pen name **Elia**)

lambast (also **lambaste**)

lambda Greek letter (compare **LAMDA**)

Lamborghini Italian motor manufacturer, or any of their vehicles (capital **L**; **-gh-**)

lambswool (also **lamb's wool** or **lamb's-wool**)

LAMDA London Academy of Music and Dramatic Art (no full stops; compare **lambda**)

lamé fabric interwoven with metal threads (not italic; acute accent)

Lamentations book of the Bible (not italic; abbreviation **Lam.**)

lamina (plural **laminae** or **laminas**)

lamington Australian cake (lower-case **l**)

Lammas August 1 (double **m**, single **s**)

lamplighter (one word)

lamppost (one word)

lampshade (one word)

Lanarkshire historical Scottish county

Lancashire English county

Lancaster English city

Lancaster, Burt US actor (not **Bert**); **Sir Osbert** English cartoonist (compare **Lanchester** and **Lankester**)

lancelet marine animal

Lancelot one of the Knights of the Round Table in Arthurian legend

lancet surgical knife

Lancet, The journal of medical profession (italics; capital *T*)

Lanchester, Frederick William English engineer (compare **Lancaster** and **Lankester**)

Lanchow variant of **Lanzhou** (also **Lan-chou**)

Lancing English town, site of **Lancing College** (compare **Lansing**)

Land any of the states of Germany or provinces of Austria (italics; capital **L**; plural *Länder*, with umlaut)

Landes department and region of France

landfill (one word)

landlocked (one word)

landlubber (one word)

landmark (one word)

land mine (two words)

land of milk and honey (lower-case **l**, **m**, & **h** in both biblical and figurative senses)

land of Nod (lower-case **l** and capital **N** in both biblical and figurative senses)

Land of the Midnight Sun any land north of the Arctic Circle, especially Lapland (capital **L**, **M**, & **S**)

Landor, Walter Savage English writer (**-or**)

landowner (one word)

Land Rover motor vehicle or manufacturer (two words; capital **L** & **R**)

landscape (*typog.*) denoting format or illustration with greater width than height (compare **portrait**)

Land's End (two words; apostrophe)

landslide (one word)

Landsmål former name for **Nynorsk**

lane narrow road (compare **lain**)

Lang, Cosmo Gordon, 1st Baron Lang of Lambeth British prelate; **Fritz** Austrian film director; **Jack** Australian politician (compare **Laing** and **Lange**)

Lange, David New Zealand statesman; **Jessica** US actress (compare **Laing**, **Lang**, and **Langer**)

Langer, Bernhard German golfer

langouste spiny lobster (not italic)

langoustine large prawn or small lobster (not italic)

Languedoc former French province (one word)

langue d'oc group of medieval French dialects spoken in S France (italics; space then apostrophe)

langue d'oïl group of medieval French dialects spoken in N France (italics; space then apostrophe; diaeresis)

languor (not **-gour**)

languorous (not **-gour-** or **-gor-**)

laniard variant of **lanyard**

Lankester, Sir Edwin Ray English zoologist (compare **Lancaster** and **Lanchester**)

Lansing US city (compare **Lancing**)

lanthanum (symbol **La**)

lanyard (also **laniard**)

Lanzhou Chinese city (also **Lanchow** or **Lan-chou**)

Lao another name for **Laotian**

Laocoon priest killed by sea serpents in Greek mythology (also **Laocoön**, with diaeresis)

Laois Irish county (also **Laoighis**)

Laos Asian country

Laotian (as noun) member of Buddhist people of Laos and NE Thailand, or the language of this people; (as adjective) of this people or language, or of Laos (also **Lao**)

Lao Zi Chinese philosopher (also **Lao-tzu**)

La Palma Atlantic island in the Canaries (compare **Las Palmas** and **Palma**)

La Paz Bolivian city (two words)

lap dancing (two words)

lapdog (one word)

Laphroaig Scotch whisky (**-oai-**)

lapis lazuli blue gemstone (two words; not italic)

Laplace, Pierre Simon, Marquis de French mathematician, physicist, and astronomer (surname is one word)

Lapland region of Europe comprising northernmost parts of Norway, Sweden, and Finland and the northwesternmost part of Russia (single **p**)

Laplander person from Lapland (compare **Sami**)

La Plata Argentine port (see also **Plata**)

Lapp see **Sami** (double **p**)

Lapsang Souchong tea (capital **L** & **S**)

lapsus linguae slip of the tongue (not italic)

laptop (one word)

laptray (one word)

lardon (the variant **lardoon** is not incorrect, but it is less common in modern usage)

lardy cake (two words)

lares and penates household gods in Roman mythology (not italic; lower-case **l** & **p**)

large-scale (hyphen)

largesse (also **largess**)

lariat (single **r**)

Larisa Greek city (also **Larissa**)

larkspur (one word)

La Rochefoucauld, François, Duc de La Rochefoucauld French writer (capital **L**; **-auld**)

La Rochelle French port

Larousse French publishing company (single **r**, double **s**)

larva immature form of insect or other animal (compare **lava** and **laver**)

laryngeal (**-ryng-**; also **laryngal**)

laryngitis (**-ryng-**, **-is**)

larynx (**-rynx**; plural **larynges**)

lasagne (**-gn-**; the spelling **lasagna** is not incorrect – it is the singular form of the Italian word – but it is less common in English)

La Salle Canadian city

La Salle, Robert Cavelier de French explorer and fur trader in North America (not **Cavalier**; surname is not one word; compare **Lassalle**)

La Scala opera house in Milan, Italy (full name **Teatro alla Scala**)

Lascaux site of cave containing Palaeolithic art, in SW France (**-aux**)

Las Palmas port on the island of Grand Canary (compare **La Palma** and **Palmas**)

La Spezia Italian port

Lassa variant of **Lhasa**

Lassa fever (capital **L**)

Lassalle, Ferdinand German socialist and writer (compare **La Salle**)

lasso (not **-oo**; plural and third person present tense **lassos** or **lassoes**)

Lassus, Roland de Flemish composer (Italian name **Orlando di Lasso**)

last (replace with **final** or **latest** where appropriate to avoid ambiguity, as in *her last novel*)

last-minute (hyphen)

Last Supper, the (capital **L** & **S**)

Las Vegas US city in Nevada, famous for casinos (not **Los**)

latchkey (one word)

late (replace with a synonym when 'former' is meant, as in *the late proprietor of the shop*, to avoid confusion with the sense 'dead')

latecomer (one word)

lateral (single **t**)

lath thin strip of wood (compare **lathe**)

lathe machine for shaping, cutting, etc. (compare **lath**)

Latinize (also **Latinise**; see **-ize/-ise**)

Latin names for the capitalization and italicization of the Latin names of plants and animals, see **binomial,**

taxonomic names, class, family, **genus**, etc.

La Tour, Georges de French painter (capital **L**, lower-case **d**; see also **de la Tour**)

Latour, Maurice Quentin de French artist (surname is one word; lower-case **d**)

latte coffee with hot milk (not italic; no accent)

latter denoting the second of two previously mentioned (compare **former**; do not use if there are more than two)

latter-day (hyphen)

Latter-day Saints official name for members of the Mormon Church (capital **L** & **S**, lower-case **d**; see **Church of Jesus Christ of Latter-day Saints**)

latticework (one word)

Latvian (as adjective) of the European country of Latvia; (as noun) the language of Latvia, or a person from Latvia (also **Lettish** for the language)

laud praise (compare **lord**)

laudable (not **-ible**)

laudanum medicine containing opium (**laud-**)

laughing stock (two words)

Launceston Australian city or English town (**-au-**, **-ces-**)

launch pad (two words)

Launderette trademark for a laundrette (capital **L**)

laundrette commercial establishment where laundry can be done in coin-operated machines

Laundromat US, Canadian, and New Zealand trademark for a laundrette (capital **L**)

Laurence, Friar character in Shakespeare's *Romeo and Juliet*; **Margaret** Canadian writer (compare **Lawrence**)

Laurentian of the St Lawrence River, or variant of **Lawrentian**

Laurentian Mountains Canada (not **Law-**)

Laurentian Shield another name for **Canadian Shield** (capital **L** & **S**; not **Law-**; also **Laurentian Plateau**)

Lautrec see **Toulouse-Lautrec**

lava volcanic rock (compare **larva** and **laver**)

lava lamp (**-va**)

lavatory (**-tory**)

laver seaweed (compare **lava** and **larva**)

laver bread (**-ver**)

Lavoisier, Antoine Laurent French chemist (surname is one word)

law-abiding (hyphen)

lawcourt (one word)

lawgiver (one word)

Law Lords (capital **L** twice)

lawn mower (two words)

Lawrence, D(avid) H(erbert) British writer; **Gertrude** British actress; **St** Roman martry; **T(homas) E(dward)** British soldier and writer (known as **Lawrence of Arabia**)

lawrencium (symbol **Lr**)

Lawrentian of D. H. Lawrence or T. E. Lawrence (also **Laurentian**)

lawsuit (one word)

lay mainly transitive verb meaning 'place', 'put in horizontal position', 'prepare', 'cause to settle', or 'produce eggs' (as in *lay the blanket on the ground, lay the table, lay the dust,* or *the hens won't lay*). The past tense and past participle is **laid**. **Lay** is also used as a noun and adjective in various senses and is the past tense of **lie** meaning 'be prostrate or horizontal', 'be situated', or 'remain' (as in *we lay in the sun, he lay low for a while,* or *the snow lay for several days*). Compare **lie**, **lain**, and **lied**. See also **ley line** and **lie of the land**.

layabout (one word)

lay-by (hyphen; plural **lay-bys**)

layette set of clothes, bedclothes, etc. for newborn baby (not italic)

layman (use **lay person** instead where appropriate)

lay-off (noun; the verb is **lay off**)

layout (noun; the verb is **lay out**)

lay person (also **layperson**; use instead of gender-specific **layman** or **laywoman** where appropriate)

laywoman (use **lay person** instead where appropriate)

lazybones (one word)

lb pound or pounds in weight (from Latin *libra*)

lbw leg before wicket

lc loco citato (see **loc. cit.**); lower-case

LCD liquid-crystal display; lowest common denominator (also **lcd**)

LCM lowest common multiple (also **lcm**)

lea meadow or field (compare **lee**)

LEA Local Education Authority

leach remove or be removed by percolation, or variant of **leech** in the sense 'edge of sail'

lead[1] go ahead, guide, first place, advantage, etc. (past tense and past participle **led**)

lead[2] (as noun) metallic element (symbol **Pb**); weight, strip, or sheet of lead; or (*typog.*) strip of metal used for interlinear spacing; (as verb) treat, surround, or space with lead (past tense and past participle **leaded**; compare **led**)

leaded past tense and past participle of **lead**[2], also used adjectivally, as in *leaded petrol, leaded lights, leaded type* (compare **lead**[2])

leader (capital **L** in the titles *Leader of the House of Commons* and *Leader of the House of Lords*)

leaders (*typog.*) dots or hyphens used to guide the reader's eye across a page

lead-in (hyphen)

leading (*typog.*) spacing between lines of type

leading edge (no hyphen unless used before another noun, as in *leading-edge technology*)

leaf (*typog.*) sheet of paper in book (compare **page**)

leafs third person present tense of **leaf** (verb; compare **leaves**)

leak escape of liquid, light, information, etc. (compare **leek**)

Leakey, Louis Seymour Bazett British anthropologist and archaeologist; **Richard** Kenyan anthropologist

leaky tending to leak

Leamington Spa English town (not **Lem-**; official name **Royal Leamington Spa**)

leaned past tense and past participle of **lean** (also **leant**)

Leaning Tower Pisa, Italy (capital **L**, & **T**)

leant variant of **leaned** (compare **lent**)

lean-to (hyphen)

leaped variant of **leapt**

leapfrog (one word)

leapfrogged, leapfrogging (double **g**)

leapt past tense and past participle of **leap** (also **leaped**)

leap year (two words)

learn acquire knowledge or skill (compare **teach**)

learned[1] past tense and past participle of **learn** (also **learnt**)

learned[2] having great knowledge, or characterized by scholarship (not **learnt**)

learning difficulties use instead of **mental handicap**, **retarded**, etc. to avoid offence, as in *people with learning difficulties, her son has learning difficulties* (also **learning disabilities**)

learnt variant of **learned**[1]

leaseback (one word)

leaseholder (one word)

leave alone refrain from bothering, or permit to be alone (also **let alone** in the sense 'refrain from bothering')

leaves plural of **leaf** (noun; compare **leafs**) or third person present tense of **leave**

Lebanon Asian country (do not use with *the*)

Lebensraum territory claimed on grounds that it is required for nation's survival (not italic; capital **L**)

Le Carré, John English novelist (real name **David John Cornwell**)

Leconte de Lisle, Charles Marie René French poet

Le Corbusier French architect (real name **Charles Édouard Jeanneret**)

Le Creuset manufacturer of enamelled cast-iron cookware

Le Creusot French town

lectern (not **-urn**)

led past tense and past participle of **lead¹** (compare **lead²**)

LED light-emitting diode

lederhosen leather shorts with braces (not italic)

ledger book used in accounting, horizontal slab or pole, or angling term (not **leg-**)

ledger line short line above or below music staff (also **leger line**)

lee sheltered side (compare **lea**)

Lee, Bruce US actor; **Gypsy Rose** US striptease artiste; **Laurie** British writer; **Robert E(dward)** American general, Confederate commander-in-chief in the Civil War (compare **Leigh**)

leech bloodsucker, or back edge of sail (also **leach** in the sense 'edge of sail')

leek vegetable (compare **leak**)

Leeuwenhoek, Anton van Dutch microscopist

Lefkoşa Turkish name for **Nicosia**

leeway (one word)

left (often **Left** in political contexts)

left-handed (hyphen)

left-hand page see **verso**

left-luggage office (one hyphen)

leftover (one word)

leftovers (one word)

left wing (noun; often capital **L** & **W** in political contexts)

left-wing (adjective)

legacy (**-acy**)

legalize (also **legalise**; see **-ize/-ise**)

legato music term (not italic; plural **legatos**)

legendary (**-dary**; beware of ambiguity when using the word with reference to real people)

Leger see **St Leger**

Léger, Fernand French painter (acute accent)

legerdemain sleight of hand or trickery (not italic; one word)

leger line variant of **ledger line**

Leghorn English name for **Livorno**, or breed of domestic fowl (capital **L**)

legible able to be read, especially because of clear handwriting or lettering (compare **readable**)

Légion d'honneur French name for Legion of Honour (capital **L**, lower-case **d** & **h**; acute accent)

legionnaire's disease (double n; also **legionnaires' disease**)

Legion of Honour (capital **L** & **H**; French name **Légion d'honneur**)

legitimize (also **legitimise**, **legitimatize**, or **legitimatise**; see **-ize/-ise**)

leg-pull (hyphen)

legroom (one word)

legwarmer (one word)

Le Havre French port

Leibnitz, Baron Gottfried Wilhelm von German philosopher and mathematician (also **Leibniz**)

Leicester English city (**-ei-**, **-ces-**)

Leiden Dutch city (also **Leyden**)

Leigh, Mike British dramatist and director; **Vivien** English actress (compare **Lee**)

Leighton Buzzard (not **Lay-**)

Leinster Irish province (not **Len-**)

leitmotif recurring phrase or theme (not italic; also **leitmotiv**)

Lely, Sir Peter Dutch-born portrait painter (Dutch name **Pieter van der Faes**)

Léman, Lac French name for Lake **Geneva** (acute accent)

Le Mans French city or its annual motor race

Lemberg German name for **Lviv**

lend give for temporary use, as in *she lent him her car* (compare **borrow**; see also **loan**)

Lenglen, Suzanne French tennis player

lengthways (also **lengthwise**)

Lenin, Vladimir Ilyich Russian statesman, first premier of Soviet Union (single **n** twice; original name **Vladimir Ilyich Ulyanov**)

Leningrad a former name (1924–91) for **St Petersburg**

Lennon, John English rock musician and songwriter, member of the Beatles (double **n** then single **n**)

lent past tens and past participle of **lend** (compare **leant**)

Lent period before Easter (capital **L**)

Leonardo da Vinci Italian painter (lower-case **d**)

Leoncavallo, Ruggiero Italian composer (surname is one word)

leopard (**leo-**; single **p**)

Léopoldville former name for **Kinshasa**

Lepanto Greek port (Greek name **Návpaktos**)

Lepanto, Gulf of another name for Gulf of **Corinth**

leprechaun (**-pre-**, **-aun**)

Le Sage, Alain-René French writer (also **Lesage**)

lesbian female homosexual (lower-case **l**)

Lesbian (as noun) person from Lesbos; (as adjective) of Lesbos, or of the poetry of Lesbos (capital **L**)

Lesbos Greek island in Aegean Sea, a centre of lyric poetry in ancient times (Modern Greek name **Lésvos**; former name **Mytilene**)

lese-majesty offence against sovereign or attack on authority (hyphen; not italic; no accents; from French *lèse-majesté*)

Lesotho African country (former name **Basutoland**)

less (use with singular nouns or with units of measurement, time, money, etc., as in *less traffic, less than five hours*; use **fewer** with plural nouns, as in *fewer cars, fewer than five people*)

lessee person to whom lease is granted (compare **lessor**)

lessen make or become less (compare **lesson**)

Lesseps, Vicomte Ferdinand Marie de French diplomat who directed the construction of the Suez Canal

lesser not as great (compare **lessor**)

lesson period of instruction (compare **lessen**)

lessor person who grants lease (compare **lesser** and **lessee**)

Lésvos Modern Greek name for **Lesbos**

let alone not to mention, or variant of **leave alone** in the sense 'refrain from bothering'

letdown (noun; the verb is **let down**)

Lethe in Greek mythology, river in Hades that caused forgetfulness

Let. Jer. Letter of Jeremiah (full stops; not italic)

let-out (noun; the verb is **let out**)

let's let us (apostrophe)

letter box (two words)

letterhead (one word)
Letter of Jeremiah book of the
Apocrypha (not italic; abbreviation
Let. Jer.)
Lettish variant of **Latvian** (the
language)
let-up (noun; the verb is **let up**)
leu monetary unit of Romania and
Moldova (plural **lei**; compare **lev**)
leucocyte white blood cell (**leuk-** in
US English)
leucotomy brain operation (**leuk-** in
US English)
leukaemia blood disease (not **leuc-**;
-kem- in US English)
Leukosia variant of **Levkosia**
Leuven Flemish name for **Louvain**
lev monetary unit of Bulgaria (plural
leva; compare **leu**)
Lev. Leviticus (full stop; not italic)
Levant, the former name for area
now occupied by Lebanon, Syria,
and Israel
levee embankment, or reception
held by sovereign (not italic; no
accent; compare **levy**)
level crossing (two words)
level-headed (hyphen)
levelled, levelling (single l in US
English)
Levi biblical patriarch
leviathan biblical monster, hence
any huge or powerful thing (lower-
case l)
Leviathan book by Thomas Hobbes
Levi's trademark for jeans (capital L;
apostrophe)
Lévi-Strauss, Claude French
anthropologist (acute accent;
hyphen)
Levi Strauss & Co. clothing
manufacturer (no accent; no
hyphen)
Leviticus book of the Bible (not
italic; abbreviation **Lev.**)
Levkosia Greek name for **Nicosia**
(also **Leukosia**)

levy impose (tax, fine, etc.) (compare
levee)
Lewes town in East Sussex
Lewis N part of Lewis with Harris
Lewis, Carl US athlete; **C(live)
S(taples)** English writer; **Sinclair** US
novelist; **Wyndham** British painter
and writer (compare **Louis**; see also
Day-Lewis)
Lewis with Harris island off
Scotland (also **Lewis and Harris**)
ley see **ley line**
Leyden variant of **Leiden**
Leyden jar (capital L; not **Lei-**)
leylandii fast-growing cypress tree
(not italic; lower-case l; also **leylandi**
or **Leyland cypress**)
ley line line joining prominent
points in landscape (not **lay**)
LGV large goods vehicle (former
name **HGV** still widely used)
lh left hand (also **LH**)
Lhasa Chinese city (also **Lassa**)
Lhasa apso breed of dog (capital L,
lower-case a; plural **Lhasa apsos**)
Li lithium (no full stop)
liaise (**-iai-**)
liaison (**-iai-**)
liana climbing plant (also **liane**)
liar person who lies (not **-er**;
compare **lyre**)
Lib Dem Liberal Democrat (no full
stops)
libel defamation in writing or other
permanent form (compare **slander**)
libelled, libelling (single l in US
English)
libellous (single l in US English)
liberalize (also **liberalise**; see **-ize/
-ise**)
Liberal Democrats British political
party (capital **L** & **D**)
Liberal Party Australian or Canadian
political party (capital **L** & **P**)
libertarian believer in freedom of
thought or expression
libertine morally dissolute person

Liberty bodice trademark for thick vest-like undergarment (capital **L**, lower-case **b**)

librarian (not **-air-**)

libretto text of opera (not italic; plural **librettos** or **libretti**)

licence (noun)

license (verb)

licensee (not **-cee**)

licentiate (not **-ciate**)

lichee variant of **lychee**

Lichfield city in Staffordshire (not **Litch-** or **Lych-**)

lich gate variant of **lych gate**

licorice US and Canadian spelling of **liquorice**

Liddell, Alice girl for whom Lewis Carroll wrote *Alice's Adventures in Wonderland*; **Eric Henry** Scottish athlete; **Henry George** English scholar, father of Alice

Liddell Hart, Sir Basil Henry British military strategist

lido public pool for swimming or water sports (lower-case **l**)

Lido Italian bathing beach (capital **L**)

lie intransitive verb meaning 'be prostrate or horizontal', 'be situated', or 'remain' (as in *don't lie in the sun, you'd better lie low for a while*, or *the snow didn't lie*). In these senses the past tense is **lay** and the past participle is **lain**. **Lie** also means 'untruth' or 'tell an untruth'; in this sense of the verb the past tense and past participle is **lied**. Compare **lay**. See also **lie of the land** and **lying**.

Liebfraumilch white wine (not italic; capital **L**)

Liechtenstein European country (**-ie-** in first syllable, **-ei-** in last)

lied[1] past tense and past participle of **lie** in the sense 'tell an untruth' (compare **lay** and **lain**)

lied[2] poem set to music for solo voice and piano (not italic; plural **lieder**)

lie-down (noun; the verb is **lie down**)

Liège Belgian city and province (grave accent; Flemish name **Luik**)

lie-in (noun; the verb is **lie in**)

lie of the land (not **lay** in UK English)

Lietuva Lithuanian name for **Lithuania**

lieu used in the phrase *in lieu (of)* (not italic)

lieutenant (**lieu-**; for capitalization see **ranks**)

life belt (two words)

lifeboat (one word)

life cycle (two words)

lifeguard person who saves people from drowning (one word)

Life Guards cavalry regiment (two words; capital **L** & **G**)

life jacket (two words)

lifeline (one word)

lifelong lasting a lifetime (compare **livelong**)

life raft (two words)

life-saver (hyphen)

life-size (hyphen; also **life-sized**)

lifestyle (one word)

lifetime (one word)

Liffey Irish river (**-ey**)

liftoff (noun; the verb is **lift off**)

ligature (*typog.*) character made up of two or more joined letters, such as *fi*, *æ* (compare **digraph** and **diphthong**)

light bulb (two words)

lighted a form of the past tense and past participle of **light**, preferred in adjectival use before a noun, as in *a lighted match* (compare **lit**)

lightening present participle of **lighten**, or a term used in obstetrics (compare **lightning**)

light-headed (hyphen)

light-hearted (hyphen)

lighthouse (one word)

lighting-up time (one hyphen)

lightning flash of light in sky (compare **lightening**)

lightship (one word)
light show (two words)
light year (two words; note that it is a unit of distance, not of time)
likable (also **likeable**)
like beware of ambiguity when using **like** in place of **such as**: the phrase *countries like Brazil* may or may not include Brazil itself. Do not use **like** in place of **as if** or **as though**, as in *it looks as if* [not *like*] *he's missed the train.*
-like (usually attached without hyphen to one- or two-syllable words unless they end in **l**, e.g. *lifelike, ladylike, snail-like*)
likeable variant of **likable**
likelihood (not **-lyhood**)
likely (do not use as adverb unless preceded by *very, most*, etc., e.g. *she has very likely forgotten* but *she has probably* [not *likely*] *forgotten*)
Lilienthal, Otto German aeronautical engineer (not **Lilli-**)
Lilliput country of tiny people in *Gulliver's Travels* by Jonathan Swift
Lilliputian very small, petty, or trivial (capital **L**)
Lilo trademark for inflatable mattress (capital **L**)
lily of the valley (no hyphens; plural **lilies of the valley**)
Limburg Belgian or Dutch province, or medieval duchy of W Europe (not **-berg**; French name **Limbourg** for the Belgian province)
limelight (one word)
limerick comic verse (lower-case **l**)
Limerick Irish county and its county town
limescale (one word)
limestone (one word)
limey US and Canadian slang word for a British person (lower-case **l**; compare **limy**)
Limousin region of France, or breed of cattle (capital **L**; **-sin**)

limousine large luxurious car (lower-case **l**; **-sine**)
limy of or resembling lime (compare **limey**)
linage number of lines of text, or payment according to number of lines (also **lineage¹**; compare **lineage²**)
linchpin (one word; also **lynchpin**)
Lincoln English or US city (**-oln**)
Lincoln, Abraham US statesman (**-oln**)
Lincoln Center for the Performing Arts New York City, USA (not **Centre**)
Lincolnshire English county
Lindbergh, Charles Augustus US aviator (**-db-, -ergh**)
linden (not **-don**)
Lindsay, Norman Alfred William Australian artist and writer; **Robert** English actor; **Vachel** US poet (**-say**; see also **Lyndsay**)
Lindsey, Parts of area of E England (**-sey**)
lineage¹ variant of **linage**
lineage² direct descent from ancestor (compare **linage**)
lineament facial feature (compare **liniment**)
line breaks see **soft hyphen**
line dancing (two words)
line drawing (two words)
line-up (noun; the verb is **line up**)
lingerie women's underwear and nightwear (not italic)
lingua franca language used for communication between native speakers of different languages (not italic; plural **lingua francas** or **linguae francae**)
liniment medicated liquid applied to the skin (compare **lineament**)
linkup (noun; the verb is **link up**)
Linnaean variant of **Linnean**
Linnaeus, Carolus Swedish botanist (**-aeus**; original name **Carl von Linné**)

Linnean of Linnaeus or the binomial system of biological nomenclature established by him (also **Linnaean**)

Linnhe, Loch Scotland (**-nnh-**)

linocut (one word; lower-case **l**)

Linotype trademark for typesetting machine that casts whole line on single piece of metal (one word; capital **L**)

lintel (not **-tle**)

Lion, Golfe du French name for Gulf of **Lions** (compare **Lyon**)

lionize (also **lionise**; see **-ize/-ise**)

Lions, Gulf of bay of Mediterranean Sea between France and Spain (French name **Golfe du Lion**; compare **Lyons**)

Lipizzaner breed of riding and carriage horse (capital **L**; also **Lippizaner**)

Lippi, Filippino and **Fra Filippo** Italian painters

Lippizaner variant of **Lipizzaner**

lip-read (hyphen)

lip service (two words)

lipstick (one word)

liquefy (not **-ify**)

liqueur flavoured sweetened spirit, or a chocolate containing this (**-ueu-**; compare **liquor**)

liquidambar tree or balsam obtained from it (one word; not **-amber**)

liquidate pay off, terminate operations of, convert into cash, or kill (compare **liquidize**)

liquidator (not **-er**)

liquidize make or become liquid (also **liquidise**, see **-ize/-ise**; compare **liquidate**)

liquidizer (not **-or**; also **liquidiser**)

liquor any alcoholic drink, or any liquid substance (compare **liqueur**)

liquorice (US and Canadian spelling **licorice**)

Lisbon capital of Portugal (Portuguese name **Lisboa**)

Lisburn city and district of Northern Ireland

lissom (the spelling **lissome** is not incorrect, but it is less common)

listeria (lower-case **l** in general use; *Listeria* is the genus name)

Liszt, Franz Hungarian composer (**-szt**)

lit a form of the past tense and past participle of **light**, preferred for most uses in UK English, as in *I lit a match, the room was lit with candles,* or *a badly lit street* (compare **lighted**)

litchi variant of **lychee**

literal in exact accordance with explicit meaning, word for word, or (*typog.*) misprint or misspelling (compare **littoral**, **literary**, and **literate**)

literally (beware of absurdity when used for emphasis, as in *we literally cried our eyes out*)

literary of literature (compare **literal** and **literate**)

literate able to read and write (compare **literal** and **literary**)

literati literary or scholarly people (not italic; single **t** twice; plural noun)

lithium (symbol **Li**)

Lithuania European country (Lithuanian name **Lietuva**)

litmus test (two words)

litre (**-er** in US English; abbreviation **l**, without full stop)

Little Bighorn US river on banks of which General Custer was defeated and killed (**Bighorn** is one word)

Littlehampton English town (one word)

Littleton, Sir Thomas English judge (compare **Lyttelton**)

littoral of the shore (compare **literal**)

livable (also **liveable**)

live-in (adjective; the verb is **live in**)

livelong used in the phrase *all the livelong day* (compare **lifelong**)

Liverpudlian of Liverpool, or a person from Liverpool (see also **Scouse** and **Scouser**)

livestock (one word)

live wire (two words)

living room (two words)

Livingston Scottish town

Livingstone, David Scottish missionary and explorer in Africa; **Ken(neth)** English politician

Livorno Italian port (English name **Leghorn**)

Livy Roman historian (Latin name **Titus Livius**)

Ljubljana capital of Slovenia (**Lj-** then **-blj-**)

Lk Luke (book of the Bible; no full stop; not italic)

LL Late Latin; Low Latin

ll. lines

'll contraction of **shall** or **will**

llama South American mammal (compare **lama**)

Llanelli Welsh town (double l twice; also **Llanelly**)

Llanfairpwllgwyngyllgogery-chwyrndrobwllllantysiliogogogoch Welsh village (shortened to **Llanfairpwllgwyngyll**, **Llanfairpwyll**, or **Llanfair P. G.**)

Llangollen Welsh town (double l twice)

llano treeless plane (not italic; double l, single **n**)

LLB Bachelor of Laws (from Latin *Legum Baccalaureus*)

LLD Doctor of Laws (from Latin *Legum Doctor*)

Llewellyn, Harry Welsh show-jumping rider; **Richard** Welsh writer (double l twice)

Llewelyn I another name for **Llywelyn ap Iorwerth** (double l then single l)

Llewelyn II another name for **Llywelyn ap Gruffudd** (double l then single l)

Llewelyn-Bowen, Laurence British interior designer (double l then single l; hyphen)

LLM Master of Laws (from Latin *Legum Magister*)

Llosa see **Vargas Llosa**

Lloyd George, David, 1st Earl Lloyd-George of Dwyfor British statesman (title is hyphenated but surname is not)

Lloyd's association of insurance underwriters (apostrophe)

Lloyds TSB bank (no apostrophe)

Lloyd Webber, Andrew, Baron Lloyd-Webber English composer (title is hyphenated but surname is not)

Llywelyn ap Gruffudd Welsh ruler (also **Llewelyn II**)

Llywelyn ap Iorwerth Welsh ruler (also **Llewelyn the Great** or **Llewelyn I**)

load (as noun) something carried, weight, or burden; (as verb) put cargo on, or put ammunition, film, etc. in (compare **lode**)

loaded past tense and past participle of **load**, used adjectivally in the neutral sense 'carrying a load' (compare **laden**) and in such phrases as *a loaded gun, a loaded question*, etc.

loadstar less common variant of **lodestar**

loadstone less common variant of **lodestone**

Loanda less common variant of **Luanda**

loan act of lending, something lent, or lend (the verb is best reserved for the lending of money by financial institutions; for spelling compare **lone**)

loan word (two words)

loath reluctant (also **loth**)

loathe hate

local (as adjective) of a particular place, or affecting a limited area; (as noun) inhabitant of a particular place, local pub, or local anaesthetic (compare **locale**)

locale place or area, especially with reference to events connected with it (compare **local**, **locality**, and **location**)

locality neighbourhood (compare **locale** and **location**)

localize (also **localise**; see **-ize/-ise**)

location position, act of locating, or place outside studio where filming is done (compare **locale** and **locality**)

loc. cit. in the place cited: used in footnotes, bibliographies, etc. to avoid repeating the page number of a source previously mentioned (not italic; from Latin *loco citato*)

loch Scottish lake or long narrow sea inlet (capital **L** as part of name, as in *Loch Ness*; compare **lough** and **lock**)

Lochgilphead Scottish town (one word)

lock (as noun) security device, section of canal or river where water level can be raised or lowered, wrestling hold, or cluster of hair; (as verb) fasten with lock, clasp, or become immovable (compare **loch** and **lough**)

Locke, John English philosopher

Lockerbie Scottish town (not **-by**)

lock-in (noun; the verb is **lock in**)

lock gate (two words)

lockjaw (one word)

lockout (noun; the verb is **lock out**)

locksmith (one word)

lockup (noun)

lock up (verb)

lock-up (adjective)

locum tenens person standing in for another, especially a doctor or pharmacist (not italic; plural **locum tenentes**; usually shortened to **locum**, plural **locums**)

locus place, or set of points in mathematics (not italic; plural **loci**)

lode deposit of ore (compare **load**)

lodestar star used in navigation, hence guide or model (one word; the spelling **loadstar** is not incorrect, but it is less common)

lodestone naturally magnetic rock, hence focus of attraction (one word; the spelling **loadstone** is not incorrect, but it is less common)

lodgment (also **lodgement**)

lodging house (two words)

Łódź Polish city

loess fine-grained accumulation of particles deposited by wind (not italic)

Lofoten and Vesterålen island group off Norway

log logarithm (no full stop)

logarithm (**-rithm**)

logbook (one word)

loge box at theatre (not italic; not **-dg-**)

loggia covered porch, or open balcony in theatre (not italic; double **g**)

Logie Australian award for achievement in television (capital **L**)

log jam (two words)

logo (plural **logos**)

Lohengrin character in German legend

Lohengrin opera by Wagner (italics)

Loire French river, or department of E central France

Loiret department of Central France

Loir-et-Cher department of N central France (two hyphens; not **Loire-**)

Lolita central character of Nabokov's novel *Lolita*, hence any sexually precocious young girl (capital **L**)

lollipop (one word; not **lolly-**)

lolloped, lolloping (not **-pp-**)

London Assembly part of Greater London Authority

Londonderry port and historical county of Northern Ireland (also

Derry, but beware of confusion with the district of that name)

lone single, solitary, or isolated (compare **loan**)

longboat (one word)

longbow (one word)

long-distance (hyphen)

long-drawn-out (two hyphens)

longhand (one word)

longitude (not **-tit-**)

long jump (two words)

Longleat House English stately home with grounds containing safari park (**-leat**)

long-range (hyphen)

long s the character ($\int$), formerly used in place of **s**

long-sighted (hyphen)

long-standing (hyphen)

long-suffering (hyphen)

longtime (one word)

longueur period of dullness or boredom (not italic; **-ueu-**)

loofah (**-ah**)

lookalike (one word)

look-in (noun; the verb is **look in**)

looking glass (no hyphen unless used before another noun, as in *a looking-glass world*, and in the title of Lewis Carroll's novel *Through the Looking-Glass*)

lookout (noun; the verb is **look out**)

lookover (noun; the verb is **look over**)

looney variant of **loony**

loonie slang word for Canadian dollar coin with loon bird on one face

loony slang word for foolish person (also **looney**)

loophole (one word)

Loos, Adolf Austrian architect; **Anita** US writer

loose (as adjective) free, not tight or compact, inexact, or promiscuous; (as verb) release, unfasten, or let fly (compare **loosen** and **lose**)

loosebox (one word)

loose cover (two words)

loosen make or become less tight, fixed, firm, or compact (compare **loose**)

loot pillage (compare **lute**)

lop-eared (hyphen)

Lope de Vega Spanish writer (full name **Lope Felix de Vega Carpio**)

lopsided (one word)

Lorca see **García Lorca**

lord person with power or authority over others, or male member of the nobility (lower-case **l**; compare **laud**)

Lord title for God or Christ, or title for earl, marquess, baron, viscount, and various others (capital **L**)

Lord Chancellor (capital **L & C**)

Lord Lieutenant (capital **L** twice)

Lord Lyon another name for **Lyon King of Arms**

Lord Mayor (capital **L & M**; note that the Lord Mayor of the City of London and the Mayor of London are separate offices held by different people)

Lord's London cricket ground (capital **L**; apostrophe)

Lords, the short for **House of Lords** (capital **L**; no apostrophe)

Lord's Prayer, the (capital **L & P**; apostrophe)

Lorelei in German legend, siren who lures Rhine boatmen to destruction

Lorentz, Hendrik Antoon Dutch physicist

Lorenz, Konrad Zacharias Austrian zoologist

lorgnette pair of spectacles or opera glasses on handle (not italic)

Lorrain see **Claude Lorrain**

Lorraine region and former province of France (German name **Lothringen**)

Los Angeles US city

lose mislay, fail to keep, fail to win, etc. (compare **loose**)

loss leader (two words)

loth variant of **loath**

Lothario character in Nicholas Rowe's play *The Fair Penitent*, hence any rake, libertine, or seducer (plural **Lotharios**; the use of lower-case **l** in the general sense is less common but not incorrect)

Lothringen German name for **Lorraine**

lotos rare variant of **lotus**

'Lotos-Eaters, The' poem by Tennyson (hyphen; **-tos-**; compare **lotus-eater**)

lotus any of various plants, or fruit that induced forgetfulness in Greek mythology (lower-case **l**; plural **lotuses**; rarely **lotos**)

Lotus motor manufacturer, or any of their vehicles (capital **L**)

lotus-eater member of people encountered by Odysseus in Greek mythology (hyphen; **-tus-**; compare **Lotos-Eaters**)

louche shifty or disreputable (not italic)

loud-hailer (hyphen)

loudspeaker (one word)

lough Irish lake or long narrow sea inlet (capital **L** as part of name, as in *Lough Neagh*; compare **loch** and **lock**)

Loughborough English town (not **-brough**)

Louis, Joe US boxer (compare **Lewis**)

Louis Quatorze of baroque style of furniture, architecture, etc. of reign of Louis XIV of France (1643–1715)

Louis Quinze of rococo style of furniture, architecture, etc. of reign of Louis XV of France (1715–74)

Louis Seize of late rococo and early neoclassical style of furniture, architecture, etc. of reign of Louis XVI of France (1774–92)

Louis Treize of style of furniture, architecture, etc. of reign of Louis XIII of France (1610–1643),

characterized by decorative features based on classical models

lounging (not **-ge-**)

lour be overcast, dark, and menacing, or scowl (also **lower**[1]; compare **lower**[2])

Lourdes French town, place of pilgrimage for Roman Catholics

Lourenço Marques former name for **Maputo**

Louvain Belgian town (Flemish name **Leuven**)

louvre sloping horizontal slat in door or window, or set of these with their supporting frame (lower-case **l**; **-er** in US English)

Louvre national museum and art gallery of France, in Paris (capital **L**)

lovable (also **loveable**)

lovebird (one word)

love-hate relationship (hyphen may be replaced by en dash)

love letter (one word)

lovesick (one word)

Love's Labour's Lost play by Shakespeare (**-'s** twice)

love song (two words)

lowbrow (one word)

Low Church (capital **L** & **C**)

Low Countries Belgium, Luxembourg, and the Netherlands (capital **L** & **C**)

lowdown (noun)

low-down (adjective)

lower[1] variant of **lour**

lower[2] comparative of **low**, or make low or lower (compare **lour**)

lower-case denoting any of the letters a, b, c, d, etc. (also **small**)

low-key (hyphen)

lowland relatively low ground (lower-case **l**)

Lowland of the Scottish Lowlands (capital **L**)

Lowlands, the central Scotland around the Forth and Clyde valleys (capital **L**)

lowlife (one word)
low-water mark (one hyphen)
LP long play; long-playing record (plural **LPs**)
LPG liquefied petroleum gas
L-plate (capital **L**; hyphen)
L'pool Liverpool (apostrophe)
Lr lawrencium (no full stop)
LRAM Licentiate of the Royal Academy of Music
LSD lysergic acid diethylamide (hallucinogenic drug; no full stops)
L.S.D. pounds, shillings, and pence (from Latin *librae, solidi, denarii*; full stops; also *£.s.d.* or **l.s.d.**)
LSE London School of Economics
L-shaped (capital **L**; hyphen)
Lt Lieutenant
Ltd limited (company)
Lu lutetium (no full stop)
Luanda (the variant **Loanda** is less common but not incorrect)
Lübeck German city (umlaut)
lubricator (not **-er**)
lubricious (the variant **lubricous** is less common but not incorrect)
lucarne dormer window
lucerne another name for the plant alfalfa (lower-case **l**)
Lucerne Swiss city and canton (German name **Luzern**)
Lucerne, Lake Switzerland (German name **Vierwaldstättersee**)
Lucknow Indian city
Luddite textile worker opposing mechanization in early 19th century, hence any opponent of industrial change or innovation (capital **L**)
Luftwaffe German air force (capital **L**; italics)
Luger trademark for automatic pistol (capital **L**)
Lughnasadh ancient Celtic festival on August 1
Luik Flemish name for **Liège**
Luke book of the Bible (not italic; abbreviation **Lk**)

lukewarm (one word)
lumbar of the lower body (compare **lumber**)
lumbar puncture (not **-ber**)
lumber timber, junk, burden with something unpleasant, or move awkwardly (compare **lumbar**)
lumberjacket (one word)
luminosity (not **-ous-**)
lumpenproletariat social group below proletariat (not italic; one word)
lunar (not **-er**)
lunging (not **-ge-**)
lupin flowering plant (**-pine** in US English)
lupine of or resembling a wolf
Lurex trademark for metallic thread or fabric containing it (capital **L**)
lustre (**-er** in US English)
lutanist variant of **lutenist**
lute ancient stringed instrument, or type of cement (compare **loot**)
lutenist (also **lutanist**)
lutetium (symbol **Lu**)
Lutine bell (capital **L**)
Luxembourg European country or its capital city
Luxemburg, Rosa German socialist leader
luxuriant abundant or lush, as in *luxuriant vegetation*
luxurious characterized by luxury, as in *a luxurious hotel suite*
Luzern German name for **Lucerne** (the city and canton)
Lviv Ukrainian city (Russian name **Lvov**, Polish name **Lwów**, German name **Lemberg**)
Lvov Russian name for **Lviv**
LW long wave; low water
Lwów Polish name for **Lviv**
lycée French secondary school (italics; acute accent)
Lyceum (not **-ium**)
lychee Chinese fruit (also **litchi** or **lichee**)

lych gate (two words; also **lich gate**)

Lycra trademark for synthetic elastic fabric (capital **L**)

lying present participle of **lie** in all senses

Lyly, John English writer

Lyme Regis English town (not **Lime**)

Lymington English town (not **Lim-**)

lymph (not **li-**, not **-mf**)

lynch hang without trial (not **li-**)

lynchpin variant of **linchpin**

Lyndsay, Sir David Scottish poet and courtier (also **Lindsay**)

Lyon French city (English name **Lyons**; compare **Lion**)

Lyon King of Arms chief herald of Scotland (capital **L**, **K**, & **A**; also **Lord Lyon**; not **Lion**)

Lyons English name for **Lyon** (compare **Lions**)

lyre ancient stringed instrument (compare **liar**)

lyrebird (one word)

Lytham St Annes English town (no apostrophe)

Lyttelton, Humphrey British jazz trumpeter and band leader (not **Lyttle-**; compare **Littleton**)

M

m metre or metres (no full stop; no **s** in plural); milli-, as in **ml** millilitre (no full stop)

M mega-, as in **MW** megawatt (no full stop); Roman numeral for 1000 (no full stop)

M. Monsieur

MA Massachusetts (US postal code); Master of Arts

Ma, Yo-Yo US cellist (hyphen in first name)

ma'am madam (apostrophe)

Maas Dutch name for **Meuse** (the river)

Maastricht (the spelling **Maestricht** is not incorrect, but it is less common)

Maastricht Treaty (capital **M** & **T**)

Mabinogion, the collection of Welsh folk tales (not italic)

mac mackintosh (no full stop; also **mack**)

Mac trademark for Apple computer (capital **M**)

Mac- (names beginning with **Mac-** and **Mc-** are alphabetized together as if they all began with **Mac-**)

macabre (not **-er**)

macadam road surface (lower-case **m**)

McAdam, John Scottish engineer

Macao special administrative region of China, a former Portuguese overseas province (Portuguese name **Macáu**)

macaroni pasta (not italic; rarely **maccaroni**)

macaroon biscuit (single **c**, single **r**)

Macarthur, John Australian entrepreneur in the wool trade

MacArthur, Douglas US general; **Ellen** British sailor

Macassar variant of **Makasar** (single **c**, double **s**)

Macassar oil (capital **M**)

Macáu Portuguese name for **Macao**

Macaulay, Dame Rose British novelist; **Thomas Babington, 1st Baron** English historian and statesman (not **-ley**)

Macc. Maccabees (full stop; not italic)

1 Maccabees book of the Apocrypha (not italic; abbreviation **1 Macc.**; also **I Maccabees**)

2 Maccabees book of the Apocrypha (not italic; abbreviation **2 Macc.**; also **II Maccabees**)

3 Maccabees book of the Apocrypha (not italic; abbreviation **3 Macc.**; also **III Maccabees**)

4 Maccabees book of the Apocrypha (not italic; abbreviation **4 Macc.**; also **IV Maccabees**)

maccaroni rare variant of **macaroni**

McCarthy, Joseph R(aymond) US politician who led investigations of alleged Communist activity

McCartney, Sir Paul English rock musician and songwriter, member of the Beatles

McCormack, John Irish-born US tenor (not **-mick**)

McCoy used in the phrase *the real McCoy*

McCullers, Carson US writer

MacDiarmid, Hugh Scottish poet (real name **Christopher Murray Grieve**)

Macdonald, Flora Scottish heroine; **Sir John Alexander** Scottish-born Canadian statesman

MacDonald, Ramsay British statesman

McDonald's multinational fast-food corporation, or one of their restaurants (not **Mac-**; apostrophe)

Macdonnell Ranges Australian mountain system (lower-case d; double **n**, double **l**)

mace club, staff of office, or spice

Mace trademark for spray used for riot control, self-defence, etc. (capital **M**)

macedoine mixture of diced vegetables or fruit (not italic; no accent)

Macedon region of the Balkans, now divided among Greece, Bulgaria, and Former Yugoslav Republic of Macedonia (also **Macedonia**)

Macedonia European country (official name **Former Yugoslav Republic of Macedonia** or **FYROM**; Serbian name **Makedonija**), area of N Greece (Modern Greek name **Makedhonia**), district of SW Bulgaria, or variant of **Macedon**

McEnroe, John US tennis player

McEwan, Ian British writer (compare **McKuen**)

Macgillicuddy's Reeks Irish mountain range

McGonagall, William Scottish writer of bad poetry (single **n**, double **l**)

McGraw-Hill publishing company (hyphen)

Mach see **Mach number**

Mach, Ernst Austrian physicist who devised the **Mach number** system of speed measurement

machete broad heavy knife (not italic)

Machiavelli, Niccolò Florentine statesman and political philosopher (single **c**, double **l**)

Machiavellian (sometimes lower-case **m** in the sense 'cunning, amoral, and opportunist'; always capital **M** in the sense 'of Machiavelli')

machine gun (noun)

machine-gun (verb)

machismo exaggerated masculine pride (not italic; **-ch-**)

Mach number ratio of speed of body to speed of sound (often shortened to **Mach** when followed by number, as in *Mach 1*; the use of lower-case **m**, especially in the shortened form, is less common but not incorrect)

macho exhibiting machismo (not italic)

machtpolitik power politics (not italic; lower-case **m**)

Machu Picchu ruined Inca city in Peru (**-ch-** then **-cch-**)

macintosh variant of **mackintosh** (lower-case **m**)

Macintosh trademark for Apple computer (capital **M**)

Macintosh, Charles Scottish inventor of mackintosh (compare **Mackintosh**)

McIntosh variety of eating apple

mack variant of **mac**

Mackay Australian port

McKellen, Sir Ian British actor (**-en**)

Mackenzie Canadian river

Mackenzie, Sir Alexander Scottish explorer in Canada; **Alexander** Canadian statesman; **Sir Compton** English author; **Sir Thomas** Scottish-born New Zealand statesman

McKinley, Mount Alaska

mackintosh raincoat, or waterproof rubberized cloth (lower-case **m**; also **macintosh**)

Mackintosh, Charles Rennie Scottish architect and artist, exponent of Art Nouveau (compare **Macintosh**)

mackle blurred impression in printing (also **macule**; compare **macle**)

McKuen, Rod US singer and songwriter (compare **McEwan**)

MacLaine, Shirley US actress (compare **Maclean**)

McLaren motor racing company, or any of their cars

macle mineral (compare **mackle**)

Maclean, Donald British civil servant who spied for the Russians (compare **MacLaine**)

McLuhan, Marshall Canadian author

Macmillan publishing company or cancer relief charity

Macmillan, Harold, 1st Earl of Stockton British statesman

MacMillan, Sir Kenneth British ballet dancer and choreographer

McMillan, Edwin M(attison) US physicist

McNaughten Rules (also **McNaghten Rules**)

MacNeice, Louis British poet (not **-Niece**)

Macon US city

Mâcon French city in Burgundy, or wine from this area (circumflex)

Macquarie Australian island and river

McQueen, Steve US actor

macramé work made by knotting thread (not italic; acute accent)

macro- large (compare **micro-**)

macroeconomics (no hyphen)

macron the symbol (¯), placed over a long vowel or used as a diacritic

macroscopic large enough to be seen by the naked eye (compare **microscopic**)

macula small spot of distinct colour, e.g. on the skin (plural **maculae**; also **macule**)

macule variant of **mackle** or **macula**

Macy's US department store (apostrophe)

Madagascar island republic off Africa (**-ar**; former name (1958–75) **Malagasy Republic**)

madam polite term of address for woman; woman who runs a brothel; precocious or pompous girl; or South African informal word for the lady of the house (sometimes capital **M** when used as title, as in *Madam Speaker*; compare **Madame**)

Madame French equivalent of **Mrs** (abbreviation **Mme**)

Madame Tussauds waxworks (no apostrophe)

mad cow disease informal name for **BSE**

Madeira island group in Atlantic Ocean, chief island of this group, Brazilian river, or fortified wine (capital **M**)

Madeira cake (capital **M**)

madeleine small sponge cake (not italic; lower-case **m**)

Mademoiselle French equivalent of **Miss** (abbreviation **Mlle**)

Madhya Pradesh Indian state

Madonna designation of the Virgin Mary, picture or statue of the Virgin Mary (also **madonna** in this sense), or US singer and actress (full name **Madonna Louise Veronica Ciccone**)

Madras Indian city (official name **Chennai**)

madrasah Islamic educational institution (also **madrasa**)

Maecenas name of Roman patron of Horace and Virgil, hence any wealthy patron of the arts (capital **M**; **-ae-** then **-e-** then **-a-**)

maelstrom large whirlpool, or any turbulent confusion (lower-case **m**; **-ae-**)

Maelstrom strong tidal current in Lofoten Islands off Norway (capital **M**; **-ae-**)

Maestricht less common variant of **Maastricht**

maestro distinguished musician (not italic; plural **maestri** or **maestros**)

Maeterlinck, Comte Maurice Belgian poet and dramatist (**-ae-**, **-er-**, **-ck**)

mae west slang name for inflatable life jacket (lower-case **m** & **w**)

Mafeking former name (until 1980) for **Mafikeng**, used in historical references, e.g. to the siege of Mafeking in the Boer War

Mafia international secret or criminal organization, or any group resembling this (capital **M**; rarely **Maffia**)

Mafikeng South African town (former name (until 1980) **Mafeking**, used in historical references)

mafioso member of the Mafia (not italic; plural **mafiosos** or **mafiosi**)

magazine titles see **titles of periodicals**

Magdalen College Oxford

Magdalene see **Mary Magdalene**

Magdalene College Cambridge

Magdeburg German city (not **-da-**, not **-berg**)

Magellan, Strait of channel between South America and Tierra del Fuego (single **g**, double **l**)

Magherafelt district of Northern Ireland

Maghreb the countries of NW Africa (also **Maghrib**)

magi plural of **magus**, or the three wise men from the East who visited the infant Jesus (often **Magi** with reference to the three wise men)

magic (not **-ck**)

magicked, magicking (**-ck-**)

Maginot line (capital **M**)

magistrates' court (**-s'** not **-'s**)

Magna Carta (capital **M** & **C**; rarely **Magna Charta**)

magnanimous (**-anim-**)

magnate powerful person (compare **magnet**)

magnesium (symbol **Mg**)

magnet something that attracts metal (compare **magnate**)

magnetize (also **magnetise**; see **-ize/ -ise**)

magneto (plural **magnetos**)

Magnificat hymn of Virgin Mary (Luke 1:46–55) used as canticle (not italic; capital **M**)

magnificent (not **-ant**)

magnolia (lower-case **m** in general use; *Magnolia* is the genus name)

magnum (plural **magnums**)

magnum opus great work of art or literature (not italic; plural **magna opera**)

Magritte, René Belgian painter (single **g**, double **t**)

magus Zoroastrian priest, or ancient astrologer or magician (plural **magi**; see also that entry)

Magyar (as noun) member of predominant ethnic group of Hungary, or the Hungarian language; (as adjective) of the Magyars or their language

Magyarország Hungarian name for **Hungary**

Mahabharata Sanskrit epic poem, containing the *Bhagavad-Gita*

maharajah Indian ruler (also **maharaja**)

maharani wife of maharajah, or woman with rank of maharajah (also **maharanee**)

maharishi Hindu teacher

mahatma Hindu sage (sometimes capital **M** when used as title, as in *Mahatma Gandhi*)

Mahayana school of Buddhism (capital **M**)

Mahdi leader expected to convert the world to Islam, or title assumed by Sudanese leader who captured Khartoum in 1885 (capital **M**; **-hd-**)

mah jong Chinese game (not italic; also **mah-jongg**)

Mahler, Gustav Austrian composer (**-hl-**)

mahogany (**-hogan-**)

Mahomet variant of **Muhammad**

Mahometan former word for **Muslim**, never used by Muslims themselves

mahonia (lower-case **m** in general use; *Mahonia* is the genus name)

mahout Indian elephant driver or keeper (not italic)

Maia mother of Hermes by Zeus in Greek mythology (compare **Maya**)

maid of honour (no hyphens)

maidservant (one word)

Maidstone English town (**-stone**)

mail post or armour (compare **male**)

mailbag (one word)

mailbox (one word)

maillot ballet tights, swimsuit, or jersey (not italic; double **l**)

mail order (no hyphen unless used before another noun, as in *a mail-order company*)

mailshot (one word)

main chief or principal; pipe for water, gas, or electricity; strength; or ocean (compare **mane**)

Main German river (compare **Maine**)

main clause see **clause**

Maine US state (compare **Main**)

Maine-et-Loire French department (not **Main-**)

mainframe (one word)

main line (noun)

mainline (verb)

main-line station (hyphen)

mainsail (one word)

mainspring (one word)

mainstay (one word)

mainstream (one word)

maintenance (not **-tain-**, not **-ence**)

Mainz German city (French name **Mayence**)

maiolica variant of **majolica**

maisonette self-contained accommodation (not italic; also **maisonnette**)

maître d'hôtel head waiter or hotel manager (not italic; two circumflexes; plural **maîtres d'hôtel**)

maize corn (compare **maze**)

majolica pottery glazed with bright metallic colours (not italic; also **maiolica**)

Majorca Mediterranean island (Spanish name **Mallorca**)

major-domo chief steward or butler (not italic; plural **major-domos**)

majority do not use to denote the greater part of something singular or uncountable (e.g. *he owns most* [not *the majority*] *of the land around here*. When followed by a plural noun it must be used with a plural verb (e.g. *the majority of the children bring packed lunches*), but when it stands alone it may be followed by a singular verb if the group it denotes is considered as a single entity (e.g. *the majority is* [or *are*] *in favour of the change*). Similar rules apply to the use of **minority**, denoting the lesser part.

Makasar another name for **Ujung Pandang** (also **Makassar** or **Macassar**)

make-believe (noun; the verb is **make believe**)

Makedhonia Modern Greek name for **Macedonia** (area of Greece)

Makedonija Serbian name for **Macedonia** (European country)

makeover (noun; the verb is **make over**)

make-ready in printing, process of preparing forme (hyphen)

makeshift (one word)

make-up cosmetics, mental or physical constitution, or arrangement of text and illustrations on page (noun; the verb is **make up**)

makeweight (one word)

Makkah Arabic name for **Mecca**

Mal. Malachi (full stop; not italic)

malacca stem of rattan palm or walking stick made from it (lower-case **m**; single **l**, double **c**)

Malacca Malaysian state (single **l**, double **c**)

Malachi book of the Bible (not italic; abbreviation **Mal.**)

maladroit clumsy or tactless (not italic)

Málaga Spanish resort, or sweet fortified dessert wine (capital **M**; acute accent)

Malagasy (as noun) a person from Madagascar or the language of Madagascar; (as adjective) of Madagascar

Malagasy Republic former name (1958–75) for **Madagascar**

malaise feeling of unease, mild sickness, or complex of problems (not italic)

malapropism use of wrong word with similar sound, e.g. *affluence* for *influence* (lower-case **m**)

malapropos inappropriate or inappropriately (not italic; one word; no accent)

Malawi African country (former name **Nyasaland**)

Malawi, Lake Malawi name for Lake **Nyasa**

Malay (as noun) member of people of Malaysian and Indonesia, or the language of this people; (as adjective) of this people or their language

Malaya the states of Malaysia on the Malay Peninsula

Malayalam Indian language (rarely **Malayalaam**)

Malayan of Malaya, or a person from Malaya

Malay Peninsula SE Asian peninsula comprising Malaya and part of Thailand

Malaysia Asian country comprising the states on the Malay Peninsula (known as **Peninsular Malaysia**) and the states of Sarawak and Sabah on Borneo

Malaysian of Malaysia, or a person from Malaysia

Malcolm X US Black civil rights leader (original name **Malcolm Little**)

malcontent discontented, or discontented person (not italic)

male of men or boys, or denoting sex of animals, plants, etc. (compare **mail** (for spelling) and **masculine** (for meaning))

male chauvinist man who believes males are superior to females (see also **chauvinist**)

Malesherbes, Chrétien de French statesman

Malherbe, François de French poet and critic

malevolent wishing evil to others (not **-ant**)

malign evil, or to defame

malignant denoting a tumour that is growing uncontrollably or resistant to therapy (not **-ent**)

Malines French name for **Mechelen**

Mallarmé, Stéphane French poet (acute accent on surname and first name)

malleable (double **l**; not **-iable**)

mallee Australian eucalyptus tree, or informal name for the Australian bush (double **l**, double **e**)

Mallorca Spanish name for **Majorca**

Malmesbury English or South African town (compare **malmsey**)

Malmö Swedish port (umlaut)

malmsey sweet Madeira wine (lower-case **m**; compare **Malmesbury**)

malpractice (not -ise)

Maltese cross (capital **M**)

Malvinas, Islas Spanish name for **Falkland Islands**

mamba snake

mambo Latin American dance

mamillary (double **l**; not -**iary**; **mamm**- in US English)

mammary (**mamm**-)

mammon wealth as source of evil, or greed (lower-case **m**)

Mammon personification of wealth and greed as a false god (capital **M**)

man to avoid controversy or offence, use an appropriate synonym with reference to people or human beings in general, e.g. *the best person* [not *man*] *for the job, the evolution of the human race* [not *man*], *to staff* [not *man*] *the call centre.* But do not replace the word **man** with **person** in well-established idiomatic phrases and compounds such as *to a man* or *manhole*.

-man see individual entries for words with this ending. As a general rule, use a gender-neutral alternative (e.g. *firefighter* for *fireman, spokesperson* for *spokesman*) where possible and appropriate, but note that indiscriminate use of -**person** in place of -**man** may have inelegant or ludicrous results.

manacle (single **n**; not -**ic**-)

manageable (**e** after **g**)

management (not -**gm**-)

manager (may be used for males and females)

manageress (use **manager** instead to avoid offence)

manakin South American bird, or rare variant of **manikin**

mañana tomorrow, or some other and later time (italics; **ñ** then **n**)

Manassas US town and battle site

Manasseh biblical patriarch (see also **Prayer of Manasseh**)

man-at-arms (plural **men-at-arms**)

manatee sea mammal (single **n**, single **t**)

Man Booker Prize official name (from 2002) of **Booker Prize**

Manche French department

Manche, La French name for **English Channel**

Manchoukuo variant of **Manchukuo**

Manchu (as noun) member of people of Manchuria who established imperial dynasty in China, or the language of this people; (as adjective) of this dynasty (compare **Manchurian**)

Manchukuo former state of E Asia (also **Manchoukuo**)

Manchuria region of NE China

Manchurian of Manchuria, or a person from **Manchuria** (compare **Manchu**)

Mancunian of Manchester, or a person from Manchester

Mandalay city in Myanmar, (all the vowels are **a**'s; compare **Manderley**)

mandamus legal writ or order (not italic; plural **mandamuses**)

mandarin citrus fruit or high-ranking official (lower-case **m**)

Mandarin official language of China (capital **M**; full name **Mandarin Chinese**)

mandatory (as adjective) compulsory, having a mandate, or having the nature of a mandate; (as noun) person or state holding a mandate (also **mandatary** for the noun only)

Manderley name of house in Daphne Du Maurier's novel *Rebecca* (compare **Mandalay**)

mandolin (also **mandoline**)

mandrel shaft or spindle (also **mandril**, with single **l**)

mandrill monkey (double **l**)

M&S Marks & Spencer (no spaces around ampersand in abbreviated form)

mane hair on animal's neck (compare **main**)

man-eater (hyphen)

manège riding school (not italic; also **manege**, without grave accent; compare **ménage**)

Manet, Édouard French painter, whose works include *Le Déjeuner sur l'herbe* (compare **Monet**)

manganese (symbol **Mn**)

mangelwurzel (one word; also **mangoldwurzel**)

mangetout pea with edible pod (not italic; one word)

mango (plural **mangoes** or **mangos**)

manhandle (one word)

Manhattan island and borough of New York City, or cocktail (capital **M**; double **t**; not **-en**)

manhole (one word)

man-hour (hyphen)

manhunt (one word)

mania mental disorder, or obsessional enthusiasm

maniac wild person or enthusiast (no longer used in psychiatry; compare **manic**)

maniacal characteristic of mania or of a maniac

manic person with mania (the mental disorder; compare **maniac**), or characteristic of or affected by mania

manic-depressive (hyphen)

Manichaeism religious system based on conflict between light and darkness or goodness and evil (also **Manicheism**)

manifesto (plural **manifestos** or **manifestoes**)

manifold (not **-ny-**)

manikin anatomical model, small person, or less common variant of **mannequin** (also **mannikin**, rarely **manakin**)

manila short for **Manila paper** (also **manilla**)

Manila capital of the Philippines, or cigar made in this city (capital **M**; single **l**)

Manila paper strong usually brown paper (capital **M**; also **Manilla paper**)

manilla early form of African currency, or variant of **manila**

Manilla paper variant of **Manila paper**

manipulator (not **-er**)

mankind (to avoid controversy or offence, use **humankind** instead with reference to the human race)

man-made (hyphen; to avoid controversy or offence, replace with **synthetic** or **artificial** where appropriate)

manna miraculous food of the Bible, sweet substance obtained from plants, or used in the phrase *manna from heaven* (compare **manner** and **manor**)

mannequin fashion model, or dummy used to display clothes (the spelling **manikin** is not incorrect, but it is less common)

manner way, style, bearing, behaviour, or type, or used in phrase *to the manner born* (compare **manor** and **manna**)

Mannheim German city (double **n**)

mannikin variant of **manikin**

manoeuvrable (**-neuver-** in US English)

manoeuvre (**-neuver** in US English)

man of straw (three words)

man-of-war (two hyphens; plural **men-of-war**)

manor house and/or estate, slang word for area of operation, or used punningly in the title of the TV sitcom *To the Manor Born* (compare **manner** and **manna**)

manor house (two words)

manpower (to avoid controversy or offence, replace with an appropriate synonym, e.g. **human resources**, **personnel**, or **staff**)

manqué would-be (italics; acute accent; used after noun)

Man Ray see **Ray**

manservant (one word; plural **menservants**)

Mansfield, Katherine New Zealand-born British writer (real name **Kathleen Mansfield Beauchamp**)

Mansion House, the residence of Lord Mayor of London or Dublin (capital **M** & **H**)

mantel frame around fireplace (the spelling **mantle** is not incorrect, but it is less common)

mantelpiece shelf above fireplace (the spelling **mantlepiece** is not incorrect, but it is less common)

mantilla Spanish woman's scarf covering head and shoulders (not italic)

mantis insect

mantissa part of logarithm

mantle cloak, covering, part of gas or oil lamp, part of earth between crust and core, or less common variant of **mantel**

mantlepiece less common variant of **mantelpiece**

Mantua Italian city (Italian name **Mantova**)

manuscript book or document written by hand, or author's original version of book or article submitted for publication

Manx cat (capital **M**)

many-sided (hyphen)

manzanilla dry sherry (not italic; lower-case **m**)

Maori (as noun) member of native people of New Zealand, or the language of this people; (as adjective) of this people or language (**-ao-**)

Mao Tse-tung Chinese statesman (Pinyin **Mao Zedong**)

Mapplethorpe, Robert US photographer (double **p**)

Maputo capital of Mozambique (former name **Lourenço Marques**)

maquis scrubby vegetation of Mediterranean coast, or French underground movement of World War II (often **Maquis** for the underground movement; compare **marquis**)

Mar. March (full stop)

marabou large stork, its feather, or fine silk

marabout Muslim holy man or shrine

Maracaibo Venezuelan port (**-aibo**)

maracas pair of percussion instruments (single **r**, single **c**)

maraschino cherry (lower-case **m**; single **r**; **-sch-**)

Marat, Jean Paul French revolutionary leader

marathon (**-thon**)

marbling mottled effect, e.g. on edges of book pages

Marburg German city, or German name for **Maribor** (**-burg**)

marc remains of pressed grapes, or brandy made from these (compare **mark** and **marque**)

MArch Master of Architecture

marchioness wife of marquess, or woman with rank of marquess (compare **marquise**)

march past (two words)

Marconi, Guglielmo Italian physicist

Mardi Gras the festival of Shrove Tuesday (capital **M** & **G**)

mare[1] female horse (compare **mayor**)

mare[2] large dry plain on surface of moon (capital **M** as part of name, as in *Mare Imbrium*; plural **maria**)

Mare see **de la Mare**

margarine (-gar-)

margarita tequila and lemon juice (compare **margarite** and **marguerite**)

margarite mineral (compare **margarita** and **marguerite**)

Margaux French red wine (-gaux)

margin (*typog.*) any of the four areas of blank space surrounding the text on a page

marginalia notes in margin of book, manuscript, etc. (not italic; plural noun)

marginalize (also **marginalise**; see -ize/-ise)

Margrethe queen of Denmark (-gr-)

marguerite flowering plant (-guer-; compare **margarite** and **margarita**)

Maria de' Medici French queen (lower-case **d**; apostrophe followed by space; also **Marie de Médicis**)

mariage de convenance marriage of convenience (italics; single **r**; plural *mariages de convenance*)

Mariánské Lázně Czech town (four diacritics; German name **Marienbad**)

Maribor Slovenian city (German name **Marburg**)

Marie Celeste spelling of *Mary Celeste* used in story by Arthur Conan Doyle

Marienbad German name for **Mariánské Lázně**

marijuana (also **marihuana**)

marinade liquid mixture with herbs or spices, or variant of **marinate**

marinate soak in marinade (also **marinade**)

marionette (single **r**, single **n**, double **t**)

marital of marriage (compare **martial**)

Maritime Provinces another name for **Atlantic Provinces**, often excluding Newfoundland (also **Maritimes**)

Marivaux, Pierre Carlet de Chamblain de French dramatist and novelist

marjoram (-jor-)

mark (the spelling used for most senses of the word with this sound, including 'model, type, or variation', in which sense it often has capital **M**, as in *a Mark 3 Cortina*: compare **marque** and **marc**)

Mark book of the Bible (not italic; abbreviation **Mk**)

markdown (noun; the verb is **mark down**)

marketed (not -tt-)

market gardening (two words)

Market Harborough English town (not -**brough**)

marketing (not -tt-)

marketplace (one word)

market research (two words)

Marks & Spencer department store (ampersand; not -'s)

mark-up (noun; the verb is **mark up**)

Marlborough English town (not -**brough**)

marlin fish, or variant of **marline**

marline rope (also **marlin**)

Marlow English town

Marlowe, Christopher English dramatist and poet (-**lowe**)

Marmara, Sea of Turkey (also **Marmora**)

marmite large cooking pot or individual covered soup dish (lower-case **m**)

Marmite trademark for yeast and vegetable extract (capital **M**)

Marmolada Italian mountain (not -**mal**-)

Marmora variant of **Marmara**

Maroc French name for **Morocco**

marque brand of product, especially a car, or emblem used to identify it, as in *the Jaguar marque* (compare **mark** and **mark**)

marquee large tent, or canopy over entrance to theatre, hotel, etc. (also **marquise** in the sense 'canopy'; compare **marquis**)

marquess British nobleman ranking between duke and earl (also **marquis**)

marquetry (the spelling **marqueterie** is not incorrect, but it is less common)

Márquez see **García Márquez**

marquis nobleman ranking above count in various countries, or variant of **marquess** (compare **marquee** and **maquis**)

marquise wife of marquis, woman with rank of marquis, gemstone, or variant of **marquee** in the sense 'canopy'

Marrakech Moroccan city (double **r**; also **Marrakesh**)

marriageable (**e** after **g**)

Marriner, Sir Neville British conductor (double **r**, single **n**)

Marriott hotel chain (double **r**, double **t**; compare **Marryat**)

marron glacé glazed sweet chestnut (italics; acute accent; plural *marrons glacés*)

marrowbone (one word)

Marryat, Frederick English novelist and naval officer (known as **Captain Marryat**; compare **Marriott**)

Marsala Sicilian port or dessert wine (the use of lower-case **m** for the wine is not incorrect, but it is less common)

Marseillaise French national anthem

Marseilles French city (French name **Marseille**)

marshal officer, arrange, assemble, or lead (single **l**; compare **martial**)

Marshall, Alfred English economist; **George Catlett** US general and statesman who proposed the Marshall Plan; **Sir John Ross** New Zealand politician (double **l**; compare **Martial**)

marshalled, marshalling (single **l** in US English)

Marshall Islands country

comprising 34 Pacific islands (not -**shal**)

Marshall Plan (capital **M** & **P**; not -**shal**)

Marshalsea former English court and prison (single **l**)

marshmallow sweet (one word)

marsh mallow plant (two words)

Martello tower (capital **M**)

marten mammal (compare **martin**)

Martens see **Doc Martens**

martial of war, soldiers, or military life (compare **marital** and **marshal**)

Martial Latin writer (full name **Marcus Valerius Martialis**; compare **Marshall**)

martial art (not **marshal**)

martial law (not **marshal**)

martin bird (compare **marten**)

Martin du Gard, Roger French writer

Martini trademark for Italian vermouth, or cocktail of gin and vermouth (the use of lower-case **m** for the cocktail is less common but not incorrect; however, the trademark must have capital **M**)

Martinique Caribbean island

Martinmas November 11 (single **s**)

martyr (-**tyr**; noun and verb: to avoid controversy, use instead of **martyrize** or **martyrise**)

marvel wonder (single **l**)

Marvell, Andrew English poet (double **l**)

marvelled, marvelling (single **l** in US English)

marvellous (single **l** in US English)

Marx, Karl German founder of modern communism

Marx Brothers family of US film comedians: **Chico** (real name **Leonard**), **Groucho** (real name **Julius**), **Harpo** (real name **Arthur**), and **Zeppo** (real name **Herbert**)

Marxism (capital **M**)

Mary biblical character, sister of

Martha (compare St **Mary** and St **Mary Magdalene**)

Mary, St biblical character, mother of Christ (see also **Our Lady** and **Virgin Mary**; compare **Mary** and St **Mary Magdalene**)

Mary I queen of England, half-sister of Elizabeth I, who succeeded her (also known as **Mary Tudor** or **Bloody Mary**; compare **Mary, Queen of Scots**)

Mary II queen of England, Scotland, and Ireland who ruled jointly with her husband William III

Mary Celeste official name of sailing ship mysteriously abandoned (see also *Marie Celeste*)

Marylebone station in London

Mary Magdalene, St biblical character, said to have been a prostitute (**-lene**; compare **Mary** and St **Mary**)

Mary, Queen of Scots Scottish monarch beheaded for plotting against English crown during reign of Elizabeth I (comma; also known as **Mary Stuart**; compare **Mary I**)

Mary Stuart see **Mary, Queen of Scots**

Mary Tudor see **Mary I**

masala mixture of spices used in Indian cookery (not italic)

Masaryk, Jan Czech statesman; **Tomáš Garrigue** Czech philosopher and statesman (**-ryk**)

masc. masculine

Mascagni, Pietro Italian composer (**-gn-**)

mascarpone Italian cream cheese (not italic)

masculine characteristic of men or boys, or denoting gender of nouns (compare **male**)

Masefield, John English poet and novelist (**Mase-**)

masjid Arab mosque (not italic; the variant **musjid** is less common but not incorrect)

mask covering for face, conceal, shield, cover, or variant of **masque**

masochism (**-soch-**)

mason person who works with stone (lower-case **m**)

Mason short for **Freemason** (capital **M**)

Masqat Arabic name for **Muscat**

masque dramatic entertainment of 16th and 17th centuries (also **mask**)

masquerade (not **mask-**)

Mass (capital **M** for religious service or choral music for this service)

Massachusetts US state (double **s** then single **s**; double **t**)

massacre (not **-er**)

Massenet, Jules Émile Frédéric French composer (double **s**, single **n**)

massif mass of rock or series of connected mountain peaks (not italic)

Massif Central mountainous region of France (capital **M** & **C**)

mass media television, radio, newspapers, and magazines as a collective means of communication reaching large numbers of people (often shortened to **media**: see that entry)

mastaba superstructure of ancient Egyptian tomb (also **mastabah**)

MasterCard trademark for credit card (one word; capital **M** & **C**)

masterclass (one word)

masterful domineering or imperious (to avoid controversy, do no use in place of **masterly**)

masterly showing exception skill, as in *a masterly performance*

mastermind (one word)

Master of the Rolls (capital **M** & **R**)

masterpiece (one word)

master plan (two words)

masterstroke (one word)

master switch (two words)

masthead (one word)

mastic (not -ick)

masturbate (not -ster-)

mat (the usual spelling for most senses of the word with this sound; see also **matt**; compare **matte**)

Matabeleland region of Zimbabwe

matador principal bullfighter, who kills bull (not italic; single **t**; -dor)

matchbox (one word)

matchlock (one word)

matchmaker (one word)

match point (two words)

matchstick (one word)

matchwood (one word)

matelot slang word for sailor (not italic)

matelote fish with wine sauce (not italic)

material substance, fabric, facts, physical, relevant, or important (compare **materiel**)

materialize (also **materialise**; see -ize/-ise)

materiel materials and equipment of organization, as opposed to **personnel** (also **matériel**; compare **material**)

matey (also **maty**)

Mathews, Charles English comedian (compare **Matthews**)

matinée daytime performance (not italic; acute accent)

matins church service (also **mattins**)

Matisse, Henri French artist (single **t**, double **s**)

matrix (plural **matrices** or **matrixes**)

matron of honour (no hyphens)

matt denoting a dull surface or finish (also **mat**, especially in US English; compare **matte**)

Matt. Matthew (full stop; not italic)

matte impure material produced during smelting, or mask used in films and television to blank out part of image (compare **mat** and **matt**)

Matterhorn mountain on border between Italy and Switzerland (French name **Mont Cervin**, Italian name **Monte Cervino**)

matter of fact (noun)

matter-of-fact (adjective)

Matthew book of the Bible (not italic; abbreviation **Mt** or **Matt.**)

Matthews, Sir Stanley English footballer (compare **Mathews**)

mattins variant of **matins**

maty variant of **matey**

matzo brittle biscuit of unleavened bread (not italic; also **matzoh**, **matza**, or **matzah**)

maudlin tearful or sentimental (compare **mawkish**)

Maudling, Reginald English politician

Maugham, W(illiam) Somerset English writer

Maulmain variant of **Moulmein**

Mau Mau secret political society in Kenya (two words)

Maundy denoting Thursday before Easter or money distributed by sovereign on that day (capital **M**; not -day)

Maupassant, Guy de French writer

Mauretania ship (compare **Mauritania**)

Maurier see **Du Maurier**

Mauritania African country (compare *Mauretania*)

Mauritius island state in Indian Ocean

Mauser trademark for gun (capital **M**; compare **mouser**)

mausoleum (plural **mausoleums** or **mausolea**)

mauvais quart d'heure brief unpleasant experience (italics)

maverick unbranded animal, or independent unorthodox person (lower-case **m**)

mawkish sentimental or nauseating (compare **maudlin**)

maximize (also **maximise**; see **-ize/ -ise**)

maximum (plural **maxima**)

may (in the sense 'be permitted', use instead of **can** for formality or politeness; see also **might**)

Maya Hindu goddess of illusion, or Central American Indian people whose ancient culture was characterized by outstanding achievements (compare **Maia**)

maybe (adverb, as in *maybe he's forgotten*)

may be (verb, as in *we may be late*)

Mayday international distress signal (one word; also **mayday**)

May Day May 1 (two words, but hyphenated when used before another noun, as in *May-Day celebrations*; capital **M** & **D**)

Mayence French name for **Mainz**

Mayer, Louis B(urt) US film producer, cofounder of **MGM** (compare **mayor**)

Mayfair district of London (one word)

mayflower (one word)

Mayflower ship in which Pilgrim Fathers sailed to America

mayfly (one word)

mayor civic head of municipal corporation, whether male or female (capital **M** in titles, as in *Mayor of London*; see also **Lord Mayor**; compare **mare** and **Mayer**)

mayoress wife or consort of mayor (note that this term is no longer officially used for a female mayor)

maypole (one word)

May queen (two words; capital **M**)

Mazarin, Jules Italian-born French cardinal and statesman (original name **Giulio Mazarini**)

maze complex network (compare **maize**)

mazurka (rarely **mazourka**)

mb millibar or millibars (no full stops)

MB Bachelor of Medicine (from Latin *Medicinae Baccalaureus*)

MBA Master of Business Administration

MBE Member of the Order of the British Empire

MC master of ceremonies

Mc- (names beginning with **Mc-** are alphabetized as if they began with **Mac-**)

MCC Marylebone Cricket Club

MCh Master of Surgery (from Latin *Magister Chirurgiae*)

MCom Master of Commerce

MCP male chauvinist pig

Md mendelevium (no full stop)

MD Doctor of Medicine (from Latin *Medicinae Doctor*); Maryland (US postal code)

MDF medium-density fibreboard

MDMA methylenedioxymeth-amphetamine (the drug ecstasy)

MDS Master of Dental Surgery

me first person singular pronoun used as object of verb or after preposition, as in *she refused to help me* or *she left with Peter and me*. In the latter case **me** is often wrongly replaced by **I**.

ME Maine (US postal code); myalgic encephalopathy (see that entry)

mea culpa acknowledgment of guilt (italics)

mead drink or meadow (compare **Mede**)

meagre (**-er** in US English)

mealie South African word for an ear of maize (also **mielie**; compare **mealy**)

meals on wheels (also **meals-on-wheels**)

mealtime (one word)

mealy resembling or containing meal or grain, mottled, or pale in complexion (compare **mealie**)

mealy-mouthed (hyphen)

mean (the spelling used for most senses of the word with this sound: compare **mien**)

means (use singular or plural verb in the sense 'medium, method, or instrument'; use plural verb in the sense 'resources or income')

means test (noun; two words)

means-tested (hyphen)

meantime (as noun) used in the phrase *in the meantime*; (as adverb) less common variant of **meanwhile**

mean time time at a particular place (capital **M** & **T** in names, as in **Greenwich Mean Time**)

meanwhile (as adverb) during the intervening period, or at the same time in another place; (as noun) less common variant of **meantime**)

measurable (not -eable)

meat animal flesh used as food (compare **meet** and **mete**)

meatball (one word)

Mecca joint capital (with **Riyadh**) of Saudi Arabia and most holy city of Islam, or any place that attracts many visitors (the use of lower-case **m** for the sense 'any place that attracts many visitors' is less common but not incorrect; Arabic name **Makkah** for the city)

mechanical another name for **camera-ready copy**

mechanize (also **mechanise**; see -ize/-ise)

Mechelen Belgian city (French name **Malines**, English name **Mechlin**)

MEd Master of Education

medal award (compare **meddle**)

medallist (single **l** in US English)

meddle interfere (compare **medal**)

meddler person who interferes (compare **medlar**)

Mede member of people who established SW Asian empire in 7th and 6th centuries B.C. (compare **mead**)

Médecins Sans Frontières international humanitarian aid organization (capital **M**, **S**, & **F**; -dec-; acute accent on first word and grave accent on last)

media a plural of **medium**, or short for **mass media** (to avoid controversy, use plural verb in all contexts, including references to the mass media as a single entity, as in *the media have been blamed for the breakdown of their marriage*)

mediaeval rare variant of **medieval**

mediate intervene in dispute (compare **meditate**)

Medicaid US health assistance programme for people of low income (capital **M**)

Medicare US, Canadian, or Australian health insurance programme (capital **M**)

Medici notable Italian family of 15th–17th centuries. Members are usually alphabetized under their first name (see **Catherine de' Medici** and **Maria de' Medici**). The Italian form of the name is **de' Medici**, with space after apostrophe; the French form of the name is **de Médicis**, with no apostrophe.

medicine (-dic-)

medieval (rarely **mediaeval**)

Medina Saudi Arabian holy city containing tomb of Mohammed (Arabic name **Al Madinah**)

mediocre (-cre)

meditate think deeply (compare **mediate**)

Mediterranean of Mediterranean Sea or surrounding area (single **t**, double **r**, -ean)

Mediterranean Sea inland sea between Europe, Africa, and Asia (capital **M** & **S**; single **t**, double **r**, -ean)

medium (plural **media** (see also that entry), which is preferred for most senses, or **mediums**, which is preferred for the sense 'spiritual intermediary')

medlar tree or its fruit (compare **meddler**)

Médoc district of France, or wine from this district (acute accent)

meerkat type of mongoose (not -cat)

meerschaum earthy mineral or tobacco pipe (not italic; lower-case m; -sch-)

meet come together, or archaic word for proper, fitting, or correct (compare **meat** and **mete**)

mega- million, as in *megahertz*; 2^{20}, as in *megabyte*; very large, as in *megalith*; or very important, as in *megastar* (abbreviation **M**)

Megaera one of the Furies in Greek mythology (compare **Megara**)

megalithic (lower-case m)

Megara Greek town (compare **Megaera**)

megaton one million tons, or explosive power equal to one million tons of TNT (not -tonne)

Mehemet Ali ruler of Egypt

Meissen German town, or porcelain made there (capital M; double s)

Meistersinger member of German guild of 15th and 16th centuries (not italic; capital M; one word; plural **Meistersinger** or **Meistersingers**)

meitnerium (symbol Mt)

Méjico Spanish name for **Mexico**

melancholy (-ch-)

Melanchthon, Philipp German Protestant reformer (-chth-; original name **Philipp Schwarzerd**)

Melanesia group of Pacific islands (not Melo-)

melange mixture (not italic; also **mélange**)

melatonin (not melo-)

Melba toast (capital M)

Melbourne Australian city (not -bur-)

Melburnian of Melbourne, or a person from Melbourne (also **Melbournian**)

melee brawl (not italic; also **mêlée**, but use both diacritics or none at all)

melodeon (also **melodion**)

melodrama (not mela-)

meltdown (noun; the verb is **melt down**)

melted past tense and usual form of the past participle of **melt**, also used adjectivally with reference to chocolate, butter, ice, snow, etc. (compare **molten**)

melting point (two words)

melting pot (two words)

Melton Mowbray English town

meltwater (one word)

Member of Parliament (capital M & P)

membranous (the variant **membraneous** is less common but not incorrect)

memento (not mom-; plural **mementos** or **mementoes**)

memento mori reminder of inevitability of death (not italic)

memo (no full stop; plural **memos**)

memoirs (not -oires)

memorabilia (plural noun)

memorandum (plural **memorandums** or **memoranda**)

memorize (also **memorise**; see -ize/-ise)

ménage people of household (not italic; acute accent; compare **manège**)

ménage à trois cohabiting couple plus lover (italics)

menagerie collection of animals (not italic; no accent; not -ery)

Mencken, H(enry) L(ouis) US journalist and literary critic (-nck-)

mendacity untruthfulness or falsehood (compare **mendicity**)

Mendel, Gregor Austrian monk and botanist

mendelevium (symbol **Md**)

Mendeleyev, Dmitri Ivanovich Russian chemist (also **Mendeleev**)

Mendelssohn, Felix German composer (double s, **-ohn**; full name **Jacob Ludwig Felix Mendelssohn-Bartholdy**)

mendicity begging (compare **mendacity**)

meneer South African title or term of address equivalent to **Mr** or **sir** (capital **M** when followed by name; **-eer**)

menhir standing stone (**-hir**)

Mennonite member of Protestant sect (double **n** then single **n**)

Menorca Spanish name for **Minorca**

Mensa constellation, or international society for people with high IQ (capital **M**)

mens rea criminal intention or knowledge that act is wrong (not italic)

menswear (one word; no hyphen)

mental handicap (use **learning difficulties** (or **learning disabilities**) instead to avoid offence)

mentholated containing menthol, as in *mentholated cigarettes* (compare **methylated**)

mentor (not **-er**)

menu (plural **menus**)

Menuhin, Yehudi US-born British violinist (**-uh-** in surname, **-hu-** in first name)

meow (also **miaow** or **miaou**)

MEP Member of the European Parliament (informal name **Euro MP**)

Mephistophelean (also **Mephistophelian**)

Mephistopheles devil to whom Faust sold his soul

Mephistophelian variant of **Mephistophelean**

Mercator projection (capital **M**; also **Mercator's projection**)

Mercedes-Benz motor manufacturer (hyphen)

mercenary (**-ary**)

mercerize (also **mercerise**; see **-ize/-ise**)

merchandise (never **-ize**)

Merchant Taylors' Company (**Tay-, -s'**)

Merchant Taylors' School (**Tay-, -s'**)

mercury (symbol **Hg**)

meretricious superficially attractive, or insincere (compare **meritorious**)

meridian (**-ian**)

meridional (**-ion-**)

Mérimée, Prosper French writer (two acute accents)

meringue (**-gue**)

merino sheep or wool (not **mar-**)

meritorious praiseworthy (compare **meretricious**)

merry-go-round (two hyphens)

merrymaking (one word)

Merthyr Tydfil Welsh town and county borough

mesmerize (also **mesmerise**; see **-ize/-ise**)

Mesolithic (capital **M**)

Mesolonghi variant of **Missolonghi**

Mesolóngion Modern Greek name for **Missolonghi**

Mesopotamia region of SW Asia (single **s**; not **Mesa-**)

Messerschmitt, Willy German aeronautical engineer (not **-idt**)

Messiaen, Olivier French composer (**-iae-**)

Messiah (capital **M**; italics as title of oratorio by Handel)

messianic (also **Messianic** with reference to the Messiah of the Bible)

Messrs plural of **Mr** (no full stop)

Met, the shortening of name

containing the word **Metropolitan**, notably the Metropolitan Police, London, or the Metropolitan Opera, New York City (capital **M**, no full stop; see also **Met Office**)

metabolize (also **metabolise**; see **-ize/-ise**)

metal hard solid substance such as iron or bronze (compare **mettle**)

metalled, metalling (single l in US English)

metallurgy (double l; -**ur**-)

metamorphosis (plural **metamorphoses**)

metastasize (also **metastasise**; see **-ize/-ise**)

mete distribute or allot, as in *mete out punishment* (compare **meat** and **meet**)

meteorology (-**eor**-)

meter measuring device, to measure with such a device, or US spelling of **metre**

Method acting (the use of lower-case **m** is less common but not incorrect)

Methodist member of Christian denomination, or denoting this denomination (capital **M**)

Methusaleh biblical patriarch, or large wine bottle (capital **M**; -**aleh**)

methylated containing methanol, as in *methylated spirits* (compare **mentholated**)

métier profession, trade, or speciality (not italic; acute accent)

Met Office the meteorological office of the UK (capital **M** & **O**; no full stop)

metre unit of length or rhythmic arrangement of syllables in verse (**meter** in US English)

metric of or involving the metre as a unit of length, as in *metric system*

metrical of or involving poetic metre, as in *metrical psalm*

metro underground railway system in various cities of the UK and elsewhere (often capital **M** in names; **métro** or **Métro** with reference to Paris or other French-speaking cities)

Metropolitan see **Met**

mettle courage or character, as in *on one's mettle* (compare **metal**)

Metz French city (-**tz**)

meunière describing fish fried in butter and served with lemon juice and parsley (not italic; grave accent)

Meurthe-et-Moselle French department (-**eur**-)

Meuse French department or European river (Dutch name **Maas** for the river)

mews stables converted into residential buildings (use singular or plural verb; compare **muse**)

Mexican wave (capital **M**)

Mexico North American country (Spanish name **Méjico**)

Mexico City capital of Mexico

mezzanine (double **z**, single **n** twice)

mezzo-soprano (hyphen; plural **mezzo-sopranos**)

mezzotint print made from engraved copper plate (one word)

MF medium frequency

mg milligram or milligrams (no full stop; no **s** in plural)

Mg magnesium (no full stop)

MGM Metro-Goldwyn-Mayer (film company)

Mgr manager; Monseigneur; Monsignor (no full stop)

MHz megahertz (capital **M** & **H**; no full stop)

MI Michigan (US postal code)

MI5 Military Intelligence, section five (no full stops or spaces)

MI6 Military Intelligence, section six (no full stops or spaces)

Miami US city and resort

Miami Beach US resort on island off Miami

miaow variant of **meow** (also **miaou**)

Mic. Micah (full stop; not italic)
Micah book of the Bible (not italic; abbreviation **Mic.**)
Micawber surname of character in Dickens' *David Copperfield*, hence any person who idles and trusts to fortune (capital **M**)
Micawberish (capital **M**)
Michaelmas September 29 (-**chael**-)
Michaelmas daisy (capital **M**)
Michelangelo Florentine artist (-**chel**-; full name **Michelangelo Buonarrotti**)
Michelin brand name of tyres, travel guides, etc. (capital **M**)
Michigan US state and lake (-**chi**-)
mickey used in the phrase *take the mickey*; Australian informal word for young bull; Canadian name for pocket-sized liquor bottle (lower-case **m**; also **micky** in phrase and in 'bull' sense)
Mickey short for **Mickey Finn** (capital **M**)
Mickey Finn drugged drink, or the drug itself (capital **M & F**)
Mickey Mouse Disney character, used figuratively in various adjectival senses, e.g. 'trivial' or 'mechanical' (not -**cky**; also **mickey mouse** in figurative use)
micky variant of **mickey** in phrase and in 'bull' sense
micro- one millionth, as in *microsecond*, or small (compare **macro-**)
microchip (no hyphen)
microclimate (no hyphen)
microeconomics (no hyphen)
microfiche sheet of film bearing miniaturized pages of books, newspapers, etc. (not italic)
microlight small aircraft (also **microlite**)
micrometer measuring instrument
micrometre one millionth of a metre (-**er** in US English;

abbreviation **μm**; former name **micron**)
microorganism (no hyphen)
microprocessor (no hyphen)
microscopic very small, or not large enough to be seen by the naked eye (compare **macroscopic**)
Microsoft trademark for computer operating system, software, etc. (capital **M**)
microwave (no hyphen)
microwaveable (also **microwavable**)
mid- attached with hyphen to words beginning with capital letter (e.g. *mid-Atlantic*), to numbers (as in *the mid-19th century*, *a man in his mid-fifties*), and in such phrases as *in mid-flight, in mid-sentence*, etc. However, there is usually no hyphen in well-established compound words (e.g. *midday, in midstream*). See also individual entries.
midair (no hyphen)
Midas in Greek legend, king with power to turn everything he touched to gold; used figuratively in the phrase *the Midas touch* (capital **M**)
mid-Atlantic (hyphen; capital **A**)
midbrain (no hyphen)
midday (no hyphen)
Middelburg Dutch city (not -**le**-, not -**berg**)
middle age (two words)
middle-aged (hyphen)
Middle Ages (broadly) the 5th–15th centuries A.D., or (narrowly) the second half of this period, the first half being called the **Dark Ages** (capital **M & A**)
middle-age spread (one hyphen; also **middle-aged spread**)
middle class (noun)
middle-class (adjective)
Middle Congo a former name for **Congo-Brazzaville**
middle distance (noun)
middle-distance (adjective)

Middle-earth fictional land created by J. R. R. Tolkien (hyphen; capital **M**, lower-case **e**)

Middle East the area around the E Mediterranean, including Israel, the Arab countries, etc. (see also **Far East** and **Near East**)

Middle England middle-class sector of English society (the use of lower-case **m** is less common but not incorrect)

Middle English English language from about 1100 to 1450 (capital **M** & **E**)

middleman (one word)

middle-of-the-road (three hyphens)

Middlesbrough English town (not **-borough**)

Middlesex former English county, now part of Greater London

Middle West another name for **Midwest**

midfield (no hyphen)

Midgard dwelling place of humankind in Norse mythology (also **Midgarth**)

Mid Glamorgan former Welsh county (two words)

midi denoting skirt or coat reaching to midcalf (see also **midi system**)

Midi the south of France

MIDI specification for electronic musical instruments, as in *MIDI synthesizer* (acronym of *musical instrument digital interface*; see also **MIDI system**)

midi system set of hi-fi equipment designed as single unit

MIDI system electronic music system with MIDI specification

midland denoting the central part of any country (lower-case **m**)

Midland of the Midlands (capital **M**)

Midlands, the central counties of England (capital **M**)

midlife crisis (no hyphen in first word)

Midlothian Scottish council area (one word)

mid-off cricket term (hyphen)

mid-on cricket term (hyphen)

Midsomer Murders TV drama series (not *-summer*)

Midsomer Norton English town (not **-summer**)

midstream (no hyphen)

midsummer middle of summer (no hyphen; lower-case **m**)

Midsummer's Day June 24 (capital **M** & **D**; also **Midsummer Day**)

midterm (no hyphen)

midway (no hyphen)

midweek (no hyphen)

Midwest N central part of USA (also **Middle West**)

midwife (no hyphen)

midwinter (no hyphen)

mielie variant of **mealie**

mien manner, bearing, or appearance (compare **mean**)

Mies van der Rohe, Ludwig German-born US architect (lower-case **v** & **d**)

MiG Soviet fighter aircraft (capital **M** & **G**, lower-case **i**)

might power, strength, or past tense of **may** (as in *they said we might leave* or *I thought it might rain*). As an indicator of possibility, **might** expresses greater doubt or less likelihood than **may** (e.g. *he might be innocent, but all the evidence is against him* versus *they may ask for proof of identity*). If the possibility no longer exists, use **might have** rather than **may have** (as in *she might have understood if you'd explained it more clearly*). For spelling, compare **mite**.

migraine (**-ne**)

migratory (not **-ery**)

mihrab niche in mosque showing direction of Mecca (not italic)

Míkonos Modern Greek name for **Mykonos** (acute accent)

milage less common variant of **mileage**

Milan Italian city (Italian name **Milano**)

milch cow source of easy income (not **milk**)

mileage (the spelling **milage** is not incorrect, but it is less common)

mileometer (the spelling **milometer** is not incorrect, but it is less common)

milestone (one word)

milieu surroundings (not italic)

militant aggressive or warring, or a militant person (lower-case **m**)

Militant short for **Militant Tendency**, or a member of Militant Tendency (capital **M**)

Militant Tendency group formerly operating within Labour Party (capital **M** & **T**)

militarize (also **militarise**; see **-ize/ -ise**)

military ranks see **ranks**

militate have influence or effect, as in *circumstances militated against our success* (compare **mitigate**)

milk float (two words)

milkman (one word)

milk round (two words)

milk shake (two words)

milksop (one word)

Milky Way band of light in night sky (capital **M** & **W**)

Millais, Sir John Everett English painter (compare **Millet** and **Millay**)

Millay, Edna St Vincent US poet (compare **Millais** and **Millet**)

millenarian (as adjective) of 1000, of a millennium, or of millenarianism; (as noun) adherent of millenarianism (double **l**, single **n**; also **millenary**)

millenarianism belief in future millennium following Christ's Second Coming (lower-case **m**)

millenary sum of 1000, or another word for **millennium** or **millenarian** (double **l**, single **n**; compare **millinery**)

millennial of a millennium (double **l**, double **n**)

millennium period of 1000 years, 1000th anniversary, or period of 1000 years following Christ's Second Coming (double **l**, double **n**; plural **millennia** or **millenniums**)

millepede variant of **millipede**

Millet, Jean François French painter (compare **Millais** and **Millay**)

milli- one thousandth, as in *milllitre* (abbreviation **m**)

millilitre (**-er** in US English; abbreviation **ml**, without full stop)

millimetre (**-er** in US English; abbreviation **mm**, without full stop)

millinery hats, or the making or selling of hats (double **l**, single **n**; compare **millenary**)

millionaire (the spelling **millionnaire** is not incorrect, but it is less common)

millipede (also **millepede**)

milometer less common variant of **mileometer**

Milošević, Slobodan Serbian politician

Milton Keynes English town and unitary authority

Milwaukee US city (single **l**; **-auk-**)

mimic (not **-ck**)

mimicked, mimicking (**-ck-**)

mimicry (**-cr-**)

mincemeat (one word)

mince pie (two words)

Mind mental health charity (not **MIND**)

Mindanao second largest island of the Philippines (**-nao**)

mind-bending (hyphen)

mind-reader (hyphen)

mind-set (hyphen)

mind's eye (two words; **-'s**)

mine detector (two words)

minefield (one word)

miner person who works in mine (compare **minor** and **mynah**)

mineralogy (not **-ology**)

minestrone soup (not italic; **-ne-** twice)

minesweeper (one word)

mini denoting something small of its kind (lower-case **m**)

Mini trademark for car (capital **M**; also **MINI**)

miniature (not **-nit-**)

miniaturize (also **miniaturise**; see **-ize/-ise**)

minibus (one word)

minicab (one word)

minimize (also **minimise**; see **-ize/-ise**)

minimum (plural **minima**)

miniseries (one word)

miniskirt (one word)

minister member of clergy, head of government department, or attend to the needs of (compare **minster**)

minke whale (**-ke**)

Minneapolis US city (double **n**; **-eap-**)

Minnelli, Liza US actress and singer (double **n**, double **l**; not **Lisa**)

Minnesota US state and river (double **n**; **-es-**)

minor lesser, person below age of legal majority, or music term (compare **miner** and **mynah**)

Minorca Mediterranean island (Spanish name **Menorca**)

minority see **majority**

Minos king of Crete in Greek mythology (**-os**)

Minotaur monster with bull's head and man's body in Greek mythology (capital **M**; **-aur**)

minster cathedral or large church (compare **minister**)

Minton denoting fine-quality porcelain (capital **M**)

minuet (not **-ette**)

minuscule (not **mini-**)

minus sign the symbol (–), usually set with a space before and after it when it indicates subtraction but with no space after it when it indicates a negative quantity, as in –5° (use **en dash** rather than **hyphen**)

minutiae (plural noun)

Mir Russian space station

mirky less common variant of **murky**

misanthrope person who dislikes other people (also **misanthropist**)

miscellaneous (**-sc-**; double **l**; not **-ious**)

mischievous (**-ie-**; not **-ious**)

misdemeanour (**-or** in US English)

mishear (no hyphen)

mishit (no hyphen)

mishmash (one word)

mislead (past tense and past participle **misled**)

misogynist person who dislikes women (**-gyn-**)

misplaced modifier participial phrase that directly precedes the subject of a verb but refers to something or somebody else, as in *born in 1940, her father was killed in action in World War II* (also **dangling participle**). The effect may be ambiguous or ludicrous, and such sentences should be rewritten. A similar error may occur with other adjectival phrases, as in *invisible to the naked eye, scientists were unaware of the existence of these organisms.*

miss (do not be tempted to add *not* after the verb in the sense 'regret loss or absence of' where it is not required, as in *people who go into residential care often miss having a home of their own*)

missal prayer book (not **-el**)

mis-sell (hyphen)

missel thrush variant of **mistle thrush**

misshapen (double **s**; no hyphen)

missionary (-ary)

missis variant of missus

Mississippi US state and river (double s twice, double p)

Missolonghi Greek town (also Mesolonghi; Modern Greek name Mesolóngion)

misspell (double s; no hyphen)

misspelt past tense and past participle of misspell (also misspelled)

misspend (double s; no hyphen)

misstate (double s; no hyphen)

missus (also missis)

mistakable (also mistakeable)

Mistinguett French entertainer (not -ette; original name Jeanne-Marie Bourgeois)

mistle thrush (two words; also missel thrush)

mistletoe (one word; not missel-)

mistral cold dry wind in S France (not italic; lower-case m)

MIT Massachusetts Institute of Technology

Mitchum, Robert US actor (-um)

mite small creature, thing, particle, or amount (compare might)

Mithras god of light in Persian mythology

Mithridates king of Pontus who waged wars against Rome

mitigate moderate, as in *mitigating circumstances* (compare militate)

Mitilíni Modern Greek name for Mytilene (the port)

mitre (-er in US English)

Mittelland Canal Germany (double t, double l)

Mitterrand, François Maurice Marie French statesman (double t, double r)

mixed metaphor incongruous combination of metaphors, often with ludicrous effect, as in *once we had cleared these hurdles it was all plain sailing*

mix-up (noun; the verb is mix up)

mizzenmast (one word; the spelling mizenmast is not incorrect, but it is less common)

Mk Mark (book of the Bible or model, type, etc.; no full stop; not italic)

mks units metric system of units based on metre, kilogram, and second, which forms the basis of SI units (see also cgs units)

ml millilitre or millilitres (no full stop; no s in plural)

MLA Member of the Legislative Assembly (of Northern Ireland)

MLitt Master of Letters (from Latin *Magister Litterarum*)

Mlle Mademoiselle (no full stop)

mm millimetre or millimetres (no full stop; no s in plural)

MM Military Medal

Mme Madame (no full stop)

MMR measles, mumps, and rubella (vaccine)

MMus Master of Music

Mn manganese (no full stop)

MN Merchant Navy; Minnesota (US postal code)

MNA Member of the National Assembly (of Quebec)

mnemonic aiding memory (compare pneumonic)

Mo molybdenum (no full stop)

MO Medical Officer; Missouri (US postal code)

moat water-filled ditch around castle (compare mote)

mobilize (also mobilise; see -ize/-ise)

Möbius strip (capital M; umlaut; -ius)

Moby-Dick novel by Herman Melville (hyphen; full title *Moby-Dick, or, The Whale*)

Moçambique Portuguese name for Mozambique

moccasin (double c, single s)

mocha dark coffee, coffee and

chocolate flavouring, or dark brown colour (lower-case **m**)

Mocha port in Yemen (also **Mokha**)

mock-heroic (hyphen)

mock turtle soup (three words)

mock-up (noun; the verb is **mock up**)

MOD Ministry of Defence

modal of mode, denoting type of verb, philosophy term, or fabric (compare **model** and **module**)

mode manner, fashion, scale of notes in music, etc. (not italic)

model (as noun) representation, standard, pattern, style, or person who poses for artist or displays clothes; (as verb) make model of or work as model (compare **modal** and **module**)

modelled, modelling (single l in US English)

Modern Greek language (capital **M** & **G**)

modernize (also **modernise**; see **-ize/-ise**)

Modigliani, Amedeo Italian artist

modiste fashionable dressmaker (not italic)

Modred rebellious knight and nephew of King Arthur in Arthurian legend (also **Mordred**)

module self-contained unit or item, unit of furniture, or course of study (compare **model**, **modal**, and **modulus**)

modulus physics or mathematics term (plural **moduli**; compare **module**)

modus operandi procedure (not italic; plural **modi operandi**)

modus vivendi compromise (not italic; plural **modi vivendi**)

Moët & Chandon champagne (diaeresis; ampersand)

Mogadishu capital of Somalia (also **Mogadiscio**)

Mogadon trademark for drug used to treat insomnia (capital **M**)

mogul important or powerful person (lower-case **m**)

Mogul member of Muslim dynasty of Indian emperors (capital **M**)

Mohammed variant of **Muhammad**

Mohammed Ali see **Mehemet Ali** (ruler of Egypt) and **Muhammad Ali** (US boxer)

Mohammedan former word for **Muslim**, never used by Muslims themselves

Mohave North American Indian people or language (also **Mojave**)

Mohave Desert variant of **Mojave Desert**

mohawk skating term, or US and Canadian name for **mohican** (lower-case **m**)

Mohawk North American Indian people or language, or US river

mohican hairstyle (lower-case **m**; US and Canadian name **mohawk**)

Mohican North American Indian people or language

Mohorovičić discontinuity boundary between earth's crust and mantle (capital **M**; diacritics)

moiety archaic word for half (**-oie-**)

moire fabric with watered pattern (not italic; no accent)

moiré (as adjective) having or denoting watered or wavelike pattern; (as noun) moiré pattern or moiré fabric (not italic; acute accent)

moisturize (also **moisturise**; see **-ize/-ise**)

Mojave variant of **Mohave**

Mojave Desert California, USA (also **Mohave Desert**)

Mokha variant of **Mocha**

molar (not **-er**)

molasses (single l)

mold US spelling of **mould**

Mold Welsh town

Moldau German name for **Moldavia** or **Vltava**

Moldavia former European principality, the W part of which remains a province of Romania (Romanian name **Moldova**, German name **Moldau**), or another name for **Moldova**

Moldova European country comprising the E part of the former principality of Moldavia (also **Moldavia**)

Molech variant of **Moloch**

molecular (not -er)

moleskin (one word)

Molière French dramatist (grave accent; real name **Jean-Baptiste Poquelin**)

mollusc (-usk in US English)

Molnár, Ferenc Hungarian writer

moloch Australian lizard (lower-case **m**)

Moloch biblical deity to whom children were sacrificed (also **Molech**)

Molotov cocktail (capital **M**)

molt US spelling of **moult**

molten a form of the past participle of **melt** chiefly used adjectivally with reference to metal, stone, etc. (compare **melted**)

Moluccas island group in Malay Archipelago (single l, double c; also **Molucca Islands**; former name **Spice Islands**)

molybdenum (symbol **Mo**)

MoMA Museum of Modern Art, New York City, USA (lower-case **o**)

Mombasa Kenyan port (single s)

momentary temporary or fleeting

momentous of great importance

momentum (not mem-)

Mona Lisa painting by Leonardo da Vinci (also *La Gioconda*)

monastery (-ery)

Mönchengladbach German city (one word; umlaut; former name **München-Gladbach**)

Monckton, Lionel English composer

Moncton Canadian city

Mondrian, Piet Dutch painter

Monegasque of Monaco, or a person from Monaco (no accent)

Monet, Claude French painter, whose works include *Water Lilies* (compare **Manet**)

monetary (-et-, -ary)

moneyed rich (also **monied**)

moneylender (one word)

moneymaking (one word)

moneys sums of money (also **monies**)

money-spinner (hyphen)

money's worth (two words; apostrophe)

mongol offensive former name for person with Down's syndrome (lower-case **m**)

Mongol person from Mongolia (capital **M**)

Mongolia Asian country (former name **Outer Mongolia**)

mongolism offensive former name for **Down's syndrome**

mongoose (plural **mongooses**)

monicker variant of **moniker**

monied variant of **moneyed**

monies variant of **moneys**

moniker slang word for name or nickname (also **monicker**)

monitor (not -er)

Monk, Thelonious US jazz pianist (not -nius)

monochrome (-chr-)

monocoque car body or aircraft fuselage (not italic)

monogram design of initials

monograph paper or book on single subject

monologue (-gue)

Monopolies and Mergers Commission former name for **Competition Commission**

monopolize (also **monopolise**; see -ize/-ise)

monopoly exclusive control of market, trade, etc. (lower-case **m**)

Monopoly trademark for board game (capital **M**)

Monro, Alexander Scottish anatomist (compare **Monroe** and **Munro**)

Monroe, James US statesman; **Marilyn** US actress (compare **Monro** and **Munro**)

Monseigneur title for French prelates and princes (italics)

Monsieur French equivalent of **Mr** (not italic; **-ieu-**; abbreviation **M.**)

Monsignor ecclesiastical title bestowed by the Pope (not italic)

montage picture composed by superimposition or juxtaposition of other elements (not italic)

Montagu family name of owners of **Beaulieu** estate

Montague family name of Romeo in Shakespeare's *Romeo and Juliet*

Montaigne, Michel Eyquem de French essayist

Mont Blanc highest mountain in Alps (not **Mount**; usually alphabetized under M rather than B)

Monte Carlo resort centre of Monaco (two words; **-te**)

Monte Cristo island featured in Dumas's *The Count of Monte Cristo* (not **Chr-**)

Montenegrin of Montenegro, or a person from Montenegro (not **-gran**)

Montenegro constituent republic of the **Union of Serbia and Montenegro** (one word)

Monterey US city in California

Monterrey city in Mexico

Montesquieu, Charles Louis de Secondat, Baron de French philosopher (**-ieu**)

Montessori method method of nursery education (capital **M** for first word; double **s**, single **r**)

Monteverdi, Claudio Italian composer (**-te-**, **-di**)

Montevideo capital of Uruguay (one word; **-te-**, **-deo**)

Montpelier US city in Vermont (single **l**)

Montpellier French city (double **l**)

Mont-Saint-Michel islet off NW France (two hyphens; compare **St Michael's Mount**)

Montserrat Caribbean island or Spanish mountain (one word; double **r**)

Moog trademark for electrophonic synthesizer (capital **M**)

moon (also **Moon** in astronomical contexts, referring to the satellite of the earth)

moonbeam (one word)

moon-faced (hyphen)

Moonie informal name for member of the **Unification Church**

moonlight (one word)

moonlighted past tense and past participle of **moonlight** (verb; compare **moonlit**)

moonlight flit (not **moonlit**)

moonlit (adjective; compare **moonlighted**)

moonshine (one word)

moonstone (one word)

Moor member of Muslim people of North Africa

Moore, Bobby British footballer; **Dudley** British actor and comedian; **Henry** British sculptor; **Sir John** British general (compare **More**)

moorhen (one word)

moose large deer (compare **mousse**)

moot point (not **mute**)

moral (as adjective) relating to distinction between right and wrong, adhering to conventional standards of conduct, or used in such phrases as *moral support* and *moral victory*; (as noun) lesson of fable (compare **morale** and **mortal**; see also **morals**)

morale spirit of optimism or

confidence, as in *boost their morale* (compare **moral**)

morals personal principles of behaviour in accordance with sense of right and wrong (compare **mores**)

morality being moral, or system of morals (compare **mortality**)

moralize (also **moralise**; see **-ize/-ise**)

Moral Rearmament former name for **Initiatives of Change** (also **Moral Re-Armament**; original name **Oxford Group**)

moratorium (plural **moratoria** or **moratoriums**)

Morava European river, or Czech name for **Moravia**

Moravia region of Czech Republic (Czech name **Morava**)

moray eel (lower-case **m**)

Moray Scottish council area

Moray Firth Scotland

mordant sarcastic, caustic, substance used to fix dye, or acid used to etch printing plate

mordent melodic ornament in music

Mordred variant of **Modred**

more see **comparative**

More, Hannah English writer; **Kenneth** English actor; **Sir Thomas** English statesman, humanist, and saint (compare **Moore**)

moreish (also **morish**)

morel edible fungus (single **r**, single **l**; compare **morrell**)

morello variety of cherry (single **r**, double **l**)

moreover (one word)

mores conventions embodying fundamental values of group (compare **morals**)

Moreton Bay Queensland, Australia (not **Morton**)

Moretonhampstead village in Devon (one word)

Moreton-in-Marsh town in Gloucestershire (not **-in-the-**)

Morgan le Fay wicked sorceress and half-sister of King Arthur in Arthurian legend (lower-case **l**; also **Morgain le Fay**)

morgue mortuary (not italic)

morgue haughtiness (italics)

MORI Market and Opinion Research Institute (no full stops; all capitals, as in *MORI poll*)

morish variant of **moreish**

Morland, George English painter (not **Moor-** or **More-**)

Mormon member of the **Church of Jesus Christ of Latter-day Saints**

morning-after pill (one hyphen)

morocco soft leather (lower-case **m**; single **r**, double **c**)

Morocco African country (capital **M**; single **r**, double **c**; French name **Maroc**)

morphine (also **morphia**)

morrell tall eucalyptus (double **r**, double **l**; compare **morel**)

Morris chair (capital **M**)

morris dance (lower-case **m**)

Morse code (capital **M**, lower-case **c**)

mortal subject to or causing death, or a human being (compare **moral**)

mortality being mortal, number of deaths, or humankind (compare **morality**)

mortar (not **-er**)

mortarboard (one word)

mortgage (**-tg-**)

mortgagee lender

mortgagor borrower (not **-er**)

mortise (the spelling **mortice** is not incorrect, but it is less common)

Morton, Jelly Roll US jazz pianist (not **Moreton**)

mosaic design made up of small coloured pieces, or plant disease (lower-case **m**)

Mosaic of Moses or his laws (capital **M**)

Moscow capital of Russia (Russian name **Moskva**)

Mosel German name for **Moselle** (the river)

Moseley, Henry Gwyn-Jeffreys English physicist (compare **Mosley**)

Moselle French department, European river, or German white wine (the use of lower-case **m** for the wine is less common but not incorrect; German name **Mosel** for the river)

Moses biblical patriarch (the possessive form is traditionally **Moses'**)

Moses basket (capital **M**; no apostrophe)

Moskva Russian name for **Moscow**

Moslem variant of **Muslim**

Mosley, Sir Oswald Ernald British politician (compare **Moseley**)

mosquito (plural **mosquitoes** or **mosquitos**)

most see **superlative**

MOT compulsory annual test for road vehicles (originally an abbreviation of Ministry of Transport, now part of the Department for Transport in the UK)

mote tiny speck (compare **moat**)

Mothering Sunday another name for **Mother's Day** in the UK and South Africa

mother-in-law (plural **mothers-in-law**)

motherland (one word)

mother-of-pearl (two hyphens)

Mother's Day fourth Sunday in Lent (in the UK and South Africa) or second Sunday in May (in the USA, Canada, and Australia) (**-'s** not **-s'**; also **Mothering Sunday** in the UK and South Africa)

Mother Teresa see **Teresa**

motif distinctive theme of composition, or decorative symbol, name, etc. added to garment

motive reason for particular course of action, or causing motion, as in *motive force*

mot juste appropriate word or expression (italics; plural *mots justes*)

motley (**-ley**)

motocross (not **motor-**)

motorbike (one word)

motorboat (one word)

motor car (the spelling **motorcar** is not incorrect, but it is less common)

motorcycle (one word)

motorize (also **motorise**; see **-ize/-ise**)

motor neurone disease (three words)

Motown trademark for type of popular music (capital **M**)

motto (plural **mottoes** or **mottos**)

moujik variant of **muzhik**

mould (**-ol-** in US English)

Moulmein port in Myanmar (also **Maulmain**)

moult (**-ol-** in US English)

mountain bike (two words)

mountebank (**-te-**)

Mountie informal name for member of Royal Canadian Mounted Police (the spelling **Mounty** is not incorrect, but it is less common)

Mourne Mountains Northern Ireland

mousaka less common variant of **moussaka**

mouse small rodent, timid person, or computer device (plural **mice** in all senses; compare **mousse**)

mouser cat (compare **Mauser**)

mousetrap (one word)

mousey variant of **mousy**

moussaka (the spelling **mousaka** is not incorrect, but it is less common)

mousse light dessert or savoury dish, bubbles on top of sparkling wine, or foamy styling or shaving product (compare **mouse** and **moose**)

Moussorgsky variant of **Mussorgsky**

moustache (**mus-** in US English)
mousy (also **mousey**)
mouthful (not **-full**; plural
   mouthfuls)
mouth organ (two words)
mouthpiece (one word)
mouthwash (one word)
mouthwatering (one word)
movable (also **moveable**, which is
   the preferred spelling in legal senses
   relating to property)
mowed past tense and past participle
   of **mow** (also **mown**)
Mozambique African country
   (Portuguese name **Moçambique**)
Mozart, Wolfgang Amadeus
   Austrian composer
mozzarella (double **z**, single **r**,
   double **l**)
MP Member of Parliament (plural
   MPs)
mpg miles per gallon
mph miles per hour
MPhil Master of Philosophy
MPV multipurpose vehicle
Mr title placed before man's name
   (no full stop)
MRCOG Member of the Royal
   College of Obstetricians and
   Gynaecologists
MRCP Member of the Royal College
   of Physicians
MRCS Member of the Royal College
   of Surgeons
MRCVS Member of the Royal
   College of Veterinary Surgeons
MRI magnetic resonance imaging
MRP manufacturers' recommended
   price
Mrs title placed before married
   woman's name (no full stop)
MRSA methicillin-resistant
   Staphylococcus aureus (the so-called
   hospital superbug)
Ms title placed before woman's name
   when marital status is unknown or
   irrelevant (no full stop)

MS manuscript (also **ms.**; plural
   MSS or **mss.**); Master of Surgery;
   Mississippi (US postal code);
   multiple sclerosis
MSc Master of Science
MS-DOS trademark for disk
   operating system developed by
   Microsoft (hyphen)
MSP Member of the Scottish
   Parliament
MSS manuscripts (also **mss.**)
Mswahili variant of **Swahili**
   (member of people; plural
   Waswahili)
Mt Matthew (book of the Bible; no
   full stop; not italic); meitnerium
   (no full stop); Mount (no full stop)
MT Montana (US postal code)
MTech Master of Technology
muckraking (one word)
mucous (adjective)
mucus (noun)
mud bath (two words)
muddleheaded (one word)
mud flat (two words)
mudguard (one word)
mudpack (one word)
mudslinging (one word)
muesli breakfast food (not italic;
   -ue-)
muezzin official at mosque (not
   italic; double **z**)
mufti civilian dress, or Muslim legal
   expert (not italic; **-ti**)
Mugabe, Robert Zimbabwean
   politician (**-be**)
Muhammad founder of Islam (also
   Mohammed or **Mahomet**)
Muhammad Ali US boxer (original
   name **Cassius Clay**)
Muhammadan former word for
   Muslim, never used by Muslims
   themselves
Mühlhausen German name for
   Mulhouse (umlaut; **-hlh-**)
mujaheddin fundamentalist Muslim
   guerrillas (plural noun; also

mujahideen or **mujahidin**; the use of capital **M** is less common but not incorrect)

mujik variant of **muzhik**

Mukden former name for **Shenyang**

mulatto (plural **mulattos** or **mulattoes**)

mulberry (single **l**)

Mulhouse French city (German name **Mühlhausen**)

mullah Muslim scholar (not italic; the spelling **mulla** is not incorrect, but it is less common)

Muller, Hermann Joseph US geneticist

Müller, Max British scholar; **Johannes Peter** German physiologist; **Paul Hermann** Swiss chemist (umlaut)

mulligatawny (-iga-)

multangular (also **multiangular**)

multi- (usually attached without hyphen)

multiaccess (no hyphen)

multiangular variant of **multangular**

multicoloured (no hyphen; -or- in US English)

multicultural (no hyphen)

multimillionaire (no hyphen)

multinational (no hyphen)

multipartite (no hyphen)

multi-part stationery (hyphen)

multiplication sign the symbol (×), usually set with a space before and after it, also used in taxonomic names to indicate a hybrid

multipurpose (one word)

multiracial (one word)

multistorey (one word)

multitasking (one word)

multi-user (hyphen)

Mumbai official name for **Bombay**

mumbo jumbo (two words)

Munch, Edvard Norwegian painter (no umlaut; not **Edward**)

Munchausen English spelling of **Münchhausen**

Munchausen's syndrome (capital **M**; no umlaut; single **h**; apostrophe)

München German name for **Munich** (umlaut)

München-Gladbach former name for **Mönchengladbach** (umlaut; hyphen)

Münchhausen, Baron German soldier famous for exaggerated tales (umlaut; double **h**; English spelling **Munchausen**, with no umlaut and single **h**)

Munich German city (German name **München**)

Munro any mountain peak over 3000 feet high (plural **Munros**)

Munro, H(ector) H(ugh) Scottish writer (pen name **Saki**; compare **Monro** and **Monroe**)

Munster Irish province

Münster German city (umlaut)

muntjac small Asian deer (also **muntjak**; not -jack)

murderer (may be used for males and females)

murderess (use **murderer** instead)

Murdoch, Dame Iris British writer; **Rupert** Australian-born US media entrepreneur (not -ock)

murky (the spelling **mirky** is not incorrect, but it is less common)

murmur (-ur- twice)

Murray Australian river

Murray, Sir Gilbert Australian-born British classical scholar; **Sir James Augustus Henry** Scottish lexicographer (compare **Murry**)

Murrumbidgee Australian river (double **r**; -ee)

Murry, John Middleton English writer (compare **Murray**)

MusB Bachelor of Music (from Latin *Musicae Baccalaureus*)

muscadel another name for **muscatel** (also **muscadelle**)

Muscadet grape or wine (the spelling **muscadet**, with of lower-case **m**, is less common but not incorrect)

muscat grape, or another name for **muscatel** (wine made from this grape) (capital **M** in wine names, e.g. *Muscat de Beaumes de Venise*)

Muscat capital of Oman (Arabic name **Masqat**)

muscatel wine, or another name for **muscat** (grape from which this wine is made) (also **muscadel** or **muscadelle** for the grape and wine; also **muscat** for the wine)

muscavado less common variant of **muscovado**

muscle body tissue (compare **mussel**)

muscovado raw sugar (the spelling **muscavado** is not incorrect, but it is less common)

muscovite mineral (lower-case **m**)

Muscovite person from Moscow, or archaic word for Russian

Muscovy former Russian principality, or archaic name for Russia or Moscow

muscular dystrophy (not **dis-**)

MusD Doctor of Music (from Latin *Musicae Doctor*)

muse ponder, or source of inspiration for creative artist (lower-case **m**; compare **mews**)

Muses nine goddesses of the arts and sciences in Greek mythology (capital **M**)

music box (also **musical box**)

music hall (no hyphen unless used before another noun, as in *a music-hall song*)

musjid less common variant of **masjid**

Muslim of Islam, or a follower of that religion (in modern use **Muslim** is generally preferred to the variant **Moslem**; see also **Mahometan**, **Mohammedan**, **Muhammadan**, and **Mussulman**)

MusM Master of Music (from Latin *Musicae Magister*)

mussel shellfish (compare **muscle**)

Mussolini, Benito Italian Fascist dictator (known as **Il Duce**)

Mussorgsky, Modest Petrovich Russian composer (**-gsky**; also **Moussorgsky**)

Mussulman archaic word for **Muslim**

mustache US spelling of **moustache**

mustachio humorous word for bushy or elaborate moustache (not **mou-**; plural **mustachios**)

mustachioed (not **-o'd**)

mustard and cress (three words)

must've contraction of **must have** (**'ve** not **of**)

mutatis mutandis the necessary changes having been made (italics)

mute (to avoid offence, do not use with reference to people who cannot speak because of physical or mental disorder; see also **deaf-and-dumb**, **deaf-mute**, and **deaf without speech**)

mutual (to avoid controversy, use **common** or **shared** instead where appropriate, but note that the phrase *a mutual friend* is sufficiently well-established to be generally acceptable)

Muybridge, Eadweard British-born US photographer (original name **Edward James Muggeridge**)

Muzak trademark for recorded light music played in shops, factories, etc. (capital **M**)

muzhik Russian peasant (not italic; also **moujik** or **mujik**)

MW medium wave; megawatt or megawatts (capitals; no full stops)

myalgic encephalopathy full name for the disorder known as **ME** (former name **myalgic encephalomyelitis**)

Myanmar SE Asian country (former name **Burma**)

Mycenae ancient Greek city (**-e-** then **-ae**)

Mycenaean of Mycenae or its ancient civilization (**-e-** then **-aea-**)

Mykonos Greek island in Aegean Sea (Modern Greek name **Míkonos**)

My Lai Vietnamese village, scene of massacre (two words)

mynah bird (also **myna**; compare **miner** and **minor**)

myopia short sight (**my-**)

myriad innumerable, as in *myriad reasons*, or an indefinitely large number, as in *a myriad of reasons* (**y** then **i**)

myrrh (**-rrh**)

Mysore former name (1956–73) for **Karnataka**

mystic person who achieves mystical experience, or variant of **mystical** (compare **mystique**)

mystical occult, metaphysical, or surpassing human understanding

mystique aura of mystery and power (compare **mystic**)

mythical imaginary, fictitious, or of a myth or myths

mythological of mythology, or of a myth or myths

Mytilene Greek port on Lesbos, or former name for **Lesbos** (Modern Greek name **Mitilíni** for the port)

myxomatosis rabbit disease (not **mix-**)

N

N nitrogen (no full stop); north or North

n. noun

'n' and, as in *fish 'n' chips* (two apostrophes, not quotation marks; sometimes no space before or after, as in *rock'n'roll*, but it is incorrect to have a space before and not after, or vice versa)

Na sodium (no full stop; from Latin *natrium*)

n/a not applicable

NAAFI organization providing canteens, shops, etc. for military personnel, or one of these canteens, shops, etc. (acronym of Navy, Army, and Air Force Institutes; no full stops; also **Naafi**)

naan another name for **nan bread**

naartjie South African word for tangerine (double **a**; **-tj-**)

Nabokov, Vladimir Vladimirovich Russian-born US novelist (not **-bak-**)

nacho Mexican snack (not italic; plural **nachos**)

nacre mother-of-pearl (not **-er**)

nacreous (not **-ious**)

nadir lowest point (compare **zenith**)

naevus birthmark (plural **naevi**; **nev-** in US English)

Nagasaki Japanese port

Nah. Nahum (full stop; not italic)

Nahuatl Central American or Mexican Indian people or language (**-uatl**)

Nahum book of the Bible (not italic; abbreviation **Nah.**)

naiad water nymph in Greek mythology, insect larva, or aquatic plant (**-aia-**)

naïf rare variant of **naive** (diaeresis)

nailbrush (one word)

nailfile (also **nail file**)

nail polish (two words)

Nairobi capital of Kenya (**Nai-**)

naive (also **naïve**, with diaeresis, but rarely **naïf**)

naivety (the variant **naïveté** – the original French spelling, with diaeresis and acute accent – is less common in English; the hybrid forms **naïvety** and **naiveté** are best avoided)

namable (also **nameable**)

namby-pamby (hyphen)

nameable variant of **namable**

namecheck (one word)

name-dropping (hyphen)

Namen Flemish name for **Namur**

nameplate (one word)

names see **aircraft**, **boat**, **ship**, **binomial**, **Latin names**, **titles of periodicals**, **titles of works**, etc.

namesake (one word)

Namibia African country (also **South West Africa**)

Namur Belgian town and province (Flemish name **Namen**)

nan bread (also **naan**)

Nanjing Chinese port (also **Nanking** or **Nan-ching**)

nano- one thousand-millionth, as in *nanosecond*, or extremely small (single **n**)

Nansen, Fridtjof Norwegian explorer, statesman, and scientist (not **-son**)

naphtha (**-phth-**)

Naples Italian city (Italian name **Napoli**; ancient name **Neapolis**)

Napoleon I emperor of France (French spelling **Napoléon**, with acute accent; see also **Bonaparte**)

Napoli Italian name for **Naples**

narcissus (lower-case **n** in general use, *Narcissus* is the genus name; plural **narcissi** or **narcissuses**)

Narcissus beautiful youth in Greek mythology

Narraganset North American Indian people or language (also **Narragansett**)

Narragansett Bay inlet of Atlantic Ocean in Rhode Island, USA (double **t**)

narrator (not **-er**)

narrow boat (two words)

narrow-minded (hyphen)

narwhal arctic whale with tusk in male (the variants **narwal** and **narwhale** are less common but not incorrect)

NASA National Aeronautics and Space Administration (no full stops; all capitals)

nasalize (also **nasalise**; see **-ize/-ise**)

Nash, John English town planner and architect; **Ogden** US poet; **Richard** English dandy (known as **Beau Nash**); **Sir Walter** New Zealand Labour statesman

Nashe, Thomas English pamphleteer, satirist, and novelist (also **Nash**)

Nassau capital of the Bahamas or region of Germany

nasturtium (not **-ian**)

NAS/UWT National Association of Schoolmasters/Union of Women Teachers

Natal former South African province, replaced by KwaZulu/Natal in 1994, or Brazilian port

National Archives, The UK government office, formed in 2003, incorporating the Public Record Office and Historical Manuscripts Commission

National Curriculum (capital **N** & **C** with reference to that of England and Wales)

National Front (capital **N** & **F**)

National Gallery London (capital **N** & **G**)

national grid (lower-case **n** & **g**)

national insurance (lower-case **n** & **i**)

nationalize (also **nationalise**; see **-ize/-ise**)

national park (capital **N** & **P** as part of name, as in *Snowdonia National Park*)

National Portrait Gallery London (capital **N** & **G**)

national service (lower-case **n** & **s**)

National Trust (capital **N** & **T**)

nation-state (hyphen)

nationwide (one word)

native (to avoid offence, do not use in the sense 'member of a non-White indigenous people')

Native American another name for **American Indian**

nativity birth or origin (lower-case **n**)

Nativity the birth of Jesus Christ (capital **N**)

Nativity play (capital **N**)

NATO North Atlantic Treaty Organization (no full stops; also **Nato**)

naturalist botanist or zoologist (compare **naturist**)

naturalize (also **naturalise**; see **-ize/ -ise**)

naturist nudist (compare **naturalist**)

NatWest National Westminster Bank (one word; capital **N** & **W**)

naught archaic or literary word for nothing or nothingness, or used in the phrase *set at naught* meaning 'disregard or disdain' (compare **nought**)

nausea (not **-ia**)

nauseate (not **-iate**)

nauseous (not **-ious**)

Nausicaä princess who helped shipwrecked Odysseus in Greek mythology (also **Nausicaa**, without diaeresis)

Navaho North American Indian people or language (also **Navajo**)

naval of a navy or ships (compare **navel**)

Navarre former European kingdom (Spanish name **Navarra**)

nave centre of church or wheel (compare **knave**)

navel depression on abdomen (compare **naval**)

navel orange (not **naval**)

navigable (not **-atable**)

navigator (not **-er**)

Návpaktos Greek name for **Lepanto** (the port)

navvy labourer (double **v**)

navy branch of armed services comprising warships and their crews (sometimes capital **N** with reference to a particular national navy as in *the Spanish Navy* or *join the Navy*, but the lower-case form is more common; always capital **N** in names, as in *the Royal Navy*)

navy blue (lower-case **n**; no hyphen unless used before another noun, as in *a navy-blue jacket*)

nay no (compare **née** and **neigh**)

Nazi (capital **N**)

Nazism (also **Naziism**)

Nb niobium (no full stop)

NB note well (from Latin *nota bene*)

NBA Net Book Agreement

NC North Carolina (US postal code)

NCO noncommissioned officer

nd no date (of publication; also **n.d.**)

Nd neodymium (no full stop)

ND North Dakota (US postal code)

Ndjamena capital of Chad (also **N'djamena**; former name **Fort Lamy**)

Ne neon (no full stop)

NE Nebraska (US postal code); northeast

né see **née**

n/e new edition

Neal, John US writer; **Patricia** US actress (compare **Neale**, **Neil**, and **Neill**)

Neale, Edward Vansittart English social reformer; **John Mason** English hymnist (compare **Neal**, **Neil**, and **Neill**)

Neanderthal man (capital **N**; not **-tal**)

Neapolis ancient name for **Naples**

Neapolitan of Naples, or a person from Naples (not **Nap-**)

Neapolitan ice cream (capital **N**)

nearby (adjective and adverb; also **near by** for the adverb)

near-death experience (one hyphen)

Near East another name for the **Middle East**, or a former name for the **Balkan States** (see also **Far East**)

nearside (one word)

NEB New English Bible (not italic)

Nebuchadnezzar biblical king, or large wine bottle (capital **N**; also **Nebuchadrezzar** for the king)

nebula (plural **nebulae** or **nebulas**)

nebulize (also **nebulise**; see **-ize/ -ise**)

necessary (single **c**, double **s**; **-ary**)

Neckar German river

Necker, Jacques French financier and statesman

nectar (-ar)

Nederland Dutch name for the **Netherlands**

née indicating maiden name of married woman, as in *Anne Smith née Jones* (not italic; also **nee**; compare **nay** and **neigh**). To avoid confusion or controversy, use **born** instead to indicate the real or original name of a woman known by a pseudonym. Derived from a feminine French word, **née** should never be used of a man; its masculine form, **né**, is also best avoided.

need want or require (compare **knead** and **kneed**)

needlecraft (one word)

needlework (one word)

ne'er-do-well (apostrophe; two hyphens)

nefarious (-fari-)

Nefertiti Egyptian queen (rarely **Nofretete**)

negative see **double negative**

Negev semidesert region of Israel (the variant **Negeb** is less common but not incorrect)

neglectful careless or heedless (compare **negligent**)

negligee (not italic; no accent)

negligence (not -ance)

negligent neglecting responsibilities or duties (compare **neglectful** and **negligible**)

negligible (not -able; compare **negligent**)

negotiable (not -cia-, not -ible)

negotiate (not -cia-)

Negress offensive former word for a female Black person

Negro (plural **Negroes**; replace with **Black person** or more specific term to avoid offence)

Negro spiritual (capital N; the use of **Negro** in this context is generally acceptable)

Neh. Nehemiah (full stop; not italic)

Nehemiah book of the Bible (not italic; abbreviation **Neh.**)

Nehru, Jawaharlal Indian statesman; **Motilal** Indian nationalist, lawyer, and journalist (known as **Pandit Nehru**)

neigh make sound of horse (compare **nay** and **née**)

neighbour (-or in US English)

neighbourhood (-or- in US English)

neighbourly (-or- in US English)

Neil, Andrew Scottish journalist and broadcaster (compare **Neill**, **Neal**, and **Neale**)

Neill, A(lexander) S(utherland) Scottish educationalist and writer (compare **Neil**, **Neal**, and **Neale**)

Neilson, Donald English murderer (known as **the Black Panther**; compare **Nilsen**, **Nielsen**, and **Nilsson**)

neither use singular verb with singular subject, as in *neither child was wearing a coat* and *neither of the children was wearing a coat*. In the **neither . . . nor** construction, use singular verb if both subjects are singular (as in *neither France nor Germany has signed the agreement*) and use plural verb if one or both subjects are plural (as in *neither her brother nor her parents were present*). Do not use **or** in place of **nor** in this construction.

nem. con. unanimously (not italic; from Latin *nemine contradicente* 'no-one contradicting')

Nemesis Greek goddess of retribution, or any agency of retribution (also **nemesis** in the sense 'any agency of retribution')

neo- (attached without hyphen, except to words beginning with **o** or capital letter; in the latter case the prefix often has capital **N**, as in *Neo-Darwinism*)

neoclassicism (no hyphen; lower-case **n**)

neocolonialism (no hyphen; lower-case **n**)

Neo-Darwinism (hyphen; capital **N** & **D**)

neodymium (symbol **Nd**)

Neo-Lamarckism (hyphen; capital **N** & **L**)

Neolithic (no hyphen; capital **N**)

neon (symbol **Ne**)

neonatal (no hyphen)

neo-orthodoxy (hyphen)

neophyte (no hyphen; not **-ite**)

Neo-Platonism (also **Neoplatonism**)

ne plus ultra the extreme or perfect point or state (italics)

neptunium (symbol **Np**)

nerd (the spelling **nurd** is not incorrect, but it is less common)

Nereid sea nymph in Greek mythology, or satellite of Neptune (capital **N**; **-eid**)

nerve-racking (hyphen; the variant **nerve-wracking** is controversial)

Nesbit, E(dith) British writer of children's books (single **t**)

Nestlé food-producing company (acute accent)

net (also **nett** in the sense 'after deductions'; lower-case **n** in all senses, including short form of Internet)

Netanyahu, Benjamin Israeli politician (also **Binyamin**)

netball (one word)

Net Book Agreement former agreement prohibiting bookshops from selling books at discount

Netherlands, the European country (lower-case **t**; also **Holland**; Dutch name **Nederland**)

netiquette informal code of behaviour on Internet (single **t** then double **t**)

nett variant of **net** in the sense 'after deductions'

nettle rash (two words)

network (one word)

Neuchâtel Swiss town and canton, or wine made there

Neufchâtel French town, or cheese made there

Neumann see **von Neumann**

neuralgia (**neur-**)

neurone (also **neuron**)

neurosis (plural **neurosis**)

neurosurgery (no hyphen)

neurotransmitter (no hyphen)

neuter (not **-re**)

neutralize (also **neutralise**; see **-ize/ -ise**)

never (do not use as emphatic substitute for **not** in formal writing)

never-ending (hyphen)

nevermore (one word)

never-never (hyphen)

Nevers French city (**-ers**)

nevertheless (one word)

new not old (compare **knew**)

New Age (capital **N** & **A**; no hyphen, even when used before another noun, as in *New Age travellers*)

Newbery, John English publisher (single **r**; compare **Newbury**)

newborn (one word)

Newbury English town (compare **Newbery**)

Newcastle-under-Lyme town in Staffordshire (two hyphens)

Newcastle upon Tyne port and unitary authority in Tyne and Wear (no hyphens; not ... **on** ...)

newcomer (one word)

New Deal domestic policies of Franklin D. Roosevelt (capital **N** & **D**)

newel post (two words)

New English Bible (not italic)

newfangled (one word)

New Forest England (capital **N** & **F**)

new-found (hyphen)

Newfoundland island and province

of Canada, or breed of dog (one word; capital **N**)

New Guinea Pacific island comprising the Indonesian province of **Irian Jaya** and the main part of **Papua New Guinea**

Newham borough of Greater London (not **-wnh-**)

Newhaven English port and resort in East Sussex

New Haven US city and port in Connecticut

New Hebrides former name for **Vanuatu**

new-laid egg (one hyphen)

newlywed (one word)

newmarket card game or 19th-century riding coat (lower-case **n**)

Newmarket English town

Newnham College Cambridge (not **-wh-**)

New Orleans US city (no accent; compare **Orléans**)

Newquay town in Cornwall (one word)

newsagency Australian name for newsagent's shop (one word)

news agency organization that collects news reports for periodicals (two words)

newsagent (one word)

newscaster (one word)

newsflash (one word)

newsgroup (one word)

newsletter (one word)

New South Wales Australian state (three words)

newspaper (one word)

newspaper titles see **titles of periodicals**

newspeak (one word; lower-case **n**)

newsprint (one word)

newsreader (one word)

newsreel (one word)

newsroom (one word)

news-sheet (hyphen)

New Style denoting date reckoned

according to **Gregorian calendar**, approximately eleven days different from **Old Style**

newsworthy (one word)

New Testament (not italic; capital **N** & **T**)

newton unit of force (lower-case **n**)

Newton surname and common place name in the British Isles (compound place names beginning with **Newton** are usually two words in England and one word in Scotland; compare **Newtown**)

Newton, Sir Isaac English mathematician and physicist

Newton Abbot English town (two words)

Newton-le-Willows English town (two hyphens; lower-case **l** in middle word)

Newtown common place name in the British Isles, notably a Welsh town in Powys (most compound place names beginning with **Newtown** are in Ireland and are one word; compare **Newton**)

Newtownabbey town and district of Northern Ireland (one word)

Newtown St Boswells Scottish village (three words)

new-variant CJD new-variant Creutzfeldt-Jakob disease: another name for **variant CJD** (abbreviation **nvCJD**)

new wave any movement in art, politics, etc. that breaks with traditional ideas (lower-case **n** & **w**)

New Wave movement in French cinema of the 1960s or rock music of the late 1970s (capital **N** & **W**)

New World the Americas (capital **N** & **W**; compare **Old World**)

New Year's Day January 1 (apostrophe)

New Year's Eve December 31, especially the evening of this day (apostrophe)

New York US city and state (also **New York City** (always capital **C**) for the city and **New York State** or **New York state** for the state)

New Zealand Australasian country (Maori name **Aotearoa**)

next door (adverb; adjective after noun)

next-door (adjective before noun)

next of kin (three words)

Nez Percé North American Indian people or language (two words; acute accent)

NFT National Film Theatre

ngaio New Zealand tree (plural **ngaios**)

NH New Hampshire (US postal code)

NHS National Health Service

Ni nickel (no full stop)

NI National Insurance; Northern Ireland; North Island (New Zealand)

niacin (not **-ine**)

Niagara river between USA and Canada

Niagara Falls falls of Niagara River, or either of two cities in USA and Canada linked by bridges (use plural verb for the falls and singular verb for the cities)

Niamey capital of Niger (**-ey**)

Nibelung any of various characters in German mythology (not italic; not **Nieb-**; plural **Nibelungs** or **Nibelungen**)

Nibelungenlied medieval German epic (italic; not *Nieb-*)

Nicaea ancient city in Asia Minor (**-aea**)

Nicaean variant of **Nicene** (**-aean**)

NICAM near-instantaneous companding system: a technique for digital coding of audio signals (no full stops)

Nicaragua Central American country (single **c**; **-ara-**; **-gua**)

Nicene of Nicaea (also **Nicaean**)

Nicene Creed (capital **N** & **C**; not **Nicaean**)

niceness quality of being pleasant, kind, good, etc.

nicety subtle point, refinement, delicacy, or precision

niche (**-che**, not **-tch**)

Nicholas usual English spelling of the first name, used for the saints, tsars, and popes of this name (French spelling **Nicolas**)

Nicholson, Ben English painter; **Jack** US actor (compare **Nicolson**)

nickel (not **-le**; symbol **Ni**)

nick-nack less common variant of **knick-knack**

nickname (one word)

Nicobar Islands island group in Indian Ocean (single **c**)

Nicolas usual French spelling of **Nicholas**

Nicolson, Sir Harold British diplomat, politician, and author, husband of Vita Sackville-West (compare **Nicholson**)

Nicosia capital of Cyprus (Greek name **Levkosia** or **Leukosia**, Turkish name **Lefkoşa**)

Niebuhr, Barthold Georg German historian; **Reinhold** US theologian (**-ie-**; **-uhr**)

niece (not **-ei-**)

Nielsen, Carl Danish composer (compare **Neilson, Nilsen**, and **Nilsson**)

Niepce, Joseph-Nicéphore French inventor who produced first photographic image

Niersteiner German white wine (capital **N**; **-ie-** then **-ei-**)

Nietzsche, Friedrich Wilhelm German philosopher (**-tzsch-**)

Niger African country and river, or Nigerian state

Nigeria African country

Nigerian of Nigeria, or a person from Nigeria (**-ian**)

Nigerien of Niger, or a person from Niger (**-ien**)

niggardly (**-ar-**)

nigger offensive word for a Black person (to avoid controversy, do not use in any context, including the phrase *nigger in the woodpile*)

night period of darkness (compare **knight**)

night blindness (two words)

nightcap (one word)

nightclub (one word)

nightdress (one word)

nightgown (one word)

nightlife (one word)

night-light (hyphen)

nightly happening at night or each night (compare **knightly**)

nightmarish (not -mareish)

night owl (two words)

night school (two words)

night shift (two words)

nightshirt (one word)

nightspot (one word)

night-time (hyphen)

night watchman (two words)

Nihon a Japanese name for **Japan**

Nijinsky, Waslaw Russian ballet dancer and choreographer (also **Vaslaw**)

Nijmegen Dutch town (**-ij-**; German name **Nimwegen**)

Nikkei denoting index of prices on Tokyo Stock Exchange (double **k**; **-ei**)

nil (single **l**)

nilgai Indian antelope (the spellings **nilghau** and **nylghau** are less common but not incorrect)

Nilsen, Dennis Scottish murderer convicted of killing a series of young men (compare **Neilson**, **Nielsen**, and **Nilsson**)

Nilsson, Birgit Swedish soprano (compare **Nilsen**, **Nielsen**, and **Neilson**)

nimbus cloud, halo, or aura (not italic; plural **nimbi** or **nimbuses**)

NIMBY not in my back yard (referring to those who object to the occurrence, siting, etc. of something undesirable in their locality; no full stops)

nimbyism (all lower-case)

Nîmes French city (circumflex)

niminy-piminy (hyphen)

Nimwegen German name for **Nijmegen**

Nin, Anaïs French-born US writer (diaeresis on first name)

ninepins (one word)

Niño see **El Niño**

niobium (symbol **Nb**)

Nippon a Japanese name for **Japan**

NIREX Nuclear Industry Radioactive Waste Executive (no full stops)

Niro see **De Niro**

nirvana in Buddhism and Hinduism, final release from cycle of reincarnation (not italic; lower-case **n**)

nisi describing court order that will come into effect on specified date unless cause is shown why it should not (not italic; used after noun, as in *decree nisi*)

Nissan Japanese motor manufacturer, or any of their vehicles (capital **N**; **-an**)

Nissen hut military shelter (capital **N**; **-en**)

nit egg or larva of louse, or foolish person (compare **knit**)

nitre (**-er** in US English)

nitrogen (symbol **N**)

nitroglycerine (one word; also **nitroglycerin**)

nitty-gritty (hyphen)

Nizhni Novgorod Russian city (former name **Gorki**)

NJ New Jersey (US postal code)

Nkrumah, Kwame Ghanaian statesman

NL New Latin

NM New Mexico (US postal code)

NMR nuclear magnetic resonance

no used to express denial, refusal, negation, lack, etc. (compare **know**)

No¹ stylized Japanese drama (also **Noh**)

No² nobelium (no full stop)

No. number (also **no.**; plural **Nos.**, **nos.**, **Nos** or **Nos**)

Noachian of Noah (**-ch-**; also **Noachic**)

Noah biblical patriarch

Noah's Ark (capital **A**)

no-ball (hyphen)

nobelium (symbol **No**)

Nobel prize (capital **N**, lower-case **p**)

nobleman (one word)

noblesse oblige supposed obligation of nobility to be honourable and generous (not italic; **-esse**)

noblewoman (one word)

nobody (interchangeable with **no-one** as pronoun)

no-claims bonus (one hyphen; also **no-claim bonus**)

nocturn section of office of matins in Roman Catholic Church (compare **nocturne**)

nocturnal (not **-ern-**)

nocturne short lyrical piece of music or painting of night scene (compare **nocturn**)

Noel male first name, or another word for Christmas (also **Noël**; compare **Noelle** and **Nowell**)

Noelle female first name (also **Noele**; compare **Noel**)

no-fly zone (one hyphen)

Nofretete rare variant of **Nefertiti**

no-go area (one hyphen)

Noh variant of **No¹**

noisome offensive or noxious

noisy making a loud noise

nolens volens whether willing or unwilling (italics)

noli-me-tangere warning against touching or interfering, work of art depicting Christ and Mary

Magdalene after the Resurrection, or variant of **touch-me-not** (not italic; two hyphens; single **l**)

nolle prosequi entry made on court record when plaintiff or prosecutor undertakes not to continue action (not italic; double **l**)

no-man's-land (two hyphens; apostrophe)

nom de guerre pseudonym (not italic; plural **noms de guerre**)

nom de plume pen name (not italic; plural **noms de plume**)

nominator person who nominates (not **-er**)

nominee person nominated (not **-atee**)

non- (usually attached without hyphen, except to words beginning with **n** or capital letter)

nonagenarian (**-age-**)

nonalcoholic (no hyphen)

nonappearance (no hyphen)

nonattendance (no hyphen)

nonbeliever (no hyphen)

nonchalant (not **-ent**)

non-Christian not of the Christian faith, or a person who is not a Christian (hyphen; capital **C**; compare **unchristian**)

noncommissioned officer (no hyphen)

noncommittal (no hyphen; double **m**, double **t**)

non compos mentis of unsound mind (italics)

nonconformist person who does not conform (no hyphen; lower-case **n**)

Nonconformist member of Protestant denomination that dissents from Church of England (no hyphen; capital **N**)

noncooperation (no hyphens)

nondescript (no hyphen; not **none-**)

nondrip (no hyphen)

none to avoid controversy, use singular verb in all contexts, e.g. *none* *of the money was stolen, none of the candidates was suitable.* However, it is not incorrect to use a plural verb in the latter example.

nonentity (no hyphen)

nonessential (no hyphen)

nonetheless (one word)

nonevent (no hyphen)

nonexistent (no hyphen; not **-ant**)

nonfattening (no hyphen)

nonfiction (no hyphen)

nonflammable not liable to catch fire (no hyphen; compare **inflammable**)

nonmember (no hyphen)

non-negotiable (hyphen)

no-nonsense (hyphen)

nonpareil peerless example (no hyphen; not italic; **-ei-**)

non-person (hyphen)

nonplus (single **s**)

nonplussed, nonplussing (double **s**; note that **nonplussed** means 'confused or at a loss' – its occasional use in the opposite sense of 'unperturbed' is controversial and may be ambiguous)

non-profit-making (two hyphens)

nonproliferation (no hyphen)

nonresident (no hyphen)

nonrestrictive relative clause see **relative clause**

non sequitur statement with little or no relevance to what went before (two words; not italic)

nonslip (no hyphen)

nonsmoker (no hyphen)

nonstarter (no hyphen)

nonstick (no hyphen)

nonstop (no hyphen)

non-U (hyphen)

nonviolence (no hyphen)

non-White (hyphen)

no-one (also **no one**; interchangeable with **nobody** as pronoun)

nor used after **neither** (e.g. *neither my mother nor my father*) or to introduce a second negative clause (e.g. *she wasn't impressed, nor was she amused*). Sometimes interchangeable with **or** in other negative contexts, as in *he has no friends or* [or *nor*] *relatives living nearby*.

Nordenskjöld, Baron Nils Adolf Erik Swedish Arctic explorer and geologist

Nord-Pas-de-Calais region of N France (three hyphens; compare **Pas de Calais** and **Pas-de-Calais**)

Nordrhein-Westfalen German name for **North Rhine-Westphalia**

Norge Norwegian name for **Norway**

normalcy (use **normality** instead)

normalize (also **normalise**; see **-ize/ -ise**)

north (as noun) direction or compass point opposite south, or area lying in this direction; (as adjective or adverb) in, to, or from the north (sometimes capital **N** in the sense 'area lying in the north'; see also **compass points**)

North northern area of England, the USA, or North America, or denoting the northern part of a particular country, continent, ocean, etc. (sometimes lower-case **n** in adjectival use, but always capital **N** in names)

Northallerton English town (one word)

North America continent comprising Canada, the USA, and Mexico (do not abbreviate **North**)

Northampton English town (single **h**)

Northamptonshire English county

Northants Northamptonshire

North Borneo former name for **Sabah** (capital **N** & **B**)

North Cape cape on Magerøy Island off Norway, or North Island, New Zealand (capital **N** & **C**; compare **Northern Cape**)

North Country northern area of England or North America (capital **N & C**)

northeast (as noun) direction or compass point between north and east, or area lying in this direction; (as adjective or adverb) in, to, or from the northeast (one word; sometimes capital **N** in the sense 'area lying in the northeast'; see also **compass points**)

Northeast northeastern area of England, or denoting the northeastern part of a particular country, continent, etc. (one word; often lower-case **n** in adjectival use, but always capital **N** in names)

North East Lincolnshire unitary authority in Lincolnshire (three words; capital **N, E, & L**)

Northeast Passage shipping route along N coast of Europe and Asia (**Northeast** is one word; capital **N & P**)

northern of, in, or to the north (lower-case **n**)

Northern of, in, or to the North (capital **N**)

Northern Cape South African province (capital **N & C**; compare **North Cape**)

Northerner person from the northern part of a particular country, especially England or the USA (the use of lower-case **n** is less common but not incorrect)

northern hemisphere (the use of capital **N & H** is less common but not incorrect)

Northern Ireland part of the **United Kingdom** and **Ireland** (do not abbreviate **Northern**; see also **Ulster**)

Northern Isles the Orkneys and Shetland (capital **N & I**)

Northern Rhodesia former name for **Zambia**

Northern Territories former British protectorate in Africa (capital **N & T**)

Northern Territory administrative division of Australia (capital **N & T**)

North Friesland region of Germany (**-ies-**)

North Island one of two main islands of New Zealand (capital **N & I**)

North Korea NE Asian country (do not abbreviate **North**; Korean name **Choson**)

north-northeast (one hyphen)

north-northwest (one hyphen)

north pole pole of magnet (lower-case **n & p**)

North Pole northernmost point on earth's axis (capital **N & P**)

North Rhine-Westphalia German state (one hyphen; German name **Nordrhein-Westfalen**)

North-Sea gas (one hyphen; capital **N & S**)

Northumberland English county

Northumbria region of NE England and former Anglo-Saxon kingdom

northward (adjective; sometimes adverb (see **-ward** and **-wards**))

northwards (adverb only)

northwest (as noun) direction or compass point between north and west, or area lying in this direction; (as adjective or adverb) in, to, or from the northwest (one word; sometimes capital **N** in the sense 'area lying in the northwest'; see also **compass points**)

Northwest northwestern area of England, Canada, or the USA; or denoting the northwestern part of a particular country, continent, etc. (one word; often lower-case **n** in adjectival use, but always capital **N** in names)

North West South African province (also **North-West**)

North-West Frontier Province province of Pakistan (one hyphen; capital **N**, **W**, **F**, & **P**)

Northwest Passage shipping route along N coast of America (**Northwest** is one word; capital **N** & **P**)

Northwest Territories territory of Canada (capital **N** & **T**)

Northwest Territory area of early USA (capital **N** & **T**)

Norway European country (Norwegian name **Norge**)

Nos. numbers (also **nos.**, **Nos**, or **nos**)

nosebag (one word)

noseband (one word)

nosebleed (one word)

nose cone (two words)

nose dive (noun)

nose-dive (verb)

nose job (two words)

nosey variant of **nosy**

no sooner (followed by *than*, not *when*, as in *no sooner had I sat down than the phone rang again*)

Nostradamus French physician and astrologer (French name **Michel de Notredame**)

nostrum medicine or remedy (not italic; plural **nostrums**)

nosy (also **nosey**)

nosy parker (lower-case **n** & **p**)

not used to form negative (compare **knot**)

nota bene note well (italics; abbreviation **NB**, which is not italic)

notable remarkable or distinguished (not **-eable**; compare **noticeable**, **noted**, and **noteworthy**)

notebook (one word)

noted famous (compare **notable**, **noteworthy**, and **noticeable**)

notepaper (one word)

noteworthy worthy of notice (compare **noticeable**, **notable**, and **noted**)

not-for-profit organization (two hyphens)

nothing but (use plural verb when followed by plural noun, as in *nothing but crumbs were left*)

noticeable perceptible (**e** after **c**; compare **notable**, **noteworthy**, and **noted**)

notice board (two words)

not only . . . but also (position these phrases so that what follows is grammatically balanced, e.g. *she has lost not only her job but also her reputation* or *she has not only lost her job but also ruined her marriage*)

notoriety (**-ie-**)

notorious (not **-our-**)

Notre Dame cathedral in Paris, France (sometimes hyphenated, e.g in the title of Victor Hugo's novel *Notre-Dame de Paris* and its English translation *The Hunchback of Notre-Dame*)

Notting Hill Carnival (capital **C**)

notwithstanding (one word)

Nouakchott capital of Mauritania

nougat hard chewy sweet (compare **nugget**)

nought zero (compare **naught**)

nous mind, reason, common sense, or intelligence (not italic)

nouveau riche person with newly acquired wealth (not italic; plural **nouveaux riches**)

nouvelle cuisine style of preparing and presenting food (not italic)

Nov. November (full stop)

nova (plural **novae** or **novas**)

Nova Scotia Canadian province (two words)

novelette short novel, or novel regarded as trivial or sentimental (single **l**, double **t**)

novella short novel or narrative tale (double **l**)

novitiate (also **noviciate**)

Novosibirsk Russian city (one word)

nowadays (one word)

Nowell archaic word for Christmas,

used in some carols (also **Nowel**; compare **Noel**)

nowhere (one word)

no-win situation (one hyphen)

noxious harmful or poisonous, as in *noxious gases* (compare **obnoxious**)

np new paragraph; no place of publication (also **n.p.**)

Np neptunium (no full stop)

NS New Style

NSPCC National Society for the Prevention of Cruelty to Children

NSU nonspecific urethritis

NSW New South Wales

NT National Trust; New Testament

nuance subtle difference (not italic)

nubile marriageable (to avoid controversy or offence, do not use in the sense 'sexually attractive'

nuclear (not **-cular**)

nuclear fission splitting of atomic nucleus (compare **nuclear fusion**)

nuclear-free zone (one hyphen)

nuclear fusion reaction in which nuclei combine (compare **nuclear fusion**)

nucleus (plural **nuclei**, which is acceptable and preferable in all senses, or **nucleuses**, which is rare and best avoided)

nugget small piece (compare **nougat**)

nuisance (**-ui-**; **-ance**)

Nuits-Saint-Georges French wine (two hyphens; also **-St-**; not **-George**)

NUJ National Union of Journalists

Nuku'alofa capital of Tonga (apostrophe; lower-case **a**)

Nullarbor Plain Australian plateau (not **-bour**)

Num. Numbers (full stop; not italic)

number use plural verb after the phrase *a number of*, as in *a number of residents have complained*; use singular verb after the phrase *the number of*, as in *the number of complaints has increased*; see also **numbers**)

numberplate (one word)

numbers use **en dash** rather than hyphen for number spans (e.g. *50–60 words*; see also **dates**). The number after the en dash is usually abbreviated (e.g. *pages 356–9*; *the period 1964–71*), but beware of possible ambiguity (see **B.C.**). Low numbers (e.g. up to *ten*, *twelve*, or *twenty*) are usually spelt out in running text, and all numbers are spelt out at the beginning of a sentence. In nontechnical text large numbers with more than three (or four) digits are usually divided by commas into thousands and millions (e.g. *1,750,000*; *45,681*; *3,906* or *3906*); in technical text thin spaces are used instead of commas to divide sets of three digits before and after the decimal point. Follow the publisher's house style in all these matters. See also **Arabic numerals, Roman numerals**, and **number**.

Numbers book of the Bible (not italic; abbreviation **Num.**)

numbskull (also **numskull**)

numerator (not **-er**)

Nunc Dimittis Canticle of Simeon (Luke 2:29–32) or a musical setting of this (not italic; capital **N** & **D**)

nuncio (plural **nuncios**)

nuptial (not **-tual**)

nurd less common variant of **nerd**

Nuremberg German city (not **-burg**; German name **Nürnberg**)

Nureyev, Rudolf Austrian ballet dancer, born in the Soviet Union

Nuri people of Nuristan and neighbouring parts of Pakistan, or the language of this people (also **Kafiri** for the language)

Nuristan region of Afghanistan (former name **Kafiristan**)

nurl less common variant of **knurl**

Nürnberg German name for
Nuremberg)

nursemaid (one word)

nursery rhyme (two words)

nutbrown (one word)

nutcracker (one word)

nutrient (not -ant)

nutshell (one word)

Nuuk capital of Greenland (double **u**; former name **Godthaab**)

nux vomica tree, its seeds, or medicine made from them (not italic; two words)

NV Nevada (US postal code)

nvCJD new-variant CJD (use **vCJD** instead)

NVQ national vocational qualification

NW northwest

NY New York (the city or state; US postal code for the state)

Nyasa, Lake central Africa (Malawi name **Lake Malawi**)

Nyasaland former name for **Malawi**

NYC New York City

nylghau less common variant of **nilgai**

nymphet sexually precocious girl (not -ette)

Nynorsk one of the official forms of written Norwegian, derived from Norwegian dialect (former name **Landsmål**; see also **Bokmål**)

NZ New Zealand

O

O¹ oxygen (no full stop)

O² variant of **oh**, or exclamation used to introduce an invocation, wish, etc., chiefly in religious or poetic contexts, as in *hear our prayer, O God* or *O for the wings of a dove!* (capital **O**)

o' of (apostrophe; usually followed by space, except in well-established words and phrases such as **o'clock**)

O' descendant of (apostrophe; capital **O**; attached without hyphen to form Irish surnames, e.g. *O'Hara*)

oak apple (two words)

Oak-apple Day May 29 (hyphen; capital **O** & **D**, lower-case **a**)

Oakham English town

oakum fibre obtained from old rope

O & M organization and method

OAP old age pensioner (no full stops; plural **OAPs**, but replace with **pensioners**, **senior citizens**, or another appropriate synonym to avoid offence)

oar device used to propel boat (compare **or** and **ore**)

oasis fertile place in desert, or place of peace, safety, etc. (lower-case **o**; plural **oases**)

Oasis trademark for porous material used as base for flower arrangements (capital **O**)

oast house (two words)

oatcake (one word)

Oates, Captain Lawrence Edward Grace English explorer (not **Laurence**); **Titus** English conspirator

oatmeal (one word)

Oaxaca Mexican city and state

Obad. Obadiah (full stop; not italic)

Obadiah book of the Bible (not italic; abbreviation **Obad.**)

obbligato music term (not italic; plural **obbligatos** or **obbligati**; the spelling **obligato** is less common but not incorrect)

OBE Officer of the Order of the British Empire

obeah variant of **obi²**

obedience act of obeying, or willingness to obey (**-bed-**; not **-ance**)

obeisance deference or homage, or gesture expressing this (**-beis-**; not **-ence**)

obelisk (*typog.*) another name for **dagger** (also **obelus**)

Oberammergau German village famous for Passion Play (double **m**)

obi¹ Japanese sash

obi² African or West Indian witchcraft (also **obeah**)

obit informal word for obituary (no full stop)

object see **direct object** and **indirect object**

objective denoting the case of pronouns such as *me* and *them* (compare **subjective**)

objet d'art small object of artistic value (italics; plural **objets d'art**)

obligated morally or legally compelled (compare **obliged**)

obligato less common variant of **obbligato**

obligatory (-tory)

obliged grateful, indebted, or compelled (compare **obligated**)

oblique (*typog.*) another name for **solidus**

oblivious (may be followed by *of* or *to*)

obnoxious extremely unpleasant (chiefly used of people; compare **noxious**)

oboe (-oe)

oboist (not -oeist)

O'Brien, Conor Cruise Irish diplomat, politician, and writer (not **Connor**); **Edna** Irish novelist (not **O'Brian**)

obscene (-sc-)

obsequies funeral rites (plural noun)

obsequious ingratiating (**-ious**)

observance compliance with law, custom, etc., ritual, or ceremony, as in *religious observances* (compare **observation**)

observant (not -ent)

observation remark, act of observing, or state of being observed, as in *under observation* (compare **observance**)

observatory (-tory)

obsessive-compulsive disorder (one hyphen)

obsolescent becoming obsolete (-sc-; -ent)

obsolete out of use or out of date

obstetrician (not -tian)

obstreperous (-per-)

Occam variant of **Ockham**

occasion (double **c**, single **s**)

occident poetic word for the west (lower-case **o**)

Occident another name for **West** in the sense 'Europe, America, etc.' (capital **O**)

Occidental of the Occident, or a person from the Occident (also **occidental**, especially for the adjective)

occult (double **c**)

occupied busy (compare **preoccupied**)

occur (double **c**, single **r**)

occurred (double **c**, double **r**)

occurrence (double **c**, double **r**; **-ence**)

occurring (double **c**, double **r**)

ocean (capital **O** as part of name, as in *Atlantic Ocean*)

ocean-going (hyphen)

ochre (**-er** in US English; not **-cr-** or **-kr-**)

Ockham, William of English philosopher (also **Occam**)

o'clock (apostrophe with no space after)

O'Connell, Daniel Irish nationalist leader and orator (double **n** and double **l** in surname)

OCR optical character reader; optical character recognition

Oct. October (full stop)

octagon (not octo-)

octahedron (not octo-; plural **octahedrons** or **octahedra**)

octaroon variant of **octoroon**

octavo book size with eight leaves (i.e. 16 pages) per sheet (also **eightvo** or **8vo**)

octodecimo another name for **eighteenmo**

octogenarian (-oge-)

octopus (plural **octopuses**)

octoroon person with one-eighth Black blood (also **octaroon**)

ocularist person who makes artificial eyes

oculist former name for **ophthalmologist**

OD overdose (third person present tense **OD's**, past tense and past participle **OD'd**)

oddball (one word)

Oddfellow member of benevolent and fraternal association (one word; capital **O**)

odds and ends (three words)

odds-on (hyphen)

Oder-Neisse Line boundary between Germany and Poland (hyphen may be replaced by en dash)

odious repugnant

odorous having characteristic smell (not **-our-**)

odour (**-or** in US English)

odourless (**-or-** in US English)

Odysseus hero in Greek mythology (Roman name **Ulysses**)

odyssey long eventful journey (double **s**; **-ey**; the use of capital **O** is not incorrect in this sense, but it is less common)

Odyssey epic poem attributed to Homer (italics; capital **O**)

oe rarely represented by the character **œ** in modern English, but note that **œ** is still sometimes used in French words and phrases. See individual entries for the use of **oe** versus **e**.

Oea ancient name for **Tripoli** (Libya)

oecumenical rare variant of **ecumenical**

OED *Oxford English Dictionary* (italics)

oedema (**ed-** in US English)

Oedipus complex sexual attachment of boy to mother (compare **Electra complex**)

oesophagus (**es-** in US English)

oestrogen (**es-** in US English)

oestrous of oestrus, as in *the oestrous cycle* (**es-** in US English)

oestrus period of sexual receptivity in female mammals (**es-** in US English)

oeuvre work of art, literature, or music, or total output of artist, writer, or composer (italics; also *œuvre*)

of (preposition; do not confuse with **'ve**, as in *you should've told me*; see also **off**)

Ofcom Office of Communications: government body regulating telecommunications industries, replacing **Oftel** (capital **O** only; single **f**)

off (not followed by **of** in standard English)

Offaly Irish county (double **f**, single **l**)

Offa's Dyke ancient earthwork between England and Wales (capital **O** & **D**; apostrophe; not **Dike**)

offbeat (one word)

off-centre (hyphen)

off colour (two words, but hyphenated when used before noun)

offcut (one word)

offence (**-ense** in US English)

offensive (not **-enc-**)

offer (double **f**, single **r**)

Offer Office of Electricity Regulation: replaced by **Ofgem** (capital **O** only; double **f**)

offered, offering (double **f**, single **r**)

offertory (**-tory**)

off guard (two words)

offhand (one word; the variant **offhanded** is less common but not incorrect)

office bearer (two words)

official of an office, sanctioned or appointed by authority, or formal (compare **officious**)

Official Receiver (capital **O** & **R**)

officious derogatory term meaning 'self-important' or 'offering unwanted help or advice', or term used in diplomacy to mean 'unofficial' (compare **official**)

off key (two words, but hyphenated when used before noun)

off-licence (hyphen; not **-ense**)

off limits (two words, but hyphenated when used before noun)

off line (adverb; adjective after noun)

off-line (adjective before noun)

off-load (hyphen)

offprint separate reprint of article that originally appeared in larger publication (one word)

off-putting (hyphen)

off-road (hyphen)

off season (two words, but hyphenated when used before noun)

offset (*typog.*) printing method in which impression is transferred via intermediate surface (one word)

offshoot (one word)

offshore (one word)

offside (one word)

offspring (one word; same form for singular and plural)

offstage (one word)

off-street parking (one hyphen)

off the cuff (three words, but hyphenated when used before noun)

off the record (three words, but hyphenated when used before noun)

off the shelf (three words, but hyphenated when used before noun)

off-the-wall (hyphenated unless used after noun, as in *his approach is rather off the wall*)

off-white (hyphen)

Ofgas Office of Gas Supply: replaced by **Ofgem** (capital **O** only; double **f**)

Ofgem Office of Gas and Electricity Markets: government body regulating power suppliers, replacing **Offer** and **Ofgas** (capital **O** only; single **f**)

Ofsted Office for Standards in Education: government body that inspects schools and colleges (capital **O** only; single **f**; not **-ead**)

OFT Office of Fair Trading

oft- (attached with hyphen, as in *oft-repeated*)

Oftel Office of Telecommunications: replaced by **Ofcom** (capital **O** only; single **f**)

Ofwat Office of Water Services: government body regulating water suppliers (capital **O** only; single **f**)

Ogaden, the region of Ethiopia, bordering on Somalia

Ogen melon (capital **O**)

Ogun Nigerian state

oh exclamation of surprise, pleasure, shock, horror, etc., or variant of **O²**

OH Ohio (US postal code)

O'Hara, Scarlett character in Margaret Mitchell's *Gone with the Wind* (not **Scarlet**)

ohm unit of electrical resistance

Ohm, Georg Simon German physicist

OHMS On Her (or His) Majesty's Service

-oholic the more common form of the suffix when added to a part word ending in **o**, as in *chocoholic* (compare **-aholic**)

oilcan (one word)

oilcloth (one word)

oil drum (two words)

oilfield (one word)

oil painting (two words)

oil rig (two words)

oil-seed rape (one hyphen)

oilskin (one word)

oil slick (two words)

oil well (two words)

Oireachtas Irish parliament, comprising **Dáil Éireann** and **Seanad Éireann**

o.i.r.o. offers in the region of

Oistrakh, David and **Igor** Russian violinists

OK¹ Oklahoma (US postal code)

OK² all right, approval, or approve (third person present tense **OK's**, past tense and past participle **OK'd**; also **okay**)

Okanagan North American river, Canadian lake, North American Indian people, or the language of this people (also **Okanogan** (for the river, people, and language) or **Okinagan** (for the people and language))

okapi (plural **okapis** or **okapi**)

okay variant of **OK²**

O'Keeffe, Georgia US painter

Okehampton English town (not **Oak-**)

Okinagan variant of **Okanagan** (the people and language)

Oklahoma US state

Oklahoma City US city (capital **C**)

okra plant with edible pods (not **-cr-** or **-chr-**)

old age pensioner (three words; see also **OAP**)

Old Bailey chief criminal court in London (capital **O** & **B**)

Oldenburg German city and former state (not **-berg**)

Old English English language until about 1100 (capital **O** & **E**)

Old English sheepdog (capital **O** & **E**)

olde-worlde pseudo-archaic variant of **old-world** in the sense 'quaint', often used facetiously

old-fashioned (hyphen)

old guard conservative element, or group working for long-established or old-fashioned cause (lower-case **o** & **g**)

Old Guard French imperial guard created by Napoleon (capital **O** & **G**)

Old Lady of Threadneedle Street, The nickname for the Bank of England (capital **O** & **L**)

old maid (two words)

old master painter or painting (lower-case **o** & **m**)

Old Peculier brand of ale (capital **O** & **P**; not **-liar**)

Old Pretender nickname of James

Francis Edward **Stuart** (capital **O** & **P**)

old school tie (three words; lower-case **o**, **s**, & **t**)

Old Style denoting date reckoned according to **Julian calendar**, approximately eleven days different from **New Style**

Old Testament (not italic; capital **O** & **T**)

old-time (hyphen)

Old World Europe, Asia, and Africa (capital **O** & **W**; compare **New World**)

old-world characteristic of former times, quaint, or traditional (lower-case **o** & **w**; hyphen; see also **olde-worlde**)

olé Spanish exclamation (not italic; acute accent)

oleaginous (**-le-**, **-gi-**)

O level (no hyphen unless used before another noun, as in *O-level maths*; replaced by **GCSE** in 1988)

olive branch (two words)

olive green (no hyphen unless used before another noun, as in *an olive-green carpet*)

olive oil (two words)

Olivier, Laurence, Baron Olivier of Brighton English actor and director (not **Lawrence**)

olla podrida Spanish dish, or miscellany (not italic)

oloroso sweet sherry (not italic; lower-case **o**)

Olympia plain in ancient Greece where original Olympic Games took place, or US port

Olympiad staging of Olympic Games, four-year period between Olympic Games, or international contest (capital **O**)

Olympian (as adjective) of Mount Olympus in Greece, godlike, or of ancient Olympia; (as noun) Greek god dwelling on Mount Olympus, person from ancient Olympia, or

competitor in Olympic Games
(capital **O**)

Olympic of Olympic Games or
ancient Olympia (capital **O**)

Olympic Games (capital **O** & **G**; use
singular or plural verb)

Olympics, the another name for the
modern Olympic Games (capital **O**)

Olympus, Mount Greek mountain
where greater gods were believed to
dwell, or US mountain

Om sacred syllable of Hinduism
(capital **O**)

OM Order of Merit

Omagh town and district in
Northern Ireland

Omaha US city

Omar Khayyám Persian poet,
mathematician, and astronomer
(double **y**; acute accent; see also
Rubáiyát of Omar Khayyám)

ombudsman (may be used for males
and females; plural **ombudsmen**;
capital **O** in titles, e.g. *Banking
Ombudsman*)

Omdurman Sudanese city (**-dur-**)

omelette (sometimes **omelet**,
especially in US English)

omertà conspiracy of silence (italics;
grave accent)

omission act of leaving out, or
something left out (compare
emission)

omit (single **m**, single **t**)

omitted, omitting (single **m**,
double **t**)

omnibus (plural **omnibuses**)

omniscient (**-sc-**, **-ient**)

on see **upon**

on appro on approval (no full stop)

once-over (hyphen)

oncoming (one word)

Ondaatje, Michael Canadian writer,
born in Sri Lanka (double **a**, **-tje**)

one use plural verb after **one of those**
. . ., as in *she is one of those people who
are* [not *is*] *always on the go*. To avoid

controversy, use singular verb after
one in . . ., as in *one in five drivers
admits* [not *admit*] *to speeding*. See
also **you**.

one another (may be used regardless
of the number of people or things
involved: synonymous with **each
other**)

one-armed bandit (one hyphen; not
-arm)

Oneida US lake, North American
Indian people, or the language of
this people (**-ei-**)

O'Neill, Eugene US dramatist
(double **l**)

one-liner (hyphen)

one-night stand (one hyphen)

one-off (hyphen)

one-parent family (one hyphen)

one-sided (hyphen)

one-stop shop (one hyphen)

one-time (hyphen)

one-to-one (two hyphens)

one-track mind (one hyphen)

one-upmanship (hyphen)

one-way (hyphen)

ongoing (one word)

online (adjective before noun; also
on-line)

on line (adverb; adjective after noun)

onlooker (one word)

only beware of ambiguity in the
positioning of this adverb: does *she
only has a copy of the document* mean
that nobody else has a copy, or that
she doesn't have the original? If
possible, place **only** directly before
the word it refers to, e.g. *only she has
a copy of the document* or *she has only
a copy of the document*. See also **not
only . . . but also**.

o.n.o. or near(est) offer

onomatopoeia (**-oeia**)

onrush (one word)

onshore (one word)

onto (one word or two words as
preposition (e.g. *he went onto* [or *on*

to] *the balcony*); two words as preposition plus infinitive marker (e.g. *he went on to* [not *onto*] *explain what had happened*))

onus (plural onuses)

onward (adjective; sometimes adverb (see **-ward** and **-wards**))

onwards (adverb only)

oolong type of tea (lower-case **o**)

Oostende Flemish name for **Ostend**

op informal word for operation (no full stop)

op. opus (often **Op.** when followed by number in names of works)

o.p. out of print

opalescent (**-sc-**; **-ent**)

op art (two words; no full stop)

op. cit. in the work cited: used in footnotes, bibliographies, etc. to avoid repeating the title of a source previously mentioned (not italic; from Latin *opere citato*)

OPEC Organization of Petroleum-Exporting Countries

open air (no hyphen unless used before another noun, as in *an open-air concert*)

open-and-shut case (two hyphens)

open door (no hyphen unless used before another noun, as in *an open-door policy*)

open-ended (hyphen)

open-heart surgery (one hyphen)

open-minded (hyphen)

open-mouthed (hyphen)

open-plan (hyphen)

Open University (capital **O** & **U**)

opera dramatic work with music (singular noun; plural **operas**), or plural of **opus**

operable (not **-atable**)

opera glasses (two words)

opera house (two words)

Operation (capital **O** for names of military and other campaigns or manoeuvres, as in *Operation Overlord*)

operetta (single **r**, double **t**)

ophthalmic (**-phth-**)

ophthalmic optician see **optician**

ophthalmologist specialist in eye diseases (**-phth-**; former name **oculist**; compare **optician**)

opinion poll (two words)

Oporto Portuguese port (Portuguese name **Pôrto**)

opossum marsupial of the Americas (single **p**, double **s**; informal name **possum**)

opponent (double **p**; not **-ant**)

opportunity (double **p**; not **-er-**)

opposition (sometimes capital **O** in the sense 'political party opposing government', especially in the official name of such a party)

oppressor (not **-er**)

optic of the eye or sense of sight, or less common variant of **optical** in its other senses (lower-case **o**)

Optic trademark for device for dispensing measured quantity from inverted bottle of whisky, gin, etc. (capital **O**)

optical of or involving light; of the eye or sense of sight; or correcting a visual disorder (the variant **optic** is less common but not incorrect in this sense)

optical illusion (not **allusion** or **delusion**)

optician person who prescribes spectacles (also **ophthalmic optician** or **optometrist**) or person who supplies and fits spectacles (also **dispensing optician**) (compare **ophthalmologist**)

optimize (also **optimise**; see **-ize/-ise**)

optometrist see **optician**

opt-out (noun; the verb is **opt out**)

opulent (not **-ant**)

opus musical work or other artistic composition (not italic; often **Opus** when followed by number in names of works; plural **opera**)

or conjunction joining alternatives (compare **oar** and **ore** (for spelling); see also **either** and **nor** (for usage))

OR operations research; Oregon (US postal code)

-or indicates performer of action, as in *lessor* (compare **-ee**). Some words end in **-er** rather than **-or**, or have both spellings with slightly different meanings: see individual entries. Where both spellings exist, the **-or** form is often more specific or specialized than the **-er** form.

Oracle former television text service of ITV and Channel 4, replaced by **Teletext**

oral of or involving the mouth, or spoken (compare **aural**; see also **verbal**)

orangeade (**-gea-**)

Orange Free State former South African province, replaced by **Free State** in 1994

Orangeism practices and principles of Orangemen (**-gei-**)

Orange Lodge group of Orangemen (capital **O** & **L**)

Orangeman member of Irish Protestant society

Orangeman's Day July 12 (capital **O** & **D**; apostrophe; not **-men's**)

orange peel (two words)

orang-utan (also **orang-utang**)

ora pro nobis pray for us (italics)

orator (not **-er**)

oratorio (plural **oratorios**)

orbited, orbiting (not **-tt-**)

Orcadian of the Orkneys, or a person from the Orkneys

orchestra (**-ch-**)

orchid (**-ch-**)

Orczy, Baroness Emmuska Hungarian-born British novelist

order in the hierarchy of **taxonomic names**, the group that comes above a family and below a class. The family name has a capital initial and is not italic.

Order of Merit (capital **O** & **M**)

Order of the Garter (capital **O** & **G**)

ordinance decree (compare **ordnance** and **ordonnance**)

ordnance artillery, munitions, or department dealing with military supplies (compare **ordinance** and **ordonnance**)

Ordnance Survey map-making body (capital **O** & **S**; not **Ordinance**)

ordonnance proper disposition of elements of building, artistic composition, etc., or decree (compare **ordinance** and **ordnance**)

ore naturally occurring mineral (compare **oar** and **or**)

oregano herb (not **ori-**; the plant is a species of the genus *Origanum*)

Oregon US state (**-reg-**, **-on**)

Øresund Danish name for the **Sound**

Öresund Swedish name for the **Sound**

organdie (**-dy** in US English)

organ-grinder (hyphen)

organism living creature, or something resembling this (compare **orgasm**)

organize (also **organise**; see **-ize/-ise**)

organon system of logical or scientific rules (also **organum**; plural **organa**, **organons**, or **organums**)

orgasm peak of sexual excitement (compare **organism**)

oriel window (lower-case **o**; not **-ial**)

Oriel College Oxford

orient (as noun) poetic word for the west; (as verb) adjust, align, or position (lower-case **o**; also **orientate** for the verb)

Orient another name for **East** in the sense 'Asia' (capital **O**)

Oriental of the Orient (also **oriental**; to avoid offence, do not use either form in the noun sense 'person from the Orient': replace with a more specific synonym, e.g. **Southeast Asian**)

orientate variant of **orient** (verb)

oriflamme scarlet flag adopted as national banner of medieval France (not italic; not **-flame**)

originator (not **-er**)

Origin of Species, On the work by Charles Darwin (not ... *the Species*; full title *On the Origin of Species by Means of Natural Selection*)

O-ring (capital **O**; hyphen)

Orinoco South American river (not **Oro-**)

Orissa Indian state (single **r**, double **s**)

Orizaba Mexican city

Orizaba, Pico de Spanish name for **Citlaltépetl**

Orkneys, the island group off Scotland (also **Orkney Islands** or **Orkney**; see also **Orcadian**)

Orléans French city (acute accent; compare **New Orleans**)

ormolu gold or gold-coloured alloy used for gilding (not italic)

Ormond the spelling used in **Great Ormond Street Hospital for Children**

Ormonde, James Butler, 1st Duke of Anglo-Irish general

Ormuz variant of **Hormuz**

orotund resonant or bombastic (compare **rotund**)

orphan (*typog.*) first line of paragraph occurring undesirably at foot of page or column

Orpheus poet and lyre-player in Greek mythology

Ortega, Daniel Nicaraguan politician

Ortega y Gasset, José Spanish essayist and philosopher

orthodox conforming with established standards (lower-case **o**)

Orthodox of Orthodox Church (always capital **O**), or relating or adhering to Orthodox Judaism (the use of lower-case **o** is not incorrect in this sense, but it is less common)

Orthodox Church collective body of Eastern Churches in communion with Greek patriarch of Constantinople, or any of these Churches (capital **O & C**; also **Eastern Orthodox Church** or **Greek Orthodox Church**)

Orthodox Judaism form of Judaism characterized by strict observance of Talmudic law (capital **O & J**)

orthopaedic of branch of surgery concerned with disorders of spine and joints (**-ped-** in US English; compare **paediatric**)

ortolan small bird eaten as delicacy (not italic)

Orvieto Italian town or wine (capital **O**)

Orwell, George English writer (real name **Eric Arthur Blair**)

Os osmium (no full stop)

OS Old Style

o.s. out of stock (also **O/S**)

Osborn, Sherard English naval officer

Osborne, John British dramatist

Osborne House Isle of Wight

Osbourne, Ozzy British rock musician (real name **John Michael Osbourne**)

Oscar statuette awarded for achievement in cinema (official name **Academy Award**)

oscillate swing or waver (compare **osculate**)

oscillator (not **-er**)

osculate kiss or touch (compare **oscillate**)

Oslo capital of Norway (former names **Christiania** (1624–1877) and **Kristiania** (1877–1924)

Osman I founder of Ottoman

Empire (the variant **Othman I** is less common but not incorrect)

osmium (symbol **Os**)

Osnabrück German city (umlaut; not **-burg**)

osseous (not **-ious**)

osso bucco veal stew (not italic; two words)

Ostend Belgian port (French name **Ostende**, Flemish name **Oostende**)

ostensible apparent (not **-able**)

ostentatious showy

osteoarthritis (no hyphen)

Österreich German name for **Austria** (umlaut; double **r**)

ostinato continuously repeated musical phrase (not italic; not **obst-**; plural **ostinatos**)

ostler archaic word for stableman (also **hostler**)

ostracize (also **ostracise**; see **-ize/ -ise**)

ostrich (not **-itch**)

Oswaldtwistle English town (**-twist-**)

Oświęcim Polish name for **Auschwitz** (the town)

OT occupational therapy; Old Testament

O tempora! O mores! exclamation at evil of times and customs (italics; not *Oh*)

otherwise as adjective and pronoun, replace with something simpler if possible, e.g. **not** (as in *please return the manuscript tomorrow, proofread or not* [not *proofread or otherwise*]) or **others** (as in *all those with an interest in the company – shareholders and others* [not *shareholders and otherwise*]). Note that as a conjunction, **otherwise** means 'or else' and should not be preceded by *or* (e.g. *hurry up, otherwise* [not *or otherwise*] *you'll miss your train*).

otherworldly (one word)

Othman less common variant of **Ottoman**

Othman I less common variant of **Osman I**

OTT over the top

Ottawa capital of Canada (not **-owa**)

ottoman padded seat or chest (lower-case **o**; plural **ottomans**)

Ottoman (as noun) member of Turkish people who invaded Near East in late 13th century; (as adjective) of this people, the Ottoman Empire, or the Turkish language (capital **O**; plural **Ottomans**; the variant **Othman** is less common but not incorrect)

Ottoman Empire former Turkish empire in Europe, Asia, and Africa (capital **O & E**)

OU Open University

Ouachita US river (also **Washita**)

Ouagadougou capital of Burkina-Faso

oubliette dungeon (not italic)

Ouessant French name for **Ushant**

ought should, as in *she ought to apologize*, or less common variant of **aught**. Note that **ought** (unlike **should**) is always followed by the infinitive with **to**, and that the negative is **ought not** or **oughtn't**, as in *they ought not to come* (not *they didn't ought …*) or *you oughtn't to have told her* (not *you hadn't ought …*).

Ouida British novelist (real name **Marie Louise de la Ramée**)

Ouija board trademark for board supposed to answer questions via spiritual forces (capital **O**, lower-case **b**)

Oujda Moroccan city

OUP Oxford University Press

our of us (compare **hour**)

Our Lady title of St **Mary**, mother of Christ (capital **O & L**)

ours (no apostrophe)

ourself used instead of **myself** or **ourselves** when **we** is used in place of **I**, e.g. by a monarch or editor

ourselves the usual reflexive form of **we** or **us** (see also **ourself**)

ousel less common variant of **ouzel**

out (do not use alone as preposition, e.g. *she ran out of the room* [not *out the room*])

out- (usually attached without hyphen)

out and about (three words)

out-and-out (two hyphens)

outback (no hyphen)

outbuilding (no hyphen)

outcast person rejected or excluded from social group, or wanderer

outcaste person expelled from caste, or person with no caste

outclass (no hyphen)

outdated (no hyphen)

outdoor (adjective before noun)

outdoors (adverb, noun; also **out-of-doors** for the adverb)

Outer Mongolia former name for **Mongolia**

outfitter (single **t** then double **t**)

outgoing (no hyphen)

out-Herod (hyphen; capital H)

outhouse (no hyphen)

outjockey (no hyphen)

outlying (no hyphen)

outmanoeuvre (no hyphen; **-neuver** in US English)

outmoded (no hyphen)

out of see **out**

out-of-body experience (two hyphens)

out of bounds (three words

out of date (three words, but hyphenated when used before noun)

out-of-doors variant of **outdoors** (adverb; two hyphens)

out of pocket (three words, but hyphenated when used before noun, as in *out-of-pocket expenses*)

out of sorts (three words)

outpatient (no hyphen)

outplacement (no hyphen)

outpouring (no hyphen)

output (the past tense and past participle is **outputted** or **output**)

outputted, outputting (single **t** then double **t**)

outrageous (**e** after **g**)

outré deviating from what is usual or proper (not italic; acute accent)

outrider (no hyphen)

outside (to avoid controversy, use alone as preposition, without *of*, e.g. *the streetlight outside* [not *outside of*] *my house*)

outspoken (no hyphen)

outstation (no hyphen)

outtake (no hyphen)

out-tray (hyphen)

outward (adjective, sometimes adverb (see **-ward** and **-wards**); compare **outwards**)

Outward Bound trademark for scheme providing adventure training (capital **O** & **B**; do not use with lower-case initials to denote a similar scheme run by another organization)

outwards (adverb only; compare **outward**)

outwitted, outwitting (single **t** then double **t**)

outwork (no hyphen)

ouzel bird (the spelling **ousel** is not incorrect, but it is less common)

ouzo Greek drink (lower-case **o**)

Oval, the cricket ground in London (capital **O**)

Oval Office, the office of US president in White House (capital **O** twice)

ovenproof (one word)

oven-ready (hyphen)

over- (usually attached without hyphen; see also **overly**)

overabundance (no hyphen)

overact (no hyphen)

overambitious (no hyphen)

overanxious (no hyphen)

overbalance (no hyphen)

overburden (no hyphen)
overcharge (no hyphen)
overcompensate (no hyphen)
overconfident (no hyphen)
overemphasize (also **overemphasise**; see **-ize/-ise**)
overexcited (no hyphen)
overgenerous (no hyphen)
Overijssel Dutch province (**-ijss-**)
overlong (no hyphen)
overly (do not use if an appropriate word with **over-** is available, e.g. *he is overdependent* [not *overly dependent*] *on his parents*; note that only a selection of **over-** words are listed here)
overmatter (*typog.*) typeset matter that cannot be used because of lack of space (no hyphen; also **overset**)
overmuch (no hyphen)
overnice (no hyphen)
overoptimistic (no hyphen)
overpass (no hyphen)
overrate (no hyphen)
overreach (no hyphen)
overreact (no hyphen)
overripe (no hyphen)
overrule (no hyphen)
overrun (*typog.*) transfer material from one column, line, or page to another (no hyphen)
oversensitive (no hyphen)
overset (*typog.*) set (type) in excess of space available, or another name for **overmatter** (no hyphen)
oversexed (no hyphen)
oversight (no hyphen)
oversimplify (no hyphen)
overspill (no hyphen)
oversubscribe (no hyphen)
over-the-counter (two hyphens)
overtone additional meaning (no hyphen; compare **undertone**)
overview (no hyphen)
overwinter (no hyphen)

overwrought (no hyphen)
Ovid Roman poet (Latin name **Publius Ovidius Naso**)
ovum (plural **ova**)
owing to (may be used instead of **due to** where appropriate, to avoid controversy, as in *the taxi arrived late owing to traffic congestion*)
Oxbridge Oxford University and/or Cambridge University (compare **Uxbridge**)
oxeye flowering plant (one word)
Oxfam Oxford Committee for Famine Relief (also **OXFAM**)
Oxford comma another name for **serial comma**
Oxford Group original name for what became **Moral Rearmament** and is now **Initiatives of Change**
Oxford Movement movement within Church of England that began in 1833 and led to Anglican High Church (also **Tractarianism**)
oxidize (also **oxidise**; see **-ize/-ise**)
oxtail (one word)
Oxon Oxfordshire
Oxon. of Oxford (from Latin *Oxoniensis*)
Oxonian of Oxford, or a person from Oxford
oxyacetylene (no hyphen)
oxygen (symbol **O**)
oxymoron rhetorical effect juxtaposing contradictory terms, as in *living death* (plural **oxymora**)
oyer legal term
oyez cry of town crier (rarely **oyes**)
oystercatcher (one word)
Ozalid trademark for method of duplicating typeset matter for proofreading, or a proof so produced (capital **O**)
ozone-friendly (hyphen)
ozone layer (two words)
'Ozymandias' sonnet by Shelley

P

P phosphorus (no full stop)
p. page (plural **pp.**)
Pa protactinium (no full stop)
PA Pennsylvania (US postal code); personal assistant; press agent; Press Association; public-address (system); Publishers Association
p.a. per annum
pace with due deference to (followed by name of someone who has expressed a different opinion; italics)
pacemaker (one word)
pacey (also **pacy**)
pacha less common variant of **pasha**
pachyderm (**-chy-**)
Pacific Ocean (capital **P** & **O**; also **the Pacific**)
pacifist (not **-ificist**)
pack drill (two words)
packed past tense and past participle of **pack** (compare **pact**)
packhorse (one word)
pack ice (two words)
packsaddle (one word)
pact agreement (compare **packed**)
pacy variant of **pacey**
paddle steamer (two words)
paddle wheel (two words)
paddymelon Australian melon, the plant on which it grows, or variant of **pademelon** (one word)
pademelon small wallaby (also **paddymelon**)
Paderewski, Ignace Jan Polish pianist, composer, and statesman (not **Pada-**)
Padova Italian name for **Padua**
padre clergyman (not italic)
Padua Italian city (Italian name **Padova**)
paean hymn, song of praise, or enthusiastic praise (compare **peon**)
paederast rare variant of **pederast**
paediatric of the branch of medical science concerned with children and their diseases (**ped-** in US English; compare **orthopaedic**)
paedophile person who is sexually attracted to children (**ped-** in US English; compare **pederast**)
paella Spanish dish (not italic; **pae-**)
paeony less common variant of **peony**
Paganini, Niccolò Italian violinist and composer (grave accent on first name)
page (*typog.*) sheet of paper in book or either of its sides (compare **leaf**; see also **recto** and **verso**)
Page, Sir Earle Australian statesman (not **Earl**); **Sir Frederick Handley** English pioneer in aircraft design (compare **Paige**)
pageant (**-gea-**)
pageboy (one word)
page numbers see **pagination**
page proof (*typog.*) proof of text made up into pages (compare **galley**)
page-turner (hyphen)

pagination numbering of pages. Numbers are usually omitted on the first page of a chapter or section or on a full-page illustration. Prelims are usually numbered with lower-case Roman numerals. In multi-volume works, numbering may or may not continue consecutively from one volume to the next.

Pago Pago port in American Samoa (former name **Pango Pango**)

Pahlavi Persian language used in Zoroastrian literature (the variant **Pehlavi** is less common but not incorrect)

Pahlavi, Mohammed Reza and **Reza** shahs of Iran

paid past tense and past participle of **pay** in all senses except 'caulk seams of vessel'

paid-up (hyphen)

Paige, Elaine English actress and singer (compare **Page**)

Paignton English town (-**gn**-)

pail bucket (compare **pale**)

paillasse less common variant of **palliasse**

pain physical discomfort (compare **pane**)

Paine, Thomas American political pamphleteer (compare **Payne**)

painkiller (one word)

painstaking (one word)

paintball (one word)

paintbox (one word)

paintbrush (one word)

paintings see **titles of works**

paint stripper (two words)

pair two things or people joined, used, or grouped together. Use singular verb if the two items form or are considered as a single entity (e.g. *a pair of scissors is required* or *a pair of socks is an unimaginative present*); use plural verb if they are considered as two individuals, or if the words *a pair of* are missing

(e.g. *a pair of troublemakers who have caused untold harm* or *scissors are required*). For spelling, compare **pare** and **pear**.

pair bonding (two words)

paisley pattern with curving shapes (lower-case **p**)

Paisley Scottish town (capital **P**)

Paisley, Bob English footballer and manager; **Rev. Ian** Northern Ireland politician and Presbyterian minister

Paiute North American Indian people or language (also **Piute**)

pajamas US spelling of **pyjamas**

Pakeha in New Zealand, person not of Maori ancestry

Paki offensive word for **Pakistani**, especially with reference to people of Pakistani descent in the UK; even more objectionable when used of people from India or Bangladesh

Pakistan S Asian country, or former S Asian country comprising two provinces, West Pakistan (which became Pakistan in 1971) and East Pakistan (which became **Bangladesh** in 1971)

Pakistani of Pakistan, or a person from **Pakistan**

Palace (capital **P** as part of name, as in *Lambeth Palace*, or in elliptical references to Buckingham Palace, as in *visitors to the Palace*)

palaeo- ancient or prehistoric, as in *palaeontology* (sometimes capital **P**, especially for nouns such as *Palaeozoic*; -**leo**- in US English)

Palaeolithic period of emergence of primitive man, or of this period (the use of lower-case **p** is confined to the adjective, and is less common even in this sense)

palatable (not -**eable** or -**ible**)

palate roof of mouth, or sense of taste (single **l**, single **t**; compare **palette** and **pallet**)

palaver (not **-va**)

pale whitish, dim, fade, wooden post, barrier, or used in the phrase *beyond the pale* (compare **pail**)

Palestine Liberation Organization (not **Palestinian**)

palette surface for mixing paint, or range of colours (single **l**, double **t**; compare **palate** and **pallet**)

palette knife (the spelling **pallet knife** is not incorrect, but it is less common)

Palgrave, Francis Turner British critic and poet

Pali language of Buddhist scriptures

palimpsest manuscript on which previous text has been erased and replaced with new text (**-imp-**, **-est**)

palish (not **-eish**)

Palladian of Palladio or his style of architecture, of Pallas Athena, or literary word for wise or learned (capital **P**)

Palladio, Andrea Italian architect

palladium (symbol **Pd**)

Pallas Athena another name for **Athena** (also **Pallas**)

pallbearer (one word)

pallet straw-filled mattress or makeshift bed (double **l**, single **t**; compare **palette** and **palate**)

pallet knife less common variant of **palette knife**

palliasse straw-filled mattress (double **l**, double **s**; **paillasse**, which is the French spelling of the word from which it is derived, is a less common variant)

palliate (double **l**)

pall-mall former ball game (hyphen)

Pall Mall street in London (two words)

pallor (not **-our**)

Palma capital of Balearic Islands, on Majorca (compare **La Palma**)

Palmas Brazilian city (compare **Las Palmas**)

Palm Beach US town in Florida (compare **Palm Springs**)

palmcorder (one word)

Palmerston former name for Darwin (the place)

Palmerston, Henry John Temple, 3rd Viscount British statesman

Palm Springs US city in California (compare **Palm Beach**)

Palm Sunday Sunday before Easter (capital **P** & **S**)

palmtop (one word)

Palo Alto US city or Mexican battlefield (two words)

Palomar, Mount USA, site of observatory (**-mar**)

palomino (lower-case **p**; plural **palominos**)

palpable (not **-ible**)

Pamplona Spanish city (former name **Pampeluna**)

panacea (not **-cia**)

Pan-African (hyphen; capital **P** & **A**)

panama variant of **Panama hat**

Panama Central American country on isthmus linking North and South America, or variant of **Panama hat**

Panama hat (also **panama** or **Panama**)

Pan-American (hyphen; capital **P** & **A**)

Pan American Union official agency of Organization of American States (no hyphen)

Pancake Day another name for **Shrove Tuesday** (capital **P** & **D**)

Panchen Lama lama ranking immediately below Dalai Lama (capital **P** & **L**; also **Tashi Lama**)

pancreas glandular organ (not **-cras**)

panda bearlike animal (compare **pander**)

pandemic affecting people over a wide area (compare **endemic** and **epidemic**)

pandemonium (**-dem-**)

pander gratify, or pimp (compare **panda**)

pandit variant of **pundit** in the sense 'learned Brahman'

Pandit, Vijaya Lakshmi Indian politician and diplomat (see also **Nehru**)

P&O shipping company (no spaces around ampersand; full name Peninsular and Oriental Steam Navigation Company)

Pandora's box (capital **P**)

p & p postage and packing

pane sheet of glass (compare **pain**)

panegyric (**e** then **y**)

panel (single **n**, single **l**)

panel beater (two words)

panelled, panelling (single **l** in US English)

panellist (single **l** in US English)

Pan-European (hyphen; capital **P** & **E**)

Pangaea ancient supercontinent (also **Pangea**)

Pango Pango former name for **Pago Pago**

panhandle (one word)

Panhellenic (no hyphen; capital **P**, lower-case **h**)

panic (not **-ck**)

panic buying (two words)

panicked, panicking (**-ck-**)

panic-stricken (hyphen)

panpipes (one word; lower-case **p**)

pantheon temple to all gods (lower-case **p**; no accent)

Pantheon church in Rome (capital **P**; no accent)

Panthéon church in Paris (capital **P**; acute accent)

pantihose (also **pantyhose**)

panzer of or denoting mechanized armoured unit used by Germans in World War II (lower-case **p**)

Papal States (capital **P** & **S**)

Papandreou, Andreas Greek economist and politician

Papanicolaou, George US anatomist who devised cervical smear, also known as **Pap test** (**-aou**)

paparazzo freelance photographer (not italic; plural **paparazzi**)

papaw North American tree or its fruit, or variant of **papaya** (also **pawpaw**)

papaya Caribbean tree or its fruit (also **papaw** or **pawpaw**)

Papeete capital of French Polynesia, on Tahiti (double **e** then single **e**)

paperback book with flexible cover, or denoting such a book or edition (also **softback** (noun) or **soft-cover** (adjective); compare **hardback**)

paperclip (one word)

paperknife (one word)

paper tiger (two words)

paperweight (one word)

paperwork (one word)

papier-mâché hard substance made from paper and paste, moulded when wet (not italic; hyphen; circumflex and acute accent; not **paper-**)

papoose (also **pappoose**)

Pap test cervical smear (capital **P**, lower-case **t**; see also **Papanicolaou**)

Papua New Guinea country in SW Pacific comprising part of New Guinea and various other islands

papyrus (**-pyr-**; plural **papyri** or **papyruses**)

par average, standard, or equality (compare **parr**)

paracetamol (lower-case **p**)

paraclete rare word for mediator or advocate (lower-case **p**)

Paraclete in Christianity, the Holy Ghost as comforter or advocate (capital **P**)

paradigm pattern, typical example, or set of all inflected forms of word (compare **paragon**)

paradise (lower-case **p** in all senses)

paradisiacal (also **paradisaical**)

paraffin (single **r**, double **f**)
paragliding (no hyphen)
paragon model of excellence
(compare **paradigm**)
paragraph subsection of text that
begins new line with left-hand
indentation or a line space above
(but rarely both). The first paragraph
following a chapter or section
heading is usually not indented.
Note that in manuscripts with
paragraphs separated by line spaces,
it may not be clear when a new
paragraph begins at the top of a
page. See also **pilcrow**, **orphan**,
widow, and **direct speech**.
Paraguay South American country
and river (**-gu-**)
parakeet (the spelling **parrakeet** is
not incorrect, but it is less common)
parallel (double **l** then single **l**)
paralleled, paralleling (double **l** then
single **l**)
parallelogram (double **l** then single **l**)
Parallel Olympics see **Paralympics**
Paralympian competitor in
Paralympics (capital **P**)
Paralympic of Paralympics (capital **P**)
Paralympics, the sporting event for
disabled people modelled on
Olympic Games (capital **P**; not **-rol-**;
short for **Parallel Olympics**)
paralyse (**-yze** in US English)
parameter variable, or limiting factor
(compare **perimeter**)
paramilitary (no hyphen)
paranoiac of or having the mental
disorder paranoia (also **paranoic**)
paranoid of, characterized by, or
resembling the mental disorder
paranoia, or showing undue
suspicion or fear of persecution
paraphernalia (**-phern-**)
Paraquat trademark for poisonous
substance used as weedkiller
(capital **P**)
parascending (**-sc-**)

par avion by airmail (italics; two
words)
Pardo palace in Madrid, Spain
(compare **Prado**)
pare peel, cut, or trim (compare **pair**
and **pear**)
parentheses the characters (and),
used to enclose incidental material
and in mathematics, logic, etc. (also
round brackets; see also **brackets**
and **square brackets**; singular
parenthesis)
Parent's Charter (**-'s** not **-s'**)
parent teacher association (three
words; capital initials with reference
to a particular association;
abbreviation **PTA**)
par excellence beyond comparison
(italics)
pariah (**-iah**)
pari-mutuel betting system (hyphen;
not italic; not **-ual**; plural **pari-
mutuels** or **paris-mutuels**)
Paris Commune council briefly
established in Paris in 1871 after
Franco-Prussian War (capital **P & C**;
see also **Commune**)
parishioner (not **-shon-**)
Parisian of Paris, or a person from
Paris (**-ian**)
Park (capital **P** as part of name, e.g.
Hyde Park)
parka hooded weatherproof coat
(not **-ker**)
Parker Bowles, Camilla name of
Prince Charles's second wife before
their marriage (no hyphen)
parking meter (two words)
parking ticket (two words)
Parkinson's disease (capital **P**;
apostrophe; named after British
surgeon James Parkinson)
Parkinson's law (capital **P**;
apostrophe; named after British
writer Cyril Northcote Parkinson)
park keeper (two words)
parlance (not **-ence**)

parlay betting system

parley discussion

parliament a legislative assembly (**-liam-**; lower-case **p**)

Parliament the legislative assembly of a particular nation, especially the UK (**-liam-**; capital **P**)

parliamentary of a parliament or Parliament (**-liam-**, **-tary**; also **Parliamentary** in the sense 'of Parliament')

parlour (**-or** in US English)

parlour game (two words)

Parma Italian or US city

Parma ham (capital **P**)

Parmesan of Parma in Italy, a person from Parma, or another name for **Parmesan cheese** (capital **P**; not **-mis-**)

Parmesan cheese (capital **P**)

Parmigiano Reggiano another name for **Parmesan cheese** (capital **P** & **R**)

Parnassus the world of poetry, or a collection of verse (capital **P**)

Parnassus, Mount Greece

paroxysm (not **-ism**)

parquet wooden floor covering (not italic)

parquetry (**-try**)

parr young salmon (compare **par**)

Parr, Catherine sixth wife of Henry VIII (not **Catharine** or **Katherine**)

parrakeet less common variant of **parakeet**

Parramatta Australian city and river (double **r**, single **m**, double **t**)

parrot-fashion (hyphen)

Parsee adherent of monotheistic religion of Zoroastrian origin, or of this religion (also **Parsi**)

Parsifal hero of Holy Grail legends in German mythology (also **Parsival**; English equivalent **Percival**)

Parsifal opera by Wagner (not *-val*)

parsimony (not **parci-**)

Parsival variant of **Parsifal**

parson's nose (apostrophe)

part. participle

partake (to avoid controversy, do not use **partake of** with reference to food and drink that is not shared with others)

parterre formal flower garden or theatre pit (not italic)

part exchange (noun)

part-exchange (verb)

Parthenon temple on the Acropolis in Athens, Greece (**-enon**)

Parthian shot hostile remark, gesture, look, etc. delivered on leaving (capital **P**; virtually synonymous with **parting shot**, which is far more frequent)

partially to some extent, as in *the house is partially obscured by trees* (compare **partly**)

participle see **misplaced modifier**, **past participle**, and **present participle**

parti-coloured (hyphen)

particularize (also **particularise**; see **-ize/-ise**)

parting shot see **Parthian shot**

Parti Québécois political party in Quebec, Canada (two acute accents)

partly used with reference to a part or parts, as in *the house is built partly of glass* (compare **partially**)

part time (adverb)

part-time (adjective)

Party (capital **P** in names of political parties, e.g. *Conservative Party*)

partygoer (one word)

party line (two words)

parvenu person who has risen socially but is considered to lack appropriate refinement (not italic; may be used for males and females)

parvenue woman who has risen socially but is considered to lack appropriate refinement (not italic)

Pasadena US city (single **s**)

pascal unit of pressure (lower-case **p**; compare **paschal**)

Pascal computer-programming language (capital **P**)

Pascal, Blaise French philosopher, mathematician, and physicist

paschal of Passover or Easter (also **Paschal**; compare **pascal**)

Pas de Calais French name for the Straits of Dover (three words)

Pas-de-Calais French department (two hyphens)

pas de deux ballet sequence for two dancers (not italic; three words; same form for singular and plural)

pasha provincial governor in Ottoman Empire (the spelling **pacha** is not incorrect, but it is less common)

Pashto language of Afghanistan and NW Pakistan (also **Pushto** or **Pushtu**)

Pasionara, La Spanish Communist leader (single **s**; real name **Dolores Ibarruri**)

paso doble ballroom dance (not italic; plural **paso dobles** or **pasos dobles**)

passable acceptable, or able to be crossed (compare **passible**)

passacaglia dance or musical composition (not italic; double **s**, **-glia**)

passbook (one word)

Passchendaele Belgian village, scene of battle in World War I (**-ssch-**, **-aele**)

passé outmoded or faded (not italic; acute accent)

passed past tense and past participle of **pass**, as in *they passed our house* or *I have passed my driving test* (verb only; compare **past**)

passe-partout gummed paper strips used to mount picture, or master key (not italic; hyphen; not **pass-**)

passer-by (hyphen; plural **passers-by**)

passible susceptible to emotion or suffering (compare **passable**)

passim throughout (italics; used instead of a more specific reference when something occurs frequently in the work cited)

Passion (capital **P** with reference to the sufferings of Christ)

passion fruit (lower-case **p**)

Passion play (capital **P** then lower-case **p**)

Passion Week (capital **P** & **W**)

passive form of verb using *be* + past participle (as in *the word is rarely used, the houses were demolished last year, she has been promoted*, etc.), as opposed to the **active** form (as in *cows eat grass, he has lost his keys*, etc.). Avoid unnecessary use of passive (e.g. replace *France was defeated by Germany* with *Germany defeated France*), but note that there are many cases where the passive is more appropriate, as in the three examples given in the opening lines, which cannot easily be converted to active form.

passkey (one word)

Passover Jewish festival (also **Pesach** or **Pesah**)

passport (one word)

password (one word)

past time that has elapsed, history, tense of verbs, finished, beyond, etc., as in *they walked past our house* or *past holders of the office* (noun, adjective, adverb, or preposition; compare **passed**)

pastel crayon or pale colour (compare **pastille**)

Pasternak, Boris Leonidovich Russian writer

paste-up (noun; the verb is **paste up**)

pasteurize (also **pasteurise**; see **-ize/-ise**)

pastiche work that mixes or imitates (not italic; the Italian form **pasticcio** is a less common variant)

pastille sweet or medicated lozenge (compare **pastel**)

pastime (single **s**)

pastis alcoholic drink (lower-case **p**)

past master (two words; not **passed**)

pastoral (as adjective) of rural life, relating to clergyman's duties to congregation, or relating to teacher's responsibility for personal development of pupils; (as noun) work of art or literature portraying rural life

pastorale musical composition evocative of rural life (not italic)

past participle part of verb that ends in **-ed** (for regular verbs) and is used with *be, have*, etc., as in *they have escaped, she will be promoted*. Past participles of irregular verbs include *broken, forgotten, swum, gone*, etc.

patchwork (one word)

pate head (compare **pâté**)

pâté spread of finely minced liver, poultry, etc. (not italic; circumflex and acute accent; compare **pate** and **patty**)

pâté de foie gras goose-liver paste (not italic; circumflex and acute accent)

patent leather (**-ent**)

Patent Office (capital **P** & **O**)

paternoster rosary beads used in reciting Lord's Prayer, fixed form of words used as prayer or charm, type of fishing tackle, or type of lift (one word; lower-case **p**)

Paternoster the Lord's Prayer, or the recital of this (one word; the use of lower-case **p** is less common but not incorrect)

Paterson US city (single **t**)

Paterson, Andrew Barton Australian poet, who wrote 'Waltzing Matilda' (known as **Banjo Paterson**); **Bill** Scottish actor; **William** Scottish banker, founder of the Bank of England (single **t**)

Pathétique sonata by Beethoven or symphony by Tchaikovsky (italics; acute accent)

pathfinder (one word)

pathos power or quality of arousing pity, sympathy, sorrow, etc. (compare **bathos**)

Patient's Charter (**-'s** not **-s'**)

patio (plural **patios**)

patisserie fancy pastries, or shop selling them (not italic; no accent; single **t**, double **s**)

Patna rice (capital **P**)

patois dialect or jargon (not italic; same form for singular and plural)

patriate bring under authority of autonomous country

patriot person who fervently supports his or her country

patrol (single **l**)

patrol car (two words)

patrolled, patrolling (double **l**)

patrolman (one word)

patronize (also **patronise**; see **-ize/-ise**)

patronymic name derived from father or ancestor (not **-nim-**)

Patton, George Smith US general (**-on**)

patty flattened cake of minced food, or small pie (compare **pâté**)

Pavarotti, Luciano Italian tenor (single **v**, single **r**, double **t**)

pavilion (single **l**)

paviour paving block, or person who lays paving (also **pavior**)

Pavlov, Ivan Petrovich Russian physiologist

pavlova meringue topped with cream and fruit (lower-case **p**)

Pavlova, Anna Russian ballerina

pawnbroker (one word)

pawnshop (one word)

pawpaw variant of **papaw** or **papaya** (one word)

pay (past tense and past participle **paid** (in most senses) or **payed** (in nautical sense 'caulk seams of vessel'))

pay-and-display (two hyphens)

payback (noun; the verb is **pay back**)

pay bed (two words)

payday (one word)

PAYE pay as you earn

paying guest (two words)

Payne, Cynthia English madam (compare **Paine**)

payoff (noun; the verb is **pay off**)

payout (noun; the verb is **pay out**)

payphone (one word)

payroll (one word)

Pb lead (no full stop; from Latin *plumbum*)

PC personal computer; Police Constable; politically correct

PCB polychlorinated biphenyl; printed circuit board

Pd palladium (no full stop)

PDSA People's Dispensary for Sick Animals

PE physical education

peace state of harmony, silence, or serenity (compare **piece**)

peaceable inclined towards peace (**e** after **c**)

peaceful calm, tranquil, or not involving violence

peacekeeping (one word)

peacemaker (one word)

peace offering (two words)

peace pipe (two words)

peacetime (one word)

peach Melba (capital **M**)

peak point, mountain, maximum, or reach peak (compare **peek** and **pique**)

Peak District England (capital **P** & **D**)

peal sound of bells, thunder, laughter, etc., or make this sound (compare **peel**)

pear fruit (compare **pair** and **pare**)

pear-shaped (hyphen)

pearl gem (compare **purl**)

Pearl Harbor Hawaiian site of US naval base attacked in World War II (not **Harbour**)

Pears, Sir Peter British tenor

Pearse, Patrick Irish nationalist (compare **Peirce** and **Pierce**)

Peary, Robert Edwin US arctic explorer

pease pudding (two words; not **peas**)

peasouper (one word)

peccadillo (double **c**, single **d**, double **l**; plural **peccadilloes** or **peccadillos**)

peccary piglike mammal (**-ary**)

peculiar (not **-lier**, but see **Old Peculier**)

pedagogue (not **paed-**; not **-gog**, except as a less common variant in US English)

pedagogy (not **-guy**)

pedal lever operated by foot (compare **peddle**)

pedalled, pedalling (single **l** in US English)

peddle sell (compare **pedal**)

peddler person who sells illegal drugs (compare **pedlar**)

pederast man who has sex with boy (rarely **paederast**; compare **paedophile**)

pedestrianize (also **pedestrianise**; see **-ize/-ise**)

pediatric US spelling of **paediatric**

pedlar person who goes from place to place selling goods (compare **peddler**)

pedophile US spelling of **paedophile**

peek glance (compare **peak** and **pique**)

peekaboo (one word)

peel skin or rind, or remove or shed surface layer (compare **peal**)

Peel, Sir Robert British statesman, founder of Metropolitan Police

Peele, George English dramatist and poet

peephole (one word)

Peeping Tom (capital **P** & **T**)

peepshow (one word)

peepul Indian tree (also **pipal** or **bo tree**)

peer member of nobility, or equal (compare **pier**)

peer group (two words)

peewit (the spelling **pewit** is not incorrect, but it is less common)

Pehlavi less common variant of **Pahlavi** (the language)

peignoir woman's dressing gown (not italic)

Peiraeus rare variant of **Piraeus**

Peirce, Charles Sanders US logician, philosopher, and mathematician (compare **Pierce** and **Pearse**)

pejorative (not **per-**)

Peking former name for **Beijing**

Pekingese breed of dog, dialect of Mandarin Chinese, or person from Beijing (capital **P**; also **Pekinese**)

pelargonium (not **perla-**; lower-case **p** in general use, *Pelargonium* is the genus name)

pell-mell (hyphen)

Peloponnese, the Greek peninsula (single **l**, single **p**, double **n**)

penalize (also **penalise**; see **-ize/ -ise**)

Penang Malaysian state and island that forms part of it, or another name for the state capital, **George Town**

pence plural of **penny** used in sums of money and to denote specific coins, usually abbreviated to *p* in speech and writing, e.g. *it cost 80p, a 50p piece* (compare **pennies**)

penchant inclination or liking (not italic)

pencil (single **l**)

pencilled, pencilling (single **l** in US English)

pendant (noun)

pendent (adjective)

pendulum (plural **pendulums**)

penetrable (not **-atable**)

penetrate (not **-ni-**)

pen friend (two words)

penicillin (single **n**, double **l**)

peninsula (noun)

peninsular (adjective)

Peninsular Malaysia see **Malaysia**

Peninsular War (capital **P** & **W**; **-ar** twice)

penknife (one word)

Penmaenmawr Welsh town

pen name (two words)

pennies plural of **penny** used with reference to the 1p coin, as in *does the machine take pennies?* (compare **pence**)

penniless (not **penny-**)

Pennsylvania US state (double **n** then single **n**)

Penny Black (capital **P** & **B**)

penny-dreadful (hyphen)

penny-farthing (hyphen)

penology (also **poenology**)

pen pal (two words)

penpusher (one word)

pension boarding house, or full board, in France (italics)

pensioners see **OAP**

penstemon variant of **pentstemon**

pentagon five-sided polygon (lower-case **p**)

Pentagon headquarters of US Department of Defense, in Virginia, or military leadership of USA (capital **P**)

pentameter line of verse (not **-tre**)

Pentateuch first five books of Old Testament (capital **P**; **-euch**; see also **Torah**)

Pentecost Jewish festival 50 days after second day of Passover, or another name for **Whit Sunday**

Pentecostal of Pentecost, or denoting charismatic Christian Church (capital **P**)

penthouse (one word)

pentstemon (also **penstemon**)

pent-up (hyphenated unless used after noun, as in *she was pent up at home all day*)

penuchle variant of **pinochle** (also **penuckle**)

peon in various countries, labourer, messenger, attendant, policeman, or soldier (compare **paean**)

peony (the spelling **paeony** is not incorrect, but it is less common)

people usual plural of **person** (compare **persons**). As a singular noun meaning 'nation' (plural **peoples**), it may be followed by a singular or plural verb (see **collective nouns**).

people carrier (two words)

People's Republic of China Asian country, third largest in the world (compare **Republic of China**)

PEP personal equity plan; political and economic planning

peppercorn (one word)

pepper mill (two words)

Pepsi-Cola trademark for carbonated drink (capital **P** & **C**; hyphen)

Pepys, Samuel English diarist and naval administrator

per annum every year or by the year (not italic; two words)

per capita of or for each person (not italic; two words)

perceive (**-ei-**)

perceivable (not **-ible**)

per cent (two words as adverb, e.g. *ten per cent*)

percentage (one word)

perceptible able to be perceived (not **-able**; compare **perceptive** and **percipient**)

perceptive quick at perceiving or able to perceive (compare **perceptible** and **percipient**)

Perceval variant of **Percival**

perchance (one word)

percipient able to perceive or quick at perceiving (compare **perceptive** and **perceptible**)

Percival Arthurian knight (also **Perceval**; see also **Parsifal**)

percolate (**-col-**)

percolator (not **-er**)

père added to French surname to specify father rather than son, as in Dumas *père* (italics; compare *fils*)

Père Lachaise cemetery in Paris, France (capital **P** & **L**; grave accent)

Perelman, S(idney) J(oseph) US humorist

peremptory urgent, commanding, decisive, or positive (compare **perfunctory**)

perennial (single **r**, double **n**)

perestroika reconstruction of Soviet economy under Mikhail Gorbachov (not italic)

Pérez de Cuéllar, Javier Peruvian diplomat (two acute accents)

perfect (do not use with *more, most,* or *very*)

perfectible (not **-able**)

perfecting (*typog.*) printing reverse side of printed sheet

perforate (**-for-**)

perforce (one word)

Performing Right Society (not **Rights**)

perfunctory cursory, superficial, careless, or indifferent (compare **peremptory**)

Pergamon Press publishing company (**-mon**)

Pergamum ancient city in Asia Minor (**-mum**)

perigee (single **r**, double **e**)

Périgord district of France (acute accent)

Perigordian period of ancient culture (no accent)

perilous (single **l**)

perimeter boundary, or line enclosing plane area (compare **parameter**)

perineum region of body between anus and genitals (compare **peritoneum**)

period US and Canadian word for **full stop**

periodic intermittent, relating to a period, or occurring in repeated cycles (adjective only)

periodical (as noun) publication issued at regular intervals; (as adjective) of a periodical, published at regular intervals, or intermittent (see also **titles of periodicals**)

peripatetic (-pate-)

peritoneum lining of abdominal cavity (compare **perineum**)

periwinkle (single **r**)

perjury (-ju-)

perk informal shortening of **percolate** or **perquisite**

permanent (-mane-)

permeable (-mea-)

Permian period of the Palaeozoic era, or of this period (-mia-)

permissible permitted (not -able)

permissive tolerant, lenient, or granting permission

permit (single **t**)

permitted, permitting (double **t**)

pernickety (-snick- in US English)

Pernod trademark for apéritif (capital **P**)

Perón, Juan Domingo Argentine statesman; **Eva (Duarte) de** Argentine actress, active in politics and social welfare as second wife of Juan Domingo (known as **Evita**) (acute accent on surname)

Peronist (as noun) supporter of Juan Domingo Perón; (as adjective) of Juan Domingo Perón or his policies (no accent)

perpetrate be responsible for, as in *perpetrate a crime*

perpetuate cause to continue, as in *perpetuate a misconception*

Perpignan French town (-gnan)

per pro per procurationem (see **pp**)

perquisite full form of **perk** in the sense 'benefit' (compare **prerequisite**)

Perrier trademark for sparkling mineral water (capital **P**)

per se by or in itself (not italic; two words)

persecute oppress (compare **prosecute**)

perseverance (not -serv-, not -ence)

Persia former name for **Iran**

Persian carpet (capital **P**)

Persian cat (capital **P**)

Persian Gulf arm of Arabian Sea between Iran and Arabia (capital **P** & **G**)

Persian rug (capital **P**)

persimmon (double **m**; -on)

persistent (not -ant)

person see **man**, **persons**, and **people**

-person see -**man**

persona (plural **personae**)

personage important person (compare **personality**)

persona grata acceptable person (italics; plural *personae gratae*)

personal private, of a particular person, of the body, etc. (compare **personnel**)

personality character, or famous person (compare **personage** and **personalty**)

personalize (also **personalise**; see -ize/-ise)

personalty legal term for personal property (compare **personality**)

persona non grata unacceptable person (italics; plural *personae non gratae*)

personate act the role of, or assume identity of (another person) for criminal purposes (compare **impersonate** and **personify**)

personify attribute human characteristics to, or represent (abstract quality) (compare **personate** and **impersonate**)

personnel people employed by organization, as opposed to **materiel**, or department that deals with employees (compare **personal**)

persons plural of **person** sometimes used in official or legal contexts but best avoided elsewhere (compare **people**)

perspective way of regarding situation, objectivity, artistic technique, or used in the phrases *in perspective, out of perspective*, etc. (compare **prospective** and **prospectus**)

Perspex trademark for clear resin used as substitute for glass (capital **P**)

perspicacious perceptive or discerning

perspicuous easily understood

persuadable (not **-dible**, but also **persuasible**, not **-sable**)

perverse wayward, contrary, or deviating from what is normal, right, good, etc. (compare perverted)

perversion state of being perverted, or something perverted

perversity state of being perverse, or something perverse

perverted gaining sexual satisfaction by abnormal means, distorted, or incorrectly interpreted (compare **perverse**)

Pesach another name for **Passover** (also **Pesah**)

Peshawar Pakistani city (**-war**)

Pestalozzi, Johann Heinrich Swiss educational reformer

Pet. Peter (books of the Bible; full stop; not italic)

Pétain, Henri Philippe Omer French marshal (acute accent)

pete (lower-case **p** in the phrase *for pete's sake*)

1 Peter book of the Bible (not italic; abbreviation **1 Pet.**; also **I Peter**)

2 Peter book of the Bible (not italic; abbreviation **2 Pet.**; also **II Peter**)

Peterborough English or Canadian city (**-borough**)

Peterhouse Cambridge college (one word)

Peterlee town in Co. Durham

Peterloo Massacre incident at St Peter's Fields, Manchester, in 1819 (capital **P & M**)

Peter Principle theory that people rise to their own level of incompetence (capital **P** twice)

petit bourgeois another name for **petite bourgeoisie**, a member of the petite bourgeoisie, or characteristic of the petite bourgeoisie (not italic; **-tit**)

petite small and slim (not italic)

petite bourgeoisie lower middle class (not italic; **-tite**; also **petit bourgeois** or **petty bourgeoisie**)

petit four small sweet cake or biscuit (not italic; plural **petits fours**)

petit larceny (also **petty larceny**)

petit mal mild form of epilepsy (not italic; compare **grand mal**)

petit point small needlepoint stitch (not italic; compare **gros point**)

Petrarch Italian poet and scholar (Italian name **Francesco Petrarca**)

petrel bird (compare **petrol**)

Petri dish (capital **P**)

petrochemical (no hyphen)

Petrograd a former name (1914–24) for **St Petersburg**

petrol fuel (compare **petrel**)

petroleum (not **-ium**)

pettifogging (double **t**, not **petty-**)

petty bourgeoisie variant of **petite bourgeoisie**

petty larceny variant of **petit larceny**

petulant (not **-ent**)

Peugeot French motor manufacturer, or any of their vehicles (capital **P**; **-eu-** then **-eo-**)

pewit less common variant of **peewit**

PG parental guidance (film classification); paying guest; postgraduate

pH potential of hydrogen (measure of acidity or alkalinity; lower-case **p**, capital **H**)

Phaedra wife of Theseus in Greek mythology (compare *Phèdre*)

Phaethon asteroid (no diaeresis; **-thon**)

Phaëthon son of Helios in Greek mythology (diaeresis; **-thon**)

phaeton horse-drawn carriage (lower-case **p**; **-ton**)

Phalangist member of Lebanese paramilitary organization (compare **Falangist**)

phalanx (plural **phalanxes** or **phalanges**)

phallic of or resembling penis (double **l**)

phantasm (archaic spelling **fantasm**)

phantasmagoria (not **fant-**; also **phantasmagory**)

phantasy archaic spelling of **fantasy**

Pharaoh title of ancient Egyptian kings (capital **P**; **-aoh**; compare **faro**)

Pharisaic of Pharisees, or self-righteously hypocritical (also **Pharisaical**; the use of lower-case **p** is confined to the meaning 'hypocritical', and is less common even in this sense)

Pharisee member of ancient Jewish sect, or self-righteous hypocrite (the use of lower-case **p** is confined to the meaning 'hypocrite', and is less common even in this sense)

pharmaceutical (**-eu-**)

pharmacopoeia (**-oeia**; capital **P** in names, e.g. **British Pharmacopoeia**)

pharyngeal (**-ryng-**; also **pharyngal**)

pharynx (**-rynx**; plural **pharynges**)

phase period or stage, introduce or remove gradually, or cause to coincide (compare **faze**)

PhD Doctor of Philosophy (from Latin *Philosophiae Doctor*; the variant **DPhil**, an abbreviation of the English form, is less common but not incorrect)

Phebe less common variant of **Phoebe** (the goddess or personification of moon)

Phèdre play by Racine (compare **Phaedra**)

Pheidippides Athenian athlete (single **d** twice, double **p**; the spelling **Phidippides** is less common but not incorrect)

phenomenon (plural **phenomena**; do not use plural form with singular meaning)

phial small bottle (also **vial**; compare **file**)

Phi Beta Kappa US honorary society based on high academic ability

Phidippides less common variant of **Pheidippides**

Phil. Philippians (full stop; not italic)

philatelist collector of postage stamps (single **l** twice, single **t**; compare **phillumenist**)

Philby, Harold Adrian Russell English double agent (known as **Kim Philby**; single **l**)

Philem. Philemon (full stop; not italic)

Philemon book of the Bible (not italic; abbreviation **Philem.**)

Philharmonic (capital **P** as part of name of orchestra, choir, or society, e.g. *Royal Liverpool Philharmonic Orchestra*)

Philip apostle of Christ; **King** various European monarchs; **Prince** another name for the Duke of **Edinburgh** (single **l**; compare **Phillip** and **fillip**)

Philippe French first name (single **l**, double **p**)

Philippi ancient city in NE Macedonia (single l, double p)

Philippians book of the Bible (not italic; single l, double p; abbreviation **Phil.**)

philippic impassioned speech of denunciation (lower-case initial p; single l then double p)

Philippics orations of Demosthenes against Philip of Macedon or Cicero against Antony (capital P)

Philippine variant of **Filipino** (adjective)

Philippines, the Asian country occupying archipelago (official name **Republic of the Philippines**; single l, double p; see also **Filipino** and **Tagalog**)

Philippopolis Greek name for **Plovdiv**

Philips company manufacturing electronic equipment (single l, single p; compare **Phillips**)

Philips, Ambrose and **John** English poets (single l, single p; compare **Phillips**)

Philistine (as noun) member of non-Semitic people of ancient Philistia in SW Palestine, or boorishly uncultured person; (as adjective) of the ancient Philistines, or boorishly uncultured (also **philistine** for the adjectival sense 'boorishly uncultured')

Phillip, Arthur English naval commander (double l, single p, no -s; compare **Philip**, **Phillips**, and **fillip**)

Phillips trademark for screw with cross-shaped slot and screwdriver that fits it (capital P; double l, single p, -s; compare **Philips**)

Phillips, Mark first husband of Princess Anne (double l, single p, -s; compare **Philips**)

Phillpotts, Eden English writer (double l, double t, -s)

phillumenist collector of matchbox labels (double l, -men-; compare **philatelist**)

philosopher's stone (-'s not -s')

philosophize (also **philosophise**; see -ize/-ise)

philtre drink supposed to arouse love or desire (-er in US English; compare **filter**)

Phiz English illustrator of Dickens' novels (real name **Hablot Knight Browne**)

phlebitis inflammation of a vein (phle-, -is)

phlegm mucus in respiratory tract (-gm)

Phnom Penh capital of Cambodia (-hn- then -nh; the spelling **Pnom Penh** is less common but not incorrect)

Phoebe girl's name, satellite of Saturn, classical goddess, or poetic personification of moon (the spelling **Phebe** is a less common variant for the goddess or moon, but it should not be used for the girl or satellite)

Phoebus Apollo as the sun god, or poetic personification of the sun

Phoenicia ancient country now occupied by parts of Lebanon, Syria, and Israel (-oe-)

phoenix (-oe-)

phone (no apostrophe)

phone book (two words)

phonecard (one word)

phone-in (hyphen)

phoney (-ny in US English)

phosphorescent (-or-, -sc-, -ent)

phosphorous (adjective)

phosphorus (noun; symbol P)

photo call (two words)

photocell (one word)

photocomposition typesetting in which photographic film or photosensitive paper is used to make printing plates (one word;

also **photosetting** or **phototype-setting**)

photocopy (one word)

photoelectric (one word)

photo finish (two words)

Photofit trademark denoting picture of police suspect built up from photographs of facial characteristics, or the method of producing such pictures (capital **P**; one word)

photojournalism (one word)

photomontage (one word)

photo-offset (hyphen)

photo opportunity (two words)

photosensitive (one word)

photosetting another name for **photocomposition** (one word)

photosynthesis (one word)

photosynthesize (also **photosynthesise**; see **-ize/-ise**)

phototypesetting another name for **photocomposition** (one word)

phraseology (**-seol-**)

Phrygian cap symbol of liberty during French Revolution (capital **P**)

phthalic acid acid used in dyes and perfumes (**phth-**; single **l**)

phthisis tuberculosis or similar disease (**phth-**)

Phuket island, province, and town in Thailand

Phyfe, Duncan US cabinet-maker (born **Duncan Fife** in Scotland)

phylactery case containing biblical passages, worn by Jewish men during prayers (**-phy-**, **-ery**)

phylloxera insect pest of plants, especially vines (**phy-**; double **l**)

phylum (plural **phyla**) in the hierarchy of **taxonomic names** of animals, the group that comes above a class and below a kingdom (compare **division**). The phylum name has a capital initial and is not italic. The term is also used to

denote a group of related language families.

physic rare or archaic word for medicine, art of healing, or physics (compare **physique**)

physical of the body, of material things, or of physics

physician doctor

physicist student of or expert in physics

physics branch of science concerned with properties of mater and energy

physiognomy (**-gn-**)

pi Greek letter used to represent ratio of circumference to diameter of circle, jumbled pile of printer's type, or slang shortening of **pious** (also **pie** in the sense 'jumbled pile'; see also **pi character**)

piano (plural **pianos**)

pianoforte (one word; use **piano** instead in all but the most formal contexts)

Pianola trademark for mechanical piano using perforated paper roll (capital **P**)

piazza open square in Italy, or covered passageway in the UK (not italic; compare **pizza** and **plaza**)

pibroch music for Scottish bagpipes (**-och**)

pica unit of measurement equal to 12 points, approximately one sixth of an inch (also **em** or **pica em**)

Picard, Jean French astronomer (compare **Piccard**)

picaresque denoting novel or story about adventures of roguish hero (compare **picturesque**)

Picasso, Pablo Spanish artist (single **c**, double **s**)

Piccadilly street or station name (double **c**, single **d**, double **l**)

piccalilli (double **c**, single **l** then double **l**; not **-y**)

piccaninny offensive name for Black or Aboriginal child (double **c**, single

n then double **n**; **picka-** or **pica-** in US English)

Piccard, Auguste Swiss physicist; **Jean Félix** Swiss-born US chemist and aeronautical engineer (compare **Picard**)

piccolo (double **c**, single **l**; plural **piccolos**)

pi character another name for **special sort**

pickaback variant of **piggyback** (one word)

pickaxe (one word)

picketed, picketing (not -tt-)

picket line (two words)

pick-me-up (two hyphens)

pickpocket (one word)

pick-up (noun and adjective; the verb is **pick up**)

picnic (not -ck-)

picnicked (-ck-)

picnicker (-ck-)

picnicking (-ck-)

picture book (two words)

picturesque attractive, striking, or vivid (compare **picaresque**)

picture window (two words)

pidgin language incorporating features from two others that is used for trade (lower-case **p**; compare **creole** (for meaning) and **pigeon** (for spelling))

pidgin English (lower-case **p**)

pie food with pastry crust, dialect name for magpie, or variant of **pi** in the sense 'jumbled pile of printer's type'

piebald denoting horse with white and black markings (compare **skewbald**)

piece part, portion, coin, object used in playing board games, etc. (compare **peace**)

pièce de résistance most outstanding item (italics; grave accent then acute accent)

piecemeal (one word)

piecework (one word)

pie chart (two words)

pied-à-terre flat or house for occasional use (not italic; two hyphens; grave accent; plural **pieds-à-terre**)

pier structure built out over water, pillar, or support (compare **peer**)

Pierce, Franklin US statesman (compare **Peirce** and **Pearse**)

Pierian Spring ancient Greek fountain of inspiration (capital **P** & **S**; -ie- then -ia-)

pierrot clown with whitened face and pointed hat (the use of capital **P** is not incorrect in this sense, but it is less common)

Pierrot character from French pantomime (capital **P**)

Piers Plowman medieval poem by William Langland (italics)

Piesporter German white wine (capital **P**; -ie-)

pietà painting or sculpture of dead Christ supported by Virgin Mary (not italic; grave accent)

Pietermaritzburg South African city (**Pie-, -burg**)

piezoelectric (no hyphen; **pie-**)

pigeon bird, dupe, or responsibility (compare **pidgin**)

pigeonhole (one word)

Piggott, Lester English jockey (double **g**, double **t**)

piggyback (one word; also **pickaback**)

piggy bank (two words)

pig-headed (hyphen)

pig iron (two words)

pigmy variant of **pygmy**

Pigmy variant of **Pygmy**

Pigott-Smith, Tim English actor (hyphen; single **g**, double **t**)

pigskin (one word)

pigsty (one word)

pigswill (one word)

pigtail (one word)

pikestaff (one word)

pilaf variant of **pilau** (the usual spelling in the phrase *rice pilaf*; also **pilaff**)

Pilate, Pontius Roman procurator who ordered Crucifixion of Christ

Pilates system of exercise (capital **P**)

pilau rice dish (the usual spelling in the phrase *pilau rice*; also **pilaf, pilaff, pilao,** or **pilaw**)

pilcrow the paragraph symbol (¶) (also **blind**)

pile-up (noun; the verb is **pile up**)

Pilgrim Fathers (capital **P** & **F**)

Pilgrim's Progress, The allegory by John Bunyan (**-'s** not **-s'**)

pill, the oral contraception (the use of capital **P** is best confined to contexts where the lower-case form would be ambiguous or unclear; it is not usually necessary in the phrase *on the pill*)

pillar (not **-er**)

pillar box (two words)

pillbox (one word)

pillowcase (one word)

pillow fight (two words)

pilot (use instead of gender-specific **airman** or **airwoman**)

piloted, piloting (not **-tt-**)

pilot light (two words)

Pils type of beer (capital **P**; single **l**)

Pilsen German name for **Plzeň**

Pilsner type of beer (capital **P**; also **Pilsener**)

Pimm's trademark for alcoholic drink (capital **P**; apostrophe)

PIN personal identification number (thus *number* in the phrase *PIN number* is redundant)

piña colada drink consisting of pineapple juice, coconut, and rum (not italic; two words; tilde)

pinball (one word)

pince-nez eyeglasses held on nose with clip (not italic; hyphen; same form for singular and plural)

pincushion (one word)

Pindar ancient Greek poet (**-ar**)

Pinero, Sir Arthur Wing English dramatist

pineapple (one word; **-ea-**)

pine cone (two words)

Ping-Pong trademark for table tennis (capital **P** twice; hyphen)

pinhole (one word)

pin money (two words)

pinochle card game (also **penuchle, penuckle,** or **pinocle**)

pinpoint (one word)

pinprick (one word)

pins and needles (three words)

pinscher see **Doberman pinscher**

pinstripe suit (**pinstripe** is one word; not **pinstriped**)

pint-size (hyphen; also **pint-sized**)

pin-up (hyphen)

Pinyin system of transliteration of Chinese, developed in 1958 and now in official use in China (compare **Wade-Giles**; see also **Chinese names**)

pious devout (compare **Pius**)

pipal variant of **peepul**

pipe cleaner (two words)

pipe dream (two words)

pipeline (one word)

piquant pleasantly pungent, tart, or stimulating (not italic; not **-cqu-**)

pique resentment, score in piquet, irritate, or excite (not italic; compare **peak** and **peek**)

piqué ribbed fabric (not italic; acute accent)

piquet card game (not italic; not **-cqu-**)

Piraeus Greek port adjoining Athens (rarely **Peiraeus**; Modern Greek name **Piraiévs**)

piraña variant of **piranha**

Pirandello, Luigi Italian writer

Piranesi, Giambattista Italian etcher and architect

piranha (not **-ana-**; also **piraña**)

pirouette (single **r**, **-oue-**)

Pisces zodiac sign (**-sc-**)

Pissarro, Camille French painter (double **s**, double **r**; compare **Pizarro**)

pistachio (not **-cho**; plural **pistachios**)

piste ski slope (not italic)

pistil part of flower

pistol gun

pistole coin

pita plant yielding fibre used to make rope and paper (compare **pitta**)

pit bull terrier (three words)

pitch-and-toss (two hyphens)

pitchblende (one word; not **-nd**)

pitchfork (one word)

piteous arousing pity (not **-ious**; compare **pitiable** and **pitiful**)

pithead (one word)

pith helmet (two words)

pitiable arousing pity or contempt (**-iable**; compare **piteous**)

pitiful arousing pity or contempt (**-tif-**; compare **piteous**)

pit stop (two words)

pitta tropical bird, or variant of **pitta bread**

pitta bread slightly leavened bread (also **pitta**)

pittance (not **-ence**)

Pittsburgh US port (double **t**, **-burgh**)

pituitary (**-ui-**, **-tary**)

Pius name of various popes (compare **pious**)

Piute variant of **Paiute**

pivoted, pivoting (not **-tt-**)

pixel (**-el**)

pixelated denoting picture in which individual pixels can be seen, or blurred with overlaid grid of squares (compare **pixilated**)

pixie (the spelling **pixy** is not incorrect, but it is less common)

pixilated eccentric, whimsical, or drunk (also **pixillated**; compare **pixelated**)

pixy less common variant of **pixie**

Pizarro, Francisco Spanish conqueror of Peru (single **z**, double **r**; compare **Pissarro**)

pizazz less common variant of **pizzazz**

pizza baked disc of dough covered with cheese, tomatoes, etc. (compare **piazza**)

pizzazz (the spelling **pizazz** is not incorrect, but it is less common)

pizzeria (not **-aria**)

placard (not **-ck-**)

place location (compare **plaice**)

placebo (plural **placebos** or **placeboes**)

place mat (two words)

place name (two words)

place setting (two words)

plagiarize (**-giar-**; also **plagiarise**; see **-ize/-ise**)

plaguing (**-gui-**)

plaice fish (compare **place**)

Plaid Cymru Welsh nationalist party

plain (as adjective) clear, simple, not decorated, patterned, etc., or unattractive; (as noun) level treeless region (compare **plane**)

plainchant (one word)

plain clothes (no hyphen unless used before another noun, as in *a plain-clothes policeman*)

plain sailing easy progress (compare **plane sailing**)

plainsong (one word)

plain-spoken (hyphen)

plaintiff person who brings action in court of law

plaintive mournful

Planck, Max German physicist (not **-nk**)

plane (as noun) aeroplane, tree, tool, or flat or level surface; (as adjective) level or flat; (as verb) glide, skim over water, or smooth or cut with plane (no apostrophe in the sense 'aeroplane'; compare **plain**)

plane figure two-dimensional shape (not **plain**)

plane sailing navigation without reference to earth's curvature (compare **plain sailing**)

plane spotter (two words)

planetarium (-net-; plural **planetariums** or **planetaria**)

Plantagenet line of English kings (-enet)

plantar of the sole of the foot, as in *plantar warts*

planter owner of plantation, settler, machine for planting seeds, or decorative pot for plants

plasterboard (one word)

plaster cast (two words)

plaster of Paris (lower-case **p** then capital **P**)

Plasticine trademark for modelling material (capital **P**; not -ene)

plasticize (also **plasticise**; see -ize/-ise)

Plata, Río de la estuary between Argentina and Uruguay (English name **River Plate**; see also **La Plata**)

plate (*typog.*) sheet of metal, plastic, rubber, etc. used as printing surface, or print produced from this

Plate, River English name for Río de la **Plata**

plateau (plural **plateaus** or **plateaux**)

plateful (not -full; plural **platefuls**)

plate glass (two words)

platen part of printing press, typewriter, or machine tool (single **t**)

Platignum pen manufacturer (capital **P**; -tign-)

platinum metallic element (-tin-; symbol **Pt**)

platonic describing a relationship that is not romantic or sexual (the use of capital **P** is not incorrect in this sense, but it is less common)

Platonic of ancient Greek philosopher Plato (capital **P**)

platypus short for **duck-billed platypus** (-ty-, -us; plural **platypuses**)

plausible (not -able)

Plautus, Titus Maccius Roman dramatist

play-act (hyphen)

playback (noun; the verb is **play back**)

playgroup (one word)

playing card (two words)

playing field (two words)

playmate (one word)

play-off (noun; the verb is **play off**)

playpen (one word)

playschool (one word)

PlayStation trademark for video game console (one word; capital **P** & **S**)

playtime (one word)

play titles see **titles of works**

playwright (-wr-; not -write)

plaza open square in Spain, or complex of shops, buildings, etc. in the USA and Canada (not italic; compare **piazza**)

plc public limited company (also **PLC** or **Plc**)

pleaded usual form of the past tense and past participle of **plead** (**pled** is a less common variant sometimes used in Scottish law and in the USA)

pleasantness the state of being pleasant

pleasantry polite, agreeable, or amusing remark

pleasurable (not -eable)

plebeian (-eian)

plebiscite (-sc-)

plectrum (plural **plectrums** or **plectra**)

pled less common variant of **pleaded** sometimes used in Scottish law and in the USA

Pleiades seven daughters of Atlas in Greek mythology, or star cluster named after them (-eia-)

Pleiocene less common variant of **Pliocene**

Pleistocene first epoch of Quaternary period, or of this epoch (**-eist-**)

plenipotentiary (not **plent-**)

plenitude (not **plent-**)

plenteous (not **-ious**)

plentiful (**-tif-**)

plethora excess, superfluity, or overabundance (do not use with reference to an abundance that is not excessive: replace *a plethora of* with *many, a large number of*, etc. where appropriate)

pleurisy (**-eu-**; **-isy**)

plimsoll canvas shoe (lower-case **p**; the spelling **plimsole** is not incorrect, but it is less common)

Plimsoll line load line on ship (capital **P**; not **-sole**)

Pliny the Elder Roman writer, known for his *Natural History* (Latin name **Gaius Plinius Secundus**)

Pliny the Younger Roman writer and statesman, known for his letters (Latin name **Gaius Plinius Caecilius**)

Pliocene last epoch of Tertiary period, or of this epoch (the spelling **Pleiocene** is not incorrect, but it is less common)

PLO Palestine Liberation Organization

Plough, the group of stars in Ursa Major (capital **P**; also **Charles's Wain**)

ploughman's lunch (apostrophe)

Plovdiv Bulgarian city (Greek name **Philippopolis**)

Plowden, Lady Bridget Hortia English educationist responsible for the **Plowden Report** into primary education (**-den**)

Plowright, Joan English actress (**-ow-**)

PLR Public Lending Right (see that entry)

plug-and-play (two hyphens)

plum fruit, tree, colour, something superior or desirable, or variant of **plumb** when used for emphasis

plumb lead weight, perpendicularity, vertically, undergo, understand, connect to water system, or used for emphasis, as in *a plumb nuisance* (also **plum** when used for emphasis)

plumb line (two words)

plum pudding (two words)

plunging (not **-geing**)

Plunket, St Oliver Irish Roman Catholic churchman and martyr (also **Plunkett**); **Sir William Lee** Governor General of New Zealand

Plunket Society Royal New Zealand Society for the Health of Women and Children (capital **P** & **S**; not **-kett**)

Plunkett variant spelling of surname of St Oliver **Plunket**

plural (see individual entries for nouns with problematic plurals; see also **singular/plural**)

pluralize (also **pluralise**; see **-ize/ -ise**)

plus as conjunction, use **and** instead in formal contexts, e.g. *they stole her passport and* (not *plus*) *her credit cards*. Prepositional use (as in *the manuscript, plus several other important documents, was destroyed in the fire*) is acceptable in all contexts, but note that the verb agrees with the noun that precedes *plus* (i.e. *manuscript*, not *documents*, in this example). The noun sense 'something good' is best restricted to informal contexts: replace with **advantage** or another appropriate synonym elsewhere. See also **plus sign**.

plus fours (two words)

plus sign the symbol (+), usually set with a space before and after it when it indicates addition but with no space after it when it indicates a positive quantity, as in $+5°$

Plutarch ancient Greek biographer and philosopher (**-arch**)

plutonium (symbol **Pu**)

Plymouth Brethren religious sect (capital **P** & **B**)

Plynlimon Welsh mountain (**-lyn-** then **-lim-**)

Plzeň Czech city (German name **Pilsen**)

Pm promethium (no full stop)

PM Prime Minister

p.m. post meridiem (full stops; used for times from midday to midnight. Note that 12 *p.m.* usually means 'midday' but may be ambiguous, and *8 p.m. in the evening* is tautological)

PMG Paymaster General; Postmaster General

PMS premenstrual syndrome

PMT photomechanical transfer; premenstrual tension

pneumatic (**pneu-**)

pneumonia (**pneu-**)

pneumonic of the lungs or pneumonia (compare **mnemonic**)

Pnom Penh less common variant of **Phnom Penh**

Po polonium (no full stop)

PO postal order; Post Office

pocketbook (one word)

pocketful (not **-full**; plural **pocketfuls**)

pocketknife (one word)

pocket money (two words)

pockmarked (one word)

Podgorica capital of Montenegro (also **Podgoritsa**; former name (1946–92) **Titograd**)

podium (plural **podiums** or **podia**)

podzol soil characteristic of coniferous forest regions (also **podsol**)

Poe, Edgar Allan US writer (not **Alan** or **Allen**)

poem titles see **titles of works**

poenology variant of **penology**

poet (may be used for males and females)

poetess (use **poet** instead to avoid offence)

poet laureate (sometimes capital **P** & **L**, especially when used with or in place of the name of the current holder of the position; plural **poets laureate**)

poetry see **verse**

Poets' Corner part of Westminster Abbey (capital **P** & **C**; **-s'** not **-'s**)

po-faced (hyphen)

pogrom persecution or extermination of ethnic group (not italic)

poignant (**-gn-**)

Poincaré, Jules Henri French mathematician, physicist, and philosopher; **Raymond** French statesman

poinsettia (not **point-**; double **t**)

point (*typog.*) unit of measurement in printing: there are approximately 72 points to the inch (see also **decimals**)

point-blank (hyphen)

pointillism painting technique (lower-case **p**; double **l**)

point of sale (no hyphens unless used before another noun, as in *point-of-sale terminal*)

point of view (three words; plural **points of view**)

point-to-point (two hyphens)

Poirot, Hercule Belgian detective in novels of Agatha Christie (not **-reau**)

poison-pen letter (one hyphen)

poitín variant of **poteen** (acute accent)

pokey variant of **pokie** or **poky**

pokie in Australia and New Zealand, a gambling machine (also **pokey**)

poky small and cramped, or US and Canadian slang word for prison (also **pokey**)

polar of a pole or poles (compare **poler**)

polar bear (two words; not **-ler**)

polarize (also **polarise**; see **-ize/-ise**)

Polaroid trademark for sunglasses or camera (capital **P**)

pole (as noun) long cylindrical piece of wood, metal, etc., extremity of magnet or earth's axis of rotation, or used in the phrases *pole position* and *poles apart*; (as verb) strike, push, mark out, or support with a pole or poles (see also **north pole**, **North Pole**, **south pole**, and **South Pole**; compare **poll**)

poleaxe (one word)

polecat (one word)

poler person who poles, e.g. person who punts a boat with a pole (compare **polar**)

pole star guiding principle (lower-case **p** & **s**)

pole vault (noun)

pole-vault (adjective)

policeman (use **police officer** instead where appropriate)

police officer (use instead of gender-specific **policeman** or **policewoman** where appropriate)

police ranks see **ranks**

police station (two words)

policewoman (use **police officer** instead where appropriate)

policyholder (one word)

poliomyelitis (one word)

Politburo executive and policy-making committee of Communist Party (capital **P**; not **-reau**)

politic shrewd, prudent, cunning, or unscrupulous

political of politics

political correctness see individual entries for terms that may cause offence. As a general rule, do not use a gender-specific word if a gender-neutral word is available and equally appropriate; do not use noun phrases such as *the blind, the disabled, the elderly*, etc.; avoid unnecessary or irrelevant references to a person's age, sex, sexual orientation, race, nationality, religion, disability, or physical characteristics; and avoid artificial coinages and euphemisms such as *vertically challenged* (unless a humorous effect is intended).

political parties see **Party**

politicize (also **politicise**; see **-ize/-ise**)

politicking (**-ck-**)

politico (plural **politicos**)

politics (use singular verb with reference to the art, science, business, or profession of government; use plural verb with reference to a person's political opinions, sympathies, etc.; use singular or plural verb with reference to the relationships of people in a particular situation, e.g. a workplace)

polka dot (no hyphen unless used before another noun, as in *polka-dot fabric*)

poll (as noun) voting, survey of opinion, counting, or head; (as verb) receive or record votes, canvass, remove or shorten horns of (compare **pole**)

pollen count (two words)

polling booth (two words)

polling station (two words)

Pollock, Jackson US painter (**-ock**)

polloi see **hoi polloi**

poll tax (two words)

Pollyanna central character of the novel *Pollyanna* by Eleanor Porter, hence anybody who is constantly or excessively optimistic (one word; capital **P**; double **l**, double **n**)

polonaise dance or music (not italic; lower-case **p**)

polonium (symbol **Po**)

Pol Pot Cambodian Communist

statesman (do not alphabetize under **Pot**)

poltergeist mischievous spirit (not italic; lower-case **p**; **-geist**)

polyanthus (single **l**; plural **polyanthuses**)

polyethylene another name for **polythene** (one word)

polygamy (not **-lig-**)

polyglot (single **t**)

Polynesia group of Pacific islands

polyp type of invertebrate organism such as sea anemone, or small growth arising from mucous membrane (not **-lip**; also **polypus** in the sense 'small growth')

polythene (**-ene**; also **polyethylene**)

polyurethane (one word)

pomegranate (single **m**, single **n**, no **i**'s)

Pomeranian of the European region of Pomerania, a person from Pomerania, or a breed of dog (capital **P**)

pomfret liquorice sweet (lower-case **p**; also **Pontefract cake**)

pommel raised part at front of saddle, knob at top of sword, or less common variant of **pummel** (double **m**, single **l**)

pommelled, pommelling (single **l** in US English)

Pompeian variant of **Pompeiian**

Pompeii ancient Italian city buried by volcanic eruption (double **i**; compare **Pompey**)

Pompeiian of Pompeii (also **Pompeian**)

Pompey Roman general and statesman (Latin name **Gnaeus Pompeius Magnus**) or informal name for **Portsmouth** (compare **Pompeii**)

Pompidou, Georges French statesman (**-dou**)

pompom ball of tufted wool, silk, etc., or globelike flower head (also **pompon**)

poncho (plural **ponchos**)

Pontefract English town (not **-tif-**)

Pontefract cake variant of **pomfret** (capital **P**)

pontiff (double **f**)

pontifical (single **f**)

Pontin's holiday company (apostrophe)

Pontypridd Welsh town (**-ty-**; **-idd**)

ponytail (one word)

pony trekking (two words)

pooh-pooh dismiss or belittle (hyphen; **-h** twice)

Poole resort and unitary authority in Dorset (**-le**)

Poona Indian city (also **Pune**)

poorhouse (one word)

pop art (two words)

pop music (two words)

pope (for capitalization see **titles of people**)

poplar tree (not **-er**; compare **popular**)

Popocatépetl Mexican volcano (acute accent; **-tl**)

poppadom (also **poppadum**)

populace inhabitants of area, or the common people (compare **populous**)

popular widely liked, or of the general public (compare **poplar** and **populist**)

popularize (also **popularise**; see **-ize/-ise**)

populist appealing to the interests or prejudices of ordinary people, or a politician who does this

populous having large population (compare **populace**)

pop-up (adjective and noun; the verb is **pop up**)

porage see **porridge**

porcelain (**-cel-**)

Porchester spelling used for Porchester Hotel and Porchester Terrace in London (compare **Portchester**)

pore small opening in skin, leaf, etc., or study, as in *I pored over the map* (compare **pour**)

porphyria disease

porphyry igneous rock

porridge (double **r**, **-idge**; the spelling **porage** is chiefly found in the brand name *Scott's Porage Oats*)

Porritt, Sir Jonathon English environmentalist (double **r**, double **t** in surname; **-thon** in first name)

Porsche motor manufacturer, or any of their vehicles (capital **P**; **-sche**)

Portakabin trademark for portable building (capital **P**; not **-cab-**)

Port-au-Prince capital of Haiti (two hyphens; not **-aux-Princes**)

Portchester spelling used for town in Hampshire and its castle (compare **Porchester**)

portcullis (one word)

portentous (not **-tious**)

portfolio (plural **portfolios**)

Porthmadog Welsh town (former name **Portmadoc**)

portico (plural **porticoes** or **porticos**)

Portland cement (capital **P**)

Portlaoise Irish town (**-aoi-**, **-se**)

Portmadoc former name for **Porthmadog**

portmanteau (plural **portmanteaus** or **portmanteaux**)

Portmeirion Welsh village, or pottery manufacturer (one word; not **-mer-**)

Port Moresby capital of Papua New Guinea (two words; **Mores-**)

Pôrto Portuguese name for **Oporto**

Portobello Road London (**Portobello** is one word)

Porto Rico former name for **Puerto Rico**

Portpatrick Scottish town (one word)

portrait (*typog.*) denoting format or illustration with greater height than width (compare **landscape**)

Port-Salut French cheese (hyphen; capital **P** & **S**)

Portsmouth English port (informal name **Pompey**)

Portuguese (**-ugu-**)

Posen German name for **Poznań**

poser person who poses, person who likes to be seen in trendy clothes and places, or baffling question

poseur person who strikes an attitude in order to impress others (not italic)

posey affectedly trendy (compare **posy**)

posited, positing (not **-tt-**)

posse body of men (compare **possie**)

possessive denoting words and phrases such as *my, mine, your, yours, his, hers, its, Julie's, the cat's*. An **apostrophe** is used with nouns only (i.e. not in *yours, hers, its,* and *theirs*). Note the use of a possessive in such phrases as *a book of my father's* or *a friend of hers*, a construction that applies to human possessives only: e.g. *all the women claimed that he was a lover of theirs*, but *don't give me chocolates, because I'm not a lover of them*. See also **-ing**.

possible (not **-able**)

possie in Australia and New Zealand, informal word for position (compare **posse**)

possum informal name for **opossum**, Australian and New Zealand name for various other marsupials, or used in the phrase *play possum*

Post see **Van der Post**

post- (usually attached without hyphen in the sense 'after', except to words beginning with **t** or capital letter; see individual entries for other exceptions)

postbag (one word)

postbox (one word)

postcode (one word)

post-colonial (hyphen)

Postcomm Postal Services Commission (double **m**)

postdate (one word)

postdoctoral (one word)

poste restante service by which mail is collected by addressee from post office (not italic; two words; **-te** twice)

postfeminist (one word)

post-free (hyphen)

postgraduate (one word)

posthaste (one word)

posthumous (-th-, -ous)

postilion (also **postillion**)

postimpressionism (one word)

postindustrial (one word)

Post-it Notes trademark for small stickers used for messages, reminders, etc. (one hyphen; capital **P** & **N**; lower-case **i**)

postmark (one word)

post meridiem full form of **p.m.** (not italic; two words; **-iem**)

postmillennial (one word)

postmodern (one word)

postmortem examination of dead body (not italic; one word; not **-um**)

postnatal (one word)

post-obit taking effect after death, or denoting bond payable after death (not italic; hyphen)

post office place offering postal and other services (lower-case **p** & **o**)

Post Office government department responsible for postal services (capital **P** & **O**)

postoperative (one word)

post-paid (hyphen)

post-Reformation (hyphen; lower-case **p**, capital **R**)

postscript (one word)

post-traumatic stress disorder (one hyphen)

post-war (hyphen)

posy small bunch of flowers (compare **posey**)

Pot see **Pol Pot**

potage thick soup, especially one made to a French recipe (italics; single *t*; compare **pottage**)

potassium (symbol **K**)

potato (plural **potatoes**)

pot-bound (hyphen)

poteen illicit spirit distilled in Ireland (also **poitín**)

pothole (one word)

pot plant (two words)

potpourri (one word; double **r**; plural **potpourris**)

potsherd fragment of pottery (one word; also **potshard**)

pottage thick meat or vegetable soup, such as that for which Esau sold his birthright to Jacob (Gen. 25:29–34) (not italic; double **t**; compare *potage*)

Potter, Beatrix British writer and illustrator of children's stories (not **Beatrice**); **Dennis** British dramatist (not **Denis**); **Stephen** British humorist and critic (not **Steven**)

Potters Bar English town (no apostrophe)

potter's wheel (-'s not -s')

potting shed (two words)

Poulenc, Francis French composer

poultice (-ou-, -ice)

pour flow or cause to flow (compare **pore**)

Poussin, Nicolas French painter

POW prisoner of war (the use of lower-case **o** is less common but not incorrect; plural **POWs**)

powder puff (two words)

powder room (two words)

Powell, Anthony British novelist; **Enoch** British politician; **Michael** British film writer, producer, and director (double **l**)

power-assisted (hyphen)

powerboat (one word)

power dressing (two words)

Powergen energy company (capital **P**, lower-case **g**)

powerhouse (one word)
power-sharing (hyphen)
power station (two words)
power steering (two words)
powwow (one word)
Powys Welsh county (**-ys**)
Powys, John Cowper British writer (**-ys**)
Poznań Polish city (German name **Posen**)
pp past participle; per procurationem (used when signing on behalf of somebody else: strictly speaking, *Mary Smith pp David Wright* means that David Wright is signing on behalf of Mary Smith, not vice versa); post-paid; prepaid
pp. pages
PPE philosophy, politics, and economics (university course)
ppm parts per million
PQ Province of Quebec; Parti Québécois
Pr praseodymium (no full stop)
PR proportional representation; public relations
practicable feasible
practical of, involving, or concerned with practice rather than theory, adapted for use, or virtual
practically (beware of possible ambiguity: e.g. *practically impossible* may mean 'almost impossible' or 'impossible to put into practice')
practice (noun)
practise (verb)
practitioner (**-tion-**)
Prado art gallery in Madrid, Spain (compare **Pardo**)
praesidium variant of **presidium**
Prague capital of Czech Republic (Czech name **Praha**)
Prairie Provinces three Canadian provinces: Manitoba, Saskatchewan, and Alberta
praseodymium (symbol **Pr**)
pratique formal permission for

vessel to use foreign port (not italic; not **pract-**)
pray address communication to deity, or implore (compare **prey**)
prayer book book of prayers (lower-case **p** & **b**)
Prayer Book another name for **Book of Common Prayer** (capital **P** & **B**)
Prayer of Manasseh book of the Apocrypha (not italic; abbreviation **Pr. Man.**)
praying mantis (not **preying**)
Pré see **du Pré**
pre- (usually attached without hyphen, except to words beginning with **e** or capital letter)
preadolescent (no hyphen)
preamplifier (no hyphen)
prearrange (no hyphen)
precarious (**-cari-**)
precautionary measure (use **precaution** instead where appropriate)
precede go before (compare **proceed**)
precedence act of preceding, or priority
precedent (as noun) example used to decide or justify later case or occurrence; (as adjective) preceding
precentor person who leads or directs singing in church or cathedral (not **-er**)
preceptor tutor or instructor (not **-er**)
precession act of preceding, or used in the phrase precession of the equinoxes (compare **procession**)
pre-Christian (hyphen; capital **C**)
pre-Christmas (hyphen; capital **C**)
precipice (**-ci-** then **-ic-**)
precipitate rash, hasty, or sudden
precipitous resembling a precipice, or very steep
precis summary of text (not italic; also **précis**)
precisian person who observes rules precisely

precision preciseness

preconceive (-ei-)

precondition (no hyphen)

precook (no hyphen)

precursor (not -er)

predate (no hyphen)

predator (not -er)

predecease (no hyphen)

predecessor (not -er)

predicate affirm

predict foretell

predictable (not -ible)

predictor (not -er)

predilection (not -deli-)

predominant (not -ent)

pre-eminent (hyphen; not -ant)

pre-empt (hyphen)

pre-exist (hyphen)

prefab prefabricated building (no full stop)

preface introductory statement written by author or editor of book (compare **foreword**)

prefer (single r at end)

preferable (single r, not -ible)

preference (single r, not -ance)

preferred, preferring (double r)

prefix word element attached at beginning, e.g. *anti-* in *antiseptic*. Usually attached without hyphen, but see entries for individual prefixes and words. Compare **suffix**.

preliminary (not -ery)

prelims the parts of a book (e.g. title page, imprint page, preface, contents, introduction) that precede the main text (also **front matter**)

premarital (no hyphen)

premier head of government, e.g. of Canadian province or Australian state, or first in importance or occurrence (do not use in place of **prime minister** for the head of the British government)

premiere first public performance (not italic; no accent)

premise statement from which conclusion is drawn (also **premiss**)

premises land and buildings, e.g. as place of business (not -isses)

premiss variant of **premise**

premium (plural **premiums**)

Premium Bonds (the use of lower-case **p** & **b** is less common but not incorrect; official name **Premium Savings Bonds**)

preoccupied absorbed in one's own thoughts (compare **occupied**)

preoccupy (no hyphen)

preordain (no hyphen)

prep informal shortening of **preparation**, **preparatory**, or **prepare** (no full stop)

prep. preposition

preparation (-ara-)

preparatory (-ara-, -ory)

preposition part of speech that usually precedes a noun or pronoun and links it to another part of the sentence or clause (e.g. *over* in *he jumped over the fence*). It is not incorrect to end a sentence or clause with a preposition: choose the solution that is most appropriate for the context (e.g. *I need a vase to put these flowers in* [... *in which to put these flowers* would be unidiomatic] but *this is the van in which the goods were smuggled into the country* [... *the van the goods were smuggled into the country in* would be inelegant]).

preproduction (no hyphen)

prep school (no full stop)

Pre-Raphaelite (hyphen; capital **P** & **R**)

prerequisite required as a prior condition, or something required as a prior condition (compare **perquisite** and **requisite**)

pre-Roman (hyphen; lower-case **p**, capital **R**)

presbyterian of Church government by lay elders (lower-case **p**)

Presbyterian denoting a Protestant Christian Church that is now largely part of the United Reformed Church in England and Wales (capital **P**)

preschool (also **pre-school**)

Prescott, John British politician (double **t**)

prescribe lay down as rule, or recommend (drug or other remedy) (compare **proscribe**)

presentiment (no hyphen)

presently (beware of ambiguity, in view of the increasing use of this adverb to mean 'at the moment' rather than 'soon')

present participle part of verb that ends in **-ing** (see that entry)

preset (no hyphen)

preshrunk (no hyphen)

president (for capitalization see **titles of people**)

presidium (plural **presidiums** or **presidia**; also **praesidium**)

press conference (two words)

press gang (noun)

press-gang (verb)

press release (two words)

press stud (two words)

press-ups (hyphen; US and Canadian name **push-ups**)

pressure (as verb) coerce or compel, or variant of **pressurize**

pressure-cook (hyphen)

pressure cooker (two words)

pressurize increase pressure in or on (enclosed space or fluid), or variant of **pressure** (verb) (also **pressurise**, see **-ize/-ise**)

Prester John legendary Christian priest and king

prestigious (**-ious**)

Prestonpans Scottish town (one word)

prestress (no hyphen)

Prestwich town in Greater Manchester

Prestwick Scottish town and airport

presumable (not **-eable**)

presume take for granted or dare (compare **assume**, which is virtually synonymous in the sense 'take for granted')

presumptive based on presumption or probability, or used in the phrase *heir presumptive*

presumptuous characterized by presumption, bold, or forward

presuppose (no hyphen)

preteen (no hyphen)

pretence act of pretending, make-believe, or pretext (**-ense** in US English)

pretension false claim to merit or importance, unfounded allegation, or pretentiousness (**-ens-**)

pretentiousness affectation or ostentation (**-tious-**)

preternatural (one word)

pretzel (**-zel**)

prevaricate be evasive (compare **procrastinate**)

preventable (the spelling **preventible** is not incorrect, but it is less common)

preventative (variant of **preventive**)

preventible less common variant of **preventable**

preventive (also **preventative**)

Prévert, Jacques French poet (acute accent)

preview (not **-vue**)

Previn, André US orchestral conductor (no accent on surname, acute accent on first name)

Prévost d'Exiles, Antoine François French novelist (known as **Abbé Prévost**)

prewar (no hyphen)

prey (as noun) animal killed by another for food, victim, or used in the phrase *bird of prey*; (as verb) kill for food, make victim of, or weigh heavily, as in *preying on my mind* (compare **pray**)

price cost (compare **prise**)

price-fixing (hyphen)

price list (two words)

pricey (also **pricy**)

prie-dieu piece of furniture for kneeling on when praying (not italic; hyphen)

priest (use this form for both males and females in Christian Church)

priestess (use this form in non-Christian contexts only)

prima donna female operatic star, or temperamental person (not italic; two words; plural **prima donnas**)

primaeval rare variant of **primeval**

prima facie at first sight (not italic; two words, but hyphenated when used before noun, as in *prima-facie evidence*)

prime (*typog.*) the symbol ('), used in mathematics

prime minister (for capitalization see **titles of people**; see also **premier**)

primeval (rarely **primaeval**)

primitive (-**mit**-)

primogenitor ancestor

primogeniture state of being first-born, or right of succession of eldest son

primula (lower-case **p** in general use; *Primula* is the genus name)

Primus trademark for portable stove (capital **P**)

prince (for capitalization see **titles of people**)

princess royal eldest daughter of monarch (lower-case **p** & **r**)

Princess Royal title of Princess **Anne** (capital **P** & **R**)

Princes Street Edinburgh (no apostrophe)

Prince's Trust (apostrophe)

Princeton University New Jersey, USA (not -**town**)

principal most important, director, head of school, leading performer, or capital or property as opposed to interest or income (adjective and noun; compare **principle**)

Principe island off W Africa, part of the country of **São Tomé e Principe**

principle standard, rule, law, morality, fundamental truth, or essence (noun only; compare **principal**)

printed circuit board (three words)

printing press (two words)

print-out (noun; the verb is **print out**)

prioritize arrange in order of priority, or give priority to (also **prioritise**, see -**ize**/-**ise**; paraphrase to avoid controversy or ambiguity)

prior to (use **before** instead where appropriate)

prise force open or obtain with difficulty (the spelling **prize** is not incorrect in this sense, but it is less common; compare **price**)

prison officer (use instead of **warder** or **wardress**)

pristine denoting something in its original state (to avoid controversy, do not use in the sense 'spotlessly clean')

Privatdocent in German-speaking countries, university lecturer who formerly received fees from students (not italic; capital **P**; one word; not -**zent**)

private personal, individual, confidential, not public, or soldier of lowest rank (compare **privet**)

privatize (also **privatise**; see -**ize**/-**ise**)

privet plant used for hedges (compare **private**)

privilege (-**vile**-; not -**dge**)

Privy Council (not -**sel**)

Privy Counsellor (not -**cillor**)

Prix Goncourt (capital **P** & **G**)

prize reward for winner, value highly, or less common variant of **prise**

prizefighter (one word)

prizewinner (one word)

Pr. Man. Prayer of Manasseh (full stops; not italic)

PRO Public Record Office (see that entry); public relations officer

pro- (usually attached without hyphen in the sense 'in favour of', except to words beginning with capital letter; see individual entries for other exceptions)

proabortion (no hyphen)

proactive (no hyphen)

pro-am (hyphen)

pro-American (hyphen)

probationary (not **-ery**)

probiotic (no hyphen)

proboscis (**-sc-**; plural **proboscises** or **proboscides**)

pro-British (hyphen)

procedure established method of doing something (not **-ceed-**; compare **proceeding** and **proceedings**)

proceed advance, undertake, institute, or arise (compare **precede**)

proceeding course of action, or step taken in legal action (compare **procedure**)

proceedings minutes of meeting, litigation, or events (compare **procedure**)

procession group moving forwards in orderly or ceremonial manner (compare **precession**)

pro-choice (hyphen)

procrastinate put off, defer, or delay (compare **prevaricate**)

Procter & Gamble company producing and marketing household cleaners, toiletries, etc. (not **-tor**; ampersand; not **-bol**)

proctor university teacher who enforces discipline (not **-er**)

procurator fiscal Scottish legal officer (two words; not **-ter**; sometimes capital **P** & **F**, especially with reference to a particular holder of the title)

prodigal recklessly extravagant or lavishly generous, or a spendthrift (to avoid controversy, do not use of somebody who is simply returning after a long absence: the *prodigal son* of the Bible (Luke 15:11–32) is so named because he has squandered his money, not because he has been away for a long time)

prodigy person with unusual talents, or any cause of wonder (compare **protégé** and **protégée**)

produce something produced, especially agricultural products regarded collectively (compare **product**)

producible (not **-able**)

product something produced, especially by personal effort or a mechanical or industrial process; result or consequence; substance formed in chemical reaction; or result of multiplying (compare **produce**)

pro-European (hyphen)

prof informal shortening of **professor** (no full stop)

Prof. Professor (used as title before name, as in *Prof. Arthur Wilson*)

professor (single **f**, double **s**, **-or**; capital **P** when used as title or part of title)

professoriate (also **professorate**)

proffer (double **f**, single **r**)

proffered, proffering (double **f**, single **r**)

proficient (not **-ant**)

profit gain (compare **prophet**)

profited, profiting (not **-tt-**)

profiterole (single **f**, single **t**)

pro forma prescribing set procedure or performed in set manner (not italic)

pro forma invoice (three words; no italics)

progenitor (not **-er**)

prognosis prediction of course or

outcome of disease, or any forecast (compare **diagnosis**)

program sequence of instructions for computer, feed program into (computer), or US spelling of **programme**

programme (as noun) list of events, performers, etc., TV or radio show, schedule, or syllabus; (as verb) schedule (**program** in US English)

programmed past tense and past participle of **program** or **programme** (the use of single **m** is confined to US English and is less common even there)

programmer person who programs or person who programmes (the use of single **m** is confined to US English and is less common even there)

programming present participle of **program** or **programme**, often used as verbal noun (the use of single **m** is confined to US English and is less common even there)

Prohibition period (1920–33) when alcohol was banned in USA (capital **P**)

projector (not **-er**)

Prokofiev, Sergei Sergeyevich Soviet composer

proletariat (not **-ate**)

pro-life (hyphen)

prolific producing something in abundance, as in *a prolific writer* (to avoid controversy, do not use in the sense 'produced in abundance', as in *prolific writings*)

PROLOG computer programming language (no full stops; also **Prolog**)

prologue (not **-log**, except as a less common variant in US English)

Prometheus Titan who stole fire for humankind in Greek mythology (not **-ius**)

promethium (symbol **Pm**)

promilitary (no hyphen)

prominent (not **-ant**)

promissory (single **m**, double **s**, **-ory**)

promoter (not **-or**)

pron. pronoun; pronunciation

prone lying face downwards, or inclined (compare **prostrate** and **supine**)

pronounceable (**e** after **c**)

pronunciation (not **-noun-**)

proof (*typog.*) trial impression or printout produced for correction of errors (see also **galley** and **page proof**)

proofread (one word)

proofreader (one word)

proofreading (one word; see Appendix i for a list of proofreading marks)

prop propeller or theatrical property (no full stop)

propaganda (singular noun; **-pag-**, **-da**)

propel (single **l**)

propellant (noun; compare **propellent**)

propelled (double **l**)

propellent (adjective; compare **propellant**)

propeller (double **l**; not **-or**)

propelling (double **l**)

property possession, land, quality, or movable object on stage set (compare **propriety**)

prophecy (noun)

prophesy (verb)

prophet person who predicts (may be used for males and females; compare **profit**)

prophetess (use **prophet** instead in modern contexts to avoid offence)

proposal act of proposing, plan, or offer of marriage

proposition (as noun) something proposed for consideration, person or matter to be dealt with, or sexual invitation; (as verb) invite to have sex

proprietary (as adjective) relating to property, privately owned, or denoting trademark or drug manufactured under trademark; (as noun) proprietary drug, proprietors collectively, or right to property (**-prie-**, **-tary**; compare **propriety**)

proprietor (may be used for males and females; not **-er**)

proprietress (use **proprietor** instead to avoid offence)

propriety appropriateness, or conformity to prevailing standard of behaviour (compare **property** and **proprietary**)

pro rata in proportion (two words; not italic)

prorate divide or assess pro rata (one word)

pros and cons arguments for and against (no italics; no full stops)

prosciutto Italian cured ham (not italic; **-sciu-**, double **t**)

proscribe prohibit or outlaw (compare **prescribe**)

prosecute bring criminal action against, engage in, or continue to do (compare **persecute**)

proselyte (**-sel-**, **yte**)

proselytize (also **proselytise**; see **-ize/-ise**)

prosody study of poetic metre and art of versification (not related to **prose**)

prospective future or likely (compare **perspective** and **prospectus**)

prospector (not **-er**)

prospectus brochure about educational institution, or statement about forthcoming share issue (plural **prospectuses**; compare **prospective** and **perspective**)

prostate gland (compare **prostrate**)

prostrate lying face downwards, exhausted, cast (oneself) down in submission or exhaust (compare

prone and **supine** (for meaning) and **prostate** (for spelling))

protactinium (symbol **Pa**)

protector (may be used for males and females; not **-er**)

protectorate territory controlled by another state, or office of protector (lower-case **p**)

Protectorate period (1653–59) in which Oliver and Richard Cromwell were heads of state (capital **P**)

protectress (use protector instead to avoid offence)

protégé person helped by another's patronage (not italic; two acute accents; may be used for males and females; compare **prodigy**)

protégée girl or woman helped by another's patronage (compare **prodigy**)

protein (**-ei-**)

pro tem for the time being (two words; not italic; no full stops; from Latin *pro tempore*)

Proterozoic division of Precambrian era (not **Proteo-**)

Protestant of any of the Christian Churches that are separated from the Roman Catholic Church, or a member of a Protestant Church (capital **P**)

protester (also **protestor**)

Proteus in Greek mythology, sea god who could change his shape at will

protocol (single **l**; all the vowels are **o**'s)

protozoan (noun and adjective; also **protozoon** (plural **protozoa**) for the noun)

protractor (not **-er**)

Proudhon, Pierre Joseph French socialist (compare **Prudhomme**)

Prov. Proverbs (full stop; not italic)

provable (not **-eable**)

proved past tense and past participle of **prove** (also **proven** for the past participle)

proven variant of **proved** (past participle), used in the Scottish legal phrase *not proven*

provenance place of origin or history of ownership of work of art, archaeological specimen, etc. (not italic; not **-ence** or **-ience**)

Provençal (as adjective) of Provence; (as noun) a language of Provence or a person from Provence (cedilla; **-al**)

Provençale culinary term (cedilla; **-ale**)

Provence former French province, now part of Provence-Alpes-Côte d'Azur

Proverbs book of the Bible (not italic; abbreviation **Prov.**)

provided variant of **providing** in the sense 'on the condition that'

provident providing for future needs, or proceeding from foresight

providential of or supposedly proceeding from divine providence (compare **provident**)

providing on the condition that (also **provided** in this sense)

proviso (plural **provisos** or **provisoes**)

Prudhomme see **Sully-Prudhomme** (compare **Proudhon**)

prurient (not **-iant**)

PS postscript

Ps. Psalms (full stop; not italic)

Psalms book of the Bible (not italic; abbreviation **Ps.**)

Psalter translation or other version of Psalms, or book containing this (capital **P**)

psaltery ancient stringed instrument

p's and q's used in the phrase *mind one's p's and q's* (apostrophes)

PSBR public sector borrowing requirement (excess of government expenditure over income from taxation, etc.)

pseud false or pretentious person (no full stop)

pseud. pseudonym

pseudo- (usually attached without hyphen)

pseudonym (ps-, -eu-, -ym)

pseudoscience (one word)

psittacosis disease transmitted by parrots (ps-, double **t**)

Pskov Russian city and lake (**Psk-**)

psych used in the phrasal verbs *psych out* and *psych up*

psyche human mind or soul

psychedelic (not **-cho-**)

psychiatrist person who treats mental disorders (compare **psychoanalyst**, **psychologist**, and **psychotherapist**)

psycho- (ps-, -ch-; usually attached without hyphen)

psychoanalyse (one word; **-yze** in US English)

psychoanalysis (one word)

psychoanalyst person who treats mental and emotional disorders by investigating unconscious mind (one word; compare **psychiatrist**, **psychologist**, and **psychotherapist**)

psychologist person who studies human or animal behaviour or attempts to modify it (compare **psychiatrist**, **psychoanalyst**, and **psychotherapist**)

psychosomatic (**-som-**)

psychotherapist person who treats nervous disorders by psychological methods (one word; compare **psychiatrist**, **psychoanalyst**, and **psychologist**)

psychotherapy (one word)

pt part; point

Pt platinum (no full stop)

PT physical training

PTA Parent Teacher Association

ptarmigan (pt-, -an)

pterodactyl (pt-, -yl)

PTO please turn over

Ptolemy ancient Greek astronomer, mathematician, and geographer

(Latin name **Claudius Ptolemaeus**), or any of various kings of ancient Egypt

ptomaine (the spelling **ptomain** is not incorrect, but it is less common)

Pty proprietary (used in names of privately owned companies in Australia, New Zealand, and South Africa

Pu plutonium (no full stop)

pub public house (no full stop)

pub. public; publication; published; publisher; publishing

pub-crawl (hyphen)

public-address system (one hyphen)

publicize (also **publicise**; see **-ize/ -ise**)

Public Lending Right right of authors to receive payment when their books are borrowed from libraries (abbreviation **PLR**)

publicly (not **-cally**)

Public Record Office (not **Records**; part of The **National Archives** since 2003)

public-spirited (hyphen)

Publishers Association (no apostrophe)

pucka less common variant of **pukka**

pucker gather or wrinkle (compare **pukka**)

Puebla Mexican city and state (compare **Pueblo**)

pueblo village or town in parts of the Americas, e.g. communal village with flat-roofed houses inhabited by American Indians (lower-case **p**)

Pueblo US city, or member of any of the American Indian peoples who live in pueblos (compare **Puebla**)

Puerto Rico Caribbean island commonwealth (former name **Porto Rico**)

puffball (one word)

puff pastry (two words)

Puglia Italian name for **Apulia**

pug-nosed (hyphen)

puissance showjumping competition (not italic; double **s**)

pukka properly done, perfect, or genuine (the spelling **pucka** is less common but not incorrect; compare **pucker**)

Pulitzer prize (capital **P** then lower-case **p**; single **l**; not **-itser**)

pull (*typog.*) proof

pull-in (noun; the verb is **pull in**)

Pullman luxurious railway coach (capital **P**; double **l**)

pull-out (noun; the verb is **pull out**)

pullover (noun; the verb is **pull over**)

pullulate (double **l** then single **l**)

pulverize (also **pulverise**; see **-ize/ -ise**)

pumice (single **m**)

pummel beat with fists (double **m**, single **l**; the variant **pommel** is less common but not incorrect)

pummelled, pummelling (single **l** in US English)

pumpernickel coarse black bread (not italic; lower-case **p**; one word)

Punch character in Punch and Judy puppet show, or used in the phrase *pleased as Punch* (capital **P**)

punchbag (one word)

punch-drunk (hyphen)

punch-up (hyphen)

punctilious paying scrupulous attention to etiquette or detail (compare **punctual**)

punctual prompt (compare **punctilious**)

punctuation see **apostrophe**, **colon**, **comma**, **full stop**, **semicolon**, and other individual entries

pundit expert, or learned Brahman (also **pandit** in the sense 'learned Brahman')

Pune variant of **Poona**

Punjab Indian state or Pakistani province

Purcell, Henry English composer (**-ur-**, double **l**)

purchasable (not **-eable**)

purdah seclusion or concealment or Muslim or Hindu women (not italic; the spelling **purda** is not incorrect, but it is less common)

purée (as noun) pulped fruit, vegetables, meat, or fish; (as verb) make into purée (not italic; **é** then **e**)

puréed, puréeing (**é** then **e**)

Purim Jewish festival in February or March (capital **P**)

puritan person with strict moral or religious principles (lower-case **p**)

Puritan extreme English Protestant in 16th and 17th centuries (capital **P**)

purl knitting stitch, or flow with rippling movement and murmuring sound (compare **pearl**)

purloin (**pur-**)

purple heart informal word for amphetamine tablet with this colour and shape (lower-case **p** & **h**)

Purple Heart US military decoration awarded to those wounded in action (capital **P** & **H**)

purposefully in a determined manner or with a definite purpose in view, as in *she strode purposefully towards the exit*

purposely deliberately or on purpose, as in *he purposely left the window open*

purr (double **r**)

purulent (**-uru-**, **-ent**)

purveyor (not **-er**)

pus fluid produced by inflammation (compare **puss**)

push-bike (hyphen)

push button (no hyphen unless used before another noun, as in *a push-button radio*)

pushchair (one word)

pushover (noun; the verb is **push over**)

Pushto variant of **Pashto** (also **Pushtu**)

push-ups US and Canadian name for **press-ups**

pusillanimous (single **s**, double **l**, single **n**, **-mous**)

puss informal name for cat (compare **pus**)

put place (compare **putt**)

putrefy (not **-ify**)

putsch political revolt (not italic; lower-case **p**; **-tsch**)

putt golfing term (compare **put**)

put-up job (one hyphen)

PVC polyvinyl chloride

Pwllheli Welsh town (double **l** then single **l**)

pygmy abnormally small person, or small example of its type (lower-case **p**; also **pigmy**)

Pygmy member of people of very small stature of Equatorial Africa (capital **P**; also **Pigmy**)

pyjamas (**paj-** in US English)

Pym, Barbara British novelist; **Francis, Baron** English politician in Margaret Thatcher's cabinet; **John** English parliamentarian during events leading up to Civil War

Pynchon, Thomas US novelist (not **Pinch-**)

Pyongyang capital of North Korea (also **P'yong-yang**)

pyramid (**py-**, **-id**)

Pyrenees mountain range between France and Spain (single **r**, single **n**; single **e** then double **e**; **Pyrénées**, with two acute accents, in names of French departments)

Pyrex trademark for heat-resistant glass (capital **P**)

pyrotechnics (**pyr-**)

Pyrrhic victory victory with great loss for the victor (also **Cadmean victory**)

Pythagoras ancient Greek philosopher and mathematician (not **Pi-**, not **-us**)

Pythagoras' theorem (**-s'** not **-s's**)

Pythias see **Damon**

Q pen name of Sir Arthur **Quiller-Couch**

Qaddafi variant of **Gaddafi**

qadi variant of **cadi**

Qaeda see **al-Qaeda**

Qantas Australian national airline (not **Qu-**; originally acronym of Queensland and Northern Territory Aerial Services)

Qatar Middle Eastern country (not **Qu-**; rarely **Katar**)

Q-boat (capital **Q**, hyphen)

QC Queen's Counsel

QED which was to be shown or proved (not italic; from Latin *quod erat demonstrandum*)

QE2 cruise ship (italics)

qi variant of **chi²**

qibla variant of **kiblah**

qigong system of breathing and exercise for physical and mental health (not **qu-**; one word; also **chi kung**)

Qingdao Chinese port (also **Tsingtao** or **Chingtao**)

Qinghai Chinese province (also **Tsinghai** or **Chinghai**)

QM Quartermaster

QMC Quartermaster Corps

Qom Iranian city and place of pilgrimage for Shiite Muslims (also **Qum** or **Kum**)

QPR Queens Park Rangers (football club)

qqv quae vide (not italic; literally, 'which (things) see', the plural of **qv**: used in cross-reference to more than one item, as in *discussed in the entries for Cézanne and Monet (qqv)*)

Q-ship (capital **Q**, hyphen)

QSO quasi-stellar object

q.t. quiet, or used in the phrase *on the q.t.*, meaning 'secretly' (full stops)

qua in the capacity of (not italic)

quad quadrangle, quadruplet, quadraphonic, (*typog.*) block of metal used for spacing, or variant of **quod** (no full stop)

quad bike (two words)

Quadragesima first Sunday in Lent

quadraphonic (the spelling **quadrophonic** is not incorrect, but it is less common)

quadrille (-**lle**)

quadriplegia (not -**dra**-; also **tetraplegia**)

quadrophonic less common variant of **quadraphonic**

quaere query (not italic)

quagga extinct horse of S Africa (double **g**)

quagmire (one word)

quahog edible clam (-**ah**-)

Quai d'Orsay site of French foreign office in Paris (-**ai** then -**ay**)

Quaker member of the Religious Society of Friends, a Christian sect founded in the mid-17th century, or of this sect (capital **Q**)

qualitative (not -**tit**-, not -**litive**)

qualm (-lm)
quandang variant of **quandong**
quandary (-dary)
quandong Australian tree, fruit, or timber (also **quandang** or **quantong**)
quango quasi-autonomous nongovernmental organization (all lower-case; plural **quangos**)
Quant, Mary British fashion designer
quantitative (the variant **quantitive** is less common but not incorrect)
quantong variant of **quandong**
quantum small quantity, especially in physics (not italic; plural **quanta**)
quantum leap sudden great advance (also **quantum jump**; the term originated in physics, where it denotes a sudden transition that is not great, and its figurative use is controversial)
quarantine (not -ren-)
quark hypothetical particle in physics, or low-fat soft cheese (lower-case **q**)
quarrel (double **r**, single **l**)
quarrelled, quarrelling (single **l** in US English)
quarrelsome (single **l**)
quartan denoting type of fever (compare **quartern**)
quarterback (one word)
quarter-binding bookbinding in which spine is bound in different material from sides (hyphen)
quarterdeck (one word)
quarterfinal (one word)
quarterlight (one word)
quartermaster (one word)
quartern denoting type of loaf (compare **quartan**)
quartet (rarely **quartette**)
quarto book size with four leaves (i.e. eight pages) per sheet (also **4to**)
quartz mineral (not -ts)
quasar quasi-stellar object (all lower-case)

quash suppress, annul, or reject as invalid (compare **squash**)
quasi- (attached with hyphen, as in *quasi-religious*; the word **quasi** can also stand alone as an adverb meaning 'as if')
Quasimodo central character of Victor Hugo's *The Hunchback of Notre-Dame* (one word)
quatercentenary 400th anniversary (not **quart-**)
Quatermass TV science-fiction series (not *Quart-*; double **s**)
Quaternary most recent period of geological time, or of this period (capital **Q**; not **Quart-**)
quattrocento 15th century, especially with reference to Italian art, literature, etc. (not italic; not **quatro-**)
quay wharf (compare **key**)
Quebec Canadian province and port
Quebecker person from Quebec, especially an English-speaking one (also **Quebecer**)
Québécois person from Quebec, especially a French-speaking one (two acute accents)
Quechua South American Indian people or language (also **Quichua**)
queen (for capitalization see **titles of people**)
Queenborough town in Kent, on the Isle of Sheppey (not **Queens-**)
Queen Mary College London (not **Mary's**)
Queens borough of New York City
Queen's Award (capital **Q** & **A**; apostrophe)
Queensberry rules code of rules used in boxing (capital **Q**, lower-case **r**; not -bury)
Queen's College Oxford (-'s not -s')
Queens' College Cambridge (-s' not -'s)
Queen's Counsel (capital **Q** & **C**; apostrophe; not -cil)

Queen's English (capital **Q** & **E**; apostrophe)

Queen's Guide (capital **Q** & **G**; apostrophe)

Queensland Australian state (one word)

Queens Park Rangers football club (no apostrophe; abbreviation **QPR**)

Queen's Scout (capital **Q** & **S**; apostrophe)

Queen's speech another name for **speech from the throne** (capital **Q**, lower-case **s**)

Queen's University Belfast and Kingston, Ontario (**-'s** not **-s'**)

queer offensive word for **homosexual** when used by heterosexuals (beware of ambiguity when using the word in other senses)

queer street used in the phrase *in queer street*, meaning 'in a difficult situation' (the use of capital **Q** & **S** is not incorrect, but it is less common)

que sera sera (line from song 'Whatever Will Be, Will Be'; compare *che sarà sarà*)

Quesnay, François French political economist, encyclopedist, and physician

question mark punctuation mark used after questions in direct speech, as in *'Who are you?' he asked* (but not in *he asked us who we were*). It may be used after a polite request in the form of a question, as in *will you shut the window, please?*, but a full stop is often preferred. Note that in Spanish questions are enclosed in a pair of marks, the first being inverted. The question mark is also used to express uncertainty, e.g. before a date.

questionnaire (double **n**)

Quetzalcoatl god of Aztecs and Toltecs (one word; **-atl**)

queue (as noun) line of people or vehicles waiting, series of items accessed in order by computer, or pigtail; (as verb) form, wait in, or arrange in a queue (compare **cue**)

queueing variant of **queuing**

queue-jumper (hyphen)

queuing (also **queueing**)

quiche savoury tart (not italic)

Quichua variant of **Quechua**

quick (use **quickly** instead as adverb in formal contexts)

quicker (use **more quickly** instead as adverb in formal contexts)

quickest (use **most quickly** instead as adverb in formal contexts)

quicklime (one word)

quickly see **quick**, **quicker**, and **quickest**

quick march (two words)

quicksand (one word)

quicksilver (one word)

quickstep (one word)

quick-tempered (hyphen)

quick-witted (hyphen)

quiddity essential nature, or trifling distinction (double **d**)

quid pro quo reciprocal exchange (not italic)

quiescent (**-sc-**, **-ent**)

quiet not loud or noisy, silence, or variant of **quieten** (compare **quite**)

quieten make or become quiet, or allay (also **quiet**)

quietus something that quashes, death, or settlement of debt (not italic; plural **quietuses**)

Quiller-Couch, Sir Arthur British critic and novelist (hyphen; pen name **Q**)

Quincey see **De Quincey**

quincunx group of five arranged like spots on dice (not italic)

Quinquagesima Sunday before Lent

quinquereme (not **-quir-**)

quinsy (not **-zy**)

quintessence (double **s**, **-ence**)

quintet (rarely **quintette**)

quire 24 or 25 sheets of paper, or 4 sheets folded once to form 16 pages (compare **choir**)

quirk (-ir-)

quisling traitor or collaborator (lower-case **q**; not **quiz-**)

quit variant of **quitted**, and the usual form of the past tense and past participle in US English

quite completely or somewhat (replace with synonym to avoid ambiguity; compare **quiet**)

quitted past tense and past participle of **quit** (also **quit**, which is the usual form in US English)

qui vive used in the phrase *on the qui vive*, meaning 'on the alert' (two words; not italic)

Quixote see **Don Quixote**

quixotic (lower-case **q**)

quiz (single **z**)

quizzed, quizzing (double **z**)

Qum variant of **Qom**

Qumran see **Khirbet Qumran**

quod slang word for prison (also **quad**)

quod erat demonstrandum full form of **QED** (italics; not *quad*)

quondam former (not italic)

Quorn trademark for vegetable protein used as meat substitute (capital **Q**)

quorum (plural **quorums**)

quotation marks the pairs of characters '' (single quotation marks) or " " (double quotation marks) used around **quotations** or **direct speech**. Either quotation marks or **italics** may be used to highlight a particular word or phrase under discussion (e.g. the word 'vulnerable' is often mispronounced/the word *vulnerable* is often mispronounced). Single quotation marks are generally preferred in UK English, and any following punctuation that does not belong to the quoted material is placed outside (e.g. *the word 'vulnerable', which is often mispronounced*); double quotation marks are used for quoted material, direct speech, highlighted words, etc. within the original quotation (e.g. *'I heard somebody calling "Help!" and went to investigate,' she said*). In US English these conventions are reversed, and the comma and full stop are always placed inside quotation marks (e.g. *the word "vulnerable," which is often mispronounced*).

quotations may be set in running text, enclosed in **quotation marks**, or as a separate block of text (see **display**), in which case quotation marks are not required. See also **ellipsis**.

Qur'an variant of **Koran**

qv quod vide (not italic; literally, 'which (thing) see', plural **qqv**: used in cross-reference to another item, as in *discussed in the entry for Cézanne (qv)*)

qwerty denoting keyboard with standard English language layout (also **QWERTY**)

R

® registered trademark (compare ™)

Ra radium (no full stop)

RA Royal Academician; Royal Academy

RAAF Royal Australian Air Force

rabbet recess cut into wood to make joint, or cut or join with rabbet (also **rebate**; compare **rabbit**)

rabbeted, rabbeting (not -tt-)

rabbi Jewish religious leader or teacher (double **b**; plural rabbis; capital **R** as title or part of title, as in *Rabbi Lionel Blue* or *Chief Rabbi*)

rabbit burrowing animal, or talk inconsequentially (compare **rabbet**)

rabbited, rabbiting (not -tt-)

rabbit warren (two words)

rabble-rouser (hyphen)

Rabelais, François French writer (note the -**'s** in *Rabelais's birthplace*, needed because the final **s** of the name is silent)

rabies disease (single **b**)

RAC Royal Automobile Club

raccoon (also **racoon**)

race (where appropriate, replace with **people**, **nation**, **ethnic group**, etc. for greater accuracy and less risk of offence)

racecard (one word)

racecourse (one word)

racegoer (one word)

racehorse (one word)

racetrack (one word)

Rachmaninoff, Sergei Vassilievich Russian composer and pianist (also **Rachmaninov**)

Rachmanism extortion or exploitation by slum landlord (capital **R**; not Rack-)

racism (also **racialism**)

rack (the usual spelling of the word with this sound in all senses and uses except 'seaweed' or 'piece of wreckage'; compare **wrack**; see also **rack and ruin**)

rack-and-pinion (two hyphens)

rack and ruin (also **wrack and ruin**: **wrack** is the original spelling of the word in this phrase but is now less common)

racket din, illegal enterprise, business, or bat used for tennis, badminton, squash, etc. (also **racquet** in the sense 'bat')

racketeer (single **t**)

racoon variant of **raccoon**

racquet variant of **racket** in the sense 'bat'

racy (not -ey)

RADA Royal Academy of Dramatic Art

radar method of detecting distant object (-**ar**)

Radcliffe, Ann British novelist (-**iffe**)

radiator (not -er)

radical (as adjective) fundamental, extreme, or of or arising from root; (as noun) person favouring extreme or fundamental change, root in mathematics or linguistics, or chemical term (compare **radicle**)

radicchio salad plant (not italic; single **d**; **-cchio**; plural **radicchios**)

radicle very small root or rootlike part (compare **radical**)

radio (plural and third person present tense **radios**, past tense and past participle **radioed**)

radioactive (one word)

radiocarbon dating (**radiocarbon** is one word; also **carbon-14 dating** or **carbon dating**)

radio-controlled (hyphen)

radio frequency (two words)

radiographer person who takes X-rays (compare **radiologist**)

radioimmunoassay (one word)

radioisotope (one word)

radiologist person who interprets X-rays (compare **radiographer**)

radiotelephone (one word)

radio telescope (two words)

radiotherapy (one word)

radio wave (two words)

radium (symbol **Ra**)

radius (plural **radii** or **radiuses**)

radon (symbol **Rn**)

Rae, John Scottish explorer (compare **Ray**)

Raeburn, Sir Henry Scottish portrait painter (compare **Rayburn**)

RAF Royal Air Force

Rafferty's rules in Australia and New Zealand, slang term for no rules at all (capital **R** then lower-case **r**)

raffia (also **raphia**)

raga Indian religious music (compare **ragga**)

ragamuffin ragged child, or variant of **ragga** (one word; single **g**, double **f**)

rag-and-bone man (two hyphens)

ragbag (one word)

rag doll soft-bodied doll made from fabric (two words)

Ragdoll breed of cat (capital **R**; one word)

ragga type of reggae (also **ragamuffin**; compare **raga**)

ragged (*typog.*) referring to lines of type that are not aligned on the specified side because interword spaces have not been adjusted to **justify** the text. Lines set *ragged right*, for example, are aligned on the left-hand side and have equal spaces between the words.

ragi cereal grass or its grain (also **raggee**)

raglan denoting sleeves that continue to the collar, or a garment that has such sleeves rather than shoulder seams and armholes (lower-case **r**)

Ragnarök twilight of the gods in Norse mythology (not italic; capital **R**; also **Ragnarok**, without umlaut)

ragout richly seasoned stew (not italic; no accent)

rag-rolling (hyphen)

ragtime (one word)

railcard (one word; capital **R** in names of specific cards, e.g. *Senior Railcard*)

railroad (one word)

raiment archaic or poetic word for clothing (not **rain-**)

rain water falling from sky (compare **rein** and **reign**)

Rainbow member of the youngest group of girls in the Guide Association (capital **R**; see also **Brownie**)

rain check (two words)

raincoat (one word)

raindrop (one word)

rainforest (one word)

rain gauge (two words)

rainmaker (one word)

rainstorm (one word)

rainwater (one word)

raise (as verb) lift, rear, cause to rise, put forward, remove, etc.; (as noun) US and Canadian word for **rise** in the sense 'pay increase' (usually transitive as verb; compare **rise** (for meaning) and **raze** (for spelling))

raisin dried grape (not **-son**)

raison d'être reason for existence (italics; circumflex; plural *raisons d'être*)

raj government or rule in India (lower-case **r**)

Raj, the the British government in India before 1947 (capital **R**)

rajah Indian ruler, or Malayan or Javanese prince or chieftain (also **raja**)

Rajasthan Indian state

Rakata another name for **Krakatoa**

rakee variant of **raki**

rake-off (noun; the verb is **rake off**)

raki spirit distilled from grain (also **rakee**)

Raleigh, Sir Walter English courtier, explorer, and writer (also **Ralegh**; compare **Rayleigh**)

RAM random access memory (no full stops)

Ramadan month of Muslim year marked by fasting from sunrise to sunset, or the fast itself (also **Ramadhan**)

Raman, Sir Chandrasekhara Indian physicist (not **Rahm-**)

Ramayana Sanskrit epic poem (italics)

ramekin (also **ramequin**)

Rameses variant of **Ramses**

Ramillies Belgian village and battle site (single **m**, double **l**)

Ramsay, Allan Scottish poet, editor, and bookseller; **Allan** Scottish portrait painter; **Sir William**, Scottish chemist (compare **Ramsey**; see also **MacDonald**)

Ramses any of various kings of ancient Egypt (also **Rameses**)

Ramsey the spelling used for various place names in England and the Isle of Man (not **-say**)

Ramsey, Sir Alf(red) English footballer and football manager; **Arthur Michael** British prelate (compare **Ramsay**)

rampant (not **-ent**)

ram raiding (two words)

ran past tense of **run**, as in *she ran all the way home* (compare **run**)

RAN Royal Australian Navy

rancour (**-or** in US English)

rancorous (not **-our-**)

rand monetary unit of South Africa (lower-case **r**)

Rand, the another name for **Witwatersrand** (capital **R**)

R & B rhythm and blues

R & D research and development

random access memory full form of **RAM** (three words)

R & R rest and recreation

ranee variant of **rani**

rang past tense of **ring** in the sense 'sound' (compare **ringed** and **rung**)

rangatira Maori chief (one word)

range (*typog.*) align with the specified margin, as in *range left*

rangefinder (one word)

Ranger Guide member of the oldest group of girls in the Guide Association (also **Ranger**)

Rangoon former name for **Yangon**

Range Rover motor vehicle (two words; capital **R** twice)

rani wife of rajah (also **ranee**)

Rank, J(oseph) Arthur, 1st Baron British film executive; **Otto** Austrian psychoanalyst

Ranke, Leopold von German historian

ranks for military or police ranks, such as *sergeant, lieutenant, commander,* etc., use capital initial (and abbreviated form if appropriate) when rank is followed by name, as in *Major Parkinson, Chief Inspector Stewart, Lt Col Harper*. When the rank is used alone, especially when it does not refer to a particular person, lower-case initials are generally preferred, as in *she was promoted to the rank of sergeant* or *the colonel of the regiment*. Do not hyphenate two-word ranks, e.g. *major general, group captain*. See also **titles of people**.

Ransom, John Crowe US poet and critic

Ransome, Arthur English writer known for his children's books, notably *Swallows and Amazons*

rap strike, utter or criticize sharply, type of pop music, or used in the phrases *not care a rap, take the rap,* and *beat the rap* (compare **wrap**)

Rapa Nui another name for **Easter Island**

Raphael Italian painter and architect (original name **Raffaello Santi** or **Sanzio**)

raphia variant of **raffia**

rapped past tense and past participle of **rap** (compare **rapt** and **wrapped**)

rapport relationship or understanding (not italic; double **p**)

rapprochement resumption of friendly relations (italics; double *p*)

rapscallion (not **rasc-** or **rabsc-**)

rapt engrossed, spellbound, showing rapture, or Australian informal word for delighted (also **wrapped** in Australian sense; compare **rapped**)

raptor (not **-er**)

rapturous (**-tur-**)

rara avis unusual or exceptional person or thing (not italic; plural **rarae aves**)

rarebit see **Welsh rabbit**

rarefaction (the variant **rarefication** is less common but not incorrect)

rarefy (not **-ify**)

rarity (not **-ety**)

raspberry (**-spb-**)

rase variant of **raze**

Rasta Rastafarian (capital **R**; compare **raster**)

Ras Tafari see **Haile Selassie** (two words)

Rastafarian member of religion of Jamaican origin, or of this religion (one word)

raster pattern of horizontal scanning lines on screen (compare **Rasta**)

ratable (also **rateable**)

ratan rare variant of **rattan**

ratatouille vegetable casserole (not italic; single **t** twice; **-oui-**)

rat-catcher (hyphen)

rateable variant of **ratable**

rather (may be preceded by *would* or *had*, as in *I would* [or *had*] *rather go by train*, but *would* is more idiomatic in modern usage; replace with *'d* where appropriate to avoid the problem, especially in direct speech)

ratio (plural **ratios**)

rational using reason, able to reason, reasonable, sane, or mathematics term

rationale reasoning behind course of action, belief, etc.

Ratisbon former English name for **Regensburg**

rat race (two words)

rat-run (hyphen)

rattan plant or its stem used for wickerwork, canes, etc. (rarely **ratan**)

rattlesnake (one word)

rat-trap (hyphen)

ravage cause extensive damage to or destroy (compare **ravish**)

ravening predatory or voracious, as in *ravening wolves* (single **n**; compare **ravenous**)

Ravenna Italian city (double **n**)

ravenous starving or voracious, as in *the children were ravenous* (single **n**; compare **ravening**)

rave-up (hyphen)

ravish enrapture or rape (compare **ravage**)

Rawalpindi Pakistani city (**-wal-**)

Rawlplug trademark for wall fixing for screw (capital **R**; one word)

Ray, John English naturalist; **Man** US photographer (real name **Emmanuel Rudnitsky**); **Satyajit** Indian film director (compare **Rae**)

Ray-Ban manufacturer of sunglasses (hyphen; capital **R & B**)

Rayburn trademark for cooking range (capital **R**; compare **Raeburn**)

Rayleigh, Lord title of **John William Strutt**, British physicist (compare **Raleigh**)

Raynaud's disease (capital **R**; apostrophe)

raze demolish completely, as in *raze to the ground* (also **rase**; compare **raise**)

razzmatazz (double **z** twice, single **t**; not **razza-**)

Rb rubidium (no full stop)

RC Roman Catholic

RCA Royal College of Art

RCAF Royal Canadian Air Force

RCMP Royal Canadian Mounted Police

RCN Royal Canadian Navy; Royal College of Nursing

Rd Road (in addresses; no full stop)

RDA recommended daily (or dietary) allowance (or amount)

RDF radio direction finder; radio direction finding

RDS radio data system (for automatic tuning of receivers)

re with reference to (not italic; best restricted to headings of letters, e-mails, etc.: replace with synonym or paraphrase in running text)

Re rhenium (no full stop)

RE religious education; Royal Engineers

re- usually attached without hyphen, except to words beginning with **e**

or sometimes **r** (as in *re-educate, re-record*) and where it is necessary to distinguish between pairs of words such as *re-form* and *reform*. Beware of tautology when using the adverbs *back* and *again* with **re-** verbs: the adverbs are redundant in *reverse back, reiterate again*, etc.

react act in response or opposition

re-act act again

read¹ understand, interpret, and/or speak aloud something written (compare **reed**)

read² past tense and past participle of **read¹** (compare **red**)

Read, Sir Herbert English critic (compare **Reade**, **Reed**, and **Reid**)

readable easy or pleasant to read (compare **legible**)

readdress (no hyphen)

Reade, Charles English novelist (compare **Read**, **Reed**, and **Reid**)

Reader's Digest periodical (**-'s** not **-s'**)

Reading town and unitary authority in Berkshire (compare **Redding**)

readjust (no hyphen)

readmission (no hyphen)

read-out (noun; the verb is **read out**)

ready-made (hyphen)

ready reckoner (two words)

reafforestation (no hyphen; double **f**; also **reforestation**)

Reagan, Ronald US actor and statesman who was President of the USA 1981–89 (compare **Regan**)

real true or genuine (compare **reel**)

realign (no hyphen)

realism acceptance of things as they are, or style of art or literature

reality the state of being real, or the state of things as they are

realize (also **realise**; see **-ize/-ise**)

real life (no hyphen unless used before another noun, as in *a real-life mystery*)

really (double **l**)

realpolitik ruthlessly realistic approach to statesmanship (not italic; one word. lower-case **r**; not **-tic**)

reappear (no hyphen)

rearguard (one word)

rearmament (no hyphen)

rearrange (no hyphen)

rear-view mirror (one hyphen)

reason replace *because* with *that* after *the reason … is/was* (e.g. *the reason he refused was that* [not *because*] *he was afraid*), or simply omit *the reason* and *is/was* (e.g. *he refused because he was afraid*). The construction *the reason why* is also controversial: omit the word *why*, use *that* instead, or paraphrase (e.g. *the reason she was absent, the reason that she was absent*, or *the reason for her absence* rather than *the reason why she was absent*)

reassemble (no hyphen)

reassure (no hyphen)

Réaumur scale denoting temperature scale in which water freezes at 0° and boils at 80° (capital **R**; acute accent; not **Réam-**)

rebate refund, or variant of **rabbet**

rebec medieval stringed instrument (also **rebeck**)

rebel (single **b**, single **l**)

rebelled, rebelling (double **l**)

rebirth (no hyphen)

rebound spring back; misfire, as in *the plan rebounded*; used in the phrase *on the rebound*; or past tense and past participle of **rebind**, meaning 'give (book) new binding' (no hyphen; compare **redound**)

rebus (plural **rebuses**)

rebut prove to be false or incorrect (single **t**; to avoid controversy, do not use in the sense 'deny')

rebuttal (double **t**)

rebutted, rebutting (double **t**)

recap informal shortening of recapitulate or recapitulation (no full stop)

recce slang shortening of reconnaissance or reconnoitre (double **c**; past tense and past participle **recced** or **recceed**)

recede withdraw, slope backwards, or start to go bald (not **-ceed**)

re-cede restore to former owner

receipt (**-ei-**, **-pt**)

receive (**-ei-**)

Received Pronunciation standard pronunciation of British English used by people without regional accents in S England (the use of lower-case **r** & **p** is less common but not incorrect; abbreviation **RP**)

receptor (not **-er**)

Rechabite total abstainer from alcoholic drink (capital **R**; not **-ck-**)

recharge (no hyphen)

recherché choice, rare, or refined (not italic; one acute accent, not **ré-**)

recidivist (**rec-**, **-div-**)

recipient (not **-ant**)

reclamation (not **-claim-**)

recognize (also **recognise**; see **-ize/ -ise**)

recommend (single **c**, double **m**)

recompense (not **-ence**)

reconnaissance act of reconnoitring (not italic; single **c**, double **n**, double **s**; rarely **reconnoissance**)

reconnoitre survey or inspect enemy's position, region of land, etc. (not italic; single **c**, double **n**; **-er** in US English; not **-aitre**)

record player (two words)

recount tell the story of

re-count count again, or a second count

recoup regain, make good, reimburse, or compensate (not italic; **-oup**)

recourse act of resorting to somebody or something, as in *have recourse to violence*; person or course of action resorted to; or used in the legal phrase *without recourse* (noun only; compare **resort** and **resource**)

recover regain or get better

re-cover cover again or provide with a new cover

recreate amuse oneself

re-create create again

recreation activity undertaken for enjoyment or relaxation

re-creation act of creating again, simulation, or re-enactment

recto front of sheet of paper, or any of the right-hand pages of a book, bearing odd numbers (compare **verso**)

recuperate (not **-coup-**)

recur (single **c** then single **r**)

recurred (single **c** then double **r**)

recurrence (single **c** then double **r**; **-ence**)

recurring (single **c** then double **r**)

red colour of blood (compare **read**)

redback (one word; also **redback spider**, not **red-backed . . .**)

redbreast (one word)

redbrick university (**redbrick** is one word)

Red Crescent Muslim branch of Red Cross (capital **R** & **C**)

Red Cross international humanitarian organization (capital **R** & **C**)

redcurrant (one word; not **-ent**)

Redding, Otis US singer and songwriter (compare **Reading**)

Redditch English town (double **d**, not **-ich**)

redeye slang name for alcoholic drink (one word)

red eye undesirable effect of flash photography (two words)

red-eye informal name for overnight flight (hyphen)

Redgauntlet novel by Sir Walter Scott (one word)

red-handed (hyphen)

redhead (one word)

red-headed (hyphen)

Red Indian offensive former name for **American Indian**

red-letter day (one hyphen)

red-light district (one hyphen)

redouble make or become much greater, or re-echo (compare **reduplicate**)

redound have good or bad effect on, as in it will redound to your credit (compare **rebound**)

redress put right, or compensation

re-dress dress again

red tape (two words)

reducible (not **-able**)

reductio ad absurdum method of disproving (or proving) a proposition by showing that its consequences (or negation) would be absurd (not italic; not **reduction . . .**)

reduplicate make or become double, or repeat (compare **redouble**)

reebok variant of **rhebok** (lower-case **r**)

Reebok sportswear manufacturer (capital **R**)

re-echo (hyphen)

reed water plant or part of musical instrument (compare **read**)

Reed, Sir Carol English film director; **Lou** US singer and songwriter (compare **Read, Reade**, and **Reid**)

re-educate (hyphen)

reek stink or smoke (compare **wreak**)

reel (as noun) cylinder holding thread, film, tape, etc., or Scottish dance; (as verb) wind onto reel, sway, stagger, or whirl (compare **real**)

re-elect (hyphen)

re-enact (hyphen)

re-enforce enforce again (hyphen; compare **reinforce**)

re-enter (hyphen)

re-examine (hyphen)

ref informal shortening of **referee** (no full stop)

ref. reference

refectory (**-tory**)

refer (single **f** then single **r**)

referee official who ensures fair play in football, boxing, etc., or person willing to supply a testimonial for another (single **f** then single **r**; compare **umpire**)

reference (single **f** then single **r**; **-ence**)

referendum (single **f** then single **r**; plural **referendums** or **referenda**)

referral (single **f** then double **r**)

referred, referring (single **f** then double **r**)

reflection (the spelling **reflexion** is not incorrect, but it is less common)

reflective thoughtful, or describing a surface that reflects light or other radiation (compare **reflexive**)

reflector (not **-er**)

reflexion less common variant of **reflection**

reflexive denoting pronoun that refers to subject of sentence (e.g. *herself*) or verb with reflexive pronoun as direct object (e.g. *perjure oneself*), or relating to a reflex (compare **reflective**)

reforestation variant of **reafforestation**

reform improve, improvement, or change for the better

re-form form again

Reformation religious and political movement of 16th century (capital **R**)

Reform Bill (capital **R** & **B**)

refractory (**-tory**)

refrigerator (not **-dg-**, not **-er**)

refuel (no hyphen)

refuelled, refuelling (single **l** in US English)

refuse collector (no hyphen; use instead of gender-specific **dustman** where appropriate)

refusenik person who refuses to cooperate, or (originally) a Jew in the Soviet Union who was refused permission to emigrate (the spelling **refusnik** is not incorrect, but it is less common)

refute prove to be false or incorrect (to avoid controversy, do not use in the sense 'deny')

regal of or befitting a king or queen (compare **regale** and **regnal**)

regale amuse, delight, or provide with fine or abundant food and drink (compare **regal**)

regalia (plural noun sometimes used with singular verb, especially when the various items are regarded as a whole)

Regan, Donald US politician who served under President Ronald **Reagan**

Regensburg German city (not **-berg**; former English name Ratisbon)

Regent's Park London (apostrophe)

reggae West Indian popular music with strongly accented upbeat (double **g**, **-ae**)

regime system of government, or variant of **regimen** (also **régime**)

regimen prescribed or recommended exercise, diet, lifestyle, etc. (also **regime**)

regiment military formation, organize into regiment, or force order or discipline on

Regina used after Latin name of queen, as in *Elizabetha Regina* (capital **R**)

register (*typog.*) correct alignment of superimposed plates in colour printing, or exact correspondence of lines of type on two sides of printed sheet

register office official name for what is more commonly called a **registry office**

Regius professor (capital **R**; lower-case **p** unless referring to a specific chair, as in *Regius Professor of Modern History*)

regnal of sovereign, reign, or kingdom, or denoted year of reign calculated from date of succession

regretful feeling or showing regret (single **t**; compare **regrettable**)

regretfully in a regretful way, as in *he nodded regretfully* or *regretfully, she rejected their offer* (i.e. she wanted to accept it but felt she should not: compare **regrettably**)

regrettable causing regret (double **t**, not **-ible**; compare **regretful**)

regrettably that is regrettable, as in *he made a regrettably hasty decision*, or it is regrettable that, as in *regrettably, she rejected their offer* (i.e. she later wished she had accepted it: compare **regretfully**)

regularize (also **regularise**; see **-ize/-ise**)

regulator (not **-er**)

rehoboam large wine bottle (lower-case **r**)

Rehoboam biblical king

Reich any of various empires, kingdoms, etc., notably the Weimar Republic (1919–33) and the **Third Reich** (the Nazi dictatorship 1933–45) (not italic; capital **R**; **-ei-**)

Reichstag German legislative assembly or the building where it meets (capital **R**; **-ei-**)

Reid, Beryl English actress and entertainer; **Sir George Houston** Scottish-born Australian statesman; **Thomas** Scottish philosopher (compare **Read**, **Reade**, and **Reed**)

Reigate English town (**-ei-**)

reign period of monarch's rule, rule as monarch, prevail, or be most recent winner, as in *the reigning champion* (compare **rein** and **rain**)

reimburse (no hyphen; **-ur-**)

Reims French city (**-ei-**; also **Rheims**)

rein (as noun) strap used to control horse or child, something that restrains or controls, or used in the phrases *give free rein to* and *keep a tight rein on*; (as verb) restrain or control, as in *rein in expenditure* (compare **reign** and **rain**)

reinforce give added strength, support, or emphasis to (no hyphen; compare **re-enforce**)

Reinhardt, Django Belgian jazz guitarist; **Max** Austrian theatre producer and director (**-ei-**, **-dt**)

reinstate (no hyphen)

reiterate (no hyphen)

Reith lecture any of annual series of lectures broadcast by BBC, named after first director general (**-ei-**; capital **R**, sometimes capital **L**, especially in plural, referring to the series as a whole)

rejoin (no hyphen)

relative clause a clause that modifies a preceding noun or pronoun, e.g. *that bit me* in *the dog that bit me was a Jack Russell*, or *who is a doctor* in *his sister, who is a doctor, lives in Australia*. The relative clause *that bit me* is **restrictive**, because it contains essential information; the relative clause *who is a doctor* is **nonrestrictive**, because it contains incidental information.

relay (as verb) pass on, spread, receive and retransmit, or broadcast (compare **re-lay**)

re-lay lay again (compare **relay**)

relevant (not **-lav-**, not **-ent**)

reliable dependable (not **-ly-**)

reliant dependent (not **-ent**)

relief (noun; **-ie-**)

relieve (verb; **-ie-**)

Religious Society of Friends see
  Quaker
reliquary receptacle for relics
  (**-quary**)
REM rapid eye movement (stage of
  sleep)
remainder in publishing, unsold
  books sold off at reduced price when
  demand ceases, or to sell off (unsold
  books) in this way
Remarque, Erich Maria German-
  born US novelist, author of *All Quiet
  on the Western Front*
rematch (no hyphen)
Rembrandt Dutch painter (**-ndt**;
  full name **Rembrandt Harmensz
  van Rijn**)
REME Royal Electrical and
  Mechanical Engineers
remediable able to be put right
remedial of or being a remedy, or
  denoting special teaching for slow
  learners
remembrance (not **-ber-**, not **-ence**)
Remembrance Sunday Sunday
  closest to November 11 (compare
  Armistice Day)
reminiscent (**-min-**, **-sc-**; not **-ant**)
remission reduction of prison
  sentence, forgiveness for sin, release
  from obligation, or abatement of
  disease
remittance payment
remitted, remitting (double **t**)
remnant part left over (**-mn-**; not
  -ent)
remodel (no hyphen)
remodelled, remodelling (single l in
  US English)
remortgage (no hyphen)
removable (not **-eable**)
renaissance revival or rebirth,
  especially of culture (lower-case **r**;
  single **n**, double **s**; **-ai-** then **-a-**;
  rarely **renascence**)
Renaissance period of European
  history following the Middle Ages,
or the spirit, culture, thought, etc.
  of this period (capital **R**)
Renaissance man (capital **R**)
renascence rare variant of
  renaissance (lower-case form only;
  -asce-)
renationalize (also **renationalise**; see
  -ize/-ise)
Renault French motor manufacturer,
  or any of their vehicles (capital **R**,
  -ault)
rendezvous meeting, appointment
  to meet, meeting place, or meet (not
  italic; same form for singular and
  plural)
renegade (**-neg-**)
renege (rarely **renegue**)
renegotiate (no hyphen)
Renoir, Jean French film director;
  Pierre Auguste French painter
renown (not **-known**)
renunciation (not **-noun-**)
reoccupy (no hyphen)
reopen (no hyphen)
reorganize (no hyphen; also
  reorganise, see **-ize/-ise**)
rep fabric, representative, repertory
  company, or repertory theatre (no
  full stop; also **repp** for the fabric)
repairable (use this form for material
  things that can be mended)
reparable (use this form for abstract
  things that can be remedied)
repartee witty remark or remarks
  (not italic)
repel drive back, disgust, dismiss, or
  resist (single **p**, single **l**; see also
  repulse)
repellant variant of **repellent** (noun)
  (single **p**, double **l**)
repelled (single **p**, double **l**)
repellent (as adjective) causing
  disgust, aversion, or distaste, or
  driving back; (as noun) substance
  that repels or increases resistance
  (single **p**, double **l**; also **repellant** for
  the noun; compare **repulsive**)

repelling (single **p**, double **l**)

repercussions (single **p**, double **s**)

repertoire all the works that a person or company can perform, or used in the phrase *in repertoire*, referring to two or more plays, ballets, etc. performed by the same company on different days during a particular period (also **repertory**)

repertory variant of **repertoire**, or used in the phrases *repertory company* and *repertory theatre*

repetitious characterized by unnecessary or tedious repetition (**e** twice then **i** twice)

repetitive characterized by repetition, which may or may not be unnecessary or tedious (**e** twice then **i** twice)

repetitive strain injury full form of **RSI** (also **repetitive stress injury**)

replace put one thing in place of (another), as in *you can replace the cream in the recipe with yogurt* (compare **substitute**)

replaceable (**e** after **c**)

replete (-ete)

reportage reporting of news or other events, style of reporting, or technique of documentary journalism using pictures alone (not italic)

reported speech another name for **indirect speech**

repp variant of **rep** (the fabric)

reprehensible (not **-able**)

represent stand in place of, portray, or typify

re-present present again

repressible (not **-able**)

reprise repeat earlier theme in music, or the repeating of a musical theme (not italic; never **-ize**)

repro reproduction or reproduction proof (no full stop)

reproducible (not **-able**)

reproduction proof (*typog.*) high-quality proof used for photographic reproduction to make printing plate

reproof a rebuke (noun; compare **reprove**)

re-proof renew waterproof or other qualities of (garment), or provide new proof of (book)

reprove to rebuke (verb; compare **reproof**)

republican of, supporting, or advocating a republic, or a supporter or advocate of a republic (lower-case **r**)

Republican of a Republican Party, of the IRA, or a member or supporter of a Republican Party or the IRA (capital **R**)

Republican Party US political party, or other political party opposed to monarchy (capital **R** & **P**)

Republic of China Asian country occupying the island of Taiwan and various other islands (also **Taiwan**; compare **People's Republic of China**)

Republic of Congo a former name for **Congo-Brazzaville**

Republic of Ireland European country occupying most of Ireland (also **Irish Republic** or **Southern Ireland**; former name **Eire**)

Republic of South Africa African country (former name **Union of South Africa**)

repulse drive back, ward off, or reject (to avoid controversy, use **repel** instead in the sense 'disgust')

repulsive causing strong disgust, loathing, or repugnance (compare **repellent**)

reputable (not **-ible**)

requisite indispensable, or something indispensable (compare **prerequisite**)

reread (no hyphen)

re-record (hyphen)

reredos screen behind altar (not **rear-**)

re-route (hyphen)

rerun (no hyphen)

reschedule (no hyphen)

rescind (**-sc-**)

resident (not **-ant**)

resign leave job, give up, or reconcile (oneself)

re-sign sign again

resilient (single **l**; not **-ant**)

resin solid or semisolid substance exuded from plants or obtained synthetically (compare **rosin**)

resistance act or resisting, ability to resist, etc. (lower-case **r**; not **-ence**)

Resistance illegal organization fighting for national liberty in occupied country (capital **R**)

resistant (not **-ent**)

resort (as verb) turn for help or use, as in *resort to violence*; (as noun) place for holidays, act of resorting, or used in the phrase *last resort*, meaning 'last possible course of action' (compare **recourse**, **resource**, and **re-sort**)

re-sort sort again (compare **resort**)

resource ingenuity, supply or source, or expedient (noun only; compare **recourse** and **resort**)

respectable worthy of respect (compare **respectful** and **respective**)

respecter (not **-or**)

respectful showing respect (compare **respectable** and **respective**)

respective belonging or relating separately to each, as in *we set out our respective requirements in a formal letter* (use only where there is a risk of ambiguity or confusion without it: e.g. *respective* is redundant in *they returned to their respective homes*; compare **respectable** and **respectful**)

Respighi, Ottorino Italian composer (**-gh-**)

respirator (not **-er**)

respiratory (**-tory**)

responsible (not **-able**)

rest relax, place, relaxation, pause, or remainder (compare **wrest**)

restaurant (**-aur-**, **-ant**)

restaurateur (not **-ant-**)

rest-cure (hyphen)

restive resisting control or authority, nervous, or uneasy

restless unable to rest or stay still, anxious, or uneasy

Restoration re-establishment of British monarchy in 1660, the subsequent reign of Charles II, or of this period, as in *Restoration drama* (capital **R**)

restrain hold back or restrict (compare **constrain**)

restrictive relative clause see **relative clause**

rest room (two words)

resume continue or take back

résumé summary, or US and Canadian word for **curriculum vitae** (not italic; two acute accents)

resurrect (single **s**, double **r**)

resurrection the act of rising from the dead, or a belief in the possibility of this (lower-case **r**)

Resurrection the rising again of Christ from the tomb or of all humankind at the Last Judgment (capital **R**)

resuscitate (**-s-** then **-sc-**)

retarded (replace with a phrase containing **learning difficulties**, e.g. *her son has learning difficulties*, to avoid offence)

retch undergo vomiting spasm (compare **wretch**)

retina (plural **retinas** or **retinae**)

retractable (not **-ible**)

retrial (no hyphen)

retrieve (**-ie-**)

retrorocket (one word)

retroussé denoting turned-up nose (not italic; acute accent)

Réunion island in Indian Ocean (acute accent)

reuse (no hyphen)

Reuters news agency (no apostrophe; not **Reuter**)

rev informal noun or verb referring to revolutions of engine (no full stop)

rev. revenue; revised; revision; revolution

Rev. Revelation (full stop; not italic); Reverend

Reval German name for **Tallinn**

rev counter (two words; no full stop)

Revd Reverend (no full stop)

reveille wake-up signal for soldiers or sailors (not italic; **-eille**)

revel (single l)

Revelation book of the Bible (not italic; not **-tions**; abbreviation **Rev.**; full name **The Revelation of St John the Divine**)

revelled (single l in US English)

reveller (single l in US English)

revelling (single l in US English)

reverberate (**-er-** twice)

revere venerate (compare **revers**)

reverend worthy of reverence, or relating to the clergy (compare **reverent**)

Reverend title of member of clergy (capital **R**; may be preceded by *the*, but should not be followed by surname alone)

Reverend Mother (capital **R & M**)

reverent feeling or showing reverence (compare **reverend**)

reverie daydreaming (not italic; rarely **revery**)

revers turned-back lining of lapel or cuff (same form for singular and plural; compare **revere** and **reverse**)

reversal act of reversing or annulling, or state of being reversed or annulled (compare **reversion**)

reverse (as verb) turn, move, etc. in opposite direction; (as noun) opposite, rear side, setback, or (*typog.*) printed matter with white lettering on black or coloured background (compare **revers**)

reverse-charge call (one hyphen; not **reversed-**)

reversible (not **-able**)

reversion act of reverting to earlier condition, practice, etc. (compare **reversal**)

revery rare variant of **reverie**

review (as noun) critical assessment, periodical containing reviews, general survey, inspection, re-examination, or less common variant of **revue**; (as verb) re-examine, look back on, inspect, or write review of

revise (never **-ize**)

Revised Standard Version revision of **American Standard Version** of Bible, published in 1946 and 1953

Revised Version revision of **Authorized Version** of Bible, published in 1881 and 1885

revitalize (also **revitalise**; see **-ize/-ise**)

revocable (the spelling **revokable** is not incorrect, but it is less common)

Revolution (capital **R** in names of significant historical events, e.g. *French Revolution* or *Russian Revolution*, and sometimes when the word stands alone with specific reference to one of these, e.g. *in Russia before the Revolution*)

Revolutionary (capital **R** with reference to a specific revolution, e.g. *in Revolutionary France*)

revolutionize (also **revolutionise**; see **-ize/-ise**)

revue show comprising sketches, songs, dances, etc. (the spelling **review** is not incorrect in this sense, but it is less common)

rewrite (no hyphen)

Rex used after Latin name of king, as in *Georgius Rex* (capital **R**)

Reykjavik capital of Iceland (**-eykj-**)

Reynard name for fox in medieval tales and fables (not **Ren-**)

Reynaud, Paul French statesman

Reynolds, Albert Irish politician; **Sir Joshua** English painter; **Osborne** British physicist

Rf rutherfordium (no full stop)

rh right hand (also **RH**)

Rh rhesus (see also that entry, **Rh factor**, **Rh negative**, and **Rh positive**); rhodium (no full stop)

rhapsodize (also **rhapsodise**; see **-ize/-ise**)

rhea flightless bird (compare **ria**)

rhebok (also **reebok**)

Rheims variant of **Reims**

Rhein German name for **Rhine**

rhenium (symbol **Re**)

rhesus (lower-case **r** in phrases such as *rhesus factor* or *rhesus baby*, but capital **R** for abbreviation **Rh**, as in **Rh factor**, **Rh negative**, and **Rh positive**)

rhesus monkey (lower-case **r** & **m**)

rhetorical (**rhet-**)

rheumatism (**rheum-**)

Rh factor agglutinogen found in human blood (capital **R**; no full stop or hyphen)

Rhine European river (German name **Rhein**, French name **Rhin**, Dutch name **Rijn**)

rhinestone (one word; lower-case **r**)

rhino (plural **rhinos** or **rhino**)

rhinoceros (**-os**; plural **rhinoceroses** or **rhinoceros**)

Rh negative denoting blood that does not contain the Rh factor, or a person with such blood (capital **R**; no full stop or hyphen)

Rhodesia former name (1964–79) for **Zimbabwe** (see also **Northern Rhodesia** and **Southern Rhodesia**)

Rhodes scholarship (capital **R**, lower-case **s**)

rhodium (symbol **Rh**)

rhododendron (**-dod-**, **-dron**; lower-case **r** in general use, *Rhododendron* is the genus name)

rhombus (plural **rhombuses** or **rhombi**)

Rhondda Valley Wales (capital **R** & **V**; double **d**)

Rhône European river or French department (circumflex)

Rh positive denoting blood that contains the Rh factor, or a person with such blood (capital **R**; no full stop or hyphen)

RHS Royal Horticultural Society

rhubarb (**rhu-**)

rhumb short for **rhumb line** (compare **rum**)

rhumba less common variant of **rumba**

rhumb line imaginary line on earth's surface, or course with uniform compass heading (**rh-**, **-mb**)

rhyme (as noun) identical sound at end of word, poem, or used in the phrase *rhyme or reason*; (as verb) have identical sound at end (archaic spelling **rime**; see also that entry)

Rhys, Jean Welsh writer (not **Rees**)

rhythm (**rh-** then **-th-**)

RI religious instruction; Rhode Island (US postal code); Royal Institution

ria long narrow inlet (compare **rhea**)

Rialto Bridge Venice, Italy (capital **R** & **B**; not **Real-**)

RIBA Royal Institute of British Architects (not **Institution**)

riband ribbon awarded for achievement (the spelling **ribband** is not incorrect, but it is less common)

ribbon strip of material

riboflavin (also **riboflavine**)

Riccio variant of **Rizzio**

Richelieu, Armand Jean du Plessis, Duc de French statesman and cardinal

Richter scale scale for expressing magnitude of earthquake (capital **R**, **-cht-**, lower-case **s**)

Richthofen, Baron Manfred von German pilot (known as **the Red Baron**; -chth-)

rick (the spelling **wrick** is not incorrect in the sense 'wrench or sprain', but it is less common and should not be used in any other sense)

rickety (single **t**)

rickshaw (the variants **jinrikisha** and **jinriksha** are less common but not incorrect)

ricocheted (also **ricochetted**)

ricocheting (also **ricochetting**)

ricotta Italian soft cheese made from sheep's milk (not italic; single **c**, double **t**)

RICS Royal Institution of Chartered Surveyors (not Institute)

rid (past tense and past participle **rid** or **ridded**)

riddance (not **-ence**)

ridded a form of the past tense and past participle of **rid**

ridden past participle of **ride**

Rider see **Haggard** and **Ryder**

ridgepole (one word)

ridge tile (two words)

riempie in South Africa, leather thong or lace used to make chair seats (**-ie-** twice)

riesling German white wine or grape (lower-case **r**; **-ie-**)

Rievaulx Abbey Yorkshire (**-ie-**, **-aulx**)

Rif member of Berber people in Morocco, or their dialect (also **Riff**)

riffle (as verb) flick through, shuffle by flicking alternate corners of cards together, ripple, or make a riffle; (as noun) rapid, rocky shoal, or ripple in water (compare **rifle**)

riffraff (one word)

rifle (as verb) search, steal, or cut spiral grooves inside (as noun) firearm (compare **riffle**)

rifle range (two words)

rigamarole less common variant of **rigmarole**

right not wrong, not left, straight, claim, privilege, put right, restore to upright position, etc. (often **Right** in political contexts; compare **rite** and **write**)

right-angled triangle (one hyphen; US and Canadian name **right triangle**)

righteous (not **-ious**)

right-hand page see **verso**

right-handed (hyphen)

Right Honourable title of respect (capital **R** & **H**)

right-thinking (hyphen)

right triangle US and Canadian name for **right-angled triangle**

right wing (noun; often capital **R** & **W** in political contexts)

right-wing (adjective)

rigmarole (the variant **rigamarole** is less common but not incorrect)

rigor rigidity, chilliness, inertia, or US spelling of **rigour**

rigor mortis rigidity of dead body (not italic; not **-gour**)

rigorous (not **-gour-**)

rigour severity, strictness, or harshness (**rigor** in US English)

rigout (noun; the verb is **rig out**)

Rig-Veda compilation of ancient Hindu poems (hyphen)

Rijn Dutch name for **Rhine**

Rijksmuseum Dutch national art gallery, in Amsterdam (one word; **-ijks-**)

Riksdag Swedish parliament (**-iks-**)

Riksmål former name for **Bokmål**

Riley the spelling of the name used in the phrase *the life of Riley*

Rilke, Rainer Maria Austro-German poet

Rimbaud, Arthur French poet

rime frost, cover with frost, or archaic spelling of **rhyme**

Rime of the Ancient Mariner, The poem by Coleridge (not *Rhyme*)

Rimsky-Korsakov, Nikolai Andreyevich Russian composer

rinderpest cattle disease (one word; lower-case **r**)

ring sound of bell, make this sound, circle, encircle, or used in the phrase *ring the changes* (compare **wring**)

ring binder (two words)

Ring des Nibelungen, Der cycle of four operas by Wagner (English name *The Ring of the Nibelung* or *The Ring*)

ringed past tense and past participle of **ring** in the sense 'encircle' (compare **rang** and **rung**)

ring fence (noun)

ring-fence (verb)

ringgit monetary unit of Malaysia (double **g**)

ringleader (one word)

Rio informal name for **Rio de Janeiro**

Río Bravo Mexican name for **Rio Grande** (the river) (acute accent)

Rio de Janeiro Brazilian port or state

Rio Grande North American river or Brazilian port (Mexican name **Río Bravo** for the river)

rioja Spanish wine (lower-case **r**)

riot act used in the phrase *read the riot act to* meaning 'warn or reprimand severely' (lower-case **r** & **a**)

Riot Act former statute in criminal law (capital **R** & **A**)

RIP rest in peace (from Latin *requiescat in pace* (for one person) or *requiescant in pace* (for more than one person))

rip-off (noun; the verb is **rip off**)

riposte (rarely **ripost**)

Rip Van Winkle character who slept for 20 years in story by Washington Irving, hence a person oblivious to change (capital **R**, **V**, & **W**)

rise (as verb) get up, ascend, increase, adjourn, etc.; (as noun) ascent, increase, upward slope (usually intransitive as verb; compare **raise**, which is used in the USA and Canada in the noun sense 'pay increase', and **arise**)

risible (not **-able**)

risky dangerous (compare **risqué**)

Risorgimento movement for Italian unification in 19th century (capital **R**)

risotto rice dish (not italic; single **s**, double **t**)

risqué bordering on indecency (not italic; acute accent; compare **risky**)

rite ceremonial act or procedure (compare **right** and **write**)

rite of passage ceremony or significant event in transitional period of life (not **right . . .**)

rival (single **l**)

rivalled, rivalling (single **l** in US English)

rivalry (single **l**)

river (*typog.*) undesirable effect of interword spacing on adjacent lines that produces twisting or vertical line of white space down body of text

River often capital **R** when used with name, as in *the River Arun* or *the Mississippi River*, but lower-case **r** is sometimes preferred: follow the publisher's house style. In UK English the word is usually placed before the name. Problems of placement and capitalization can be avoided by using the name alone, as in *a bridge over the Seine.*

riveted, riveting (not **-tt-**)

Riviera Mediterranean coastal region of France and Italy (capital **R**; **-ier-**)

Riyadh joint capital (with **Mecca**) of Saudi Arabia (**-iy-**, **dh**)

Rizzio, David Italian musician and courtier who became favourite of Mary, Queen of Scots (also **Riccio**)

RM Royal Mail; Royal Marines

Rn radon (no full stop)

RN Royal Navy

RNA ribonucleic acid

RNIB Royal National Institute of the Blind (not **Institution**; not . . . **for the Blind**)

RNID Royal National Institute for Deaf People (not **Institution**; not . . . **for the Deaf**)

RNLI Royal National Lifeboat Institution (not **Institute**)

RNZAF Royal New Zealand Air Force

RNZN Royal New Zealand Navy

road thoroughfare (capital **R** as part of name; compare **rode** and **rowed**)

roadblock (one word)

roadholding (one word)

road map (two words)

road rage (two words)

roadrunner (one word)

road tax (two words)

road test (noun)

road-test (verb)

roadworks (one word)

roadworthy (one word)

Roanoke Island island off North Carolina, USA (**-oa-** then **-o-**)

rob take something unlawfully from, as in *rob a bank, they robbed me of my wallet* (the direct object is the person or place from which the thing or things are taken; compare **steal**)

Robert I king of Scotland (known as **Robert the Bruce** or **Robert Bruce**)

Robespierre, Maximilien François Marie Isidore de French revolutionary leader

Robinson, Edward G. US actor (real name **Emanuel Goldenberg**);

(William) Heath British cartoonist (see also **Heath Robinson**)

Rob Roy Scottish outlaw (real name **Robert Macgregor**)

roc enormous bird in Arabian legend (compare **rock**)

Rochefoucauld see **La Rochefoucauld**

Rochelle see **La Rochelle**

rock (the usual spelling for most senses of the word with this sound; compare **roc**)

rock and roll (no hyphens unless used before another noun, as in *rock-and-roll music*; also **rock'n'roll**)

rock bottom (no hyphen unless used before another noun, as in *rock-bottom prices*)

rock cake (two words)

rock climbing (two words)

Rockefeller, John D(avison) US industrialist and philanthropist (or his son, grandson, etc.); **Nelson** US politician (not **Rocka-**)

rocketed, rocketing (not **-tt-**)

rock face (two words)

rock garden (two words)

Rockies another name for **Rocky Mountains**

rock'n'roll variant of **rock and roll** (two apostrophes, not quotation marks)

Rock of Gibraltar (capital **R & G**)

rock plant (two words)

rockrose (one word)

Rocky Mountains North America (capital **R & M**; also **Rockies**)

rococo highly ornamented style of art, architecture, or music (single **c** twice; also **Rococo**)

rode past tense of **ride**, or nautical word for anchor rope or chain (compare **road** and **rowed**)

rodeo (plural **rodeos**)

Rodgers, Richard US composer of musical comedies (compare **Rogers**)

roe fish eggs, or short for **roe deer** (compare **row**)

roebuck (one word)

Roedean School English public school for girls, in East Sussex (**-oe-** then **-ea-**)

roe deer (two words)

roentgen unit of dose of electromagnetic radiation (lower-case **r**; also **röntgen**)

Roentgen, Wilhelm Konrad German physicist (also **Röntgen**)

Roeselare Belgian city (not **-sl-**; French name **Roulers**)

Roger de Coverley see **Sir Roger de Coverley**

Rogers, Ginger US actress and dancer (real name **Virginia McMath**); **Richard, Baron Rogers of Riverside** British architect (compare **Rodgers**)

Roget, Peter Mark English physician noted for his *Thesaurus of English Words and Phrases* (usually called *Roget's Thesaurus*), compiled in retirement (do not use *Roget* in connection with any modern thesaurus that does not have this name in its title)

rogues' gallery (**-s'** not **-'s**)

roguish (not **-uei-**)

role part played by person, or function (the spelling **rôle**, with circumflex, is less common in modern usage but not incorrect; compare **roll**)

role model (two words)

role-playing (hyphen)

roll turn over and over, move on wheels, coil, reverberate, cylinder, list of names, small loaf or pastry, rapid beating on drum, etc. (compare **role**)

roll call (two words)

Rollerblade trademark for in-line skate (capital **R**; one word)

roller coaster (two words)

roller skate (noun)

roller-skate (verb)

rollick (double **l**, **-ick**)

rolling pin (two words)

rollmop (one word)

roll-on/roll-off denoting type of ferry or cargo ship (two hyphens)

rollover (noun; the verb is **roll over**)

Rolls-Royce motor manufacturer, or a luxurious and prestigious car made by this company (hyphen; note that the global company with this name is also involved in other fields of engineering, aerospace, energy, etc.)

roll-top (hyphen)

roly-poly (hyphen; single **l** twice)

rom. roman (type)

Rom. Romans (book of the Bible; full stop; not italic)

Roma Italian name for **Rome**, another name for **Romany** (the language), or a collective word for the **Gypsy** people

Romains, Jules French writer (**-ains**; real name **Louis Farigoule**)

roman describing the standard vertical type used for most text, as in these words (lower-case **r**; compare **italic**)

Roman of Rome (capital **R**)

Roman Catholic (capital **R** & **C**; see also **Catholic**)

Romance group of languages derived from Latin, e.g. French, Italian, Portuguese, and Spanish, or denoting any of these languages (capital **R**)

Romanes variant of **Romany** (the language)

Romanesque denoting style of architecture, painting, or sculpture (capital **R**)

roman-fleuve novel or series of novels about several generations of same family (italics; plural *romans-fleuves*)

Romani variant of **Romany**

Romania European country (the spellings **Rumania** and **Roumania** are less common, especially in modern usage, but not incorrect)

Roman numerals the symbols I (= 1), V (= 5), X (= 10), L (= 50), etc. (capital **R**; compare **Arabic numerals**)

Romanov surname of Russian imperial dynasty ruling from 1613 to 1917 (**-ov**)

Romans book of the Bible (not italic; abbreviation **Rom.**)

Romansch group of dialects spoken in Switzerland (also **Romansh**)

romantic of love, idealistic, or a romantic person (lower-case **r**)

Romantic denoting movement in art, music, and literature of 18th–19th centuries, or a poet, composer, etc. of this period (the use of lower-case **r** is not incorrect in this sense, but it is less common and may be ambiguous)

romanticize (also **romanticise**; see **-ize/-ise**)

Romany the language of the Gypsy people, or another name for **Gypsy** (also **Romani** in both senses; also **Roma** or **Romanes** for the language)

Rome capital of Italy (Italian name **Roma**)

Romeo Shakespearean hero, hence any male lover (capital **R**; plural **Romeos**)

Rommel, Erwin German field marshal (double **m**, single **l**; known as **the Desert Fox**)

Romney Marsh area of SE England, in Kent, or sheep from this area (capital **R** & **M**)

Romsey English town (**-sey**)

Ronaldsay part of name of two islands of the Orkneys, **North Ronaldsay** and **South Ronaldsay**

Ronaldsway airport of Isle of Man

rondeau poem (not italic; plural **rondeaux**)

rondo piece of music (not italic; plural **rondos**)

röntgen variant of **roentgen** (umlaut)

Röntgen variant of **Roentgen** (umlaut)

roo Australian informal word for kangaroo (no apostrophe; compare **roux** and **rue**)

rood crucifix, as in *rood screen*, or unit of area (compare **rude** and **rued**)

roof (plural **roofs**)

roof rack (two words)

rooftop (one word)

Rook, Jean English journalist

Rooke, Sir George English admiral

roomful (not **-full**; plural **roomfuls**)

roommate (one word)

room service (two words)

Roosevelt, Franklin Delano 32nd president of USA; **Theodore** 26th president of USA

root part of plant, tooth, etc., origin, base form of word, mathematics term, dig, or search (compare **route**)

root and branch (adverb)

root-and-branch (adjective)

rope ladder (two words)

ropewalk (one word)

ropey (also **ropy**)

Roquefort cheese (capital **R**; not **-cqu-**)

Rorschach test ink-blot test used in psychology (capital **R**, lower-case **t**; **-sch-** then **-ch**)

rosary prayers counted on beads, or the beads themselves (compare **rosery**)

Roscommon Irish county and its county town

rosé pink wine (not italic; acute accent)

rosebay willowherb (two words)

Rosebery, Earl of title of **Archibald Philip Primrose**, British statesman (not **-berry** or **-bury**)

rosebud (one word)

rosebush (one word)

rose-coloured glasses variant of **rose-tinted glasses** (one hyphen; also **rose-coloured spectacles**)

rosehip (one word)

Rosencrantz character in Shakespeare's *Hamlet* (**-ntz**)

rosery bed or garden of roses (compare **rosary**)

rose-tinted glasses used in the phrase **see through rose-tinted glasses**, meaning 'view in excessively optimistic light' (also **rose-tinted spectacles**, **rose-coloured glasses**, or **rose-coloured spectacles**)

Rosetta stone (capital **R**, lower-case **s**; single **s**, double **t** in first word)

rose-water (hyphen)

rose window (two words)

rosewood (one word)

Rosh Hashanah Jewish New Year (also **Rosh Hashana**)

Rosicrucian member of esoteric religious society (capital **R**)

rosin substance rubbed on bows of stringed instruments, used in varnishes, etc. (compare **resin**)

RoSPA Royal Society for the Prevention of Accidents (lower-case **o**; no full stops)

Rossellini, Roberto Italian film director (double **s**, double **l**, single **n**; not **Rosso-**)

Rossetti, Christina Georgina British poet; **Dante Gabriel** British poet and painter (double **s**, double **t**)

Rostand, Edmond French playwright and poet (**-and** in surname, **-ond** in first name)

roster (not **-ta**)

Rostock German port

Rostov Russian port (also **Rostov-on-Don**)

Rostropovich, Mstislav Leopoldovich Soviet cellist, composer, and conductor (not **-stra-**)

rostrum (plural **rostrums** or **rostra**)

rosy (not **-ey**)

Rotarian member of Rotary Club (capital **R**)

rotary relating to or operating by rotation, or able to rotate (**-ary**; compare **rotatory**)

Rotary Club any of the local clubs that form Rotary International (capital **R** & **C**)

Rotary International international association of professional and business people (capital **R** & **I**)

rotator (not **-er**)

rotatory relating to or causing rotation, or able to rotate (**-ory**; compare **rotary**)

Rotavator trademark for machine used to break up soil (capital **R**)

rote routine, or used in the phrase *learn by rote* (compare **wrote**)

Rothesay Scottish town, on the island of Bute (**-esay**)

Rothschild surname of family of bankers (**-thsch-**)

rotor (not **-er**)

Rotorua New Zealand city (not **Rota-**)

Rottweiler breed of dog (capital **R**; double **t**; **-ei-**)

rotund rounded or plump (compare **orotund**)

Rouault, Georges French artist (**-ouau-**)

rouble monetary unit of Russia and Belarus (also **ruble**)

rouche less common variant of **ruche**

roué debauched man (not italic; acute accent)

Rouget de Lisle, Claude Joseph French army officer who composed the Marseillaise (not **L'Isle**)

rough not smooth; harsh; approximate; unfinished; ground covered with scrub, boulders, long grass, etc.; preliminary sketch; or used in the phrases *sleep rough, rough it*, etc. (compare **ruff**)

roughage dietary fibre (not **ruff-**)

rough-and-ready (two hyphens)

rough-and-tumble (two hyphens)
roughcast (one word)
rough-hew (hyphen)
roughshod (one word)
Rougon-Macquart surname of family of characters in cycle of novels by Zola (hyphen; **-gon, -cqu-**)
Roulers French name for **Roeslare**
roulette gambling game (not italic; single **l**, double **t**)
Roumania less common variant of **Romania**
roundabout (noun)
round about (adverb and preposition)
round brackets another name for **parentheses**
Roundhead supporter of Parliament against Charles I in Civil War (capital **R**; one word)
round table meeting of people on equal terms for discussion (lower-case **r** & **t**; no hyphen unless used before another noun, as in *round-table conference*)
Round Table table for Arthurian knights, or organization of professional and business people (capital **R** & **T**)
round trip (no hyphen unless used before another noun, as in *round-trip ticket*)
roundup (noun; the verb is **round up**)
rouse wake or stir (compare **arouse**)
rouseabout in Australia and New Zealand, unskilled labourer in shearing shed (one word; also **roustabout**)
Rousseau, Henri French painter (known as **le Douanier**); **Jean Jacques** French philosopher and writer; **Théodore** French painter (double **s**)
roustabout unskilled labourer on oil rig; in the USA and Canada, circus or fairground labourer; or variant of **rouseabout** (one word)

rout defeat, drive out, gouge, dig over, or search (compare **route**)
route roads or paths used to reach destination, course, journey, means, or send by particular route (compare **root** and **rout**)
routeing present participle of **route** (use this form to prevent ambiguity or confusion; also **routing**)
routemarch (one word)
routing present participle of **rout**, or less desirable variant of **routeing**
roux mixture of fat and flour used to make sauce (not italic; compare **roo** and **rue**)
row line of people, seats, houses, squares, etc., or propel boat with oars (compare **roe**)
rowboat US and Canadian name for **rowing boat** (one word)
rowed past tense and past participle of row (compare **road** and **rode**)
rowing boat (two words; US and Canadian name **rowboat**)
rowlock device holding oar on rowing boat (not **roll-**)
royal (lower-case **r** in general use, e.g. *royal family, royal jelly*; capital **R** in titles, names of institutions, etc., e.g. *Royal Highness, Royal Society*)
Royal Academy (full name **Royal Academy of Arts**)
Royal Air Force (capital **R, A,** & **F**)
Royal Albert Hall full name for **Albert Hall**
royal family (lower-case **r** & **f**)
Royal Festival Hall full name for **Festival Hall**
Royal Highness (capital **R** & **H**)
Royal Institution society for dissemination of scientific knowledge (capital **R** & **I**)
royal jelly (lower-case **r** & **j**)
Royal Leamington Spa official name for **Leamington Spa**
Royal Mint (capital **R** & **M**)
Royal Navy (capital **R** & **N**)

Royal Society society founded to promote scientific research (capital **R** & **S**)

Royal Welch Fusiliers (not **Welsh**)

RP Received Pronunciation (see that entry)

RPI retail price index

rpm revolutions per minute

RS Royal Society

RSA Republic of South Africa

RSC Royal Shakespeare Company

RSFSR Russian Soviet Federative Socialist Republic

RSI repetitive strain (or stress) injury

RSJ rolled-steel joist

RSM regimental sergeant major

RSPB Royal Society for the Protection of Birds

RSPCA Royal Society for the Prevention of Cruelty to Animals

RSV Revised Standard Version (of the Bible)

RSVP please reply (from French *répondez s'il vous plaît*)

Rt Hon. Right Honourable (one full stop)

Ru ruthenium (no full stop)

Ruanda former name for **Rwanda**

Rubáiyát of Omar Khayyám, The Edward Fitzgerald's translation of poems by Omar Khayyám (italics)

rubberize (also **rubberise**; see **-ize/ -ise**)

rubberneck (one word)

rubber stamp (noun)

rubber-stamp (verb)

rubdown (noun; the verb is **rub down**)

rubella German measles (single **b**, double **l**; used in technical and general contexts; compare **rubeola**)

Rubens, Sir Peter Paul Flemish painter (not **Reu-**)

rubeola measles (used in technical contexts only; compare **rubella**)

Rubicon, cross the (capital **R**)

rubidium (symbol **Rb**)

Rubinstein, Anton Grigorevich Russian composer and pianist; **Artur** Polish-born US pianist (not **-bin-**)

ruble variant of **rouble**

ruche frill (not italic; the spelling **rouche** is not incorrect, but it is less common)

rucksack (one word)

rude impolite, vulgar, or rough (compare **rued** and **rood**)

rudimentary (**-tary**)

rue regret, or plant (compare **roux** and **roo**)

rued past tense and past participle of **rue** (compare **rude** and **rood**)

ruff circular pleated collar, hair or feathers around neck, or bird (compare **rough**)

Rugbeian of Rugby School, or former pupil of Rugby School

rugby ball game (lower-case **r**; also **rugby football**; see also **rugby league** and **rugby union**)

Rugby English town (see also **Rugby School**)

rugby league form of rugby with 13 players in each team

Rugby School English public school for boys and girls

rugby union form of rugby with 15 players in each team

Ruhr German river and industrial region (**-uh-**)

rule (*typog.*) line or dash

rule of thumb (no hyphens unless used before another noun, as in *rule-of-thumb decision*)

rum alcoholic drink, or strange (compare **rhumb**)

Rumania less common variant of **Romania**

rumba (the spelling **rhumba** is not incorrect, but it is less common)

ruminant (**-in-** then **-ant**)

rumour (**-or** in US English)

Rumpelstiltskin dwarf in German legend (**-pel-**)

run past participle of **run**, as in *she had run all the way home* (compare **ran**)

runabout (noun; the verb is **run about**)

run-around (noun; the verb is **run around**)

runaway (noun; the verb is **run away**)

rundown (noun)

run down (verb)

run-down (adjective)

rung past participle of **ring** in the sense 'sound' (compare **ringed** and **rang** (for usage) and **wrung** (for spelling))

run-in (noun; the verb is **run in**)

runner-up (hyphen; plural runners-up)

running head (also **running title** or **running headline**) heading printed at the top of every page of a book (except title pages, chapter openings, etc.), often bearing the title of the book or of a major division of the book on the verso (left-hand page) and the title of the chapter or other subdivision on the recto (right-hand page). In the prelims and back matter both verso and recto usually bear the same running head. In reference books the running head on the verso is usually the first headword on that page and the running head on the recto is usually the last headword on that page.

running mate (two words)

running title another name for **running head**)

Runnymede place where King John set his seal on Magna Carta (not **-ni-**, not **-mead**)

runoff (noun; the verb is **run off**)

run-of-the-mill (three hyphens)

run on (*typog.*) set (text) without indentation or paragraph break (two words as verb)

run-on (*typog.*) denoting text set without indentation or paragraph break, or a derived word added at the end of a dictionary entry (hyphen)

run-through (noun; the verb is **run through**)

run-up (noun; the verb is **run up**)

runway (one word)

Runyon, Damon US writer (not **Damian** or **Damien**)

rupee monetary unit of India, Nepal, Pakistan, Sri Lanka, Mauritius, and the Seychelles

rupiah monetary unit of Indonesia

rural of the countryside as opposed to the town, as in *rural life* (compare **rustic**)

Ruritania imaginary European kingdom, the setting of Anthony Hope's novel *The Prisoner of Zenda* and other works

rush hour (two words)

Russell, Bertrand, 3rd Earl British philosopher and mathematician; **George William** Irish poet and journalist (pen name **A.E.**); **Ken** British film director

Russia Eurasian country, or another name for the former **Russian Soviet Federative Socialist Republic** or the former **Soviet Union** (official name **Russian Federation**)

Russian (use **Soviet** instead for the period 1922–91)

Russian Federation official name for **Russia**

Russian roulette (capital **R** then lower-case **r**)

Russian Soviet Federative Socialist Republic largest administrative division of the former Soviet Union (abbreviation **RSFSR**; also **Russia**)

rustic (as adjective) of the countryside, or having qualities associated with the countryside or country people, as in *rustic charm*; (as noun) a country person, especially one considered to be unsophisticated or simple (compare **rural**)

Ruth book of the Bible (not italic; not abbreviated)

ruthenium (symbol **Ru**)

Rutherford, Ernest, 1st Baron British physicist; **Dame Margaret** British actress; **Mark** British writer (original name **William Hale White**)

rutherfordium (symbol **Rf**)

RV Revised Version (of the Bible)

Rwanda African country (former name **Ruanda**)

RYA Royal Yachting Association

Ryder, Susan, Baroness Ryder of Warsaw British philanthropist, founder of the charity Sue Ryder Care (not **Rider**)

Ryder Cup golfing championship or trophy (capital **R** & **C**; not **Rider**)

rye cereal grass or its grain (compare **wry**)

Ryukyu Islands part of Japan

S

S south or South; sulphur (no full stop)

s' see **apostrophe**

's see **apostrophe** and **contraction**

SA Salvation Army; *Sociedad Anónima* (used in Spanish company names); *Société anonyme* (used in French company names); South Africa

Saab motor manufacturer, or any of their vehicles (capital **S**; double **a**)

Saar European river (French name **Sarre**)

Saarbrücken German city (double **a**, umlaut)

Saatchi Gallery London (double **a**, -tch-)

Saba Caribbean island, or another name for **Sheba**

Sabaean (as noun) a person from Sheba or the language of Sheba; (as adjective) of Sheba (also **Sabean**)

Sabah Malaysian state, on Borneo (former name **North Borneo**)

sabbat variant of **Sabbath** in the sense 'meeting of witches, etc.'

Sabbatarian person advocating or practising observance of Sabbath (double **b**, single **t**)

sabbath period of rest (lower-case **s**)

Sabbath day of worship in Judaism (Saturday) and Christianity (Sunday), or meeting of witches, sorcerers, devil-worshippers, etc. (capital **S**; also **sabbat** in the sense 'meeting of witches, etc.')

sabbatical denoting period of leave (lower-case **s**)

Sabbatical of the Sabbath (capital **S**)

Sabean variant of **Sabaean**

Sabine member of ancient Italian people

Sabin vaccine oral vaccine against polio (not -**bine**)

sabotage (single **b**, single **t**)

sabre (-**er** in US English)

sabre-rattling (hyphen)

sabre-toothed tiger (one hyphen; also **sabre-toothed cat**)

sac baglike part in animal or plant (compare **sack**)

saccharin (noun)

saccharine (adjective)

Sachs, Andrew German-born actor who played Manuel in the BBC TV sitcom *Fawlty Towers*; **Hans** German shoemaker and Meistersinger; **Julius von** German botanist; **Leonard** South African-born actor who hosted the BBC TV variety show *The Good Old Days*; **Nelly** German poet and dramatist (compare **Sacks, Sax,** and **Saxe**)

Sachsen German name for **Saxony**

sack (as noun) large bag used as container, dismissal from employment, slang word for bed, plundering of place, or wine; (as verb) dismiss from employment or plunder (compare **sac**)

sackcloth (one word)

sack race (two words)

Sacks, Jonathan English rabbi; **Oliver** English neurologist (compare **Sachs**, **Sax**, and **Saxe**)

Sackville-West, Victoria British writer and gardener (hyphen; known as **Vita Sackville-West**)

sacrament (not **-crem-**)

Sacramento US city and river (not **-crem-**)

sacrilegious (not **-reli-**)

SAD seasonal affective disorder

Saddam Hussein see **Hussein**

saddhu variant of **sadhu**

saddlebag (one word)

saddler person who makes or repairs saddles (double **d**)

saddle soap (two words)

saddle-sore (hyphen)

Sadducee member of ancient Jewish sect (double **d**)

sadhu Hindu wandering holy man (not italic; also **saddhu**)

Sadler's Wells London theatre (single **d**; apostrophe)

sadomasochism (one word)

s.a.e. stamped addressed envelope (also **SAE** or **sae**)

safari (plural **safaris**)

safe-breaker (hyphen)

safe-conduct (hyphen)

safe-cracker (hyphen)

safe-deposit box (one hyphen; also **safety-deposit box**)

safeguard (one word)

safe house (two words)

safekeeping (one word)

safe sex (two words)

safety belt (two words)

safety catch (two words)

safety-deposit box variant of **safe-deposit box** (one hyphen)

safety net (two words)

safety pin (two words)

Saffron Walden English town (**-on** then **-en**)

S.Afr. South Africa; South African

saga heroic narrative, series of novels, or series of events over long period (lower-case **s**)

Saga company providing services for over-50s (capital **S** only)

Sagittarius (single **g**, double **t**)

Sahara African desert (from Arabic word for desert, so the phrase *Sahara desert* is tautological)

Saigon former name for **Ho Chi Minh City**

sail piece of fabric used to propel boat or ship, journey by boat or ship, part of windmill, travel by boat or ship, or move smoothly or effortlessly (compare **sale**)

sailboard (one word)

sailboat US and Canadian name for **sailing boat** (one word)

sailcloth (one word)

sailer vessel that sails (compare **sailor**)

sailing boat (two words; US and Canadian name **sailboat**)

sailor person who sails (compare **sailer**)

Sainsbury, John, Baron Sainsbury of Drury Lane English grocer (compare **Saintsbury**)

Sainsbury's supermarket (apostrophe; note that the company name is **J Sainsbury plc**)

Saint names and phrases beginning with **Saint** and **St** are alphabetized together as if they all began with **Saint**. The two forms are usually interchangeable in place names but not in surnames. English place names beginning with **Saint** or **St** are not hyphenated; French ones are. The saints themselves are alphabetized under their personal names.

St Agnes's Eve January 20 (**-s's** not **-s'**)

St Albans English city (no apostrophe; Latin name **Verulamium**)

St Andrews Scottish city and university (no apostrophe)

St Anthony's fire another name for **ergotism** or **erysipelas** (not **Antony's**; lower-case **f**)

St Austell English town (double **l**)

St Bartholomew's Day August 24

St Bartholomew's Day Massacre murder of Huguenots in Paris in 1572 (capital **M**)

St Bernard breed of dog

St Bernard Pass either of two Alpine passes (capital **P**)

St Catharines Canadian city in Ontario (no apostrophe; not -**ther**-)

St Catharine's College Cambridge

St Catherine's College Oxford

St Christopher another name for **St Kitts**

St Christopher-Nevis official name for **St Kitts-Nevis** (one hyphen)

St Davids Welsh city (no apostrophe)

St David's Day March 1

Sainte-Beuve, Charles Augustin French literary critic (not **Saint-**)

St Elmo's fire luminous region around spires, masts, etc. (lower-case **f**)

Saint-Émilion red wine (hyphen; acute accent)

Saint-Exupéry, Antoine de French novelist and aviator (hyphen; acute accent)

St George's Channel strait between Wales and Ireland (apostrophe; capital C)

St George's Day April 23

St Giles' Oxford street name (-**s'** not -**s's**)

St Gotthard mountain range in Swiss Alps (double **t**)

St Helena volcanic island in SE Atlantic

St Helens English town and unitary authority, or volcanic peak in USA (no apostrophe)

St Helier town on Jersey (single **l**)

St Ive village in Cornwall

St Ives town in Cambridgeshire or Cornwall (no apostrophe)

St James's Palace London (-**s's** not -**s'**)

St John Canadian port in New Brunswick, Caribbean island, or North American river (compare St John's)

St John Ambulance first aid charity (not **John's**)

St John's Canadian port in Newfoundland, or capital of Antigua and Barbuda (apostrophe; compare **St John**)

St John's wort plant (apostrophe; lower-case **w**)

Saint-Just, Louis Antoine Léon de French revolutionary leader (hyphen)

St Katharine Docks London (not **Cath**-, not -**ther**-; also **St Katharine's**)

St Kitts Caribbean island (also **St Christopher**)

St Kitts-Nevis Caribbean country comprising islands of St Kitts and Nevis (one hyphen; official name **St Christopher-Nevis**)

Saint Laurent, Yves French fashion designer (no hyphen)

St Lawrence Canadian river (not **Laurence**)

St Lawrence Seaway inland waterway of North America (not **Laurence**; capital **S** twice)

St Leger English horse race run at Doncaster (not -**dg**-)

St-Lô French town (hyphen; circumflex)

St Luke's summer period of unusually warm weather in October (compare **St Martin's summer**)

St Martin Caribbean island (Dutch name **Sint Maarten**)

St Martin-in-the-Fields London church (three hyphens)

St Martin's summer period of unusually warm weather in November (compare **St Luke's summer**)

St Michael's Mount islet off S Cornwall (compare **Mont-Saint-Michel**)

St Moritz Swiss resort (no hyphen)

St-Nazaire French port (hyphen)

St Neot village in Cornwall

St Neots town in Cambridgeshire (no apostrophe)

St Pancras station in London (not **-creas**)

St Patrick's Day March 17

saintpaulia (lower-case **s** in general use; *Saintpaulia* is the genus name)

St Paul's London cathedral (apostrophe)

St Peter Port town on Guernsey (not **Peter's**)

St Peter's basilica of Vatican City (apostrophe)

St Petersburg Russian city (former names **Petrograd** (1914–24) and **Leningrad** (1924–91))

St-Quentin French town (hyphen)

Saint-Saëns, Camille French composer (hyphen; diaeresis)

Saintsbury, George Edward Bateman British literary critic (compare **Sainsbury**)

saint's day (**-'s** not **-s'**)

Saint-Simon, Claude Henri de Rouvroy, Comte de French social philosopher (hyphen)

St Swithin's Day July 15

St Valentine's Day February 14 (also **Valentine's Day**)

St Valentine's Day Massacre murder of gangsters in Chicago in 1929 (capital **M**)

St Vitus's dance disorder of central nervous system (**-s's** not **-s'**; lower-case **f**)

sake¹ see **apostrophe**, **conscience**, **goodness**, **heaven**, and **pete**

sake² Japanese alcoholic drink (not italic; also **saké** or **saki**)

Sakharov, Andrei Soviet physicist and human-rights campaigner (**-kh-**)

saki variant of **sake²**

Saki pen name of H. H. **Munro**

salaam Muslim salutation (single **a** then double **a**)

salable US spelling of **saleable**

salami highly seasoned sausage (single **a** twice)

salary payment for professional or office work, usually monthly (compare **wage**)

sale act of selling, amount sold, or event at which goods are sold (compare **sail**)

saleable (**salable** in US English)

saleroom auction room (one word; compare **salesroom**)

salesman (use **salesperson** instead where appropriate)

salesperson (use instead of gender-specific **salesman** or **saleswoman** where appropriate)

salesroom room for display of merchandise, e.g. cars (one word; compare **saleroom**)

saleswoman (use **salesperson** instead where appropriate)

salient (not **-ant**)

Salinger, J(erome) D(avid) US writer (single **l**)

Salisbury English or Australian city, or former name for **Harare**

Salisbury Plain England (capital **P**)

salivary (not **-ery**)

Salmanazar biblical king, or large wine bottle (capital **S**)

salmonella (lower-case **s** in general use; Salmonella is the genus name)

salon assembly of guests in fashionable household; commercial establishment where hairdressers, beauticians, etc. work; or art exhibition (compare **saloon**)

Salonika English name for **Thessaloníki** (also **Salonica**)

saloon lounge bar; large public room, e.g. on ship; or type of car (compare **salon**)

Salop former name for **Shropshire**

salopettes skiing garment (not italic; single **l**, single **p**, double **t**)

SALT Strategic Arms Limitation Talks (or Treaty) (thus *talks* and *treaty* in the phrases *SALT talks* and *SALT treaty* are redundant, strictly speaking, but their omission would be unidiomatic and could cause confusion)

saltcellar (one word)

saltpetre (one word; **-er** in US English)

salt pork (two words)

saltwater (adjective)

salt water (noun)

salubrious wholesome or favourable to health (compare **salutary**)

Saluki breed of dog (capital **S**)

salutary intended to have beneficial effect or promote health (not **-ory**; compare **salubrious** and **salutatory**)

salutatory of or resembling a salutation (not **-ary**; compare **salutary**)

Salvador Brazilian port (compare **El Salvador** and **San Salvador**)

Salvadorian of Salvador or El Salvador, or a person from Salvador or El Salvador (also **Salvadorean** or **Salvadoran** for El Salvador)

Salvation Army (capital **S** & **A**)

salver tray, or variant of **salvor**

salvo (plural **salvos** (in all senses) or **salvoes** (in the senses 'discharge of fire' or 'outburst'))

sal volatile ammonium carbonate or smelling salts (not italic; two words)

salvor person who salvages vessel or cargo (also **salver**)

Salzburg Austrian city (**-lz-**, **-burg**)

Sam. Samuel (books of the Bible; full stop; not italic)

S.Am. South America; South American

samarium (symbol **Sm**)

Samarkand city in Uzbekistan (**-mark-**)

sambuca liqueur (lower-case **s**; single **c**)

sambucus plant (lower-case **s** in general use, *Sambucus* is the genus name; single **c**)

samey (not **-my**)

Samhain ancient Celtic festival on November 1

Sami (as noun) member of nomadic indigenous people of Lapland, or the language of this people; (as adjective) of this people or language (also **Lapp**, which remains in widespread use, though **Sami** is preferred by the people themselves)

samizdat clandestine printing and publication in former Soviet Union (not italic)

Samoa group of Pacific islands, or country occupying nine of these (also **Samoa Islands** (for the archipelago); former name **Western Samoa** (for the country))

Samoyed member of group of Russian peoples, their languages, or breed of dog (capital **S**)

sampan (**-am-** then **-an**)

Samson biblical character (not **Samp-**)

1 Samuel book of the Bible (not italic; abbreviation **1 Sam.**; also **I Samuel**)

2 Samuel book of the Bible (not italic; abbreviation **2 Sam.**; also **II Samuel**)

samurai (lower-case **s**; same form for singular and plural)

San'a administrative capital of Yemen (also **Sanaa**)

sanatorium (plural **sanatoriums** or **sanatoria**; **sanitarium** in US English)

sanctum sacred place or place of privacy (not italic; plural **sanctums** or **sancta**)

sanctum sanctorum holy of holies, or especially private place (not italic)

Sand, George French novelist (not **Georges**; real name **Amandine Aurore Lucie Dupin**)

sandal (single **l**)

sandalled (single **l** in US English)

sandbag (one word)

sandbank (one word)

sand bar (two words)

sandblast (one word)

Sandburg, Carl US poet (not **-berg**)

sand castle (two words)

San Diego US port in California (two words)

Sandinista member of revolutionary group in Nicaragua (one word)

sandpaper (one word)

sandpit (one word)

Sandringham House royal residence in Norfolk, England (**-gh-**)

sandstone (one word)

sandstorm (one word)

SANE mental health charity (no full stops; all capitals)

sang past tense of **sing** (compare **sung**)

sang-froid composure (not italic; hyphen)

sangria Spanish drink of wine, fruit juice, soda, etc. (not italic; lower-case **s**)

sanguine (**-ui-**)

Sanhedrin supreme council of Jews in ancient times (capital **S**; **-nh-**)

sanitarium US name for **sanatorium** (plural **sanitariums** or **sanitaria**)

sanitary (not **-nat-**, not **-ory**)

sanitation (not **-nat-**)

sanitize (not **-nat-**; also **sanitise**, see **-ize/-ise**)

San Jose US city in California (no accent)

San José capital of Costa Rica (acute accent)

sank past tense of **sink** (compare **sunk**)

San Salvador capital of El Salvador (compare **Salvador** and **El Salvador**)

Sanskrit ancient Indian language (not **-scr-**)

sans serif typeface without serifs, as in **these words** (also **sanserif**)

Santa Ana city in El Salvador or California, USA (not **Anna**)

Santa Fe US city in New Mexico, or Argentine port (no accent)

Santander Spanish port (one word)

Santayana, George US philosopher, poet, and critic

Santiago capital of Chile (official name **Santiago de Chile**) or city in Dominican Republic (official name **Santiago de los Caballeros**)

Santiago Bernabéu Stadium full name for **Bernabéu**

Santiago de Chile official name for **Santiago** (in Chile)

Santiago de Compostela Spanish city

Santiago de Cuba Cuban port

Santiago del Estero Argentine city

Santiago de los Caballeros official name for **Santiago** (in Dominican Republic)

Santo Domingo capital of Dominican Republic, or a former name for **Hispaniola** or **Dominican Republic**

Saône French river (circumflex)

São Paulo Brazilian city and state (tilde; not **Paolo**)

São Tomé island off W Africa, part of the country of **São Tomé e Principe** (tilde and acute accent)

sapient (not **-ant**)

Sappho ancient Greek poet (double **p**)

sarabande dance or music (also **saraband**)

Saragossa English name for Zaragoza

Sarajevo capital of Bosnia-Herzegovina (rarely **Serajevo**)

Sarawak Malaysian state, on Borneo

sarcophagus (plural **sarcophagi** or **sarcophaguses**)

Sardinia Mediterranean island, a region of Italy (Italian name **Sardegna**)

saree less common variant of **sari**

Sargent, Sir Malcolm English conductor; **John Singer** US painter (compare **Sergeant**)

sari Indian and Pakistani women's garment (the spelling **saree** is not incorrect, but it is less common)

SARS severe acute respiratory syndrome; South African Revenue Service

sarsaparilla plant, its roots, or drink prepared from them (not **sasp-**, not **-ella**)

Sarre French name for **Saar**

Sartre, Jean-Paul French philosopher, novelist, and dramatist

SAS Special Air Service

sashay move or walk in casual or showy manner (**s-** then **-sh-**; do not use in formal text)

sash cord (two words)

sashimi Japanese dish of thin fillets of raw fish (not italic)

sash window (two words)

Saskatchewan Canadian province and river

Saskatoon Canadian city

sassafras tree or its aromatic root bark (double **s** in middle, single **s** at end)

Sassenach Scottish word for English person or Lowland Scot (**-en-**, **-ach**)

sat past tense and past participle of **sit**, as in *they sat on the floor* or *I had sat for too long* (do not use in place

of **sitting** in contexts similar to the examples at that entry)

satai less common variant of **satay**

Satan (capital **S**)

satanic (lower-case **s**)

Satanism (capital **S**)

satay barbecued spiced meat on skewers (the spellings **saté** and **satai** are less common but not incorrect)

satchel (**-tch-**)

saté less common variant of **satay**

satellite (single **t** then double **l**)

satiety (**-ety**)

satire use of ridicule, irony, etc. (compare **satyr**)

satirize (also **satirise**; see **-ize/-ise**)

satsuma fruit or tree (lower-case **s**)

Satsuma former Japanese province

Satsuma ware pottery or porcelain from Satsuma (capital **S**, lower-case **w**; two words)

Saturnalia ancient Roman festival renowned for merrymaking, or any time of wild revelry (also **saturnalia** in the sense 'wild revelry')

Saturnian of the god or planet Saturn (capital **S**)

saturnine gloomy or taciturn (lower-case **s**)

satyagraha policy of nonviolent resistance (not italic; **-aha**)

satyr deity in Greek mythology, man with strong sexual desires, or butterfly (compare **satire**)

sauce liquid eaten with food, or impudence (compare **source**)

sauce boat (two words)

saucepan (one word)

Sauchiehall Street Glasgow

Saudi of Saudi Arabia, or a person from Saudi Arabia (also **Saudi Arabian**)

Saudi Arabia SW Asian country occupying most of Arabian peninsula

Saudi Arabian variant of **Saudi**

sauerkraut pickled cabbage (not italic; one word; lower-case **s**; not **sour-**)

sausage dog (two words)

sausage meat (two words)

sausage roll (two words)

Saussure, Ferdinand de Swiss linguist

sauté fry quickly, or denoting food cooked in this way (not italic; acute accent; past tense and past participle **sautéed**)

Sauternes sweet white wine (not **-erne**; the spelling **sauternes**, with lower-case **s** is less common but not incorrect)

savanna open grassland (lower-case **s**; also **savannah**)

Savannah US port and river (**-ah**)

savant man of great learning (not italic)

savante woman of great learning (not italic)

Savile, Sir Henry English scholar and courtier; **Jimmy** English broadcaster and charity worker (full name **Sir James Wilson Vincent Savile**) (single **l**)

Savile Row London (single **l**)

Saville Theatre London (double **l**)

saviour rescuer (lower-case **s**; **-or** in US English; compare **savour**)

Saviour Jesus Christ as rescuer of humankind (capital **S**; **-or** in US English)

Savoie French department, or French name for **Savoy**

savoir-faire ability to do the right thing in any situation (not italic; hyphen)

savoir-vivre familiarity with customs of good society (not italic; hyphen)

Savonarola, Girolamo Italian reformer (**-vona-**)

savory plant or its leaves used in cookery, or US spelling of **savoury**

savour taste, smell, or relish (**-or** in US English; compare **saviour**)

savoury not sweet; pleasant; respectable; or savoury dish (**savory** in US English)

savoy cabbage (lower-case **s**)

Savoy area of France (French name **Savoie**)

saw past tense of **see**, cutting tool, cut with saw, or proverb (compare **seen** (for usage) and **soar** and **sore** (for spelling))

sawdust (one word)

sawed past tense and past participle of **saw** (also **sawn** for the past participle)

sawmill (one word)

sawn variant of **sawed** (past participle)

sawn-off (hyphen)

Sax, Adolphe Belgian inventor of the saxophone (**-phe** in first name; compare **Saxe**, **Sachs**, and **Sacks**)

Saxe French name for **Saxony**

Saxe, Hermann Maurice, Comte de French marshal (compare **Sax**, **Sachs**, and **Sacks**)

saxe blue (not **sax**; no hyphen unless used before another noun, as *a saxe-blue blazer*)

Saxe-Coburg-Gotha German duchy and name of British royal family 1901–17 (not **Sax-**)

Saxony German state or former duchy (German name **Sachsen**, French name **Saxe**)

saxophone (not **saxa-**)

sayid variant of **sayyid**

say-so (hyphen)

sayyid Muslim title (also **sayid**)

Sb antimony (no full stop; from Latin *stibium*)

sc small capitals

Sc scandium (no full stop)

SC South Carolina (US postal code)

sc. scene; scilicet (see that entry)

scabbard (double **b**, **-ard**)

scabious (as adjective) of scabies, or covered with scabs; (as noun) plant

scabrous scaly, salacious, or difficult to deal with

Sca Fell mountain in Cumbria (two words)

Scafell Pike highest mountain in England, in Cumbria (**Scafell** is one word)

scagliola imitation marble (not italic; **-glio-**)

Scala see **La Scala**

scalable (not **-eable**)

scalar denoting quantity that has magnitude but not direction (compare **scaler**)

scalawag variant of **scallywag**

scaler person or thing that scales (compare **scalar**)

Scalextric trademark for toy cars and track (capital **S**; not **-ectrix**)

scallawag variant of **scallywag**

scallop (double **l**, single **p**; rarely **escallop** or **scollop**)

scalloped, scalloping (not **-pp-**)

scallywag (also **scallawag** or **scalawag**)

scaly (not **-ley**)

scandalize (also **scandalise**; see **-ize/ -ise**)

scandalmonger (one word)

Scandinavia European peninsula occupied by Norway and Sweden, or the countries of Norway, Sweden, Denmark, Finland, and Iceland considered as a cultural unit (not **-dan-**)

scandium (symbol **Sc**)

scant limited, or slightly less than (used before abstract nouns or units of measurement, as in *scant attention* or *a scant half litre*)

scanty limited, inadequate, or small (used before or after noun, as in *our resources were scanty* or *scanty underwear*)

Scapa Flow anchorage in Orkneys (two words; single **p**)

Scaramouch boastful coward in commedia dell'arte (also **Scaramouche**)

Scarborough English resort (not **-brough**)

scarecrow (one word)

scaremonger (one word)

scarf (plural **scarves** or **scarfs** in the sense 'cloth worn around neck or head'; plural **scarfs** in the sense 'timber joint')

Scarfe, Gerald British cartoonist (**-fe**)

scarify scratch surface of, break up (soil), or make small incisions in (skin) (to avoid controversy, do not use in the sense 'scare')

scarlatina scarlet fever (not **-let-**)

Scarlatti, Alessandro Italian composer regarded as founder of modern opera; **Domenico** Italian composer and harpsichordist

Scarlett O'Hara see **O'Hara**

scary (not **-rey**)

scatterbrained (one word)

scavenge (not **-inge**)

SCE Scottish Certificate of Education

scenario (plural **scenarios**)

scene setting, subdivision of play, landscape, or display of emotion (compare **seen**)

scenery (not **-ary**)

scent smell (compare **cent** and **sent**)

sceptic doubter (**sk-** in US English; compare **septic**)

sceptre (**-er** in US English)

Schadenfreude pleasure gained from others' misfortune (italic; capital **S**)

Scheherazade character in *The Arabian Nights' Entertainments* (**-che-** then **-he-**)

Scheldt European river (Flemish and Dutch name **Schelde**, French name **Escaut**)

schema (plural **schemata**)

schematize (also **schematise**; see **-ize/-ise**)

scherzo (plural **scherzos** or **scherzi**)

Schiller, Johann Christoph Friedrich von German poet and dramatist (**Sch-**)

Schiphol Amsterdam airport (**Sch-**, **-ph-**)

schizophrenic (to avoid offence, use only with reference to the mental disorder and only as adjective in that context: replace the noun with a phrase such as *person with schizophrenia*, and do not use the word in the informal adjectival sense 'having contradictory attitudes or emotions')

schlep drag with difficulty (not italic; not **shl-**)

Schlesinger, John British film director (**Schl-**)

Schleswig-Holstein German state (hyphen)

schlock cheap inferior goods (not italic; not **shl-**)

schmaltz sentimentality (not italic; not **shm-**; also **schmalz**)

Schmidt, Helmut German statesman (not **-itt**)

schmooze chat (not italic; not **shm-**)

schnapps alcoholic spirit (not italic; lower-case **s**; also **schnaps**)

schnauzer breed of dog (not italic; lower-case **s**)

schnitzel thin slice of meat (not italic; lower-case **s**)

schnorkel rare variant of **snorkel**

Schoenberg, Arnold Austrian composer (also **Schönberg**)

scholarship (not **-er-**)

Schönberg variant of **Schoenberg**

schoolboy (one word)

school bus (two words)

schoolchild (one word)

school day hours of day spent at school (two words)

schooldays period of life spent at school (one word)

schoolgirl (one word)

schoolhouse (one word)

school-leaver (hyphen)

school-leaving age (hyphen)

schoolroom (one word)

schoolteacher (one word)

school year (two words)

Schopenhauer, Arthur German philosopher (**-pen-**)

Schrödinger, Erwin Austrian physicist (umlaut)

Schubert, Franz Austrian composer

Schumacher, Ernst Friedrich German-born British economist; **Michael** and **Ralf** German racing drivers

Schuman, Robert French statesman; **William** US composer

Schumann, Elisabeth German soprano (not **Elizabeth**); **Robert Alexander** German composer

schuss downhill run in skiing (not italic; **sch-**)

schwa the vowel sound of the unstressed first and last syllables of *production, atrocious, America*, etc., or its symbol (ə) (the spelling **shwa** is not incorrect, but it is less common)

Schwaben German name for **Swabia**

Schwarzenegger, Arnold Austrian-born US actor (not **-tz-**; the last three vowels are **e**'s)

Schwarzkopf, Dame Elisabeth Austro-British soprano (not **Elizabeth**); **Norman** US general (not **-tz-**)

Schwarzwald German name for the **Black Forest** (one word; not **-tz-**)

Schweitzer, Albert Franco-German medical missionary, philosopher, and theologian (**-eitz-**)

Schweiz German name for Switzerland (**-eiz**)

science fiction (two words)

Science Museum London (capital **S** & **M**)

Scientology philosophy of the nondenominational Church of Scientology (capital **S**)

sci-fi (hyphen)

scilicet namely, or that is (used to introduce missing word or explanation of obscure text; not italic; abbreviation **sc.**)

Scilly Isles island group off SW England (also **Scilly Islands** or **Scillies**)

scimitar (rarely **simitar**)

scintillate (**sc-**, double **l**)

scion descendant, or shoot of plant used for graft (**sc-**)

scissors (**sc-** then **-ss-**)

sclerosis (plural **scleroses**)

scollop rare variant of **scallop**

Scope charity for people with cerebral palsy (not **SCOPE**; former name **Spastics Society**)

scoreboard (one word)

scorecard (one word)

Scot person from Scotland (use instead of gender-specific **Scotsman** and **Scotswoman** where appropriate)

scotch put an end to, or wedge (lower-case **s**)

Scotch whisky made in Scotland (capital **S**; also **Scotch whisky**). See following entries for other fixed phrases; use **Scots** or **Scottish** instead for general references to Scotland, its people, or their language.

Scotch broth (capital **S**)

Scotch egg (capital **S**)

Scotchman (one word; use **Scot** or **Scotsman** instead to avoid offence)

Scotch mist (capital **S**)

Scotch pancake (capital **S**)

Scotch pine another name for **Scots pine** (capital **S**)

Scotch tape trademark for adhesive tape (capital **S**)

Scotch terrier another name for **Scottish terrier** (capital **S**)

Scotch whisky another name for **Scotch** (capital **S**; **-ky**)

Scotchwoman (one word; use **Scot** or **Scotswoman** instead to avoid offence)

scot-free (hyphen; lower-case **s**)

Scotism doctrines of John Duns Scotus (single **t**)

Scotland part of **Great Britain** and the **United Kingdom**

Scots (as adjective) of Scotland, its people, their dialects, or their Gaelic language; (as singular noun) any of the dialects spoken in Scotland; (as plural noun) the people of Scotland (see also **Scottish** and **Scotch**)

Scots Guards British regiment (capital **S** & **G**; no apostrophe)

Scotsman (one word; use instead of **Scotchman** to avoid offence, but replace with gender-neutral **Scot** where appropriate)

Scots pine (also **Scotch pine**)

Scotswoman (one word; use instead of **Scotchwoman** to avoid offence, but replace with gender-neutral **Scot** where appropriate)

Scotus see **Duns Scotus**

Scott, Sir George Gilbert British architect who designed the Albert Memorial in London; **Sir Giles Gilbert** British architect who designed the Anglican cathedral in Liverpool; **Sir Peter** British naturalist and wildlife artist; **Robert Falcon** British naval officer and Antarctic explorer; **Sir Walter** Scottish novelist and poet

Scott Fitzgerald see **Fitzgerald**

Scotticism Scottish word or phrase (double **t**)

Scottie another name for **Scottish terrier** (also **Scotty**)

Scottish (as adjective) of Scotland, its people, their dialects, or their Gaelic language; (as plural noun) the people

of Scotland (see also **Scots** and
Scotch)

Scottish terrier (also **Scotch terrier**,
Scottie, or **Scotty**)

scouse stew made from left-over
meat (lower-case **s**)

Scouse informal word for
Liverpudlian (adjective) or the
dialect of Liverpool (capital **S**)

Scouser informal word for a person
from Liverpool, especially one with
a strong accent (capital **S**; use
Liverpudlian instead in formal
contexts or to avoid offence)

Scout member of the senior branch
of the Scout Association (the use
of lower-case **s** in this sense is not
incorrect but may cause confusion
with other senses of **scout**; see also
Explorer Scout)

Scout Association worldwide youth
movement

SCR senior common room

Scrabble trademark for board game
in which players form interlocking
words (capital **S**)

scrapbook (one word)

scrapheap (one word)

scratchcard (one word)

screenplay (one word)

screen test (two words)

screenwriter (one word)

screwdriver (one word)

screw top (noun)

screw-top (adjective; also **screw-
topped**)

screw-up (noun; the verb is **screw
up**)

Scriabin, Aleksandr Nikolayevich
Russian composer (also **Skryabin**
or **Skriabin**)

scrimmage disorderly struggle, or
term used in American football (also
scrummage)

scripture sacred, solemn, or
authoritative book or writing (lower-
case **s**)

Scripture the Christian Bible, or any
body of writings regarded as sacred
by a particular religious group
(capital **S**)

scriptwriter (one word)

Scrooge character in Dickens'
A Christmas Carol, hence any mean
or miserly person (capital **S**)

scrum disorderly struggle, or term
used in rugby (also **scrummage**)

scrummage variant of **scrimmage**
or **scrum**

scrutinize (also **scrutinise**; see **-ize/
-ise**)

scuba diving (two words)

Scud missile (capital **S**)

sculpt practise sculpture, or variant
of **sculpture** (verb)

sculptor (not **-er**; may be used for
males and females)

sculptress (use **sculptor** instead to
avoid offence)

sculpture (as noun) three-
dimensional art; (as verb) carve or
cast, portray by means of sculpture,
shape by erosion, or decorate with
sculpture (also **sculpt** for the verb)

Scunthorpe English town (not
-thorp)

scurrilous (double **r**, single **l**)

Scutari former name for **Üsküdar**,
or Italian name for **Shkodër**

scutcheon less common variant of
escutcheon

Scylla rock or sea monster in
classical mythology (compare
Charybdis)

SD South Dakota (US postal code)

SDLP Social Democratic and Labour
Party (Northern Ireland political
party)

SDP Social Democratic Party (former
British political party)

Se selenium (no full stop)

SE southeast

sea body of water on earth, dry plain
on moon, or vast expanse, as in *a sea*

of faces (compare **see**; capital **S** as part of name, as in *Caspian Sea* or *Sea of Tranquillity*)

sea bird (two words)

seaborgium (symbol **Sg**)

sea change (two words)

seacoast (one word)

seafaring (one word)

seafood (one word)

seafront (one word)

seagull (one word)

sea horse (two words)

sea legs (two words)

sea level (two words)

sealing present participle of **seal** (compare **ceiling**)

sealing wax (two words)

sea lion (two words)

Sea Lord either of two naval officers on admiralty board of Ministry of Defence: the **First Sea Lord** and the **Second Sea Lord** (capital initials)

sealskin (one word)

seam (as noun) line where edges are joined, wrinkle, or stratum; (as verb) join with seam (compare **seem**)

Séamas Irish spelling of **Seamus**

seamless without seams, as in *seamless stockings*, or continuous or flowing, as in *a seamless transition* (not **seem-**)

Seamus male first name of Irish origin (phonetic spelling **Shamus**; Irish spelling **Séamas**)

seamy sordid (not **seem-**)

Sean male first name of Irish origin (phonetic spelling **Shaun**)

Seanad Éireann upper chamber of Irish parliament (acute accent; compare **Dáil Éireann**; see also **Oireachtas**)

seance meeting, e.g. to attempt to contact spirits of dead people (not italic; also **séance**)

seaport (one word)

sear burn or wither, or variant of

sere in the sense 'dried up or withered' (compare **seer**)

searchlight (one word)

search party (two words)

seashell (one word)

seashore (one word)

seasick (one word)

seasonable suitable for the season, as in *seasonable clothing*, or taking place at the appropriate time, as in *seasonable advice*

seasonal of or occurring at a particular time or season of the year, as in *seasonal labour*

seat belt (two words)

sea wall (two words)

seaweed (one word)

sebaceous (not **-cious**)

Sebastopol English name for **Sevastopol**

sec informal shortening of **second** (no full stop)

secateurs (single **c**, single **t**; **-eur-**)

secede (not **-ceed**)

second see **first**

secondary (**-dary**)

second best (noun; adjective after noun)

second-best (adjective before noun)

second class (noun; adverb; adjective after noun)

second-class (adjective before noun)

Second Coming (capital **S** & **C**)

second hand pointer on clock or watch

second-hand (adjective; adverb)

secondly see **first**

second-rate (hyphen)

Second Sea Lord see **Sea Lord** (capital initials)

second sight (two words)

second-sighted (hyphen)

Second World War another name for **World War II**

secrecy (not **-sy**)

secret hidden, private, or something unrevealed (compare **secrete**)

secretaire writing desk (not italic; compare **secretary**)

secretariat clerical or administrative office or its staff (not italic; not -**tair**-)

secretary person who does clerical or administrative work (compare **secretory** and **secretaire**)

secretary-general (hyphen)

secretary of state (lower-case **s** twice)

secrete synthesize and release, or hide (compare **secret**)

secretory of or producing a secretion (compare **secretary**)

secret service any government agency involved in intelligence or counterintelligence (lower-case **s** twice)

Secret Service US government agency responsible for protecting the president (capital **S** twice)

sector (not -**er**)

secular (not -**er**)

secularize (also **secularise**; see -**ize**/ -**ise**)

Seder ceremonial meal in Jewish home at beginning of Passover (not italic; capital **S**)

Sedgemoor English plain and battle site (not -**dgm**-)

see (as verb) perceive with eyes, understand, consider, undergo, etc.; (as noun) diocese of bishop (compare **sea**)

seed (as noun) part of plant, source, beginning, offspring, or high-ranking sports player; (as verb) plant, form seeds, remove seeds from, rank (sports players), or put substance in (clouds) to cause rain (compare **cede**)

seedbed (one word)

seed pod (two words)

Seeland German name for **Zealand** (not **Sea**-)

seem appear (compare **seam**)

seemly proper or fitting (not **seam**-)

seen past participle of **see** (compare **saw** (for usage) and **scene** (for spelling))

seer prophet (compare **sear** and **sere**)

seersucker crinkled fabric (one word; not **sear**-)

seesaw (one word)

seethe (-**the**)

see-through (adjective; the verb is **see through**)

segregate (not -**grig**-)

seicento 17th century, especially with reference to Italian art, literature, etc. (not italic)

seigneur French feudal lord (not italic; see also **droit du seigneur**)

seignior English feudal lord

Seine French river (-**ei**-)

seismogram record produced by seismograph (-**ei**-)

seismograph instrument that records earthquakes (-**ei**-)

seize (-**ei**-)

Sekt German sparkling wine (not italic; capital **S**)

Selangor Malaysian state (-**gor**)

Selassie see **Haile Selassie**

Selborne English village (not -**bourne**)

selector (not -**er**)

selenium (symbol **Se**)

self- (always attached with hyphen, as in *self-conscious*, *self-service*, etc.)

Selfridges department store (no apostrophe)

sell put on sale or dispose of by sale (compare **cell** and **cel**)

Sellafield site of atomic power station and nuclear reprocessing plant in Cumbria (former name **Windscale**)

Sellars, Peter US stage director (compare **Sellers**)

sell-by date (one hyphen)

seller person who sells (compare **cellar**)

Sellers, Peter English actor and comedian (compare **Sellars**)

sellers' market (**-s'** not **-'s**)

Sellotape trademark for adhesive tape (capital **S**)

sellout (noun; the verb is **sell out**)

Selsey Bill English headland (not **-sea**)

Seltzer effervescent mineral water (capital **S**; **-ltz-**; also **Seltzer water**)

selvage finished edge of woven fabric (also **selvedge**)

semblance (not **-ence**)

semester division of academic year (not **sim-**, not **-tre**)

semi- (usually attached without hyphen)

semiautomatic (no hyphen)

semicolon punctuation mark used to separate two clauses, each of which could form a sentence in its own right (e.g. *They squandered their winnings; their children never forgave them.*). Semicolons are also used to separate divisions of a complex list that are further subdivided by commas (e.g. *I had cereal, toast, and coffee for breakfast; soup and sandwiches for lunch; and chicken, pasta, and salad for dinner*)

semiconductor (no hyphen)

semiconscious (no hyphen)

semidetached (no hyphen)

semifinal (no hyphen)

semiprecious (no hyphen)

semper fidelis always faithful (italics)

Semtex plastic explosive (capital **S**; **-mt-**)

senate legislative body, or governing body of college or university (lower-case **s**)

Senate upper chamber of US, Canadian, or Australian legislature, or legislative council of ancient Rome (usually capital **S**)

senator (not **-er**; for capitalization see **titles of people**)

Sendak, Maurice US artist and illustrator of children's books (**-ak**)

sendoff (noun; the verb is **send off**)

send-up (noun; the verb is **send up**)

Seneca, Lucius Annaeus Roman philosopher, statesman, and dramatist (known as **Seneca the Younger**); **Marcus Annaeus** Roman writer on oratory and history (known as **Seneca the Elder** or **Seneca the Rhetorician**)

Senegal African country (French name **Sénégal**)

Senhor Portuguese equivalent of **Mr**

Senhora Portuguese equivalent of **Mrs**

Senhorita Portuguese equivalent of **Miss**

Senior (used to distinguish father from son; usually preceded by comma and abbreviated to **Snr** or **Sr**, as in *Douglas Fairbanks, Snr*)

Senlac English hill, site of Battle of Hastings (**-ac**)

Senna, Ayrton Brazilian racing driver (double **n**)

Sennacherib Assyrian king (not **-char-**)

Señor Spanish equivalent of **Mr**

Señora Spanish equivalent of **Mrs**

Señorita Spanish equivalent of **Miss**

sensible showing good sense, practical, perceptible, or having capacity for sensation

sensitive having capacity for sensation; responsive to feelings, moods, etc.; affected by external stimuli; or easily irritated or offended

sensitize (also **sensitise**; see **-ize/-ise**)

sensor (not **-er**)

sensory (not **-ary**)

sensual relating to any of the senses, strongly inclined to gratification of the senses, or arousing sexual and other bodily appetites

sensuous aesthetically pleasing, appreciative of qualities perceived by the senses, or relating to any of the senses

sent past tense and past participle of **send** (compare **cent** and **scent**)

sentient (not **-ant**)

sentimentalize (also **sentimentalise**; see **-ize/-ise**)

Seoul capital of South Korea (**-eou-**)

Sep. September (full stop)

separable (not **-per-**)

separate (not **-per-**)

separator (not **-ter**)

Sept. September (full stop)

septet (rarely **septette**)

septic of or caused by the presence of pus-forming bacteria (compare **sceptic**)

septicaemia (**-cem-** in US English)

septuagenarian (not **-ta-**)

Septuagesima third Sunday before Lent (capital **S**)

Septuagint ancient Greek version of Old Testament and Apocrypha (capital **S**)

sepulchre (**-cher** in US English)

seq. the following (one) (from Latin *sequens*)

seqq. the following (ones) (from Latin *sequentia*)

sequoia (lower-case **s** in general use; *Sequoia* is the genus name)

seraglio Muslim harem (not italic; single **r**; plural **seraglios**; also **serail**)

Serajevo rare variant of **Sarajevo**

seraph (plural **seraphim** or **seraphs**)

Serb another name for **Serbian**

Serbia constituent republic of the **Union of Serbia and Montenegro** (former name **Servia**; Serbian name **Srbija**)

Serbian (as adjective) of Serbia; (as noun) a person from Serbia or the dialect of Serbo-Croat used in Serbia (also **Serb**)

Serbo-Croat language of Serbs and Croats (also **Serbo-Croatian** or **Croato-Serb**)

sere changes in ecological community, or archaic word meaning 'dried up or withered' (also **sear** in the sense 'dried up or withered'; compare **seer**)

serf slave (compare **surf**)

serge fabric (compare **surge**)

sergeant officer in armed forces, police, or court (rarely **serjeant**)

sergeant at arms officer who maintains order in legislative or fraternal body (three words; the spelling **serjeant at arms** is not incorrect, but it is less common)

sergeant at law less common variant of **serjeant at law**

Sergeant, John British broadcaster (compare **Sargent**)

serial (as noun) novel, play, etc. in instalments, or publication regularly issued; (as adjective) of a series or serial, or doing the same thing repeatedly, as in *serial killer* (compare **cereal**)

serial comma (also **Oxford comma** or **series comma**) comma preceding *and* or *or* in lists of three or more items, as in *men, women, and children*. This practice is favoured by many publishers, but not all: be aware of the house style of the publication for which you writing and follow it consistently.

serialize (also **serialise**; see **-ize/-ise**)

series (same form for singular and plural)

series comma another name for **serial comma**

serif small line at end of stroke in typeface, as in p, I, v, etc (as opposed to p, l, v, etc.: see **sans serif**)

serjeant rare variant of **sergeant**

serjeant at arms less common variant of **sergeant at arms**

serjeant at law formerly, English barrister of special rank (the spelling **sergeant at law** is not incorrect, but it is less common)

SERPS state earnings-related pension scheme (no full stops; also **Serps**)

serrated (double **r**)

Servia former name for **Serbia**

serviceable (**e** after **c**)

servo (plural **servos**)

servomechanism (one word)

servomotor (one word)

sesame (not **-ss-**, not **-mi**)

sestet six lines of poetry, or rare variant of **sextet**

session meeting or period (compare **cession**)

set the spelling used for most senses of the word with this sound, or variant of **sett**

set-aside (noun; the verb is **set aside**)

setback (noun; the verb is **set back**)

set piece (two words)

set square (two words)

sett paving block, badger's burrow, or square in tartan (also **set**)

settler person who settles in new country

settlor legal term denoting person who settles property on another

set-to (noun; the verb is **set to**)

setup (noun)

set up (verb)

set-up (adjective)

Seurat, Georges French painter (**-eur-**)

Seuss, Dr pen name of US children's author and illustrator **Theoder Seuss Giesel**

Sevastopol Ukrainian port (English name **Sebastopol**)

Sevenoaks English town (one word)

seven seas (lower-case **s** twice)

Seventh-Day Adventist member of Protestant Christian group (hyphen; capital **S**, **D**, & **A**)

Seven Wonders of the World (capital **S** & **W** twice)

seven-year itch (one hyphen)

Seven Years' War Britain and Prussia against France and Austria, 1756–63 (capital **S**, **Y**, & **W**; apostrophe)

severance (**-vera-**)

Severn British or Canadian river (**-ern**)

Seville Spanish port (Spanish name **Sevilla**)

Seville orange (capital **S**)

Sèvres French town or porcelain made there (grave accent; **-s**)

sew join with thread (compare **so** and **sow**)

sewage waste matter (compare **sewerage**)

sewed past tense of **sew** or variant of **sewn** (compare **sowed**)

sewer[1] drain for sewage or surface water

sewer[2] person or thing that sews (compare **sower**)

sewerage system of sewers, or removal of sewage and surface water (compare **sewage**)

sewn past participle of **sew** (also **sewed**; compare **sown**)

sex see **gender**

sexagenarian (**-age-**)

Sexagesima second Sunday before Lent (capital **S**)

sex appeal (two words)

sex change (two words)

sexism see **gender**

sex symbol (two words)

sextant navigation instrument, or sixth part of circle (compare **sexton**)

sextet group of six musicians, or music written for them (rarely **sextette** or **sestet**)

sexto another name for **sixmo**

sextodecimo another name for **sixteenmo**

sexton church caretaker (compare **sextant**)

Seychelles island group in Indian Ocean (**Sey-**)

Seymour, Jane third wife of Henry VIII (**-our**)

SF science fiction

Sg seaborgium (no full stop)

sgian-dhu Scottish dirk carried in stocking (not italic; also **skean-dhu**)

SGML standard generalized mark-up language

's Gravenhage a Dutch name for The Hague (apostrophe; lower-case **s**; not **-hague**)

Shaanxi NW Chinese province (also **Shensi**)

Shabuoth variant of **Shavuot**

shadoof mechanism for raising water (also **shaduf**)

Shaftesbury English town (**-tes-**)

shah Middle Eastern ruler (for capitalization see **titles of people**)

shakedown (noun; the verb is **shake down**)

shake-out (noun; the verb is **shake out**)

Shakespeare, William English dramatist and poet (**-kes-**, **-eare**)

Shakespearean (also **Shakespearian**)

Shakespeareana (also **Shakespeariana**)

Shakespearian variant of **Shakespearean**

Shakespeariana variant of **Shakespeareana**

shake-up (noun; the verb is **shake up**)

shako military headdress (plural **shakos** or **shakoes**)

shaky (not **-key**)

shall according to traditional grammar, **shall** is used in the first person to express futurity (as in *we shall see*) and in the second and third persons to express determination, obligation, etc. (as in *they shall apologize*); compare **will**. In modern usage **shall** is often replaced by **will** or shortened to **'ll**.

shallot vegetable (double **l**, single **t**)

shalom aleichem peace be to you (used by Jews as greeting or farewell; italics for full form, but the short form **shalom** is usually not italic)

Shalott, The Lady of poem by Tennyson (italics; single *l*, double *t*)

shaman (plural **shamans**)

shamefaced (one word)

shammy leather less common variant of **chamois leather**

Shamus phonetic spelling of **Seamus**

Shan phonetic spelling of **Sian¹**

Shandong Chinese province (also **Shantung**)

shanghai kidnap for naval service, force or trick into doing something, or Australian and New Zealand word for catapult (lower-case **s**)

Shanghai Chinese port

Shangri-la imaginary utopia (capital **S**, lower-case **l**; hyphen)

Shankill Road Belfast (not **-hill**)

shanks's pony (**-s's** not **-s'**; the variant **Shanks's pony** is less common but not incorrect; also **shanks's mare** or **Shanks's mare**, especially in US and Canadian English)

Shansi variant of **Shanxi**

shan't contraction of **shall not**

shantung heavy fabric with knobbly surface

Shantung variant of **Shandong**

shantytown (one word)

Shanxi N Chinese province (also **Shansi**)

shapable (also **shapeable**)

shareholder (one word)

sharia body of Muslim law (thus *law* in the phrase *sharia law* is redundant, strictly speaking)

Sharp, Becky character in Thackeray's *Vanity Fair*; **Cecil** British musician and editor of folk songs

Sharpe, Richard title character in series of novels about Napoleonic Wars by Bernard Cornwell; **Tom** English novelist

Sharpeville South African town and scene of riots (not **Sharpes-** or **Sharp-**)

sharpshooter (one word)

sharp-witted (hyphen)

Shatt-al-Arab Iraqi river (two hyphens; lower-case **a** for middle word)

Shaun phonetic spelling of **Sean**

shaved past tense or past participle of **shave** (also **shaven** for the past participle)

shaven variant of **shaved** (past participle) chiefly used as adjective meaning 'closely shaved' (as in *shaven head*) or in combination (as in *clean-shaven*)

Shavian of George Bernard **Shaw**

shaving cream (two words)

Shavuot Hebrew name for **Pentecost** (also **Shabuoth**)

Shaw, George Bernard Irish dramatist and critic; **Richard Norman** English architect (compare **Shore**)

she (when gender is unspecified, use **he or she** in formal contexts and **they** elsewhere, or rephrase to avoid the problem; do not use **s/he**)

sheaf (plural **sheaves**)

shear remove fleece of, cut with shears, deform or fracture (as in *the bolt sheared off*), or strip or divest (compare **sheer**)

sheared past tense and past participle of **shear** (also **shore** for the past tense in Australia and New Zealand; also **shorn** for the past participle, especially with reference to sheep or in the sense 'stripped or divested'; compare **sheered**)

shearlegs variant of **sheerlegs**

shears cutting tool (not **-ee-**)

shearwater bird (one word; not **sheer-**)

sheath (noun)

sheathe (verb)

Sheba ancient Arabian country (also **Saba**)

shebang situation or affair, as in *the whole shebang*

shebeen place where alcohol is consumed, often illegally (also **shebean**)

sheep-dip (hyphen)

sheepdog (one word)

sheepskin (one word)

sheer (as adjective) very steep, almost transparent, or absolute; (as verb) deviate or avoid, as in *the car sheered away from the tree* (compare **shear**)

sheered past tense and past participle of **sheer** (compare **sheared**)

sheerlegs lifting device (one word; also **shearlegs**)

Sheerness English port (not **Shear-**)

sheet (*typog.*) piece of printed paper before folding or binding

sheet metal (two words)

sheet music (two words)

sheikh Muslim leader (also **sheik**)

shekel monetary unit of Israel (also **sheqel**)

shelduck (single **l**)

shelf (noun; compare **shelve**)

shelf life (two words)

shelf-stacker (hyphen)

shellac resin, or coat with varnish containing shellac (not **-ack**)

shellacked, shellacking (**-ck-**)

Shelley, Mary British author; **Percy Bysshe** British poet (**-ey**)

shellfire (one word)

shellfish (one word)

shell-like (hyphen)

shell shock (two words)

shell-shocked (hyphen)

shell suit (two words)

sheltie another name for **Shetland pony** or **Shetland sheepdog** (lowercase **s**; also **shelty**)

shelve (verb; compare **shelf**)

Shensi variant of **Shaanxi**

Shenyang Chinese city (former name **Mukden**)

Shepard, Alan Bartlett, Jr US astronaut; **E(rnest) H(oward)** English artist and illustrator; **Sam** US dramatist, actor, and director (compare **Shephard, shepherd**, and **Sheppard**)

Shephard, Gillian English politician (not **-erd**; compare **Shepard, shepherd**, and **Sheppard**)

shepherd person who tends sheep (compare **Shepard, Shephard**, and **Sheppard**)

Shepherds Bush London (no apostrophe)

shepherd's pie (apostrophe)

shepherd's purse (apostrophe)

Sheppard, David English prelate; **Jack** English criminal celebrated in 18th-century ballads and plays (compare **Shepard, Shephard**, and **shepherd**)

Sheppey, Isle of island in Thames estuary (**-ey**)

sheqel variant of **shekel**

Sheraton, Thomas English furniture maker (compare **Sheridan**)

sherbet (not **-ert**)

Sherborne town in Dorset (not **-bourne**)

Sheridan, Philip Henry American cavalry commander in the Civil War; **Richard Brinsley** Irish dramatist (compare **Sheraton**)

sheriff law-enforcement officer or court officer (single **r**, double **f**)

sherpa official who assists delegate at summit meeting (lower-case **s**)

Sherpa member of Himalayan people noted as mountaineers (capital **S**; see also **Tenzing Norgay**)

's Hertogenbosch Dutch city (also **Den Bosch**)

Shetland island group off N Scotland (also **Shetland Islands**; former official name **Zetland**)

Shetland pony (capital **S**; also **sheltie**)

Shetland sheepdog (capital **S**; also **sheltie**)

Shevaun phonetic spelling of **Siobhan**

Shiah (as noun) one of the two main branches of Islam, or a member of this group; (as adjective) of or belonging to Shiah (also **Shia**; compare **Sunni**; use **Shiah Muslim** or **Shiah** in place of **Shiite**)

shiatsu acupressure (compare **shih-tzu**)

shibboleth (double **b**, single **l**)

shih-tzu breed of dog (hyphen; compare **shiatsu**)

shiitake mushroom (also **shitake**)

Shiite (use **Shiah Muslim** or **Shiah** instead)

shillelagh (rarely **shillala**)

shillyshally (one word)

shined past tense and past participle of **shine** in the sense 'polish' (compare **shone**)

shiny (not **-ney**)

ship large seagoing vessel (compare **boat**; use italics for names of individual ships, e.g. the *Titanic*, but note that HMS is not italic, e.g. HMS *Sheffield*)

shipbuilding (one word)

shipowner (one word)

ship's biscuit (apostrophe)

shipshape (one word)

shipwreck (one word)

shipwright (one word)

shipyard (one word)

Shiraz Iranian city, or Australian name for **Syrah** grape or wine

shirtsleeves (one word)

shirt-tail (hyphen)

shish kebab (two words)

shitake variant of **shiitake**

Shiva variant of **Siva**

Shkodër Albanian town and lake (Italian name **Scutari**)

shock absorber (two words)

shock wave (two words)

shoe covering for foot, something resembling this in form or functions, or fit or furnish with shoes (compare **shoo** and **choux**)

shoeing (-oei-)

shoehorn (one word)

shoelace (one word)

shoe leather (two words)

shoestring (one word)

shogun Japanese military commander or dictator (-un)

shone past tense and past participle of shine in all senses except 'polish' (compare **shined**)

shoo (as interjection) go away!; (as verb) drive away (compare **shoe** and **choux**)

shoot (as verb) fire weapon, injure or kill with weapon, go quickly, germinate, photograph, or inject; (as noun) new plant growth, hunting party, or photographic assignment (compare **chute**)

shooting star (two words)

shooting stick (two words)

shoot-out (noun; the verb is **shoot out**)

shopaholic (not -oholic)

shop floor (no hyphen unless used before another noun, as in *shop-floor workers*)

shopkeeper (one word)

shoplifting (one word)

shopping bag (two words)

shopsoiled (one word)

shop steward (two words)

shoptalk (one word)

shopwalker (one word)

shop window (two words)

shore beach, prop, or variant of

sheared (past tense) in Australia and New Zealand (compare **sure**)

Shore, Peter, Baron English politician (compare **Shaw**)

shore bird (two words)

shorn variant of **sheared** (past participle), especially with reference to sheep or in the sense 'stripped or divested'

short-change (hyphen)

short circuit (noun)

short-circuit (verb)

shortcoming (one word)

shorthand (one word)

short-handed (hyphen)

short list (noun)

short-list (verb)

short-lived (hyphen)

short-sighted (hyphen)

Shostakovich, Dmitri Dmitriyevich Soviet composer

shotgun (one word)

should past tense of **shall**, also used to express obligation (as in *you should apologize*), in questions (as in *should I bring a packed lunch?*), and in some conditional constructions (as in *should they fail, the mission will have to be aborted*). According to traditional grammar, **should** is used in the first person in reported speech (as in *we said we should be late*) and in polite expressions of desire or preference (as in *I should like an explanation*), but in modern usage it is often replaced by **would** in these contexts. See also **subjunctive**.

shoulder pad (two words)

should've contraction of **should have** ('**ve** not **of**)

shovel (single l)

shoveler species of duck, or US spelling of **shoveller**

shovelled (single l in US English)

shoveller person or thing that shovels (US spelling **shoveler**)

shovelling (single l in US English)

showcase (one word)

showdown (one word)

showed past tense of **show** or variant of **shown**

showground (one word)

showjumping (one word)

shown past participle of **show** (also **showed**)

show-off (noun; the verb is **show off**)

showpiece (one word)

showroom (one word)

shrank past tense of **shrink** (also **shrunk**)

shrink-wrap (hyphen)

shrivel (single l)

shrivelled, shrivelling (single l in US English)

Shropshire English county (former name **Salop**)

Shrove Tuesday last day before Lent (capital **S** & **T**; also **Pancake Day**)

shrunk past participle of **shrink** or variant of **shrank** (also **shrunken** for the past participle)

shrunken variant of **shrunk** (past participle) chiefly used as adjective, as in *a shrunken head*

shutdown (noun; the verb is **shut down**)

Shute, Nevil English novelist (not Neville; real name **Nevil Shute Norway**)

shuttlecock (one word)

shwa less common variant of **schwa**

Si¹ variant of **Xi**

Si² silicon (no full stop)

SI South Island (New Zealand); Système International (see **SI units**)

Siam former name for **Thailand**

Siamese cat (capital **S**)

Siamese twins nontechnical name for **conjoined twins** (capital **S**)

Sian¹ female first name of Welsh origin (phonetic spelling **Shan**; Welsh spelling **Siân**)

Sian² variant of **Xi An**

Siang variant of **Xiang**

Siangtan variant of **Xiangtan**

sibling (single **b**)

sibyl oracle, fortune-teller, or witch (compare **Sybil**)

sic so or thus: chiefly used when quoting to indicate that the preceding word or phrase is what was actually said or written and is not an error of transcription, as in *he described it as 'a shot across the bowels [sic] of the government'*. It is traditionally enclosed in square brackets and is sometimes italic.

Sichuan Chinese province (also **Szechwan**)

sickbay (one word)

sickbed (one word)

sick building syndrome (three words)

sic transit gloria mundi thus passes the glory of the world (italics)

Siddhartha personal name of the **Buddha** (double **d**)

sideboard (one word)

side dish (two words)

side effect (two words)

sidekick (one word)

sidelight (one word)

sideline (one word)

side-saddle (hyphen)

sideshow (one word)

side-splitting (hyphen)

sidestep (one word)

side street (two words)

sidetrack (one word)

Sidney, Sir Philip English poet, courtier, and soldier (compare **Sydney**)

SIDS sudden infant death syndrome

siege (-ie-)

Siegfried in German mythology, prince who wins Brunhild for Gunther (-ie- twice; compare **Sigurd**)

Sieg Heil hail to victory: a Nazi salute (italics; -ie- then -ei-)

siemens unit of electrical conductance (lower-case **s**)

Siemens electronics company (capital **S**)
Siena Italian city (single **n**)
sienna pigment (lower-case **s**; double **n**)
sierra mountain range (capital **S** in names, e.g. *Sierra Madre* or *Sierra Nevada*)
Sierra Leone African country
sight vision, glimpse, view, spectacle, alignment device on gun, or see (compare **cite** and **site**)
sight-read (hyphen)
sightseeing (one word)
sigla list of symbols used in book
sign indication, signal, gesture, placard, symbol, write one's name, or make signal or gesture (compare **sine**)
signal box (two words)
signalled (single **l** in US English)
signaller (single **l** in US English)
signalling (single **l** in US English)
signatory (**-tory**)
signature (*typog.*) sheet of paper bearing a number of printed pages (usually 16 or 32) that is folded to form a section of a book
signet seal or impression made by it (compare **cygnet**)
significant (not **-ent**)
Signor Italian equivalent of **Mr**
Signora Italian equivalent of **Mrs**
Signorita Italian equivalent of **Miss**
signpost (one word)
Sigurd in Norse mythology, hero who wins Brynhild for Gunnar (compare **Siegfried**)
Sikes, Bill character in Dickens' *Oliver Twist* (compare **Sykes**)
Sikh adherent of Indian religion that separated from Hinduism in the 16th century, or of this religion (**-kh**)
Siking former name for **Xi An**
Sikorski, Władysław Polish general and statesman

Sikorsky, Igor Russian-born US aeronautical engineer
silhouette (**-lh-**, **-ou-**)
silicon chemical element used e.g. in alloys and electronics, as in *silicon chip* (symbol **Si**; compare **silicone**)
silicone synthetic material used e.g. in polishes and rubber, as in *silicone breast implants* (compare **silicon**)
silk-screen printing (one hyphen)
silkworm (one word)
sillabub less common variant of **syllabub**
silo (plural **silos**)
silvan less common variant of **sylvan**
silver (symbol **Ag**)
silverfish (one word)
silviculture (the spelling **sylviculture** is not incorrect, but it is less common)
s'il vous plaît if you please (italics)
simitar rare variant of **scimitar**
Simla Indian city (single **m**)
simnel cake (lower-case **s**)
Simon's Town South African port (also **Simonstown**)
simoom sand-laden desert wind (also **simoon**)
simplistic extremely or excessively simple (the word implies naivety or oversimplification: do not use in place of **simple** in neutral senses such as 'uncomplicated' or 'easy to understand')
simulacrum (plural **simulacra**)
simulate feign, imitate, or reproduce conditions of (compare **dissimulate** and **stimulate**)
simultaneous (not **-ious**)
Sinbad see **Sindbad**
sincerely (**-rely**)
Sindbad character in *The Arabian Nights' Entertainments* who undertakes a number of sea voyages (not **Sinbad**, although that spelling is used in some adaptations of the story (e.g. the 1947 film *Sinbad the*

Sailor) and as a general nickname for a sailor)

sine trigonometric function (compare **sign**)

sine die without a (fixed) day (italics)

sine prole without issue (i.e. childless; italics)

sine qua non essential condition or requirement (literally 'without which not'; italics)

singeing present participle of **singe** (compare **singing**)

Singer Sargent see **Sargent**

Singhalese variant of **Sinhalese**

singing present participle of **sing** (compare **singeing**)

single-handed (hyphen)

single-minded (hyphen)

single parent (no hyphen unless used before another noun, as in *single-parent family*)

Sing Sing US prison (two words)

singular/plural (for the use of singular or plural verb see **collective nouns**, **either**, **neither**, **none**, **one**, **acoustics**, **graphics**, **data**, **graffiti**, and other individual entries)

Sinhalese people living chiefly in Sri Lanka; their language, which is the official language of Sri Lanka; or of this people or language (also **Singhalese**; compare **Sri Lankan**)

Sining variant of **Xining**

sink go down, or basin used for washing (compare **sync**)

Sinn Féin Irish republican political movement (acute accent)

Sint Maarten Dutch name for **St Martin**

sinuous curving, twisting, devious, or lithe

sinus bodily cavity (plural **sinuses**)

Siobhan female first name of Irish origin (phonetic spelling **Shevaun**; Irish spelling **Siobhán**)

Sion Swiss town, or less common variant of **Zion**

Sioux North American people or language (**-iou-**)

siphon (also **syphon**)

Sir. Sirach (full stop; not italic)

Sirach book of the Apocrypha (not italic; abbreviation **Sir.**; also **Ecclesiasticus**)

siren (also **Siren** in the sense 'sea nymph in Greek mythology')

Sir John Soane's Museum London (not **Soane**, not **Sloane's**)

sirloin (not **sur-**)

sirocco hot southerly wind (single **r**, double **c**; plural **siroccos**)

Sir Roger de Coverley traditional English country dance or fictitious character in 18th-century *Spectator* essays (**-ley**)

sirup rare variant of **syrup**

sissy (also **cissy**)

sister-in-law (plural **sisters-in-law**)

Sistine Chapel (capital **S** & **C**; not **Cist-**)

Sisyphus character in Greek mythology who was punished in Hades by eternally having to roll a heavy stone up a hill (**i** then **y**)

sitar Indian musical instrument (single **t**)

sitcom (one word)

sit-down (noun and adjective; the verb is **sit down**)

site location on land or Internet, or locate (compare **cite** and **sight**)

sit-in (noun; the verb is **sit in**)

sitting present participle of **sit**, as in *they were sitting on the floor* or *I had been sitting for too long* (do not replace with **sat** in contexts similar to the examples here)

sitting room (two words)

situation (avoid vague or unnecessary use, e.g. in phrases such as *crisis situation*)

Sitwell, Dame Edith English poet and critic; **Sir Osbert** English writer; **Sir Sacheverell** English poet and writer of books on art, music, etc.

sitz bath (two words; lower-case **s**; not **sits**)

SI units Système International d'Unités: international system of units used in science and technology. The SI units are the metre, kilogram, second, ampere, kelvin, candela, mole, radian, and steradian. Their abbreviations take the same form for singular and plural and do not have full stops. See also **cgs units, fps units,** and **units of measurement.**

Siva Hindu god (also **Shiva**)

Six Day War Israel against Egypt, Jordan, and Syria, June 1967 (capital **S, D,** & **W**; not **Days'**)

sixmo book size with six leaves (i.e. twelve pages) per sheet (also **6mo** or **sexto**)

six-pack (hyphen)

sixteenmo book size with 16 leaves (i.e. 32 pages) per sheet (also **16mo** or **sextodecimo**)

sixty-fourmo book size with 64 leaves (i.e. 128 pages) per sheet (also **64mo**)

sizable (also **sizeable**)

-size (also **-sized**)

SJ Society of Jesus (religious order of the Jesuits)

Sjælland Danish name for **Zealand** (-æ- not **-ae-**)

sjambok heavy whip used in South Africa (**sj-, -ok**)

Skagerrak arm of North Sea between Denmark and Norway (single **g**, double **r**)

skateboard (one word)

skean-dhu variant of **sgian-dhu**

skein (-ei-)

skeletonize (also **skeletonise**; see **-ize/-ise**)

Skelmersdale English town (-mers-)

skeptic US spelling of **sceptic**

sketchbook (one word)

skewbald denoting horse marked with white and any colour except black (compare **piebald**)

skied past tense and past participle of **ski** (also **ski'd**)

skies plural of **sky** (compare **skis**)

skiing present participle of **ski**

ski jump (noun)

ski-jump (verb)

skilful (single **l** twice in UK English; double **l** then single **l** in US English)

ski lift (two words)

skin-deep (hyphen)

skin diving (two words)

skinflint (one word)

skin graft (two words)

skinhead (one word)

skin test (two words)

skintight (one word)

skipping-rope (hyphen)

skirting board (two words)

skis plural and third person present tense of **ski** (compare **skies**)

skivvy (double **v**)

skol drinking toast (not italic; also **skoal**)

Skopje capital of (Former Yugoslav Republic of) Macedonia (**-pje**)

Skryabin variant of **Scriabin** (also **Skryabin**)

skulduggery (single **l**, double **g**)

skullcap (one word)

skydiving (one word)

Skye island off NW Scotland (**-ye**)

Skye terrier (capital **S**)

skylark (one word)

skylight (one word)

skyrocket (one word)

skyscraper (one word)

slàinte drinking toast (not italic; grave accent)

slander defamation in speech or other transient form (compare **libel**)

slanging match (two words)

slapdash (one word)

slap-happy (hyphen)

slapstick (one word)
slap-up (hyphen)
slash another name for **solidus**
slaughterhouse (one word)
Slav speaker of Slavonic language
Slavic variant of **Slavonic**
Slavonia region of Croatia
Slavonian of Slavonia, or a person from Slavonia
Slavonic (as noun) group of languages spoken in E Europe and NW Asia, including Russian, Serbo-Croat, Polish, etc.; (as adjective) of these languages, or of the people who speak them (also Slavic)
slay kill (compare **sleigh**)
sleazy (-eaz-)
sled US and Canadian name for **sledge**
sledge vehicle drawn by dogs or horses over snow, toboggan, or go by sledge (also **sleigh** for the vehicle; US and Canadian name **sled**)
sledgehammer (one word)
sleepover (one word)
sleigh variant of **sledge** (the vehicle) (compare **slay**)
sleight used in the phrase *sleight of hand* (compare **slight**)
sleuth (-eu-)
slew past tense of **slay**, twist sideways, or great number (the spelling **slue** is not incorrect in the senses 'twist sideways' and 'great number', but it is less common in these senses and should not be used as the past tense of **slay**)
slight small or snub (compare **sleight**)
slimline (one word)
slipknot (one word)
slip road (two words)
slipshod (one word)
slipstream (one word)
slip-up (noun; the verb is **slip up**)
Sloan, John US artist (compare **Sloane** and **Soane**)

Sloane, Sir Hans British naturalist (compare **Sloan** and **Soane**)
Sloane Ranger (capital **S** & **R**; also **Sloane**)
Sloane Square London
sloe small sour blue-black fruit (compare **slow**)
sloe-eyed (hyphen)
Slough English town and unitary authority
Slovak (as adjective) of Slovakia, its people, or their language; (as noun) language of Slovakia, or a person from Slovakia
Slovakia European country
Slovakian of Slovakia, or a person from Slovakia
Slovene (as adjective) of Slovenia, its people, or their language; (as noun) language of Slovenia, or a person from Slovenia
Slovenia European country
Slovenian of Slovenia, or a person from Slovenia
slow lacking speed, promptness, etc. (compare **sloe**)
slowworm (one word)
SLR single-lens reflex
slue less common variant of **slew** in the senses 'twist sideways' and 'great amount'
sluicegate (one word)
slush fund (two words)
Sm samarium (no full stop)
small another word for **lower-case** (see also **small capital**)
small capital a character with the form of a capital letter but the size of a lower-case letter, as in THESE WORDS. Small capitals are used for **A.D.** and **B.C.**, and sometimes for other abbreviations, to avoid littering text with full capitals; for characters' names in plays; for authors' names in bibliographies; and in cross-references. They are indicated with a double underline

in proofreading and editing. See also **capital letter** and **full capital**.

smallholding (one word)

small-minded (hyphen)

small print (two words)

smart aleck (lower-case **a**; also **smart alec**)

smart card (two words)

smash-up (noun; the verb is **smash up**)

smelled variant of **smelt** (past tense and past participle)

smelling salts (two words)

smelt past tense and past participle of **smell**, extract metal from, or fish (also **smelled** for the past tense and past participle)

Smetana, Bedřich Czech composer (diacritic on first name)

smidgen (also **smidgin**)

smiley (not **-ly**)

Smith, Adam Scottish economist and philosopher; **Delia** British cookery writer and broadcaster; **Harvey** British showjumper; **Ian** Zimbabwean statesman; **Joseph** US religious leader, founder of the Mormon Church; **Dame Maggie** British actress; **Stevie** British poet (real name **Florence Margaret Smith**); **Sydney** British clergyman and writer (not **Sidney**) (compare **Smyth**; see also **WHSmith**)

Smithsonian Institution Washington, DC (not Institute)

smokable (also **smokeable**)

smoke screen (two words)

smokestack (one word)

Smollett, Tobias George Scottish novelist (double l, double t)

smooth (noun and verb; not **-the**)

smorgasbord Scandinavian buffet (not italic; not **-board**)

smoulder (**-old-** in US English)

Smyrna ancient city in Asia Minor

Smyth, Dame Ethel British composer (compare **Smith** and **Smythe**)

Smythe, Pat(ricia) English showjumper and writer (compare **Smyth**)

Sn tin (no full stop; from Latin *stannum*)

snapdragon (one word)

snarl-up (noun; the verb is **snarl up**)

sneaked past tense and past participle of **sneak** (see also **snuck**)

snivel (single v, single l)

snivelled, snivelling (single l in US English)

snorkel (rarely **schnorkel**)

snorkelled, snorkelling (single l in US English)

Snorri Sturluson Icelandic historian and poet

snowball (one word)

snow-blind (hyphen)

snowcapped (one word)

snowdrift (one word)

snowflake (one word)

snowplough (one word)

snowstorm (one word)

SNP Scottish National Party

Snr Senior

snub-nosed (hyphen)

snuck nonstandard past tense and past participle of **sneak** (use **sneaked** instead in formal contexts)

snuffbox (one word)

so (the spelling used for the word with this sound in all parts of speech except the verbs **sew** and **sow**[1])

so-and-so (two hyphens; plural **so-and-sos**)

Soane, Sir John British architect (compare **Sloane** and **Sloan**; see also **Sir John Soane's Museum**)

soapbox (one word)

soapsuds (one word)

soar rise or fly upwards (compare **sore** and **saw**)

Soave Italian white wine (capital **S**; **-oa-**)

sobriquet nickname (not italic; also **soubriquet**)

sob story (two words)

so-called (hyphen; note that there is no need for quotation marks around the word or phrase that follows)

soccer (not **-ck-**)

sociable friendly or convivial

social of society, living in a community, of human interaction, or promoting companionship

Social Chapter part of Maastricht Treaty (capital **S** & **C**)

socialist (also capital **S** with reference to a particular political party)

socialize (also **socialise**; see **-ize/-ise**)

social worker (two words)

Society of Friends see **Quaker**

socioeconomic (no hyphen)

sociopolitical (no hyphen)

Socotra island in Indian Ocean, administratively part of Yemen (also **Sokotra** or **Suqutra**)

sodium (symbol **Na**)

Sodom biblical city destroyed by God in the Old Testament, hence any place of vice or depravity (**-om**)

Sod's law (capital **S**, lower-case **l**)

sofa bed (two words)

soffit (double **f**, single **t**)

Sofia capital of Bulgaria (Bulgarian name **Sofiya**)

softback another word for **paperback** (noun) (one word)

soft-boiled (hyphen)

soft-centred (hyphen)

soft-cover another word for **paperback** (adjective) (hyphen)

softhearted (one word)

soft hyphen hyphen used to break a word at the end of a line. In modern style, words are usually broken according to phonetic rather than etymological principles (e.g. *photo-graph* but *photog-raphy*). Never break a syllable, never leave a single letter at the beginning or end of the line, and beware of unfortunate breaks

such as *the-rapist*. When editing typewritten or word-processed copy containing soft hyphens, highlight any end-of-line hyphens that are not soft (i.e. that must remain in the printed text). See also **hyphen**.

softly-softly (hyphen)

soft pedal (noun)

soft-pedal (verb)

soft sell (two words)

soft soap (noun)

soft-soap (verb)

software computer programs (not **-wear**)

Soho district of London

SoHo district of Manhattan, New York City (one word, capital **H**)

soi-disant self-styled (not italic; hyphen)

soiree evening party (not italic; no accent)

sojourn (not **-jurn**)

Sokotra variant of **Socotra**

solar (not **-er**)

sola topee Indian pith helmet (not **solar**; also **sola topi**)

solder alloy for joining metal, bond, or join with solder

soldier member of army, diligent worker, or serve as soldier

sole only, underside of foot or shoe, bottom of oven, or flatfish (compare **soul**)

solecism (not **-lic-**)

solemn (**-mn**)

solemnize (also **solemnise**; see **-ize/-ise**)

solenoid (not **-lin-**)

sol-fa (hyphen)

solicitor (not **-er**)

Solicitor General (two words; capital **S** & **G**)

solicitude (single **l**)

solid (*typog.*) with no space between characters or lines

solidus (also **slash** or **oblique**) the

symbol (/), used in dates (e.g. 21/10/06), in fractions (e.g. 13/16), to separate alternatives (e.g. and/or), on the Internet (e.g. www.bbc.co.uk/weather), etc. In computing it is sometimes called **forward slash** to distinguish it from **backslash**.

soliloquy (-lilo-)

soliloquize (also **soliloquise**; see -ize/-ise)

solitary (-tary)

solo (plural **solos** (in all senses) or **soli** (in music sense only))

solstice (not -ise)

Solti, Sir Georg Hungarian-born British conductor (not **George**)

soluble able to be dissolved or able to be solved

solvable able to be solved

solvent (not -ant)

Solzhenitsyn, Alexander Isayevich Russian novelist

Somalia African country

Somaliland former region of Africa

sombre (-er in US English)

sombrero (plural **sombreros**)

some unspecified, or an unspecified amount or number of, as in *some people* (compare **sum**)

somebody (one word; interchangeable with **someone**)

someday (one word)

someone (one word; interchangeable with **somebody**)

somersault (not -alt; rarely **summersault**)

Somerset English county (not **Summer-**)

sometime at some unspecified time (as in *come up and see me sometime*) or former (as in *the sometime president*)

some time a relatively long period of time (as in *she has been away for some time*)

sometimes occasionally (as in *he sometimes wears a hat*)

sommelier wine steward (not italic; double **m**, single **l**)

son male offspring (compare **sun**)

son et lumière entertainment with sound and lighting effects at night (not italic; three words; grave accent)

songbird (one word)

song cycle (two words)

Song of Solomon book of the Bible (not italic; abbreviation **SS**; also **Song of Songs** or **Canticle of Canticles**)

Song of Thr. Song of Three Jews (full stop; not italic)

Song of Three Jews book of the Apocrypha (not italic; abbreviation **Song of Thr.**)

song titles see **titles of works**

songwriter (one word)

son-in-law (plural **sons-in-law**)

Son of Man title of Jesus Christ (capital **S & M**)

sonorous (not -ner-)

Sophocles ancient Greek dramatist (-phoc-)

soporific (not -per-)

soprano (plural **sopranos** or **soprani**)

Sorbonne part of University of Paris

sorcerer (-or- in first syllable only)

sore painful, annoying, or urgent (compare **soar** and **saw**)

sorghum cereal grass (not -gum)

sort (*typog.*) variant of **character** (see also **special sort**). In the general sense 'kind or type', use *this/that sort of book*, *these/those sorts of books*, or *these/those sorts of book*, but do not use plural *these* or *those* with singular *sort*.

sort code (two words)

sortie military term (not italic; -ie)

sortilege divination by drawing lots (not italic; -ege)

SOS distress signal (all capitals; plural **SOSs**)

so-so (hyphen)

Sotheby's auction house (apostrophe; not -ther-)

Soubirous, Marie Bernarde original name of St **Bernadette of Lourdes** (**-ou-** twice)

soubriquet variant of **sobriquet**

souchong tea (not **soo-**)

Soudan French name for **Sudan**

soufflé light sweet or savoury dish (not italic; acute accent)

souk marketplace in Muslim countries (not italic; also **suq**)

soul spirit, person, or type of Black music (compare **sole**)

soul-destroying (hyphen)

soulless (double **l**; no hyphen)

soul mate (two words)

soul-searching (hyphen)

Sound, the strait between Sweden and Denmark (Swedish name **Öresund**, Danish name **Øresund**)

soundalike (one word)

sound bite (two words)

sound effect (two words)

soundtrack (one word)

sound wave (two words)

soupçon slight amount (italics; cedilla)

source origin (compare **sauce**)

sour cream (two words; also **soured cream**)

Sousa, John Philip US bandmaster and composer (**-ou-**)

south (as noun) direction or compass point opposite north, or area lying in this direction; (as adjective or adverb) in, to, or from the south (sometimes capital **S** in the sense 'area lying in the south'; see also **compass points**)

South southern area of England or the USA, or denoting the southern part of a particular country, continent, ocean, etc. (sometimes lower-case **s** in adjectival use, but always capital **S** in names)

South Africa see **Republic of South Africa** (do not abbreviate **South**)

South America continent linked to North America by Central America (do not abbreviate **South**)

Southampton English port and unitary authority (single **h**)

South Australia Australian state (do not abbreviate **South**)

southeast (as noun) direction or compass point between south and east, or area lying in this direction; (as adjective or adverb) in, to, or from the southeast (one word; sometimes capital **S** in the sense 'area lying in the southeast'; see also **compass points**)

Southeast southeastern area of England, or denoting the southeastern part of a particular country, continent, etc. (one word; often lower-case **s** in adjectival use, but always capital **S** in names)

Southeast Asia region including Brunei, Cambodia, Indonesia, Laos, Malaysia, Myanmar, the Philippines, Thailand, and Vietnam

Southend-on-Sea English town and unitary authority (two hyphens)

southern of, in, or to the south (lower-case **s**)

Southern of, in, or to the South (capital **S**)

Southerner person from the southern part of a particular country, especially England or the USA (the use of lower-case **s** is less common but not incorrect)

southern hemisphere (the use of capital **S** & **H** is less common but not incorrect)

Southern Ireland another name for **Republic of Ireland**

Southern Ocean another name for **Antarctic Ocean**

Southern Rhodesia former name (until 1964) for **Zimbabwe**

Southey, Robert English poet (not
-thy)
South Island one of two main
islands of New Zealand (capital **S**
& **I**)
South Korea NE Asian country (do
not abbreviate **South**; Korean name
Hanguk)
south pole pole of magnet (lower-
case **s** & **p**)
South Pole southernmost point on
earth's axis (capital **S** & **P**)
South Sea Bubble financial crash
of 1720 (capital **S** twice, capital **B**)
South Sea Islands islands of S
Pacific, including Melanesia,
Micronesia, and Polynesia (capital **S**
twice, capital **I**)
South Seas seas south of the equator
(capital **S** twice)
south-southeast (one hyphen)
south-southwest (one hyphen)
southward (adjective; sometimes
adverb (see **-ward** and **-wards**))
southwards (adverb only)
Southwark (-wa-)
southwest (as noun) direction or
compass point between south and
west, or area lying in this direction;
(as adjective or adverb) in, to, or
from the southwest (one word;
sometimes capital **S** in the sense
'area lying in the southwest'; see
also **compass points**)
Southwest southwestern part of
England, comprising Cornwall,
Devon, and Somerset; or denoting
the southwestern part of a particular
country, continent, etc. (one word;
often lower-case **s** in adjectival use,
but always capital **S** in names)
South West Africa another name for
Namibia (three words)
southwester wind or storm from the
southwest
sou'wester waterproof hat
(apostrophe)

sovereign (-eign)
Soviet (use instead of **Russian** for the
period 1922–91)
Soviet Union former federal
republic in Europe and Asia,
established in 1922 and disbanded
in 1991 to form Armenia, Azerbaijan,
Belarus, Estonia, Georgia,
Kazakhstan, Kyrgyzstan, Latvia,
Lithuania, Moldova, Russia,
Tadzhikistan, Turkmenistan,
Ukraine, and Uzbekistan (official
name **Union of Soviet Socialist
Republics** (abbreviation **USSR**); also
Russia)
sow[1] scatter seed (compare **sew** and
so)
sow[2] female pig
sowed past tense of **sow** or variant of
sown (compare **sewed**)
sower person or thing that sows
(compare **sewer2**)
Soweto group of Black African
townships in South Africa
sown past participle of **sow** (also
sowed; compare **sewn**)
soya bean (US and Canadian name
soybean)
soy sauce (also **soya sauce**)
sp. species (singular; plural **spp.**)
SpA *Società per Azioni* (used in Italian
company names; lower-case **p**)
space age (no hyphen unless used
before another noun, as in *space-age
technology*)
spacecraft (one word)
spaceship (one word)
space shuttle (two words)
space station (two words)
space-time (hyphen)
spacial rare variant of **spatial**
spaghetti (-gh-; double **t**)
spaghetti bolognese (lower-case **s** &
b; -gnese)
spaghetti western (lower-case **s** & **w**)
Spain European country (Spanish
name **España**)

Spalato Italian name for **Split** (compare **Spoleto**)

spam unsolicited e-mail (lower-case **s**)

Spam trademark for tinned luncheon meat (capital **S**)

span archaic past tense of **spin** (use **spun** instead)

Spanish Inquisition (capital **S** & **I**)

sparerib (one word)

sparking plug (also **spark plug**)

spastic (to avoid offence, do not use with reference to people with cerebral palsy)

Spastics Society former name for **Scope**

spatial (rarely **spacial**)

SPCK Society for Promoting Christian Knowledge

speakeasy (one word)

speaker person who speaks (lower-case **s**)

Speaker presiding officer of legislative body, e.g. the House of Commons or House of Representatives (capital **S**)

Speakers' Corner Hyde Park, London (capital **S** & **C**; **-s'** not **-'s**)

spearhead (one word)

spec informal shortening of **specification** or **speculative**, or used in the phrase *on spec* (no full stop)

Special Branch department of British police force concerned with political security (capital **S** & **B**)

speciality special interest or skill, service or product specialized in, or distinguishing feature (**specialty** in US and Canadian English)

specialize (also **specialise**; see **-ize/-ise**)

specially in a special way, as in *he doesn't expect to be treated specially*, or for a particular purpose, as in *specially made* (compare **especially**)

special sort (*typog.*) special character, e.g. accented letter or mathematical symbol, not found in standard fonts or on standard keyboards (also **pi character**)

specialty US and Canadian word for **speciality**, or legal term for formal contract or obligation expressed in deed

specie money in the form of coins as opposed to notes or bullion

species (same form for singular and plural) in the hierarchy of **taxonomic names**, the group that comes above a subspecies or variety and below a genus. The species name has a lower-case initial and is italic (see also **binomial**).

spectator (not **-er**)

spectre (**-er** in US English)

spectrum (plural **spectra**)

speculator (not **-er**)

sped past tense and past participle of **speed** (also **speeded**, see also **speed up**)

speech see **direct speech** and **indirect speech**

speech day (two words)

speech from the throne speech at opening of parliamentary session in the UK and Commonwealth countries (the use of capital **S** & **T** is less common but not incorrect; also **Queen's speech** or **King's speech**, especially in the UK)

speedboat (one word)

speeded variant of **sped** (see also **speed up**)

speed trap (two words)

speed up (verb; past tense and past participle **speeded** [not **sped**] **up**)

speed-up (noun)

speleology scientific study of caves, or pastime of exploring caves (also **spelaeology**)

spellbound (one word)

spellchecker (one word; beware of overreliance on spellcheckers: they will not pick up errors such as *rein* for *reign*, *that* for *than*, *form* for *from*, or *pubic* for *public*)

spelled variant of **spelt**

spelt past tense and past participle of **spell** (also **spelled**)

Spence, Sir Basil Scottish architect

Spencer, Lady Diana Frances maiden name of **Diana, Princess of Wales**; **Herbert** English philosopher; **Sir Stanley** English painter

Spenser, Edmund English poet

spew (archaic spelling **spue**)

Spezia see **La Spezia**

sphinx any of various Egyptian statues with lion's body and man's head, or an inscrutable person (not **sphy-**; lower-case **s**)

Sphinx monster in Greek mythology with lion's body and woman's head, or the sphinx near the pyramids at El Gîza in Egypt (not **Sphy-**; capital **S**)

sphygmomanometer instrument for measuring blood pressure (**sphygm-**, **-er**)

spic-and-span less common variant of **spick-and-span**

Spice Islands former name for **Moluccas**

spick-and-span (two hyphens; the spelling **spic-and-span** is not incorrect, but it is less common)

spicy (not **-cey**)

Spielberg, Steven US film director (**-ie-**, **-er-**; not **Stephen**)

spiky (not **-key**)

spilled variant of **spilt**

spillover (noun; the verb is **spill over**)

spilt past tense and past participle of **spill** (also **spilled**)

spina bifida congenital disorder of backbone (two words; single **f**)

spinach (**-ach**)

spin doctor (two words)

spin-dry (hyphen)

spine-chilling (hyphen)

spinnaker sail (double **n**; **-ak-**)

spinney small wood (double **n**; **-ey**)

spinning jenny (two words; lower-case **j**)

spin-off (noun; the verb is **spin off**)

Spinoza, Baruch Dutch philosopher

spiny (not **-ney**)

spiralled, spiralling (single **l** in US English)

spiritualism (lower-case **s**; the variant **spiritism** is less common but not incorrect)

spirt rare variant of **spurt**

spit and image original form of **spitting image**, now a rare variant

spitfire person (lower-case **s**)

Spitfire aeroplane or car (capital **S**)

Spitsbergen another name for **Svalbard** (not **-itz-**, not **-urg-**)

spitting image (originally and now rarely **spit and image**)

splashdown (noun; the verb is **splash down**)

splendour (**-or** in US English)

Split Croatian port and resort (Italian name **Spalato**)

split infinitive infinitive in which an adverb (or other word) is placed between *to* and the verb, as in *to boldly go*. Split infinitives are best avoided if the adverb can be placed elsewhere without ambiguity or inelegance.

spoiled variant of **spoilt**

spoilsport (one word)

spoilt past tense and past participle of **spoil** (also **spoiled**)

spoke past tense of **speak**

spoken past participle of **speak**

spokesman (use **spokesperson** instead where appropriate)

spokesperson (use instead of gender-specific **spokesman** or **spokeswoman** where appropriate)

spokeswoman (use **spokesperson** instead where appropriate)

Spoleto Italian town (compare **Spalato**)

spoliation (not **spoil-**)
sponge bag (two words)
sponge cake (two words)
spoonerism transposition of initial letters of pair of words, e.g. *bat flattery* for *flat battery* (lower-case **s**)
spoon-feed (hyphen)
spoonful (not **-full**; plural **spoonfuls**)
sportsman (use **sportsperson** instead where appropriate)
sportsperson (use instead of gender-specific **sportsman** or **sportswoman** where appropriate)
sportswoman (use **sportsperson** instead where appropriate)
spot check (noun)
spot-check (verb)
spp. species (plural; singular **sp.**)
SPQR the Senate and People of Rome (from Latin *Senatus Populusque Romanus*)
Sprachgefühl instinctive feeling for a language (italics; capital *S*; umlaut)
sprang past tense of **spring** (also **sprung**)
sprightly (not **sprite-**)
springbok antelope (lower-case **s**; the variant **springbuck** is less common but not incorrect)
Springbok member of South African sports team (capital **S**; not **-buck**)
springbuck less common variant of **springbok**
spring-clean (hyphen)
springtide season of spring (one word)
spring tide tide occurring at new moon and full moon (two words)
spritzer white wine with soda (not italic; lower-case **s**; **-tz-**)
sprung past participle of **spring** or variant of **sprang**
spue archaic spelling of **spew**
spun past tense and past participle of **spin** (see also **span**)
spurt (rarely **spirt**)
spyglass (one word)

spyhole (one word)
sq. square
squalor (never **-our**)
square brackets the characters [and], used to enclose editorial interpolations in quoted text (as in *'What kind of people do they [the Japanese] think we are?' asked Churchill*) and for various other purposes, e.g. in mathematics and logic
square dance (noun)
square-dance (verb)
square-rigger (hyphen)
square root (two words)
squash press, squeeze, cram, crush, or suppress (compare **quash**)
squeaky-clean (hyphen)
squirrel (double **r**, single **l**)
squirrelled, squirrelling (single **l** in US English)
Sr Senior; strontium (no full stop)
Srbija Serbian name for **Serbia**
Sri Lanka island republic in S Asia (former name **Ceylon**)
Sri Lankan of Sri Lanka, or a person from Sri Lanka (compare **Sinhalese**)
Srinagar Indian city (**Sr-**, **-ar**)
SS *Schutzstaffel* (Nazi paramilitary organization); Song of Solomon (no full stops; not italic); steamship
SS. Saints
SSSI site of special scientific interest
ssp. subspecies
St Saint (names beginning with this abbreviation are alphabetized as if they began with the full form); Street (in addresses)
Sta *Santa* (used before name of female saint in Italy, Spain, and Portugal)
stabilize (also **stabilise**; see **-ize/-ise**)
stabilizer (not **-or**)
staccato denoting short, clipped sounds in music or speech (not italic; double **c**)
staddlestone (one word)

stadholder chief magistrate of former Dutch republic in 17th and 18th centuries, or governor of a province (not italic; also **stadtholder**)

stadium (plural **stadiums** or **stadia**)

stadtholder variant of **stadholder**

staff (also **stave** in the sense 'set of lines used in writing music; plural **staffs** in senses referring to a body of people, plural **staffs** or **staves** in senses referring to a stick, pole, or rod and in music sense)

Staffordshire bull terrier (capital **S**, lower-case **b** & **t**)

stagecoach (one word)

stage door (two words)

stage fright (two words)

stagehand (one word)

stage-manage (hyphen)

stage manager (two words)

stage-struck (two words)

stagy (not **-gey**)

staid sedate (compare **stayed**)

stained glass (no hyphen unless used before another noun, as in *stained-glass window*)

Staines English town (**-ai-**, **-es**)

stair step (compare **stare**)

staircase (one word)

stairwell (one word)

stake (as noun) post, money bet, financial interest, or used in the phrase *at stake*; (as verb) gamble or invest (compare **steak**)

stakeholder (one word)

stakeout (noun; the verb is **stake out**)

stalactite mass hanging from roof of cave

stalagmite mass rising from floor of cave

stalemate (one word)

Stalin, Joseph Soviet leader (original name **Iosif Vissarionovich Dzhugashvili**)

Stalinabad former name (1929–61) for **Dushanbe**

Stalingrad former name (1925–61) for **Volgograd**

stalk plant stem, follow, or walk haughtily (compare **stork**)

stalking-horse (hyphen)

stalwart (single **l**)

stamp collecting (two words)

stamping ground (two words)

stanch stem or prevent flow of (also **staunch**)

stand-alone (hyphen)

standard-bearer (hyphen)

standardize (also **standardise**; see **-ize/-ise**)

stand-by (noun and adjective; the verb is **stand by**)

stand-in (noun; the verb is **stand in**)

standing present participle of **stand**, as in *they were standing by the door* or *I had been standing for too long* (do not replace with **stood** in contexts similar to the examples here)

standoff (noun; the verb is **stand off**)

standoffish (one word)

standpipe (one word)

standstill (one word)

stank past tense of **stink** (also **stunk**)

Stansted Airport near London (not **Stand-**, not **-stead**)

star-crossed (hyphen)

stare gaze (compare **stair**)

starfish (one word)

star fruit (two words)

Stars and Stripes US national flag (capital **S** twice; also **Star-Spangled Banner**)

Star-Spangled Banner US national anthem, or another name for **Stars and Stripes**

START Strategic Arms Reduction Talks (or Treaty) (thus *talks* and *treaty* in the phrases *START talks* and *START treaty* are redundant, strictly speaking, but their omission would be unidiomatic and could cause confusion)

state (lower-case **s** in most senses; often capital **S** with reference to a particular state, e.g. of the USA, and with reference to the body politic of a particular sovereign power, as in *the conflict between Church and State*)

State Department US government department in charge of foreign affairs

Staten Island borough of New York (capital **S** & **I**; not **-att-** or **-aat-**)

state of the art (noun)

state-of-the-art (adjective)

stateroom (one word)

States, the informal name for the USA (capital **S**)

stateside of, in, or to the USA (lower-case **s**)

stationary not moving

stationery writing materials

Stationery Office see **HMSO** and **TSO**

statistics (use plural verb in the sense 'quantitative data', use singular verb with reference to the study or interpretation of such data)

status (plural **statuses**)

status quo existing state of affairs (not italic)

statutory (not **-ary**)

staunch loyal, dependable, solid, or variant of **stanch**

stave variant of **staff** in music sense, strip of wood forming barrel or boat hull, crosspiece bracing chair legs, or used in the phrasal verbs *stave in* (meaning 'break, crush, or make hole in') and *stave off* (meaning 'avert')

staved past tense and past participle of **stave** (also **stove**, especially for the phrasal verb *stave in*)

stay-at-home (two hyphens)

stayed past tense and past participle of **stay** (compare **staid**)

STD sexually transmitted disease; subscriber trunk dialling

Ste *Sainte* (used before name of female saint in France)

steadfast (the spelling **stedfast** is not incorrect, but it is less common)

steak piece of meat or fish (compare **stake**)

steakhouse (one word)

steal take unlawfully, as in *they stole my wallet* (the direct object is the thing or things taken; compare **rob** (for meaning) and **steel** and **stele** (for spelling)

steam-engine (hyphen)

steamroller (one word)

steamship (one word)

Stearn, William Thomas English botanist (compare **Stern** and **Sterne**)

stedfast less common variant of **steadfast**

steel metal, hardness, fit with steel, or make hard and unfeeling (compare **steal** and **stele**)

Steel, Baron David British politician

Steele, Sir Richard British essayist and dramatist; **Tommy** English actor and singer (original name **Thomas Hicks**)

steelworks (one word; use singular or plural verb)

steenbok antelope (also **steinbok**)

steeplechase (one word)

steeplejack (one word)

Steinbeck, John US writer

steinbock ibex

steinbok variant of **steenbok**

stele upright slab or column with inscription or decoration (plural **stelae** or **steles**; compare **steal** and **steel**)

stencil (single **l**)

stencilled, stencilling (single **l** in US English)

Stendhal pen name of French writer **Marie Henri Beyle**

Sten gun (two words; capital **S**)

stentor person with unusually loud voice (lower-case **s**)

Stentor herald with powerful voice in Greek mythology (capital **S**)

stentorian (lower-case **s**)

step movement made in walking, dancing, etc. (compare **steppe**)

stepbrother son of step-parent by a partner other than one's parent (no hyphen; compare **half-brother**)

stepchild (no hyphen)

stepdaughter (no hyphen)

stepfather (no hyphen)

Stephen, Sir Leslie English biographer and critic (compare **Stephens**); **St** first Christian martyr (not **Steven**)

Stephens, Alexander Hamilton US politician; **James** Irish poet (compare **Stephen** and **Stevens**)

Stephenson, George English railway engineer; **Robert** English railway and structural engineer (compare **Stevenson**)

stepladder (one word)

stepmother (no hyphen)

step-parent person who has married one of one's parents after the death or divorce of the other (hyphen)

steppe grassy treeless plain (lower-case **s**; compare **step**)

Steppes, the grasslands of Eurasia (capital **S**; plural noun)

stepping stone (two words)

stepsister daughter of step-parent by a partner other than one's parent (no hyphen; compare **half-sister**)

stepson (no hyphen)

step-up (noun and adjective; the verb is **step up**)

stereo (plural **stereos**)

sterilize (also **sterilise**; see **-ize/-ise**)

sterling British money, genuine, reliable, or first-class (not **stir-**)

sterling silver (not **stir-**)

Sterling, John Scottish writer (compare **Stirling**)

Stern, Isaac Soviet-born US violinist;

Otto German-born US physicist (compare **Stearn** and **Sterne**)

Sternberg see **von Sternberg**

Sterne, Laurence English novelist (compare **Stern** and **Stearn**)

stet let it stand: typographical mark indicating that something deleted is to be retained (not italic; the deleted material is usually marked with dots underneath and a circled tick or the word 'stet' above or in the margin)

Stetson trademark for cowboy hat (capital **S**)

Stettin German name for **Szczecin**

stevedore (-**ved**-, -**ore**)

Stevenage English town (-**vena**-)

Stevens, Thaddeus US politician; **Wallace** US poet (compare **Stephens**)

Stevenson, Adlai Ewing US statesman; **Juliet** English actress; **Robert** Scottish lighthouse engineer; **Robert Louis** Scottish writer (compare **Stephenson**)

steward (may be used for males and females)

stewardess (replace with **steward** or other appropriate gender-neutral alternative, e.g. **flight attendant**)

Stewart usual spelling of royal house before mid-16th century (compare **Stuart**)

Stewart, Jackie Scottish racing driver (full name **John Young Stewart**); **James** US actor; **Rod** British rock singer (compare **Stuart**)

stick-in-the-mud (three hyphens)

stick-up (noun; the verb is **stick up**)

stigma (plural **stigmas** (for most senses) or **stigmata** (for the sense 'marks resembling the wounds of Christ'))

stigmatize (also **stigmatise**; see **-ize/-ise**)

stile set of steps used to cross fence (compare **style**)

stiletto (single **l**, double **t**; plural **stilettos**)

stillbirth (one word)

stillborn (one word)

still life (plural **still lifes**)

Stilton trademark for cheese (capital **S**)

stimulant drug that increases physiological activity, or something that stimulates (compare **stimulus**)

stimulate inspire, excite, or encourage (compare **simulate**)

stimulus something that causes response in organism, incentive, or something perceived by senses (plural **stimuli**; compare **stimulant**)

stir-fry (hyphen)

Stirling Scottish city and council area (not **Ster-**)

Stirling, James Scottish mathematician; **Robert** Scottish minister and inventor (compare **Sterling**)

stirrup (double **r**, single **p**)

stockbreeder (one word)

stockbroker (one word)

stock exchange (two words; also capital **S** & **E**, especially with reference to a particular stock exchange)

Stockhausen, Karlheinz German composer (**-au-** in surname; first name is one word)

Stockholm capital of Sweden (**-holm**)

stockinet (not **-ing-**, not **-ette**)

stocking filler (two words)

stock in trade (three words)

stock market (two words; lower-case **s** & **m**)

stockpile (one word)

stock-still (hyphen)

stocktaking (one word)

stodgy (not **-ey**)

stoep (in South Africa) veranda (compare **stoop**)

stoic stoical person, or variant of **stoical** (lower-case **s**)

Stoic member of ancient Greek school of philosophy, or of the doctrines of this school (capital **S**)

stoical impassive or resigned (lower-case **s**; also **stoic**)

stoicism indifference to pleasure and pain (lower-case **s**)

Stoicism philosophy of the Stoics (capital **S**)

Stoke-on-Trent English city and unitary authority (two hyphens; not **-upon-**)

Stone Age (capital **S** & **A** and no hyphen unless used before another noun, as in *Stone-Age culture* or *stone-age tools*)

stone-cold (hyphen)

stoneground (one word)

stonemason (one word)

stonewall (one word)

stony (the spelling **stoney** is not incorrect, but it is less common)

stood past tense and past participle of **stand**, as in *they stood by the door* or *I had stood for too long* (do not use in place of **standing** in contexts similar to the examples at that entry)

stoop bend body forward and downward, deign, swoop, stooping posture, (in USA and Canada) platform with steps at entrance to building (compare **stoep**), or less common variant of **stoup**

stopcock (one word)

stopgap (one word)

stopover (noun; the verb is **stop over**)

stop press (two words)

stopwatch (one word)

storable (not **-eable**)

storage heater (two words)

storeroom (one word)

storey floor of building (**story** in US English)

stork bird (compare **stalk**)

storm petrel (also **stormy petrel**)

storm trooper (two words)

stormy petrel variant of **storm petrel**

Stornoway Scottish port on Lewis in the Outer Hebrides (not **-away**)

Storting Norwegian parliament (also **Storthing**)

story piece of fiction, or US spelling of **storey**

storyboard (one word)

storybook (one word)

storyteller (one word)

stoup basin for holy water (the spelling **stoop** is not incorrect in this sense, but it is less common)

stove (as noun) cooker or heating apparatus; (as verb) variant of **staved**, especially for the phrasal verb *stave in*

Stow, John English antiquary (compare **Stowe**)

stowaway (noun; the verb is **stow away**)

Stowe, Harriet Elizabeth Beecher US writer

Stow-on-the-Wold English town (three hyphens; not **Stowe-**)

Strachey, Lytton English biographer and critic

Stradivarius violin made by Italian violin maker Antonio Stradivari (not **-ious**)

Strafford, Thomas Wentworth English statesman (not **-tf-**)

straight not curved or bent, direct, honest, level, upright, continuous, undiluted, or heterosexual. (compare **strait**)

straightaway (also **straight away**)

straighten make or become straight, tidy, or less confused (compare **straiten**)

straight-faced (hyphen)

straightforward (one word)

straightjacket less common variant of **straitjacket** in the sense 'jacket for binding prisoner or patient' (one word)

straight-laced less common variant of **strait-laced** (hyphen)

strait narrow channel; difficult position (as in *dire straits*); or archaic word for narrow, tight, limiting, or strict (compare **straight**)

straiten embarrass or distress financially (as in *straitened circumstances*), or limit (compare **straighten**)

straitjacket jacket for binding violent prisoners or mental patients, severe restriction, or confine (one word; sometimes **straightjacket**, especially in the sense 'jacket for binding prisoner or patient')

strait-laced (hyphen; the spelling **straight-laced** is not incorrect, but it is less common)

Stranraer Scottish town (**-raer**)

Strasbourg French city (not **-burg**; German name **Strassburg**)

strata plural of **stratum** (do not use with singular meaning)

stratagem plan or trick

strategy art or science of planning and waging war, or long-term plan for success

Stratford (the name of the town is **Stratford-upon-Avon**; the name of the constituency and district is **Stratford-on-Avon**)

stratum layer (plural **strata**; do not use plural form with singular meaning)

stratus cloud (plural **strati**)

Straus, Oscar French composer

Strauss, David Friedrich German theologian; **Johann** Austrian composer; **Richard** German composer (see also **Lévi-Strauss**)

Stravinsky, Igor Fyodorovich Russian-born US composer

stream of consciousness (no hyphens unless used before another noun, as in *the stream-of-consciousness technique*)

streetlight (one word; also **streetlamp**)

Street-Porter, Janet British broadcaster (hyphen)

streetwise (one word)

Streisand, Barbra US singer (**-ei-**; not **Barbara**)

strew (not **strow**)

strewed past tense of **strew** or variant of **strewn**

strewn past participle of **strew** (also **strewed**)

stricken variant of **struck** (past participle) in the abstract sense 'rendered incapable', chiefly used as adjective (as in *stricken by disease*) or in combination (as in *grief-stricken*)

strife (noun; compare **strive**)

strikebreaker (one word)

stringed having strings, as in *stringed instrument* (compare **strung**)

stripey variant of **stripy**

strip lighting (two words)

strip-search (hyphen)

striptease (one word)

stripy (also **stripey**)

strive (verb; compare **strife**)

striven past participle of **strive** (compare **strove**)

stroganoff short for **beef stroganoff** (lower-case **s**, **-gan-**, **-off**)

Stroheim see **von Stroheim**

strong-arm (hyphen)

strongroom (one word)

strontium (symbol **Sr**)

Strood town in Kent

Stroud town in Gloucestershire or village in Hampshire

strove past tense of **strive** (compare **striven**)

struck past tense and past participle of **strike** (also **stricken** in the abstract sense 'rendered incapable')

strung past tense and past participle of **string** (compare **stringed**)

strychnine (**-ych-**, **-ine**)

Stuart usual spelling of royal house after mid-16th century (compare **Stewart**)

Stuart, Gilbert Charles US painter; **John McDouall** Australian explorer (compare **Stewart** and **Sturt**; see also **Mary, Queen of Scots**, **Old Pretender**, and **Young Pretender**)

Stubbs, George English painter (**-bbs**)

stucco (plural **stuccoes** or **stuccos**)

studio (plural **studios**)

stumbling block (two words)

stunk past participle of **stink** or variant of **stank**

stupefy (not **-pif-**)

stupor (never **-our**)

Sturluson see **Snorri Sturluson**

Sturm und Drang German literary movement (italics; not ***and***)

Sturt, Charles Australian explorer (compare **Stuart**)

Stuttgart German city (double **t** in middle)

Stuyvesant, Peter Dutch colonial administrator in America (**-uy-**)

sty pen for pigs, or variant of **stye**

stye inflammation of eyelid (also **sty**)

Stygian of Styx, dark, gloomy, or inviolable (capital **S**; **-yg-**)

style design, type, manner, elegance, pointed instrument, or botanical or zoological term (compare **stile**)

stylize (also **stylise**; see **-ize/-ise**)

stylus (plural **styli** or **styluses**)

stymie (rarely **stymy**)

Styx river in Hades in Greek mythology

suave (**-ua-**)

sub informal shortening of **subedit**, **subeditor**, **submarine**, **subscription**, **substitute**, etc. (no full stop)

sub- (usually attached without hyphen, except to words beginning with capital letter, as in *sub-Saharan*, and some compounds, as in *sub-post office*)

Subbuteo trademark for table football game with toy players flicked by fingers (capital **S**; double **b**, single **t**)

subcategory (no hyphen)

subcommittee (no hyphen)

subcontinent (no hyphen)

subcontract (no hyphen)

subculture (no hyphen)

subdivision (no hyphen)

subedit (no hyphen)

subeditor (no hyphen)

subfusc formal academic dress at Oxford University (not italic; one word)

subheading (no hyphen)

subhuman (no hyphen)

subject person or thing that performs action of verb and usually precedes it, e.g. *they* in *they gave me a present* (compare **direct object** and **indirect object**)

subjective denoting the case of pronouns such as *I* and *they* (compare **objective**)

sub judice under judicial consideration (not italic; two words)

subjunctive the form of the verb used in fixed phrases such as *far be it from me* and *as it were*, and in formal English after verbs such as *demand, insist, suggest, recommend*, etc., as in *I demand that she apologize* and *they suggested that we leave by the back door*. For most verbs the subjunctive takes the same form as the infinitive (minus *to*) in both present and past tense, the only exception being the verb *be*, which has *were* as its past subjunctive. The subjunctive is sometimes replaced by **should** + infinitive, as in *they suggested that we should leave by the back door*.

sublet (no hyphen)

sub-machine-gun (two hyphens)

submersible (not **-able**)

subordinate clause see **clause**

subplot (no hyphen)

subpoena writ requiring person to appear before court, or serve with such a writ (not italic; one word; **-oe-**)

subpoenaed (not **-a'd**)

sub-post office (one hyphen)

sub rosa in secret (not italic; two words)

sub-Saharan (hyphen; lower-case **s** then capital **S**)

subscript denoting a character written or printed below the line, as is the number in H_2O (also **inferior**)

subsection (no hyphen)

subsequent following or succeeding (compare **consequent**)

subsidence (not **-ance**)

subsidiary (not **-uary**)

subsidize (also **subsidise**; see **-ize/ -ise**)

subspecies (same form for singular and plural) in the hierarchy of **taxonomic names**, a subdivision of a species. The subspecies name follows the genus and species names (see **binomial**) in italics with lower-case initial, as in *Motacilla alba yarrellii* (pied wagtail); for plants it is preceded by the abbreviation **ssp.**, which is not italic, as in *Lavatera triloba* ssp. *pallescens*.

substandard (no hyphen)

substitute put (one thing) in place of another, as in *you can substitute yogurt for the cream in the recipe* (compare **replace**)

subtext (no hyphen)

subtile rare variant of **subtle**

subtitle (no hyphen; see also **titles of works**)

subtle (**-bt-**; rarely **subtile**)

subtotal (no hyphen)

subtropical (no hyphen)

succès de scandale success due to notoriety (italics; grave accent; same form for singular and plural)

successfully with success

successively in succession
succinct (double **c** then **-nct**)
Succoth variant of **Sukkoth**
succour (**-or** in US English)
succulent (double **c**; **-ent**)
such as see **like**
suchlike (one word)
sucking pig (not **-ling**)
Sudan African country (French name **Soudan**)
Sudan, the region of Africa between Sahara and tropical zone
suede leather with nap (compare **swayed** and **swede**)
Suetonius Roman biographer and historian (full name **Gaius Suetonius Tranquillus**)
Suez Canal Egypt (capital **S** & **C**)
suffix word element attached at end, e.g. *-less* in *helpless*. May cause spelling problems (e.g. *-able* versus *-ible*, *-ent* versus *-ant*): see entries for individual suffixes and words. Compare **prefix**.
Sufi adherent of Muslim mystical order (single **f**)
sugar beet (two words)
sugar cane (two words)
Sugar Loaf Mountain Brazil (three words; capital **S**, **L**, & **M**)
suggestible (not **-able**)
sui generis unique (not italic)
suing (not **-uei-**)
Suisse French name for **Switzerland**
suit set of clothes, armour, sails, or playing cards; litigation; petition, courtship; or be appropriate or acceptable (compare **suite**)
suite set of furniture, rooms, or pieces of music (compare **suit** and **sweet**)
suitor (not **-er**)
sukiyaki Japanese dish of thinly sliced meat and vegetables quickly cooked (not italic; one word)
Sukkoth Jewish harvest festival (also **Succoth**)

Sulawesi Indonesian island (also **Celebes**)
sulfa drug any of a group of antibacterial drugs (not **-lph-**, not **-ur**; note that the **-lf-** spelling is also used in the names of individual drugs, e.g. **sulfadiazine**)
sulfur spelling of **sulphur** used in US English and in technical scientific writing in UK English
Sully-Prudhomme, René François Armand French poet
sulphur (symbol **S**; **sulfur** in US English and in technical scientific writing in UK English)
sum total, calculation, quantity, essence, or add (compare **some**)
sumach (also **sumac**; not **-ack**)
summarize (also **summarise**; see **-ize/-ise**)
summary (as noun) account giving main points; (as adjective) done quickly, arbitrarily, and without formality (compare **summery**)
summerhouse (one word)
summersault rare variant of **somersault**
summertime period or season of summer
summer time daylight-saving time (capital **S** & **T** in names, as in *British Summer Time*)
summery characteristic of summer (compare **summary**)
summon send for, call, or muster (verb only; past tense **summoned**)
summons (as noun) call or order to do something, e.g. to attend court, or writ requiring somebody to attend court; (as verb) take out a summons against (plural **summonses**; past tense **summonsed**)
summum bonum highest or supreme good (italics)
sun (also **Sun** in astronomical contexts, referring to star at the

centre of our solar system; compare **son**)

sunbathe (one word)

sun block (two words)

sunburn (one word)

sunburnt (also **sunburned**)

sundae ice cream topped with sauce, nuts, etc.

Sunday day of week

Sunday school (no hyphen unless used before another noun, as in *a Sunday-school teacher*)

sundial (one word)

sung past participle of **sing** (compare **sang**)

sunglasses (one word)

sun-god (hyphen)

sunhat (one word)

sunk past participle of sink (also **sunken**; compare **sank**)

sunken variant of **sunk** chiefly used as adjective, as in *sunken cheeks, a sunken bath, sunken treasure*, etc.

Sunni (as noun) one of the two main branches of Islam, or a member of this group; (as adjective) of or belonging to Sunni (compare **Shiah**; use **Sunni Muslim** or **Sunni** in place of **Sunnite**)

Sunnite (use **Sunni Muslim** or **Sunni** instead)

sunscreen (one word)

sunspot (one word)

suntan (one word)

suntrap (one word)

Sun Yat-sen Chinese statesman

Suomi Finnish name for **Finland**

Super Bowl main championship game of American football (capital **S** & **B**)

supercilious (single **c**)

superconductivity (one word)

superglue (one word)

superhighway (one word)

superhuman (one word)

superior (*typog.*) another word for **superscript**

superkingdom another name for **domain** (in taxonomy)

superlative denoting the form of an adjective or adverb marked by the addition of **-est** or the use of **most** before the word. Most one-syllable and some two-syllable words take **-est** (e.g. *straightest, cleverest*); others take **most** (e.g. *most honest, most probably*). Do not use **most** and **-est** together, and do not use either with *unique, perfect, complete, equal, impossible,* etc. (compare **comparative**)

supermodel (one word)

superpower (one word)

superscript denoting a character written or printed above the line, as are the letters in 5th (also **superior**)

supersede (not **-cede**)

superstructure (one word)

supertanker (one word)

supervise (never **-ize**)

supervisor (not **-er**)

supine lying face upwards, or lethargic (compare **prone** and **prostrate**)

supplement (as noun) addition; (as verb) add to or make up for a deficiency in (compare **complement**)

supposititious hypothetical

supposititious substituted with intent to mislead or deceive

suppository medication for insertion into vagina or rectum (not **-ary**)

Supreme Court (capital **S** & **C**)

supremo (plural **supremos**)

suq variant of **souk**

Suqutra variant of **Socotra**

Sur Arabic name for **Tyre**

sure certain (compare **shore**)

sure-fire (hyphen)

surety (not **-ity**)

surf waves breaking on shore; ride on crest of wave; or move rapidly from site to site on the Internet, from channel to channel on the TV, etc. (compare **serf**)

surfboard (one word)

surge rush, sudden increase, rolling motion, or move with or undergo a surge (compare **serge**)

Surinam South American country (not **-name**; former name **Dutch Guiana**)

surmise (never **-ize**)

surplice liturgical vestment

surplus excess

surprise (not **sup-**; never **-ize**)

surreal (double **r**)

surveillance close observation or supervision (not italic; **-eill-**)

surveyor (not **-er**)

survivor (not **-er**)

Sus. Susanna (full stop; not italic)

Susanna book of the Apocrypha (not italic; abbreviation **Sus.**)

susceptible (not **-able**)

sushi Japanese dish of small cakes of rice topped with raw fish (not italic)

suspense insecurity, uncertainty, or excitement at approach of climax

suspension act of suspending or state of being suspended, interruption, deferment, temporary revocation or debarment, system of springs and shock absorbers supporting vehicle, or dispersion of particles in fluid

Sussex former English county, divided in 1974 into the counties of **East Sussex** and **West Sussex**

suttee former Hindu custom in which widow burnt herself to death on husband's funeral pyre (not italic; double **t**, double **e**)

Sutton Coldfield English town (not **Coal-**)

SUV sport (or sports) utility vehicle

Suwannee US river (also **Swanee**: see that entry)

sv sub verbo (or voce): used in references to a particular entry in a dictionary, encyclopedia, etc. (also **s.v.**)

Svalbard Norwegian archipelago (also **Spitsbergen**)

svelte slim or sophisticated (not italic; **sv-**, **-te**)

Svengali character in the novel *Trilby* by George Du Maurier, hence a person who controls another's mind with sinister intentions (capital **S**)

Sverige Swedish name for **Sweden**

Svizzera Italian name for **Switzerland**

SW southwest

swab (rarely **swob**)

Swabia region of Germany (German name **Schwaben**)

Swahili African language (also **Kiswahili**), member of people speaking this language (also **Mswahili**, plural **Waswahili**), or of this language or people

swam past tense of **swim** (compare **swum**)

swami Hindu saint or religious teacher (not italic; plural **swamies** or **swamis**)

Swanee variant of **Suwanee**, and the form used in the song 'Old Folks at Home'

Swansea Welsh port and county (**-sea**)

swan song (two words)

swan-upping (hyphen)

swap (also **swop**)

swat strike sharply, as in *swat a fly*, or less common variant of **swot** (also **swot**)

swath strip cut in scything or mowing, or used figuratively in the phrase *cut a swath through* (also **swathe**)

swathe bandage, wrap, envelop, or variant of **swath**

swayed past tense and past participle of **sway** (compare **suede**)

swearword (one word)
sweatband (one word)
sweatshirt (one word)
sweatshop (one word)
swede root vegetable (lower-case **s**; compare **suede**)
Swede person from Sweden (capital **S**)
Sweden European country (Swedish name **Sverige**)
Swedenborg, Emanuel Swedish scientist and theologian (**-borg**)
sweepstake (one word; **sweepstakes** in singular and plural in US English)
sweet tasting like sugar, pleasant, not rancid, piece of confectionery, or dessert (compare **suite**)
sweet-and-sour (two hyphens)
sweetbread (one word)
sweet talk (noun)
sweet-talk (verb)
sweet william flowering plant (lower-case **w**)
swelled past tense of swell or variant of **swollen**
sweptwing (one word)
swimming pool (two words)
swimsuit (one word)
Swinburne, Algernon Charles English poet and critic (**-ne**)
Swindon town and unitary authority in Wiltshire (not **-ton**, not **-den**)
swing door (two words)
swingeing severe or punishing (present participle of archaic verb **swinge**)
swinging present participle of **swing**, or slang word meaning 'modern and lively'
swing-wing (hyphen)
Swiss cheese plant (three words; capital **S**)
Swiss Guard pope's bodyguard (capital **S & G**)
swiss roll (two words; lower-case **s**)
switchblade (one word)

switchboard (one word)
Swithin, St English ecclesiastic (also **Swithun**)
Switzerland European country (German name **Schweiz**; French name **Suisse**; Italian name **Svizzera**; Latin name **Helvetia**)
swivel (single **v**, single **l**)
swivelled, snivelling (single **l** in US English)
swob rare variant of **swab**
swollen past participle of **swell** (also **swelled**)
swop variant of **swap**
sword dance (two words)
Sword of Damocles (capital **S & D**)
swore past tense of **swear** (compare **sworn**)
sworn past participle of **swear**, or bound by an oath (compare **swore**)
swot study hard, person who swots, or less common variant of **swat** (also **swat**)
swum past participle of **swim** (compare **swam**)
swung dash the symbol (~), used for various purposes, e.g. in place of an omitted word or part of a word to avoid repetition (see also **tilde**)
Sybil female first name (compare **sibyl**)
sycamore Eurasian maple tree, American plane tree, or African and Asian tree with figlike fruit (also **sycomore** for the African and Asian tree)
Sydney Australian or Canadian city (compare **Sidney**)
Sykes, Eric English comedy actor and writer (compare **Sikes**)
syllabub (the spelling **sillabub** is not incorrect, but it is less common)
syllabus (plural **syllabuses** or **syllabi**)
sylvan (the spelling **silvan** is not incorrect, but it is less common)
sylviculture less common variant of **silviculture**

symbol something that represents something else (compare **cymbal**)

symbolize (also **symbolise**; see -ize/ -ise)

symmetry (double **m**)

sympathize (also **sympathise**; see -ize/-ise)

symposium (plural **symposiums** or **symposia**)

synagogue (-gue)

sync informal shortening of **synchronize** or **synchronization**, as in *out of sync* (also **synch**; compare **sink**)

synchronize (also **synchronise**; see -ize/-ise)

synonym (-yn- then -ym)

synopsis (plural **synopses**)

synoptic Gospels Matthew, Mark, and Luke (often capital **S**, always capital **G**)

synthesize (also **synthesise**; see -ize/ -ise)

syphon variant of **siphon**

Syrah grape or wine (Australian name **Shiraz**)

syringe (**y** then **i**)

syrup (rarely **sirup**)

systematic methodical, as in *a systematic approach* (compare **systemic**)

systematize (also **systematise**; see -ize/-ise)

Système International see **SI units**

systemic affecting the whole body or plant, as in *systemic pesticides* (compare **systematic**)

syzygy alignment of celestial bodies (all the vowels are **y**'s)

Szczecin Polish port (German name **Stettin**)

Szechwan variant of **Sichuan**

Szent-Györgyi, Albert Hungarian-born US biochemist (hyphen; -gy- twice; diaeresis)

T

-t/-ed (see individual entries for the use of **-ed** versus **-t** to form the past tense and past participle of verbs such as *burn, dream, leap,* and *spell*)

Ta tantalum (no full stop)

TA Territorial Army

TAB Totalizator Agency Board (in Australia and New Zealand); typhoid-paratyphoid A and B (vaccine)

tabard (single **b**; **-ard**)

Tabasco Mexican state, or trademark for very hot red sauce (capital **T**)

tableau dramatic group or scene (not italic; plural **tableaux** or **tableaus**)

tableau vivant representation of scene, sculpture, etc. by silent and motionless person or people (plural *tableaux vivants*)

tablecloth (one word)

table dancing (two words)

table d'hôte with set number of courses, limited choice of dishes, and fixed price (not italic; circumflex)

Table Mountain South Africa (capital **T** & **M**)

tablespoon (one word)

table tennis (two words)

table top (two words)

table-turning (hyphen)

taboo (the spelling **tabu** is not incorrect, but it is less common)

tabor small drum (also **tabour**; compare **tambour**)

tabu less common variant of **taboo**

tabular in form of table (**-ar**)

tabula rasa mind in original state, or opportunity for fresh start (not italic; not **-lar**; plural **tabulae rasae**)

tabulator (not **-er**)

tacheometer surveying instrument (also **tachymeter**; compare **tachometer**)

tachogram record produced by tachograph

tachograph instrument that records speed and distance covered by vehicle

tachometer rev counter (compare **tacheometer**)

tachymeter variant of **tacheometer**

taco filled rolled tortilla (not italic; plural **tacos**)

tactics (use singular verb in the sense 'art and science of military manoeuvres', use plural verb in the sense 'manoeuvres used to achieve an aim')

Tadzhikistan variant of **Tajikistan** (also **Tadjikistan**)

taedium vitae feeling that life is boring (not italic; not **ted-**)

tae kwon do Korean martial art (not italic; three words)

taffeta (double **f**, single **t**)

Tagalog official language of the Philippines

tagliatelle (not **-lli**)

Tagore, Rabindranath Indian poet and philosopher

Tagus European river (Spanish name **Tajo**; Portuguese name **Tejo**)

t'ai chi Chinese system of callisthenics (apostrophe; full name **t'ai chi ch'uan**)

tail appendage on animal's body, rear part, end, line, or track (compare **tale**)

tailback (one word)

tail coat (two words)

tail end (two words)

tailgate door or board at rear of vehicle, or drive very close behind (one word)

tail gate gate at lower end of lock (two words)

tail-light (hyphen)

tailor (not **-er**)

tailor-made (hyphen)

tailpiece (*typog.*) decorative design at foot of page or end of chapter (one word)

tailpipe (one word)

tailspin (one word)

Taine, Hippolyte Adolphe French literary critic and historian

Taipei capital of the Republic of China (also **T'ai-pei**)

Tait, Archibald Campbell Scottish prelate; **Peter Guthrie** Scottish mathematician; **William** Scottish publisher (compare **Tate**)

Taiwan island occupied by the **Republic of China**, or another name for that country (former name **Formosa**)

Tajikistan central Asian country (also **Tadzhikistan** or **Tadjikistan**)

Taj Mahal marble mausoleum in Agra, India (two words; capital **T** & **M**)

Tajo Spanish name for **Tagus**

takable (also **takeable**)

takeaway (adjective and noun; the verb is **take away**)

take back (*typog.*) move (text) to previous line

take-home pay (one hyphen)

taken past participle of **take** (compare **took**)

takeoff (noun; the verb is **take off**)

takeout (adjective and noun; the verb is **take out**)

takeover (noun)

take over (*typog.*) move (text) to following line (verb)

talcked, talcking (also **talced, talcing**)

tale story (compare **tail**)

Taleban variant of **Taliban**

talebearer (one word)

Tales of Hoffmann opera by Offenbach (double *f*, double *n*; see also **Hoffmann**)

taleteller (one word)

Taliban (also **Taleban**)

Taliesin Welsh bard (**-ie-**)

talisman (plural **talismans**)

talk speak or speech (compare **torque**)

talkback (noun; the verb is **talk back**)

talking-to (hyphen)

talk show (two words)

Tallahassee US city (double **l**, double **s**)

tallboy (one word)

Talleyrand-Périgord, Charles Maurice French statesman

Tallinn capital of Estonia (also **Tallin**; German name **Reval**)

tally-ho (hyphen)

Talmud primary source of Jewish religious law (capital **T**)

tamable (also **tameable**)

tamarin monkey

tamarind tropical evergreen tree, its acid fruit, or its wood

tamarisk ornamental tree or shrub with feathery clusters of flowers

tambour embroidery frame, sliding door made of strips of wood on desk or cabinet, or drum (never **-or**; compare **tabor**)

Tamburlaine variant of **Tamerlane**

tameable variant of **tamable**

Tamerlane Mongol ruler (also **Tamburlaine**)

Tameside unitary authority in Greater Manchester (not **Th-**)

Tamil (as noun) member of people of India and Sri Lanka, or the language of this people; (as adjective) of this people or language

Tamil Tigers Sri Lankan Tamil separatist movement (capital **T** twice)

Tammerfors Swedish name for **Tampere**

tam-o'-shanter brimless wool cap (lower-case **t**, **o**, & **s**; two hyphens; apostrophe)

'Tam o' Shanter' poem by Robert Burns (quotation marks; three words; capital **T** & **S**, lower-case **o**; space after apostrophe)

Tampa US city

Tampere Finnish city (Swedish name **Tammerfors**)

tandoori (double **o**)

tangible (not **-able**)

Tangier Moroccan port (not **-giers**)

tango (plural **tangos**)

Tannhäuser character in German legend (double **n**; umlaut)

Tannhäuser opera by Wagner (italics; double **n**; umlaut)

tannin (double **n** then single **n**)

Tannoy trademark for public-address system (capital **T**)

tantalize (also **tantalise**; see **-ize/ -ise**)

tantalum (symbol **Ta**)

Tanzania African country formed in 1964 by the union of Tanganyika and Zanzibar

Taoiseach prime minister of the Republic of Ireland (capital **T**; **-aoi-** then **-ea-**)

Taoism philosophy of Lao Zi (capital **T**)

tapas light snacks or appetizers (not italic; plural noun)

tap dance (noun)

tap-dance (verb)

tap-dancing (hyphen)

tape-record (hyphen)

tape recording (two words)

taper make or become narrower

tapir mammal with elongated snout

tappet mechanical part that transmits motion (double **p**, **-et**)

taproom (one word)

taproot (one word)

tap water (two words)

Tarabulus el Gharb Arabic name for **Tripoli** (Libya)

Tarabulus esh Sham Arabic name for **Tripoli** (Lebanon)

taramasalata pink pâté made from fish roe (not italic; all the consonants are single, all the vowels are **a**'s)

tarantella dance or music for it

tarantula spider (plural **tarantulas** or **tarantulae**)

tare plant, or weight of wrapping, container, or empty vehicle (compare **tear**)

targeted, targeting (not **-tt-**)

tariff (single **r**, double **f**)

Tarmac (as noun) trademark for paving material, or name of company; (as verb) apply Tarmac to (always capital **T** for the company, but often lower-case **t** with reference to the material or a road or runway surfaced with it (or something similar), and usually lower-case **t** for the verb)

tarmacked, tarmacking (**-ck-**)

taro plant or its edible rootstock

tarot denoting cards used for fortune-telling (lower-case **t**)

tarpaulin (not **-ing**)

Tarpeian Rock cliff in ancient Rome from which traitors were thrown (capital **T** & **R**; **-eian**)

tartar deposit on teeth, deposit in wine, or formidable person (also **Tartar** in the sense 'formidable person')

Tartar variant of **Tatar**, especially in historical contexts, or of **tartar** in the sense 'formidable person'

tartare sauce (also **tartar sauce**)

Tartuffe central character in the play *Tartuffe* by Molière, hence any religious hypocrite (capital **T**)

Tashi Lama another name for **Panchen Lama** (capital **T** & **P**)

task force (two words)

Tasmania Australian island state (former name **Van Diemen's Land**)

TASS Soviet news agency, replaced in 1992 by **ITAR-TASS** (acronym of *Telegrafnoye Agenstvo Sovetskovo Soyuza*)

taste bud (two words)

tasteful showing good taste

tasty having a pleasant flavour

ta-ta informal word for goodbye (hyphen)

Tatar member of Mongoloid people of central Asia led by Genghis Khan; descendant of this people, now living in Russia; or any of the languages of the present-day Tatars (also **Tartar**, especially in historical contexts)

Tatar Republic constituent republic of Russia (not **Tartar . . .**)

Tate, Sir Henry British sugar refiner, philanthropist, and art collector; **Nahum** British poet and dramatist (compare **Tait**)

Tate Collection art collection originally displayed at the **Tate Gallery** (Millbank, London), which is now called **Tate Britain** and contains British art of the 16th–early 20th centuries; modern art is housed at the **Tate Modern** (Bankside, London), the **Tate Liverpool**, and the **Tate St Ives** (Cornwall)

Tatler periodical (single **t** in middle; compare **tattler**; see also **titles of periodicals**)

tattersall checked fabric (lower-case **t**)

Tattersall's London horse market, or Australian lottery (apostrophe)

tattler person who gossips (double **t** in middle; compare *Tatler*)

tattoo (double **t** in middle, double **o**)

taught past tense and past participle of **teach**

taut tightly stretched or tense

tautological (also **tautologous**)

tawny (rarely **tawney**)

tax avoidance reduction of tax liability by lawful methods

tax evasion reduction of tax liability by unlawful methods

tax-free (hyphen)

taxi see following entries

taxied (not **-i'd**)

taxies third person present tense of **taxi**, or less common variant of **taxis**

taxiing (the spelling **taxying** is not incorrect, but it is less common)

taxis plural of **taxi** (the spelling **taxies** is not incorrect, but it is less common)

taxonomic names the hierarchical classifications used for living organisms: domain, kingdom, phylum or division, class, order, family, genus, species, subspecies or variety. Names from domain to genus (inclusive) have capital initial; names from domain to family (inclusive) are not italic. See also **binomial** and individual entries.

taxpayer (one word)

taxying less common variant of **taxiing**

Tb terbium (no full stop)

TB tuberculosis

Tbilisi capital of Georgia (Russian name **Tiflis**)

T-bone steak (capital **T**, one hyphen)

Tc technetium (no full stop)

Tchad French name for **Chad** (the country)

Tchaikovsky, Pyotr Ilyich Russian composer

Te tellurium (no full stop)

tea drink or meal (compare **tee**)

tea bag (two words)

teach impart knowledge or skill (compare **learn**)

tea chest (two words)

teach-in (hyphen)

teacup (one word)

tea leaf (two words)

team group of people or animals working together (compare **teem**; see **collective nouns**)

team-mate (hyphen)

team spirit (two words)

teamwork (one word)

TEAP Teaching of English for Academic Purposes

teapot (one word)

tear¹ drop of water in eye (compare **tier**)

tear² rip or rush (compare **tare**)

tearaway (noun; the verb is **tear away**)

tear gas (two words)

tear-jerker (hyphen)

teasel (the spellings **teazel** and **teazle** are less common but not incorrect)

teaspoon (one word)

tea towel (two words)

Teatro alla Scala full name for **La Scala**

teazel less common variant of **teasel** (also **teazle**)

technetium (symbol **Tc**)

technical (-ch-)

Technicolor trademark for colour film process (capital **T**, never **-our**)

technicolour brightly coloured (lower-case **t**; **-or** in US English)

technology (-ch-)

techy less common variant of **tetchy**

tectonics (not -ch-)

teddy bear (two words; lower-case **t**)

teddy boy (two words; lower-case **t**)

tee (as noun) T-shaped part, support for golf ball, or area of golf course where first stroke is played; (as verb) position or strike (golf ball) at beginning of game (compare **tea**)

teem abound or pour (compare **team**)

teenage (also **teenaged** when used of a person)

teepee variant of **tepee**

tee shirt variant of **T-shirt** (two words)

Teesside industrial region in NE England (double **s**)

teeth (plural noun)

teethe (verb)

teetotal (double **e**, single **l**)

teetotaller (single **l** in US English)

TEFL Teaching (of) English as a Foreign Language (see **EFL**)

Teflon trademark for nonstick material (capital **T**)

Tehran capital of Iran (also **Teheran**)

Teignmouth resort in SW England (compare **Tynemouth**)

Tejo Portuguese name for **Tagus**

telamon column in form of male figure (plural **telamones** or **telamons**; compare **caryatid**)

Tel Aviv city in Israel (two words)

teleconference (no hyphen)

telemarketing (no hyphen)

telesales (no hyphen)

Teletext television text service of ITV and Channel 4, replacing **Oracle** (compare **Ceefax**; capital **T**, but also used generically with lower-case **t**)

Teletubbies characters in children's TV show (capital **T**; not **Telly-**)

televise (never -ize)

Telford English town (single **l**)

telltale (one word)

tellurium (symbol **Te**)

Téméraire see *Fighting Téméraire*

temerity rashness or boldness (compare **timidity**)

tempera painting medium or technique (compare tempura)

tempestuous (not **tempt-**)

Templar member of military religious order (capital **T**; not **-er**; also **Knight Templar**)

template (rarely **templet**)

tempo (plural **tempos** or **tempi**)

temporal of time, of secular rather than religious affairs, or of grammatical tense

temporary not permanent, or lasting only a short time

temporize delay, act evasively, or adapt oneself to the circumstances or occasion (also **temporise**, see **-ize/-ise**; compare **extemporize**)

tempura Japanese dish of battered and deep-fried seafood or vegetables (compare **tempera**)

Ten Commandments (capital **T** & **C**; also **Decalogue**)

tenderhearted (one word)

tenderize (also **tenderise**; see **-ize/-ise**)

tendril (single **l**)

Tenerife Atlantic island in the Canaries (**-ner-**; single **f**)

tenet (single **n**)

Teng Hsiao-Ping variant of **Deng Xiaoping**

tenner ten-pound note (compare **tenor**)

Tennessee US state and river (double **n**, double **s**)

Tenniel, Sir John English cartoonist and illustrator (double **n**, single **l**)

Tennyson, Alfred, Lord English poet (double **n**, **-ys-**)

tenor male voice or singer, general drift of thought, or exact words of deed (compare **tenner** and **tenure**)

tenpin bowling (**tenpin** is one word)

tenure holding or term of office or position, right to permanent employment, or occupation of property in return for services rendered (compare **tenor**)

Tenzing Norgay Nepalese mountaineer (not **Tens-**; known as **Sherpa Tenzing**)

tepee (also **teepee**)

tequila alcoholic spirit (lower-case **t**)

Tequila region of Mexico

terbium (symbol **Tb**)

Terence Roman comic dramatist (single **r**; Latin name **Publius Terentius Afer**)

Teresa, St Spanish nun and mystic (known as **St Teresa of Ávila**; also **Theresa**); **Mother** Indian missionary (original name **Agnes Gonxha Bojaxhiu**; not **Theresa**)

tergiversate (**-er-** twice)

teriyaki Japanese dish basted with soy sauce and rice wine (not italic; one word)

termagant (not **-ent**)

terminal (as adjective) situated at end, of a term, or terminating in death; (as noun) electrical connection, device linked to computer, or access point for air or rail passengers (compare **terminus**)

terminator (not **-er**)

terminus either end of railway or bus route, final part or point, or goal aimed for (plural **termini** or **terminuses**; compare **terminal**)

Terpsichorean of dancing, or a dancer (capital **T**; not **-ian**)

terraced house (the variant **terrace house** is less common but not incorrect)

terracotta earthenware or reddish-brown colour (not italic; one word; double **r**, double **t**)

terra firma solid earth or firm ground (not italic; two words)

terrain ground with particular physical character or military potential, or variant of **terrane**

terrane series of rock formations (also **terrain**)

Terrence Higgins Trust HIV and AIDS charity (double **r** in first name; no apostrophe in surname)

terrible very bad or serious

terrific very good or great

Territorial member of Territorial Army (capital **T**; compare **Territorian**)

Territorial Army (capital **T** & **A**)

Territorian in Australia, person from Northern Territory (capital **T**; compare **Territorial**)

terrorize (also **terrorise**; see -ize/-ise)

TES *Times Educational Supplement* (italics)

Tesco supermarket (not -'s)

TESL Teaching (of) English as a Second Language (see **ESL**)

TESOL Teaching (of) English to Speakers of Other Languages (see **ESOL**)

tessellate (double **s**, double **t**)

Tess of the D'Urbervilles novel by Thomas Hardy (italics; capital **D**; apostrophe; *-ber-*)

Test (often capital **T** with reference to cricket test matches, as in *the third Test, a Test cricketer*, etc.)

test case (two words)

test drive (noun)

test-drive (verb)

testimonial recommendation of person, product, etc., statement of truth or fact, or tribute for services or achievements

testimony declaration of truth or fact, evidence given by witness, or evidence testifying to something, as in *her success is a testimony to her hard work*

testis (plural **testes**)

test match international match, especially one of a series in cricket (see also **Test**)

test pilot (two words)

test tube (two words)

test-tube baby (one hyphen)

tetchy (the spelling **techy** is not incorrect, but it is less common)

tête-à-tête private conversation (not italic; two hyphens; three diacritics; plural **tête-à-têtes** or **tête-à-tête**)

Tetragrammaton Hebrew name for God consisting of four letters YHVH or YHWH, transliterated as **Jehovah** or **Yahweh** (capital **T**; double **m**)

tetralogy group of four related works (not **-ology**)

tetraplegia variant of **quadriplegia**

Teutonic (-eu-)

Tevere Italian name for **Tiber**

Tewkesbury English town (**Tew-**, **-kes-**)

textbook (one word)

text messaging (two words)

TGV *train à grande vitesse*: high-speed French passenger train

Th thorium (no full stop)

Thailand SE Asian country (former name **Siam**)

Thaïs Athenian courtesan (diaeresis)

thalidomide (lower-case **t**)

thallium (symbol **Tl**)

Thames Barrier (capital **B**)

Thames estuary (lower-case **e**)

than (in formal English, use subjective case for following pronoun if it is the subject of the unexpressed verb (as in *we are older than they (are)*) and use objective case for following pronoun if it is the object of the unexpressed verb (as in *I like her more than (I like) him*))

thane member of aristocratic class in Anglo-Saxon England, or person of rank in medieval Scotland (also **thegn**)

thankfully (the controversial use of this adverb in the sense 'fortunately', as in *thankfully it didn't rain*, is now acceptable in informal contexts)

Thanksgiving holiday in USA on fourth Thursday of November and in Canada on second Monday of October (capital **T**; full name **Thanksgiving Day**)

thank you (two words as interjection or noun)

Thant, U Burmese diplomat (no full stop after **U**, as it is not an initial)

that (usually used to introduce restrictive **relative clause** (as in *the dog that bit me was a Jack Russell*) but never used to introduce nonrestrictive relative clause in place of **which**)

Thatcher, Margaret, Baroness British stateswoman

theatre (**-er** in US English; capital **T** as part of name, as in *Chichester Festival Theatre*)

theatregoer (one word)

theatre-in-the-round (three hyphens; plural **theatres-in-the-round**)

thegn variant of **thane**

their of them (compare **there** and **they're**). Use **their** instead of **his** when gender is unspecified and **his or her** is inappropriately formal or unwieldy (as in *anybody who hates their job*) or rephrase to avoid the problem, e.g. by changing singular to plural (as in *people who hate their jobs*). Do the same for **theirs, them, themselves**, and **they**.

theirs of them (no apostrophe; see **their**)

them see **their**

theme park (two words)

themselves (also **themself** when used instead of **himself or herself**; see **their**)

thence thereafter, therefore, or from that place (thus *from* in the phrase *from thence* is redundant and should be avoided)

theodolite (**-dol-**)

theorize (also **theorise**; see **-ize/-ise**)

therapeutic (**-eu-**)

there in that place (compare **their** and **they're**). Use **there is/was** or **there's** when the following noun phrase would normally take a singular verb (as in *there is £500 left in the account* or *there's no excuse*) and use **there are/were** when the following noun phrase would normally take a plural verb (as in *there were several people waiting*).

thereabouts (one word)

thereafter (one word)

there are see **there**

therein (one word)

thereinafter (one word)

thereinbefore (one word)

there is see **there**

there's see **there**

Theresa variant of (St) **Teresa** (of Ávila)

Thérèse de Lisieux, St French nun noted for her autobiography, *The Story of a Soul* (acute accent then grave accent)

thereupon (one word)

therewith (one word)

thermonuclear (no hyphen)

Thermopylae battle site in ancient Greece (**-pyl-**)

Thermos trademark for vacuum flask (capital **T**)

Theroux, Paul US novelist and travel writer (compare **Thoreau**)

thesaurus (plural **thesauruses** or **thesauri**)

thesis (plural **theses**)

thespian of drama, or an actor (lower-case **t**)

Thess. Thessalonians (full stop; not italic)

1 Thessalonians book of the Bible (not italic; abbreviation **1 Thess.**; also **I Thessalonians**; full name

The First Epistle of Paul the Apostle to the Thessalonians)

2 Thessalonians book of the Bible (not italic; abbreviation **2 Thess.**; also **II Thessalonians**; full name **The Second Epistle of Paul the Apostle to the Thessalonians**)

Thessaloníki Greek port (acute accent; Latin name **Thessalonica**, English name **Salonika** or **Salonica**)

they see **their**

they're contraction of **they are** (compare **their** and **there**)

thiamine (also **thiamin**)

thickset (one word)

thick-skinned (hyphen)

thief (noun; plural **thieves**)

thieve (verb)

thighbone (one word)

thingumabob (also **thingamabob**, **thingumajig**, **thingamajig**, or **thingummy**)

think-tank (hyphen)

thin space (*typog.*) one fifth of an **em space**, slightly smaller than a standard word space but larger than a **hair space**. It is used for various purposes, e.g. instead of a comma to divide long numbers into sets of three digits.

third see **first**

third class (noun; adverb; adjective after noun)

third-class (adjective before noun)

Third International another name for **Comintern**

thirdly see **first**

third-rate (hyphen)

Third Reich see **Reich** (no italics; capital **T** & **R**; **-ei-**)

Third World (capital **T** & **W**; to avoid offence, use *developing countries* or *less-developed* countries instead)

Thirty-nine Articles set of formulas defining doctrinal position of Church of England (capital **T** & **A**,

the use of capital **N** is less common but not incorrect)

thirty-twomo book size with 32 leaves (i.e. 64 pages) per sheet (also **32mo**)

Thirty Years' war European conflict of 1618–48 (capital **T**, **Y**, & **W**; apostrophe)

Thompson, Daley British athlete; **Emma** British actress; **Flora** British writer

Thomson, Sir George Paget and **Sir Joseph John** British physicists; **Virgil** US composer and conductor

Thoreau, Henry David US writer (compare **Theroux**)

thorium (symbol **Th**)

thorn (*typog.*) the character (þ) or (Þ), representing the initial consonant sound of *thin* in Icelandic and formerly in phonetics, or the initial consonant sound of *this* in Old and Middle English

thorough utter, complete, careful, or painstaking (compare **through**)

thoroughbred purebred, or purebred animal (lower-case **t**)

Thoroughbred breed of horse (capital **T**)

thoroughfare (not **through-**)

thoroughgoing (one word)

Thorshavn capital of the Faeroes (not **-ven**)

Thousand and One Nights, The another name for *The **Arabian Nights' Entertainments***

Thousand Island dressing (three words; capital **T** & **I**, lower-case **d**)

thraldom (double l in US English)

thrall (double l)

threadbare (one word)

Threadneedle Street London (see also **Old Lady of Threadneedle Street**)

three-point turn (one hyphen)

three Rs, the (no apostrophe)

threshold (single **h** in middle)

threw past tense of **throw** (compare **through** (for spelling) and **thrown** (for usage))

thrips insect (same form for singular and plural)

thrived past tense and past participle of **thrive** (also **throve** for the past tense or **thriven** for the past participle)

thriven variant of **thrived** (past participle)

Throckmorton, Francis English conspirator against Elizabeth I (also **Throgmorton**)

throes violent pangs, as in *death throes*, or used in the phrase *in the throes of*, meaning 'struggling with' (compare **throws**)

Throgmorton variant of **Throckmorton**

throne seat of monarch (compare **thrown**)

through from one side to the other, during, by means of, etc. (compare **thorough** and **threw**; also **thru** in US English)

Through the Looking-Glass novel by Lewis Carroll (hyphen; not *Alice through . . .*: the full title is *Through the Looking-Glass and What Alice Found There*)

throve variant of **thrived** (past tense)

throwaway (adjective and noun; the verb is **throw away**)

throwback (noun; the verb is **throw back**)

throw-in (noun; the verb is **throw in**)

thrown past participle of **throw** (compare **threw** (for usage) and **throne** (for spelling))

throws plural or third person present tense of **throw** (compare **throes**)

thru US variant of **through**

Thucydides ancient Greek historian and politician (**y** then **i**)

Thule region believed by ancient geographers to be northernmost inhabited land, or Eskimo settlement in NW Greenland (also **ultima Thule** in ancient sense)

thulium (symbol **Tm**)

thumb index (noun)

thumb-index (verb)

thumbscrew (one word)

thunderbolt (one word)

thundercloud (one word)

thunderstruck (one word; rarely **thunder-stricken**)

Thuringia German state (German name **Thüringen**, with umlaut)

thyme herb (compare **time**)

Ti titanium (no full stop)

Tia Maria trademark for coffee-flavoured liqueur (capital **T** & **M**)

Tiananmen Square Beijing, China (**-anmen**)

Tianjin Chinese city (also **Tientsin**)

tiaraed wearing a tiara or tiaras (not **-a'd**)

Tiber Italian river (Italian name **Tevere**)

Tiberias Israeli resort

Tiberius Roman emperor

tibia one of two bones between knee and ankle (compare **fibula**)

tic twitch

tick sound of clock, moment, mark indicating correctness, parasite, covering of pillow or mattress, or informal word for credit

ticketed, ticketing (not **-tt-**)

tick-over (noun; the verb is **tick over**)

ticktack sign language used by bookmakers (one word; **-ck-** twice)

Ticonderoga US village and battle site (**-der-**)

tidal wave unusually large incoming wave caused by high wind and spring tide (compare **tsunami**)

tidbit US word for **titbit**

tiddlywinks (one word)

tide rise and fall of sea, current, tendency, or used to form words such as *Christmastide* (compare **tied**)

tidemark (one word)

tide table (two words)

tie (present participle **tying**)

tie-and-dye (two hyphens)

tieback (one word)

tie-break (hyphen; also **tie-breaker**)

tied past tense and past participle of **tie**, or used in compounds such as *tied cottage* and *tied house* (compare **tide**)

tie-dyed (hyphen)

tie-in (noun; the verb is **tie in**)

Tientsin variant of **Tianjin**

tiepin (one word)

tier row, layer, or rank (compare **tear**)

Tierra del Fuego South American archipelago (lower-case **d**)

tie-up (noun; the verb is **tie up**)

Tiffany, Louis Comfort US glass-maker (double **f**, single **n**)

Tiflis Russian name for **Tbilisi**

tightrope (one word)

tigress (not -ger-)

tikka term used in Indian cookery (double **k**)

tilde the diacritic used on ã, ñ, etc. (see also **swung dash**)

till short for **until** (double **l**, no apostrophe)

Till Eulenspiegel peasant in German legend

Tim. Timothy (books of the Bible; full stop; not italic)

timber wood

timbre tone quality

Timbuktu town in Mali, or any distant place (French name **Tombouctou** (for the town); the spelling **Timbuctoo** is used in Tennyson's poem of that name)

time (the spelling used for most senses of the word with this sound: compare **thyme**)

time and motion study (four words)

time bomb (two words)

time-honoured (hyphen)

timekeeper (one word)

time lag (two words)

time-out (noun; the verb is **time out**)

timepiece (one word)

Times, The (italic *The* with capital *T*; see also **titles of periodicals**)

timescale (one word)

time-share (hyphen)

time sharing (no hyphen unless used before another noun, as in *a time-sharing system*)

time switch (two words)

timeworn (one word)

time zone (two words)

timidity shyness or fear (compare **temerity**)

1 Timothy book of the Bible (not italic; abbreviation **1 Tim.**; also **I Timothy**; full name **The First Epistle of Paul the Apostle to Timothy**)

2 Timothy book of the Bible (not italic; abbreviation **2 Tim.**; also **II Timothy**; full name **The Second Epistle of Paul the Apostle to Timothy**)

timpani kettledrums (also **tympani**, but never -ny; plural noun, sometimes used with singular verb, especially when the drums are regarded as a set)

tin (symbol **Sn**)

Tindal, Matthew English theologian (compare **Tindale** and **Tyndall**)

Tindale variant of **Tyndale**

tinfoil (one word)

tingeing (also **tinging**)

Tin Pan Alley any district where popular music is produced (originally a district of New York), or derogatory term for the commercial side of show business (three words; capital **T**, **P**, & **A**)

tin soldier (two words)

tintinnabulation (single **n** then double **n**)

tip-off (noun; the verb is **tip off**)

Tipperary Irish county (double **p**; **-er-** then **-ar-**)

Tipp-Ex trademark for correction fluid (capital **T** & **E**; hyphen)

tiptoeing (**-oei-**)

tip-up (adjective; the verb is **tip up**)

Tirana capital of Albania (also **Tiranë**)

tire make or become weary, or US spelling of **tyre**

tiro variant of **tyro**

Tirol variant of **Tyrol**

'tis poetic contraction of **it is** (apostrophe; one word)

Tit. Titus (full stop; not italic)

titanic colossal, or of titanium (lower-case **t**)

Titanic ill-fated ship (italics; capital *T*)

titanium (symbol **Ti**)

titbit (**tidbit** in US English)

tit for tat (three words)

Titian Italian painter (original name **Tiziano Vecellio**), or of the reddish-gold hair colour used in his works (also **titian** or **Titian red** for the colour)

titillate arouse, interest, or excite (single **t** three times, double **l**)

titivate smarten up (the spelling **tittivate** is not incorrect, but it is less common)

title deed (two words)

titleholder (one word)

title page (also **full-title page**) page bearing full title of book (including any subtitle), name of author or editor, publisher's imprint, etc. It is usually the right-hand page following the **half-title page**.

titles of people for titles such as *earl, duke, duchess, baron, king, queen, pope, president, prime minister, senator*, etc., use capital initial when title is followed by name, as in *Queen Anne, Pope John Paul II*. Where titles of nobility are followed by a place name (as in *the Duke of Kent*), or where the title is used alone with reference to a particular person (as in *the President's address to the nation on September 11*), capitalization depends on the publisher's house style, but capital initials are usually preferred in English. Where the title does not refer to a particular person, as in *the country residence of the British prime minister*, lower-case initials are used. See also **ranks**.

titles of periodicals for capitalization, follow the principles outlined at **titles of works**. Use italics for titles of newspapers, magazines, journals, and other periodicals; use quotation marks and roman type for titles of individual articles within a periodical. As a general rule, do not use capital **T** or italics for the word 'the', even if it appears on the front page or cover (e.g. the *Daily Telegraph*), with the exception of *The Times* (and sometimes other periodicals with single-word titles, e.g. *The Economist*).

titles of works for capitalization, follow publisher's house style. The usual convention in English is to capitalize the first word and all nouns, verbs, adjectives, and adverbs. Other languages have other conventions and these are usually followed when foreign titles are mentioned in English texts (see **foreign titles of works**). Subtitles are usually preceded by a colon and follow the same capitalization conventions as the main title. Use italics for titles and subtitles of books (except the Bible, the Koran, etc. and subdivisions of these); long poems (e.g. Milton's *Paradise Lost*); plays; films; television and radio series; operas, ballets, and descriptive titles of other musical compositions (e.g. Handel's *Water Music*, but not Beethoven's Fifth Symphony); and albums of recorded music (e.g. the Beatles' *Abbey Road*). Use quotation marks and roman type for titles of short stories, articles, and essays collected within a larger publication; chapters in books; short poems (e.g. Shelley's 'To a Skylark'); episodes of television and radio series; songs and album tracks (e.g. the Beatles' 'Nowhere Man'); and the popular titles of musical compositions (e.g. Mozart's 'Jupiter' Symphony).

Tito, Marshal Yugoslav statesman (original name **Josip Broz**)

Titograd former name (1946–92) for **Podgorica**

tittivate less common variant of **titivate**

Titus book of the Bible (not italic; abbreviation **Tit.**)

T-junction (capital **T**; hyphen)

Tl thallium (no full stop)

TLS *Times Literary Supplement* (italics)

Tm thulium (no full stop)

TM transcendental meditation

™ unregistered trademark (compare **®**)

TN Tennessee (US postal code)

TNT trinitrotoluene

to preposition used to indicate destination or limit (as in *going to school*, *Monday to Friday*, to mark infinitive or indirect object (as in *to be or not to be*, *give it to me*), etc. (compare **too** and **two**)

toad-in-the-hole (three hyphens)

toadstool (one word)

to and fro (three words, but hyphenated when used before noun)

toast rack (two words)

Tob. Tobit (full stop; not italic)

tobacco (single **b**, double **c**; plural **tobaccos** or **tobaccoes**)

tobacconist (single **b**, double **c**, single **n**)

Tobago see **Trinidad and Tobago**

Tobit book of the Apocrypha (not italic; abbreviation **Tob.**)

toboggan (single **b**, double **g**)

tobogganing (single **b**, double **g**, single **n**)

toby jug (two words; lower-case **t**)

Toc H society encouraging Christian comradeship (no full stops)

Tocqueville, Alexis Charles Henri Maurice Clérél de French politician and writer (**-cqu-**)

tocsin alarm bell (compare **toxin**)

today (no hyphen)

to-do (hyphen; plural **to-dos**)

toe part of foot, shoe, or sock; something resembling this in shape or position; touch or strike with toe; or used in the phrase *toe the line* (compare **tow**)

toecap (one word)

toeing (**-oei-**)

toenail (one word)

toffee (rarely **toffy**)

together with (use singular verb if the preceding noun is singular, as in *the Queen, together with several other members of the royal family, was in the palace when the fire broke out*)

toilet lavatory, or old-fashioned word for the act of washing, dressing, etc. (compare **toilette**)

toilet roll (two words)

toilette literary or affected word for the act of washing, dressing, etc. (not italic)

toilet water (two words; also **eau de toilette**)

toing and froing (three words; no apostrophes)

Tokaj Hungarian town or region where Tokay is made

Tokay sweet wine made in Tokaj, or similar wine made elsewhere

Tokyo capital of Japan (not **-kio**)

tolbooth less common variant of **tollbooth**

tolerance state of being tolerant, permitted variation in measurement, or capacity to endure effects of poison, drug, etc.

toleration act of tolerating, or freedom to hold religious opinions that differ from those of the established religion

Tolkien, J(ohn) R(onald) R(euel) British writer (not **-ein**)

tollboth (one word; the spelling **tolbooth** is not incorrect, but it is less common)

Tolstoy, Leo Russian writer (Russian name **Count Lev Nikolayevich Tolstoy**)

tomahawk (not **-mo-**)

tomato (plural **tomatoes**)

Tombouctou French name for **Timbuktu** (the town)

tombstone (one word)

tomcat (one word)

Tom, Dick, and Harry used in the phrase *every Tom, Dick, and Harry*

Tom, Dick, or Harry used in the phrase *any Tom, Dick, or Harry*

tomfoolery (one word)

tomorrow (single **m**, double **r**; no hyphen)

tom-tom (hyphen)

ton unit of weight equal to 2240 lb (in UK) or 2000 lb (in US) (compare **tonne** and **tun**)

Tonbridge town in Kent (compare **Tunbridge Wells**)

tongue mass of tissue in mouth (**-gue**)

tongue-tied (hyphen)

tongue twister (two words)

tonguing (**-gui-**)

tonight (no hyphen)

tonne unit of weight equal to 1000 kg (compare **ton** and **tun**)

tonneau cover protecting open car (not italic; plural **tonneaus** or **tonneaux**)

tonsil (single **l**)

tonsillitis (double **l**)

too also or excessively (compare **to** and **two**)

took past tense of **take** (compare **taken**)

toolkit (one word)

tool shed (two words)

toothache (one word)

toothbrush (one word)

toothcomb see **fine-tooth comb**

toothpick (one word)

tootsy child's word for foot or toe (also **tootsie**; compare **Tutsi**)

topee pith helmet (also **topi**; compare **toupee**)

top hat (two words)

top-heavy (hyphen)

topi variant of **topee**

topknot (one word)

topsoil (one word)

topsy-turvy (hyphen; lower-case **t** twice)

top-up (noun; the verb is **top up**)

tor hill or prominent rock (compare **tore**)

Torah Jewish word for the **Pentateuch**, the scroll on which it is written, or the whole body of traditional Jewish teaching (capital **T**)

torc variant of **torque** (the necklace)

tore past tense of **tear²** (compare **tor** (for spelling) and **torn** (for usage))

Torino Italian name for **Turin**

tormentor (also **tormenter**)

torn past participle of **tear** (compare **tore**)

tornado (plural **tornadoes** or **tornados**)

torpedo (plural **torpedoes**)

torpor (never **-our**)

torque force that causes rotation, or ancient necklace made of twisted metal (also **torc** for the necklace; compare **talk**)

Torquemada, Tomás de Spanish monk, first Inquisitor-General of Spain (acute accent on first name)

torso (plural **torsos** or **torsi**)

tort civil wrong (not italic)

torte rich cake or tart (not italic)

tortilla Mexican pancake (not italic; double **l**)

tortoiseshell (one word)

tortuous twisted, winding, devious, or intricate, as in *a tortuous road* or *a tortuous explanation*

torturous involving great pain or anguish, as in *a torturous experience*

Torvill, Jayne British ice dancer, partner of **Christopher Dean** (not -**ville**, not **Jane**)

Tory (always capital **T** in the political sense 'Conservative', sometimes lower-case **t** in the extended sense 'reactionary')

Toscana Italian name for **Tuscany**

Toscanini, Arturo Italian conductor (single **n** twice)

toss-up (noun; the verb is **toss up**)

total (single **l**)

totalled, totalling (single **l** in US English)

totem pole (two words; not -**tum**)

touch and go (three words, but hyphenated when used before noun)

touchdown (noun; the verb is **touch down**)

touché used to acknowledge a hit in fencing, or in figurative senses (not italic; acute accent)

touchline (one word)

touch-me-not plant with seed pods that open when touched (two hyphens; also **noli-me-tangere**)

touchpaper (one word)

touch-type (hyphen)

Toulouse-Lautrec, Henri de French artist (hyphen)

toupee wig or hairpiece (not italic; no accent; compare **topee**)

tour de force brilliant stroke or accomplishment (italics; plural *tours de force*)

Tournai Belgian city (Flemish name **Doornik**)

tournedos steak (not italic; same form for singular and plural)

tourniquet device to control bleeding (not italic; not **torn-**)

Tours French town (-**rs**)

Toussaint L'Ouverture, Pierre Dominique Haitian revolutionary leader (double **s**; **L'Ou-**)

tovarisch comrade (not italic; also **tovarich** or **tovarish**)

tow pull, act of pulling, or fibres of hemp, flax, etc. (compare **toe**)

toward (adjective; sometimes adverb (see -**ward** and -**wards**))

towards (adverb only)

towel (single **l**)

towelled, towelling (single **l** in US English)

Tower of Babel biblical tower where the language of the builders was confused (Gen. 11)

town hall (two words)

town house (two words)

Townsend, Francis Everett US reformer

Townshend, Charles, 2nd Viscount English politician and agriculturist (nicknamed **Turnip Townshend**); **Pete** British rock musician

toxaemia (-**xem-** in US English)

toxin poison (compare **tocsin**)

toy boy (two words)

Toys 'R' Us retail company selling toys (quotation marks, not apostrophes; the **R** is reversed and in double quotation marks in the company logo, on shop fronts, etc., but **'R'** is acceptable in textual references in UK English)

tr. transitive; translated

Trabzon Turkish port (also
  Trebizond)
traceable (always **-ceable**)
trachea (**-ch-**; plural **tracheae**)
track record (two words)
tracksuit (one word)
tractable (not **-ible**)
Tractarianism another name for
  Oxford Movement
tractor (not **-er**)
tradable (also **tradeable**)
Trade Descriptions Act (capital **T, D,**
  & **A**; not **Trades . . .**)
trade-in (noun; the verb is **trade in**)
trademark (one word) name or
  symbol used to identify products,
  services, slogans, etc. of a particular
  commercial enterprise. Use capital
  initial for trademarks and
  acknowledge proprietary status (e.g.
  with ® or ™) where appropriate.
  Avoid using a trademark as a generic
  noun or verb, i.e. replace *Hoover*
  with *vacuum*, replace *Xerox* with
  photocopy, etc.
trade name name under which
  commercial enterprise operates
  (two words)
tradescantia (not **trand-**; lower-case **t**
  in general use, *Tradescantia* is the
  genus name)
trades union less common variant of
  trade union
Trades Union Congress association
  of British trade unions (not **Trade
  . . .**; abbreviation **TUC**)
trade union (the variant **trades union**
  is less common but not incorrect)
trade wind (two words)
traffic (not **-ck**)
trafficked (**-ck-**)
trafficker (**-ck-**)
trafficking (**-ck-**)
tragicomedy (no hyphen)
trail (as verb) drag, follow, lag, or tow
  (as noun) path or track (compare
  trial)

trailblazer (one word)
train spotter (also **trainspotter**)
Trainspotting novel by Irvine Welsh
  and film (one word)
traipse (rarely **trapes**)
trait characteristic feature (compare
  tray)
tramlines (one word)
trampoline (not **-lin**)
tranche portion or instalment (not
  italic)
tranquil (single **l**)
tranquillity (the use of single **l** is
  confined to US English, and is less
  common even there)
tranquillize (also **tranquillise**, see
  -ize/-ise; single **l** in US English)
transatlantic (no hyphen, no capital
  letters)
transcendent (not **-ant**)
transexual less common variant of
  transsexual
transfer (single **r** at end)
transferable (single **r**, not **-ible**)
transference (single **r**, not **-ance**)
transferred, transferring (double **r**)
transgressor (not **-er**)
tranship less common variant of
  transship
transistor (not **-er**)
transistorize (also **transistorise**; see
  -ize/-ise)
transitive denoting verb used with
  direct object, e.g. *bring* (compare
  intransitive)
Transkei former Bantu homeland
  in South Africa (**-kei**)
translate express in another
  language (compare **transliterate**)
translator (not **-er**)
transliterate transcribe in another
  alphabet (compare **translate**; see
  also Appendix iii)
transmissible (not **-able**)
transmittable (the spelling
  transmittible is not incorrect, but
  it is less common)

transmitter (not **-or**)

transpacific (no hyphen, no capital letters)

transparent (not **-ant**)

transpire (to avoid controversy, do not use in the sense 'happen')

transpose (*typog.*) interchange characters, words, or lines, as in correcting *form* to *from*

transsexual (no hyphen; the spelling **transexual** is not incorrect, but it is less common)

transship (no hyphen; the spelling **tranship** is not incorrect, but it is less common)

Trans-Siberian Railway (capital **T**, **S**, & **R**; hyphen)

transubstantiation (single **s**)

Transvaal former province of South Africa (single **a** then double **a**)

transverse crossing from side to side (compare **traverse**)

Transylvania region of Romania (single **s**; not **-sil-**)

trap door (two words)

trapes rare variant of **traipse**

trapezium (**-zi-**; plural **trapeziums** or **trapezia**)

trattoria Italian restaurant (not italic; double **t** in middle)

traumatize (also **traumatise**; see **-ize/-ise**)

travel (single **l**)

travelled (single **l** in US English)

traveller (single **l** in US English; the use of capital **T** in the sense 'member of itinerant people' is less common but not incorrect)

traveller's cheque (**-'s** not **-s'**)

travelling (single **l** in US English)

travel-sick (hyphen)

traverse (as verb) cross or obstruct; (as noun) something that lies or goes across, or obstruction (compare **transverse**)

tray board or plate for carrying

things, or shallow receptacle (compare **trait**)

treadmill (one word)

treasure-trove (hyphen)

treasury place where treasure is stored, funds or revenues of government or private organization, or source of something valuable (lower-case **t**)

Treasury government department in charge of finance (capital **T**)

treaties plural of **treaty**

treatise formal written work on subject

treaty formal agreement or contract

Trebizond variant of **Trabzon**

trecento 14th century, especially with reference to Italian art, literature, etc. (not italic)

trek (not **-ck**)

trekked, trekking (double **k**)

tremolo music term (not italic; not **-mul-**; plural **tremolos**)

tremor (never **-our**)

trench coat (two words)

Trent English river, or a German name for **Trento**

Trento Italian city (German name **Trent** or **Trient**; see also **Council of Trent**)

trepan tool for cutting circles or grooves, or instrument formerly used in surgery to remove circular sections of bone

trepang sea cucumber (also **bêche-de-mer**)

trephine instrument used in surgery to remove circular sections of bone

Trèves French name for **Trier**

triad group of three (lower-case **t**)

Triad Chinese secret society (capital **T**)

triage sorting of casualties, or allocating of limited resources (not italic)

trial test, judicial examination,

trouble, or competition (compare **trail**)

tricolour (**-or** in US English)

Trient a German name for **Trento**

Trier German city (French name **Trèves**)

Trieste Italian port (Slovene and Serbo-Croat name **Trst**)

trig point (no full stop)

trillion one million million (formerly, one million million million; compare **billion**)

trimaran (not **-mer-**)

Trinidad and Tobago Caribbean country occupying islands of Trinidad and Tobago in Lesser Antilles

trinity group of three (lower-case **t**)

Trinity union of Father, Son, and Holy Spirit in Christian theology (capital **T**)

Trinity College Dublin (no comma)

Tripoli capital of Libya (Arabic name **Tarabulus el Gharb**, ancient name **Oea**) or Lebanese port (Arabic name **Tarabulus esh Sham**, ancient name **Tripolis**)

triptych set of three pictures (**i** then **y**)

triptyque customs permit for temporary importation of motor vehicle (not italic)

tripwire (one word)

Tristan character in Arthurian legend who fell in love with **Iseult** (also **Tristram**)

Tristan and Isolde English title of *Tristan und Isolde*

Tristan da Cunha group of four Atlantic islands (not **de**; **-nh-**)

Tristan und Isolde opera by Wagner (English title *Tristan and Isolde*)

Tristram variant of **Tristan**

triumphal celebrating or resembling triumph

triumphant experiencing or displaying triumph

triumvir (plural **triumvirs** or **triumviri**)

trivet (**i** then **e**)

trivia (plural noun sometimes used with singular verb, especially when the things, facts, etc. are considered as a whole)

trivialize (also **trivialise**; see **-ize/ -ise**)

trod past tense of **tread** or variant of **trodden**

trodden past participle of **tread** (also **trod**)

Troilus and Cressida play by Shakespeare

Troilus and Criseyde poem by Chaucer

trolley (**-ey**)

trollop promiscuous woman, prostitute, or slattern (**-op**)

Trollope, Anthony and **Joanna** British novelists (**-ope**)

trompe l'oeil painting or decoration giving illusion of reality (not italic)

Trondheim Norwegian port (**-ei-**)

troop large group of people or animals, specifically of soldiers or Scouts; move in a crowd; or parade ceremonially (compare **troupe**)

trooper soldier (compare **trouper**)

Trooping the Colour ceremony in London to mark official birthday of sovereign (capital **T** & **C**; not . . . **of the** . . .)

tropic of Cancer line of latitude north of equator (the use of capital **T** is less common but not incorrect)

tropic of Capricorn line of latitude south of equator (the use of capital **T** is less common but not incorrect)

Trotsky, Leon Russian revolutionary (original name **Lev Davidovich Bronstein**)

troubadour (**-ou-** twice)

troublemaker (one word)

troubleshooter (one word)

trouble spot (two words)

troupe company of actors or other performers (compare **troop**)

trouper member of troupe, or dependable worker (compare **trooper**)

trousseau clothes, linen, etc. collected by bride-to-be (not italic; plural **trousseaux** or **trousseaus**)

Trowbridge English town (**-ow-**)

troy system of weights (lower-case **t**)

Troy ancient city of Asia Minor (Greek name **Ilion**, Latin name **Ilium**)

Troyes French city

Trst Slovene and Serbo-Croat name for **Trieste**

Trucial States former name for **United Arab Emirates**

truculent (not **-ant**)

Trudeau, Pierre Elliott Canadian statesman (**-eau**)

Trueman, Freddy English cricketer (compare **Truman**)

Truffaut, François French film director (**-aut**)

truly (not **true-**)

Truman, Harry S. US statesman (compare **Trueman**; the middle initial **S** is not short for anything and therefore sometimes has no full stop)

trumpeted (not **-tt-**)

trumpeter (not **-tt-**)

trumpeting (not **-tt-**)

trustee person who administers property in trust

trusty (as adjective) faithful or reliable; (as noun) prisoner with special privileges

try (use **try to**, not **try and**, as in *try to* [not *and*] *take more exercise*)

try-on (noun; the verb is **try on**)

tryout (noun; the verb is **try out**)

tsar Russian emperor, tyrant, autocrat, or public official responsible for a particular issue, as in *drugs tsar* (also **czar**)

tsarevitch son of Russian tsar (also **czarevitch**)

tsarevna daughter of Russian tsar (also **czarevna**)

tsarina wife of Russian tsar (also **czarina**, **tsaritsa**, or **czaritza**)

Tsaritsyn former name (until 1925) for **Volgograd**

tsetse fly (rarely **tzetze fly**)

T-shirt (capital **T**; hyphen; also **tee shirt**)

Tsinghai variant of **Qinghai**

Tsingtao variant of **Qingdao**

TSO The Stationery Office (former name **HMSO**)

tsunami large wave produced by earthquake in sea floor (compare **tidal wave**; plural **tsunamis** or **tsunami**)

TT teetotal; Tourist Trophy (motorcycle races); tuberculin-tested

Tübingen German town (umlaut)

TUC Trades Union Congress (not **Trade** . . .)

tuck shop (two words)

Tucson US city in Arizona (**-cs-**)

tug-of-war (two hyphens)

tulle fine net fabric (not italic; double **l**)

tumbledown (one word)

tumbrel (also **tumbril**)

tumour (**-or** in US English)

tumulus (plural **tumuli**)

tun beer cask (compare **ton** and **tonne**)

Tunbridge Wells town in Kent (compare **Tonbridge**)

tune-up (noun; the verb is **tune up**)

tungsten (symbol **W**)

tunnel (double **n**, single **l**)

tunnelled, tunnelling (single **l** in US English)

Tupperware trademark for range of plastic food containers and other products (capital **T**)

turbid muddy or cloudy (compare **turgid** and **turbulent**)

turbo-charge (hyphen)

turbocharger (one word)

turbulent in state of confusion, movement, or agitation (compare **turbid**)

turf (plural **turfs** or **turves**)

Turgenev, Ivan Sergeyevich Russian writer

turgid swollen, congested, or bombastic (compare **turbid**)

Turin Italian city (Italian name **Torino**)

Turkestan region of central Asia (also **Turkistan**)

Turkish bath (capital **T**)

Turkish delight (capital **T**)

Turkistan variant of **Turkestan**

Turkman variant of **Turkoman**

Turkmen language of the Turkomans

Turkmenistan central Asian country

Turkoman member of central Asian people now living chiefly in Turkmenistan and NE Iran (plural **Turkomans**; also **Turkman**, plural **Turkmans**)

Turku Finnish city (Swedish name **Åbo**)

turmeric (-**ur**- then -**er**-)

turnaround (also **turnround**; noun, the verb is **turn around** or **turn round**)

turndown (adjective; the verb is **turn down**)

turned comma the opening quotation mark ('), as opposed to the **apostrophe** (')

Turner, J(oseph) M(allord) W(illiam) British painter (not **Mallard**)

turning point (two words)

turnkey (one word)

turn-line (*typog.*) overlong line of text that finishes on the line below, often with an indent (also **turnover line**)

turn-off (noun; the verb is **turn off**)

turn-on (noun; the verb is **turn on**)

turnout (noun; the verb is **turn out**)

turnover (noun and adjective; the verb is **turn over**)

turnover line variant of **turn-line**

turnround variant of **turnaround**

turnstile (one word)

turntable (one word)

turn-up (noun; the verb is **turn up**)

turtledove (one word)

turtleneck (one word)

Tuscany region of central Italy (Italian name **Toscana**)

Tussaud, Marie Swiss modeller in wax (see also **Madame Tussauds**)

Tutankhamen ancient Egyptian king (also **Tutankhamun**)

Tutsi member of people of Rwanda and Burundi (compare **tootsy**)

tutti-frutti ice cream containing small pieces of fruit (not italic; hyphen)

tutu ballet dancer's skirt (not italic; one word)

Tutu, Desmond South African clergyman

Tuvalu country comprising nine Pacific islands (former names **Lagoon Islands** and **Ellice Islands**)

tuxedo (plural **tuxedos**)

TV television; transvestite (no full stops)

Twain, Mark pen name of Samuel Langhorne **Clemens**

'twas poetic contraction of **it was** (apostrophe; one word)

Twelfth Day January 6

Twelfth Night the evening of January 5 or January 6

twelvemo another name for **duodecimo** (also **12mo**)

'twill poetic contraction of **it will** (apostrophe; one word)

'twixt poetic contraction of **betwixt** (the variant **twixt**, with no apostrophe, is less common but not incorrect)

two the number 2 (compare **to** and **too**)

two-faced (hyphen)
two-time (hyphen)
TX Texas (US postal code)
tying present participle of **tie**
Tyler, John US statesman; **Wat** English leader of the Peasants' Revolt
Tylor, Sir Edward Burnett British anthropologist
tympani variant of **timpani**
Tyndale, William English translator of the Bible (also **Tindale**; compare **Tyndall** and **Tindal**)
Tyndall, John Irish physicist (compare **Tindal** and **Tyndale**)
Tyne and Wear metropolitan county of NE England (three words; not **Weir**)
Tynemouth port in NE England (compare **Teignmouth**)
Tynwald Manx parliament (-**yn**-, -**al**-)

type (use *this/that type of book*, *these/those types of books*, or *these/those types of book*, but do not use plural *these* or *those* with singular *type*)
typecast (one word)
typeface another name for **face**
typescript (one word)
typesetting (one word)
typify (not -**efy**)
typo informal word for typographical error (no full stop; plural **typos**)
Tyr variant of **Tyre**
tyranny (single **r**, double **n**)
tyre rubber or metal ring around wheel (**tire** in US English)
Tyre Lebanese port (also **Tyr**; Arabic name **Sur**)
tyro novice (also **tiro**; plural **tyros** or **tiros**)
Tyrol Austrian state (also **Tirol**)
tzetze fly rare variant of **tsetse fly**
Tzigane Hungarian Gypsy (capital **T**)

439

U

U uranium (no full stop)
UAE United Arab Emirates
U-bend (capital **U**; hyphen)
uber- indicating the greatest or most extreme example of something, as in *uberachiever* or *ubercool computer games* (sometimes attached with hyphen; also **über-**; not italic)
ubiquitous (not **-ious**)
U-boat (capital **U**; hyphen)
UCAS Universities and Colleges Admissions Service (no apostrophes)
UCCA Universities Central Council on Admissions (replaced by **UCAS**)
UCL University College London
UCLA University of California, Los Angeles
Udaipur Indian city
Udall, Nicholas English dramatist (also **Uvedale**)
UDI Unilateral Declaration of Independence
UDR Ulster Defence Regiment
UEA University of East Anglia
UEFA Union of European Football Associations
Uffizi art gallery in Florence, Italy (double **f**, single **z**)
UFO unidentified flying object (plural **UFOs**)
ufology study of UFOs (lower-case **ufo-**)
UGLI trademark for hybrid citrus fruit (all capitals)

ugly unattractive or unpleasant
UHT ultra heat treated (milk, cream, etc.)
Uigur member of people of China, Uzbekistan, Kyrgyzstan, and Kazakhstan, or the language of this people (also **Uighur**)
uitlander South African word for foreigner (also **Uitlander**)
Ujung Padang Indonesian port (also **Makasar**, **Makassar**, or **Macassar**)
UK United Kingdom (used as noun or adjective; see also entry for full form)
ukelele variant of **ukulele**
ukiyo-e school of Japanese painting depicting everyday life (not italic; hyphen)
Ukraine European country (not **the . . .**)
ukulele (also **ukelele**)
Ulan Bator capital of Mongolia (former name **Urga**; Chinese name **Kulun**)
Ullswater English lake (double **l**; note that the name is not preceded by **Lake**)
ulster heavy overcoat (lower-case **u**)
Ulster province of Ireland comprising the six counties of Northern Ireland and three counties of the Republic of Ireland, or informal name for Northern Ireland
ultima Thule variant of **Thule** (in

ancient sense), any distant or unknown region, or a remote goal or aim (lower-case **u**, capital **T**)

ultimatum (plural **ultimatums** or **ultimata**)

ultraconservative (one word)

ultramodern (one word)

ultrasound (one word)

ultraviolet (one word)

ultra vires beyond legal power or authority of person or corporation (not italic; two words)

Uluru Australian monolith (former name **Ayers Rock**)

Ulysses Roman name for **Odysseus**

Ulysses novel by James Joyce (italics)

UMIST University of Manchester Institute of Science and Technology (formerly a separate institution, now part of the University of Manchester)

umlaut the diacritic used on **ä**, **ö**, etc. in German and other languages, indicating a change in the vowel sound (compare **diaeresis**). A vowel with an umlaut can sometimes be replaced by vowel + **e** in English, as in *Führer* or *Fuehrer*.

umpire official who ensures fair play in tennis, cricket, baseball, etc. (compare **referee**)

UN United Nations (used as noun or adjective)

un- (usually attached without hyphen, except to words beginning with capital letter)

'un informal word for **one**, as in *young 'un* (the variant **un**, with no apostrophe, is less common but not incorrect)

un-American (hyphen)

unanimous (-**nim**-)

unaware (adjective, or less common variant of the adverb **unawares**)

unawares (adverb only; the variant **unaware** is less common but not incorrect)

unbeknown (-**kn**- in middle; also **unbeknownst**)

unbiased (also **unbiassed**)

uncalled-for (one hyphen)

uncared-for (one hyphen)

uncharted not mapped or surveyed, as in *uncharted waters*

unchartered having no charter, or unauthorized, as in *unchartered guilds*

unchristian not in accordance with the principles of Christianity (no hyphen; lower-case **c**; compare **non-Christian**)

unconscionable unscrupulous or immoderate

unconscious lacking awareness or insensible

uncooperative (no hyphen)

uncoordinated (no hyphen)

unctuous (not -**tious**)

under- (usually attached without hyphen)

underage (one word)

undercarriage (no hyphen)

undercurrent (no hyphen)

underdeveloped (no hyphen)

underestimate (no hyphen)

underhand (also **underhanded**)

underlay (as verb) place underneath, or past tense of **underlie**; (as noun) something placed underneath, e.g. felt or rubber under a carpet (past tense and past participle **underlaid**)

underlie lie underneath, or be the foundation, cause, or root of (past tense **underlay**, past participle **underlain**)

underlining use single straight underline for *italic*, double for small capitals, triple for CAPITALS, and wavy underline for **bold**. Underlines may be combined, e.g. wavy and straight for ***bold italic***. See also Appendix i.

undermentioned (no hyphen)

Under Milk Wood play by Dylan Thomas (italics; three words)

underprivileged (no hyphen)
underrate (no hyphen)
undersecretary (no hyphen)
understaffed (no hyphen)
undertone underlying meaning (compare **overtone**)
underwater (one word)
under way (two words)
undiscriminating lacking good taste or judgment (compare **indiscriminate**)
undoubtedly (not **-ably**)
uneatable not fit to be eaten, especially in the sense 'unpleasant to eat' (**-able**; compare **inedible**)
un-English (hyphen)
unequivocal (not **-cable**)
UNESCO United Nations Educational, Scientific, and Cultural Organization (all capitals; no full stops)
unexceptionable beyond criticism
unexceptional ordinary
unheard-of (one hyphen)
unhoped-for (one hyphen)
UNICEF United Nations Children's Fund (acronym of its former name, United Nations International Children's Emergency Fund; all capitals; no full stops)
Unification Church religious sect (see also **Moonie**)
uninterested indifferent or unconcerned (compare **disinterested**)
Union, the in history, the union of England and Wales, England and Scotland, Great Britain and Ireland, or Great Britain and Northern Ireland; the USA or the northern states of the USA in the American Civil War; or the **Union of South Africa** (capital **U**)
Union flag official name for the national flag of the United Kingdom (capital **U**, lower-case **f**; common name **Union Jack**)

unionize (also **unionise**; see **-ize/-ise**)
Union Jack common name for **Union flag**, or official name for this flag flown at bow of ship (capital **U** & **J**)
Union of Serbia and Montenegro European country, formed in 2002
Union of South Africa former name for **Republic of South Africa**
Union of Soviet Socialist Republics official name for former **Soviet Union** (abbreviation **USSR**)
unique (do not use with *more*, *most*, or *very*)
UNISON trade union representing workers in local government, health care, etc. (all capitals; no full stops)
unitary authority district administered independently of county council
United Arab Emirates SW Asian country comprising seven emirates (former name **Trucial States**)
United Kingdom European country comprising England, Wales, Scotland, and Northern Island. The term came into use in this sense in 1922; it formerly referred to Great Britain alone (from 1707) and to Great Britain and all Ireland (from 1801). See also **Great Britain** and **British Isles**.
United Nations international organization of independent states (abbreviation **UN**)
United Reformed Church Protestant denomination formed from the union of the Presbyterian Church and the Congregational Church in England and Wales (not **Reform**)
United States of America country comprising 50 states and the District of Columbia, mainly in North America (also **United States**)
units of measurement for the use

of metric versus imperial units, and for spacing between number and abbreviated unit (as in *20 kg, 5lb 2oz*, etc.), follow publisher's house style. Abbreviated units usually have same form for singular and plural and no full stop. See also **SI units**, **cgs units**, and **fps units**.

unit trust (two words)

Univers typeface (capital **U**; not **-se**)

universal time see **UTC**

University (capital **U** in names, as in *University of Exeter* or *Brunel University*)

University College Dublin (no comma)

University College London (no comma)

unjustified (*typog.*) denoting text in which lines are of uneven length (usually aligned on the left-hand side) because the interword spaces are of equal size

Unknown Soldier unidentified soldier whose tomb is a national memorial (capital **U** & **S**)

unlicensed (not **-ced**)

unlooked-for (one hyphen)

unlovable (also **unloveable**)

unmistakable (also **unmistakeable**)

unnecessary (double **n**, single **c**, double **s**)

UNO United Nations Organization (use **UN** instead)

unpalatable (**-lat-**)

unparalleled (double **l** then single **l**)

unpractised (**-ced** in US English)

unprecedented (not **-cid-**)

unputdownable (no hyphens)

unravel (single **l**)

unravelled, unravelling (single **l** in US English)

unreadable difficult or impossible to read, especially because of poor content, complex wording, etc. (compare **illegible**)

unselfconscious (no hyphens)

unshakable (also **unshakeable**)

unsociable not inclined to socialize (compare **unsocial**, **asocial**, and **antisocial**)

unsocial preventing social activity, as in *unsocial hours* (compare **unsociable**, **asocial**, and **antisocial**)

until (single **l**; short form **till**, with double **l** and no apostrophe)

unwanted not desired (compare **unwonted**)

unwieldy (**-ie-**; the spelling **unwieldly** is not incorrect, but it is less common)

unwonted unusual (compare **unwanted**)

up-and-coming (two hyphens)

upbeat (one word)

upbringing (one word)

Updike, John US writer (not **-dyke**)

upgrade (one word)

upkeep (one word)

uplift (one word)

up-market (also **upmarket**)

upon (use **on** instead except in the sense of imminence, as in *Christmas is upon us*, and in fixed phrases such as *once upon a time* or *take it upon oneself*)

Upper Volta former name for **Burkina-Faso**

upper-case denoting a **capital letter**

upper class (noun)

upper-class (adjective)

Uppsala Swedish city

upriver (one word)

Upsala variant of **Uppsala** or place name in USA and Canada

upside down (two words, but hyphenated when used before noun, as in *upside-down cake*)

upstage (one word)

upstairs (adverb, adjective, and noun; never **-stair**)

up-to-date (hyphenated unless used after noun, as in *the catalogue is up to date*)

upturn (one word)

UPVC unplasticized polyvinyl chloride

upward (adjective; sometimes adverb (see **-ward** and **-wards**))

upwards (adverb only)

upwards of (usually means 'more than', but can occasionally mean 'less than', 'almost', or 'approximately'; replace with appropriate synonym to avoid ambiguity)

upwind (one word)

Ural Mountains Russia (capital **U** & **M**; also **Urals**)

uranium (symbol **U**)

urban of a town or city

urbane elegant or sophisticated

urbanize (also **urbanise**; see **-ize/ -ise**)

Urdu official language of Pakistan, also spoken in India

ureter tube conveying urine from kidney to bladder

urethra tube conveying urine from bladder out of the body

Urfé, Honoré d' French writer (lower-case **d'**; acute accent)

Urfey see **D'Urfey**

Urga former name for **Ulan Bator**

URL uniform resource locator (website address)

Urquhart, Sir Thomas Scottish writer (**-quh-**)

Uruguay South American country (**-gu-**)

Urundi former name for **Burundi**

US United States (used as noun or adjective; also **U.S.**)

USA United States of America (also **U.S.A.**)

usable (also **useable**)

USB Universal Serial Bus (standard for connection sockets on computers)

used to (in formal English, the negative is **used not to**)

user-friendly (hyphen)

Ushant island off NW France (French name **Ouessant**)

usher (may be used for males and females)

usherette (use **usher** instead to avoid offence)

Üsküdar Turkish town (former name **Scutari**)

usquebaugh Irish former name for whiskey, Scottish former name for whisky, or Irish liqueur flavoured with coriander (not italic)

USSR Union of Soviet Socialist Republics (see **Soviet Union**)

UT universal time (see **UTC**); Utah (US postal code)

UTC universal time coordinated (international system of civil timekeeping that corresponds with **Greenwich Mean Time** (**GMT**) and is also called **universal time** (**UT**), though the latter term has other specialist uses; variants of the full form have 'coordinated' before 'universal' or before 'time')

U Thant see **Thant**

utilitarian (**-tilit-**)

utilize (also **utilise**; see **-ize/-ise**)

Utopia ideal place or society (the use of lower-case **u** is less common but not incorrect)

Utrecht Dutch province or its capital city

Uttar Pradesh Indian state (not **Utter**)

U-turn (capital **U**; hyphen)

UV ultraviolet

Uvedale variant of **Udall**

Uxbridge English town (compare **Oxbridge**)

Uzbekistan central Asian country (**-bek-**)

V

V Roman numeral for 5; vanadium; volt or volts (no full stop)

v. verb; verse (plural **vv.**); versus (also **v.**); vide (see that entry)

V-1 robot bomb used by Germans in World War II (hyphen; also **doodlebug**)

V-2 rocket-powered ballistic missile used by Germans in World War II (hyphen)

V6 car or engine with six cylinders arranged in form of V (no hyphen)

V8 car or engine with eight cylinders arranged in form of V (no hyphen)

VA Virginia (US postal code)

vacation holiday (compare **vocation**)

vaccinate introduce vaccine into body to induce immunity (double **c**, single **n**; compare **inoculate**)

vacuum (single **c**, double **u**; plural **vacuums** (in all senses) or **vacua** (in scientific senses))

vacuum cleaner (two words)

vacuum flask (two words)

vacuum-packed (hyphen)

vade mecum handbook carried on the person (not italic; plural **vade mecums**)

vagary (not **-iary**)

vain conceited, worthless, futile, or used in the phrase *in vain* (compare **vane** and **vein**)

vainglorious (one word)

Vaishnava member of Hindu sect devoted to cult of Vishnu (not **Vish-**)

valance drapery hung around bed, along shelf, etc. (compare **valence**)

Val d'Isère French ski resort (lower-case **d**; grave accent)

vale valley (compare **veil**)

valedictory (not **vali-**)

valence scientific term, or variant of **valency** (compare **valance**)

Valence French town (not **-ance**)

Valenciennes French town or type of lace originally made there (capital **V**; **-iennes**)

valency term used in chemistry and linguistics (also **valence**)

valentine card sent on St Valentine's Day, or person to whom it is sent (lower-case **v**)

Valentine, St Christian martyr

Valentine's Day variant of **St Valentine's Day**

Valentino, Rudolph Italian-born US actor (not **Rudolf**)

Valera see **de Valera**

valet manservant, act as valet for, or clean (car) inside and out (not italic; compare **varlet**)

valeta ballroom dance (also **veleta**)

valeted, valeting (not **-tt-**)

Valetta variant of **Valletta**

Valhalla in Norse mythology, great hall where dead heroes of battle dwell eternally (single **l** then double l; the variant **Walhalla** is less common but not incorrect)

Valium trademark for diazepam used as tranquillizer (capital **V**)

Valkyrie in Norse mythology, beautiful maiden who takes dead heroes of battle to Valhalla (the variants **Walkyrie** and **Valkyr** are less common but not incorrect)

Valladolid Spanish city (double l then single l)

Valletta capital of Malta (also **Valetta**)

Valois, Dame Ninette de British ballet dancer and choreographer (original name **Edris Stannus**)

valorous (not **-our-**)

valour (**-or** in US English)

Valparaíso Chilean port (acute accent)

Valpolicella Italian red wine (single l twice then double l)

value-added tax see VAT

van, Van chiefly used in surnames of Dutch or Flemish origin (compare **von**). For capitalization and alphabetization of names containing **van** or **Van** as a separate word, see individual entries. Note that **van** and **Van** are usually followed by **der** rather than **de**.

vanadium (symbol **V**)

Van Allen, James Alfred US physicist (capital **V**; **-an** then **-en**)

Vanbrugh, Sir John English dramatist and architect (surname is one word; not **-burgh**)

Van Buren, Martin US statesman (capital **V**)

Vancouver system another name for **author–number system**

V&A Victoria and Albert (Museums), London (no spaces around ampersand)

vandal person who deliberately damages or destroys private or public property (lower-case **v**)

Vandal member of Germanic people that raided Rome, Gaul, etc. in 3rd–6th centuries (capital **V**)

vandalize (also **vandalise**; see **-ize/-ise**)

Van de Graaff, Robert J(emison) US physicist (capital **V**; lower-case **d**; not **der**; double **a**, double **f**)

Vanderbilt, Cornelius US magnate and philanthropist (surname is one word)

Van der Post, Sir Laurens South African writer and traveller (capital **V**; lower-case **d**)

van der Rohe see **Mies van der Rohe**

van der Waals, Johannes Diderik Dutch physicist (lower-case **v** & **d**)

van de Velde, Adriaen, Esaias, and **Willem** Dutch painters (lower-case **v** & **d**; not **der**; sometimes alphabetized under **Velde**)

Van Diemen's Land former name for **Tasmania**

Van Dyck, Sir Anthony Flemish painter (capital **V**; also **Vandyke**)

Vandyke beard (capital **V**; not **Van Dyck**)

vane flat plate or blade indicating wind direction, forming part of windmill, etc. (compare **vain** and **vein**)

van Eyck, Jan Flemish painter (lower-case **v**)

Van Gogh, Vincent Dutch painter (capital **V**)

vanilla (single **n**, double **l**)

van't Hoff, Jacobus Hendricus Dutch physical chemist (lower-case **v**; apostrophe)

Vanuatu country comprising a group of Pacific islands (former name **New Hebrides**)

vaporize (not **-our-**; also **vaporise**, see **-ize/-ise**)

vapour (**-or** in US English)

Varanasi Indian city (former name **Benares** or **Banaras**)

Varèse, Edgar(d) French-born US composer (grave accent)

Vargas Llosa, Mario Peruvian novelist

variant CJD variant Creutzfeldt-Jakob disease: the form of the disease that is thought to be linked to eating contaminated beef (abbreviation **vCJD**; also **new-variant CJD**)

varicose veins (not **-cous**)

variegated (**-ie-**)

variety in the hierarchy of **taxonomic names**, a subdivision of a plant species. The variety name follows the species name in italics with lower-case initial, preceded by the abbreviation var., which is not italic, as in *Artemisia ludoviciana* var. *latiloba.*

variorum denoting edition containing notes by various scholars or various versions of the text (not italic)

varlet archaic word for menial servant or rascal (compare **valet**)

Vasco da Gama see **Gama**

vas deferens duct conveying sperm to urethra (not italic; plural **vasa deferentia**)

Vaseline trademark for petroleum jelly (capital **V**)

Västerås Swedish city (diacritics)

VAT value-added tax (no full stops; note hyphen in full form, which is rarely used)

Vatican palace or authority of pope (capital **V**)

Vatican City independent state in Rome (capital **V & C**)

Vaughan Williams, Ralph English composer (no hyphen)

vb verb

VC Vice Chancellor; Victoria Cross

vCJD variant CJD

vd various dates (also **v.d.**)

VD venereal disease

VDU visual display unit

've have, as in *you should've told me* (do not confuse with **of**)

V-E Day (one hyphen; capital D)

Veda any or all of the ancient sacred writings of Hinduism

Vedanta one of the philosophical schools of Hinduism

vedette small naval patrol vessel (not italic; single **d**, double **t**)

veg informal shortening of vegetable or vegetables (no full stop)

Vega Carpio see **Lope de Vega**

Vegas see **Las Vegas**

Vegemite in Australia, trademark for vegetable extract used as spread (capital **V**)

vegetable (**-get-**)

vehement (all the vowels are **e**'s)

veil (as noun) covering for face, something that conceals, or used in the phrase *take the veil* meaning 'become a nun'; (as verb) cover or conceal (compare **vale**)

veiled disguised, as in *a veiled threat*, or muffled (not **val-**)

vein blood vessel, strand of tissue in leaf, streak, distinctive quality, or mood (compare **vain** and **vane**)

Velázquez, Diego Rodríguez de Silva y Spanish painter (two acute accents; also **Velásquez**)

Velcro trademark for fastening with tiny hooks and threads (capital **V**)

veld elevated open grassland in Africa (also **veldt**)

Velde see **van de Velde**

veldt variant of **veld**

veleta variant of **valeta**

vellum fine parchment or paper resembling this (compare **velum**)

velour velvet-like fabric (not italic; also **velours**)

velouté rich white sauce or soup (not italic; acute accent)

velum membrane or veil-like bodily structure (compare **vellum**)

velvety (single **t**)

vena cava large vein conveying blood to heart (not italic; plural **venae cavae**)

venal open to or characterized by bribery or corruption (compare **venial**)

Vendée French department (acute accent)

vender less common variant of **vendor**

vendetta feud (not italic)

vendor (the spelling **vender** is not incorrect, but it is less common)

venerable (**-era-**)

venereal disease (not **-rial**)

Venetian blind (capital **V**; not **-tion**)

Venezia Italian name for **Venice**

vengeance (not **-ence**)

venial easily excused or forgiven (compare **venal**)

Venice (Italian name **Venezia**)

venin poisonous constituent of **venom**

Venn diagram diagram with overlapping circles used in mathematics and logic (capital **V**)

venom poisonous fluid secreted by snakes, scorpions, etc., or spite (not **-um**; see also **venin**)

venose having veins

venous of the veins or the blood circulating in them

ventilator (not **-er**)

ventricle chamber of heart or cavity in brain (not **-cal**)

Venture Scout former name for **Explorer Scout**

Venus de Milo statue of Aphrodite found in Melos, Greece (not italic; lower-case **d**)

Venus's-flytrap insectivorous plant (also **Venus flytrap**)

veracity truthfulness or accuracy (compare **voracity**)

veranda (also **verandah**)

verbal expressed in words, especially spoken (although rarely used with reference to written words, beware of possible ambiguity in such phrases as *verbal agreement* and use **oral** instead if necessary)

verbalize (also **verbalise**; see **-ize/-ise**)

verbatim word for word (not italic)

verboten forbidden (italics)

verb. sap. a word is enough to the wise (two full stops; from Latin *verbum sapienti sat est*; also **verb. sat.**)

Verde, Cape westernmost point of Africa (see also **Cape Verde**)

verdigris patina on metal (not italic; not **vir-**)

Vereeniging South African city (single **e** then double **e**; **-ig-** then **-ing**)

verger (the spelling **virger** is used at St Paul's and Winchester Cathedral)

Vergil variant of **Virgil**

verkrampte in South Africa during apartheid, Afrikaner Nationalist opposing liberalization (not italic; compare **verligte**)

Verlag German name for publishing house (italics; capital **V**)

verligte in South Africa during apartheid, member of White political party supporting liberalization (not italic; compare **verkrampte**)

Vermeer, Jan Dutch painter (**-er-** then **-eer**; full name **Jan van der Meer van Delft**)

vermilion (also **vermillion**)

vermin (**e** then **i**; same form for singular and plural)

vermouth (lower-case **v**)

vernacular (**-ar**)

vernier movable scale on measuring instrument, or device for making fine adjustment to instrument (lower-case **v**; **-ier** at end)

Veronese, Paolo Italian painter (original name **Paolo Cagliari**)

verruca (double **r**, single **c**; plural **verrucae** or **verrucas**)

Versailles French city, site of royal residence (**-ailles**)

verse lines of verse may be aligned left or indented according to the writer's or publisher's style. In the traditional setting of a poem with alternate rhyming lines, the second, fourth, sixth, etc. lines have a greater indent than the first, third, fifth, etc. Where a verse quotation is set in running text, line breaks are usually indicated with a solidus.

versicle short verse, or short sentence to which congregation makes response in liturgical ceremony (not **-cal**; compare **vesicle**)

vers libre free verse (italics)

verso back of sheet of paper, or any of the left-hand pages of a book, bearing even numbers (compare **recto**)

versus against (not italic; abbreviation **v.** or **vs**)

vertebra (plural **vertebrae** or **vertebras**)

vertex highest point (plural vertexes or vertices; compare **vortex**)

vertical (not **-cle**)

vertiginous (**-gin-**)

vertigo (not **vir-**)

Verulamium Latin name for **St Albans**

Verwoerd, Hendrik Frensch Dutch-born South African statesman (**-er-** then **-oer-**)

Very light signal flare (capital **V**)

vesical of the bladder (compare **vesicle**)

vesicle small sac or cavity (compare **vesical** and **versicle**)

Vespucci, Amerigo Florentine navigator after whom America was named (double **c**; Latin name **Americus Vespucius**)

vestigial (**-gial**)

Vesuvius Italian volcano (Italian name **Vesuvio**)

veteran car car constructed before 1919 (compare **vintage car**)

veterinary (**-eri-**, **-ary**)

veto (plural and third person present tense **vetoes**)

Veuve Clicquot champagne (**-cqu-**)

VHF very high frequency

via by way of (not italic)

viable (to avoid controversy, do not use in the sense 'feasible')

vial variant of **phial** (compare **viol** and **vile**)

Viborg Danish town, or Swedish name for **Vyborg**

vibrato music term (not italic; plural **vibratos**)

vibrator (not **-er**)

vice immoral or wicked habit or practice, failing or imperfection, tool, or serving as deputy for (**vise** in US English for the tool; sometimes attached with hyphen in the sense 'serving as deputy for': see individual entries)

vice chancellor (also **vice-chancellor**)

vicegerent deputy with administrative powers, or representative of God or Christ on earth (one word; not **-reg-**)

vice president (also **vice-president**)

vicereine wife of viceroy or female viceroy (one word)

viceroy governor of colony, province, etc. who rules in the name of his sovereign or government (one word)

vice versa the other way around (not italic)

Vichy French town and spa (**-chy**)

vichyssoise thick soup served cold (not italic; double **s** then single **s**)

vicious wicked or ferocious (compare **viscous**)

vicious circle (the variant **vicious cycle** is less common but not incorrect)

vicissitude (single **c**, double **s**)

victimize (also **victimise**; see **-ize/ -ise**)

victoria plum, carriage, or giant water lily (lower-case **v**)

victualled (single **l** in US English)

victualler (single **l** in US English)

victualling (single **l** in US English)

vicuña cud-chewing animal or cloth made from its wool (also **vicuna**, without tilde)

vide see (used in references; not italic; abbreviation **v.**)

videlicet full form of **viz**

video cassette (two words)

video cassette recorder (three words)

video conferencing (two words)

video game (two words)

videophone (one word)

video tape (noun)

video-tape (verb)

vie (present participle **vying**)

Vienna capital of Austria (German name **Wien**)

Vienne French department and river

Vierwaldstättersee German name for Lake **Lucerne**

Vietcong guerrilla force fighting for reunification of North and South Vietnam in Vietnam War (1954–75) (also **Viet Cong**)

Vietminh Vietnamese organization fighting for national independence (1941–54) (also **Viet Minh**)

Vietnam SE Asian country (the variant **Viet Nam** is less common in English but not incorrect)

vieux jeu old-fashioned (italics)

viewfinder (one word)

viewpoint (one word)

vigilance (not **-ence**)

vigilant alert

vigilante one of group of citizens who take it upon themselves to protect their district

vignette small illustration at beginning or end of book or chapter; short literary essay; photograph or drawing with edges shaded off; or any small endearing scene, picture, etc. (not italic; **-gn-**)

vigorous (not **-our-**)

vigour (**-or** in US English)

Viipuri Finnish name for **Vyborg**

vilayet administrative division of Turkey (not italic)

vile wicked, evil, disgusting, or unpleasant (compare **vial**)

vilify (single **l**)

villain bad person, or less common variant of **villein**

Villa-Lobos, Heitor Brazilian composer (hyphen; not **Hector**)

villanella song (not italic)

villanelle verse form (not italic)

villein medieval peasant (the spelling **villain** is not incorrect in this sense, but it is less common)

Vilnius capital of Lithuania (also **Vilnyus**; Russian name **Vilna**, Polish name **Wilno**)

Viña del Mar Chilean city (lower-case **d**; tilde)

vinaigrette salad dressing (not italic; **-aigr-**)

Vinci see **Leonardo da Vinci**

vineyard (**-ney-**)

vinho verde wine made from early-picked grapes (not italic; **-nh-**)

vintage car car constructed between 1919 and 1930 (compare **veteran car**)

vintner wine merchant (**-ntn-**)

vinyl (**i** then **y**)

viol musical instrument (compare **vial**)

Viollet-le-Duc, Eugène Emmanuel French architect (two hyphens; not **Violet-**)

violoncello (one word; not **-lin-**; use **cello** instead in all but the most formal contexts; plural **violoncellos**)

VIP very important person (plural **VIPs**)

virago (plural **viragoes** or **viragos**)

virger the spelling of **verger** used at St Paul's and Winchester Cathedral

Virgil Roman poet (also **Vergil**; Latin name **Publius Vergilius Maro**)

Virginia creeper (capital **V**)

Virgin Mary title of St **Mary**, mother of Christ (capital **V** & **M**)

virility (single **l**)

virtue (not **ver-**)

virtuoso person with masterly skill or technique (not italic; plural **virtuosos** or **virtuosi**)

virus (plural **viruses**)

visa (plural **visas**, past tense and past participle **visaed**)

vis-à-vis regarding or opposite (not italic; two hyphens; grave accent)

viscera internal organs (plural noun; singular **viscus**)

viscous thick and sticky (compare **viscus** and **vicious**)

viscus singular of **viscera**

vise US spelling of **vice** (the tool)

Vishnu Hindu deity (see also **Vaishnava**)

visible (not **-able**)

visionary (**-nary**)

visitor (not **-er**, except in the title of *The Young Visiters*)

visitors' book (**-s'** not **-'s**)

visor (the spelling **vizor** is not incorrect, but it is less common)

visualize (also **visualise**; see **-ize/-ise**)

vitalize (also **vitalise**; see **-ize/-ise**)

vitamin (lower-case **v** in names, e.g. **vitamin C**)

Viti Levu largest island of Fiji

Vitoria Spanish city and battle site (single **t**)

vitriol (**-iol**)

viva[1] long live or up with (the specified person or thing) (not italic unless part of Italian phrase)

viva[2] oral examination, e.g. for postgraduate student (not italic; full form **viva voce**)

vivarium (plural **vivariums** or **vivaria**)

viva voce by word of mouth, or full form of **viva**[2] (not italic)

vive long live or up with (the specified person or thing) (not italic unless part of French phrase)

Viyella trademark for soft fabric (capital **V**; **-iy-**)

viz namely (full form **videlicet**)

vizier official in former Ottoman Empire and some other Muslim countries (not **vis-**, not **-ir**)

vizor less common variant of **visor**

V-J Day (one hyphen; capital D)

vlei area of marshy ground in South Africa (not italic; **-ei**)

Vlissingen Dutch name for **Flushing**

Vltava Czech river (**Vlt-**; German name **Moldau**)

V neck (noun)

V-neck (adjective; also **V-necked**)

vocalise[1] variant of **vocalize**

vocalise[2] musical exercise (never **-ize**)

vocalize express or articulate with the voice (also **vocalise**; see **-ize/-ise**)

vocation occupation, profession, calling, or career (compare **vacation**)

Vodafone telecommunications company (capital **V**; not **-phone**)

voice mail (two words)

voice-over (hyphen)

voile light semitransparent fabric (not italic)

Voiotia Greek department (Greek name **Boeotia**)

vol. volume

Volapuk artificial language (also **Volapük**)

vol-au-vent small filled pastry (not italic; two hyphens; plural **vol-au-vents**)

volcano (plural **volcanoes** or **volcanos**)

volcanology (also **vulcanology**)

Volgograd Russian port (former names **Tsaritsyn** (until 1925) and **Stalingrad** (1925–61))

Volkswagen motor manufacturer, or any of their vehicles (not **-on**)

volley (**-ey**)

volleyball (one word)

vols. volumes

volt unit of electric potential (lower-case **v**, but abbreviation is **V**)

Voltaire pen name of French writer **François Marie Arouet**

volte-face reversal of opinion, policy, etc., or change of position (not italic; hyphen; same form for singular and plural)

voluminous (**-min-**)

voluntary (**-tary**)

vomited, vomiting (not **-tt-**)

von, Von chiefly used in surnames of German or Swiss origin (compare **van**). For capitalization and alphabetization of names containing **von** or **Von** as a separate word, see individual entries; most have lower-case **von** and are alphabetized under the following capital initial.

von Braun, Werner German-born US rocket engineer (lower-case **v**)

von Neumann, John Hungarian-born US mathematician (lower-case **v**; **-mann**)

von Sternberg, Joseph Austrian-born US film director (lower-case **v**; **-berg**)

von Stroheim, Erich Austrian-born US film director and actor (lower-case **v**; real name **Erich Maria Stroheim von Nordenwall**)

voodoo (one word; double **o** twice)

Voortrekker any of original Afrikaner settlers of Transvaal and Orange Free State, or member of Afrikaner youth movement (not italic; capital **V**; double **o**, double **k**)

voracity great hunger or eagerness (compare **veracity**)

vortex whirling mass of liquid, gas, etc. (plural **vortexes** or **vortices**; compare **vertex**)

Vosges French mountain range and department (**-sg-**, **-es**)

vouchsafe (one word)

vox pop TV or radio interviews with members of the public (two words; no full stop)

vox populi the voice of the people, i.e. popular opinion (not italic; two words)

voyeur person who watches others undressing, having sex, etc. (not italic)

VR Queen Victoria (from Latin *Victoria Regina*); variant reading; virtual reality

vs versus

V-sign (capital **V**; hyphen)

VSO Voluntary Service Overseas

VT Vermont (US postal code)

vulcanize (also **vulcanise**; see **-ize/ -ise**)

vulcanology variant of **volcanology**

vulgar (**-ar**)

vulgarize (also **vulgarise**; see **-ize/ -ise**)

Vulgate Latin version of Bible produced by St Jerome in 4th century (capital **V**)

vulnerable (not **vun-**)

vv. verses

Vyatka Russian river and former name for **Kirov**

Vyborg Russian port on an inlet of the Gulf of Finland (Finnish name **Viipuri**, Swedish name **Viborg**)

vying present participle of **vie**

W

W tungsten (no full stop; from former name *wolfram*); watt or watts (no full stop); west or West

WA Washington (US postal code)

Waals see **van der Waals**

wacky (not **wh-**)

Waddenzee part of North Sea between Dutch mainland and Frisian islands (one word; see also **Zuider Zee**)

waddy heavy wooden club used as Aboriginal weapon (compare **wadi**)

Wade-Giles system of transliteration of Chinese, dating from 1859 and characterized by the use of hyphens and apostrophes (compare **Pinyin**; see also **Chinese names**)

wadi usually dry watercourse in N Africa and Arabia (also **wady**; compare **waddy**)

wage payment for manual work, domestic service, etc., usually weekly (compare **salary**). Use singular form before another noun, as in *wage freeze*, and in general references, as in *minimum wage*. Use plural form with reference to a person's actual pay packet, as in *he gives half his wages to his mother.*

wage earner (two words)

Wagga Wagga Australian city (two words)

waggon less common variant of **wagon**

waggoner less common variant of **wagoner**

wagon (the spelling **waggon** is not incorrect, but it is less common)

wagoner (single **n**; the spelling **waggoner** is not incorrect, but it is less common)

Wahhabi member of strictly conservative Muslim sect (also **Wahabi**)

wail cry (compare **wale** and **whale**)

Wailing Wall another name for **Western Wall**

Wain, John British writer (compare **Wayne**)

waist narrow part of body, or something resembling this (compare **waste**)

waistband (one word)

waistcoat (one word)

waistline (one word)

wait (as verb) stay in one place, hold oneself in readiness, delay, or serve at tables in restaurant; (as noun) period of waiting (the verb is usually intransitive, as in *waiting for a bus*: compare **await** (for usage) and **weight** (for spelling))

Waitangi Day February 6, national day of New Zealand (capital **W** & **D**)

waiter (may be used for males and females)

waiting list (two words)

waiting room (two words)

waitress (use **waiter** as gender-neutral alternative if required)

waive set aside or refrain from enforcing (compare **wave**)

waiver relinquishment of claim or right (compare **waver**)

wake rouse or become roused from sleep (often followed by *up*; the variant **waken** is less common but not incorrect; compare **awake**)

waken less common variant of **wake** (not followed by *up*; compare **awaken**)

Walachia former European principality, now part of Romania (also **Wallachia**)

Waldorf salad (capital **W**)

wale raised mark or ridge (compare **whale** and **wail**)

Wales part of **Great Britain** and the **United Kingdom** (Welsh name **Cymru**)

Wałęsa, Lech Polish statesman

Walhalla less common variant of **Valhalla**, or place name in Australia and USA

walkabout (noun; the verb is **walk about**)

walkie-talkie (hyphen; also **walky-talky**)

walking stick (two words)

Walkman trademark for small portable cassette player with headphones (capital **W**)

walk-on (noun and adjective; the verb is **walk on**)

walkout (noun; the verb is **walk out**)

walkover (noun; the verb is **walk over**)

walk-through (noun; the verb is **walk through**)

walkway (one word)

Walkyrie less common variant of **Valkyrie**

walky-talky variant of **walkie-talkie**

wallaby (double **l**, single **b**)

Wallace, Alfred Russel British naturalist (not **Russell**); **Edgar** English crime novelist; **Sir Richard** English art collector and philanthropist; **Sir William** Scottish patriot (compare **Wallis**)

Wallachia variant of **Walachia**

Wallasey English town (**-sey**)

walleye (one word)

walleyed (one word)

wallflower (one word)

Wallis, Sir Barnes English aeronautical engineer (compare **Wallace**)

Wallis and Futuna Islands French overseas territory in SW Pacific (not **Wallace**)

wallop (double **l**, single **p**)

walloped, walloping (double **l**, single **p**)

wallpaper (one word)

Wall's brand of ice cream, sausages, etc. (apostrophe)

wall-to-wall (two hyphens)

Wal-Mart retail company (single **l**; hyphen; capital **W & M**)

walnut (single **l**)

Walpurgis Night eve of May 1 (German name *Walpurgisnacht*)

walrus (single **l**)

Walsall English town (single **l** then double **l**)

Walt Disney World full name of **Disney World**

Walton, Izaak English writer, known for *The Compleat Angler* (not **Isaac**); **Sir William** English composer

waltz (**-ltz**)

wander move or travel without definite purpose, go astray, or lose concentration (compare **wonder**)

wanderlust desire to travel (not italic; one word)

wannabe (double **n**; also **wannabee**)

want wish, need, or desire (compare **wont**)

wanted past tense and past participle

of **want**, or being searched for by the police in connection with a crime (compare **wonted**)

WAP Wireless Application Protocol (enabling users of mobile phones to access the Internet)

war armed conflict (compare **wore**; capital **W** in names, e.g. *Vietnam War, War of the Spanish Succession*)

war cry (two words)

-ward in UK English, attached to form adjectives and variants of adverbs; in US English, attached to form adjectives and adverbs (see individual entries and compare **-wards**)

war dance (two words)

warden person in charge of something, e.g. a building or park

warder officer in charge of prisoners in jail (may be used for males and females, but **prison officer** is preferred form for both sexes in modern usage)

wardress (use **prison officer** instead)

-wards in UK English, attached to form adverbs; in US English, attached to form variants of adverbs (see individual entries and compare **-ward**)

-ware used to form names of articles of the specified kind or material, as in *hardware, glassware*, etc. (usually attached without hyphen, but sometimes two words, as in *jasper ware*; compare **-wear**)

war game (two words)

warhorse (one word)

Warks Warwickshire

warlock sorcerer or magician (not **wor-**)

Warlock, Peter British composer (real name **Philip Arnold Heseltine**; compare **Worlock**)

warm-up (noun; the verb is **warm up**)

warn make aware of danger, or inform in advance (compare **worn**)

War of American Independence (also **American War of Independence**; US name **American Revolution**)

war paint (two words)

warpath (one word)

Warsaw capital of Poland (Polish name **Warszawa**)

Warsaw Pact military treaty and association of E European countries (1955–91) (capital P)

warship (one word)

Warszawa Polish name for **Warsaw**

warthog (one word)

wartime (one word)

was past tense of **be** used with *I, he, she*, and *it* (compare **were**)

washbasin (one word)

wash house (two words)

washing machine (two words)

Washington US state on W coast, capital of USA on E coast, or English town (also **Washington, DC** for the US city: see **DC** and **District of Columbia**)

washing-up (hyphen)

Washita variant of **Ouachita**

washout (one word)

washroom (one word)

Wasp White Anglo-Saxon Protestant: person of European ancestry in USA, forming part of privileged or influential group (also **WASP**)

waste (as verb) use carelessly or to no avail, fail to take advantage of, or decline physically; (as noun) act of wasting, state of being wasted, or anything rejected as useless, worthless, surplus, etc.; (as adjective) discarded, produced in excess, not cultivated or inhabited, or used in the phrase *lay waste* (compare **waist**)

waste disposal unit (three words)

wasteland (one word)

Waste Land, The poem by T. S. Eliot (*Waste Land* is two words)

wastepaper basket (two words)

Waswahili plural of **Mswahili** (see **Swahili**)

watchdog (one word)

watchstrap (one word)

watchtower (one word)

watchword (one word)

water bird (two words)

watercolour (one word; **-or** in US English)

watercress (one word)

waterfowl (one word)

water hole (two words)

watering can (two words)

water lily (two words)

water main (two words)

watermark (one word)

watermelon (one word)

water-ski (hyphen for both verb and noun, but also **water ski** for the noun)

Waterstone's bookseller (apostrophe)

water tower (two words)

waterway (one word)

waterworks (use singular verb in the sense 'establishment for purifying water', use plural verb in the senses 'fountain', 'urinary system', or 'tears')

Watford town in Hertfordshire or village in Northamptonshire

Watford Gap motorway service area in Northamptonshire

Watling Street Roman road from Kent to Shropshire (single **t** in first word)

watt unit of power (lower-case **w**, but abbreviation is **W**; compare **what**)

Watteau, Jean-Antoine French painter (double **t**; **-eau**)

Waugh, Auberon English journalist and novelist; **Evelyn** English novelist

waul (also **wawl**)

wave move to and fro, curve, undulation, oscillation, or prolonged spell (compare **waive**)

wavelength (one word)

waver be irresolute, hesitate, fluctuate, or flicker (compare **waiver**)

wawl variant of **waul**

waxwork (one word)

way method, style, route, distance, or journey (compare **weigh** and **whey**)

Wayne, John US actor (real name **Marion Michael Morrison**; compare **Wain**)

-ways used to form words indicating position or direction (as in *lengthways*), some of which have variants ending in **-wise**. See also individual entries.

WC water closet (i.e. toilet)

WEA Workers' Educational Association (note position of apostrophe in full form)

weak not strong (compare **week**)

weak-kneed (hyphen)

weakly in a weak manner (compare **weekly**)

weal raised mark on skin, or archaic word for prosperity or wellbeing (also **wheal** in the sense 'raised mark'; compare **wheel**)

Weald, the region of SE England between North Downs and South Downs (capital **W**; compare **wield**)

wear have on body as clothing or ornament; deteriorate or cause to deteriorate by use, rubbing, etc.; tire; weaken; state of being worn; something worn (see also **-wear**); or used in the phrase *wear and tear* (compare **were** and **where**)

Wear English river (compare **weir**; see also **Tyne and Wear**)

-wear used to form names of things worn, as in *footwear, knitwear, sportswear*, etc. (usually attached without hyphen, but sometimes two words, as in *leisure wear*; compare **-ware**)

weather meteorological conditions (thus *conditions* in the phrase *weather conditions* is redundant; compare **wether** and **whether**)

weathercock (one word)

weather vane (two words)

weaved variant of **wove** or **woven**, especially with reference to making one's way by moving from side to side

weaver person who weaves (compare **weever**)

weaverbird (one word; not **wee-**)

web (also **Web** as short form of **World Wide Web**, but lower-case **w** in compounds such as **webcam** and **website**)

Webb, Sir Aston British architect; **Beatrice** British writer on social and economic problems; **Mary** British novelist; **Sidney, Baron Passfield** British economist and social historian (double **b**)

webcam (one word; lower-case **w**)

Weber, Baron Carl Maria Friedrich Ernst von German composer and conductor; **Ernst Heinrich** German physiologist and anatomist; **Max** German economist and sociologist; **Wilhelm Eduard** German physicist

Webern, Anton von Austrian composer

web-fed (*typog.*) denoting printing press that receives paper from reel rather than in sheets (hyphen)

web page (two words; lower-case **w**)

website (one word; lower-case **w**)

wedded past tense and past participle of **wed** (also **wed**)

Weddell Sea part of Atlantic Ocean in Antarctica (double **d**, double **l**; capital **S**)

wedding cake (two words)

wedding ring (two words)

Wedgwood trademark for pottery (capital **W**; not **Wedge-**)

Wednesday (**-nes-**)

week period of seven days (compare **weak**)

weekly once a week or every week, happening weekly, calculated by the week, or periodical issued weekly (compare **weakly**)

weever fish (compare **weaver**)

weevil beetle (**-ee-**, **-il**)

Weidenfeld & Nicolson publishing company (**-eid-** then **-eld**; ampersand; not **Nichol-**)

weigh measure weight of, have weight, consider, be influential, or raise (anchor) (compare **way** and **whey** (for spelling) and **weight** (for meaning))

weighbridge (one word)

weigh-in (noun; the verb is **weigh in**)

weight (as noun) heaviness, heavy object or load, oppressive force, or importance; (as verb) add weight to, burden, oppress, or bias (compare **wait** (for spelling) and **weigh** (for meaning))

weights and measures see **units of measurement**

Weihai Chinese port (also **Wei-hai** or **Weihaiwei**)

Weil, Simone French philosopher and mystic

Weill, Kurt German composer

Weil's disease (capital **W**; single **l**; apostrophe)

Weimar German city

Weimaraner breed of dog (capital **W**; **-ar-** then **-er**)

Weimar Republic German republic from 1919 to 1933

weir low dam across river (**-ei-**; compare **Wear**)

weird (**-eir-**)

Weismann, August German biologist

Weizmann, Chaim Russian-born Israeli statesman

welch variant of **welsh**

Welch archaic variant of **Welsh**, still used in the name **Royal Welch Fusiliers**

welfare state (lower-case **w** & **s**)

well- (compound adjectives are usually hyphenated when used before noun and two words when used after noun: see **well-known** for example)

wellbeing (no hyphen)

Welles, Orson US film director, actor, and screenwriter (compare **Wells**)

Wellesley family name of 1st Duke of **Wellington** (three **e**'s)

Wellingborough English town (not **-brough**)

wellington short for **Wellington boot** (lower-case **w**)

Wellington capital of New Zealand

Wellington, 1st Duke of title of Arthur **Wellesley**, British soldier and statesman

Wellington boot (capital **W**, but short form **wellington** has lower-case **w**)

well-known (hyphenated before noun (as in *a well-known author*) and two words after noun (as in *the author is well known*); the same principle applies to other **well-**compounds)

well-nigh (hyphen)

Wells, Henry US businessman who founded express mail service with William Fargo; **H(erbert) G(eorge)** British writer (compare **Welles**)

well-to-do (always two hyphens)

well-wisher (hyphen)

welsh fail to pay a debt or fail to fulfil an obligation (lower-case **w**; also **welch**)

Welsh (as adjective) of Wales; (as noun) the language or people of Wales (see also **Welch**)

Welsh dresser (capital **W**)

Welsh rabbit cheese on toast (capital **W**; the variant **Welsh rarebit** (or simply **rarebit**) is more frequent in modern times, but **Welsh rabbit** is the original name)

Weltanschauung personal philosophy of life and the universe (italics; capital **W**; double **u**)

Weltpolitik policy of participation in world affairs (italics; one word; capital **W**)

Weltschmerz world-weariness (italics; capital **W**; **-tsch-**; **-rz**)

Welwyn Garden City English town (**-lw-**; capital **G** & **C**)

were past tense of **be** used with *you*, *we*, and *they*, or past subjunctive of **be** surviving only in conditional clauses or fixed phrases such as *if I were you* and *as it were* (compare **was** (for usage) and **wear** and **where** (for spelling))

we're contraction of **we are**

werewolf (not **-rw-**; plural **werewolves**)

west (as noun) direction or compass point opposite east, or area lying in this direction; (as adjective or adverb) in, to, or from the west (sometimes capital **W** in the sense 'area lying in the west'; see also **compass points**)

West Europe, America, etc., regarded as culturally distinct from Asia; formerly, the non-Communist countries; or denoting the western part of a particular country (sometimes lower-case **w** in adjectival use, but always capital **W** in names; also **Occident** in the sense 'Europe, America, etc.')

West, Mae US actress (not **May**); **Nathanael** US novelist (not **Nathaniel**; real name **Nathan Weinstein**)

West Bank, the disputed region in Middle East beside River Jordan (capital **W** & **B**)

West Country, the SW England, especially Cornwall, Devon, and Somerset (capital **W** & **C**)

West End part of London containing

main shopping and entertainment areas (capital **W** & **E**)

western of, in, or to the west (lower-case **w**)

Western (as adjective) of, in, or to the West; (as noun) film or book about life in western USA in pioneering times (capital **W**)

Western Australia Australian state (do not abbreviate **Western**)

Western Cape South African province (capital **W** & **C**; also **Western Province**)

Western Ghats Indian mountain range

Western Isles another name for the **Hebrides**, or an island authority comprising the **Outer Hebrides**

westernize (also **westernise**; see -ize/ -ise)

Western Province variant of **Western Cape**

Western Samoa former name for **Samoa** (the country)

Western Wall part of Temple of Herod in Jerusalem, a place of prayer for Jews (also **Wailing Wall**)

West Germany former European country, created in 1949 and reunited with **East Germany** in 1990 (do not abbreviate **West** in this sense; see also **FRG**)

West Indies archipelago off Central America, separating Caribbean Sea from Atlantic Ocean and comprising the Greater Antilles, the Lesser Antilles, and the Bahamas

West Irian English name for **Irian Jaya**

Westminster London borough containing the Houses of Parliament and Westminster Abbey (not **-mini-**)

Westmorland former English county (**-morl-**)

west-northwest (one hyphen)

Weston-super-Mare English town and resort (two hyphens; not **Western**; lower-case **s** on middle word)

west-southwest (one hyphen)

westward (adjective; sometimes adverb (see **-ward** and **-wards**))

westwards (adverb only)

wet moist, saturate, feeble, foolish, wetness, or make or become wet (past tense and past participle **wet** or **wetted**; compare **whet**)

wether castrated male sheep (compare **weather** and **whether**)

wet suit (two words)

wetted variant of **wet** (past tense and past participle)

wf wrong font

whale large sea mammal, or used in the phrase *a whale of a time* (compare **wail** and **wale**)

whalebone (one word)

wharf (plural **wharves** or **wharfs**)

what used to ask a question or make an exclamation (compare **watt**). Do not use as relative pronoun in place of **that** or **who**, as in *the car that* [not *what*] *caused the accident*). Use **what** instead of **which** to ask about a particular item when the range of possibilities is large or unlimited, as in *what tool* [i.e. of all the things available for the purpose] *should I use?* To avoid controversy, use singular verb in sentences such as *what they need is* [not *are*] *better facilities*.

whatever (also two words as emphatic form of **what**, as in *what ever does it mean?*; always one word in the senses 'no matter what', 'everything that', etc.)

whatnot (one word)

whatsoever (one word)

wheal variant of **weal** in the sense 'raised mark', or Cornish name for a mine (compare **wheel**; capital **W** in names of Cornish tin mines, e.g. *Wheal Jane*)

wheel rotating disc or ring, anything resembling this in form or function, roll, turn, or used in the phrase *wheel and deal* (compare **weal** and **wheal**)

wheelbarrow (one word)

wheelchair (one word; do not mention a disabled person's use of a wheelchair unless relevant, and avoid compounds such as *wheelchair-bound*)

wheel clamp (two words)

wheeler-dealer (hyphen)

wheelhouse (one word)

wheelwright (not -lr-)

whelk (**wh-**)

whence from what place or origin (thus *from* in the phrase *from whence* is redundant and should be avoided)

whenever (also two words as emphatic form of **when**, as in *when ever will we get there?*; always one word in the senses 'no matter when', 'every time that', etc.)

where at or to which place (compare **were** and **wear**). The use of **where** instead of **in which** in contexts such as *a situation where* [or *in which*] *it is impossible to please all parties* was formerly controversial but is now generally acceptable.

whereabouts (one word)

whereas (one word)

whereby (one word)

whereupon (one word)

wherever (also two words as emphatic form of **where**, as in *where ever did I put my keys?*; always one word in the senses 'no matter where', 'everywhere that', etc.)

wherewithal (one word; single l)

whet sharpen or stimulate, as in *whet the knife, whet your appetite* (compare **wet**)

whether if (compare **weather** and

wether). Note that the addition of *or not* is optional in contexts such as *she was not sure whether to accept* (*or not*) but is obligatory in contexts such as *you must go, whether you want to or not.*

whey watery liquid that separates from curd when milk is clotted (compare **way** and **weigh**)

which used in questions and relative clauses (compare **witch**). Always used to introduce a nonrestrictive **relative clause** (as in *the dog, which belongs to my neighbour, bit me on the leg*) and sometimes used in place of **that** to introduce a restrictive relative clause, e.g. to avoid inelegant repetition or overuse of the word (as in *she said that that was the dog which had bitten her son*). Use **which** instead of **what** to ask about a particular item when the range of possibilities is small or limited, as in *which tool* [e.g. of the three or four in front of me] *should I use?*

Which? consumer magazine (italics, question mark)

Whig member of political party that developed into Liberal Party in the UK (capital **W**; compare **wig**)

while (as conjunction) at the same time that, in spite of the fact that, or whereas; (as noun) period of time, or used in the phrase *worth one's while* (**whilst** is a less common variant for the conjunction, but should not be used for the noun; compare **wile**)

whimsy (also **whimsey**)

whine high-pitched cry or sound, peevish complaint, or make such a sound or complaint (compare **wine**)

whinge (**wh-**)

whingeing (**e** after **g**)

whiplash (one word)

whippersnapper (one word)

whippoorwill (one word)

whip-round (noun; the verb is whip round)

whir (also **whirr**)

whirligig spinning toy, or anything that whirls or spins (**-li-**)

whirlybird informal name for helicopter (**-ly-**)

whirr variant of **whir**

whiskey alcoholic spirit distilled in Ireland or the USA

whisky alcoholic spirit distilled in Scotland

whistle-blower (hyphen)

Whistler, James Abbott McNeill US artist (double **t** & double **l** at end of forenames)

whistle-stop tour (one hyphen)

whit smallest particle or amount, as in *not a whit* (compare **wit**)

Whit of **Whitsuntide**, as in *Whit Monday*

Whitaker's Almanack (single **t**; apostrophe; **-ack**)

White (as adjective) of a light-skinned race, or of European ancestry; (as noun) a White person (capital **W**; also **Caucasian** or **Caucasoid** in the sense 'of a light-skinned race')

whitebait (one word)

Whitechapel district of London (one word)

white-collar of professional and clerical workers (hyphen; compare **blue-collar**)

Whitefield, George English Methodist preacher (not **Whitfield**)

white horse outline carved into chalk hill, or broken crest of wave (two words)

Whitehorse Canadian town (one word)

White House, the official residence of US president in Washington (two words; capital **W** & **H**)

white-knuckle ride (one hyphen)

whitewash (one word)

whither archaic or poetic word meaning 'to what place' (compare **wither**)

whitish (not **-te-**)

Whitley Bay English resort (not **-ly**)

Whitsun another name for **Whitsuntide**

Whit Sunday seventh Sunday after Easter, observed as Christian festival commemorating descent of Holy Spirit on apostles (two words; also **Pentecost**)

Whitsuntide days following **Whit Sunday** (one word; also **Whitsun**)

whittle (**wh-**)

whiz variant of **whizz**

whiz kid variant of **whizz kid**

whizz (also **whiz** in all senses or **wiz** in the sense 'person with great skill')

whizz kid (two words; also **whiz kid** or **wiz kid**)

who used for subject of verb, as in *who wrote that song?*, *the people who live next door*, or *the man who they say was responsible for the accident* (compare **whom**). Note that **who**, not **whom**, is required in the last of these examples: *who* is the subject of *was responsible*, not the object of *they say*.

WHO World Health Organization

whodunnit (one word; also **whodunit**)

whoever (also two words as emphatic form of **who**, as in *who ever told you that?*; always one word in the senses 'no matter who', 'anyone who', etc.)

whole complete, undamaged, healthy, complete thing, unit, or used in the phrases *as a whole* and *on the whole* (compare **hole**)

wholefood (one word)

wholehearted (one word)

wholemeal (one word)

wholly entirely or exclusively (double **l**; not **-lely**; compare **holy** and **holey**)

whom in formal English, used for

object of verb or preposition, as in *the woman whom he married, the people to whom we sold the house,* or *the children, some of whom are orphans* (compare **who**). In the first example **whom** may be replaced by **who** in informal English or simply dropped altogether; in the second example it cannot be replaced by **who**, even in informal English, unless the preposition is moved to the end, as in *the people (who) we sold the house to*; in the third example **whom** must remain.

whoop cry of enthusiasm or excitement, characteristic sound of whooping cough, utter such a cry, or make such a sound (compare **hoop**)

whoopee (**-pee**)

whooping cough (not **hoop-**)

whore (**wh-**)

who's contraction of **who is** or **who has**, as in *anyone who's late* or *the player who's won*

whose of whom or of which, as in *whose jacket is this?* or *the car whose alarm went off*

who's who any book or list giving names and short biographies of famous people (not italic; lower-case **w** twice)

Who's Who annual publication (italics; capital **W** twice)

why ever (two words)

WH Smith retail company selling books, stationery, etc. (no full stops; also **WH Smith**)

WI West Indies; Wisconsin (US postal code); Women's Institute

Wichita US city (not **-taw**)

wicketkeeper (one word)

Wickliffe variant of **Wycliffe** (also **Wiclif**)

Widdecombe, Ann British politician (not **Anne**; double **d** and **-ec-** in surname)

'Widdicombe Fair' song (double **d**, **-ic-**)

Widecombe in the Moor English village (single **d**, **-ec-**)

widgeon variant of **wigeon**

widow (*typog.*) short last line of paragraph, especially when occurring undesirably at top of page or column

widow's cruse unfailing supply (alluding to I Kgs 17:10–16; **-'s** not **-s'**; **-use**)

wield handle, use, or exert (**-ie-**; compare **Weald**)

Wien German name for **Vienna**

Wiener schnitzel veal escalope coated in breadcrumbs (not italic; capital **W**, lower-case **s**)

Wiesbaden German city (**-ie-**)

wig artificial hair (compare **Whig**)

wigeon (also **widgeon**)

Wight, Isle of island off S England

wild card (two words)

wildcat (one word)

Wilde, Oscar (Fingal O'Flahertie Wills) Irish writer and wit (**-de**)

wildebeest (not **-beast**)

wildfire (one word)

wildfowl (one word)

wild-goose chase (one hyphen)

Wild West (capital **W** twice)

wile cunning or trick (compare **while**)

wilful (single **l** twice in UK English, but **will-** in US English)

Wilhelmstrasse Berlin street where government buildings were formerly situated (one word)

will according to traditional grammar, **will** (as a form of the verb **be**) is used in the first person to express determination, obligation, etc. (as in *I will never surrender*) and in the second and third persons to express futurity (as in *you will be late*); compare **shall**. In modern usage **will** is often used in all persons for all meanings, or shortened to **'ll**. See also **would**. The verb **will** meaning 'exercise faculty of volition' (as in *I willed them to lose*), 'bequeath' (as in *she willed us her house*), 'decree' (as in *he wills that they shall die*), or 'wish' (as in *wander where you will*) is perfectly regular, with **wills** for the third person present tense and **willed** for the past tense and past participle

Willkie, Wendell US politician (double **l** in surname and first name)

will-o'-the-wisp (three hyphens; apostrophe)

willpower (one word)

willy-nilly (hyphen)

Wilno Polish name for **Vilnius**

Wimpey construction company

Wimpy chain of fast-food restaurants

winceyette (-ey-)

Winckelmann, Johann Joachim German archaeologist and art historian (**-ckel-**; double **n** at end of surname and first name)

windbreak (one word)

Windermere English lake or town on its shore (**-der-**; use **Lake Windermere** only if there is a risk of confusion with the town)

wind farm (two words)

Windhoek capital of Namibia (not **-hook**)

window box (two words)

window-dressing (hyphen)

window-shopping (hyphen)

windowsill (one word)

Windscale former name for **Sellafield**

windscreen (one word)

windshield (one word)

Windsor official name of British royal family from 1917

windsurfing (one word)

wine alcoholic drink or dark red colour (compare **whine**)

wine bar (two words)

wineglass (one word)

winepress (one word)

wineskin (one word)

winey (also **winy**)

wingspan (one word)

Winnebago North American Indian people or language, or US lake (double **n**; **e** in middle

Winnie-the-Pooh character in children's stories and poems by A. A. Milne (two hyphens)

Winnipeg Canadian city and lake (double **n**; **i** in middle)

wintry (also **wintery**)

winy variant of **winey**

wipeout (noun; the verb is **wipe out**)

WIPO World Intellectual Property Organization (no full stops; also **Wipo**)

Wirral peninsula and unitary authority in NW England (double **r**, single **l**)

Wis. Wisdom of Solomon (full stop; not italic)

Wisbech English town (not **-beach**)

Wisden Cricketers' Almanack (often shortened to *Wisden* or **Wisden**; **-s'** not **-'s**; **-ack**)

Wisdom of Solomon book of the Apocrypha (not italic; abbreviation **Wis.**)

-wise used to form words indicating position or direction (as in *crosswise*), some of which have variants ending in **-ways**. Also means 'in the manner of' (as in *crabwise*) or 'with reference to' (as in *careerwise*); the coining of new words in the latter category is best avoided. See also individual entries.

wishbone (one word)

wish list (one word)

wishy-washy (hyphen)

wisteria (lower-case **w** in general use, *Wisteria* is the genus name; the spelling **wistaria** is not incorrect, but it is less common)

wit humour, witty person, intelligence, or used in the phrase *to wit* meaning 'namely' (compare **whit**)

witch female who casts spells (compare **which**)

witch-elm variant of **wych-elm**

witchetty grub (**witch-**)

witch hazel (also **wych-hazel**)

witch-hunt (hyphen)

wither shrivel, fade, or decline (compare **whither**)

withers part of horse's back between shoulders (not **wh-**)

withhold (double **h**)

wits mind (not **wh-**)

wits' end used in the phrase *at one's wits' end* (**-ts'** not **-t's**)

Witt, Johan de Dutch statesman (double **t**; also **Jan**; lower-case **d**)

Wittenberg German city (double **t**; not **-burg**)

Witwatersrand rocky ridge in South Africa containing rich gold deposits (one word; also **the Rand**)

wivern less common variant of **wyvern**

wiz variant of **whizz** in the sense 'person with great skill'

wizened (single **z**, single **n**)

Wobegon see **Lake Wobegon** (compare **woebegone**)

Woburn Abbey England (**-ur-**)

Wodehouse, Sir P(elham) G(renville) English-born US author (compare **Woodhouse**)

woebegone sorrowful (compare **Wobegon**)

woke past tense of **wake**

woken past participle of **wake**

Wolf, Hugo Austrian composer (compare **Wolfe**, **Wolff**, **Woolf**, and **Woulfe**)

Wolf Cub former name for **Cub**

Wolfe, James English soldier;

Thomas US novelist (compare **Wolf**, **Wolff**, **Woolf**, and **Woulfe**)

Wolfenden Report study produced in 1956 recommending legalization of homosexual relations between consenting adults (capital **W** & **R**; **-en-** twice)

Wolff, Kaspar Friedrich German embryologist (compare **Wolf**, **Wolfe**, **Woolf**, and **Woulfe**)

wolfhound (one word)

wolf whistle (noun)

wolf-whistle (verb)

Wollongong Australian city (single **o** three times; double **l**)

Wollstonecraft, Mary British feminist and writer (single **o** twice; double **l**; **-ne-**)

Wolseley former motor manufacturer, or any of their vehicles

Wolsey, Thomas English cardinal and statesman

woman (avoid using before another noun in the sense 'female' (as in *woman doctor*) unless absolutely necessary; and do not use the plural form **women** before a singular noun)

womanize (also **womanise**; see **-ize/ -ise**)

women's lib (lower-case **w** & **l**; no full stop)

Women's Liberation (capital **W** & **L**)

Women's Movement (capital **W** & **M**)

wonder speculate, marvel, or feeling of surprise or awe (compare **wander**)

wont habit, as in *as is her wont*, or accustomed, as in *he is wont to be late* (compare **want** and **won't**)

won't contraction of **will not** (compare **wont**)

wonted accustomed or usual (compare **wanted**)

wood timber, or a collection of trees (compare **would**)

woodcut print made from block of wood cut along the grain (one word)

wood engraving print made from block of wood cut across the grain (two words)

Woodhouse, Barbara Irish dog trainer (compare **Wodehouse**)

woodlouse (one word; plural **woodlice**)

woodpecker (one word)

woodshed (one word)

woodworm (one word)

Wookey Hole English village and nearby cave with prehistoric remains (not **-ky**)

Woolf, Virginia English novelist (compare **Wolf, Wolfe, Wolff**, and **Woulfe**)

Woollcott, Alexander US writer and critic (double **o** then single **o**; double **l**; double **t**)

woollen (single **l** in US English)

Woolley, Sir Leonard British archaeologist (**-ey**)

woolly (double **l**)

woolsack (one word; also **Woolsack** for seat of Lord Chancellor in House of Lords)

Woolworths retail company (no apostrophe)

Wootton, Barbara, Baroness of Abinger English economist, educationalist, and social scientist (compare **Wotton**)

Worcester English city, US city, or South African town

Worcester sauce (capital **W**; also **Worcestershire sauce**)

Worcestershire English county

Worcestershire sauce variant of **Worcester sauce** (capital **W**)

word division see **soft hyphen**

Worde, Wynkyn de English printer, born in Alsace (sometimes alphabetized under **Wynkyn**)

word-perfect (hyphen)

wordplay (one word)

word processor (two words)

wore past tense of **wear** (compare **war** (for spelling) and **worn** (for usage))

workaday (one word)

workaholic (not **-oholic**)

workbench (one word)

workforce (one word)

workhorse (one word)

workhouse (one word)

work-in (noun; the verb is **work in**)

working class (noun)

working-class (adjective)

workmate (one word)

work-out (noun; the verb is **work out**)

workshop (one word)

worktop (one word)

work-to-rule (noun; the verb is **work to rule**)

World Bank (capital **W** & **B**; official name **International Bank for Reconstruction and Development**, abbreviation **IBRD**)

World Cup (capital **W** & **C**)

World Trade Center US building destroyed in terrorist attack on September 11, 2001 (capital **W**, **T**, & **C**; not **Centre**)

World War I 1914–18 (also **First World War**)

World War II 1939–45 (also **Second World War**)

world-weary (hyphen)

worldwide (one word)

World Wide Fund for Nature see **WWF** (not **Worldwide**)

World Wide Web (not **Worldwide**; capital **W** three times)

World Wildlife Fund see **WWF**

Worlock, Derek English Roman Catholic prelate (compare **Warlock**)

worn past tense of **wear** (compare **warn** (for spelling) and **wore** (for usage))

Worrall Thompson, Antony British chef (double **r**, double **l**; no hyphen; not **Thomson**, not **Anthony**)

worry beads (two words)
worshipped (single **p** in US English)
worshipper (single **p** in US English)
worshipping (single **p** in US English)
worthwhile (one word)
Wotton, Henry English poet and diplomat
would past tense of **will** (as a form of the verb **be**), also used in polite requests (as in *would you close the door, please?*), to express habitual past action (as in *she would take the dog for a walk every day*), and in the sense 'I wish' (as in *would that I had accepted their offer*). According to traditional grammar, **would** is used in the second and third persons in reported speech (as in *she said she would be late*) and in polite expressions of desire or preference (as in *they would like an explanation*), but in modern usage it is often used in all persons (i.e. replacing **should** in the first person) in these contexts. For spelling, compare **wood**.
would-be (hyphen)
would've contraction of **would have** ('ve not of)
Woulf, Peter English chemist (compare **Wolf, Wolfe, Wolff**, and **Woolf**)
wove past tense of **weave** (also **weaved**, especially with reference to making one's way by moving from side to side)
woven past participle of weave (also **weaved**, especially with reference to making one's way by moving from side to side)
wove paper paper with faint mesh impressed on it that is not visible when held to the light (compare **laid paper**)
Woyzeck play by Georg Büchner
Wozzeck opera by Alban Berg

wpm words per minute
WRAC Women's Royal Army Corps (disbanded in early 1990s)
wrack seaweed, piece of wreckage, or variant of **rack** in the sense 'destruction' (see **rack and ruin**). The use of **wrack** in place of **rack** is controversial in the senses 'cause to suffer' or 'strain' (as in *racked by guilt* or *rack one's brains*) and is wrong in other senses.
WRAF Women's Royal Air Force (disbanded in early 1990s)
wrap fold paper, cloth, etc. around; envelop; surround; garment wrapped round body; tortilla wrapped round filling; or end of filming (compare **rap**)
wraparound automatic shifting of word to new line to keep within margins, or variant of **wrapround** (one word)
wrapped past tense and past participle of **wrap**, or variant of **rapt** in Australian informal sense 'delighted' (compare **rapped**)
wrapround made to be wrapped round something, curving round, surrounding, printed sheet folded round section for binding, or slip of paper folded round jacket of book (one word; also **wraparound**)
wrath anger (compare **wroth**)
wreak inflict, cause, or express (compare **reek**)
wreaked past tense and past participle of **wreak**, as in *the storm wreaked havoc* (see also **wrought**)
wreath (noun; plural **wreaths**)
wreathe (verb)
wren small bird (lower-case **w**)
Wren informal name for member of **WRNS** (capital **W**)
wrest obtain by violence or effort (compare **rest**)
wretch despicable or pitiable person (compare **retch**)

wrick less common variant of **rick** in the sense 'wrench or sprain'

wring twist, squeeze, or obtain with difficulty or force (compare **ring**)

wristband (one word)

wristwatch (one word)

writable (not **-eable**)

write mark (letters, words, etc.) on surface, or compose (compare **rite** and **right**)

write-off (noun; the verb is **write off**)

writer's cramp (**-'s** not **-s'**)

write-up (noun; the verb is **write off**)

written past participle of **write** (compare **wrote**)

WRNS Women's Royal Naval Service (disbanded in early 1990s; see also **Wren**)

Wrocław Polish city (German name **Breslau**)

wrongdoer (one word)

wrong-foot (hyphen)

wrote past tense of **write** (compare **rote** (for spelling) and **written** (for usage))

wroth archaic word for angry (compare **wrath**)

wrought archaic past tense and past participle of **work**, now used as adjective (as in *wrought iron*) or in combination (as in *well-wrought*) (to avoid controversy, do not use in place of **wreaked**)

wrung past tense and past participle of **wring** (compare **rung**)

WRVS Women's Royal Voluntary Service (former name (until 1966) **WVS**)

wry twisted, contorted, or sardonic (compare **rye**)

Württemberg former German state, now part of **Baden-Württemberg** (umlaut, double **t**, **-berg**)

Wuthering Heights novel by Emily Brontë (**-*uth*-**)

WV West Virginia (US postal code)

WVS Women's Voluntary Service: former name (until 1966) for **WRVS**

WWF international conservation charity (short for **World Wildlife Fund**; the name was changed to **World Wide Fund for Nature** in 1986 but the charity now uses the original initials only)

WWW World Wide Web

WY Wyoming (US postal code)

wych-elm (also **witch-elm**)

Wycherley, William English dramatist (**-ych-**, **-er-**, **-ey**)

wych-hazel variant of **witch hazel**

Wycliffe, John English religious reformer (also **Wyclif**, **Wickliffe**, or **Wiclif**)

Wycombe see **High Wycombe**

Wykeham, William of English prelate and statesman (not **Wickham** or **Wycombe**)

Wyndham, John pen name of British novelist **John Wyndham Parkes Lucas Beynon Harris** (not **Wind-**)

Wynkyn de Worde see **Worde**

WYSIWYG what you see is what you get (i.e. computer print-out will match screen display)

wyvern heraldic beast (the spelling **wivern** is not incorrect, but it is less common)

X

X symbol for Christ (from form of initial letter of Greek name); Roman numeral for 10

Xanthippe wife of Socrates, hence any nagging or irritable woman (capital **X**; the spelling **Xantippe** is not incorrect, but it is less common)

Xavier, St Francis Spanish missionary

x-axis horizontal axis of graph (first letter is lower-case italic; hyphen)

X-chromosome (capital **X**; hyphen)

Xe xenon (no full stop)

xebec small Mediterranean sailing boat (also **zebec**)

xenon (symbol **Xe**)

xenophobia (not **zeno-**)

Xenophon Greek general and historian

Xeres former name for **Jerez**

xerography photocopying process (lower-case **x**)

Xerox trademark for a photocopying process (capital **X**, sometimes lower-case when used as a verb; in generic use better replaced by a synonym)

Xerxes Persian king (the possessive form is traditionally **Xerxes'**)

x-height (*typog.*) height of lower-case letters without ascenders or descenders

Xhosa S African people or their language (see also **Kaffir**)

Xi Chinese river (also **Hsi** or **Si**)

Xi An Chinese city (also **Hsian** or **Sian**; former name **Siking**)

Xiang either of two Chinese rivers (also **Hsiang** or **Siang**)

Xianggang Pinyin name for **Hong Kong**

Xiangtan Chinese city (also **Siangtan**)

Xiaoping see **Deng Xiaoping**

Ximenes de Cisneros variant of **Jiménez de Cisneros** (also **Ximenez de Cisneros**)

Xining Chinese city (also **Hsining** or **Sining**)

Xmas Christmas (see also **X**)

XML extended mark-up language

Xn Christian (see also **X**)

Xnty Christianity (see also **X**)

X-rated (capital **X**; hyphen; note that British films now have the rating **18** rather than **X**)

X-ray (also **x-ray**)

Xtian Christian (see also **X**)

Xty Christianity (see also **X**)

xylophone (not **zylo-**)

Y

Y yttrium (no full stop)

yabby small Australian crayfish (also **yabbie**)

yacht (-cht)

yack variant of **yak** in the sense 'chatter'

Yafo Hebrew name for **Jaffa** (the port)

yahoo brutish or coarse person (lower-case **y**)

Yahoo any of a race of brutish creatures in Swift's *Gulliver's Travels* (capital **Y**)

Yahoo! Internet company (capital **Y**; exclamation mark)

Yahweh see **Tetragrammaton** (the variants **Yahveh**, **Jahweh**, and **Jahveh** are less common but not incorrect)

yak Tibetan cattle, or chatter (also **yack** in the sense 'chatter')

Yale trademark for a type of lock (capital **Y**)

Yamoussoukro administrative capital of Côte d'Ivoire (-**ou**- twice then -**o**; double **s**; compare **Abidjan**)

Yang see **Yin and Yang**

Yangon capital of Myanmar (former name **Rangoon**)

Yangtze Chinese river (also **Yangtze Jiang**; Pinyin **Chang** or **Chang Jiang**)

Yanina variant of **Ioánnina**

Yankee person from the USA, person from New England, or person from the northern USA, especially a soldier in the American Civil War (often disparaging, and therefore best avoided, in the sense 'person from the USA')

Yaoundé capital of Cameroon (acute accent; also **Yaunde**)

yardarm (one word)

Yardie member of Black criminal syndicate (capital **Y**; -**die**)

yardstick (one word)

Yarmouth port and resort on the Isle of Wight, or shortening of **Great Yarmouth** (see that entry)

yarmulke skullcap worn by Jews (not italic)

Yates, Dornford pen name of English novelist **Cecil William Mercer** (compare **Yeats**)

Yaunde variant of **Yaoundé**

y-axis horizontal axis of graph (first letter is lower-case italic; hyphen)

Yb ytterbium (no full stop)

Y-chromosome (capital **Y**; hyphen)

yd yard or yards (also **yd.**)

yearbook (one word)

years see **dates**

Yekaterinburg Russian city (also **Ekaterinburg**)

Yekaterinodar former name for **Krasnodar**

yellowhammer (one word)

Yellowknife Canadian city (one word)

Yellow Pages trademark for classified telephone directory (capital **Y** & **P**)

Yellow River China (Chinese name **Hwang Ho**, Pinyin **Huang Ho**)

Yellow Sea part of Pacific Ocean between Korea and China (Chinese name **Hwang Hai**, Pinyin **Huang Hai**)

Yellowstone US river and national park

Yemen Arabian country (not **the** ...)

yeoman (-eo-)

yeoman of the guard member of Yeomen of the Guard (lower-case **y** & **g**)

Yeomen of the Guard bodyguard of the monarch, now with ceremonial functions only (capital **Y** & **G**)

Yerevan capital of Armenia (also **Erevan**)

yes man (two words)

yesteryear (one word)

Yevtushenko, Yevgeny Aleksandrovich Russian poet

yeti abominable snowman (lower-case **y**)

yew tree (compare **ewe** and **you**)

Y-fronts trademark for underpants with inverted Y-shaped front opening (capital **Y**, hyphen)

Ygdrasil less common variant of **Yggdrasil**

Ygerne less common variant of **Igraine**

Yggdrasil ash tree in Norse mythology that was thought to bind earth, heaven, and hell together (the spelling **Ygdrasil** is not incorrect, but it is less common)

YHA Youth Hostels Association

Yin and Yang complementary principles of Chinese philosophy, **Yin** being negative, dark, and feminine and **Yang** being positive, bright, and masculine (capital **Y** twice)

YMCA Young Men's Christian Association

Ymuiden less common variant of **IJmuiden**

Ynys Môn Welsh name for **Anglesey**

yodel (rarely **yodle**)

yodelled (single **l** in US English)

yodeller (single **l** in US English)

yodelling (single **l** in US English)

yodle rare variant of **yodel**

yogurt (also **yoghurt**)

Yogyakarta Indonesian city (also **Jogjakarta**)

yoke frame attached to necks of pair of draught animals or fitting over person's shoulders, fitted part of garment, oppressive burden, put a yoke on, join with a yoke, or link (compare **yolk**)

yokel (-kel)

yolk nourishing substance in egg (compare **yoke**)

Yom Kippur Jewish holiday observed with fasting and prayers of penitence (also **Day of Atonement**)

Yonge, Charlotte M(ary) British novelist (compare **Young**)

yore time long past, as in *days of yore* (compare **your** and **you're**)

York English city or royal house of the 15th century

Yorkshire former English county, divided in 1974 into the counties of **North Yorkshire**, **South Yorkshire**, and **West Yorkshire**

Yorkshire Dales (capital **Y** & **D**; also **the Dales**)

Yorkshire pudding (capital **Y**, lower-case **p**)

Yorkshire terrier (capital **Y**, lower-case **t**)

Yosemite US national park

you second person pronoun, also increasingly used in place of **one** with reference to an unspecified person or people in general (compare **yew** and **ewe**)

Young, Brigham US Mormon leader; **Edward** English poet and dramatist; **Neil** Canadian rock musician; **Thomas** English physicist, physician, and Egyptologist (compare **Yonge**)

young offender institution place for detention and instruction of young offenders (no **s** at end of middle word; former name **borstal**)

Young Pretender nickname of Charles Edward **Stuart**, also known as **Bonnie Prince Charlie** (capital **Y** & **P**)

Young Turk member of organization or party agitating for radical reform, or (originally) member of abortive reform movement in Ottoman Empire (capital **Y** & **T**)

Young Visiters, The story by Daisy Ashford (not **-tors**)

your of you (compare **you're** and **yore**)

you're contraction of **you are** (compare **your** and **yore**)

yours of you (no apostrophe)

yo-yo (hyphen; plural **yo-yos**)

Ypres Belgian town (Flemish name **Ieper**)

Yquem French vineyard in Sauternes region, or the sweet white wine

produced there (also **Château d'Yquem**, especially for the wine)

yr year; your

yrs years; yours

-yse/-yze for words such as *analyse, paralyse,* etc., use the **-yse** form in UK English and the **-yze** form in US English. See also **-ize/-ise.**

Yseult variant of **Iseult**

Yssel less common variant of **IJssel**

Ysselmeer less common variant of **IJsselmeer**

ytterbium (symbol **Yb**)

yttrium (symbol **Y**)

Yucatán Mexican state or Central American peninsula (**a** then **á**)

yucca (lower-case y in general use, *Yucca* is the genus name; double **c**)

Yugoslavia former European country

yule Christmas (also **Yule**)

yuppie (lower-case y; also **yuppy**)

Yves Saint Laurent fashion house (no hyphens; not **St**)

YWCA Young Women's Christian Association

-yze/yse see **-yse/-yze**

Z

zabaglione foamy dessert (not italic; not **-ni**)

Zabrze Polish city (German name **Hindenburg**)

Zacharias father of John the Baptist (also **Zachariah** or **Zachary**; compare **Zechariah**)

Zagreb capital of Croatia (German name **Agram**)

Zaïre former name for **Congo** (the river) and **Democratic Republic of Congo** (diaeresis)

Zambezi African river (the spelling **Zambese** is not incorrect, but it is less common)

Zambia African country (former name **Northern Rhodesia**)

zamindar owner of agricultural estate in India (also **zemindar**)

Zangwill, Israel British writer

Zanu(PF) Zimbabwe African National Union (Patriotic Front) (less common variants have all capitals, and/or a hyphen or space instead of brackets)

Zanzibar African island and former country, now part of Tanzania

Zappa, Frank US rock musician

ZAPU Zimbabwe African People's Union

Zaragoza Spanish city (English name **Saragossa**)

Zarathustra Avestan name for **Zoroaster** (**-thu-**, **-tra**)

Zealand largest island of Denmark (Danish name **Sjælland**, German name **Seeland**; compare **Zeeland**)

zealous (**-eal-**)

zebec variant of **xebec**

Zech. Zechariah (full stop; not italic)

Zechariah Hebrew prophet and book of the Bible (not italic; abbreviation **Zech.**; compare **Zacharias**)

Zedong see **Mao Tse-tung**

Zeebrugge Belgian port (not **Zea-**)

Zeeland Dutch province (compare **Zealand**)

Zeitgeist spirit of a particular time or period (italics; capital **Z**; **-ei-** twice)

zemindar variant of **zamindar**

Zen form of Buddhism (capital **Z**)

zenith highest point (compare **nadir**)

Zeph. Zephaniah (full stop; not italic)

Zephaniah book of the Bible (not italic; abbreviation **Zeph.**)

zephyr gentle breeze (**-yr**)

zeppelin airship (double **p**, single **l**; the use of capital **Z** is not incorrect in this sense, but it is less common)

Zermatt Swiss village and resort (double **t**)

zeroes third person present tense of **zero**, or variant of **zeros**

zeros plural of **zero** (also **zeroes**)

zero tolerance (no hyphen unless used before another noun, as in *a zero-tolerance policy*)

Zeta-Jones, Catherine Welsh actress (hyphen; not **Katherine** or **Catharine**)

Zetland former official name for **Shetland**

Zhou Enlai Pinyin form of **Chou En-lai**

Ziegfeld, Florenz US theatrical producer (**-ie-** then **-e-**)

ziggurat ancient Mesopotamian temple (rarely **zikkurat** or **zikurat**)

zigzag (no hyphen)

zigzagged, zigzagging (double **g**)

zikkurat rare variant of **ziggurat** (also **zikurat**)

Zimbabwe African country (former names **Southern Rhodesia** (until 1964) and **Rhodesia** (1964–79))

Zimmer trademark for walking frame (capital **Z**; also **Zimmer frame**)

zinc (symbol **Zn**)

Zion hill on which Jerusalem stands; in Judaism, ancient Israelites, modern Jewish nation, or Israel as home of Jewish people; in Christianity, heaven (the spelling **Sion** is not incorrect, but it is less common)

zip code US postal code (two words; **ZIP Code** in the USA, where it is a trademark)

zirconium (symbol **Zr**)

zloty monetary unit of Poland

Zn zinc (no full stop)

zodiac (lower-case **z**)

zoetrope cylinder with pictures inside producing illusion of animation when rotated (not **zeo-**)

Zoffany, John German-born British painter (double **f**, single **n**; first name also **Johann**)

zombie (lower-case **z**; rarely **zombi**)

zoological name see **binomial** and **taxonomic names**

Zoroaster Persian prophet (Avestan name **Zarathustra**)

Zoroastrianism (also **Zoroastrism**)

Zr zirconium (no full stop)

zucchini US, Canadian, and Australian name for **courgette** (**-cch-**; plural **zucchini** or **zucchinis**)

Zuider Zee former inlet of North Sea in Netherlands, now dammed to form **IJsselmeer** and **Waddenzee** (two words; the spelling **Zuyder Zee** is not incorrect, but it is less common)

Zuleika Dobson novel by Max Beerbohm (**-ei-**)

Zulu member of SE African people, or the language of this people (plural **Zulus** or **Zulu**)

Zululand region of South Africa partly corresponding to **KwaZulu/Natal**

Zürich Swiss city, canton, and lake (umlaut)

Zuyder Zee less common variant of **Zuider Zee**

zwieback type of rusk (not italic; lower-case **z**; **-ie-**)

Zwingli, Ulrich Swiss leader of the Reformation (first name also **Huldreich**)

Appendices

Appendix i:
Proofreading marks

Group A: General

No.	Instruction	Textual mark	Marginal mark	Notes
A1	End of change	None	/ or solidus followed by a circled number bottom right /⊗	P Make after every change that is not an insertion or deletion, i.e. followed by B1 (This is identical to B4) Use circled number to indicate number of times same change is repeated in the same line without interruption
A2	Leave unchanged	— — — — — — under characters to remain	⟨✓⟩	M P
A3	Push down risen spacing material	Circle blemish	⊥	P For hot metal only
A4	Refer to appropriate authority anything of doubtful accuracy	Circle word(s) affected	⟨?⟩	P

Group B: Deletion, insertion and substitution

B1	Insert in text the matter indicated in the margin	⋏	New matter followed by ⋏ or ⋏⊗	M P Use circled number to indicate number of times same insert is repeated in the same line without interruption
B2	Insert additional matter identified by a letter in a diamond	⋏	⋏ preceded by, for example, ⟨A⟩	M P The relevant section of the copy should be supplied with the corresponding letter marked on it in a diamond, e.g. ⟨A⟩

Proofreading marks - *cont.*

No.	Instruction	Textual mark	Marginal mark	Notes
B3	Delete	/ through single character, rule or underline or ⊢————⊣ through all characters to be deleted	⌀ or ⌀ (x2)	M P Use for deletion at the beginning or end of a word and where no space is to be left in place of deletion. Use circled number to indicate number of deletions in the same line without interruption
B4	Substitute character or substitute part of one or more word(s)	/ through character or ⊢————⊣ through all characters	new character / or new characters /	M P
B5	Wrong font. Replace by character(s) of correct font	Circle character(s) to be changed	⊗	P Use to indicate wrong typeface or size
B6	Change damaged character(s) or remove extraneous marks	Circle character(s) to be changed or mark(s) to be removed	✕	P
B7	Set in or change to italic	_____ under character(s) to be set or changed	⌒	M P Where space does not permit textual marks, or for clarity, circle the affected area instead
B8	Change italic to roman/vertical type	Circle character(s) to be changed	⊥	M P
B9	Set in or change to bold type	〜〜〜〜〜 under character(s) to be set or changed	〜	M P Where space does not permit textual marks, or for clarity, circle the affected area instead
B10	Change bold to non-bold type	Circle character(s) to be changed	⋀〜	M P
B11	Set in or change to bold italic type	〜〜〜〜〜 under character(s) to be set or changed	⇜	M P Where space does not permit textual marks, or for clarity, circle the affected area instead

Proofreading marks - *cont.*

No.	Instruction	Textual mark	Marginal mark	Notes
B12	Change to non-bold and non-italic	Circle character(s) to be changed		M P
B13	Set in or change to capital letters	═════ under character(s) to be set or changed	═	M P Where space does not permit textual marks, or for clarity, circle the affected area instead
B14	Set in or change to small capital letters	──── under character(s) to be set or changed	══	
B15	Set in or change to capital letters for initial letters and small capital letters for the rest of the words	═══ under initial letters and ──── under rest of words	══	
B16	Change capital letters to lower case letters	Circle character(s) to be changed	≢	P
B17	Change small capital letters to lower case letters	Circle character(s) to be changed	╪	P
B18	Turn type or figure	Circle type or figure to be altered	⑱ ↻	P Use circled number to give number of degrees of rotation, e.g. 180
B19	Substitute or insert character in 'superior' position	/ through character or ⋀ where required	⋎ or ⋋ under character e.g. ²⋎ or ⋌²	P Do not use additional insert or substitute mark with these marks
B20	Substitute or insert character in 'inferior' position	/ through character or ⋀ where required	⋀ over character e.g. ⋀₂	
B21	Substitute ligature, e.g. ffi, for separate letters	├───────┤ through characters affected	⌒ e.g. ﬃ	P
B22	Substitute separate letters for ligature	├───────┤ through characters affected	Write out separate letters	P

Proofreading marks - *cont.*

No.	Instruction	Textual mark	Marginal mark	Notes
B23	Substitute or insert full stop or decimal point	/ through character or ⋏ where required	⊙	M P
B24	Substitute or insert colon	/ through character or ⋏ where required	⊙	M P
B25	Substitute or insert semi-colon	/ through character or ⋏ where required	⁏	M P
B26	Substitute or insert comma	/ through character or ⋏ where required	،	M P
B27	Substitute or insert apostrophe	/ through character or ⋏ where required	ỿ or ⋋	M P Do not use additional insert or substitute mark with these marks
B28	Substitute or insert single quotation marks	/ through character or ⋏ where required	ỿ or ⋋ and/or ỿ or ⋋	
B29	Substitute or insert double quotation marks	/ through character or ⋏ where required	ỿ or ⋋ and/or ỿ or ⋋	
B30	Substitute or insert ellipsis or leader dots	/ through character or ⋏ where required	⊙⋯	M P When used as leader, give the measure
B31	Substitute or insert hyphen	/ through character or space or ⋏ where required	⊢⊣	M P

Proofreading marks - *cont.*

No.	Instruction	Textual mark	Marginal mark	Notes
B32	Substitute or insert rule	/ through character or ⋀ where required	⊢⊣	M P Give the size of the rule in the margin mark e.g. ⊢①N⊣ ⊢4mm⊣
B33	Substitute or insert oblique	/ through character or ⋀ where required	⊘	M P
B34	Insert underline	Circle characters/words	Circle horizontal line	M P

Group C: Positioning

No.	Instruction	Textual mark	Marginal mark	Notes
C1	Start new paragraph			M P
C2	Run on (no new paragraph, no new line)			M P
C3	Transpose characters or words	between characters or words		M P
C4	Transpose a number of characters or words	③②①	①②③	M P Use when the sequence cannot be clearly indicated by the use of C3 Circle numbers to prevent them being typeset
C5	Transpose lines			M P Extend rules the full length of matter being transposed
C6	Transpose a number of lines	③ ② ①		P Use when the sequence cannot be clearly indicated by the use of C5 Circle numbers to prevent them being typeset

Proofreading marks - *cont.*

No.	Instruction	Textual mark	Marginal mark	Notes
C7	Centre	enclosing matter to be centred		M P
C8	Indent or move beginning of line(s) to the right			M P Draw vertical lines of mark to show position to which character(s) are moved
C9	Cancel indent or move end of line(s) to the left			
C10	Set line justified to specified measure	⊢ [and/or] ⊣	↦←	P Give the exact dimensions when necessary
C11	Set column justified to specified measure	⊢⟶⊣	↦⊣	M P Give the exact dimensions when necessary
C12	Unjustify		or	M P Use mark on side of line/column to be unjustified
C13	Move specified matter to the right	enclosing matter to be moved to the right		P Draw vertical line to show position to which matter is moved
C14	Move specified matter to the left	← enclosing matter to be moved to the left		
C15	Take over character(s), word(s) or line to next line, column or page			P The textual mark surrounds the matter to be taken over and extends into the margin

Proofreading marks - *cont.*

No.	Instruction	Textual mark	Marginal mark	Notes
C16	Take back character(s), word(s), or line to previous line, column or page			P The textual mark surrounds the matter to be taken back and extends into the margin
C17	Raise matter	over matter to be raised under matter to be raised		P Give the exact dimensions when necessary (Use D8 for insertion of space between lines or paragraphs in text)
C18	Lower matter	over matter to be lowered under matter to be lowered		P Give the exact dimensions when necessary (Use D9 for reduction of space between lines or paragraphs in text)
C19	Move matter to position indicated	Enclose matter to be moved and indicate new position		P Give the exact dimensions when necessary
C20	Correct vertical alignment			P
C21	Correct horizontal alignment	Single line above and below misaligned matter e.g. mis͟a͟l͟i͟g͟n͟e͟d͟		P The marginal mark is placed level with the head and foot of the relevant line

Group D: Spacing

No.	Instruction	Textual mark	Marginal mark	Notes
D1	Close up. Delete space between characters or words	linking characters		M P
D2	Insert or substitute space between characters or words	/ through character or ⋏ where required		M P Give the size of the space to be inserted when necessary

Proofreading marks - *cont.*

No.	Instruction	Textual mark	Marginal mark	Notes
D3	Reduce space between characters or words	| between characters or words affected	⌒	M P Give amount by which the space is to be reduced when necessary
D4	Make space equal between characters or words in entire line	| between characters or words affected	⊔	M P
D5	Insert or substitute thin space	/ through character or ⋏ where required	⊖	M P
D6	Insert or substitute fixed space	/ through character or ⋏ where required	(2pt) Y or Y	M P Circle numbers to prevent them being typeset
D7	Close up to normal interline spacing		(each side of column linking lines)	M P The marks are in the margin
D8	Insert space between lines or paragraphs	—⊂ or)——		M P The mark extends between the lines of text. Give the size of the space to be inserted when necessary
D9	Reduce space between lines or paragraphs	—⊃ or ⊂—		M P The mark extends between the lines of text. Give the amount by which the space is to be reduced when necessary

Appendix ii:
Mathematical and scientific symbols

+ plus sign
− minus sign
× multiplication sign
÷ division sign
± plus or minus
· centred dot
= equal to
≠ not equal to
≡ identical to
~ equivalent to
≈ approximately equal to
< less than
> greater than
≤ less than or equal to
≥ greater than or equal to
↓ tends down to
↑ tends up to
∞ infinity
√ square root
^{2} squared or square (in names of units)
^{3} cubed or cubic (in names of units)
μ micro- (in names of units)
° degree
Ω ohm
π pi
∂ partial derivative
∫ integral
Δ increment
Σ summation
Π product
∩ intersection
♀ female
♂ male

Appendix iii:
Transliteration of Greek, Cyrillic, and Hebrew alphabets

Greek

A α	alpha	a
B β	beta	b
Γ γ	gamma	g
Δ δ	delta	d
E ε	epsilon	e
Z ζ	zeta	z
H η	eta	e *or* ē
Θ θ	theta	th
I ι	iota	i
K κ	kappa	k
Λ λ	lambda	l
M μ	mu	m
N ν	nu	n
Ξ ξ	xi	x
O o	omicron	o
Π π	pi	p
P ρ	rho	r *or* rh
Σ σ ς	sigma	s
T τ	tau	t
Y υ	upsilon	u
Φ φ	phi	ph
X χ	chi	kh
Ψ ψ	psi	ps
Ω ω	omega	o *or* ō

Cyrillic

А а	a
Б б	b
В в	v
Г г	g
Д д	d
Е е	e *or* ye
Ё ё	yo
Ж ж	zh
З з	z
И и	i
Й й	ĭ
К к	k
Л л	l
М м	m
Н н	n
О о	o
П п	p
Р р	r
С с	s
Т т	t
У у	u
Ф ф	f
Х х	kh
Ц ц	ts
Ч ч	ch
Ш ш	sh
Щ щ	shch
Ъ ъ	(hard sign)
Ы ы	y
Ь ь	(soft sign)
Э э	e
Ю ю	yu
Я я	ya

Hebrew

א	aleph *or* alef	ʾ
ב	beth	b
ג	gimel	g *or* gh
ד	daleth	d *or* dh
ה	he	h
ו	vav *or* waw	v *or* w
ז	zayin	z
ח	heth *or* cheth	h
ט	teth	t
י	yod *or* yodh	y
ך כ	kaph	k *or* kh
ל	lamed *or* lamedh	l
ם מ	mem	m
ן נ	nun	n
ס	samekh	s
ע	ayin	ʿ
ף פ	pe	p *or* ph
ץ צ	sadhe, sade, *or* tsade	s *or* ts
ק	koph *or* qoph	q
ר	resh	r
שׂ	sin	s
שׁ	shin	sh
ת	tav *or* taw	t *or* th

Appendix iv:
Beaufort scale

Category	Description
0	Calm
1	Faint air just not calm
2	Light airs
3	Light breeze
4	Gentle breeze
5	Moderate breeze
6	Fresh breeze
7	Gentle steady gale
8	Moderate gale
9	Brisk gale
10	Fresh gale
11	Hard gale
12	Hard gale with heavy gusts
13	Storm

Appendix v:
Diacritics used in European languages

All letters have corresponding capital forms, with the exception of German ß (same form for lower-case and capital) and Czech and Slovak ď and ť, for which the corresponding capital forms are Ď and Ť.

Albanian: ç ë
Czech: á č ď Ď é ě í ň ó ř š ť Ť ú ü ý ž
Danish: å æ ø
Dutch: é ë ó
French: à â ç é è ê ë î ï ô ù û ÿ
German: ä ö ß ü
Italian: à é è í ì ò ú ù
Norwegian: å æ ø
Polish: ą ć ę ł ń ó ś ź ż
Portuguese: á à â ã é ê í ó ô õ ú ü
Romanian: ă â î ş ţ
Slovak: á ä č ď Ď é í ĺ ľ ň ó ô ŕ š ť Ť ú ý ž
Spanish: á é í ñ ó ú ü
Swedish: å ä ö